Collins Concise School Dictionary

Collins

Collins Concise School Dictionary

First published 2001
This edition published 2005

10 9

ISBN-13 978-0-00-720388-8 hardback
ISBN-10 0-00-720388-8 hardback
ISBN-13 978-0-00-720389-5 paperback
ISBN-10 0-00-720389-6 paperback

A catalogue record for this book is available from the British Library.

Published by Collins
A division of HarperCollins*Publishers* Ltd
77-85 Fulham Palace Road
Hammersmith
London W6 8JB
www.collins.co.uk

Browse the complete Collins Education catalogue at:
www.collinseducation.com

Editor John McIlwain
Consultant editor Betty Kirkpatrick
Consultant teacher Ruth Grainger
Literacy consultants Kay Hiatt, Rosemary Boys
Numeracy consultants Jan Henley, Karen Pegram, Jayne Spiller
Science consultant Rona Wyn Davies
Cover designer Nicola Croft
Design Wigwam Digital, Wordcraft and DSM Partnership

Adapted by John McIlwain from the text of the Collins New School Dictionary

Acknowledgements
The publishers would like to thank all the staff, teachers and pupils who contributed to this book:

Schools
Aberhill Primary, Fife; ASDAC, Fife; Canning St Primary, Newcastle upon Tyne; Cowgate Primary, Newcastle upon Tyne; Crombie Primary, Fife; the Literacy Team at Dryden Professional Development Centre, Gateshead; Dunshalt Primary, Fife; Ecton Brook Lower, Northampton; English Martyrs RC Primary, Newcastle upon Tyne; Hotspur Primary, Newcastle upon Tyne; John Betts Primary School, London; Lemington First, Newcastle upon Tyne; LMTC Education Centre, Northumberland, Melcombe Primary, London; Methihill Primary, Fife; Newcastle Literacy Centre, Newcastle upon Tyne; Northampton High, Northampton; Pitcoudie Primary, Fife; Pitreavie Primary, Fife; Ravenswood Primary, Newcastle upon Tyne; St Andrew's CE Primary, London; Simon de Senlis Lower, Northampton; Sinclairtown Primary, Fife; Standens Barn Lower, Northampton; Touch Primary, Fife; Towcester Infants, Northampton; Wooton Primary, Northampton.

Special thanks to Fiona McIlwain.

How to use this dictionary

The main part of a dictionary tells you what words mean, how to spell them and other facts about them. Useful information is also contained at the front and back of the dictionary.

How to find a word

Words are arranged in alphabetical order. On each page is an **alphabet line**. The shaded box highlights the first letter of words on that page. The **guide words** at the top of each page tell you the first and last words on that page. Both of these will help you to find the word you want quickly.

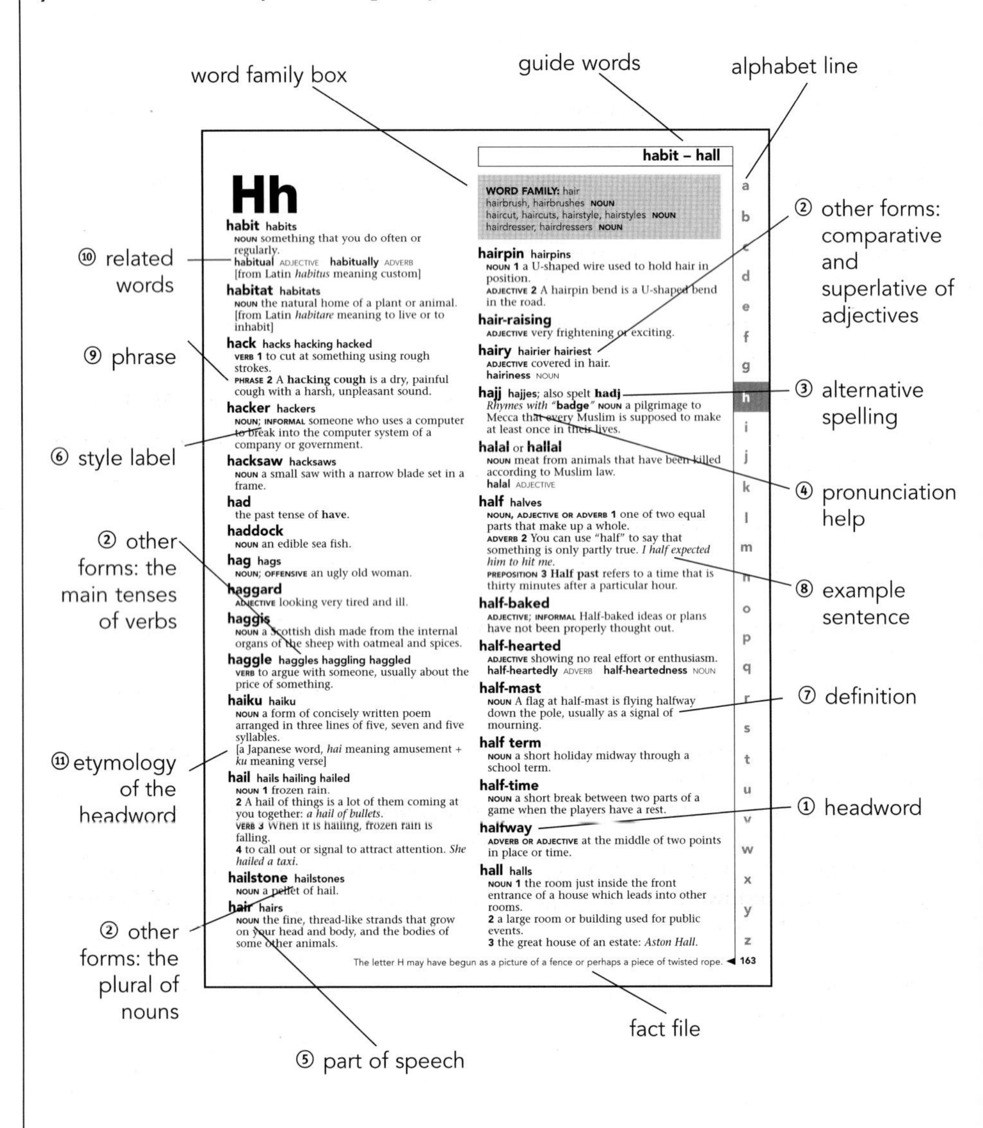

Finding out about a word

① The **headword** is the main word for each definition.

② On the same line as the headword are **other forms of the word**, such as plural nouns, verb tenses and the comparative and superlative forms of adjectives.

③ **Alternative spellings** for headwords are provided.

④ Where the **pronunciation** of a headword may be unclear from its spelling, this is given separately.

⑤ The **part of speech** tells you what type of word the headword is, such as noun, verb, adjective and so on.

⑥ Some definitions include a **style label** which tells you more about how the word is usually used. See page x.

⑦ The main part of the entry is the **definition**, which tells you what the headword means. The definitions are numbered if a word has more than one meaning.

⑧ Some headwords have an **example sentence** in *italics*. This shows you how the word might be used in speech or writing.

⑨ A **phrase** may also be included. For example, below the headword "hack" is a definition of the phrase "hacking cough".

⑩ Sometimes **related words** from the same root are given at the end of an entry.

⑪ Modern English words come from many sources. Some entries have an **etymology** (or word history) showing the origin of the headword.

Other features of this dictionary

Throughout the dictionary, there are a range of other features to help you understand more about the English language.

- **Grammar boxes** contain general rules and advice on English grammar and punctuation.
- **Usage notes** (4) provide tips on spelling and advice on when to use a word or particular phrase.
- **Word family boxes** list a group of words that are derived from a single root word, see for example the box for "hair".
- **Synonyms** (words with a similar meaning) and **antonyms** (words with an opposite meaning) are given for some headwords.
- **Fact files**, at the foot of each page, contain a fascinating language fact or puzzle linked with a headword on that page. Answers to fact file questions can be found at the back of the dictionary.

★ **The Collins Word Wizard section** at the end of the dictionary provides grammar help, word banks, abbreviations, puzzles, quizzes and answers to the fact file questions.

Parts of speech

Every word in every sentence can be classified into one of the eight parts of speech (sometimes also called word classes). These are:

- verb
- noun
- pronoun
- adjective
- adverb
- conjunction
- preposition
- interjection

Many words can be more than one part of speech, depending on how they are used. The word "round" can be an adjective, adverb, verb, noun or preposition:
Circles are round. (adjective)
Run round the block. (adverb)
We watched the car round the bend. (verb)
She did a paper round. (noun)
The shop was round the corner. (preposition)

Try this

Use each of these words in at least two sentences, using the word as a different part of speech every time:

cheer aged park brown match love tomorrow common horse glass

Verbs

Verb is from the Latin *verbum* meaning word. Every sentence must have a verb before it can "say" anything. Verbs are "doing" or "being" words.

The **tense** of a verb tells us whether the action is in the past, the present or the future. The main tenses are as follows:

present	past	future	conditional
I do I am doing	I did I was doing I used to do I have done I have been doing I had done I had been doing	I shall do, I will do I shall be doing I shall have done I shall have been doing	I would do I should do

When the verb has "to" before it, such as "to run" and "to cry", it is called an **infinitive**. Placing a word between to and its verb is called "splitting the infinitive". Some people think that split infinitives should be avoided if possible.

Participles are forms of the verb used in forming certain tenses. For each verb in this dictionary, two participles are listed:

- the **present participle** which ends in "-ing", such as *looking, breaking, thinking*
- the **past participle** which usually ends in "-ed", "-en" or "-t", such as *looked, broken, thought.*

Irregular verbs are normal in their "-s" form and their "-ing" form, but have an unusual past tense, past participle or both. The main types of irregular verb are:

verb has	present		past tense		past participle
the same past tense and past participle	have	→	had	→	had
	keep	→	kept	→	kept
	send	→	sent	→	sent
an irregular past tense and an "-n" ending for the past participle	blow	→	blew	→	blown
	see	→	saw	→	seen
	take	→	took	→	taken
the same form for present, past tense and past participle	cut	→	cut	→	cut
	let	→	let	→	let
	shut	→	shut	→	shut
the vowel changes with each form	begin	→	began	→	begun
	swim	→	swam	→	swum

Nouns

Nouns are the names given to all the things we can experience or identify.

- **Common nouns** are words which indicate every example of a certain type of thing, such as table, boy, apple, ship or town.
- **Proper nouns** name particular persons, places or objects, such as Peter, Buckingham Palace or Aberdeen. They begin with capital letters.
- **Concrete nouns** indicate things you can touch, such as tree, bike or house.
- **Abstract nouns** indicate things you can experience through your mind and emotions, but not through the five senses, such as love, hope or friendship.
- **Collective nouns** name groups of things, such as a flock of birds.

Try this

Can you name a common noun and a proper noun beginning with each letter of the alphabet?

Try the same for collective and abstract nouns. How many letters can you do?

Pronouns

Pronouns are words that can be used instead of nouns. The main pronouns are:

I	she	one	nobody
me	us	someone	none
you	we	somebody	both
him	it	anyone	all
her	they	anybody	everyone
he	them	no one	everybody

Pronouns cut down repetition of the same words. Look at this sentence:

Mrs Brown cleaned Mrs Brown's car then drove Mrs Brown's car to pick up Mrs Brown's son Philip from Philip's football match.

Now look at the same sentence when pronouns are used:

*Mrs Brown cleaned **her** car then drove **it** to pick up **her** son Philip from **his** football match.*

Parts of speech

Adjectives

Adjectives add descriptive force to a noun. They can affect the meaning of a sentence:
The man knocked at the door.
*The **desperate** man knocked at the **barred** door.*
*The **sleepy** man knocked at the **moonlit** door.*

Note that adjectives of nationality (such as Welsh, American, Dutch, etc.) normally begin with a capital letter. There are exceptions, such as "french window".

Try this

Write the story of a picnic using the word "nice" as often as possible. Exchange it with a partner, and rewrite their story, replacing "nice" throughout with more precise adjectives.

Comparative adjectives tell you more about the noun. They are usually formed by adding add "-er" to the adjective:
*a **smaller** dog; a **sillier** game.*

Some adjectives have the word "more" in front of them to make them comparative:
*a **more gifted** writer; a **more cheerful** expression.*

Superlative adjectives tell the most that a noun can have. They are usually formed by add "-est" to the adjective:
*the **smallest** dog; the **silliest** game.*

Some adjectives have the word "most" in front of them to make them superlative:
*the **most gifted** writer; the **most cheerful** expression.*

Adverbs

An **adverb** adds to the sense of a verb or of another adverb. It usually answers one of the questions "how", "when" or "where" about the verb:
*She ran **well**. She ran **yesterday**. She ran **home**.*

Many adverbs end with the letters "-ly". The letters "-ly" are added to the adjective to form the adverb, for example, "quick" changes to "quickly". If the adjective ends in "-y", you take off the "-y" and add "-ily", for example, "happy" changes to "happily".

Adverbs of manner answer the question "How?".
*She runs **quickly**. He sings **badly**.*

Adverbs of place answer the question "Where?".
*He travelled **northwards**. We live **here**.*

Adverbs of time answer the question "When?".
*You must answer **soon**. They arrived **yesterday**.*

Adverbs of degree answer the question "To what extent?".
*I **almost** caught the bus. She **quite** likes her new teacher.*

Adverbs of frequency answer the question "How often?".
*We **sometimes** play hockey. He **never** answers my questions.*

Try this

Explain how the meaning of this sentence is changed if the word "only" is used in different places in the sentence:
Only boxers may enter the ring.

Conjunctions

A **conjunction** is a word used to link sentences or clauses, or to link words within the same phrase. A conjunction is a type of connective. Conjunctions can be used to indicate:

- cause, such as *because, therefore*
- opposition, such as *however*
- addition, such as *furthermore*
- time, such as *later*.

A **connective** is a word or phrase used to link the different parts of a text, such as clauses, sentences, paragraphs or chapters. They maintain the cohesiveness of the text. Connectives can be:

- conjunctions, such as *and, but*
- adverbs, such as *finally*
- prepositional expressions, such as *in other words*
- pronouns, such as *he, they*.

If you use too many simple conjunctions in your writing, it can become monotonous: ***then** he did that **and** she did this **so** he went **and**...* You can use other connectives which make the relationships between your ideas clearer. Try using conjunctions such as "when", "before", "because", "as", "if", "whether", "although" and "while" in your sentences. For example, instead of *He was tired and went to bed,* you could say *As he was tired, he went to bed.*

Try this

Make up eight answers to this question, each containing a different conjunction.
Are you coming out this evening?

Prepositions

A **preposition** shows the relationship of one noun to another. The most common ones are:

after	between	off	to
around	by	on	under
at	from	over	up
beside	in	through	with

Certain words always take the same preposition:
different ***from*** (not "than" or "to")
I live ***in*** *Southampton* (not "at")
We went ***to*** *Manchester* (not "up" or "over")

Interjections

An **interjection** is the only part of speech that stands alone, grammatically unconnected with the words around it. Examples are:

Hello.	Alas!	Pooh!	Encore!
Ha ha!	Oh!	Wow!	Hear, hear!
Hurray!	Phew!	Hush!	Whoops!

Terms used in this dictionary

antonym
A word meaning the opposite of another word.
For example, **strong** is an antonym of **weak**.

formal
Likely to be used in writing and official language rather than in everyday speech.
See entries for **adjacent**, **resolute**.

homonym
1 A word that has the same spelling but a different meaning as another word, such as **right** meaning correct, and **right** meaning opposite of left (also called **homograph**).
2 A word that sounds the same as another but is spelled differently, such as **hare** and **hair**.

informal
Used in everyday speech but not in serious speech or official language.
See entries for **awesome**, **telly**.

literary
Used in traditional stories, poetry and songs.
See entries for **rove**, **slay**.

plural noun
Not generally used in the singular form.
See entries for **trousers**, **pyjamas**.

phrase
For words used together, often with a non-literal meaning, such as **on the other hand**.

prefix
A letter or group of letters added at the beginning of a word or root to form a new word.
See entries for **centi-**, **trans-**.

suffix
A letter or group of letters, such as **-ology** or **-graph**, added at the end of a word or root to form a new word.

comparative
The form of an adjective or adverb used when two things are being compared, such as **better** or **worse**.

superlative
The form of an adjective or adverb used to show that something is at the extreme when *more than two* things are being compared, such as **best** or **worst**.

synonym
A word having the same or similar meaning to another word.
For example, **brainy** and **clever** are synonyms of **intelligent**.

trademark
The name of a particular product.
See entries for **Rollerblade**, **Velcro**.

a an
INDEFINITE ARTICLE **1** "a" is used mostly before words beginning with a consonant. *A dog ate a bone.*
2 "an" is used mostly before words beginning with a vowel. *An elephant ate an apple.*

aback
ADVERB If you are taken aback, you are very surprised.

abacus abacuses
NOUN a frame with beads that slide along rods, used for counting.

abandon abandons abandoning abandoned
VERB If you abandon someone or something, you leave them or give them up for good. *The sailors abandoned the sinking ship.*

Synonyms: desert, forsake, leave

abattoir abattoirs
Said "**ab**-a-twah" NOUN a place where animals are killed for meat.

abbey abbeys
NOUN a church with buildings attached to it in which monks or nuns live and worship God.

abbot abbots
NOUN the monk or priest in charge of an abbey or monastery.

abbreviate abbreviates abbreviating abbreviated
VERB to write something in a shorter form.

abbreviation abbreviations
NOUN a short form of a word or phrase. *EU is an abbreviation of the European Union.*

abdicate abdicates abdicating abdicated
VERB If a king or queen abdicates, they give up being on the throne.
abdication NOUN

abdomen abdomens
NOUN the front part of your body below your chest, containing your stomach and intestines; your belly.
abdominal ADJECTIVE

abduct abducts abducting abducted
VERB to take someone away by force, to kidnap.
abduction NOUN

abide abides abiding abided
VERB **1** If you abide by the rules, you accept them and behave properly.
2 If you can't abide something, you dislike it very much.

ability abilities
NOUN the intelligence or skill needed to do something: *the ability to get on with others; children of mixed abilities.*

Synonyms: capability, proficiency, skill

ablaze
ADJECTIVE on fire.

able
ADJECTIVE **1** If you are able to do something, you can do it.
2 Someone who is able is very clever or talented.

abnormal
ADJECTIVE not normal or usual.
abnormally ADVERB **abnormality** NOUN

aboard
PREPOSITION OR ADVERB on a ship or plane.

abolish abolishes abolishing abolished
VERB to do away with something: *the campaign to abolish hunting.*

Synonyms: eliminate, end

abolition
NOUN the act of a government in doing away with something: *the abolition of the death penalty.*

abominable
ADJECTIVE very unpleasant or shocking.
abominably ADVERB

Aborigine Aborigines
Said "ab-or-**rij**-in-ee" NOUN the people who lived in Australia before Europeans arrived, and their descendants.
Aboriginal ADJECTIVE

abort aborts aborting aborted
VERB If a plan or activity is aborted, it is stopped before it is finished.

abortion abortions
NOUN If a woman has an abortion, her pregnancy is ended deliberately.

abound abounds abounding abounded
VERB If things abound, there are very large numbers of them.

about
PREPOSITION OR ADVERB **1** of or concerning: *a book about London.*
2 approximately, not exactly: *about two o'clock.*
ADVERB **3** in different directions. *The dogs ran about in the garden.*
ADJECTIVE **4** present or in a place. *Is Jane about?*
PHRASE **5** If you are **about to** do something, you are just going to do it. *He was about to leave.*

above
PREPOSITION OR ADVERB **1** directly over or higher than something.
2 greater than something in level or amount: *above freezing point.*

Antonym: below

abrasion abrasions
NOUN an area where your skin has been broken.

The letter A began as a picture of an ox head. Look at A upside down.

abrasive
ADJECTIVE **1** An abrasive substance is rough and can be used to clean hard surfaces.
2 someone who is abrasive is unpleasant and rude.

abreast
ADJECTIVE side by side.

abridge **abridges abridging abridged**
VERB To abridge a piece of writing means to make it shorter.
abridged ADJECTIVE **abridgement** NOUN

abroad
ADVERB in a foreign country.

abrupt
ADJECTIVE **1** sudden and quick.
2 impolite, sharply spoken and unfriendly.
abruptly ADVERB **abruptness** NOUN

abscess **abscesses**
Said "**ab**-sess" NOUN a painful, infected swelling.

abseil **abseils abseiling abseiled**
Said "**ab**-sayl" VERB to go down a cliff, mountain or tall building by sliding down a rope in a special harness.

absent
ADJECTIVE not present in a place or situation.
absence NOUN

absentee **absentees**
NOUN someone who is not present when they should be.

absent-minded
ADJECTIVE forgetful.
absent-mindedly ADVERB
absent-mindedness NOUN

absolute
ADJECTIVE total and complete.

absolutely
ADVERB totally, completely.

absorb **absorbs absorbing absorbed**
VERB If something absorbs a liquid or gas, it soaks the liquid or gas up.
absorption NOUN

absorbent
ADJECTIVE Something which is absorbent soaks up liquid easily.
absorbency NOUN

abstain **abstains abstaining abstained**
VERB If you abstain from something, you do not do it or have it. *I abstained from voting.*
abstention NOUN **abstainer** NOUN

Synonyms: forbear, keep from, refrain

abstract
ADJECTIVE based on thoughts and ideas rather than physical objects or events.

Antonym: concrete

absurd
ADJECTIVE ridiculous and stupid.
absurdly ADVERB **absurdity** NOUN

Synonyms: ludicrous, preposterous, ridiculous

abundance
NOUN Something that exists in abundance exists in large amounts or numbers.

Synonyms: plenty, profusion

abundant
ADJECTIVE existing in large amounts or numbers, plentiful.
abundantly ADVERB

abuse **abuses abusing abused**
Said "ab-**yoos**" NOUN **1** cruel physical treatment of someone.
2 rude and unkind remarks directed towards someone.
3 misuse of something: *the abuse of power; alcohol abuse.*
Said "ab-**yooze**" VERB **4** to treat cruelly.
5 to speak insultingly to someone.
6 to use something wrongly or for a bad purpose.

Synonyms: (sense 1) ill-treatment, injury, maltreatment

abusive
ADJECTIVE rude and insulting.
abusively ADVERB

abysmal
Said "ab-**biz**-mul" ADJECTIVE very bad indeed.
abysmally ADVERB

abyss **abysses**
NOUN a very deep hole.

academic
ADJECTIVE **1** Academic work is work done in a school, college or university.
2 of no real importance, theoretical. *She had passed her exam – her actual mark was academic.*
academically ADVERB

academy **academies**
NOUN a school or college, usually one that specializes in one particular subject.

accelerate **accelerates accelerating accelerated**
VERB to speed up.

acceleration
NOUN the rate at which the speed of something increases.

accelerator **accelerators**
NOUN a pedal you press to make something go faster.

accent **accents**
NOUN **1** the way a language is pronounced. *She spoke with an Australian accent.*
2 a mark placed above or below a letter in some languages, which affects the way it is pronounced. *The word "café" has an accent on the last letter.*

 ► *Ab seil* in German means down rope. Many English words come directly from foreign words.

accentuate **accentuates accentuating accentuated**
VERB To accentuate a feature of something is to make it more noticeable.

accept **accepts accepting accepted**
VERB **1** If you accept something, you say yes to it or take it from someone.
2 If you accept a situation, you realize that it cannot be changed.
3 If you accept a statement or story, you believe it is true.
4 If a group accepts you, they treat you as one of the group.
acceptance NOUN

acceptable
ADJECTIVE good enough to be accepted.
acceptability NOUN

access **accesses accessing accessed**
NOUN **1** the right or opportunity to use something or to enter a place.
VERB **2** If you access information from a computer, you find it.

accessible
ADJECTIVE easily reached or obtained.
accessibility NOUN

accession
NOUN the time when a king or queen begins their reign.

accessory **accessories**
NOUN an extra part or item.

accident **accidents**
NOUN **1** an unexpected event in which something unfortunate happens.
PHRASE **2** Something that happens **by accident** happens without being intended.

accidental
ADJECTIVE happening by chance, not deliberate.
accidentally ADVERB

Synonyms: inadvertent, unintentional, unplanned

acclaim **acclaims acclaiming acclaimed**
VERB **1** FORMAL to praise someone or something a lot.
NOUN **2** great praise.
acclamation NOUN

accommodate **accommodates accommodating accommodated**
VERB **1** If you accommodate someone, you provide them with a place to sleep, live or work.
2 If a place can accommodate a number of things or people, it has enough room for them.
✔ *Accommodate* has two *c*s and two *m*s.

accommodation
NOUN somewhere for someone to stay or live.

accompany **accompanies accompanying accompanied**
VERB **1** If you accompany someone, you go with them.
2 If one thing accompanies another, the two things go together. *The pain was accompanied by fever.*
3 to play an instrument with another person who is singing or playing the main part of the music.
accompanying ADJECTIVE **accompanist** NOUN

accomplice **accomplices**
NOUN a person who helps someone else to commit a crime.

accomplish **accomplishes accomplishing accomplished**
VERB If you accomplish something, you succeed in doing it.

accomplished
ADJECTIVE very talented at something.

accomplishment **accomplishments**
NOUN an achievement, something done well.

accord
NOUN **1** agreement.
PHRASE **2** If you do something **of your own accord**, you do it willingly.

accordingly
ADVERB **1** in a suitable way. *The actress changed her costume, and her character changed accordingly.*
2 therefore. *Our bus was delayed, and accordingly we missed the first act.*

according to
PREPOSITION **1** If something is true according to a particular person, that person says it is true.
2 If something is done according to a plan, that plan is used as the basis for it.

accordion **accordions**
NOUN a box-like musical instrument you squeeze in and out while pressing keys.

account **accounts accounting accounted**
NOUN **1** a written or spoken report of something.
2 If you have a bank account, you can leave money in the bank and take it out when you need it.
PLURAL NOUN **3** Accounts are records of money spent and received by a person or business.
VERB **4** To account for something is to explain it. *It's her birthday, which accounts for her excited behaviour.*
PHRASE **5** If you **take something into account**, you consider it.
6 **On account of** means because of.

accountant **accountants**
NOUN a person who keeps or inspects financial accounts.

accumulate **accumulates accumulating accumulated**
VERB to collect or gather over a period of time. *Dead leaves accumulate on the ground in the autumn. We accumulated a lot of drawings over the year.*
accumulation NOUN

Accumulate comes from *cumulus*, the Latin word for a heap. Cumulus clouds are big and fluffy.

accurate
ADJECTIVE completely correct or precise.
accurately ADVERB **accuracy** NOUN

accusation **accusations**
NOUN **1** the act of accusing someone.
2 the charge brought against someone who is accused of an offence.

accuse **accuses accusing accused**
VERB If you accuse someone of doing something wrong, you say they have done it.
accuser NOUN

accustomed
ADJECTIVE If you are accustomed to something, you are used to it.

ace **aces**
NOUN **1** a playing card with a single symbol on it.
2 in tennis, a serve that the other player cannot return.
ADJECTIVE **3** INFORMAL good or skilful.

ache **aches aching ached**
VERB to feel a continuous dull pain.
ache NOUN

achieve **achieves achieving achieved**
VERB to do something successfully or to cause it to happen.
achievement NOUN
✔ The *i* comes before the *e* in *achieve*.

Synonyms: accomplish, attain, fulfil

acid **acids**
NOUN **1** a chemical substance that turns litmus paper red. Strong acids can damage skin, cloth and metal.
ADJECTIVE **2** acid tastes are sharp or sour.
acidic ADJECTIVE

Antonym: alkali

acid rain
NOUN rain polluted by acid in the atmosphere which has come from factories, power stations, car exhausts, etc. It can damage buildings and may kill plants and fish.

acknowledge **acknowledges acknowledging acknowledged**
VERB **1** If you acknowledge something, you admit it is true.
2 If you acknowledge a message, you tell the sender you have received it.
acknowledgment or **acknowledgement** NOUN

Synonyms: (sense 1) accept, admit, grant

acne
Said "**ak**-nee" NOUN lumpy spots on the face and neck.

acorn **acorns**
NOUN the fruit of the oak tree, an oval nut in a cup-shaped base.

acoustic
Said "a-**koo**-stik" ADJECTIVE **1** relating to sound or hearing.
2 an acoustic guitar is not made louder through an amplifier.

acoustics
PLURAL NOUN The acoustics of a room are its structural features, which are responsible for how clearly you can hear sounds made in it.

acquaintance **acquaintances**
NOUN someone you know slightly but not well.

acquainted
ADJECTIVE having knowledge of someone or something.

acquire **acquires acquiring acquired**
VERB to obtain something.
acquisition NOUN

acquit **acquits acquitting acquitted**
VERB To acquit someone is to find them not guilty in a court.
acquittal NOUN

acre **acres**
NOUN a unit for measuring areas of land. One acre is 4840 square yards, 4047 square metres, or 0·4 of a hectare.

acrobat **acrobats**
NOUN an entertainer who performs gymnastic tricks.
acrobatic ADJECTIVE **acrobatically** ADVERB
acrobatics PLURAL NOUN
[from Greek *akrobatos* meaning walking on tiptoe]

acronym **acronyms**
NOUN a word made up of the initial letters of a phrase, for example, *scuba* comes from "self-contained underwater breathing apparatus", as in scuba diving.

across
PREPOSITION OR ADVERB from one side of something to another.

acrostic **acrostics**
NOUN **1** a number of lines of writing, such as poem, where the first letter of the first word in each new line forms a word, proverb, etc.
2 a word puzzle such as a crossword.

acrylic **acrylics**
Said "a-**kril**-ik" NOUN a type of man-made cloth or paint.

act **acts acting acted**
VERB **1** to do something. *The barn's caught fire, we must act quickly.*
2 to behave in a particular way. *Stop acting daft!*
3 to perform a role in a play or film.
NOUN **4** a single thing which someone does: *an act of kindness.*
5 An Act of Parliament is a law passed by the government.

Synonyms: (sense 4) action, deed
(sense 5) bill, decree, law

► Well-known acronyms include "laser", "radar" and "PIN" number. Find out what they stand for.

action actions
NOUN **1** a physical movement.
2 something you do for a particular purpose or occasion. *Her swift action prevented the fire from spreading.*

activate activates activating activated
VERB to make something start working.

active
ADJECTIVE An active person is full of energy and does a lot of things.
actively ADVERB

Antonym: passive

THE ACTIVE VOICE
When information is written in the **active voice** the subject of the verb is doing the action:
The boy kicked the ball.
Also look at the grammar box at **passive**.

activist activists
NOUN An activist is a person who tries to bring about change for a particular cause, such as politics or environmental issues.

activity activities
NOUN **1** lots of things happening at the same time.
2 something you do. *Making pottery was his favourite activity.*

actor actors
NOUN a man or woman who performs in plays or films.

actress actresses
NOUN a woman who performs in plays or films.

actual
ADJECTIVE real, not made up or guessed at.
actually ADVERB

acupuncture
NOUN the ancient Far Eastern treatment of illness or pain by sticking small needles into specific places in a person's body.

acute
ADJECTIVE **1** severe or intense: *an acute pain.*
2 An acute angle is one that is less than 90°.
3 In French, an acute accent is a forward-sloping line over a vowel to indicate a change in pronunciation, as in the word "café". See **obtuse**, **reflex**.

AD
You use AD in dates to indicate the number of years after the birth of Jesus Christ.

adamant
ADJECTIVE determined not to change your mind.
adamantly ADVERB

Adam's apple
NOUN the larynx, a lump that sticks out at the front of men's necks.

adapt adapts adapting adapted
VERB **1** If you adapt to a new situation, you change so you can deal with it successfully.
2 If you adapt something, you change it so it is suitable for a new purpose or situation.
adaptable ADJECTIVE **adaptation** NOUN

adaptor adaptors; also spelt **adapter**
NOUN a type of electric plug which can be used to connect two or more plugs to one socket.

add adds adding added
VERB **1** In mathematics if you add numbers together, you count them up to get the total.
2 If you add one thing to another, you put them together.

adder adders
NOUN a small poisonous snake.

addict addicts
NOUN a person who cannot stop doing or taking something, often used when referring to something harmful.
addicted ADJECTIVE **addiction** NOUN

addictive
ADJECTIVE If a drug or drink is addictive, the people who take it cannot give it up.

addition additions
NOUN **1** In mathematics, addition is the process of adding numbers together.
2 something that has been added to something else: *a last-minute addition.*

Synonyms: (sense 2) extra, supplement

additional
ADJECTIVE extra, more, added on.
additionally ADVERB

additive additives
NOUN an ingredient which is added to something else.

address addresses addressing addressed
NOUN **1** the written location of a particular place.
2 an e-mail address is the location of a computer site on the World Wide Web.
VERB **3** To address a letter is to write the name and location of the recipient on it.
4 If you address a group of people, you give a speech to them.

adenoids
PLURAL NOUN the two soft lumps of tissue at the back of your throat.

adequate
ADJECTIVE sufficient, enough.
adequately ADVERB **adequacy** NOUN

adhere adheres adhering adhered
VERB to stick firmly to something.
adherence NOUN

adhesive adhesives
NOUN a substance that sticks things together, such as glue.

AD is short for the Latin phrase *anno Domini* meaning in the year of Our Lord.

a b c d e f g h i j k l m n o p q r s t u v w x y z

adjacent
Said "ad-**jay**-sent" ADJECTIVE adjacent things are positioned next to each other.

adjective **adjectives**
NOUN a word that describes a noun. For example, in "they live in a large white house", "large" and "white" are both adjectives.
adjectival ADJECTIVE

ADJECTIVES
Adjectives are sometimes called describing words.
They may indicate how many:
three men, some fish.
They may describe feelings or qualities:
a happy child, a strange girl.
They may describe size, age, measurement:
a huge marrow, an old coat.
They may indicate colour:
red socks, dark hair.
They may describe nationality or origin:
my Indian cousin, a northern accent.
They may indicate what something is made of:
a wooden box.

adjourn **adjourns adjourning adjourned**
VERB If a meeting or trial is adjourned, it stops for a time.
adjournment NOUN

adjust **adjusts adjusting adjusted**
VERB **1** If you adjust something, you change its position or alter it in some other way.
2 If you adjust to a new situation, you get used to it.
adjustment NOUN **adjustable** ADJECTIVE

ad-lib **ad-libs ad-libbing ad-libbed**
VERB to say something that has not been prepared beforehand. *I use a script on TV but ad-lib on radio.*
ad-lib NOUN

administer **administers administering administered**
VERB **1** To administer an organization is to be responsible for managing it.
2 To administer the law or justice is to put it into practice.
3 To administer a medicine is to give it to someone.
administrator NOUN **administrative** ADJECTIVE

administration
NOUN the work of organizing and supervising an organization.

admirable
ADJECTIVE very good, deserving to be admired.
admirably ADVERB

admiral **admirals**
NOUN the highest ranking commander of a navy.

admire **admires admiring admired**
VERB to respect and approve of something or someone.
admiration NOUN **admirer** NOUN
admiring ADJECTIVE **admiringly** ADVERB

admission **admissions**
NOUN **1** If you are granted admission to a place, you are allowed to go in.
2 a confession or reluctant agreement that something is true.

admit **admits admitting admitted**
VERB **1** to allow someone or something to enter a place or organization.
2 to confess or agree reluctantly that something is true.

admittance
NOUN the right to enter a place.

adolescent **adolescents**
NOUN a young person who is no longer a child but who is not yet an adult.
adolescence NOUN

adopt **adopts adopting adopted**
VERB **1** When someone adopts a child they take them into their family as a son or daughter.
2 FORMAL If you adopt a particular attitude, you start to behave with that attitude.
adoption NOUN

adorable
ADJECTIVE sweet, attractive and worthy of love.

adore **adores adoring adored**
VERB If you adore someone, you feel deep love and admiration for them.
adoration NOUN **adoring** ADJECTIVE

adorn **adorns adorning adorned**
VERB to decorate. *The church is adorned with flowers.*
adornment NOUN

adrenalin or **adrenaline**
Said "a-**dren**-al-in" NOUN a substance which is produced by your body when you are angry, scared or excited, and which makes your heart beat faster.

adrift
ADJECTIVE OR ADVERB floating on water without being controlled.

adult **adults**
NOUN a mature and fully developed human or other animal.
adult ADJECTIVE **adulthood** NOUN

adultery
NOUN sexual intercourse between a married person and someone they are not married to.

advance **advances advancing advanced**
VERB **1** to move forward.
NOUN **2** progress in something. *Steam power was a great scientific advance.*
ADJECTIVE **3** happening before an event. *The show received little advance publicity.*
PHRASE **4** If you do something **in advance** you do it before something else happens.

advanced
ADJECTIVE being ahead or at a high level in knowledge or technology, etc.

► A is an Anglo-Saxon prefix meaning on, in, at: for example, abed, aboard, around, asleep, apiece.

advantage advantages
NOUN **1** a benefit or something that puts you in a better position.
PHRASE **2** If you **take advantage of** someone, you treat them unfairly for your own benefit.
3 If you **take advantage of** something, you make use of it.
advantageous ADJECTIVE

Advent
NOUN the season just before Christmas in the Christian calendar.

adventure adventures
NOUN a series of events that are unusual and exciting.
adventurous ADJECTIVE

adverb adverbs
NOUN a word that adds information about a verb or a following adjective or other adverb. For example, "slowly", "now", and "here", which say how, when or where something is done.
[from Latin *adverbium* meaning added word]

ADVERBS
Many adverbs end with the letters -ly, but this is not always the case.
Adverbs of manner answer the question "How?"
She runs quickly.
Adverbs of place answer the question "Where?"
He travelled northwards.
Adverbs of time answer the question "When?"
You must answer soon.
They arrived yesterday.
Adverbs of degree answer the question "To what extent?"
I almost caught the bus.
She quite likes her new teacher.
Adverbs of frequency answer the question "How often?"
We sometimes play hockey.
He never answers my questions.

adverse
ADJECTIVE unfavourable, opposite to what you want or need: *adverse weather conditions.*
adversely ADVERB

adversity adversities
NOUN a time of danger or difficulty.

advert adverts
NOUN; INFORMAL an advertisement.

advertise advertises advertising advertised
VERB to tell people about something through a newspaper, poster, on television or radio, or via the Internet.
advertising NOUN **advertiser** NOUN

advertisement advertisements
Said "ad-**ver**-tiz-ment" NOUN an announcement about something in a newspaper, on a poster, on television or radio, or on the Internet.

Synonyms: ad, advert, commercial

advice
NOUN a suggestion from someone about what you should do.

Synonyms: counsel, guidance, suggestion

advisable
ADJECTIVE sensible and likely to achieve the result you want.
advisably ADVERB **advisability** NOUN

advise advises advising advised
VERB to suggest to someone that they should act in a certain way.
adviser NOUN **advisory** ADJECTIVE

Synonyms: counsel, recommend, suggest

advocate advocates advocating advocated
VERB **1** to be in favour of something publicly. *Caesar advocated the reform of the Roman laws.*
NOUN **2** someone who speaks for someone or in favour of something.

aerial aerials
Said "**air**-ee-al" ADJECTIVE **1** happening in the air: *aerial combat.*
NOUN **2** a wire or device for receiving television or radio signals.

aero-
PREFIX relating to the air or to flight.

aerobatics
NOUN skilful movements by a small aeroplane, for example diving and making loops.
aerobatic ADJECTIVE

aerobics
NOUN a type of fast physical exercise which increases the amount of oxygen in your blood and strengthens your heart and lungs.
aerobic ADJECTIVE

aeroplane aeroplanes
NOUN a flying vehicle with an engine, wings and a tail.

aerosol aerosols
NOUN a small metal container in which liquid is kept under pressure so that it can be forced out as a spray.

aerospace
ADJECTIVE involved in making and designing aircraft or spacecraft.

aesthetic
Said "eess-**thet**-ik" ADJECTIVE; FORMAL relating to the appreciation of beauty or art.

affair affairs
NOUN **1** an event or series of events. *The wedding was a quiet affair.*
2 a romantic relationship between two people, often secret.
PLURAL NOUN **3** Your affairs are your private and personal life.

affect affects affecting affected
VERB to influence or change something or somebody else.

Adverbs end "-lly" only if the original adjective ends with "l": faithfully, really BUT sincerely, clearly. ◀

affection affections
NOUN a feeling of fondness or love for someone.

affectionate
ADJECTIVE full of fondness or love for someone.
affectionately ADVERB

afflict afflicts afflicting afflicted
VERB If something afflicts someone, they suffer from it. *She was afflicted by depression.*
affliction NOUN

affluent
ADJECTIVE having a lot of money and possessions.
affluence NOUN

afford affords affording afforded
VERB **1** If you can afford something, you have enough money to pay for it.
2 If you cannot afford something to happen, it would be harmful to you if it happened. *We can't afford to waste any more time.*

afloat
ADVERB OR ADJECTIVE floating on water.

afraid
ADJECTIVE **1** frightened.
2 worried, concerned.

Synonyms: (sense 1) fearful, scared
(sense 2) anxious

aft
ADVERB OR ADJECTIVE towards the back of a ship or boat.

after
PREPOSITION **1** later than a particular time or event.
2 following someone or something. *The police ran after him.*
after ADVERB

afternoon afternoons
NOUN the part of the day between 12 noon and about six o'clock.

afterwards
ADVERB after an event, date or time.

again
ADVERB **1** happening one more time.
2 returning to the same state or place as before. *Her back began to hurt again.*

against
PREPOSITION **1** touching or leaning on. *He propped the ladder against the wall.*
2 in opposition to: *the match against the USA.*

age ages ageing or aging aged
NOUN **1** the length of time someone or something has existed: *a boy ten years of age.*
2 the quality of being old. *Wine improves with age.*
3 a particular period in history: *the Iron Age.*
PLURAL NOUN **4** INFORMAL a very long time. *She's been ages.*
VERB **5** to grow old or to appear older.
✔ *Ageing* and *aging* are both correct spellings.

aged
*Rhymes with "***raged***"* ADJECTIVE **1** having a particular age: *people aged 16 to 24.*
*Said "***ay***-jid"* **2** very old: *an aged lady.*

agency agencies
NOUN an organization or business which provides certain services: *a detective agency.*

agenda agendas
NOUN a list of items to be discussed at a meeting.

agent agents
NOUN **1** someone who arranges work or travel for other people.
2 a secret agent is a spy.

aggravate aggravates aggravating aggravated
VERB **1** to make a situation or injury worse.
2 INFORMAL If someone or something aggravates you, they make you annoyed.
aggravating ADJECTIVE **aggravation** NOUN

aggregate aggregates
NOUN a total that is made up of several smaller amounts.

aggression
NOUN violent and hostile behaviour.

aggressive
ADJECTIVE full of hostility and violence.
aggressively ADVERB

aghast
*Said "a-***garst***"* ADJECTIVE shocked and horrified.

agile
ADJECTIVE able to move quickly and easily.
agilely ADVERB **agility** NOUN

agitate agitates agitating agitated
VERB **1** to upset or disturb someone.
2 to move or shake something vigorously.
agitated ADJECTIVE **agitation** NOUN

agnostic agnostics
NOUN a person who believes we cannot know definitely whether God exists or not. See **atheist**.
agnostic ADJECTIVE **agnosticism** NOUN

ago
ADVERB in the past. *I bought this bike three years ago.*

agony
NOUN very great physical or mental pain.
agonizing ADJECTIVE

Synonyms: pain, suffering, torment

agree agrees agreeing agreed
VERB **1** to have the same opinion as someone else.
2 If you agree to do something, you mean that you will do it.

agreeable
ADJECTIVE **1** prepared to say yes. *She was agreeable to the idea.*
2 pleasant. *The climate was agreeable.*

▶ "A" before a word beginning with a vowel becomes "an": for example, an agency, an umbrella.

agreement agreements
NOUN 1 a situation where people agree.
2 a document that confirms a formal arrangement.

agriculture
NOUN farming.
agricultural ADJECTIVE

aground
ADVERB If a boat runs aground, it becomes stuck in a shallow stretch of water.

ahead
ADVERB 1 in front.
2 more advanced than someone or something else. *Our research is ahead of everyone else's.*
3 in the future. *We must plan ahead.*

aid aids
NOUN 1 money, equipment, or services provided for people in need.
2 help or support: *the aid of experts.*
3 something that makes a task easier: *visual aids.*
aid VERB

AIDS
NOUN a disease which destroys the body's natural resistance to diseases. AIDS is an abbreviation for Acquired Immune Deficiency Syndrome.

ailing
ADJECTIVE sick or ill, and not getting better.

ailment ailments
NOUN a minor illness.

aim aims aiming aimed
VERB 1 If you aim an object or weapon, you point it at someone or something.
2 If you aim to do something, you plan or hope to do it.
NOUN 3 Your aim is what you intend to achieve.

aimless
ADJECTIVE having no clear purpose or plan.
aimlessly ADVERB **aimlessness** NOUN

air
NOUN 1 the mixture of oxygen and other gases which we breathe and which forms the earth's atmosphere.
2 a mood, feeling or impression: *an air of mystery.*
PHRASE 3 **by air** refers to air travel.

airborne
ADJECTIVE in the air and flying.

air-conditioning
NOUN a system of providing cool, clean air in buildings.
air-conditioned ADJECTIVE

aircraft
NOUN any vehicle which can fly.

airfield airfields
NOUN an open area of ground where small aircraft take off and land.

air force air forces
NOUN the part of a country's armed services that fights using aircraft.

air gun air guns
NOUN a gun which uses air pressure to fire pellets.

airline airlines
NOUN a company which provides air travel.

airmail
NOUN the system of sending letters and parcels by air.

airman airmen
NOUN a man who serves in his country's air force.

airport airports
NOUN a place where people go to travel by air.

air raid air raids
NOUN an attack by enemy aircraft, in which bombs are dropped.

airship airships
NOUN a large, light aircraft consisting of a rigid balloon filled with gas and powered by an engine, with a passenger compartment underneath.

airtight
ADJECTIVE not letting air in or out.

airy airier airiest
ADJECTIVE full of fresh air and light.

aisle aisles
*Rhymes with "***mile***"* NOUN a long narrow gap between rows of seats or shelves that you can walk along.

ajar
ADJECTIVE A door or window that is ajar is slightly open.

alarm alarms alarming alarmed
NOUN 1 a feeling of fear and worry.
2 an automatic device used to warn people of something.
VERB 3 If something alarms you, it makes you worried and anxious.
alarming ADJECTIVE

alas
ADVERB; OLD-FASHIONED unfortunately, sadly. *Alas, sir, the dog ate my homework.*

albatross albatrosses
NOUN a large white sea bird.

albino albinos
NOUN a human or other animal with very white skin, white hair and pink eyes.

album albums
NOUN 1 a book for displaying things such as photographs or stamps.
2 a CD, cassette or record with a number of songs on it.

alcohol
NOUN drink that can make people drunk.

What's wrong: my cat am poorly; that are a great bike. Make sure your nouns and verbs agree.

a b c d e f g h i j k l m n o p q r s t u v w x y z

A B C D E F G H I J K L M N O P Q R S T U V W X Y Z

alcoholic alcoholics
ADJECTIVE **1** If a drink is alcoholic, it contains alcohol.
NOUN **2** someone who is addicted to alcohol.
alcoholism NOUN

alcove alcoves
NOUN an area of a room which is set back slightly from the main part.

ale ales
NOUN a type of beer.

alert alerts alerting alerted
ADJECTIVE **1** paying full attention to what is happening. *The criminal was spotted by an alert member of the public.*
NOUN **2** a situation in which people prepare for danger. *The troops were on war alert.*
VERB **3** to warn someone of a problem or danger.
alertness NOUN

Synonyms: (sense 1) vigilant, watchful

algae
Said "**al**-jee" PLURAL NOUN moss-like plants that grow in water or on damp surfaces.

algebra
NOUN the branch of mathematics in which symbols and letters are used instead of numbers to express relationships between quantities.
algebraic ADJECTIVE

alias aliases
Said "**ay**-lee-ass" NOUN a false or alternative name. *The crook used an alias on his passport.*

alibi alibis
Said "**al**-li-bye" NOUN evidence proving you were somewhere else when a crime was committed.

alien aliens
Said "**ay**-lee-an" NOUN **1** a fictional creature from outer space.
2 someone who is not a citizen of the country where they live.
ADJECTIVE **3** not part of one's normal experience: *a totally alien culture.*

alight alights alighting alighted
ADJECTIVE **1** burning.
VERB **2** FORMAL to get out of a vehicle at the end of a journey.
3 to land on. *The bird alighted on the branch.*

alike
ADJECTIVE **1** very similar.
ADVERB **2** If people or things are treated alike, they are treated in the same way.

alive
ADJECTIVE living.

alkali alkalis
Said "**al**-kal-eye" NOUN a chemical substance that turns litmus paper blue.
alkaline ADJECTIVE **alkalinity** NOUN

Antonym: acid

all
ADJECTIVE, PRONOUN, OR ADVERB the whole of something, everything.

Allah
NOUN the Muslim name for God.

allege alleges alleging alleged
Said "a-**lej**" VERB If you allege something, you say it is true but do not provide any proof. *It is alleged that you were at the scene of the robbery.*
allegation NOUN **alleged** ADJECTIVE
allegedly ADVERB

allegiance allegiances
Said "al-**lee**-jenss" NOUN loyal support for a person or organization.

allegory allegories
Said "**al**-lig-or-ee" NOUN a piece of writing in which the events or characters are symbols for a hidden meaning.
allegorical ADJECTIVE

allergic
ADJECTIVE If you are allergic to something, you become ill when you eat it or touch it.

allergy allergies
Said "**al**-er-jee" NOUN A sensitivity someone has to something, which makes them ill.

alley alleys
NOUN a narrow passage between buildings.

alliance alliances
NOUN a group of people, organizations or countries working together for similar aims.

Synonyms: association, league, union

alligator alligators
NOUN a large amphibious animal, similar to a crocodile.
[from Spanish *el lagarto* meaning the lizard]

alliteration
NOUN; LITERARY the use of several words together which all begin with the same sound, for example, "the forest's ferny floor".
alliterative ADJECTIVE

allotment allotments
NOUN a piece of land which someone rents to grow vegetables on.

allow allows allowing allowed
VERB **1** to permit.
2 to set aside something for a particular purpose. *Allow four hours for the paint to dry.*
allowable ADJECTIVE

allowance allowances
NOUN **1** money given regularly to someone for a particular purpose: *a clothing allowance.*
PHRASE **2** If you **make allowances** for something you take it into consideration.

alloy alloys
NOUN a mixture of two or more metals.

► Many poets use alliteration by repeating an initial consonant several times. ◄

all right or **alright**
ADJECTIVE **1** satisfactory, but not especially good.
2 safe and not harmed.
3 You say "all right" to agree to something.

ally **allies**
NOUN a person or country that helps and supports another.
ally VERB **allied** ADJECTIVE

Synonyms: friend, helper, partner

almighty
ADJECTIVE **1** very great or serious.
NOUN **2** The Almighty is another name for God.

almond **almonds**
NOUN a pale brown oval nut.

almost
ADVERB very nearly.

Synonyms: just about, virtually, practically

alone
ADJECTIVE OR ADVERB not with others.

along
PREPOSITION **1** running the length of something: *along the road.*
ADVERB **2** moving forward. *We marched along.*
3 with. *Bring it along.*

alongside
PREPOSITION OR ADVERB beside, next to.

aloof
ADJECTIVE distant from other people, unwilling to get involved.

aloud
ADVERB When you read or speak aloud, you speak loudly enough for other people to hear you.

alphabet **alphabets**
NOUN a formal arrangement of all the letters in a language.
[from *alpha* + *beta*, the first two letters of the Greek alphabet]

alphabetical
ADJECTIVE related to the order of the alphabet.
alphabetically ADVERB

already
ADVERB having happened before.

Alsatian **Alsatians**
NOUN a breed of dog, also called a German shepherd.

also
ADVERB in addition, as well.

altar **altars**
NOUN the raised table in a church or temple where religious ceremonies are performed.

alter **alters altering altered**
VERB to change.
alteration NOUN

alternate **alternates alternating alternated**
Said "**ol**-ter-nayt" VERB **1** to happen in turns. For example, if A alternates with B, the sequence is ABABAB, and so on.
Said "ol-**ter**-nut" ADJECTIVE **2** If something happens on alternate days, it happens on the first day but not the second, and happens again on the third day but not the fourth, and so on.
alternately ADVERB **alternation** NOUN

alternative **alternatives**
NOUN **1** something you can do or have instead of something else.
ADJECTIVE **2** other: *an alternative method of travel.*
alternatively ADVERB
✔ *Alternative* implies a choice between two things. For more than two, use the word *choice.*

although
CONJUNCTION in spite of the fact that. *He wasn't well-known, although he had made several films.*

altitude **altitudes**
NOUN the height of something above sea level.

altogether
ADVERB **1** entirely. *She wasn't altogether sorry to be leaving.*
2 in total (used of amounts). *You will need 3 kg of mince altogether.*

aluminium
NOUN a lightweight silvery-white metal.

always
ADVERB all the time, for ever.

am
the first person singular, present tense of **be**.

a.m.
used to specify morning times, that is, between 12 midnight and 12 noon.
[abbreviation of Latin *ante meridiem* meaning before noon]

amateur **amateurs**
NOUN someone who does something as a hobby rather than as a job.

amaze **amazes amazing amazed**
VERB to astonish or astound.
amazement NOUN

Synonyms: stun, surprise

amazing
ADJECTIVE very surprising or remarkable.
amazingly ADVERB

ambassador **ambassadors**
NOUN a person sent to a foreign country as the representative of their own government.

amber
ADJECTIVE **1** yellowish brown in colour.
NOUN **2** fossilized resin.

Repeat quickly: it took twenty talented teachers to teach him his ten times table.

A B C D E F G H I J K L M N O P Q R S T U V W X Y Z

ambiguous
ADJECTIVE A word or phrase that is ambiguous has more than one meaning.
ambiguously ADVERB **ambiguity** NOUN

ambition **ambitions**
NOUN something that you want very much to achieve. *Her ambition was to climb Everest.*

ambitious
ADJECTIVE **1** having a strong desire for success, power or wealth.
2 an ambitious plan is a large one which requires a lot of work.

amble **ambles ambling ambled**
VERB to walk slowly in a relaxed manner.

ambulance **ambulances**
NOUN a vehicle for taking sick and injured people to hospital.

ambush **ambushes ambushing ambushed**
VERB To ambush someone is to lie in wait for them and attack them.
ambush NOUN

amen
INTERJECTION a word said by Christians at the end of a prayer.
[a Hebrew word meaning truly, so be it]

amend **amends amending amended**
VERB **1** to alter slightly, especially speech or writing.
PLURAL NOUN **2** If you make amends for something bad you have done, you say you are sorry and try to make up for it.
amendment NOUN

amiable
ADJECTIVE pleasant and friendly.
amiably ADVERB **amiability** NOUN

amicable
ADJECTIVE fairly friendly, without bad feeling. *Their divorce was an amicable one.*
amicably ADVERB

amid or **amidst**
PREPOSITION surrounded by.
✔ *Amidst* is old fashioned; *amid* is more common.

ammonia
NOUN a colourless strong smelling gas or liquid used in industry, and in some hair colouring products.

ammunition
NOUN anything that can be used in fighting, particularly explosive materials such as bullets and shells.

amnesty **amnesties**
NOUN an official pardon for political or other prisoners.
[from Latin *amnestia* meaning forgetfulness]

amoeba **amoebas** or **amoebae**; also spelt **ameba**
Said "am-**mee**-ba" NOUN a tiny living organism. Amoebas consist of one cell, which reproduces by dividing into two.

among or **amongst**
PREPOSITION surrounded by, in the midst of.
✔ For more than two things, use *among(st)*. For only two things, use *between*. *Amongst* is rather old-fashioned and *among* is more often used.

amount **amounts amounting amounted**
NOUN **1** An amount of something is how much there is of it.
VERB **2** If something amounts to a particular total, all the parts of it add up to that total. *Her vocabulary amounted to only 50 words.*

Synonyms: (sense 1) extent, number, quantity

amphibian **amphibians**
NOUN an animal that lives both on land and in water, such as a frog or a newt.
amphibious ADJECTIVE

ample
ADJECTIVE enough, adequate.
amply ADVERB

amplifier **amplifiers**
NOUN a piece of equipment in a radio or stereo system which causes sounds or signals to become louder.

amplify **amplifies amplifying amplified**
VERB If you amplify a sound, you make it louder.
amplification NOUN

amputate **amputates amputating amputated**
VERB to cut off a body part in a surgical operation.
amputation NOUN

amuse **amuses amusing amused**
VERB **1** If something amuses you, you think it is funny.
2 If you amuse yourself, you find things to do which stop you from being bored.
amused ADJECTIVE **amusing** ADJECTIVE

amusement **amusements**
NOUN **1** the state of thinking something is funny.
PLURAL NOUN **2** Amusements are fairground rides or electronic machines for entertainment or gambling, such as video games and fruit machines.

an
INDEFINITE ARTICLE "An" is used instead of "a" in front of words that begin with a vowel sound: *an apple*.

anaemia
Said "a-**nee**-mee-a" NOUN a medical condition resulting from too few red cells in a person's blood. People with anaemia look pale and feel very tired.
anaemic ADJECTIVE

 ► Curiously, the word "ambulance" comes from the Latin *ambulo* meaning I walk.

anaesthetic anaesthetics
Said "an-niss-**thet**-ik" NOUN a substance given to prevent you from feeling pain. General anaesthetics put you to sleep; local anaesthetics make just one body part go numb.
anaesthetist NOUN

anagram anagrams
NOUN a word or phrase formed by changing the order of the letters of another word or phrase, for example, "astronomers" is an anagram of "moon-starers".

analogue
ADJECTIVE an analogue clock or watch has a dial and hands to measure the time. See **digital**.

analogy analogies
Said "an-**al**-o-jee" NOUN a comparison showing that two things are similar in some ways. *The teacher drew an analogy between our behaviour and a chimpanzees' tea party.*
analogous ADJECTIVE

analyse analyses analysing analysed
VERB to investigate something carefully in order to understand it or find out what it consists of.

analysis analyses
NOUN the process of investigating something to understand it or find out what it is made of.

anarchy
Said "**an**-nar-kee" NOUN a situation where nobody obeys laws or rules.

anatomy anatomies
NOUN **1** the study of the structure of the body of a human or other animal.
2 the structure of the body of a human or other animal.
anatomical ADJECTIVE **anatomically** ADVERB

ancestor ancestors
NOUN A member of your family who lived many years ago.
ancestral ADJECTIVE

Synonyms: forebear, forefather

anchor anchors
NOUN a heavy, hooked object attached to a boat by a chain and dropped into the water to keep the boat in one place.
anchor VERB

ancient
Said "**ayn**-shent" ADJECTIVE **1** existing or happening in the distant past.
2 very old or having a very long history.

and
CONJUNCTION You use "and" to link two or more words or phrases together.

anecdote anecdotes
NOUN a short, entertaining description of a person or event.
anecdotal ADJECTIVE

anemone anemones
Said "an-**em**-on-ee" NOUN a plant with red, purple or white flowers.

angel angels
NOUN Angels are believed by some people to be beautiful and good beings who live in heaven and act as messengers for God.
angelic ADJECTIVE

anger angers angering angered
NOUN **1** the strong feeling you get when you feel someone has behaved in an unfair or cruel way.
VERB **2** If something angers you, it makes you feel angry.

Synonyms: (sense 1) fury, rage, wrath
(sense 2) enrage, infuriate, madden

angle angles
NOUN **1** The distance between two straight lines that join together. Angles are measured in degrees.
2 a point of view. *He had painted the vase from all angles. She considered the matter from a financial angle.*

angler anglers
NOUN someone who fishes with a fishing rod as a hobby.
angling NOUN

Anglican Anglicans
NOUN OR ADJECTIVE a member of the Church of England or one of its associated churches throughout the world.

Anglo-Saxon Anglo-Saxons
NOUN **1** The Anglo-Saxons were people who settled in England from the 5th century AD and were dominant until the Norman invasion in 1066. They were composed of three West Germanic tribes, the Angles, Saxons and Jutes.
2 Anglo-Saxon is another name for the Old English language.

angry angrier angriest
ADJECTIVE very annoyed.
angrily ADVERB

Synonyms: enraged, furious, mad

anguish
NOUN extreme suffering.
anguished ADJECTIVE

angular
ADJECTIVE Angular things have straight lines and sharp points.

animal animals
NOUN any living being except a plant. Sometimes the word animal is used but is not meant to include humans: *animals are not allowed in this shop.*
[from Latin *anima* meaning life or soul]

animated
ADJECTIVE **1** lively and interesting.
2 An animated film is one made by creating and shooting individual frames of film, such as a cartoon.
animatedly ADVERB

animation
NOUN **1** a method of film-making based on drawings, models or computer images.
2 Someone who shows animation is lively in the way they speak.

ankle ankles
NOUN the joint which connects your foot to your leg.

annex annexes; also spelt **annexe**
NOUN an extra building which is joined to a larger main building.

annihilate annihilates annihilating annihilated
Said "an-**nye**-ill-ate" VERB to destroy completely.
annihilation NOUN

anniversary anniversaries
NOUN a date which is remembered because something special happened on that date in a previous year.

annotate annotates annotating annotated
VERB to write notes explaining or commenting on a book, document, etc.

announce announces announcing announced
VERB to tell people publicly or officially about something.
announcement NOUN

Synonyms: broadcast, make known, proclaim

announcer announcers
NOUN a person who introduces television or radio programmes, or who makes other public announcements.

annoy annoys annoying annoyed
VERB If someone or something annoys you, they make you angry or impatient.
annoyance NOUN **annoying** ADJECTIVE

Synonyms: bother, exasperate, irritate

annual annuals
ADJECTIVE **1** once a year.
NOUN **2** a book which is published in a new edition each year.
3 a plant that has a cycle of less than 12 months.
annually ADVERB

anonymous
ADJECTIVE If something is anonymous, nobody knows who is responsible for it; if someone is anonymous, nobody knows who they are. *The police received an anonymous phone call.*
anonymously ADVERB

anorak anoraks
NOUN a warm waterproof jacket, usually with a hood.

anorexia
NOUN a psychological illness in which a person refuses to eat.
anorexic ADJECTIVE OR NOUN

another
ADJECTIVE OR PRONOUN one more.

answer answers answering answered
VERB **1** to reply to someone in speech, writing or action.
NOUN **2** a reply, in any form.
3 a solution to a problem.

Synonyms: (sense 1) reply, respond, retort

ant ants
NOUN a small insect that lives in large groups.

antagonize antagonizes antagonizing antagonized; also spelt **antagonise**
VERB to make someone feel angry or bitter.

Antarctic
ADJECTIVE relating to Antarctica.

antelope antelopes
NOUN a mammal of Africa and Asia which is similar to the deer.

antenna antennae or antennas
NOUN **1** The antennae of insects are the two long, thin parts attached to their heads which they use to sense things.
2 a radio or television aerial. The plural is "antennas".

anthem anthems
NOUN a song or hymn written for a special occasion.

anther anthers
NOUN the end of a flower's stamen, where pollen matures.

anthology anthologies
NOUN a collection of writings by various authors published in one book.

anti-
PREFIX against, opposed to or opposite to something.

antibiotic antibiotics
NOUN a drug or chemical used in medicine to kill bacteria and cure infections.

anticipate anticipates anticipating anticipated
VERB If you anticipate something, you are expecting it and are prepared for it.
anticipation NOUN

anticlimax anticlimaxes
NOUN If something is an anticlimax, it disappoints you because it is not as exciting as you expected.

 ▶ Batty books: *The Unknown Woman* by Ann Onymous. Invent some others.

anticlockwise
ADJECTIVE OR ADVERB moving in the opposite direction to the hands of a clock.

antics
PLURAL NOUN funny or silly ways of behaving.

antidote antidotes
NOUN a chemical substance that acts against the effect of a poison.

antiperspirant antiperspirants
NOUN a substance you put on your skin to stop you from sweating.

antique antiques
Said "an-**teek**" NOUN 1 an object from the past that is collected because of its value or beauty.
ADJECTIVE 2 from or concerning the past: *antique furniture.*

antiseptic antiseptics
NOUN 1 a substance used to kill germs, particularly in the treatment of wounds.
ADJECTIVE 2 acting to kill germs, particularly in wounds.

antler antlers
NOUN one of the branched horns on a deer's head.

antonym antonyms
NOUN a word which means the opposite of another word, for example, "hot" is the antonym of "cold".
[from Greek *anti-* meaning opposite + *onoma* meaning name]

anus anuses
NOUN the hole between the buttocks.

anvil anvils
NOUN a heavy iron block on which hot metal is beaten into shape.

anxiety anxieties
NOUN a nervous or worried feeling.

anxious
ADJECTIVE 1 nervous or worried.
2 If you are anxious to do something, you very much want to do it.
anxiously ADVERB

any
ADJECTIVE OR PRONOUN 1 some, several. *Do you have any paperclips I could borrow?*
2 even the smallest amount. *I haven't got any.*
3 whatever, whichever. *Any type of cooking oil will do.*

anybody
PRONOUN any person.

anyhow
ADVERB 1 in any case.
2 in a careless way: *they were all shoved in anyhow.*

anyone
PRONOUN any person.

anything
PRONOUN any object, event, situation, or action.

anyway
ADVERB in any case.

anywhere
ADVERB in, at or to any place.

apart
ADVERB OR ADJECTIVE 1 When something is apart from something else, there is a space or a distance between them.
ADVERB 2 If you take something apart, you separate it into pieces.
PHRASE 3 **Apart from** means except for, or in addition to. *Apart from Jim, no one had a bat.*

apartheid
Said "ap-**par**-tide" NOUN In South Africa, apartheid was the government policy and laws which kept people of different races apart. It was abolished in 1994.
[an Afrikaans word meaning separateness]

apartment apartments
NOUN a set of rooms for living in, usually on one floor of a building.

apathy
Said "**ap**-path-ee" NOUN a state of mind in which you do not care about anything.
apathetic ADJECTIVE **apathetically** ADVERB

ape apes aping aped
NOUN 1 Apes are mammals which are closely related to man. They include chimpanzees, gorillas and gibbons.
VERB 2 If you ape someone's speech or behaviour, you imitate it.

apex apexes or apices
NOUN The apex of something is its pointed top.

aphid aphids
Said "**ay**-fid" NOUN a small insect that feeds by sucking the juices from plants.

apiece
ADVERB If people have a particular number of things apiece, they have that number each.

apologetic
ADJECTIVE showing or saying you are sorry.
apologetically ADVERB

apologize apologizes apologizing apologized; also spelt **apologise**
VERB to say you are sorry for something you have said or done.
apology NOUN

apostle apostles
NOUN The Apostles were the 12 disciples, or special followers, chosen by Christ.

apostrophe apostrophes
Said "ap-**poss**-troff-ee" NOUN a type of punctuation mark.

a b c d e f g h i j k l m n o p q r s t u v w x y z

What is the antonym of "synonym"?

THE APOSTROPHE
An apostrophe is used for two things.
First, it is used to show where letters have been omitted:
he's (he is or he has),
rock'n'roll (rock and roll)
I'm hungry (I am hungry)
Second, it is used to show who owns something:
Fiona's bag
the children's play area
To place the apostrophe correctly, ask yourself who the thing belongs to and place the apostrophe directly after the owner, for example:
the dog's kennel (the kennel of the dog)
the dogs' kennel (the kennel of the dogs)
Never use apostrophes to make plural words, for example, the plural of tomato is *tomatoes*, not tomato's.

appal appals appalling appalled
VERB If something appals you, it shocks you because it is very bad.

apparatus
NOUN the equipment used for a particular task.

apparent
ADJECTIVE **1** clear and obvious. *It was apparent that she wasn't interested.*
2 seeming real rather than definitely being real. *The expedition was an apparent failure.*
apparently ADVERB

appeal appeals appealing appealed
VERB **1** to make an urgent request.
2 If something or someone appeals to you, you find them attractive or interesting.
NOUN **3** a formal or serious request.
4 being attractive or interesting.
appealing ADJECTIVE

appear appears appearing appeared
VERB **1** to move into view.
2 If something appears to be a certain way, it seems or looks that way. *She appeared to be enjoying herself.*
3 To appear in a film, etc. is to take part in it.

appearance appearances
NOUN **1** the act of coming into sight.
2 the way someone or something looks.
3 a part in a film or show.

appendicitis
Said "app-end-i-**site**-uss" NOUN a painful illness in which a person's appendix becomes infected.

appendix appendices or appendixes
NOUN **1** a small closed tube forming part of your digestive system.
2 An appendix to a book is extra information placed after the end of the main text.
✔ The plural of the part of the body is *appendixes*. The plural of the extra section in a book is *appendices*.

appetite appetites
NOUN the desire to eat.

appetizing or **appetising**
ADJECTIVE Food that is appetizing looks and smells tasty.

applaud applauds applauding applauded
VERB **1** to clap your hands in approval or praise.
2 to praise someone's action or attitude.
applause NOUN

apple apples
NOUN a crisp, round, red or green or yellow fruit used for cooking and eating.

appliance appliances
NOUN any machine in your home used to do a job such as cleaning or cooking.

application applications
NOUN **1** a formal request for something, usually in writing.
2 The application of a rule, system or skill is the use of it in a particular situation. *Mathematics has many practical applications.*

apply applies applying applied
VERB **1** to ask for something formally, usually by writing a letter.
2 to put a rule or system into practice. *She applied her mind to the problem.*
3 to be relevant to a person or situation. *The law applies only to people living in England and Wales.*
4 to put something on to a surface. *She applied her lipstick.*

appoint appoints appointing appointed
VERB If you appoint someone to a job or position, you formally choose them for it.

appointment appointments
NOUN **1** an arrangement you have with someone to meet them.
2 The appointment of a person to do a job is the employment of that person to do it.

Synonyms: (sense 1) date, engagement, meeting

appreciate appreciates appreciating appreciated
VERB **1** to like something because of its good qualities.
2 to understand a situation or problem and know what it involves.
3 to be grateful for what someone has done for you.
appreciation NOUN

Synonyms: (sense 1) prize, rate highly, value

appreciative
ADJECTIVE grateful.
appreciatively ADVERB

apprehensive
ADJECTIVE afraid that something bad may happen.
apprehensively ADVERB

 ► Apostrophes are *only* used when a letter has been omitted or to show ownership. ◄

apprentice apprentices
NOUN a young person who works with a craftsman in order to learn a skill or trade.
apprenticeship NOUN

approach approaches approaching approached
VERB **1** to come near or nearer.
2 to tackle a situation in a particular way.
NOUN **3** a way of tackling a situation. *She used a commonsense approach.*

appropriate
ADJECTIVE suitable or acceptable for a particular situation.
appropriately ADVERB **appropriateness** NOUN

approval
NOUN **1** agreement given to a plan or request.
2 admiration. *She looked at James with approval.*

Synonyms: (sense 1) agreement, consent, permission

approve approves approving approved
VERB **1** If you approve of something or someone, you think that thing or person is acceptable or good.
2 to give formal agreement to a plan, treaty, etc.

Synonyms: (sense 2) authorize, pass, permit

approximate approximates approximating approximated
Said "app-**rox**-i-mut" ADJECTIVE **1** nearly exact.
Said "app-**rox**-i-mate" VERB **2** to be or make close to.
approximately ADVERB **approximation** NOUN

Synonyms: (sense 1) close, near

apricot apricots
NOUN a small, soft, yellowish-orange fruit.

April
NOUN the fourth month of the year.

apron aprons
NOUN a piece of clothing worn over the front of normal clothing to protect it, for example, when cooking.

apt
ADJECTIVE **1** suitable or relevant: *a very apt description.*
2 having a particular tendency. *She is apt to be rather giggly at times.*
aptly ADVERB **aptness** NOUN

aptitude
NOUN the ability to learn something quickly and to do it well.

aquarium aquaria or aquariums
NOUN a glass fish tank.

aquatic
ADJECTIVE **1** An aquatic animal or plant lives or grows in water.
2 involving water: *aquatic sports.*

aqueduct aqueducts
NOUN a bridge which carries water.

arable
ADJECTIVE Arable land is used for growing crops.

arbitrary
ADJECTIVE An arbitrary decision or action is not based on any plan or system.
arbitrarily ADVERB

arc arcs
NOUN **1** a smoothly curving line.
2 An arc is a section of the circumference of a circle.

arcade arcades
NOUN **1** a covered passageway where there are shops or market stalls.
2 An amusement arcade is a room or building filled with electronic machines for entertainment or gambling.

arch arches arching arched
NOUN **1** a structure that has a curved top supported on either side by a pillar or wall.
VERB **2** If something arches, it forms a curved line or shape.

archaeology or **archeology**
Said "ar-kee-**ol**-loj-ee" NOUN the study of the past by digging up and examining the remains of buildings, tools, etc.
archaeological ADJECTIVE **archaeologist** NOUN

archbishop archbishops
NOUN in a Christian church, the chief bishop of an area.

archery
NOUN a sport in which people shoot at a target with a bow and arrow.

architect architects
Said "**ar**-kit-tekt" NOUN a person who designs buildings.

architecture
NOUN the design of buildings.
architectural ADJECTIVE

Arctic
ADJECTIVE **1** belonging or relating to the Arctic region north of the Arctic Circle.
2 very cold indeed.
[from Greek *arktos* meaning bear; originally it referred to the northern constellation of the Great Bear]

are
the plural form of the present tense of **be**.

area areas
NOUN **1** a particular part of a place, country or the world.
2 a particular kind of subject or activity. *Computers affect almost every area of our lives.*
3 The area of a piece of ground or surface is the amount of space it covers, measured in square metres (m^2) or square feet (ft^2).

Synonyms: (sense 1) district, region, zone

a b c d e f g h i j k l m n o p q r s t u v w x y z

Never use an apostrophe for a simple plural.

A B C D E F G H I J K L M N O P Q R S T U V W X Y Z

arena arenas
NOUN a place where sports and other large public events take place.
[from Latin *harena* meaning sand, and referring to the sandy centre of an area where gladiators fought, the sand being used to soak up the blood]

aren't
contraction of **are not**.

argue argues arguing argued
VERB **1** to disagree with someone in an angry way.
2 to give a reasoned, logical statement of why you think something is true.

argument arguments
NOUN **1** a disagreement between two people which causes a quarrel.
2 a point or a set of reasons you use to try to convince people about something.
argumentative ADJECTIVE

arid
ADJECTIVE Arid land is very dry because it has very little rain.
aridity NOUN

arise arises arising arose arisen
VERB **1** When something arises, such as an opportunity or a problem, it appears or begins to exist.
2 FORMAL to stand up.

aristocracy
NOUN a general word for people of high social rank and with a title, such as "Sir", "Lady" or "Lord", before their name.

aristocrat aristocrats
NOUN someone whose family has a high social rank, and who has a title, such as "Sir", "Lady" or "Lord", before their name.
aristocratic ADJECTIVE

arithmetic
NOUN the branch of mathematics which is to do with the addition, subtraction, multiplication and division of numbers.
arithmetical ADJECTIVE **arithmetically** ADVERB
[from Greek *arithmos* meaning number]

ark
NOUN **1** In the Bible, the ark was the boat built by Noah for his family and the animals during the flood.
2 The Ark of the Covenant was a holy golden box, the symbol of the presence of God to the Hebrew people.

arm arms arming armed
NOUN **1** the part of your body between your shoulder and your wrist.
VERB **2** To arm someone is to provide them with weapons.

armada armadas
Said "ar-**mar**-da" NOUN a large fleet of warships.

armadillo armadillos
NOUN a mammal from South America, covered with strong bony plates like armour.
[a Spanish word meaning little armed man]

armament armaments
NOUN armaments are the weapons and military equipment of a particular country.

armchair armchairs
NOUN a large comfortable chair with a support on each side for your arms.

armed forces
PLURAL NOUN a general word for the army, navy and air force of a country.

armistice armistices
Said "**ar**-miss-tiss" NOUN an agreement in a war to stop fighting in order to discuss peace.

armour
NOUN In the past, armour was metal clothing worn for protection in battle.
armoured ADJECTIVE

armpit armpits
NOUN the area under your arm where your arm joins your shoulder.

arms
PLURAL NOUN weapons used in a war.

army armies
NOUN a large group of soldiers trained to fight on land.

aroma aromas
NOUN a strong, pleasant smell.
aromatic ADJECTIVE

arose
past tense of **arise**.

around
PREPOSITION **1** from place to place. *There were empty seats all around the ground.*
2 about. *See you at around half past three.*
ADVERB **3** here and there. *Scatter the seed around.*

arouse arouses arousing aroused
VERB **1** If something arouses a feeling in you, it stirs up that feeling in you.
2 to wake someone up.
arousal NOUN

arrange arranges arranging arranged
VERB **1** If you arrange objects, you set them out in a particular position.
2 to make plans for something to happen.
arrangement NOUN

array arrays arraying arrayed
VERB to display things in an attractive way.
array NOUN

arrest arrests arresting arrested
VERB **1** If the police arrest someone, they take them to a police station because they believe they may have committed a crime.
NOUN **2** the act of arresting someone.

► Army words: regiment, arms, squad, parade, drill, platoon, cavalry, infantry.

arrive **arrives arriving arrived**
VERB **1** to reach the place at the end of your journey.
2 When you arrive at a decision or conclusion, you reach it.
arrival NOUN

arrogant
ADJECTIVE An arrogant person behaves as if they are better than other people.
arrogance NOUN **arrogantly** ADVERB

arrow **arrows**
NOUN **1** a long thin pointed weapon, shot from a bow.
2 a symbol used to show direction.

arsenal **arsenals**
NOUN a place where weapons and ammunition are stored or produced.

arsenic
NOUN a very strong poison which can kill people.

arson
NOUN the crime of deliberately setting fire to someone else's property.
arsonist NOUN

art **arts**
NOUN **1** the creation of objects such as paintings and sculptures; also the objects themselves.
2 An activity is called an art when it requires special skill or ability: *the art of cookery*.
PLURAL NOUN **3** The arts are literature, music, drama, painting and sculpture.

artefact **artefacts**
Said "**ar**-tif-fact" NOUN any object made by people.

artery **arteries**
NOUN Arteries are tubes through which blood flows from your heart to the rest of your body. See **vein**.

artful
ADJECTIVE; OLD-FASHIONED clever and skilful, often in a cunning way; crafty.
artfully ADVERB

arthritis
NOUN a condition in which the joints of the body become swollen and painful.
arthritic ADJECTIVE

article **articles**
NOUN **1** a particular object or item: *an article of clothing*.
2 a piece of writing in a newspaper or magazine.

artificial
ADJECTIVE created or carried out by people rather than occurring naturally.
artificially ADVERB

artillery
NOUN **1** Artillery consists of large, powerful guns such as cannons.
2 the branch of an army which uses large, powerful guns.

artist **artists**
NOUN a person who draws or paints, or produces other works of art such as novels or music.

artistic
ADJECTIVE **1** having creative and visual skill.
2 performed, made or arranged decoratively or tastefully.
artistically ADVERB **artistry** NOUN

as
CONJUNCTION **1** at the same time that. *She waved at fans as she arrived for the concert.*
2 in the same way that. *She behaved towards him as she did to everyone.*
3 because. *The first lesson is important, as it introduces all the main ideas.*
4 You use the structure **as ... as** when you are comparing things that are similar. *It was as tall as four houses.*
PREPOSITION **5** You use "as" when saying what role someone has. *She worked as a waitress.*

asbestos
NOUN a grey heat-resistant material used in the past to make fireproof articles.
[a Greek word meaning inextinguishable]

ascend **ascends ascending ascended**
Said "ass-**end**" VERB; FORMAL to move or lead upwards.
ascent NOUN

ash **ashes**
NOUN the grey or black powdery remains of anything that has been burnt.

ashamed
ADJECTIVE feeling embarrassed or guilty.

ashore
ADVERB on land or onto land.

ashtray **ashtrays**
NOUN a small dish for ash from cigarettes and cigars.

aside
ADVERB to one side.

ask **asks asking asked**
VERB to put a question or request to someone.

asleep
ADJECTIVE sleeping.

aspect **aspects**
NOUN An aspect of something is one of its features. *They considered all aspects of the party: the food and drink, the decorations, the entertainment.*

asphalt
NOUN a black substance used to make road surfaces and playgrounds.

aspirin **aspirins**
NOUN a common pain-relieving drug.

a b c d e f g h i j k l m n o p q r s t u v w x y z

Some words from Arabic: assassin, orange, algebra, zero, alcohol, sofa, magazine.

A B C D E F G H I J K L M N O P Q R S T U V W X Y Z

ass asses
NOUN 1 a donkey.
2 INFORMAL a stupid person.

assassin assassins
NOUN someone who has murdered a public figure, especially a political or religious leader or royalty.

assassinate assassinates assassinating assassinated
VERB to murder a political or religious leader.
assassination NOUN

assault assaults assaulting assaulted
VERB To attack someone violently.
assault NOUN

assemble assembles assembling assembled
VERB 1 to gather together.
2 to fit the parts of something together.

assembly assemblies
NOUN 1 a group of people gathered together for a meeting or service.
2 The assembly of an object is the fitting together of its parts.

assent assents assenting assented
Said "as-**sent**" VERB 1 to agree to something.
NOUN 2 agreement.

assert asserts asserting asserted
VERB 1 If you assert something, you insist on it firmly and positively.
2 If you assert yourself, you speak and behave in a confident and direct way, so that people pay attention to you.

assertive
ADJECTIVE speaking and behaving in a confident and direct way, so that people pay attention to you.
assertively ADVERB **assertiveness** NOUN

assess assesses assessing assessed
VERB to consider something carefully and make a judgement about it.
assessment NOUN

Synonyms: appraise, judge, size up

asset assets
NOUN 1 a useful person or thing. *You are an asset to the school.*
PLURAL NOUN 2 The assets of a person or company are all the things they own that could be sold to raise money.

assign assigns assigning assigned
VERB If someone is assigned to do something, they are officially told to do it.

assignment assignments
NOUN a job someone is given to do.

assist assists assisting assisted
VERB to help.
assistance NOUN

assistant assistants
NOUN someone whose job is to help another person.

associate associates associating associated
VERB 1 If you associate one thing with another, you connect the two things in your mind.
2 If you associate with a group of people, you spend a lot of time with them.
NOUN 3 Your associates are the people you work with or spend a lot of time with.

association associations
NOUN 1 an organization for people who have similar interests, jobs or aims.
2 An association between two things is a link you make in your mind between them.

assonance
NOUN Assonance is the use of similar vowel or consonant sounds in words near to each other or in the same word: *a deep, dreamy, peaceful sleep*.

assorted
ADJECTIVE of several different types.

assortment assortments
NOUN a group of similar things that are different sizes, shapes or colours.

assume assumes assuming assumed
VERB If you assume that something is true, you accept it is true even though you have not thought about it.

Synonyms: believe, presume, take for granted

assumption assumptions
NOUN a belief that something is true, without checking the facts; taking something for granted.

assure assures assuring assured
VERB If you assure someone that something is true, you tell them firmly it is true.

asterisk asterisks
NOUN the symbol (*) used in printing and writing.
[from Greek *asteriskos* meaning small star]

asteroid asteroids
NOUN one of the large number of very small rocky bodies that move around the sun between the orbits of Mars and Jupiter.

asthma
Said "**ass**-ma" NOUN a disease of the chest which causes wheezing and difficulty in breathing.
asthmatic ADJECTIVE

astonish astonishes astonishing astonished
VERB If something astonishes you, it surprises you very much.
astonished ADJECTIVE **astonishing** ADJECTIVE **astonishingly** ADVERB **astonishment** NOUN

astound astounds astounding astounded
VERB If something astounds you, it shocks and amazes you.
astounded ADJECTIVE **astounding** ADJECTIVE

► Assonance: the lonely gnome moaned in his hole.

astray
PHRASE **1** If something **goes astray** it gets lost.
2 To **lead someone astray** is to influence them to do something wrong.

astride
PREPOSITION with one leg on either side of something.

astrology
NOUN the study of the sun and moon and other stars and planets in order to predict the future. See **astronomy**.
astrological ADJECTIVE **astrologer** NOUN

astronaut **astronauts**
NOUN a person who operates a spacecraft.
[from Greek *astron* meaning a star + *naute* meaning a sailor]

astronomy
NOUN the scientific study of stars and planets. See **astrology**.
astronomer NOUN

asymmetrical or **asymmetric**
Said "ay-sim-**met**-ri-kl" ADJECTIVE unbalanced or with one half not exactly the same as the other half.
asymmetry NOUN

at
PREPOSITION used to say where or when. *Bert met us at the airport. The baby threw her plate at the wall. The game starts at 3 o'clock.*

ate
past tense of **eat**.

atheist **atheists**
Said "**ayth**-ee-ist" NOUN someone who believes there is no God. See **agnostic**.
atheistic ADJECTIVE **atheism** NOUN

athlete **athletes**
NOUN **1** someone who is naturally good at sport and physical activity.
2 someone who takes part in running, jumping and throwing events at a track.

athletic
ADJECTIVE strong, healthy, and good at sports.
athletically ADVERB

athletics
NOUN Sporting events such as running, jumping and throwing.

Atlantic
ADJECTIVE relating to the Atlantic Ocean.

atlas **atlases**
NOUN a book of maps.
[from the giant *Atlas* in Greek mythology who supported the sky on his shoulders]

atmosphere **atmospheres**
NOUN **1** the air and other gases that surround a planet.
2 the general mood of a place.
atmospheric ADJECTIVE

atom **atoms**
NOUN **1** the smallest part of an element that can take part in a chemical reaction.
2 a tiny amount of something. *There's not an atom of truth in what he says.*

atomic
ADJECTIVE relating to atoms or the immense power released by splitting atoms.

atomic bomb **atomic bombs**
NOUN an extremely powerful and destructive bomb which explodes because of the energy created by splitting atoms.

atrocious
ADJECTIVE extremely bad.
atrociously ADVERB

atrocity **atrocities**
NOUN an extremely cruel and shocking act.

attach **attaches attaching attached**
VERB to join or fasten one thing to another.

attached
ADJECTIVE If you are attached to someone or something, you are very fond of them or it.

attachment **attachments**
NOUN **1** Attachment to someone is a feeling of love and affection for them.
2 A piece of equipment attached to a tool or machine to do a particular job.

attack **attacks attacking attacked**
VERB **1** to use violence against someone to hurt or kill them.
2 to criticize strongly.
3 In sport, to attack is to move forward.
attack NOUN **attacker** NOUN

attain **attains attaining attained**
VERB; FORMAL If you attain something, you achieve it.
attainable ADJECTIVE **attainment** NOUN

attempt **attempts attempting attempted**
VERB **1** to try.
NOUN **2** an act of trying: *an attempt to escape.*

attend **attends attending attended**
VERB **1** If you attend an event or place, you go there.
2 If you attend to something, you deal with it.

attendance **attendances**
NOUN **1** the condition of being where you are asked or told to be.
2 the number of people attending an event.

attendant **attendants**
NOUN someone whose job is to serve people in a place such as a petrol station or cloakroom.

attention
NOUN intense concentration or care.

attentive
ADJECTIVE paying close attention to something.
attentively ADVERB **attentiveness** NOUN

attic **attics**
NOUN a room at the top of a house immediately below the roof.

a b c d e f g h i j k l m n o p q r s t u v w x y z

attitude attitudes
NOUN Your attitude to someone or something is the way you think about them and behave towards them.

attract attracts attracting attracted
VERB **1** If something attracts people, it interests them and makes them want to go to it.
2 If someone attracts you, you like and admire them.
3 Magnets attract other magnets and magnetic materials.

attraction attractions
NOUN **1** a feeling of liking someone or something very much.
2 something people visit for interest or pleasure. *The funfair was a big tourist attraction.*
3 a force by which one object attracts another, for example, magnetic attraction.

attractive
ADJECTIVE **1** pleasant to look at or be with.
2 desirable. *A holiday was an attractive idea.*
attractively ADVERB **attractiveness** NOUN

Synonyms: (sense 1) charming, lovely
(sense 2) appealing, tempting

aubergine aubergines
Said "**oh**-ber-jeen" NOUN a dark purple, pear-shaped vegetable. It is also called an eggplant.

auburn
ADJECTIVE Auburn hair is reddish brown.

auction auctions auctioning auctioned
NOUN **1** a public sale in which goods are sold to the person who offers the highest price.
VERB **2** To auction something is to sell it in an auction.
auctioneer NOUN

audible
ADJECTIVE loud enough to be heard.
audibly ADVERB **audibility** NOUN

audience audiences
NOUN a group of people who are watching or listening to a performance. See **crowd**.

audio
ADJECTIVE used in recording and reproducing sound.
[from Latin *audire* meaning to hear]

audition auditions
NOUN a short piece given by a performer as a trial, so a director can decide whether they are suitable for a place in the performance.

auditorium auditoriums or auditoria
NOUN the part of a theatre where the audience sits.

August
NOUN the eighth month of the year.
[from the name of the first Roman emperor, Augustus Caesar]

aunt or **auntie** or **aunty** aunts aunties
NOUN Your aunt is the sister of your mother or father, or the wife of your uncle.

au pair au pairs
Said "oh **pair**" NOUN a young foreign person who lives with a family to help with the children and housework while learning the local language.

austere
ADJECTIVE plain and simple, and without luxury.
austerity NOUN

authentic
ADJECTIVE real and genuine.
authentically ADVERB **authenticity** NOUN

author authors
NOUN a person whose job is writing, the writer of a book.

authority authorities
NOUN **1** the right to control other people.
2 Someone who is an authority on something knows a lot about it. *She's the world's leading authority on fashion.*

authorize authorizes authorizing authorized; also spelt **authorise**
VERB To authorize something is to give official permission for it to happen.
authorization NOUN

autistic
ADJECTIVE If someone is autistic, they have a medical condition which means they are unable to relate to other people and the world around them in the usual way.
autism NOUN

auto-
PREFIX self or same.

autobiography autobiographies
NOUN Someone's autobiography is an account of their life which they have written themselves.
autobiographical ADJECTIVE

autograph autographs
NOUN the signature of a famous person.

automatic
ADJECTIVE **1** An automatic machine is programmed to perform tasks without needing a person to operate it.
2 Automatic actions or reactions take place without requiring any conscious thought.
automatically ADVERB

automation
NOUN the use of automatic machinery instead of people to carry out industrial work.

automobile automobiles
NOUN; FORMAL a car.

autumn autumns
NOUN the season between summer and winter.

available
ADJECTIVE **1** Something that is available can be obtained.
2 Someone who is available is ready for work or free for people to talk to.

 ► Pun. Why is "o" the only vowel that is sounded? All the others are inaudible.

avalanche avalanches
Said "**av**-a-lahnsh" NOUN a huge mass of snow and ice that falls down a mountainside.

avenge avenges avenging avenged
VERB If you avenge something harmful someone has done to you or your family, you punish or harm the other person in return.
avenger NOUN

avenue avenues
NOUN a street, especially one with trees along it.

average averages
NOUN **1** a result obtained by adding several amounts together and then dividing the total by the number of the amounts. *Ten pupils got a total of 85 marks, an average of 8·5 marks per pupil.*
ADJECTIVE **2** standard or normal. *The pupil's work was about average for her age.*
PHRASE **3** You say **on average** when mentioning what usually happens in a situation. *Men are, on average, taller than women.*

avert averts averting averted
VERB If you avert an unpleasant event, you prevent it from happening.

aviary aviaries
NOUN a large cage or group of cages in which birds are kept.

aviation
NOUN the science of flying aircraft.

avid
ADJECTIVE eager and enthusiastic for something.
avidly ADVERB

avocado avocados
NOUN a pear-shaped fruit, with dark green skin, soft greenish yellow flesh and a large stone.

avoid avoids avoiding avoided
VERB **1** If you avoid doing something, you make an effort not to do it.
2 If you avoid someone, you keep away from them.
avoidance NOUN

Synonyms: (sense 1) dodge, refrain from, shirk
(sense 2) dodge, evade, keep away from

await awaits awaiting awaited
VERB **1** If you await something, you expect it.
2 If something awaits you, it will happen to you in the future.

awake awakes awaking awoke awoken
ADJECTIVE **1** not sleeping.
VERB **2** to wake up.

awaken awakens awakening awakened
VERB **1** to wake up.
2 to arouse an emotion or interest in someone.

award awards awarding awarded
NOUN **1** a prize or certificate for doing something well.
VERB **2** If you award someone something, you give it to them formally or officially.

aware
ADJECTIVE If you are aware of something, you already know about it, or can see, hear, smell or feel it.
awareness NOUN

Synonyms: conscious of, knowing about, mindful of

away
ADVERB **1** going from a place. *I saw them walk away.*
2 at a distance. *Our nearest supermarket is 8 miles away.*
3 in its proper place. *He put his textbook away.*
4 not present. *She had been away from home for years.*
5 continuing. *He continued to scribble away.*

awe
NOUN; FORMAL a feeling of great respect mixed with amazement and sometimes slight fear.

awesome
ADJECTIVE **1** impressive and rather frightening.
2 INFORMAL excellent, really good. *This new computer game is awesome!*

awful
ADJECTIVE **1** very unpleasant or very bad.
2 INFORMAL very great. *The trip will cost an awful lot of money.*
awfully ADVERB

Synonyms: (sense 1) appalling, dreadful, terrible

awhile
ADVERB for a brief period.

awkward
ADJECTIVE **1** difficult to deal with.
2 clumsy and uncomfortable.

awoke
past tense of **awake**.

awoken
past participle of **awake**.

axe axes
NOUN a tool with a handle and a sharp blade, used for chopping wood.

axis axes
Said "**ak**-siss" NOUN **1** an imaginary line through the centre of something, around which it moves.
2 one of the two sides of a graph.

axle axles
NOUN the bar that connects a pair of wheels on a vehicle.

aye or **ay**
INTERJECTION yes.

Words from the USA: automobile, movie, bulldozer, elevator, skyscraper. ◀

A B C D E F G H I J K L M N O P Q R S T U V W X Y Z

Bb

babble babbles babbling babbled
VERB 1 to talk in a confused or excited way.
2 to make a continuous bubbling sound.

baboon baboons
NOUN an African monkey with a pointed face, large teeth and a long tail.

baby babies
NOUN a child in the first year or two of its life.
babyhood NOUN

babyish
ADJECTIVE behaving in a very childish way.

baby-sit baby-sits baby-sitting baby-sat
VERB to look after someone's children while they are out.
baby-sitter NOUN **baby-sitting** NOUN

bachelor bachelors
NOUN a man who has never married.

back backs backing backed
NOUN 1 the rear part of your body.
2 the part of something that is behind the front. *You write on the back of a postcard.*
ADJECTIVE 3 The back part of something is the part near the rear: *the back seat.*
ADVERB 4 When people or things move back, they move in the opposite direction to the one they are facing.
5 When people go back to a place or situation, they return to it.
6 If you get something back, it is returned to you.
7 **back** also means in the past. *It happened back in the early 1980s.*
back down VERB to withdraw and give up.
back out VERB to decide not to do what you had agreed to do.
back up VERB 1 to help or support someone.
2 to save a copy of a computer file, in case the original is lost.

backbone backbones
NOUN 1 the column of linked bones along the back of a human or other vertebrate.
2 If you say that someone has backbone, you mean that they have great strength of character.

Synonym: (sense 1) spine

backfire backfires backfiring backfired
VERB 1 If a plan backfires, it fails.
2 When a car backfires, there is a small but noisy explosion in its exhaust pipe.

background backgrounds
NOUN 1 the things in a picture or scene that are less noticeable than the main things.
2 Your background is the kind of family you come from and your education.
3 the circumstances which help to explain an event or caused it to happen.

backing
NOUN support or help. *The expedition had the backing of several big companies.*

backpack backpacks
NOUN a large bag with straps that hikers or campers carry on their backs.

Synonyms: knapsack, rucksack

backstroke
NOUN a type of swimming you do floating on your back.

backward
ADJECTIVE 1 directed behind you: *a backward glance.*
2 OLD-FASHIONED A backward child is one who is unable to learn as quickly as other children of the same age.
backwardness NOUN

backwards
ADVERB 1 towards the back.
2 If you do something backwards, you do it the opposite of the usual way. *I counted backwards.*

bacon
NOUN meat from the back or sides of a pig, which has been salted or smoked.

bacteria
PLURAL NOUN very tiny organisms which can cause disease.
bacterial ADJECTIVE
✔ The singular form is *bacterium.*

bad worse worst
ADJECTIVE 1 not good: *bad news.*
2 A bad person is naughty or wicked.
3 Bad language consists of swearwords.
4 If you have a bad temper, you become angry easily.

Synonyms: (sense 2) evil, sinful

badge badges
NOUN a piece of plastic or metal, etc. with a design or message on it, that you can pin to your clothes.

badger badgers badgering badgered
NOUN 1 a nocturnal, black-and-white mammal.
VERB 2 to pester someone.

badly worse worst
ADVERB 1 not good, poor in quality. *The script was badly written.*
2 seriously. *She was badly hurt in the accident.*

badminton
NOUN a game for two or four, played with rackets, a shuttlecock and a high net.

baffle baffles baffling baffled
VERB If something baffles you, you cannot understand or explain it.
baffled ADJECTIVE **baffling** ADJECTIVE

bag bags
NOUN a cloth container for carrying things.

 ► The letter B probably began as a picture of a house. "Beth" was a word for house.

baggage
NOUN the suitcases and bags that you take on a journey.

baggy **baggier baggiest**
ADJECTIVE Baggy clothing hangs loosely.

bagpipes
PLURAL NOUN a musical instrument played by squeezing air out of a leather bag and through pipes.

baguette **baguettes**
NOUN a long, crusty bread roll.

bail **bails bailing bailed**
NOUN **1** a sum of money paid to a court to allow an accused person to go free until the time of the trial.
2 In cricket, the bails are the two small pieces of wood placed on top of the stumps to form the wicket.
VERB **3** If you bail water from a boat, you scoop it out; also spelt **bale**.
bail out VERB To bail out of an aircraft means to jump out of it with a parachute.

bait **baits**
NOUN a small amount of food placed on a hook or in a trap, to attract a fish or wild animal so that it gets caught.
bait VERB

bake **bakes baking baked**
VERB to cook in an oven without using liquid or fat.
baking NOUN

baker **bakers**
NOUN a person who makes and sells bread and cakes.
bakery NOUN

balance **balances balancing balanced**
VERB **1** to remain steady and not fall over.
2 In mathematics, balance is used when weighing and comparing two weights: if two weights are equal, they balance.
NOUN **3** the state of being upright and steady.
4 The balance in someone's bank account is the amount of money in it.

balcony **balconies**
NOUN **1** a platform on the outside of a building with a wall or railing round it.
2 an area of upstairs seats in a theatre or cinema.

bald **balder baldest**
ADJECTIVE A bald person has little or no hair on their head.
baldly ADVERB **baldness** NOUN

bale **bales baling baled**
NOUN **1** a large bundle of something, such as hay or straw, tied tightly.
VERB **2** If you bale water from a boat, you scoop it out; also spelt **bail**.
bale out VERB To bale out of an aircraft means to jump out of it with a parachute.

ball **balls**
NOUN **1** a round object used in games such as soccer and tennis.
2 a large formal dance.

ballad **ballads**
NOUN a long song or poem which tells a story.

ballerina **ballerinas**
NOUN a principal woman ballet dancer.

ballet
Said "**bal**-lay" NOUN a highly skilled type of artistic dancing.

balloon **balloons**
NOUN **1** a small, inflatable, coloured rubber bag used as a decoration.
2 a large, strong bag filled with gas or hot air, which travels through the air carrying passengers in a basket underneath it.

ballot **ballots**
NOUN a secret vote to choose a candidate in an election, or express an opinion about something.

ballpoint **ballpoints**
NOUN a pen with a small metal ball at the end which transfers the ink onto the paper.

ballroom **ballrooms**
NOUN a very large room used for dancing or formal balls.

balsa
NOUN a very lightweight wood often used for models.

bamboo
NOUN a tall tropical plant with hard, hollow stems.

ban **bans banning banned**
VERB **1** If something is banned, or if you are banned from doing it, you are not allowed to do it.
NOUN **2** If there is a ban on something, it is not allowed.

Synonyms: (sense 1) forbid, prohibit

banana **bananas**
NOUN a long curved fruit with a yellow skin.

band **bands**
NOUN **1** a group of musicians who play together.
2 a group of people who share a common purpose: *a band of outlaws*.
3 a narrow strip of something used to hold things together.

bandage **bandages**
NOUN a strip of fabric for wrapping around a wound.

bandit **bandits**
NOUN a member of an armed gang who rob travellers.

bandstand **bandstands**
NOUN a platform, usually with a roof, where a band plays.

a b c d e f g h i j k l m n o p q r s t u v w x y z

A baker's dozen is 13. Bakers gave an extra loaf when giving short weight was a criminal offence.

A B C D E F G H I J K L M N O P Q R S T U V W X Y Z

bang bangs banging banged
VERB **1** to hit something noisily.
2 to bump against something accidentally.
NOUN **3** a sudden, short, loud noise.
4 a hard or painful bump against something.

bangle bangles
NOUN an ornamental wrist or ankle band.
[from Hindi *bangli* meaning glass bracelet]

banish banishes banishing banished
VERB To banish someone or something means to send them away forever.
banishment NOUN

Synonyms: exile, expel, outlaw

banister banisters; also spelt **bannister**
NOUN a rail along the side of a staircase.

banjo banjos or banjoes
NOUN a musical instrument like a small guitar with a round body.

bank banks banking banked
NOUN **1** a business that looks after people's money.
2 the raised ground along the edge of a river or lake.
VERB **3** to use a bank or to put money in it.
PHRASE **4** If you **bank on** something happening, you expect it and rely on it.
banker NOUN **banking** NOUN

bankrupt
ADJECTIVE People or organizations that go bankrupt do not have enough money to pay their debts.
bankruptcy NOUN

banner banners
NOUN a long strip of cloth with a message or slogan on it.

bannister bannisters.
See **banister**.

banquet banquets
NOUN a grand formal dinner, often followed by speeches.

baptism baptisms
NOUN the ceremony in which someone is baptized.

baptize baptizes baptizing baptized; also spelt **baptise**
VERB When someone is baptized, water is sprinkled on them or they are immersed in water, as a sign that they have become a Christian.

bar bars barring barred
NOUN **1** a long, straight piece of metal.
2 a counter or room where alcoholic drinks are served.
3 a rectangular piece of something: *a bar of chocolate.*
VERB **4** If you bar someone's way, you stop them going somewhere by standing in front of them.

barbarian barbarians
NOUN a member of a wild or uncivilized people.

barbaric
ADJECTIVE cruel or brutal.
barbarity NOUN

barbecue barbecues
NOUN **1** a grill with a charcoal fire on which you cook food.
2 an outdoor party where you eat food cooked on a barbecue.
[from a Caribbean word meaning framework]

barbed wire
NOUN strong wire with sharp spikes, used to make fences.

barber barbers
NOUN a person who cuts men's hair.

bar chart bar charts
NOUN a kind of graph where the information is shown in vertical or horizontal rows or bars.

bar code bar codes
NOUN a small pattern of lines on something which can be electronically scanned to give information on a computer.

bare
ADJECTIVE **1** not covered with clothes: *bare legs.*
2 If something is bare it has nothing on top of it or in it: *bare floorboards; bare cupboards.*
3 The bare minimum or the bare essentials means the very least that is needed.

Synonyms: (sense 1) naked, nude, uncovered

barefoot
ADJECTIVE OR ADVERB not wearing anything on your feet.

barely
ADVERB only just. *I had barely made it to school when the storm broke.*

bargain bargains bargaining bargained
NOUN **1** a deal between two people or groups.
2 something which is very good value when you buy it.
VERB **3** When people bargain with each other, they discuss and agree terms about what each will do, pay or receive.

barge barges barging barged
NOUN **1** a boat with a flat bottom used for carrying heavy loads, especially on canals.
VERB **2** INFORMAL If you barge into a place or situation, you push into it in a rough or rude way.

bark barks barking barked
VERB **1** When a dog barks, it makes a short, loud noise several times.
NOUN **2** the tough material that covers the outside of a tree.

barley
NOUN a cereal grown for food and also used for making beer and whisky.

 ► Bank words: account, cashpoint, cheque, deposit, balance, overdraft, loan.

bar mitzvah
NOUN a ceremony that takes place on a Jewish boy's 13th birthday, after which he is regarded as an adult.

barmy barmier barmiest
ADJECTIVE; INFORMAL mad or very foolish.

barn barns
NOUN a large farm building used for storing crops or animal food.

barnacle barnacles
NOUN a small shellfish that fixes itself to rocks and the bottom of boats.

barometer barometers
NOUN an instrument that measures air pressure and shows when the weather is changing.

baron barons
NOUN a male member of the lowest rank of the nobility. Barons are called "Lord".

baroness baronesses
NOUN a woman who has the rank of baron, or who is the wife of a baron.

barracks
NOUN a building where soldiers live.

barrage barrages
NOUN 1 continuous questions, complaints or gunfire.
2 A barrage across a river is an artificial barrier to control the flow of water.

barrel barrels
NOUN 1 a wooden container with rounded sides and flat ends.
2 The barrel of a gun is the long tube through which the bullet is fired.

barren
ADJECTIVE not capable of growing anything: *barren land.*
barrenness NOUN

Synonym: infertile

barricade barricades barricading barricaded
NOUN 1 a temporary barrier put up to block the way.
VERB 2 If you barricade yourself inside a room or building, you put something heavy against the door to stop people getting in.

barrier barriers
NOUN a fence or wall that prevents people, vehicles, etc. getting from one area to another.

barrister barristers
NOUN a lawyer who is qualified to represent people in the higher courts.

barrow barrows
NOUN 1 a wheelbarrow.
2 a large cart from which fruit or other goods are sold in the street.
3 a mound of earth or stones built over a grave in ancient times.

barter barters bartering bartered
VERB If you barter goods or services, you exchange them for other goods and services, rather than selling them for money.
barter NOUN

base bases basing based
NOUN 1 the lowest part of something, often on which it rests.
2 the headquarters of an organization.
3 a number used as the main unit for a pattern of counting. *Base 10.*
VERB 4 If one thing is based on another thing, it is developed from it. *The show West Side Story is based on Shakespeare's Romeo and Juliet.*
5 If you are based somewhere, you live there or work from there.

Synonyms: (sense 1) bottom, stand, support

baseball
NOUN an American team game played with a bat and a ball, similar to rounders.

basement basements
NOUN a floor of a building built completely or partly below the ground. See **cellar**.

bash bashes bashing bashed
VERB 1 INFORMAL to hit.
NOUN 2 a hard blow.
PHRASE 3 INFORMAL If you **have a bash** at something, you try to do it.

bashful
ADJECTIVE shy and easily embarrassed.
bashfully ADVERB **bashfulness** NOUN

basic
ADJECTIVE 1 The basic aspects of something are the most important or the essential ones.
2 having only simple, necessary features. *The holiday cottage was pretty basic.*
basically ADVERB

Synonyms: (sense 1) essential, necessary, vital

basin basins
NOUN 1 a sink.
2 a deep food bowl.

basis bases
NOUN 1 the essential main principle from which something can be developed. *Red was used as the basis for the colour scheme.*
2 The basis for a belief is the facts which support it. *What is the basis for your argument?*

Synonyms: (sense 1) base, foundation

bask basks basking basked
VERB If you bask in the sun, you sit or lie in it, enjoying its warmth.

basket baskets
NOUN a container made of woven cane.

basketball
NOUN a fast-moving game where two teams try to throw a large ball through a hoop.

a b c d e f g h i j k l m n o p q r s t u v w x y z

Use an adult dictionary to find out what these measure: barometer, thermometer, pedometer, odometer. ◀

bass
Rhymes with "lace" **ADJECTIVE** A bass musical instrument or voice is one that produces a very deep sound.

bassoon **bassoons**
NOUN a large woodwind instrument.

bastard **bastards**
NOUN 1 OFFENSIVE People sometimes call someone a bastard if they dislike them or are very angry with them.
2 OLD-FASHIONED someone whose parents were not married when they were born.

bat **bats batting batted**
VERB 1 in certain team games such as cricket or rounders, to try to hit the ball in order to score.
NOUN 2 a specially-shaped piece of wood used for hitting a ball in a game.
3 a small flying mammal, active at night, that looks like a mouse with wings.

batch **batches**
NOUN a group of things made or dealt with together.

bath **baths**
NOUN 1 a tub which you fill with water and sit in to wash yourself.
PLURAL NOUN 2 another term for a public indoor swimming pool.

bathe **bathes bathing bathed**
VERB to swim or play in water.
bather NOUN

bathroom **bathrooms**
NOUN a room for bathing or washing yourself in.

baton **batons**
NOUN 1 In athletics, the baton is a short stick passed from one runner to another in a relay race.
2 a light, thin stick that a conductor uses to direct an orchestra or choir.

batsman **batsmen**
NOUN In a ball game such as cricket, the batsman is the person who is batting.

battalion **battalions**
NOUN an unit of soldiers, bigger than a platoon or company but usually smaller than a regiment.

batten **battens battening battened**
NOUN 1 A strip of wood that is fixed to something to strengthen it or hold it firm.
VERB 2 If you batten down something which is loose, you make it secure by fixing something strong across it.

batter **batters battering battered**
VERB 1 to hit heavily many times.
NOUN 2 a mixture of flour, eggs and milk used to coat food, such as fish, before frying it, or to make pancakes, etc.

battering ram **battering rams**
NOUN a large wooden beam carried by several people and used to break down doors or walls.

battery **batteries**
NOUN 1 a device for storing and producing electricity, for example, in a torch or a car.
ADJECTIVE 2 A battery hen is one of a large number of hens kept in small cages for the mass production of eggs.

battle **battles**
NOUN 1 a fight between armed forces.
2 a struggle between two people or groups with different aims.

battlefield **battlefields**
NOUN a place where a battle is or has been fought.

battlements
PLURAL NOUN The wall at the top of a castle which has gaps through which guns or arrows were fired.

battleship **battleships**
NOUN a large, heavily armoured warship.

bawl **bawls bawling bawled**
VERB; INFORMAL to shout or cry loudly and harshly.

bay **bays**
NOUN 1 a part of a coastline where the land curves inwards.
2 a space specially divided off for a particular purpose: *a loading bay.*

Synonyms: (sense 1) cove, gulf, inlet

bayonet **bayonets**
NOUN a sharp blade that can be fixed to the end of a rifle and used for stabbing.

bazaar **bazaars**
NOUN 1 a sale to raise money for charity.
2 a Middle Eastern market.

BC
abbreviation of before Christ.

BCE
abbreviation of before common era, used as a non-Christian alternative to BC.

be **am is are; being; was were; been**
VERB 1 "Be" is used to give more information about the subject of a sentence. *Her name is Fiona.*
AUXILIARY VERB 2 "Be" is used with participles to form other tenses, voices and moods. *We are going to America next month. We were beaten by the second team.*

beach **beaches**
NOUN an area of sand or pebbles beside the sea.

Synonyms: shore, seashore, seaside

beacon **beacons**
NOUN In the past, a beacon was a light or fire on a hill, which acted as a signal or warning.

 ► Joke. The police caught one man swallowing batteries and another eating fireworks. ►

bead beads
NOUN **1** Beads are small hollow pieces of coloured glass or wood, strung together to make necklaces.
2 Beads are drops of liquid.

beady
ADJECTIVE Beady eyes are small and bright like beads.

beagle beagles
NOUN a short-haired dog with long ears and short legs.

beak beaks
NOUN the hard part of a bird's mouth that sticks out.

beaker beakers
NOUN **1** a tall drinking cup.
2 a glass container with a lip which is used in laboratories.

beam beams beaming beamed
NOUN **1** a ray of light shining from something such as a torch or the sun.
2 a broad smile.
3 a long, thick bar of wood or metal, especially one that supports a roof.
VERB **4** to smile broadly.

bean beans
NOUN Beans are the edible seeds or pods of certain plants.

bear bears bearing bore borne
NOUN **1** a large, strong mammal with thick fur and sharp claws.
VERB **2** To bear something means to carry it or support its weight. *The ice was not thick enough to bear our weight.*
3 If you bear something difficult, you accept it and are able to deal with it.
4 If something bears a mark or typical feature, it has that mark or feature.
bear down VERB If something bears down on you, it moves quickly and menacingly towards you.
bear up VERB If you bear up when you are having problems, you remain brave and cheerful.
bear with VERB If someone asks you to bear with them, they want you to understand their difficulties and be patient with them.

bearable
ADJECTIVE If a situation is bearable, you can put up with it.

Synonyms: tolerable, endurable

beard beards
NOUN the hair that grows on the lower part of a man's face.

bearing bearings
NOUN the direction in which something lies.

beast beasts
NOUN **1** OLD-FASHIONED a large wild animal.
2 INFORMAL If you call someone a beast, you mean that they are cruel or spiteful.

beastly
ADJECTIVE; OLD-FASHIONED cruel or spiteful.

beat beats beating beat beaten
NOUN **1** a regular rhythm or stroke, such as your heart makes when it pumps blood or in music.
VERB **2** To beat someone or something means to hit them hard and repeatedly.
3 If you beat someone in a race or game, you win.
4 to mix food with a fork or whisk.
beat up VERB To beat someone up means to hit or kick them repeatedly.

Synonyms: (sense 3) conquer, defeat

beautiful
ADJECTIVE very attractive or pleasing.
beautifully ADVERB **beauty** NOUN

Synonyms: attractive, gorgeous, lovely

beaver beavers beavering beavered
NOUN **1** an animal with a big, flat tail and webbed hind feet that builds dams.
VERB **2** If you beaver away at a task, you work very hard and steadily at it.

became
past tense of **become**.

because
CONJUNCTION "Because" is used with a clause to give the reason for something. *I went home because I was feeling ill.*

beckon beckons beckoning beckoned
VERB to signal that you want someone to come to you.

become becomes becoming became become
VERB To become something means to start feeling or being that thing. *I became very angry. He became an actor.*

bed beds
NOUN **1** a piece of furniture for sleeping on.
2 an area in a garden where plants are grown.
3 The bed of a sea or river is the ground at the bottom of it.

bedclothes
PLURAL NOUN the sheets and covers on a bed.

bedding
NOUN a general word for bedclothes and mattresses.

bedraggled
ADJECTIVE in a messy and untidy state.

bedridden
ADJECTIVE too ill or disabled to get out of bed.

bedroom bedrooms
NOUN a room used for sleeping in.

bedspread bedspreads
NOUN a cover put over a bed, on top of the sheets and blankets.

bedtime bedtimes
NOUN the time when a person goes to bed.

a b c d e f g h i j k l m n o p q r s t u v w x y z

bee **bees**
NOUN a winged insect that lives in large groups and makes honey.

beech **beeches**
NOUN a tree with a smooth grey trunk and shiny leaves.

beef
NOUN the meat of a cow, bull or ox.

beefy **beefier beefiest**
ADJECTIVE; INFORMAL A beefy person is strong and muscular.

beehive **beehives**
NOUN a container in which bees live and make their honey.

been
past participle of **be**.

beer **beers**
NOUN an alcoholic drink made from malt and flavoured with hops.

beetle **beetles**
NOUN a flying insect with hard wings which cover its body when it is not flying.

beetroot **beetroots**
NOUN a round, dark red root of a type of beet, eaten as a vegetable.

before
ADVERB **1** previously. *Have you been to Greece before?*
2 earlier than. *She arrived before he did.*
PREPOSITION **3** FORMAL in front of. *They stopped before a large white villa.*

beforehand
ADVERB earlier, in advance.

beg **begs begging begged**
VERB **1** to ask for money or food.
2 If you beg someone to do something, you ask them very anxiously to do it.

Synonyms: (sense 2) beseech, implore, plead

began
past tense of **begin**.

beggar **beggars**
NOUN someone who lives by asking people for money or food.

begin **begins beginning began begun**
VERB to start, to commence.

beginner **beginners**
NOUN someone who has just started learning to do something.

Synonyms: learner, novice

beginning **beginnings**
NOUN the start of something.

begun
past participle of **begin**.

behalf
PHRASE To do something **on behalf of** someone or something means to do it for their benefit or as their representative.

behave **behaves behaving behaved**
VERB **1** If you behave in a particular way, you act in that way.
2 To behave yourself means to act correctly or properly.

behaviour
NOUN the way in which someone behaves.

behead **beheads beheading beheaded**
VERB to cut someone's head off.

behind
PREPOSITION **1** at the back of. *The moon disappeared behind a cloud.*
2 supporting someone. *The whole country was behind him as he went for the gold medal.*
ADVERB **3** If you stay behind, you remain after other people have gone.
4 If you leave something behind, you do not take it with you.

beige
Said "**bayj**" NOUN OR ADJECTIVE creamy-brown.

being **beings**
NOUN **1** the state or fact of existing. *The organization came into being in 1923.*
2 a living creature, either real or imaginary. See **be**.

belch **belches belching belched**
VERB **1** to burp loudly.
2 If something belches smoke or fire, it sends it out in large amounts.

belief **beliefs**
NOUN **1** a feeling of certainty that something is true.
2 one of the principles of a religion or moral system.

Synonyms: (sense 2) creed, doctrine, faith

believe **believes believing believed**
VERB **1** If you believe something, you think very firmly that it is true.
2 If you believe someone, you accept that they are telling the truth.
3 If you believe in something, you think that it exists or is important.
believable ADJECTIVE **believer** NOUN

bell **bells**
NOUN a cup-shaped metal object with a clapper that makes a ringing sound when shaken.

belligerent
ADJECTIVE aggressive and keen to start a fight or an argument.
belligerence NOUN

bellow **bellows bellowing bellowed**
VERB **1** to shout in a loud, deep voice.
NOUN **2** a loud, deep roar.
PLURAL NOUN **3** Bellows are a piece of equipment used for blowing air into a fire to make it burn more fiercely.

 ► Before, after, up, down, over, under, off, on are all prepositions.

belly **bellies**
NOUN 1 Your belly is your stomach or the front of your body below your chest.
2 An animal's belly is the underneath part of its body.

belong **belongs belonging belonged**
VERB 1 If something belongs to you, you own it.
2 To belong to a group means to be a member of it.
3 If something belongs in a particular place, that is where it should be.

belongings
PLURAL NOUN Your belongings are the things that you own.

beloved
Said "bil-**luv**-id" **ADJECTIVE** A beloved person or thing is one that you feel great affection for.

Synonyms: adored, dear, precious

below
PREPOSITION OR ADVERB under, at a lower point than.

belt **belts**
NOUN a strip of leather or cloth that you fasten round your waist to hold your trousers or skirt up.

bench **benches**
NOUN 1 a long seat that two or more people can sit on.
2 a long, narrow worktable.

bend **bends bending bent**
VERB 1 to make a straight thing curved or angular.
2 If you bend, you move your head and shoulders forwards and downwards.
NOUN 3 a curved part of something.

Synonyms: (sense 1) arch, bow, curve

beneath
PREPOSITION, ADJECTIVE AND ADVERB; OLD-FASHIONED underneath.

benefactor **benefactors**
NOUN a person who helps to support a person or organization by giving money.

beneficial
ADJECTIVE good for you or for others: *exercise has beneficial effects.*
beneficially ADVERB

Synonyms: advantageous, favourable, helpful

benefit **benefits benefiting benefited**
NOUN 1 The benefit of something is the advantage that it brings to people: *the benefits of a good education.*
2 a regular payment received from the government to help in particular circumstances.
VERB 3 If you benefit from something, it helps you.

benevolent
ADJECTIVE kind and helpful.
benevolence NOUN **benevolently** ADVERB

bent
the past participle and past tense of **bend**.

bequeath **bequeaths bequeathing bequeathed**
VERB; FORMAL If someone bequeaths money or property to you, they give it to you in their will, so that it is yours after they have died.
bequest NOUN

bereaved
ADJECTIVE; FORMAL You say that someone is bereaved when a close relative of theirs has recently died.
bereavement NOUN

beret **berets**
Said "**ber**-ray" **NOUN** a circular, soft, flat hat with no brim.

berry **berries**
NOUN Berries are small, round fruits that grow on bushes or trees.

berserk
PHRASE If someone **goes berserk** they lose control of themselves and become very violent.
[from Icelandic *berserkr*, a kind of Viking who wore a shirt made from the skin of a bear. They worked themselves into a frenzy before battle]

berth **berths**
NOUN 1 a space in a harbour where a ship stays when it is being loaded or unloaded.
2 In a boat, train or caravan, a berth is a bed.
PHRASE 3 If you **give something a wide berth**, you avoid it because it is unpleasant or dangerous.

beside
PREPOSITION next to.

Synonyms: adjacent to, alongside

besides
PREPOSITION 1 in addition to, apart from. *What languages do you know besides English?*
ADVERB 2 anyway. *I don't need any help. Besides, I'm nearly finished.*

besiege **besieges besieging besieged**
VERB When soldiers besiege a place, they surround it and wait for the people inside to surrender. See **siege**.

best
ADJECTIVE, ADVERB OR NOUN the superlative of **good** and **well**. *Jim was good, I was better, but Tess was the best.*

Synonyms: finest, supreme, top

best man
NOUN The best man at a wedding is a friend or relative of the bridegroom who acts as his attendant.

a b c d e f g h i j k l m n o p q r s t u v w x y z

A B C D E F G H I J K L M N O P Q R S T U V W X Y Z

bestseller bestsellers
NOUN a book which sells a very large number of copies.

bet bets betting bet
VERB **1** If you bet on the result of an event, you will win money if something happens and lose money if it does not.
NOUN **2** the money that you gamble when you bet.

betray betrays betraying betrayed
VERB **1** If you betray someone who trusts you, you do something which harms them, such as helping their enemies.
2 If you betray a secret, or a feeling or thought, you give it away.
betrayal NOUN **betrayer** NOUN

better
ADJECTIVE OR ADVERB the comparative of **good** and **well**. *She's better than me at maths. These apples are better than those.*

Synonyms: finer, greater, superior

between
PREPOSITION OR ADVERB something that is between is in the middle of two things or somehow links two things together. *They built two houses with a garage between. She was headteacher between 1993 and 1999.*

beverage beverages
NOUN; FORMAL a drink.

beware
VERB a word used to warn people of something dangerous or harmful.

bewilder bewilders bewildering bewildered
VERB to confuse, to baffle.
bewildered ADJECTIVE **bewildering** ADJECTIVE

bewitch bewitches bewitching bewitched
VERB to cast a spell on someone.
bewitched ADJECTIVE **bewitching** ADJECTIVE

beyond
PREPOSITION on the other side of, after.

bi-
PREFIX twice or two.

bias
NOUN Someone who shows bias favours one person or thing unfairly.

Synonyms: favouritism, partiality, prejudice

bib bibs
NOUN a piece of cloth or plastic which very young children wear under their chin when they are eating, to keep their clothes clean.

Bible Bibles
NOUN the sacred book of the Christian religion.
biblical ADJECTIVE
[from Greek *biblia* meaning the books]

bibliography bibliographies
NOUN a list of books or articles on a particular subject.

biceps
NOUN Your biceps are the large muscles on the front of your upper arms.

bicker bickers bickering bickered
VERB to argue or quarrel about unimportant things.

bicycle bicycles
NOUN a two-wheeled vehicle you ride by pedalling.

bid bids bidding bid
NOUN **1** an attempt to obtain or do something. *He made a bid for freedom.*
2 an offer to buy something for a certain sum of money, especially at an auction.
VERB **3** to offer to pay a certain sum of money for something, especially at an auction.
bidder NOUN

bide bides biding bided
PHRASE If you **bide your time**, you wait for a good opportunity before doing something.

big bigger biggest
ADJECTIVE large or important.

Synonyms: enormous, huge, massive

bike bikes
NOUN; INFORMAL a bicycle or motorcycle.

bikini bikinis
NOUN a two-piece swimming costume worn by women.

bilge bilges
NOUN **1** the lowest part of a ship where dirty water collects.
2 If you say that someone is talking bilge, you disagree strongly with what they are saying.

bilingual
ADJECTIVE involving or using two languages: *bilingual street signs.*
bilingually ADVERB **bilingualism** NOUN

bill bills
NOUN **1** a written statement of how much is owed for goods or services.
2 a formal statement of a proposed new law that is discussed and then voted on in Parliament.
3 a bird's beak.

billiards
NOUN a game similar to snooker, played with a cue and three balls.

billion billions
NOUN a thousand million (1 000 000 000).
✔ Formerly in Britain, a billion was a million million.

billow billows billowing billowed
VERB **1** When things made of cloth billow, they fill out and flap in the wind.
2 When smoke or cloud billows, it spreads upwards and outwards.

 ► Colossal, gigantic, vast and immense are further synonyms for "big".

billy goat billy goats
NOUN a male goat.

Antonym: nanny goat

bin bins
NOUN a container, especially one which you put rubbish in.

binary
Said "**by**-nar-ee" ADJECTIVE The binary, or Base 2, system expresses numbers using only two digits, 0 and 1.

bind binds binding bound
VERB **1** to hold something firmly by tying it round.
2 If something binds you to a course of action, it makes you act in that way.

bingo
NOUN a game in which players aim to match numbers that someone calls out with numbers on a card they have been given.

binoculars
PLURAL NOUN an instrument with lenses for both eyes, which you look through in order to see objects far away.

biodegradable
ADJECTIVE capable of being rotted down into its natural elements by the action of bacteria.
biodegradability NOUN

biography biographies
NOUN the history of someone's life, written by someone else.
biographical ADJECTIVE

biology
NOUN the study of living things.
biological ADJECTIVE **biologist** NOUN
biologically ADVERB

bionic
ADJECTIVE having a part or parts of the body that work electrically.

birch birches
NOUN a tall deciduous tree with thin branches and thin bark.

bird birds
NOUN an animal with two legs, two wings and feathers.

birth births
NOUN When a baby is born, you refer to this event as its birth.

birthday birthdays
NOUN the anniversary of the date on which someone or something was born.

birthmark birthmarks
NOUN a mark on someone's skin that has been there since they were born.

biscuit biscuits
NOUN a small flat cake that is crisp and usually sweet.
[from Latin *bis* meaning twice + Old French *pain bescuit* bread which was baked twice]

bisect bisects bisecting bisected
VERB To bisect a line or area means to divide it in half.

bishop bishops
NOUN **1** a high-ranking clergyman in some Christian churches.
2 In chess, a bishop is a piece that is moved diagonally across the board.

bison
NOUN a large hairy animal, related to cattle.

bit bits **1** the past tense of **bite**.
NOUN **2** a small piece of something.
PHRASE **3** INFORMAL slightly or to a small extent. *That sum's a bit difficult.*

Synonyms: (sense 2) fragment, part, piece

bitch bitches
NOUN a female dog.

bite bites biting bit bitten
VERB **1** to cut through something with your teeth.
NOUN **2** a small amount of something that you cut off with your teeth.
3 the injury you get when something bites you.

bitter bitterest
ADJECTIVE **1** sharp and unpleasant to taste.
2 If someone is bitter, they feel angry and resentful.
3 In a bitter argument or war, people argue or fight fiercely and angrily.
bitterly ADVERB **bitterness** NOUN

bizarre
Said "biz-**zahr**" ADJECTIVE odd or unusual, strange, weird.
bizarrely ADVERB

blab blabs blabbing blabbed
VERB; INFORMAL to give away secrets by talking carelessly.

black blacker blackest; blacks
NOUN OR ADJECTIVE **1** the darkest possible colour.
2 Someone who is Black is a member of a dark-skinned ethnic group.
blackness NOUN

blackberry blackberries
NOUN Blackberries are small black fruits that grow on prickly bushes called brambles.

blackbird blackbirds
NOUN a common European bird, the male of which has black feathers and a yellow beak.

blackboard blackboards
NOUN a dark-coloured board in a classroom, on which teachers write using chalk.

blackcurrant blackcurrants
NOUN Blackcurrants are very small dark purple fruits that grow in bunches on bushes.

blacken blackens blackening blackened
VERB to make something black or dirty.

a b c d e f g h i j k l m n o p q r s t u v w x y z

Idioms. What are black sheep, black holes, black looks, black marks?

A B C D E F G H I J K L M N O P Q R S T U V W X Y Z

black eye black eyes
NOUN a bruise round the eye caused by being hit in the face.

black hole black holes
NOUN a region of space where the gravity is so intense that no matter, light or other form of radiation can escape from it.

blackmail blackmails blackmailing blackmailed
VERB If someone blackmails another person, they threaten to reveal an unpleasant secret about them unless that person gives them money or does something for them.
blackmail NOUN **blackmailer** NOUN

black market
NOUN If something is bought or sold on the black market, it is bought or sold illegally.

blackout blackouts
NOUN If you have a blackout, you lose consciousness for a short time.
black out VERB

blacksmith blacksmiths
NOUN a person whose job is making things out of iron, such as horseshoes.

bladder bladders
NOUN a bag-like organ inside your body where urine is held until it leaves your body.

blade blades
NOUN 1 the sharp part of a knife, saw, etc.
2 a single piece of grass.

blame blames blaming blamed
VERB 1 If someone blames you for something bad that has happened, they believe you caused it.
NOUN 2 the responsibility for letting something bad happen.

Synonyms: (sense 1) accuse, hold responsible

bland blander blandest
ADJECTIVE plain, dull, unexciting: *a bland diet.*
blandly ADVERB

blank blanker blankest
ADJECTIVE Something that is blank has nothing on it: *a blank piece of paper. She wore a blank expression.*
blankly ADVERB

blanket blankets
NOUN a thick cloth which is put on a bed for warmth.

blank verse
NOUN poetry in which the lines do not rhyme.

blare blares blaring blared
VERB to make a loud, unpleasant noise.

blasphemous
ADJECTIVE disrespectful to God or religion.
blaspheme VERB **blasphemy** NOUN

blast blasts blasting blasted
VERB 1 to make a hole with an explosion.
NOUN 2 an explosion.
3 a strong rush of air or wind.

blastoff
NOUN the moment when a rocket leaves the ground and rises into the air.

blatant
ADJECTIVE clear and obvious in an unpleasant way. *The blatant foul deserved a penalty.*
blatantly ADVERB

blaze blazes blazing blazed
NOUN 1 a large, hot fire.
2 a great or strong amount of something: *a blaze of colour.*
VERB 3 to burn or shine brightly.

blazer blazers
NOUN a kind of jacket, often in the colours of a school or sports team.

bleach bleaches bleaching bleached
VERB 1 To bleach material or hair means to make it white, usually by using a chemical.
NOUN 2 a strong chemical usually used to clean thoroughly and kill germs or to make something white or whiter.

bleak bleaker bleakest
ADJECTIVE 1 If a place is bleak, it is cold, bare and exposed to the wind.
2 If a situation is bleak, it is bad and seems unlikely to improve.
bleakly ADVERB **bleakness** NOUN

bleat bleats bleating bleated
VERB 1 When sheep or goats bleat, they make a high-pitched cry.
NOUN 2 the high-pitched cry that a sheep or goat makes.

bleed bleeds bleeding bled
VERB to lose blood.

bleep bleeps
NOUN a short high-pitched sound made by an electrical device such as an alarm.

blemish blemishes
NOUN a mark that spoils the appearance of something.

blend blends blending blended
VERB 1 When you blend things, you mix them together to form a single thing.
2 When colours or sounds blend, they combine in a pleasing way.

bless blesses blessing blessed
VERB When a priest blesses people or things, he or she asks God to make them holy.
blessed ADJECTIVE **blessedly** ADVERB

blessing blessings
NOUN 1 something good that you are thankful for. *Good health is the greatest blessing.*
PHRASE 2 If something is done **with someone's blessing**, they approve of it and support it.

► Blank verse was Shakespeare's favourite form for his plays.

blew
the past tense of **blow**.

blight **blights blighting blighted**
NOUN 1 something that damages or spoils other things. *The blight of violence in the inner cities.*
VERB 2 When something is blighted, it is seriously harmed.

blind **blinds blinding blinded**
ADJECTIVE 1 unable to see.
VERB 2 to make someone unable to see, either for a short time or permanently.
NOUN 3 a roll of cloth or paper that you pull down over a window to keep out the light.
blinding ADJECTIVE **blindly** ADVERB
blindness NOUN

blindfold **blindfolds**
NOUN a strip of cloth tied over someone's eyes so that they cannot see.

blink **blinks blinking blinked**
VERB to close your eyes quickly for a moment.

bliss
NOUN complete happiness.
blissful ADJECTIVE **blissfully** ADVERB

blister **blisters**
NOUN a small bubble on your skin containing watery liquid, caused by a burn or rubbing.
blistering ADJECTIVE

blitz
NOUN a bombing attack by enemy aircraft on a city.
[from German *Blitzkrieg* meaning lightning war]

blizzard **blizzards**
NOUN a heavy snowstorm with strong winds.

bloated
ADJECTIVE Something that is bloated is much larger than normal, often because there is a lot of liquid or gas inside it.

blob **blobs**
NOUN a small amount of a thick or sticky substance.

block **blocks blocking blocked**
NOUN 1 a large rectangular piece of something.
2 a large building containing flats or offices.
VERB 3 To block a road or channel means to put something across it so that nothing can get through.

Synonyms: (sense 1) bar, chunk, piece
(sense 3) bar, obstruct

blockade **blockades**
NOUN an action that prevents goods or people from reaching a place.

blockage **blockages**
NOUN When there is a blockage in a pipe or tunnel, something is clogging it up.

Synonyms: impediment, obstruction, stoppage

block capitals or **block letters**
PLURAL NOUN Block capitals are capital letters all the same size.

bloke **blokes**
NOUN; INFORMAL a man.

blonde **blondes**; also spelt **blond**
ADJECTIVE 1 Blonde hair is pale yellow in colour.
NOUN 2 a girl or woman with light-coloured hair.
✔ The spelling *blond* is used when referring to men.

blood
NOUN the red liquid that is pumped by the heart round the bodies of humans and other mammals.

bloodshed
NOUN When there is bloodshed, people are killed or wounded.

bloodshot
ADJECTIVE If a person's eyes are bloodshot, the white parts have become red.

bloodstream
NOUN the flow of blood through your body.

bloodthirsty
ADJECTIVE Someone who is bloodthirsty enjoys using or watching violence.

blood vessel **blood vessels**
NOUN Blood vessels are the narrow tubes in your body through which your blood flows.

bloody **bloodier bloodiest**
ADJECTIVE 1 A bloody event is one in which a lot of people are killed.
2 covered in or smeared with blood.
ADJECTIVE OR ADVERB 3 a common swearword.

bloom **blooms blooming bloomed**
VERB 1 To grow and blossom.
NOUN 2 a flower.

blossom **blossoms blossoming blossomed**
NOUN 1 the growth of flowers that appears on a tree before the fruit.
VERB 2 When a tree blossoms, it grows flowers.

blot **blots blotting blotted**
NOUN 1 a drop of spilled ink.
2 A blot on someone's record is a mistake or piece of bad behaviour that spoils their reputation.
blot out **VERB** to prevent something from being seen by being in front of it. *The smoke blotted out the hills behind.*

blotch **blotches**
NOUN a discoloured patch or stain.
blotchy ADJECTIVE

blouse **blouses**
NOUN a light shirt, worn by a girl or a woman.

A B C D E F G H I J K L M N O P Q R S T U V W X Y Z

blow blows blowing blew blown
VERB **1** to breathe air at, through or into something, such as a candle, a musical instrument or a balloon.
2 When the wind blows, the air moves around.
NOUN **3** If you receive a blow, someone or something hits you.
4 something that makes you very disappointed or unhappy. *Failing the exam was a bit of a blow.*
blow over VERB If a situation blows over, it gradually ends.
blow up VERB to destroy something with an explosion.

blubber
NOUN The blubber of mammals such as whales and seals is the layer of fat that protects them from the cold.

blue bluer bluest
ADJECTIVE OR NOUN the colour of the sky on a clear, sunny day.
bluish or **blueish** ADJECTIVE

bluebell bluebells
NOUN a woodland plant with blue, bell-shaped flowers.

blues
PLURAL NOUN **1** a feeling of depression or deep unhappiness.
2 a type of music.

bluff bluffs bluffing bluffed
NOUN **1** an attempt to make someone believe that you will do something when you do not really intend to do it.
VERB **2** If you are bluffing, you are trying to make someone believe that you are in a stronger position than is actually true.

blunder blunders blundering blundered
VERB **1** to make a stupid or clumsy mistake.
2 to move around clumsily.
NOUN **3** a stupid or clumsy mistake.

blunt blunter bluntest
ADJECTIVE **1** If an object is blunt, it is not sharp.
2 If you are blunt, you say exactly what you think, without trying to be polite.
bluntly ADVERB **bluntness** NOUN

Synonyms: (sense 2) forthright, outspoken, straightforward

blur blurs
NOUN a shape or area which you cannot see clearly. *From the train, the countryside was a blur.*
blur VERB **blurred** ADJECTIVE

blurb
NOUN The blurb about a product is information about it, written to make people interested in it.

blurt out blurts out blurting out blurted out
VERB to say something suddenly, after trying to keep it a secret.

blush blushes blushing blushed
VERB If you blush, your face becomes red, because you are embarrassed or ashamed.

blustery
ADJECTIVE Blustery weather is rough and windy.

boa boas
NOUN **1** A boa, or boa constrictor, is a large snake that kills its prey by coiling round it and crushing it.
2 a type of long scarf of feathers or fur worn by women, popular in the 1920s.

boar boars
NOUN a male wild pig, or a male domestic pig used for breeding.

board boards boarding boarded
NOUN **1** a flat piece of wood, plastic or cardboard.
2 the group of people who control a company or organization.
VERB **3** to get on a ship or aircraft.
4 to be a live-in pupil at a boarding school.
PHRASE **5** If you are **on board** a ship or aircraft, you are on it or in it.

boarder boarders
NOUN a pupil who lives at a boarding school during term.

boarding school boarding schools
NOUN a school where the pupils live during the term.

boast boasts boasting boasted
VERB to talk proudly about your possessions or achievements.
boastful ADJECTIVE **boastfulness** NOUN

Synonyms: blow your own trumpet, brag, crow

boat boats
NOUN a floating vehicle for travelling on water.

bob bobs bobbing bobbed
VERB **1** to move up and down.
NOUN **2** a woman's hair style in which her hair is cut level with her chin.

bobsleigh bobsleighs; also spelt **bobsled**
NOUN a racing sledge for two or more people.

bodice bodices
NOUN the upper part of a dress.

bodily
ADVERB **1** relating to the body.
2 involving the whole of someone's body. *They carried me bodily up the stairs.*

body bodies
NOUN **1** Your body is either all your physical parts, or just the main part not including your head, arms and legs.
2 A body is a corpse, or dead person.
3 the main part of something, without any additional bits: *the body of the car was sound, but the engine was rusted.*

Synonyms: (sense 1) figure, form, physique

► Quote from supermodel: "I used to be boastful, but now I'm perfect."

bodyguard bodyguards
NOUN a person employed to protect someone.

bog bogs
NOUN an area of land which is always wet and spongy.
boggy ADJECTIVE
[from Gaelic *bogach* meaning a swamp]

bogus
ADJECTIVE not genuine.
[from the name of a machine which made counterfeit money]

boil boils boiling boiled
VERB **1** to heat a liquid until bubbles appear in it and it starts to give off steam.
2 to cook food in boiling water.
NOUN **3** a red swelling on your skin.

boiler boilers
NOUN a piece of equipment which burns fuel to provide hot water or steam.

boiling
ADJECTIVE; INFORMAL very hot indeed.

boisterous
ADJECTIVE noisy and lively.
boisterously ADVERB **boisterousness** NOUN

Synonyms: loud, rowdy, unruly

bold bolder boldest
ADJECTIVE **1** brave or confident.
2 clear and noticeable.
boldly ADVERB **boldness** NOUN

bollard bollards
NOUN a short, thick post used to keep vehicles out of a road or off a traffic island.

bolt bolts bolting bolted
NOUN **1** a metal object which screws into a nut and is used to fasten things together.
2 a sliding metal bar used to fasten doors, gates and windows.
3 a flash of lightning.
VERB **4** to run away unexpectedly.
5 To bolt food means to eat it quickly.

bomb bombs bombing bombed
NOUN **1** a container filled with explosive material, designed to explode when detonated or when dropped to the ground.
VERB **2** When a place is bombed, it is attacked with bombs.
[from Greek *bombos* meaning a booming sound]

bombard bombards bombarding bombarded
VERB to issue a constant, heavy attack, usually of gunfire. *We were bombarded with paperwork.*
bombardment NOUN

bond bonds bonding bonded
NOUN **1** a close relationship between people.
VERB **2** When two things bond or are bonded, they become closely linked or attached.

Synonyms: (sense 1) connection, link, tie

bondage
NOUN Bondage is the condition of being someone's slave.

bone bones
NOUN Bones are the hard parts that form the framework of the body of a human or other animal.

bonfire bonfires
NOUN a large fire made outdoors.
[from *bone* + *fire*; bones were used as fuel in the Middle Ages]

bonnet bonnets
NOUN **1** a baby's or woman's hat tied under the chin.
2 the metal cover over a car's engine.

bonus bonuses
NOUN **1** a good thing that you get in addition to something else.
2 an amount of money added to your usual pay.

bony bonier boniest
ADJECTIVE A bony person is thin with prominent bones.

boo boos booing booed
VERB to shout to show disapproval.
boo NOUN

booby prize booby prizes
NOUN a consolation prize given to the person who comes last in a competition.

booby trap booby traps
NOUN a trap or bomb which is hidden or disguised.
booby-trapped ADJECTIVE

book books booking booked
NOUN **1** a number of pages held together inside a cover.
VERB **2** to make an arrangement to have or use something at a particular time, for example, a train, a meal, an appointment, a theatre ticket.
3 to record that someone has committed an offence. *He was booked for speeding in a built-up area.*
booking NOUN

bookcase bookcases
NOUN a piece of furniture with shelves for books.

booklet booklets
NOUN a small, thin book with a paper cover.

bookmaker bookmakers
NOUN a person who makes a living from taking people's bets, paying them when they win.

bookmark bookmarks
NOUN a piece of card or cloth which you put between the pages of a book to mark your place.

a b c d e f g h i j k l m n o p q r s t u v w x y z

A B C D E F G H I J K L M N O P Q R S T U V W X Y Z

boom **booms booming boomed**
NOUN **1** a loud, deep echoing sound.
2 a rapid increase in something. *There was a boom in rail travel when the fares were reduced.*
VERB **3** to make a loud deep echoing sound.
4 to increase rapidly.

boomerang **boomerangs**
NOUN a curved wooden missile that can be thrown so that it returns to the thrower, originally used as a weapon by Australian Aborigines.

boost **boosts boosting boosted**
VERB **1** To boost something means to cause it to improve or increase. *The advertising campaign boosted sales.*
NOUN **2** an improvement or increase.

boot **boots**
NOUN **1** Boots are strong shoes that cover your ankle and sometimes calf.
2 the covered space in a car for carrying things in.
boot up VERB to switch on a computer.

booth **booths**
NOUN a small open cubicle: *a telephone booth.*

border **borders bordering bordered**
NOUN **1** the dividing line between two countries.
2 a strip or band round the edge of something.
VERB **3** to form a boundary along the side of something.
PHRASE **4** If an action **borders on** something, it is almost that thing. *The clever decision bordered on genius.*

borderline
ADJECTIVE only just acceptable.

bore **bores boring bored**
1 the past tense of **bear**.
VERB **2** If something bores you, you find it dull and uninteresting.
3 to drill a hole in something.
NOUN **4** someone or something that bores you.

bored
ADJECTIVE If you are bored you are impatient because you find something uninteresting or because you have nothing to do.
boredom NOUN
✔ You can say that you are *bored with* or *bored by* something, but avoid *bored of*, which is incorrect.

boring
ADJECTIVE dull, tedious, uninteresting.
boringly ADVERB

born
VERB When a baby is born, it comes out of its mother's womb at the beginning of its life.

borough **boroughs**
Said "**bur**-uh" NOUN a town, or a district within a large town, that has its own council.

borrow **borrows borrowing borrowed**
VERB If you borrow something that belongs to someone else, they let you have it for a period of time.

Antonym: lend

bosom **bosoms**
NOUN A woman's bosom is her breasts.

boss **bosses bossing bossed**
NOUN **1** Someone's boss is the person in charge of the place where they work.
VERB **2** If someone bosses you around, they keep telling you what to do.

bossy **bossier bossiest**
ADJECTIVE A bossy person tries to tell other people what to do.
bossily ADVERB **bossiness** NOUN

Synonyms: dictatorial, domineering, overbearing

botany
NOUN the scientific study of plants.
botanic or **botanical** ADJECTIVE **botanist** NOUN

both
ADJECTIVE AND PRONOUN this word refers to two things or people together. *Both recipes were equally delicious. Both boys and girls play this game.*
✔ You can use *of* after *both*, but it is not essential. *Both the puppies* means the same as *both of the puppies.*

bother **bothers bothering bothered**
VERB **1** If you do not bother to do something, you do not do it because it takes too much effort or it seems unnecessary.
2 If something bothers you, you are worried or concerned about it.
3 If you bother someone, you interrupt them when they are busy.
NOUN **4** trouble, fuss or difficulty.
bothersome ADJECTIVE **bothered** ADJECTIVE

bottle **bottles**
NOUN a glass or plastic container for keeping liquids in.

bottleneck **bottlenecks**
NOUN a section of road where traffic has to slow down or stop.

bottom **bottoms**
NOUN **1** Your bottom is the part of your body that you sit on.
NOUN AND ADJECTIVE **2** the lowest part of something.

bottomless
ADJECTIVE having no visible bottom. *The millionaire seemed to have bottomless pockets.*

bough **boughs**
Rhymes with "**now**" NOUN a large branch of a tree.

► Some words from Ireland: boycott, shamrock, galore, tory. ►

bought
the past tense and past participle of **buy**.
✔ Do not confuse *bought* and *brought*. *Bought* comes from *buy* and *brought* comes from *bring*.

boulder boulders
NOUN a large rounded rock.

bounce bounces bouncing bounced
VERB When an object bounces, it springs back from something after hitting it.

Synonyms: rebound, recoil, ricochet

bouncy bouncier bounciest
ADJECTIVE **1** easily bounced.
2 Bouncy people are lively and enthusiastic.

bound bounds bounding bounded
1 the past tense and past participle of **bind**.
ADJECTIVE **2** If you say that something is bound to happen, you mean that it is certain to happen.
3 If a person or a vehicle is bound for a place, they are going there.
VERB **4** When people or animals bound, they move quickly with large leaps.
NOUN **5** a large leap.
PLURAL NOUN **6** Bounds are limits which restrict or control something.
PHRASE **7** If something is **out of bounds**, you are forbidden to go there.

boundary boundaries
NOUN something that indicates the farthest limit of anything.

bouquet bouquets
Said "boo-**kay**" NOUN an attractively arranged bunch of flowers.

bout bouts
NOUN a short period of something.

boutique boutiques
Said "boo-**teek**" NOUN a small shop that sells fashionable clothes.

bow bows bowing bowed
Rhymes with "**now**" VERB **1** to bend your body or lower your head as a sign of respect or greeting.
NOUN **2** the front part of a ship.
Rhymes with "**go**" NOUN **3** a long thin piece of wood with horsehair stretched along it, which is used to play a violin.
4 a long flexible piece of wood used for shooting arrows.
5 a knot with two loops and two loose ends.

bowel bowels
Rhymes with "**towel**" NOUN Your bowels are the tubes leading from your stomach, through which waste passes before it leaves your body. [from Latin *botellus* meaning little sausage]

bowl bowls bowling bowled
Rhymes with "**mole**" NOUN **1** a deep dish.
VERB **2** To bowl a ball is to throw it in a game.

bowling
NOUN a game in which you roll a heavy ball down a narrow track towards skittles to try to knock them down.

bowls
PLURAL NOUN a game where you roll heavy black balls as near as possible to a white ball called the jack.

bow tie bow ties
Rhymes with "**go**" NOUN a man's tie in the form of a bow, often worn at formal occasions.

box boxes
NOUN **1** a firm cube or cuboid container, usually with a lid.
2 a rectangular space on a printed form.

boxer boxers
NOUN **1** a person who takes part in the sport of boxing.
2 a type of medium-sized, smooth-haired dog with a fairly flat face.

Boxing Day
NOUN a public holiday which is nearly always the first day after Christmas.

box office box offices
NOUN the place where tickets are sold in a theatre or cinema.

boy boys
NOUN a male child.

Synonyms: lad, youth

boycott boycotts boycotting boycotted
VERB **1** to have nothing to do with something, as a protest.
NOUN **2** a protest which takes the form of a general refusal to do or buy something.

boyfriend boyfriends
NOUN a man or boy with whom someone is having a romantic relationship.

bra bras
NOUN a piece of underwear worn by a woman to support her breasts.

brace braces bracing braced
VERB **1** When you brace yourself, you stiffen your body in order to steady yourself or avoid falling.
NOUN **2** an object fastened to something in order to straighten or support it.
PLURAL NOUN **3** Braces are a pair of straps to hold up trousers.

bracelet bracelets
NOUN a chain or band worn around someone's wrist as an ornament.

bracken
NOUN a plant like a large fern that grows on hills and in woods.

bracket brackets
NOUN Brackets are a pair of written marks, ( ), [ ] or { }.

a b c d e f g h i j k l m n o p q r s t u v w x y z

Irish people refused to pay rent to Captain Boycott, an unreasonable and hated land agent. ◀

WHAT DO BRACKETS DO?
Brackets ( ) enclose words in a sentence which are extra to the main sentence and which could be omitted:
It cost the coachman a guinea (£1.05 in today's money) to feed the horses.
They are also used to make an aside:
George went home (and he never did it again).
Square brackets [ ] are used in quotations where an editor has inserted words that are not part of the original quotation to make it clearer or explain something:
The minister said, "I think that five million [pounds] should do it."

brag **brags bragging bragged**
VERB When someone brags, they boast about themselves.

braid **braids braiding braided**
NOUN 1 a strip of decorated cloth used to decorate clothes or curtains.
2 a length of hair which has been plaited or tied.
VERB 3 To braid hair or thread means to plait it.

Braille
NOUN a system of printing for blind people in which letters are represented by raised dots that can be felt with the fingers.
[named after the inventor Louis Braille (1809–52)]

brain **brains**
NOUN 1 the organ inside your head that controls your body and enables you to think and feel.
2 your mind and the way that you think.

brainstorm
NOUN intensive discussion to solve a question or problem, where people are encouraged to give ideas spontaneously.

brainwave **brainwaves**
NOUN; INFORMAL a clever, sudden idea.

brainy **brainier brainiest**
ADJECTIVE; INFORMAL clever.

brake **brakes**
NOUN a device for making a vehicle stop or slow down.
brake VERB

bramble **brambles**
NOUN a wild, thorny bush that produces blackberries.

branch **branches branching branched**
NOUN 1 the parts of a tree that grow out from its trunk.
2 A branch of a business is one of its offices or shops.
branch off **VERB** to branch off is to split off into a different direction.
branch out **VERB** to branch out is to start doing something new.

brand **brands branding branded**
NOUN 1 a particular kind or make of a product.
VERB 2 When an animal is branded, a mark is burned on its skin to show who owns it.

brandish **brandishes brandishing brandished**
VERB; LITERARY to wave something vigorously.
Wallace brandished his sword above his head.

brand-new
ADJECTIVE completely new.

brandy
NOUN a strong alcoholic drink.

brass
NOUN AND ADJECTIVE 1 a yellow-coloured metal made from copper and zinc.
2 In an orchestra, the brass section consists of brass wind instruments such as trumpets, trombones and horns.

brat **brats**
NOUN; INFORMAL a badly behaved child.

brave **braver bravest; braves braving braved**
ADJECTIVE 1 courageous.
VERB 2 to face up to an unpleasant or dangerous situation.
bravely ADVERB **bravery** NOUN

Synonyms: (sense 1) daring, fearless, plucky

brawl **brawls brawling brawled**
VERB to take part in a rough fight.
brawl NOUN **brawler** NOUN

brawn
NOUN physical strength.
brawny ADJECTIVE

bray **brays braying brayed**
VERB When a donkey brays, it makes a loud, harsh sound.
bray NOUN

brazen
ADJECTIVE When someone behaves in a brazen way, they do not care if other people think they are behaving wrongly.
brazenly ADJECTIVE

breach **breaches breaching breached**
VERB 1 To breach a barrier means to break through it.
2 FORMAL To breach an agreement or law means to break it.
breach NOUN

bread
NOUN a food made from flour, water and often yeast, and baked in an oven.

breadth
NOUN The breadth of something is the distance between its two sides. See **width**.

 ► Brand names of goods begin with capital letters: Microsoft, Sellotape, Sony.

break breaks breaking broke broken
NOUN **1** a short rest from something.
VERB **2** If you break an object, you damage it so it is useless, often in pieces.
3 If you break a rule or a promise, you fail to keep it.
4 When a boy's voice breaks, it becomes permanently deeper.
break down VERB to stop working.
break up VERB If something breaks up, it ends.

Synonyms: fracture, separate

breakable
ADJECTIVE easily broken.

Synonym: fragile

breakage breakages
NOUN the act of breaking something, or the thing that has been broken.

breakdown breakdowns
NOUN **1** the failure of something such as machinery, a system, a plan or negotiations.
2 If you have a breakdown, you become so anxious or depressed that you cannot cope with life.

breaker breakers
NOUN Breakers are big sea waves.

breakfast breakfasts
NOUN the first meal of the day.

break-in break-ins
NOUN the illegal entering of a building, especially by a burglar.

breakthrough breakthroughs
NOUN a sudden important development.

breakwater breakwaters
NOUN a wall extending into the sea which protects the coast from the force of the waves.

breast breasts
NOUN A female's breasts are the parts of her body which produce milk.

breaststroke
NOUN a frog-like swimming stroke.

breath breaths
NOUN **1** the air you take into your lungs and let out again when you breathe.
PHRASE **2** If you are **out of breath**, you are breathing with difficulty after doing something energetic.
3 If you say something **under your breath**, you say it very quietly.

breathe breathes breathing breathed
VERB to take air into your lungs and let it out again.

breathless
ADJECTIVE to breathe very rapidly or with difficulty.
breathlessly ADVERB **breathlessness** NOUN

breathtaking
ADJECTIVE A breathtaking view is exciting and beautiful.

bred
past tense and past participle of **breed**.

breeches
Said "**brit**-chiz" PLURAL NOUN trousers reaching to just below the knee.

breed breeds breeding bred
NOUN **1** one particular type of a species of domestic animal.
VERB **2** When animals breed, they mate and produce offspring.
3 to keep animals or plants especially for mating and reproduction.

breeze breezes
NOUN a gentle wind.

brew brews brewing brewed
VERB **1** If you brew tea or coffee, you make it in a pot by pouring hot water over it.
2 To brew beer means to make it, by boiling and fermenting malt.

brewery breweries
NOUN a place where beer is made, or a company that makes it.

bribe bribes
NOUN a gift or money given to an official or other person in an influential situation, to persuade them to do what you want.
bribe VERB **bribery** NOUN

brick bricks
NOUN Bricks are rectangular blocks of baked clay used in building.

bride brides
NOUN a woman on her wedding day.
bridal ADJECTIVE

bridegroom bridegrooms
NOUN a man on his wedding day.

bridesmaid bridesmaids
NOUN a woman or girl who helps and accompanies a bride on her wedding day.

bridge bridges
NOUN **1** a structure built over a river, road or railway so that vehicles and people can cross.
2 a card game for four players based on whist.
3 the control room of a ship.

bridle bridles
NOUN a set of straps round a horse's head and mouth, which the rider uses to control the horse.

brief briefer briefest; briefs briefing briefed
ADJECTIVE **1** lasting only a short time.
VERB **2** When you brief someone on a task, you give them all the necessary instructions or information about it.
briefly ADVERB **brevity** NOUN

Synonyms: (sense 1) fleeting, momentary, quick

A B C D E F G H I J K L M N O P Q R S T U V W X Y Z

briefcase **briefcases**
NOUN a case for carrying papers.

briefs
PLURAL NOUN Briefs are underpants.

brigade **brigades**
NOUN 1 a group of people organized to do a particular task: *the fire brigade.*
2 a large army unit containing several battalions.

bright **brighter brightest**
ADJECTIVE 1 Bright colours are strong and noticeable.
2 clever.
3 cheerful and brisk.
brightly ADVERB **brightness** NOUN

Synonyms: (sense 1) brilliant, dazzling, vivid

brighten **brightens brightening brightened**
VERB to make something brighter or to become brighter.

brilliant
ADJECTIVE 1 very bright indeed.
2 extremely clever or skilful.
3 INFORMAL extremely good or enjoyable.
brilliantly ADVERB **brilliance** NOUN

brim **brims brimming brimmed**
NOUN 1 the part of a hat that sticks outwards at the bottom.
VERB 2 To brim with a liquid means to be full of it. *Her eyes brimmed with tears.*
PHRASE 3 If a container is filled **to the brim**, it is filled right to the top.

brine
NOUN salt water.

bring **brings bringing brought**
VERB If you bring something or someone, you take them with you.
bring about **VERB** to cause to happen.
bring up **VERB** to look after children while they grow up.

brink **brinks**
NOUN 1 the edge of a high place. *He stood on the brink of the cliffs.*
PHRASE 2 If you are **on the brink** of doing something, you are just about to do it.

brisk **brisker briskest**
ADJECTIVE 1 quick and energetic: *a brisk walk.*
2 quick and efficient. *Service in the take-away was brisk.*
briskly ADVERB **briskness** NOUN

bristle **bristles bristling bristled**
NOUN 1 Bristles are strong animal hairs used to make brushes.
VERB 2 If the hairs on an animal's body bristle, they rise up because it is frightened.
bristly ADJECTIVE

brittle
ADJECTIVE hard but easily broken.
brittleness NOUN

broad **broader broadest**
ADJECTIVE 1 wide.
2 general rather than detailed. *We must take a broad view.*
3 A broad accent is one that makes it obvious where a person has come from.
broadly ADVERB

broadcast **broadcasts**
NOUN a programme or announcement on radio or television.
broadcast VERB **broadcaster** NOUN

broaden **broadens broadening broadened**
VERB to become broader, or make something broader.

broccoli
NOUN a green vegetable, similar to cauliflower.

brochure **brochures**
Said "**broh**-sher" **NOUN** a booklet which gives information about a product or service.

broke **1** the past tense of **break**.
ADJECTIVE 2 INFORMAL If you are broke, you have no money.

broken
the past participle of **break**.

bronchitis
NOUN an illness in which the tubes which take air to your lungs become obstructed, making you cough.

brontosaurus **brontosauruses**
NOUN a very large, plant-eating dinosaur.

bronze
NOUN AND ADJECTIVE a yellowish-brown metal made from copper and tin; also the colour of this metal.

brooch **brooches**
Rhymes with "**coach**" **NOUN** a piece of jewellery with a pin at the back for attaching to clothes.

brood **broods brooding brooded**
NOUN 1 a family of baby birds.
VERB 2 to keep thinking about something in a serious or unhappy way.

brook **brooks**
NOUN a stream.

broom **brooms**
NOUN a long-handled brush.

broth
NOUN a type of soup, usually with vegetables in it.

brother **brothers**
NOUN a boy or man who has the same parents as you.
brotherly ADJECTIVE

brother-in-law **brothers-in-law**
NOUN Someone's brother-in-law is the brother of their husband or wife, or their sister's husband.

 ► Joke. If a girl can't do her homework, why can't her brother help? ►

brought
past tense and past participle of **bring**.
✔ Do not confuse *brought* and *bought*. *Brought* comes from *bring* and *bought* comes from *buy*.

brow **brows**
NOUN **1** the forehead.
2 Your brows are your eyebrows.
3 The brow of a hill is the top of it.

brown **browner brownest**
ADJECTIVE OR NOUN the colour of earth or wood.

Brownie **Brownies**
NOUN a junior member of the Guides.

browse **browses browsing browsed**
VERB **1** If you browse through a shop, a book or text on the Internet, you look through it in a casual way.
2 When animals such as deer are browsing, they are nibbling at the young shoots and leaves of trees.

browser **browsers**
NOUN a software package, especially on the World Wide Web, that allows you to move directly to related websites by clicking on highlighted text.

bruise **bruises**
NOUN a purple mark that appears on your skin after something has hit it.
bruise VERB

brunette **brunettes**
NOUN a girl or woman with dark brown hair.

brush **brushes brushing brushed**
NOUN **1** an object with bristles used for cleaning things, painting or tidying your hair.
VERB **2** to clean or tidy something with a brush.
3 to touch something lightly while passing it.

brussels sprout **brussels sprouts**
NOUN Brussels sprouts are vegetables that look like tiny cabbages.

brutal
ADJECTIVE cruel and violent.
brutally ADVERB **brutality** NOUN

brute **brutes**
NOUN **1** a rough, insensitive person.
ADJECTIVE **2** Brute force is the use of strength alone without any skill.

bubble **bubbles bubbling bubbled**
NOUN **1** a ball of gas in a liquid, particularly soapy liquid.
VERB **2** When a liquid bubbles, bubbles form in it.

bubbly **bubblier bubbliest**
ADJECTIVE **1** full of bubbles.
2 A bubbly person has a lively personality.

buck **bucks bucking bucked**
NOUN **1** the male of various animals, including the deer and the rabbit.
VERB **2** If a horse bucks, it jumps and kicks.
PHRASE **3** INFORMAL If you **pass the buck**, you pass the responsibility or blame for something to someone else.

bucket **buckets**
NOUN a deep round container with an open top and a handle.

buckle **buckles buckling buckled**
NOUN **1** a fastening on the end of a belt or strap.
VERB **2** to fasten a belt or strap.
3 to become bent because of severe heat or pressure.

bud **buds budding budded**
NOUN **1** a small, tight swelling on a tree or plant, which develops into a flower or a cluster of leaves.
VERB **2** When a tree or plant buds, new buds appear on it.
PHRASE **3** To **nip something in the bud** is to put an end to it at an early stage.

Buddhist **Buddhists**
NOUN a person who follows the religious teachings of Buddha.

budding
ADJECTIVE **1** beginning to sprout blooms or leaves.
2 just beginning to develop and showing promise. *She was a budding artist.*

budge **budges budging budged**
VERB to move slightly or give way.

budgerigar **budgerigars**
NOUN a small, brightly coloured pet bird.
[an Australian Aboriginal name, from *budgeri* meaning good + *gar* meaning cockatoo]

budget **budgets budgeting budgeted**
NOUN **1** a plan showing how much money will be available and how it will be spent.
VERB **2** If you budget for something, you plan your money carefully, so you can afford it.

budgie **budgies**
NOUN; INFORMAL a budgerigar.

buffalo **buffaloes**
NOUN a wild animal like a large cow with long curved horns, also called a bison.

buffer **buffers**
NOUN **1** Buffers on a train or at the end of a railway line are metal discs on springs that reduce shock when they are hit.
2 something that prevents something else from being harmed. *Keep savings as a buffer against unexpected cash needs.*

buffet **buffets**
*Said "***boof***-ay"* NOUN **1** a café at a station.
2 a meal at which people serve themselves from a separate table.

a b c d e f g h i j k l m n o p q r s t u v w x y z

A B C D E F G H I J K L M N O P Q R S T U V W X Y Z

bug bugs bugging bugged
NOUN **1** a general name for a type of insect with piercing and sucking mouth parts.
2 a small error in a computer program which means that the program will not work properly.
3 INFORMAL a virus or minor infection.
VERB **4** If a room is bugged, tiny microphones are hidden there to record what people are saying.

bugle bugles
NOUN a brass instrument that looks like a small trumpet.
bugler NOUN

build builds building built
VERB **1** to make something from its parts.
2 to develop gradually: *building a fairer society.*
NOUN **3** Your build is the shape and size of your body.

Synonyms: (sense 1) assemble, construct, erect

builder builders
NOUN a person who makes his living by constructing or repairing buildings.

building buildings
NOUN a structure with walls and a roof.

bulb bulbs
NOUN **1** an onion-shaped root from which a flower or plant grows. Tulips and daffodils are grown from bulbs.
2 the glass part of an electric lamp.

bulge bulges bulging bulged
VERB **1** If something bulges, it swells out from a surface.
NOUN **2** a lump on a normally flat surface.

bulk bulks
NOUN **1** a large mass of something. *The encyclopedia is more impressive for its bulk than its content.*
2 The bulk of something is most of it.
PHRASE **3** To buy something **in bulk** means to buy it in large quantities.

bulky bulkier bulkiest
ADJECTIVE large and heavy.

bull bulls
NOUN the male of some species of animals, including the cow family, elephants and whales.

bulldog bulldogs
NOUN a squat dog with a broad head and muscular body.

bulldozer bulldozers
NOUN a powerful tractor with a broad blade in front, used for moving earth, rocks, etc.

bullet bullets
NOUN **1** a small piece of metal fired from a gun.
2 a bullet point is a dark spot that appears next to each entry in a list to mark them out clearly.

bulletin bulletins
NOUN **1** a leaflet or small newspaper regularly produced by a group or organization.
2 a short news report on radio or television.

bullion
NOUN gold or silver in the form of bars.

bullock bullocks
NOUN a young neutered bull.

bull's-eye bull's-eyes
NOUN the small central disc of a target.

bully bullies bullying bullied
NOUN **1** someone who uses their strength or power to hurt or frighten other people.
VERB **2** If someone bullies you into doing something, they make you do it by using force or threats.

bum bums
NOUN; INFORMAL **1** your bottom.
2 In American English, a bum is a tramp.

bumblebee bumblebees
NOUN a type of bee.

bump bumps bumping bumped
VERB **1** to knock into something with a jolt.
NOUN **2** a raised, uneven part of a surface.
PHRASE **3** To **bump into someone** is to meet them by chance.

bumper bumpers
NOUN Bumpers are protective bars on the front and back of a vehicle.

bumpy bumpier bumpiest
ADJECTIVE If you experience a bumpy ride, your vehicle bumps up and down.

bun buns
NOUN a small, round cake.

bunch bunches
NOUN **1** a group of people or things. *There was a bunch of people waiting at the bus stop.*
2 A bunch of bananas or grapes is a group of them growing on the same stem.

bundle bundles bundling bundled
NOUN **1** a number of things tied or wrapped up together.
VERB **2** to push someone or something quickly and roughly. *They bundled him into the police van.*

bung bungs bunging bunged
NOUN **1** a stopper used to close holes in barrels, pipes, etc.
VERB **2** INFORMAL If you bung something somewhere, you put it there quickly and carelessly.

bungalow bungalows
NOUN a one-storey house.
[from Hindi *bangla* meaning house of Bengal, and so of a house in the Bengal style]

bungle bungles bungling bungled
VERB to fail to do something properly.
bungler NOUN

 ► What kind of person is a bull in a china shop, a wolf in sheep's clothing, a dog in the manger?

bunk **bunks**
NOUN **1** a bed fixed to a wall in a ship or caravan, or with another bed on top of it; short for bunk bed.
PHRASE **2** INFORMAL If someone **does a bunk**, they leave without telling anyone.

bunker **bunkers**
NOUN **1** On a golf course, a bunker is a hole full of sand which golfers try to avoid.
2 A coal bunker is a storage place for coal.
3 an underground shelter with strong walls to protect it from bombing.

buoy **buoys**
Said "**boy**" NOUN a floating object anchored to the bottom of the sea, marking a channel or warning of danger.

buoyant
Said "**boy**-unt" ADJECTIVE **1** able to float.
2 lively and cheerful.
buoyancy NOUN

burden **burdens**
NOUN **1** a heavy load to carry.
2 If something is a burden to you, it causes you a lot of worry or hard work.
burdensome ADJECTIVE

bureau **bureaux**
Said "**byoo**-roh" NOUN **1** an office that provides a service: *an employment bureau.*
2 a writing desk with shelves and drawers.

burger **burgers**
NOUN a beefburger or hamburger.

burglar **burglars**
NOUN a thief who breaks into a building.
burglary NOUN

burgle **burgles burgling burgled**
VERB If your house is burgled, someone breaks into it and steals things.

burly **burlier burliest**
ADJECTIVE having a broad, strong body.

burn **burns burning burned** or **burnt**
VERB **1** If something is burning, it is on fire.
2 To burn something means to destroy it by fire.
3 If you burn yourself or are burned, you are injured by fire or by something hot.
NOUN **4** an injury caused by fire or by something hot.
✔ You can write either *burned* or *burnt* as the past form of *burn.*

burp **burps burping burped**
VERB to make a noise because air from your stomach has been forced up through your throat.

burrow **burrows burrowing burrowed**
NOUN **1** a tunnel or deep hole in the ground dug by a small animal.
VERB **2** to dig a tunnel or deep hole in the ground.

burst **bursts bursting burst**
VERB **1** to split open suddenly.
2 To burst means to happen suddenly and with force. *We burst through the door.*
NOUN **3** a sudden short period of an activity: *a burst of speed.*

bury **buries burying buried**
VERB **1** to bury someone is to put their dead body into a grave.
2 to bury something is to put it into a hole in the ground and cover it with earth.

bus **buses**
NOUN a large motor vehicle that carries passengers.
[buses were originally called omnibuses, from Latin *omnibus* meaning for all]

bush **bushes**
NOUN **1** a thick plant with many stems branching out from ground level.
2 The wild uncultivated part of some countries is known as the bush.

bushy **bushier bushiest**
ADJECTIVE Bushy hair or fur grows very thickly.

business **businesses**
NOUN **1** work relating to the buying and selling of goods and services.
2 an organization which produces or sells goods or provides a service.
3 Business is a general word for any event, situation or activity. *This whole business has upset me.*

busker **buskers**
NOUN someone who plays music or sings in public places in the hope of receiving money from passers-by.

bus stop **bus stops**
NOUN a place on a bus route where passengers may get on or off the bus.

bust **busts busting bust** or **busted**
VERB **1** INFORMAL to break something.
PHRASE **2** INFORMAL To **go bust** is to be bankrupt.
NOUN **3** A woman's bust is her chest and breasts.
4 a statue of someone's head and shoulders: *a bust of Beethoven.*

bustle **bustles bustling bustled**
VERB **1** to move in a busy, hurried way.
NOUN **2** busy, noisy activity.

busy **busier busiest**
ADJECTIVE **1** doing something and not free to do anything else.
2 full of people doing things or moving about.
busily ADVERB

busybody **busybodies**
NOUN someone who interferes in other people's affairs.

but
CONJUNCTION **1** "But" is used when you are saying something which contrasts with something else that has been said. *He was small but very strong.*
2 except. *We had nothing but sunshine.*

Like bureau, we take gateau and plateau direct from French. ◀

butcher **butchers**
NOUN a shopkeeper who sells meat; also the shop itself.

butler **butlers**
NOUN the chief male servant in a rich household.

butt **butts butting butted**
VERB 1 If you butt something, you ram it with your head.
NOUN 2 If you are the butt of teasing, you are the target of it.
butt in VERB If you butt in, you join in a private conversation or activity without being asked to.

butter
NOUN a soft, fatty food made from cream, which is spread on bread and used in cooking.

buttercup **buttercups**
NOUN a wild plant with bright yellow flowers.

butterfly **butterflies**
NOUN a type of insect that develops from a caterpillar and has large white or coloured wings.

butterscotch
NOUN a kind of hard toffee made mainly of butter and sugar.

buttocks
PLURAL NOUN Your buttocks are the part of your body you sit on.

button **buttons buttoning buttoned**
NOUN 1 a small, hard object sewn on to clothing to act as a fastener.
2 a small object on a piece of equipment that you press to make it work.
VERB 3 to fasten clothing using buttons.

buy **buys buying bought**
VERB to obtain something by paying money for it.
buyer NOUN

buzz **buzzes buzzing buzzed**
VERB to make a humming sound, like a bee.
buzz NOUN

buzzard **buzzards**
NOUN a large brown and white bird of prey.

buzzer **buzzers**
NOUN a device that makes a buzzing sound to attract attention.

by
PREPOSITION 1 used to indicate why, when, how, who or what: *She was very pleased by his kind action. The flowers would bloom by next summer. The statement was issued by their solicitor.*
2 next to or near. *I sat by her bed.*
ADVERB 3 going past. *We walked by her house.*

by-election **by-elections**
NOUN an election held to choose a new Member of Parliament.

bypass **bypasses**
NOUN a main road which takes traffic round a town rather than through it.

bystander **bystanders**
NOUN someone who sees something happen but does not take part in it.

byte **bytes**
NOUN a unit of storage in a computer.

 ► Joke. What's white and yellow with greasy wings? A bread and butterfly.

Cc

cab **cabs**
NOUN 1 a taxi.
2 the part of a truck where the driver sits.
[from French *cabriolet* meaning a light two-wheeled carriage]

cabbage **cabbages**
NOUN a large, green, leafy vegetable.

cabin **cabins**
NOUN 1 a room in a ship where a passenger sleeps.
2 a small wooden house, usually in the country.

cabinet **cabinets**
NOUN 1 a small cupboard.
2 The cabinet of a government is a group of senior ministers who advise the leader and decide policies.

cable **cables**
NOUN 1 a strong, thick rope or chain.
2 a bundle of electricity wires with a rubber covering.

cable car **cable cars**
NOUN a vehicle pulled by a moving cable, for taking people up and down mountains.

cable television
NOUN a television service which people receive from underground wires.

cackle **cackles cackling cackled**
VERB to laugh harshly.
cackle NOUN

cactus **cacti** or **cactuses**
NOUN a thick, fleshy plant that grows in deserts and is usually covered in spikes.

cadet **cadets**
NOUN a young person being trained in the armed forces or police.

cadge **cadges cadging cadged**
VERB If you cadge something from someone, you get it from them and don't give them anything in return. *I cadged a lift into town.*
cadger NOUN

café **cafés**
Said "**kaf**-fay" **NOUN** a place where you can buy light meals and drinks.

cafeteria **cafeterias**
Said "kaf-fit-**ee**-ree-ya" **NOUN** a restaurant where you serve yourself.

caffeine
Said "**kaf**-feen" **NOUN** a chemical in coffee and tea which makes you more active.

cage **cages**
NOUN a box made of wire or bars in which birds or other animals are kept.
caged ADJECTIVE

cagey **cagier cagiest**
Said "**kay**-jee" **ADJECTIVE; INFORMAL** cautious and not open. *She was very cagey about where she had been.*
cagily ADVERB **caginess** NOUN

cagoule **cagoules**
Said "ka-**gool**" **NOUN** a lightweight waterproof jacket with a hood.

cake **cakes**
NOUN a sweet food made by baking flour, eggs, fat and sugar.

caked
ADJECTIVE If you are caked in mud, you are covered in it.

calamity **calamities**
NOUN an event that causes disaster or distress.
calamitous ADJECTIVE

calcium
Said "**kal**-see-um" **NOUN** a soft white mineral that builds bones and teeth.

calculate **calculates calculating calculated**
VERB to work something out, usually by doing some mathematics.

calculator **calculators**
NOUN a small electronic machine used for doing mathematical calculations.
calculation NOUN
[from Latin *calculus* meaning a pebble; the Romans used pebbles to help them count]

calendar **calendars**
NOUN a chart showing the date of each day in a particular year.

calf **calves**
NOUN 1 a young cow or bull.
2 Your calves are the backs of your legs between your ankles and knees.

call **calls calling called**
VERB 1 to call is to shout out.
2 If you call someone, you telephone them.
3 If you call on someone, you pay them a visit.
4 If you call someone something, you are saying that they are like that. *They called Columbus crazy when he said the earth was round.*
5 The name that someone is called is their name. *I am called Vicky.*
NOUN 6 If you get a call from someone, they telephone you or pay you a visit.
7 a cry or shout for help.
8 a demand for something: *the call for good teachers.*
call off **VERB** to cancel something.

calligram **calligrams**
NOUN a poem in which the calligraphy, the formation of the letters, or the font selected, represents an aspect of the poem's subject: *growth.*

A B C D E F G H I J K L M N O P Q R S T U V W X Y Z

callous
ADJECTIVE cruel and not concerned with other people's feelings.
callously ADVERB **callousness** NOUN

Synonyms: hardhearted, heartless, unfeeling

calm **calmer calmest; calms calming calmed**
ADJECTIVE **1** quiet and not showing any worry or excitement.
2 If the sea is calm, the water is not moving very much.
VERB **3** If you calm someone down, you help make them less upset or excited.

Synonyms: (sense 1) composed, cool, self-possessed
(sense 3) quieten, soothe

calorie **calories**
NOUN a unit of measurement for the energy that food gives you.

calves
the plural of **calf**.

calypso **calypsos**
Said "kal-**lip**-soh" NOUN a type of song from the West Indies.

camcorder **camcorders**
NOUN a camera for taking home videos.

came
the past tense of **come**.

camel **camels**
NOUN a large desert mammal with one or two humps on its back.

camera **cameras**
NOUN a piece of equipment used for taking photographs or for filming.

camouflage **camouflages camouflaging camouflaged**
Said "**kam**-mof-flahj" NOUN **1** a way of avoiding being seen by having the same colour or appearance as the surroundings.
VERB **2** to hide something by using camouflage.

camp **camps camping camped**
VERB **1** If you camp or go camping, you stay in a tent.
NOUN **2** a place where people live or stay in tents or caravans.
3 a collection of buildings for a particular group of people such as soldiers or prisoners.

campaign **campaigns**
Said "kam-**pane**" NOUN a set of actions intended to achieve a particular result.
campaign VERB

campus **campuses**
NOUN the area of land and the buildings that make up a university or college.

can **could**
VERB to be able to do something.

can **cans**
NOUN a metal container, often a sealed one with food or drink inside.

canal **canals**
NOUN a long, narrow man-made stretch of water.

canary **canaries**
NOUN a small yellow bird.
[named after the Canary Islands where they are found]

cancel **cancels cancelling cancelled**
VERB **1** If you cancel something that has been arranged, you stop it from happening.
2 If you cancel a fraction, you reduce it to its lowest terms by dividing the numerator and denominator by the same number.
cancellation NOUN

cancer **cancers**
NOUN **1** a serious disease in which abnormal cells in a part of the body increase rapidly, causing growths.
2 Cancer is also a sign of the zodiac, represented by a crab. People born between 21 June and 22 July are born under this sign.
cancerous ADJECTIVE

candid
ADJECTIVE honest and frank.
candidly ADVERB **candour** NOUN

candidate **candidates**
NOUN a person who is entering an exam or being considered for a job.

candle **candles**
NOUN a stick of wax with a piece of string called a wick through the middle, that can be set alight to produce light.

candlestick **candlesticks**
NOUN a holder for a candle.

candy **candies**
NOUN an American word for sweets and chocolates.

cane **canes caning caned**
NOUN **1** a cane is a long, hollow stem of a plant such as bamboo.
2 a long narrow stick, often one used to beat people as a punishment.
VERB **3** to beat someone with a cane as a punishment.

canine **canines**
Said "**kay**-nine" ADJECTIVE **1** relating to dogs.
NOUN **2** A canine tooth is one of the pointed teeth near the front of the mouth in humans and some other animals. See **incisor**, **molar**.

cannibal **cannibals**
NOUN a person who eats other human beings.
cannibalism NOUN

cannon **cannons cannoning cannoned**
NOUN **1** a large gun, usually on wheels, used in battles to fire heavy metal balls.
VERB **2** To cannon into people or things means to bump into them with force.

 ► Camcorder is a portmanteau word: it is a combination of the words "camera" and "recorder".

cannonball cannonballs
NOUN a heavy round piece of metal made to be fired from a cannon.

cannot
VERB a word meaning the same as **can not**.

canoe canoes
Said "ka-**noo**" NOUN a small, narrow boat that you propel using a paddle.
canoeing NOUN **canoeist** NOUN

canopy canopies
NOUN a cover used for shelter or decoration.

can't
the contraction of **cannot**.

canteen canteens
NOUN the part of a workplace where the workers can go to eat.

canter canters cantering cantered
VERB When a horse canters, it moves at a speed between a gallop and a trot.

canvas canvases
NOUN 1 a strong, heavy cloth used for making things such as sails and tents.
2 a piece of cloth on which an artist does a painting.

canvass canvasses canvassing canvassed
VERB 1 If you canvass people, you go round trying to persuade them to vote for a particular candidate or party in an election.
2 If you canvass opinion, you ask what people think about a particular subject.
canvasser NOUN

canyon canyons
NOUN a narrow river valley with steep, rocky sides.

cap caps capping capped
NOUN 1 a soft, flat hat, often with a peak at the front.
2 the top of a bottle.
VERB 3 If you cap something that has just been done or said, you do better. *Sue capped my joke with her own hilarious story.*

capable
ADJECTIVE 1 If you are capable of doing something, you are able to do it.
2 skilful or talented.
capably ADVERB **capability** NOUN

capacity capacities
Said "kap-**pas**-sit-tee" NOUN 1 the maximum amount that something can hold or produce.
2 a person's power or ability to do something. *He had a great capacity for remembering names.*
3 someone's position or role. *She attended the meeting in her capacity as director.*

cape capes
NOUN 1 a short cloak with no sleeves.
2 a large piece of land sticking out into the sea: *the Cape of Good Hope.*

capillary capillaries
Said "kap-**pill**-lar-ree" NOUN Capillaries are very thin-walled blood vessels.

capital capitals
NOUN 1 The capital of a country is the city where the government meets.
2 A capital letter is a larger letter used at the beginning of a sentence or a name.

capitalism
NOUN Capitalism is an economic and political system where businesses and industries are not owned and run by the government, but by individuals who can make a profit from them.
capitalist ADJECTIVE OR NOUN

capital punishment
NOUN a punishment whereby the convicted criminal is put to death.

capsize capsizes capsizing capsized
VERB If a boat capsizes, it turns upside down.

capsule capsules
NOUN 1 a small container with medicine inside which you swallow.
2 the part of a spacecraft in which astronauts travel.

captain captains captaining captained
NOUN 1 the person in charge of a ship or aeroplane.
2 the leader of a sports team.
3 an army or navy officer.
VERB 4 If you captain a group of people, you lead them.

caption captions
NOUN a title or short explanatory phrase printed underneath a picture or photograph.

captivate captivates captivating captivated
VERB to fascinate or attract someone so much that they cannot take their attention away. *The crowd was captivated by the firework display.*

captive captives
NOUN 1 a person who has been captured and kept prisoner.
ADJECTIVE 2 imprisoned or enclosed.
captivity NOUN

captor captors
NOUN someone who has captured a person or an animal.

capture captures capturing captured
VERB to take someone or something prisoner.

car cars
NOUN a four-wheeled road vehicle for a small number of passengers.
[from Latin *carrus* meaning wagon]

caramel caramels
NOUN a chewy sweet made from sugar, butter, and milk.

carat carats
NOUN 1 a unit for measuring the weight of diamonds and other precious stones.
2 a unit for measuring the purity of gold.

a b c d e f g h i j k l m n o p q r s t u v w x y z

caravan caravans
NOUN 1 a vehicle usually pulled by a car in which people live or spend their holidays.
2 a group of people and their animals travelling together across a desert.

carbohydrate carbohydrates
NOUN a substance found in foods like sugar and bread which gives you energy.

carbon
NOUN a chemical element which all living things contain. It is pure in diamonds and also found in coal.

carbon dioxide
NOUN a gas without colour or smell that humans and some other animals breathe out. It is used in making fizzy drinks and fire extinguishers.

carbon monoxide
NOUN a colourless, poisonous gas that is emitted by car exhausts.

carburettor carburettors
Said "**kahr**-bur-ret-ter" NOUN the part of a vehicle engine in which air and petrol are mixed together.

carcass carcasses; also spelt **carcase**
NOUN the body of a dead animal.

card cards
NOUN 1 a piece of stiff paper or plastic.
2 a playing card.
3 a greetings card.

cardboard
NOUN thick, stiff paper.

cardigan cardigans
NOUN a knitted jacket that fastens up the front.

cardinal cardinals
NOUN 1 a high-ranking member of the Roman Catholic clergy who chooses and advises the Pope.
2 a cardinal number is a number expressing quantity not order, such as 256, 6, 34, etc.
ADJECTIVE 3 extremely important: *a cardinal principle of law.*

care cares caring cared
VERB 1 If you care about something, you are concerned about it and interested in it.
2 to feel affection towards someone.
3 to look after someone.
NOUN 4 Your cares are your concerns or worries.
5 If you do something with care, you do it with great attention to avoid mistakes.
caring ADJECTIVE

career careers
NOUN the series of jobs that someone has, usually in the same occupation: *a career in journalism.*

carefree
ADJECTIVE having no worries or responsibilities.

careful
ADJECTIVE 1 If you are careful, you pay attention to what you are doing so as to avoid mistakes; cautious.
2 Something that is careful shows a concern for detail: *careful planning.*
carefully ADVERB

careless
ADJECTIVE not paying enough attention to what you are doing.
carelessly ADVERB **carelessness** NOUN

Synonyms: slapdash, sloppy

caress caresses caressing caressed
VERB to stroke in a gentle and affectionate way.
caress NOUN

caretaker caretakers
NOUN a person who looks after a large building such as a school.

cargo cargoes
NOUN the goods carried on a ship or plane.

Caribbean
ADJECTIVE related to the islands of the West Indies in the Caribbean Sea, east of Central America.

caricature caricatures
NOUN a drawing or description of someone that exaggerates the more obvious features of their appearance or personality.
caricature VERB

carnation carnations
NOUN a plant with a long stem and most commonly white, pink, or red flowers which often have a sweet smell.

carnival carnivals
NOUN a public festival with music, processions and dancing.

carnivore carnivores
NOUN an animal that eats meat.
carnivorous ADJECTIVE

carol carols
NOUN a religious song sung at Christmas time.

carp carps carping carped
NOUN 1 a large edible freshwater fish.
VERB 2 to complain about unimportant things.

car park car parks
NOUN an area or building for parking cars.

carpel carpels
NOUN the female part of a flower that contains the seed.

carpenter carpenters
NOUN a person who makes and repairs wooden things.
carpentry NOUN

carpet carpets carpeting carpeted
NOUN 1 a thick, cloth covering for a floor.
VERB 2 to cover a floor with a carpet.

 ► What have cardigans, sandwiches and diesel engines got in common?

carriage carriages
NOUN 1 a horse-drawn passenger vehicle.
2 one of the sections of a passenger train.

carriageway carriageways
NOUN one side of the road, where traffic travels in one direction only.

carrier carriers
NOUN 1 a vehicle used for carrying things: *a troop carrier.*
2 a carrier of a germ or a disease is someone that can pass it on to others.

carrier bag carrier bags
NOUN a plastic or paper bag with handles, used for carrying shopping.

carrot carrots
NOUN a thin, orange-coloured root vegetable.

carry carries carrying carried
VERB 1 To carry something is to hold it and take it somewhere.
2 If sound carries, it can be heard a long way away.
3 A human or other animal carrying a germ can pass it on to other people.
carry on VERB to continue doing something.
carry out VERB To carry something out means to do it and complete it.

Synonyms: (sense 1) bear, convey, take

cart carts
NOUN an old-fashioned wooden vehicle, usually pulled by an animal.

cartilage
NOUN a strong, flexible substance found around your joints and in your nose and ears.

carton cartons
NOUN a cardboard or plastic container for milk, cream, fruit juice, etc.

cartoon cartoons
NOUN 1 a humorous topical drawing in a newspaper or magazine.
2 a film in which all the characters and scenes are drawn.

cartridge cartridges
NOUN 1 a thin plastic tube of ink for a fountain pen.
2 a tube containing a bullet for a gun.

cartwheel cartwheels
NOUN an acrobatic movement in which you move sideways on your hands then feet.

carve carves carving carved
VERB 1 To carve an object means to cut it out of a substance such as stone or wood.
2 To carve meat means to cut slices from it.

cascade cascades cascading cascaded
NOUN 1 a waterfall or group of waterfalls.
VERB 2 to flow downwards quickly.

case cases
NOUN 1 a container for something.
2 a particular situation, event or example. *This causes problems in some cases.*
3 a crime, or a trial that takes place after a crime. *Police have re-opened the case.*
4 If something is the case, it is true.
5 In an argument, the case for an idea is the reasons used to support it.
PHRASE 6 you say **in case** to explain something that you do because a particular thing might happen. *I didn't want to shout in case I frightened you.*

Synonyms: (sense 2) circumstance, instance, situation

cash cashes cashing cashed
NOUN 1 money in the form of notes and coins.
VERB 2 If you cash a cheque or a postal order, you exchange it for cash.
[from Italian *cassa* meaning money-box]

cashier cashiers
NOUN the person who you get money from in a bank, or who you pay money to in a shop.

cash register cash registers
NOUN a machine in a shop where the money received is put and which records each sale.

casino casinos
Said "kass-**ee**-noh" NOUN a place where people go to play gambling games.

cask casks
NOUN a wooden barrel.

casket caskets
NOUN a small box for jewellery or other valuables.

casserole casseroles
NOUN a dish made by cooking a mixture of meat and vegetables slowly in an oven; also the pot this is cooked in.

cassette cassettes
NOUN a flat plastic container with tape inside, used for recording and playing back sounds or pictures.

cast casts casting cast
NOUN 1 all the people who act in a play or film.
VERB 2 To cast something somewhere is to throw it carelessly.
3 When people cast their votes in an election, they vote.
4 To cast doubt or suspicion on something is to make people unsure about it.

castanets
PLURAL NOUN a Spanish musical instrument consisting of two small round pieces of wood that are clicked together with the fingers.

castaway castaways
NOUN a person who has been shipwrecked.

caster sugar or **castor sugar**
NOUN very fine white sugar used in cooking.

castle castles
NOUN a large ancient building with walls or ditches round it to protect it from attack.

Cassette is a French word meaning small box.

A B C D E F G H I J K L M N O P Q R S T U V W X Y Z

castor castors; also spelt **caster**
NOUN a small wheel fitted to furniture so that it can be moved easily.

casual
ADJECTIVE **1** Casual clothes are suitable for informal occasions.
2 happening by chance and without planning: *a casual remark*.
3 careless or without interest.
casually ADVERB

Synonyms: (sense 3) nonchalant, offhand

casualty casualties
NOUN a person killed or injured in an accident or war.

cat cats
NOUN **1** a furry mammal often kept as a pet.
2 any of the family of mammals that includes lions and tigers.

catalogue catalogues cataloguing catalogued
NOUN **1** a list of things, such as the goods you can buy from a company, the objects in a museum, or the books in a library.
VERB **2** To catalogue a collection of things is to list them in a catalogue.

catalyst catalysts
Said "**kat**-a-list" NOUN a substance that speeds up a chemical reaction without changing itself.

catamaran catamarans
NOUN a sailing boat with two hulls connected to each other.
[from Tamil *kattumaram* meaning tied logs]

catapult catapults
NOUN a Y-shaped object with a piece of elastic tied between the two top ends, used for shooting small stones.

catarrh
Said "kat-**tahr**" NOUN mucus in your nose and throat.

catastrophe catastrophes
Said "kat-**tass**-truf-fee" NOUN a terrible disaster.
catastrophic ADJECTIVE

catch catches catching caught
VERB **1** to grasp something that is falling.
2 to capture something or someone.
3 If you catch someone doing something they should not be doing, you discover them doing it.
4 to board and travel on a bus, train or plane.
5 If you catch a cold, you become infected with it.
6 If something catches on an object, it sticks to it or gets entrapped by it.
NOUN **7** a hook that fastens or locks a door or window.
8 a problem or hidden complication in something.

catch up VERB If you catch up with someone, you move forwards to reach the same place they are in or the same level they are at.

catching
ADJECTIVE tending to spread very quickly. *Measles is catching.*

catch phrase catch phrases
NOUN; INFORMAL a phrase that is often used, especially by a famous person, and is therefore popular and well-known.

catchy catchier catchiest
ADJECTIVE If a tune is catchy, it is pleasant and easily remembered.

category categories
NOUN a set of things with a particular characteristic in common.
categorize VERB

cater caters catering catered
VERB to provide people with the things they need, especially food.

caterer caterers
NOUN a person or business that provides food for groups or parties.

caterpillar caterpillars
NOUN the larva of a butterfly or moth.
[from Old French *chatepelose* meaning hairy cat]

cathedral cathedrals
NOUN the main church in an area, with a bishop in charge of it.

Catherine wheel Catherine wheels
NOUN a firework which spins round.
[after St Catherine who, for her Christian beliefs, was tortured on a spiked wheel]

Catholic Catholics
NOUN OR ADJECTIVE someone who belongs to the Roman Catholic church.
Catholicism NOUN

catkin catkins
NOUN a downy or silky spike of male or female flowers on trees such as willow and hazel.

cattle
PLURAL NOUN cows and bulls kept by farmers.

caught
the past tense and past participle of **catch**.

cauldron cauldrons
NOUN a large, round metal cooking pot, especially one that sits over a fire.

cauliflower cauliflowers
NOUN a large, round, white vegetable with green leaves.

cause causes causing caused
NOUN **1** The cause of something is the thing that makes it happen.
2 an aim or principle which a group of people are working for. *The money went to a good cause.*
VERB **3** to make something happen. *Road works often cause delays.*

 ► Proverbs: when the cat's away the mice will play; every dog has its day.

caution cautions cautioning cautioned
NOUN **1** great care you take to avoid danger.
2 an official warning. *The policeman let the driver off with a caution.*
VERB **3** to warn people not to do something again.

cautious
ADJECTIVE acting carefully in order to avoid danger, trouble or disappointment.

cavalry
NOUN the part of an army that uses horses or armoured vehicles.

cave caves
NOUN a large hole in the side of a cliff or under the ground.
cave in VERB to collapse inwards.

caveman cavemen
NOUN Cavemen were people who lived in prehistoric times.

cavern caverns
NOUN a large cave.
cavernous ADJECTIVE

cavity cavities
NOUN a small hole in something solid, such as a tooth.

CD CDs
NOUN a compact disc.

CD-ROM CD-ROMs
NOUN a method of storing video, sound or text on a compact disc, which can be played on a computer using a laser. CD-ROM is an abbreviation for compact disc read-only memory.

CE
abbreviation for Common Era, the last two thousand years.

cease ceases ceasing ceased
VERB to stop.
cessation NOUN

cease-fire cease-fires
NOUN an agreement between two groups who are fighting to stop for a period and discuss peace.

ceaseless
ADJECTIVE going on without stopping.
ceaselessly ADVERB

cedar cedars
NOUN a large evergreen tree with wide branches and needle-shaped leaves.

ceiling ceilings
NOUN **1** the top inside surface of a room.
2 the top limit for things such as prices.

celebrate celebrates celebrating celebrated
VERB to do something enjoyable because of a special event.
celebration NOUN **celebratory** ADJECTIVE

celebrity celebrities
NOUN a famous person.

celery
NOUN a vegetable with long, pale green stalks.

cell cells
NOUN **1** In biology, a cell is the smallest part of an animal or plant that can exist by itself.
2 a small room in which a prisoner is locked up.

cellar cellars
NOUN a room underneath a building. See **basement**.

cello cellos
Said "**chel**-loh" NOUN a large, stringed musical instrument.
cellist NOUN

Celsius
Said "**sel**-see-yuss" NOUN a scale for measuring temperature in which water freezes at 0 degrees (0 °C) and boils at 100 degrees (100 °C). It is the same scale as Centigrade. [named after Anders Celsius (1701–1744), who invented it]

Celtic
ADJECTIVE
Said "**kel**-tik" relating to the languages, culture and people of Ireland, Scotland, Wales and Brittany.

cement cements cementing cemented
NOUN **1** a grey powder which is mixed with sand, water and gravel to make mortar and concrete.
VERB **2** Something that cements a relationship seals it and makes it stronger. *The trade agreement cemented the link between the economies of the two countries.*

cemetery cemeteries
NOUN an area of land where dead people are buried.

censor censors censoring censored
VERB **1** If someone censors a book or film, they cut or ban parts of it that they consider unsuitable for its audience.
NOUN **2** a person whose job it is to censor films.
censorship NOUN

censure censures censuring censured
VERB to express strong disapproval of something.
censure NOUN

census censuses
NOUN an official survey of the population of a country.

cent cents
NOUN a unit of currency in the USA and in some other countries. In the USA, 100 cents are worth one dollar.

centenary centenaries
Said "sen-**teen**-er-ee" NOUN the 100th anniversary of something.

a b c d e f g h i j k l m n o p q r s t u v w x y z

The word cemetery comes from the Greek word *koimeterion* meaning a sleeping room.

centi-
PREFIX one hundred.
[from Latin *centum* meaning hundred]

Centigrade
NOUN another name for the **Celsius** temperature scale.
✔ Scientists say and write *Celsius* rather than *Centigrade*.

centilitre centilitres
NOUN A unit of liquid volume equal to one hundredth of a litre. Centilitre is abbreviated to "cl".

centimetre centimetres
NOUN A unit of length equal to ten millimetres or one hundredth of a metre. Centimetre is abbreviated to "cm".

centipede centipedes
NOUN a long, thin insect with many pairs of legs.

central
ADJECTIVE in or near the centre.

central heating
NOUN a heating system in which water or air is heated in one place and passed round a building through pipes and radiators.

centre centres
NOUN **1** the middle.
2 a building where people go for activities, meetings or help: *a health centre*.

centurion centurions
NOUN a Roman officer in charge of 100 soldiers.

century centuries
NOUN a period of 100 years.

ceramic ceramics
Said "sir-**ram**-mik" NOUN **1** a hard material made by baking clay to a very high temperature.
2 Ceramics is the art of making objects out of clay.

cereal cereals
NOUN a food made from grain, often eaten with milk for breakfast.

ceremony ceremonies
NOUN a formal ritual, such as performed at a wedding or funeral.
ceremonial ADJECTIVE OR NOUN
ceremonially ADVERB

certain
ADJECTIVE **1** definite and with no doubt at all.
2 particular. *Certain parts of your essay look as if they have been copied.*
certainty NOUN

certainly
ADVERB without doubt, definitely.

certificate certificates
NOUN a document stating particular facts, for example, that you have passed an examination.

certify certifies certifying certified
VERB to declare formally that something is true.

chaffinch chaffinches
NOUN a small European bird with black and white wings.

chain chains chaining chained
NOUN **1** a number of metal rings connected together in a line.
2 a number of things in a series or connected to each other: *a chain of shops*.
VERB **3** If you chain two things together, you fasten them with a chain.

chain saw chain saws
NOUN a large, motorized saw.

chair chairs chairing chaired
NOUN **1** a seat with a back and four legs.
VERB **2** to be in charge of a meeting.

chair lift chair lifts
NOUN a line of chairs that hang from a moving cable and carry people up and down a mountain.

chairperson chairpersons
NOUN **1** a person in charge of a meeting.
2 the head of a company or committee.
You can also say chair, chairman or chairwoman.

chalet chalets
Said "**shall**-lay" NOUN a wooden house with a sloping roof, especially in a mountain area or a holiday camp.

chalk
NOUN a soft white rock, often used for writing on a blackboard.
chalky ADJECTIVE

challenge challenges challenging challenged
NOUN **1** something that is new and exciting but requires a lot of effort.
2 a suggestion from someone to compete with them.
VERB **3** to suggest to someone that you compete with them.
4 to question whether something is correct or true. *She challenged the suggestion that boys might be better at maths.*
challenger NOUN

chamber chambers
NOUN a large room, especially one used for formal meetings.

chameleon chameleons
Said "kam-**ee**-lee-on" NOUN a lizard which is able to change the colour of its skin to match its surroundings.

champagne champagnes
Said "sham-**pain**" NOUN a sparkling white wine made in France.

champion champions
NOUN a person who wins a competition.

 ► Find out what's happening in this word chain and add another 10 words: ►

championship championships
NOUN a competition to find the champion of a sport.

chance chances chancing chanced
NOUN **1** the possibility of something happening.
2 an opportunity to do something.
3 Something that happens by chance happens unexpectedly.
VERB **4** to take a risk.

Synonyms: (sense 3) accident, coincidence, luck

chancellor chancellors
NOUN the head of government in some European countries.

Chancellor of the Exchequer
NOUN in Britain, the government minister responsible for finance and taxes.

chandelier chandeliers
Said "shan-del-**leer**" NOUN an ornamental light fitting which hangs from the ceiling.

change changes changing changed
NOUN **1** a difference or alteration in something.
2 a swap or replacement.
3 Change is money you get back when you have paid more than the actual price of something.
VERB **4** to make different or alter.
5 to swap or replace.
6 to change money means to exchange it for smaller coins of the same total value, or to exchange it for foreign currency.

changeable
ADJECTIVE likely to change all the time.

Synonyms: erratic, inconstant, variable

channel channels channelling channelled
NOUN **1** a passage along which water flows or along which something is carried.
2 a wavelength on which television programmes are broadcast; also the television station itself.
VERB **3** To channel something such as money or energy means to direct it in a particular way.

chant chants chanting chanted
VERB to repeat a group of words over and over again.
chant NOUN

Chanukah
NOUN another spelling of Hanukkah, a Jewish religious festival.

chaos
Said "**kay**-oss" NOUN a state of complete disorder.
chaotic ADJECTIVE

chap chaps
NOUN; INFORMAL a man.
[from *chapman*, an old word meaning customer or buyer]

chapel chapels
NOUN a type of small church.

chapter chapters
NOUN one of the parts into which a book is divided.

char chars charring charred
VERB If something chars it gets partly burned and goes black.

character characters
NOUN **1** all the qualities which combine to form the personality or atmosphere of a person or place.
2 the fictional people in a film, play or book.
3 an unusual person. *He's an odd character.*

Synonyms: (sense 1) nature, personality, quality

characteristic characteristics
NOUN **1** a quality that is typical of a particular person or thing.
ADJECTIVE **2** typical of a particular person or thing. *Telling the carol singers off was very characteristic of Scrooge.*

charades
PLURAL NOUN a party game in which people try to guess what others are acting or miming.

charcoal
NOUN a black form of carbon made by burning wood without air, used as a fuel and also for drawing.

charge charges charging charged
VERB **1** If someone charges you money, they ask you to pay for something you have bought.
2 When the police charge someone, they formally accuse them of having committed a crime.
3 To charge a battery means to pass an electrical current through it to make it store electricity.
4 to rush forward, often to attack someone.
NOUN **5** the price that you have to pay for something.
6 a formal accusation that a person is guilty of a crime and has to go to court.
7 To have charge or be in charge of someone or something means to be responsible for them.

chariot chariots
NOUN a two-wheeled open vehicle pulled by horses.

charity charities
NOUN an organization that raises money to help a good cause.
charitable ADJECTIVE

A B C D E F G H I J K L M N O P Q R S T U V W X Y Z

charm charms charming charmed
NOUN 1 the quality of being attractive and pleasant.
VERB 2 If you charm someone, you use your charm to please them.

charming
ADJECTIVE very pleasant and attractive.
charmer NOUN

chart charts charting charted
NOUN 1 a diagram or table showing information.
VERB 2 If you chart something, you observe and record it carefully.

charter charters chartering chartered
VERB to hire transport for private use.

chase chases chasing chased
VERB 1 to run after someone or something in order to catch them.
NOUN 2 the activity of hunting or pursuing someone or something.

Synonyms: (sense 1) hunt, pursue

chasm chasms
Said "**kazm**" NOUN a deep crack in the earth's surface.

chat chats chatting chatted
VERB to have a friendly, informal conversation.
chat up VERB; INFORMAL If you chat up someone, you talk to them in a friendly way because you are attracted to them romantically.
chat NOUN

Synonyms: gossip, natter, talk

chatter chatters chattering chattered
VERB 1 to talk very fast.
2 If your teeth are chattering, they are knocking together because you are cold.
NOUN 3 very fast talk.

chatty chattier chattiest
ADJECTIVE pleasantly talkative.

chauffeur
Said "**show**-fur" NOUN a person whose job is to drive another person's car.
chauffeur-driven ADJECTIVE

cheap cheaper cheapest
ADJECTIVE costing very little money, and sometimes of poor quality.
cheaply ADVERB **cheapness** NOUN

cheat cheats cheating cheated
VERB 1 If someone cheats, they do wrong or unfair things to win or get what they want.
2 If you are cheated out of something, you do not get what you are entitled to.
NOUN 3 a person who cheats.

Synonyms: (senses 1 and 2) con, deceive, swindle

check checks checking checked
VERB 1 to examine something in order to make sure that everything is all right.
NOUN 2 an inspection to make sure that everything is all right.
ADJECTIVE 3 Check or checked means marked with a pattern of squares.
check in VERB to sign in or show your ticket at a hotel, airport, etc.
check out VERB If you check something out, you inspect it and find out whether everything about it is right.
check up on VERB to find out information about someone, or what they are doing.

checkmate
NOUN In chess, a situation where a player cannot stop their king being captured and so loses the game.
[from Arabic *sah mat* meaning the king is dead]

checkout checkouts
NOUN a counter in a supermarket where customers pay for their goods.

checkup checkups
NOUN a regular examination by a dentist, doctor, etc.

cheek cheeks
NOUN 1 Cheeks are the sides of your face below your eyes.
2 Cheek is speech or behaviour that is rude or disrespectful.

Synonyms: (sense 2) impertinence, impudence, insolence

cheeky cheekier cheekiest
ADJECTIVE rather rude or disrespectful, often in an amusing way.

cheer cheers cheering cheered
VERB 1 to shout with approval or in order to show support for a person or team.
NOUN 2 a shout of approval or support.
cheer up VERB When you cheer up, you feel more cheerful.

cheerful
ADJECTIVE happy and smiling.
cheerfully ADVERB **cheerfulness** NOUN

cheerio
INTERJECTION a friendly way of saying goodbye.

cheery cheerier cheeriest
ADJECTIVE happy and cheerful.

cheese cheeses
NOUN a solid food made from milk.

cheetah cheetahs
NOUN a large, wild, cat-like animal with black spots.

chef chefs
NOUN a cook in a restaurant, hotel, etc.

chemical chemicals
NOUN 1 Chemicals are elements and compounds used or produced in chemistry.
ADJECTIVE 2 involved in chemistry or using chemicals.

 ► Some words from French: chef, ballet, chalet, brunette, fiancé, garage.

chemist **chemists**
NOUN **1** a shop where medicines and cosmetics are sold.
2 a person who is qualified to make up drugs and medicines prescribed by a doctor.

chemistry
NOUN the scientific study of substances and the ways in which they change when they are combined.

cheque **cheques**
NOUN a printed form on which you instruct your bank to pay someone a certain amount of money from your account.

chequered
Said "**chek**-kerd" ADJECTIVE **1** covered with a pattern of squares.
2 If someone has a chequered history, both good and bad things have happened to them.

cherish **cherishes cherishing cherished**
VERB to love and care deeply about someone or something.

cherry **cherries**
NOUN a small, juicy fruit with a red or black skin and a hard stone in the centre.

chess
NOUN a board game for two people.

chest **chests**
NOUN **1** the front part of your body between your shoulders and your waist.
2 a large wooden box with a hinged lid.

chestnut **chestnuts**
NOUN **1** a reddish brown nut inside a prickly green covering, grown on the horse chestnut tree.
ADJECTIVE **2** of a reddish-brown colour.

chest of drawers **chests of drawers**
NOUN a piece of furniture with drawers in it, used for storing clothes.

chew **chews chewing chewed**
VERB to break something up in your mouth using your teeth.
chewy ADJECTIVE

chewing gum
NOUN a kind of sweet which you chew but do not swallow.

chick **chicks**
NOUN a young bird.

chicken **chickens**
NOUN a bird kept on a farm for its eggs and meat; also the meat of this bird.

chickenpox
NOUN an illness which produces a fever and blister-like spots on the skin.

chief **chiefs**
NOUN **1** the leader of a group or organization.
ADJECTIVE **2** most important.

chiefly
ADVERB mainly.

chieftain **chieftains**
NOUN the leader of a tribe or clan.

chilblain **chilblains**
NOUN a sore, itchy swelling on a finger or toe.

child **children**
NOUN a young person who is not yet an adult.

Synonyms: kid, youngster

childhood **childhoods**
NOUN the time when you are a child.

childish
ADJECTIVE immature and foolish.
childishly ADVERB **childishness** NOUN

childminder **childminders**
NOUN a person paid to look after other people's children while they are at work.

childproof
ADJECTIVE A childproof device is designed to stop children from hurting themselves on it or damaging it.

children
the plural of **child**.

chill **chills chilling chilled**
VERB **1** to make something cold.
NOUN **2** a feverish cold.
3 a feeling of cold.

chilli **chillies**
NOUN the red or green seed pod of a type of pepper which has a very hot spicy taste.

chilly **chillier chilliest**
ADJECTIVE rather cold.

chime **chimes chiming chimed**
VERB When a bell chimes, it makes a clear ringing sound.

chimney **chimneys**
NOUN a funnel above a fire through which smoke escapes.

chimpanzee **chimpanzees**
NOUN a small ape with dark fur that lives in forests in Africa.

chin **chins**
NOUN the part of your face below your mouth.

china
NOUN China is pottery made from thin, baked clay.

chink **chinks**
NOUN a small, narrow opening.

chip **chips chipping chipped**
NOUN **1** Chips are thin strips of fried potato. They are also called French fries.
2 In electronics, a chip is a tiny piece of silicon inside a computer which is used to form electronic circuits.
3 a small piece broken off an object, or the mark it leaves.
VERB **4** If you chip an object, you break a small piece off it.

a b c d e f g h i j k l m n o p q r s t u v w x y z

The letters "ch" can represent three different sounds, as in chorus, champion, chef. ◀

chirp **chirps chirping chirped**
VERB When a bird chirps, it makes a short, high-pitched sound.

chirpy **chirpier chirpiest**
ADJECTIVE; INFORMAL lively and cheerful.

chisel **chisels chiselling chiselled**
NOUN **1** a tool used for cutting and shaping wood, stone or metal.
VERB **2** to cut or shape using a chisel.

chivalry
Said "**shiv**-val-ree" NOUN polite and helpful behaviour.
chivalrous ADJECTIVE

chlorine
Said "**klaw**-reen" NOUN a poisonous greenish-yellow gas with a strong, unpleasant smell. It is used as a disinfectant for water, and to make bleach.

chlorophyll
Said "**klor**-rof-fil" NOUN the green pigment in plants that is needed for photosynthesis to take place. Chlorophyll absorbs light energy from the sun.

chock-a-block or **chock-full**
ADJECTIVE completely full.

chocolate **chocolates**
NOUN a sweet food made from cocoa beans. [from Aztec *xococ* + *atl* meaning bitter water]

choice **choices**
NOUN **1** an option.
2 something that you choose.

choir **choirs**
Said "**kwire**" NOUN a group of singers.

choke **chokes choking choked**
VERB to prevent or be prevented from breathing properly.

cholera
Said "**kol**-ler-a" NOUN a serious disease causing diarrhoea and sickness, caught from infected food or water.

cholesterol
Said "kol-**less**-ter-rol" NOUN a substance found in all animal fats, tissues, and blood.

choose **chooses choosing chose chosen**
VERB to decide to have or do something.

Synonyms: opt for, pick, select

chop **chops chopping chopped**
VERB **1** to cut something with quick, heavy strokes using an axe or a knife.
NOUN **2** a small piece of lamb or pork containing a bone, usually cut from the ribs.

chopper **choppers**
NOUN; INFORMAL a helicopter.

choppy **choppier choppiest**
ADJECTIVE Choppy water has a lot of small waves because it is windy.

chopsticks
PLURAL NOUN Chopsticks are a pair of thin wooden or plastic sticks used by people in the Far East for eating food.

choral
ADJECTIVE relating to singing by a choir, or speaking by a group of people together.

chord **chords**
NOUN a group of three or more musical notes played together.

chore **chores**
NOUN an uninteresting job that has to be done.

chorus **choruses**
NOUN a part of a song which is repeated after each verse.

chose
the past tense of **choose**.

chosen
the past participle of **choose**.

christen **christens christening christened**
VERB When a baby is christened, it is made a member of the Christian church.
christening NOUN

Christian **Christians**
NOUN **1** a person who believes in Jesus Christ and his teachings.
ADJECTIVE **2** relating to Jesus Christ and his teachings.
Christianity NOUN

Christmas **Christmases**
NOUN the period around 25 December, when Christians celebrate the birth of Jesus Christ.

chrome
Said "**krome**" NOUN metal plated with chromium, having a shiny silver finish.

chromosome **chromosomes**
NOUN In biology, a chromosome is a part of a cell which contains genes that determine the characteristics of an animal or plant.

chronic
Said "**kron**-nik" ADJECTIVE **1** A chronic illness lasts a very long time and is unlikely to get better.
2 INFORMAL very bad, severe, or unpleasant.
chronically ADVERB

chronicle **chronicles**
NOUN a record of events described in the order in which they happened.

chronological
Said "kron-nol-**loj**-i-kl" ADJECTIVE arranged in the order in which things happened.
chronologically ADVERB

chronology **chronologies**
NOUN the arrangement of dates or events in sequence.

 ► Past participles ending in "-en", such as beaten, and "-t", such as slept, come from Anglo-Saxon.

chrysalis chrysalises
Said "**kriss**-sal-liss" **NOUN** a butterfly or moth when it is developing from caterpillar to fully grown adult.

chrysanthemum chrysanthemums
Said "kriss-**an**-thim-mum" **NOUN** a plant with large brightly coloured flowers.

chubby chubbier chubbiest
ADJECTIVE plump and round.
chubbiness NOUN

chuck chucks chucking chucked
VERB; INFORMAL to throw something casually.

chuckle chuckles chuckling chuckled
VERB to laugh quietly.

chug chugs chugging chugged
VERB When a machine or engine chugs, it makes a continuous dull thudding sound.

chum chums
NOUN; INFORMAL a friend.

chunk chunks
NOUN a thick piece of something.
chunky ADJECTIVE

Synonyms: hunk, lump, piece

church churches
NOUN 1 a building where Christians go for religious services.
2 In the Christian religion, a church is one of the groups with their own particular beliefs, customs and ministers: *the Catholic Church.*

churchyard churchyards
NOUN the area around a church, usually in which people are buried.

churn churns churning churned
VERB 1 to move about in a vigorous way. *My stomach was churning before the exam.*
NOUN 2 a container used for making milk or cream into butter.

chute chutes
Said "**shoot**" **NOUN** a steep slope or tunnel used to slide things down.

chutney
NOUN a strong-tasting thick sauce made from fruit, vinegar and spices.

cider
NOUN an alcoholic drink made from apples.

cigar cigars
NOUN a roll of dried tobacco leaves for smoking.

cigarette cigarettes
NOUN a thin tube of paper containing tobacco for smoking.

cinder cinders
NOUN Cinders are small pieces of burnt coal left after a fire has gone out.

cinema cinemas
NOUN a place where people go to watch films.

cinquain cinquains
NOUN a poem with five lines of 2, 4, 6, 8 and 2 syllables respectively.

circle circles circling circled
NOUN 1 a perfectly round two-dimensional shape.
2 a group of people, usually with the same interests. *He has a large circle of friends.*
3 The circle is an area of seats on the first upper floor of a theatre.
VERB 4 to move round something in a circle.

circuit circuits
Said "**sir**-kit" **NOUN 1** any circular line or path, for example a racing track; also the distance round this path. *I want you to do three circuits of the track.*
2 An electrical circuit is a complete route around which an electric current can flow.

circulate circulates circulating circulated
VERB 1 to move around an area.
2 to distribute something around a group of people.

circulation circulations
NOUN 1 the action of something circulating.
2 Your circulation is the movement of blood through your body.
3 A newspaper's circulation is the number of copies it sells at each issue.

circum-
PREFIX around, surrounding.

circumference circumferences
NOUN the outer line of a circle, and its length.

circumstance circumstances
NOUN The circumstances of a situation or event are the conditions that affect what happens. *She did well under the circumstances.*

circus circuses
NOUN a show, often performed in a large tent, with performers such as clowns, acrobats and trained animals.

cistern cisterns
NOUN a tank in which water is stored, for example, one in a roof or above a toilet.

citizen citizens
NOUN the people who live in or belong to a city or country.
citizenship NOUN

citrus fruit citrus fruits
NOUN Citrus fruits are juicy, sharp-tasting fruits such as oranges, lemons and grapefruit.

city cities
NOUN a large town with a special status where many people live and work.

civic
ADJECTIVE relating to a city or citizens.

a b c d e f g h i j k l m n o p q r s t u v w x y z

Some words from Spanish: cigar, patio, cockroach, cork, potato, sherry, mosquito, cargo.

A B C D E F G H I J K L M N O P Q R S T U V W X Y Z

civil
ADJECTIVE **1** related to the lives of ordinary citizens, not the business of the forces, the law or the church.
2 polite.
civilly ADVERB **civility** NOUN

civilian civilians
NOUN a person who is not in the armed forces.

civilization civilizations; also spelt **civilisation**
NOUN a society which has a highly developed organization and culture.

civilized or **civilised**
ADJECTIVE **1** A civilized society is one with a developed social and political organization and culture.
2 A civilized person is polite and reasonable.

civil rights
PLURAL NOUN the rights of a citizen to be treated equally and fairly in a society.

civil service
NOUN the government departments responsible for the administration of a country.
civil servant NOUN

civil war civil wars
NOUN a war between forces within a single country.

claim claims claiming claimed
VERB **1** to say that something is a fact. *She claimed she climbed to the top.*
2 If you claim something, you ask for it because you believe you have a right to it.
NOUN **3** a statement that something is the case, or that you have a right to something.
claimant NOUN

Synonyms: (sense 1) allege, assert, maintain

clam clams
NOUN a type of shellfish.

clamber clambers clambering clambered
VERB to climb with difficulty.

clammy clammier clammiest
ADJECTIVE unpleasantly damp and sticky.

clamp clamps clamping clamped
NOUN **1** a device that holds something firmly in place: *a wheel clamp.*
VERB **2** When you clamp something, you stop it from moving by using a clamp.

clan clans
NOUN a group of families related to each other by being descended from the same ancestor.

clang clangs clanging clanged
VERB When something metal clangs, or when you clang it, it makes a loud deep sound.

clank clanks clanking clanked
VERB If something metal clanks, it makes a loud noise.

clap claps clapping clapped
VERB **1** to hit your hands together making a loud noise, to show your appreciation for something.
NOUN **2** the action of clapping your hands.
3 a clap of thunder is a sudden loud noise of thunder.

clarify clarifies clarifying clarified
VERB to make something clear and easier to understand.
clarification NOUN

clarinet clarinets
NOUN a woodwind instrument.
clarinettist NOUN

clarity
NOUN clearness. *The clarity of the pictures from space was amazing.*

clash clashes clashing clashed
VERB **1** If people clash with each other, they fight or argue.
2 Colours that clash do not go well together.
3 If one event clashes with another, they happen at the same time, so that you cannot go to both.
NOUN **4** a fight or argument.

clasp clasps clasping clasped
VERB **1** to hold something tightly.
2 to fasten two things together.
NOUN **3** a fastening such as a hook or catch.

class classes classing classed
NOUN **1** A class of people or things is a group of a particular type.
2 a group of pupils or students taught together, or a lesson that they have together.
VERB **3** If someone or something is classed as a particular thing, they are considered as belonging to that group of things. *At 19 you're still classed as a teenager.*

Synonyms: (sense 1) category, kind, sort

classic classics
ADJECTIVE **1** typical and therefore a good model or example of something: *a classic day out at the seaside.*
2 of very high quality: *a classic car.*
NOUN **3** something of the highest quality. *The race was a classic.*

classical
ADJECTIVE traditional in style, form or content: *classical music.*
classically ADVERB

classified
ADJECTIVE Classified information has been officially declared secret.

classify classifies classifying classified
VERB To classify things is to arrange them into groups with similar characteristics or properties.
classification NOUN

 ► Clang, smack, neigh and hiss are examples of onomatopoeia. What does it mean?

classroom classrooms
NOUN a room in a school where lessons take place.

clatter clatters clattering clattered
VERB to make a loud rattling noise.
clatter NOUN

clause clauses
NOUN 1 In grammar, a clause is a group of words with a subject and a verb, which may be a complete sentence or one of the parts of a sentence.
2 a section of a legal document.

claustrophobia
Said "klos-trof-**foe**-bee-ya" **NOUN** a fear of being in enclosed spaces.
claustrophobic ADJECTIVE

claw claws
NOUN the hard, curved nails at the end of an animal's feet.

clay
NOUN a type of earth used to make pottery and bricks.

clean cleans cleaning cleaned; cleaner cleanest
VERB 1 to remove dirt from something.
ADJECTIVE 2 free from dirt or unwanted marks.
cleaner NOUN

cleanliness
Said "**klen**-lin-ness" **NOUN** the habit of keeping yourself and your surroundings clean.

cleanse cleanses cleansing cleansed
Said "**klenz**" **VERB** to make something completely free from dirt.
cleanser NOUN

clear clearer clearest; clears clearing cleared
ADJECTIVE 1 easy to understand, see or hear.
2 see-through: *a clear liquid.*
3 free from obstructions or unwanted things. *The runway was clear so the plane landed.*
VERB 4 to remove unwanted things from a place.
5 If you clear a fence or other obstacle, you jump over it without touching it.
6 When fog or mist clears, it disappears.
7 If someone is cleared of a crime, they are proved to be not guilty.
clear up VERB 1 to tidy a place and put things away.
2 When a problem or misunderstanding is cleared up, it is solved or settled.
clearance NOUN

Synonyms: (clear, sense 1) evident, obvious, plain

clearing clearings
NOUN an area of bare ground in a forest.

clench clenches clenching clenched
VERB 1 When you clench your fist, you curl your fingers up tightly.
2 If you clench your teeth, you bite them hard together.

clergy
NOUN The clergy are the ministers of the Christian church.

clerical
ADJECTIVE relating to work done in an office, often by clerks.

clerk clerks
Said "**klahrk**" **NOUN** a person who keeps records or accounts in an office, bank or law court.

clever cleverer cleverest
ADJECTIVE 1 intelligent and quick to understand things.
2 very effective or skilful: *a clever plan.*
cleverly ADVERB **cleverness** NOUN

Synonyms: (sense 1) bright, intelligent, smart

cliché clichés
Said "**klee**-shay" **NOUN** an idea or phrase which is no longer effective because it has been used so much, for example, "at the end of the day".
clichéd ADJECTIVE

click clicks clicking clicked
VERB 1 to make a short snapping sound.
2 INFORMAL When something clicks, you suddenly understand it.
NOUN 3 a short snapping sound.

client clients
NOUN someone who pays a professional person or company to receive a service.

cliff cliffs
NOUN a high area of land with a very steep side, usually next to the sea.

cliffhanger cliffhangers
NOUN; INFORMAL a book, film or series with exciting scenes that leave you not sure what will happen next.

climate climates
NOUN the general long-term weather conditions that are typical of an area.
climatic ADJECTIVE

climax climaxes
NOUN The climax of something is the most exciting moment in it, usually near the end.

climb climbs climbing climbed
VERB 1 to move upwards.
2 If you climb in or out of somewhere, you move there with difficulty.
NOUN 3 a movement upwards: *the long climb.*
climber NOUN

cling clings clinging clung
VERB If you cling to something, you hold onto it tightly.

clingfilm
NOUN a clear, thin plastic used for wrapping food.

clinic clinics
NOUN a building where people go for medical treatment.

"Last but not least", "at this moment in time" and "over the moon" are all clichés. Think of some more.

A B C D E F G H I J K L M N O P Q R S T U V W X Y Z

clink clinks clinking clinked
VERB When glasses clink they make a light, sharp, ringing sound.

clip clips clipping clipped
NOUN 1 a small metal or plastic object used for holding things together.
VERB 2 to fasten things together, using clips.
3 to cut small pieces from something in order to shape it.
clipper NOUN

clippers
PLURAL NOUN tools used for cutting.

clipping clippings
NOUN extracts cut from a newspaper or magazine.

cloak cloaks
NOUN a wide, loose coat without sleeves.

cloakroom cloakrooms
NOUN a room for hanging coats, possibly with toilets and washbasins.

clock clocks
NOUN a device that measures and shows the time.

clockwise
ADVERB movement in the same direction as the hands on a clock.

Antonym: anticlockwise

clockwork
NOUN 1 Toys that work by clockwork move when they are wound up with a key.
PHRASE 2 If something happens **like clockwork**, it happens with no problems or delays.

clog clogs clogging clogged
VERB 1 to block up.
NOUN 2 Clogs are heavy wooden shoes.

cloister cloisters
NOUN a covered area in a monastery or a cathedral around a square garden.

clone clones cloning cloned
NOUN 1 an animal or plant that has been produced artificially from the cells of another animal or plant and is therefore identical to it.
VERB 2 To clone an animal or plant is to produce it as a clone.

close closer closest; closes closing closed
Rhymes with "**dose**" ADJECTIVE 1 near, nearby.
2 People who are close to each other are very friendly and know each other well.
3 very equally contested: *a close race.*
4 A close inspection of something is very careful and thorough.
Said "**cloze**" VERB 5 to shut.
close down VERB If an organization closes down, it shuts permanently.
closely ADVERB **closeness** NOUN

close-up close-ups
NOUN a detailed close view of something.

clot clots clotting clotted
NOUN 1 a lump formed when liquid solidifies, particularly blood.
2 INFORMAL If you call someone a clot, you mean that they have done something stupid.
VERB 3 When a liquid clots, it thickens and forms a lump.
clotted ADJECTIVE

cloth cloths
NOUN fabric made by a process such as weaving.

clothe clothes clothing clothed
VERB to give someone clothes to wear.

clothes
PLURAL NOUN the things people wear.

clothing
NOUN a general word for clothes.

cloud clouds clouding clouded
NOUN 1 a mass of water vapour that is seen as a white or grey patch in the sky.
2 a mass of smoke, dust, etc. floating in the air.
VERB 3 If something clouds or is clouded, it becomes cloudy or difficult to see through.
4 Something that clouds an issue makes it more confusing.

cloudy
ADJECTIVE 1 full of clouds.
2 If a liquid goes cloudy it becomes difficult or impossible to see through.

Synonyms: (sense 1) dull, overcast

clout clouts clouting clouted
VERB 1 to hit.
NOUN 2 a hit.
3 INFORMAL someone who has clout has influence and power.

clover
NOUN a small plant with leaves made up of three similar parts.

clown clowns
NOUN an amusing circus performer.

club clubs clubbing clubbed
NOUN 1 an organization of people with a particular interest, who meet regularly; also the place where they meet.
2 a nightclub.
3 a thick, heavy stick used as a weapon.
4 one of the sticks that a golfer uses to hit the ball.
5 Clubs are one of the four suits in a pack of playing cards.
VERB 6 To club someone is to hit them hard with a heavy object.

Synonyms: (sense 1) association, group, society

cluck clucks clucking clucked
VERB to make a short, repeated, high-pitched sound like a hen.
cluck NOUN

 ► More examples of onomatopoeia: clink, squelch, jingle, buzz, clang, splatter, hoot, boom.

clue clues
NOUN a hint that helps to solve a problem or mystery.

clueless
ADJECTIVE; INFORMAL helpless or stupid.

clump clumps clumping clumped
NOUN **1** a small group of things close together.
VERB **2** If you clump about, you walk with heavy footsteps.

clumsy clumsier clumsiest
ADJECTIVE **1** moving awkwardly and carelessly.
2 said or done without thought or tact.
clumsily ADVERB **clumsiness** NOUN

Synonyms: (sense 1) awkward, gauche, ungainly

clung
the past tense of **cling**.

cluster clusters clustering clustered
NOUN **1** A cluster of things is a group of them together.
VERB **2** If people cluster together, they stay together in a close group.

clutch clutches clutching clutched
VERB **1** If you clutch something, you hold it tightly or seize it.
NOUN **2** In a car, the clutch is the foot pedal that you press when changing gear.

clutter clutters cluttering cluttered
NOUN **1** Clutter is an untidy mess.
VERB **2** Things that clutter a place fill it and make it untidy.

co-
PREFIX Co- means together. *Paula is now co-writing a book with Pierre.*
[from Latin *com* meaning together]

coach coaches coaching coached
NOUN **1** a large bus that takes passengers on long journeys.
2 a section of a train that carries passengers.
3 someone who coaches a person or sports team.
VERB **4** If someone coaches you, they help you to get better at a sport or a subject.

Synonyms: (sense 3) instructor, trainer

coal
NOUN Coal is a hard black rock taken from underground and burned as a fuel.

coarse coarser coarsest
ADJECTIVE **1** Something that is coarse is rough in texture, often consisting of large particles.
2 Someone who is coarse talks or behaves in a rude or rather offensive way.
coarsely ADVERB **coarseness** NOUN

coast coasts coasting coasted
NOUN **1** the edge of the land where it meets the sea.
VERB **2** If a vehicle coasts somewhere, it moves there with the engine switched off.
coastal ADJECTIVE

coastguard coastguards
NOUN an official who watches the sea near a coast to get help for sailors when they need it, and to prevent smuggling.

coastline coastlines
NOUN the outline of a coast, especially its appearance as seen from the sea or air.

coat coats coating coated
NOUN **1** a piece of clothing which you wear over your other clothes.
2 An animal's coat is the fur or hair on its body.
3 A coat of paint or varnish is a layer of it.
VERB **4** To coat something means to cover it with a thin layer of something.

coating coatings
NOUN a substance applied to something as an outer layer.

coax coaxes coaxing coaxed
VERB If you coax someone to do something, you gently persuade them to do it.

Synonyms: cajole, talk into, wheedle

cobbler cobblers
NOUN a person whose job it is to mend shoes.

cobbles
PLURAL NOUN Cobbles or cobblestones are stones with a rounded surface that were used in the past for making roads.

cobra cobras
Said "**koh**-bra" NOUN a type of large poisonous snake from Africa and Asia.

cobweb cobwebs
NOUN the very thin net that a spider spins for catching insects.

cock cocks
NOUN an adult male chicken; also used of any male bird.

cockerel cockerels
NOUN a young cock.

cockle cockles
NOUN a small, edible seashore animal.

cockney cockneys
NOUN; INFORMAL a person born in or near London.

cockpit cockpits
NOUN the place in a small plane where the pilot sits.

cockroach cockroaches
NOUN a large dark-coloured insect often found in dirty rooms.

cocky cockier cockiest
ADJECTIVE; INFORMAL cheeky or too self-confident.
cockily ADVERB **cockiness** NOUN

These words come from the Viking invasions: clumsy, fellow, knife, outlaw, hit, clip.

cocoa
NOUN Cocoa is a brown powder made from the seeds of a tropical tree and used for making chocolate; also a hot drink made from this powder.

coconut coconuts
NOUN a very large nut with white flesh, milky juice, and a hard hairy shell.

cocoon cocoons
NOUN a silky covering over the larvae of moths and some other insects.

cod
NOUN a large edible fish.
✔ The plural of *cod* is also *cod*.

code codes
NOUN **1** a system of replacing the letters or words in a message with other letters or words, so that nobody can understand the message unless they know the system.
2 a group of numbers and letters which is used to identify something: *the telephone code for Melbourne*.

coeducation
NOUN Coeducation is the system of educating boys and girls together at the same school.
coeducational ADJECTIVE

coffee
NOUN Coffee is the roasted beans of the coffee plant; also a hot drink made from this substance.

coffin coffins
NOUN a box in which a dead body is buried or cremated.
[from Greek *kophinos* meaning basket]

cog cogs
NOUN a wheel with teeth which turns another wheel or part of a machine.

coil coils coiling coiled
NOUN **1** a length of rope or wire wound into a series of loops; also one of the loops.
2 The coil is a contraceptive device placed inside a woman's womb.
VERB **3** If something coils, it turns into a series of loops.

coin coins coining coined
NOUN **1** a small metal disc which is used as money.
VERB **2** If you coin a word or a phrase, you invent it.

coincide coincides coinciding coincided
VERB **1** If two events coincide, they happen at about the same time.
2 When two people's ideas or opinions coincide, they agree.

coincidence coincidences
NOUN A coincidence is when two or more things occur at the same time by chance.

coke
NOUN Coke is a grey fuel produced from coal.

cola colas
NOUN a fizzy soft drink such as Coca Cola or Pepsi Cola.

colander colanders
Said "**kol**-an-der" NOUN a bowl-shaped container with holes in it, used for washing or draining food.

cold colder coldest; colds
ADJECTIVE **1** Something or someone that is cold has a very low temperature.
2 If someone is said to be a cold person, they do not show much affection.
NOUN **3** You can refer to cold weather as the cold.
4 a minor illness in which you sneeze and may have a sore throat.

cold-blooded
ADJECTIVE **1** Someone who is cold-blooded does not show any feeling or pity.
2 A cold-blooded animal has a body temperature that changes according to the surrounding temperature.
cold-bloodedly ADVERB
cold-bloodedness NOUN

coleslaw
NOUN Coleslaw is a salad of chopped cabbage and other vegetables in mayonnaise.

collaborate collaborates collaborating collaborated
VERB When people collaborate, they work together to produce something.
collaboration NOUN **collaborator** NOUN

collage collages
Said "**kol**-lahj" NOUN a picture made by sticking pieces of paper, cloth or other objects onto a surface.

collapse collapses collapsing collapsed
VERB **1** If something such as a building collapses, it falls down suddenly.
2 If a person collapses, they fall down suddenly because they are ill.
3 If something such as a system or a business collapses, it suddenly stops working.
NOUN **4** The collapse of something is what happens when it stops working: *the collapse of the peace talks*.
[from Latin *collapsus* meaning fallen in ruins]

collapsible
ADJECTIVE A collapsible object can be folded flat when it is not in use.

collar collars
NOUN **1** The collar of a shirt or coat is the part round the neck which is usually folded over.
2 a band around the neck of a dog or cat.

colleague colleagues
NOUN A person's colleagues are the people they work with.

 ▶ Try and crack this coded message: EBIM FJ QOXMMBA FKPFAB QEFP AFZQFLKXOV.

collect collects collecting collected
VERB **1** To collect things is to gather them together for a special purpose or as a hobby.
2 If you collect someone or something from a place, you call there and take them away.
3 When things collect in a place, they gather there over a period of time.
collector NOUN

collection collections
NOUN **1** the act of collecting something.
2 a group of things acquired over a period of time.
3 money that has been collected.

Synonyms: (sense 2) accumulation, compilation, set

collective noun
NOUN A collective noun is a single word for a group of things. Examples include a "litter" of pups, a "flock" of sheep and a "clump" of trees.

college colleges
NOUN a place where students study after they have left school.

collide collides colliding collided
VERB If a moving object collides with something, it hits it.

collie collies
NOUN a dog that is used for rounding up sheep.

collision collisions
NOUN A collision occurs when a moving object hits something.

Synonyms: crash, impact, smash

colloquial
Said "kol-**loh**-kwee-al" ADJECTIVE Colloquial words and phrases are informal and used especially in conversation.
colloquially ADVERB **colloquialism** NOUN

colon colons
NOUN the punctuation mark (:).

WHAT DOES THE COLON DO?
The colon (:) and the semicolon (;) are often confused and used incorrectly. The colon is used to introduce a list.
I bought fruit: pears, apples, grapes and plums.
The colon can also be used to introduce a quotation.
He received a message which read: "You can't fool all of the people all of the time."
The colon can be used to introduce an explanation of a statement.
They did not enjoy the meal: the food was cold.
Also look at the grammar box at semicolon.

colonel colonels
Said "**kur**-nl" NOUN an army officer with a fairly high rank.

colony colonies
NOUN **1** a country controlled by a more powerful country.
2 a group of the same type of animal or plant living or growing together: *a colony of bees.*

colossal
ADJECTIVE very large indeed.
colossally ADVERB

Synonyms: enormous, massive

colour colours colouring coloured
NOUN **1** the appearance something has as a result of relecting light. *My car is a bright red.*
2 Someone's colour is the normal colour of their skin.
VERB **3** to give something a colour by using paints or crayons, etc.
colouring NOUN

colour blind
ADJECTIVE not able to distinguish between colours.
colour blindness NOUN

colourful
ADJECTIVE having attractive and bright or varied colours.

colourless
ADJECTIVE having a dull colour or no colour.

colt colts
NOUN a young male horse.

column columns
NOUN **1** a tall solid upright cylinder, especially one supporting a part of a building.
2 In a newspaper or magazine, a column is a vertical piece of writing; also a regular piece of writing by the same person.
columnist NOUN

coma comas
NOUN a state of deep unconsciousness.
comatose ADJECTIVE

comb combs combing combed
NOUN **1** a flat object with pointed teeth, used for tidying your hair.
VERB **2** to tidy your hair with a comb.
3 to search. *Police combed the area for the missing child.*

combat combats combating combated
NOUN **1** Combat is fighting.
VERB **2** To combat something means to try to stop it happening or developing. *We should help combat crime.*
combatant NOUN

combination combinations
NOUN a mixture of things.

combine combines combining combined
VERB to join things together to make a single thing.

combine harvester combine harvesters
NOUN a machine that cuts, threshes and cleans a crop of grain at the same time.

a b c d e f g h i j k l m n o p q r s t u v w x y z

Some collective nouns: a "clowder" of cats, a "kindle" of kittens, a "murder" of crows.

A B C D E F G H I J K L M N O P Q R S T U V W X Y Z

combustion
NOUN the act of burning something, or the process of burning.
combustible ADJECTIVE

come comes coming came come
VERB **1** To come to something is to move there or reach there. *I will come to see you. Have you come to a decision? The water came up to her waist.*
2 If you come from a place, you were born there or it is your home.
3 A time or event to come is in the future.
come about VERB to happen.
come across VERB to find something by chance.
come off VERB to succeed. *The rescue plan came off.*
come on VERB If something is coming on, it is making progress.
come up VERB If something comes up in a conversation or meeting, it is mentioned or discussed.
come up with VERB to suggest something. *They came up with a daring rescue plan.*

comeback comebacks
NOUN To make a comeback means to be popular or successful again.

comedian comedians
NOUN an entertainer whose job is to make people laugh.

comedy comedies
NOUN a humorous play, film, television programme or other entertainment.

comet comets
NOUN an object made of rocks and ice that orbits the sun, leaving a bright trail behind it.

comfort comforts comforting comforted
NOUN **1** the state of being physically or mentally relaxed.
PLURAL NOUN **2** Comforts are things which make your life easier and more pleasant.
VERB **3** To comfort someone is to make them less worried or unhappy.

comfortable
ADJECTIVE **1** physically or mentally relaxed.
2 Something that is comfortable makes you feel relaxed: *a comfortable bed.*
comfortably ADVERB

comic comics
ADJECTIVE **1** funny.
NOUN **2** a magazine that contains stories told in pictures.
3 a comedian.

comical
ADJECTIVE funny.
comically ADVERB

comma commas
NOUN the punctuation mark (,).

WHAT DOES THE COMMA DO?
The comma (,) indicates a short pause between different elements within a sentence, for example:
Fiona likes swimming, but Tony prefers fishing.
After a month of sunshine, it rained on Thursday.
If the introductory phrase is short, it does not need to be followed by a comma:
After lunch the classes continued.
The comma also separates items in a list or series:
I made this soup with carrots, leeks, onions and potatoes.
Commas separate the name of a person or people being addressed from the rest of the sentence:
Thank you, ladies and gentlemen, for your attention.

command commands commanding commanded
VERB **1** to order someone to do something.
2 to be in charge of a ship or a military unit.
3 If you command respect, you receive it because you are popular or important.
NOUN **4** an order to do something.
5 Your command of something is your knowledge of it and your ability to use this knowledge: *a good command of English.*

commander commanders
NOUN **1** the person in charge of a large military group or operation.
2 a officer of the navy immediately below the rank of captain.

commandment commandments
NOUN The commandments are ten rules of behaviour that, according to the Old Testament of the Bible, people should obey.

commando commandos
NOUN a soldier who has been specially trained to carry out raids.

commemorate commemorates commemorating commemorated
VERB to remind people of a person or event in a special and formal way. *The statue commemorates the D-day landings of 1944.*
commemorative ADJECTIVE
commemoration NOUN

commence commences commencing commenced
VERB; FORMAL to begin.
commencement NOUN

commend commends commending commended
VERB to praise someone or something, often in a formal way.
commendation NOUN **commendable** ADJECTIVE

comment comments commenting commented
VERB **1** to make a remark.
NOUN **2** a remark.

commentary commentaries
NOUN a spoken description of an event, piece of film, etc.

► Comedy words: parody, humour, wit, farce, slapstick, sketch, pantomime.

commentator **commentator**
NOUN a person whose job it is to describe an event as it happens.

commerce
NOUN a general word for the buying and selling of goods.

commercial **commercials**
ADJECTIVE **1** relating to the buying and selling of goods. *Any market is a hive of commercial activity.*
2 involving the production of goods or provision of services in order to make money. *Breeding hamsters was OK as a hobby but a failure as a commercial venture.*
NOUN **3** an advertisement on television or radio.

commit **commits committing committed**
VERB **1** To commit a crime or sin is to do it.
2 If you commit yourself to something, you accept it fully or state that you will do it.
3 to send someone officially to a hospital or prison.

Synonyms: (sense 1) do, perform, perpetrate

commitment **commitments**
NOUN something that you are obliged to do, that is scheduled to take up some of your time. *I have several business commitments today.*

committee **committees**
NOUN a group of people elected to make decisions on behalf of a larger group.

common **commoner commonest; commons**
ADJECTIVE **1** existing in large numbers or happening often.
2 If something is common to two or more people, they all have it or use it. *English is a language that is common to many countries.*
3 If you describe someone as common, you mean they do not have good taste or good manners.
NOUN **4** a common noun refers to a whole class of things or people, for example, city, day, building. Common nouns always start with a small letter.
5 an area of grassy land where everyone can go.
PHRASE **6** If two things or people have something **in common**, they both have it.

common denominator
NOUN a fraction that two or more fractions will all divide into exactly. For example, a common denominator for halves [$\frac{1}{2}$] and thirds [$\frac{1}{3}$] is sixths [$\frac{1}{6}$], because 2 and 3 divide exactly into 6. In this case, sixths [$\frac{1}{6}$] can be called the **lowest common denominator**, because 6 is the lowest number that 2 and 3 will divide exactly into.

common factor
NOUN Common factors are whole numbers which will all divide exactly into another number. For example, 3, 4 and 6 are common factors of 12.

commonplace
ADJECTIVE Something that is commonplace happens often.

common sense
NOUN the natural ability to behave sensibly and appropriately and to make good judgements.

Commonwealth
NOUN The Commonwealth is an association of countries that used to be ruled by Britain.

commotion
NOUN a lot of noise and excitement.

communal
Said "com-**yoo**-nul" ADJECTIVE shared by a group of people.
communally ADVERB

communicate **communicates communicating communicated**
VERB to exchange information, usually by talking or writing.
communicative ADJECTIVE

communication **communications**
NOUN **1** the process by which people or animals exchange information.
PLURAL NOUN **2** Communications are the systems by which people communicate or broadcast information, especially using electricity or radio waves.

communion
NOUN **1** the sharing of thoughts and feelings.
2 In Christianity, Communion is a religious service in which people share bread and wine in remembrance of the death and resurrection of Jesus Christ.

communism
NOUN the political belief that all people are equal and that workers should control society.

community **communities**
NOUN **1** all the people living in a particular area.
2 a particular group within a society: *the Asian community.*

commuter **commuters**
NOUN a person who regularly travels a long distance to work each day.

compact **compacts**
ADJECTIVE **1** taking up very little space.
NOUN **2** a small flat round case containing face-powder and a mirror.
compactly ADVERB **compactness** NOUN

compact disc **compact discs**
NOUN a digital audio recording read by a laser; a CD.

companion **companions**
NOUN someone you spend time with.
companionship NOUN

Most "com-" words derive from *cum*, the Latin for with.

a b c d e f g h i j k l m n o p q r s t u v w x y z

A B C D E F G H I J K L M N O P Q R S T U V W X Y Z

company companies
NOUN **1** a business that sells goods or provides a service.
2 If you have company, you have a friend or visitor with you.
PHRASE **3** If you **keep someone company**, you spend time with them.

comparable
Said "**kom**-pra-bl" ADJECTIVE similar in size or quality.
comparably ADVERB **comparability** NOUN

comparative comparatives
ADJECTIVE **1** You add comparative to indicate that something is true only when compared with what is normal. *A bitter war was followed by six years of comparative calm.*
NOUN **2** In grammar, the comparative is the form of an adjective which indicates that the person or thing described has more of a particular quality than someone or something else, for example, "quicker", "better", "easier". See **superlative**.
comparatively ADVERB

compare compares comparing compared
VERB to consider things together and see in what ways they are similar.

comparison comparisons
NOUN the act of comparing things.

compartment compartments
NOUN one of the separate parts of an object. *The secret documents were in a special compartment in his briefcase.*

compass compasses
NOUN **1** an instrument with a magnetic needle for finding directions.
PLURAL NOUN **2** Compasses are a hinged instrument for drawing circles. (The proper name for this instrument is **a pair of compasses**.)

compassion
NOUN pity and sympathy for someone who is suffering.
compassionate ADJECTIVE
compassionately ADVERB

compass point compass points
NOUN the directions marked on a compass, for example north, north-east, north-north-east, etc.

compatible
ADJECTIVE If people or things are compatible, they go well together.
compatibility NOUN

compel compels compelling compelled
VERB to force someone to do something.

compensate compensates compensating compensated
VERB **1** to give someone money to replace something lost or damaged.
2 If one thing compensates for another, it makes up for the bad effects of the other. *The posh new hotel we were sent to compensated for the awful time we had at the Hotel Grotty.*
compensation NOUN **compensatory** ADJECTIVE

compete competes competing competed
VERB **1** to take part in a contest or game.
2 If two things such as businesses are competing, they are rivals.

competent
ADJECTIVE able to do something satisfactorily.
competently ADVERB **competence** NOUN

competition competitions
NOUN **1** an event in which people take part to find who is best at something.
2 When there is competition between people or groups, they are all trying to get something that not everyone can have. *Competition was keen for places at the school.*

compile compiles compiling compiled
VERB When someone compiles a book or report, they make it by putting together several items.
compilation NOUN

complacent
ADJECTIVE to be too relaxed about a serious situation and do nothing about it.
complacently ADVERB **complacency** NOUN

complain complains complaining complained
VERB **1** to say that you are not satisfied with something.
2 to have the symptoms of illness. *She complained of shortage of breath.*

Synonyms: (sense 1) find fault, grumble, moan

---

complaint complaints
NOUN **1** the act of complaining about something.
2 an illness. *Arthritis is often a very painful complaint.*

complement complements complementing complemented
VERB If two things complement each other, they go well together.
complementary ADJECTIVE
✔ Do not confuse *complement* with *compliment*.

complete completes completing completed
VERB **1** to finish a task.
ADJECTIVE **2** finished, done.
3 If something is complete, none of it is missing.
4 to the greatest degree possible: *a complete surprise.*

Synonyms: (sense 3) entire, full, whole
(sense 4) absolute, thorough, total

---

completely
ADVERB totally, utterly, absolutely.

 ► Computer words: keyboard, cursor, printer, backup, word processing, software...

complex complexes
ADJECTIVE **1** having many different parts and being hard to understand, complicated.
NOUN **2** a group of buildings used for a particular purpose: *a hotel and restaurant complex.*
complexity NOUN

complexion complexions
NOUN the quality of the skin on your face.

complicated
ADJECTIVE Something that is complicated has so many parts or aspects that it is difficult to understand or deal with.

complication complications
NOUN something that makes a situation more difficult to deal with.

compliment compliments complimenting complimented
NOUN **1** If you pay someone a compliment, you tell them you admire something about them.
VERB **2** to pay a compliment.
✔ Do not confuse *compliment* with *complement.*

complimentary
ADJECTIVE **1** If you are complimentary about something, you praise it.
2 A complimentary seat, ticket, etc. is given to you free.
✔ Do not confuse *complimentary* with *complementary.*

component components
NOUN The components of something are the parts it is made of.

compose composes composing composed
VERB **1** If something is composed of particular things or people, they are its parts or members.
2 To write a letter, message, piece of music, etc.

composer composers
NOUN someone who writes music.

composition compositions
NOUN **1** a piece of music or writing.
2 The composition of something is the things it consists of: *the composition of the ozone layer.*
3 the act of creating a new piece of music or writing.

compost
NOUN a mixture of decaying plants and manure added to soil to help plants grow.

compound compounds
NOUN **1** an enclosed area of land with buildings used for a particular purpose.
2 In grammar, a compound is a word which combines two words or parts of words, for example, "handbag".
3 In chemistry, a compound is a substance consisting of two or more different substances or chemical elements.
ADJECTIVE **4** consisting of two or more parts.

comprehend comprehends comprehending comprehended
VERB; FORMAL to understand or appreciate something.
comprehensible ADJECTIVE

comprehension
NOUN **1** a language exercise in which you have to read a text and answer questions on it to show that you understand it.
2 understanding.

comprehensive comprehensives
ADJECTIVE **1** including everything necessary or relevant: *a comprehensive guidebook.*
NOUN **2** a secondary school where children of all abilities are taught together.
comprehensively ADVERB
comprehensiveness NOUN

compress compresses compressing compressed
VERB to squeeze something so that it takes up less space.
compression NOUN

comprise comprises comprising comprised
VERB to include, to contain, to consist of. *The district then comprised 66 villages.*
✔ You do not need *of* after *comprise.* For example, you say: "The library comprises 500 000 books".

compromise compromises compromising compromised
NOUN **1** an agreement in which disagreeing people settle their dispute by accepting less than they originally wanted. *We reached a compromise: I had the rabbit and she had the guinea pig.*
VERB **2** to agree to accept less than you originally wanted.

compulsory
ADJECTIVE If something is compulsory, you have to do it.
compulsorily ADVERB

computer computers
NOUN an electronic machine that can quickly make calculations or store and find information.
computing NOUN

computerize computerizes computerizing computerized; also spelt **computerise**
VERB When a system or process is computerized, the work is done by computers.
computerization NOUN

comrade comrades
NOUN; OLD-FASHIONED a friend or colleague.
comradeship NOUN

con cons conning conned
VERB; INFORMAL to trick someone into doing or believing something.
con NOUN **con artist** NOUN

CD-ROM, modem, website, e-mail, database, spreadsheet, games console. ◀

A B C D E F G H I J K L M N O P Q R S T U V W X Y Z

con-
PREFIX with, together.

concave
ADJECTIVE A concave surface curves inwards.

Antonym: convex

conceal **conceals concealing concealed**
VERB To conceal something is to hide it.
concealed ADJECTIVE **concealment** NOUN

conceited
ADJECTIVE too proud of your appearance or your abilities.
conceitedly ADVERB **conceit** NOUN

conceivable
ADJECTIVE able to be imagined or believed. *It's conceivable that you saw her.*

conceive **conceives conceiving conceived**
VERB **1** to think up an idea, plan, invention, etc.
2 to imagine or believe something. *He couldn't conceive of anyone arguing with his results.*
3 to become pregnant.

concentrate **concentrates concentrating concentrated**
VERB **1** to give something all your attention.
2 When something is concentrated in one place, it is all there rather than spread out.

concentrated
ADJECTIVE A concentrated liquid has been made stronger by having water removed from it.

concentration
NOUN the act of giving something your complete attention.

concentric
ADJECTIVE Concentric circles share the same centre.

concept **concepts**
NOUN an abstract or general idea: *the concept of free public transport.*

conception **conceptions**
NOUN **1** Your conception of something is the idea you have of it.
2 Conception is the process by which a woman becomes pregnant.

concern **concerns concerning concerned**
NOUN **1** Concern is worry about something or someone.
2 If something is your concern, it is your duty or responsibility.
VERB **3** If you are concerned about something, it worries you.
4 If something concerns you it affects or involves you.

concerning
PREPOSITION You use "concerning" to show what something is about. *I wrote to you recently concerning the money you owe me.*

concert **concerts**
NOUN a public performance by musicians.

concertina **concertinas**
NOUN a small musical instrument held in the hands and played by pressing buttons while squeezing the sides in and out.

concerto **concertos** or **concerti**
Said "kon-**cher**-toe" NOUN a piece of music for a solo instrument and an orchestra.

concession **concessions**
NOUN If you make a concession, you agree to let someone have or do something. *As a special concession, the children were allowed to stay up late.*

concise
ADJECTIVE Concise writing or speech says what it needs to without wasting words.

Synonyms: brief, short, succinct

conclude **concludes concluding concluded**
VERB **1** If you conclude something, you decide that it is true using the facts you know.
2 to finish something.

conclusion **conclusions**
NOUN **1** the finish of something.
2 the decision that is reached after considering the facts.

concrete
NOUN **1** a building material made by mixing cement, gravel and water.
2 A concrete poem is one where the lines form a shape which helps to convey the poem's meaning.
ADJECTIVE **3** real and physical, rather than abstract.

Antonym: (sense 3) abstract

concussion
NOUN the condition of being confused or unconscious because of a blow to the head.
concussed ADJECTIVE

condemn **condemns condemning condemned**
VERB **1** If someone is condemned to a punishment, they are given it.
2 to say something is bad and unacceptable. *The Prime Minister condemned the terrorist attack.*

condensation
NOUN a coating of tiny drops of liquid formed on a surface by cooling gas or vapour.

condense **condenses condensing condensed**
VERB **1** When a gas or vapour condenses, it changes into a liquid.
2 to shorten a piece of writing or a speech.

► Concrete poems use words and letters to make patterns, shapes and pictures. Try one.

condition conditions
NOUN **1** the state someone or something is in.
2 a requirement that must be carried out in order for something else to happen. *Mum let us stay up on the condition that we went to bed straight afterwards.*
3 an illness or other medical problem. *She had a heart condition.*
PLURAL NOUN **4** The conditions in which people live or do things are the factors that affect their comfort, safety or success.

condom condoms
NOUN a rubber sheath worn by a man on his penis or by a woman inside her vagina as a contraceptive.

conduct conducts conducting conducted
Said "con-**duct**" VERB **1** When you conduct an activity, you do it. *I decided to conduct an experiment.*
2 When a substance conducts heat or electricity, it allows it to pass through.
3 FORMAL The way you conduct yourself is the way you behave.
4 to beat time for an orchestra or choir, using a baton.
Said "**con**-duct" NOUN **5** Your conduct is your behaviour.

conduction
NOUN the process by which heat travels through solids.

conductor conductors
NOUN **1** someone who rehearses and conducts an orchestra or choir.
2 someone who moves round a bus or train selling or checking tickets.
3 a substance that conducts heat or electricity.

cone cones
NOUN **1** a regular three-dimensional shape with a circular base and a point at the top.
2 the fruit of a fir or pine tree.

confectionery
NOUN sweets and chocolates.

confer confers conferring conferred
VERB to discuss something with others in order to make a decision.

conference conferences
NOUN a meeting at which formal discussions take place.

confess confesses confessing confessed
VERB to admit that you have done something wrong.

Synonyms: admit, own up

confession confessions
NOUN If you make a confession, you admit you have done something wrong.

Synonyms: acknowledgement, admission

confetti
NOUN small pieces of coloured paper thrown over the bride and groom at a wedding.

confide confides confiding confided
VERB If you confide in someone, you tell them a secret which you do not wish them to pass on.

confidence confidences
NOUN **1** If you have confidence in someone, you trust them to do what you expect of them.
2 If you are full of confidence, you are sure of your own abilities or qualities.

confident
ADJECTIVE **1** If you are confident about something, you are sure it will happen the way you want it to.
2 Someone who is confident is sure of their own abilities or qualities.
confidently ADVERB

Synonyms: (sense 1) certain, positive, sure
(sense 2) assured, self-assured

confidential
ADJECTIVE Confidential information is meant to be kept secret.
confidentially ADVERB

confine confines confining confined
VERB **1** If you are confined to a place, you cannot leave it.
2 If something is confined to a particular place or group, it exists only there.
confinement NOUN

confirm confirms confirming confirmed
VERB **1** To confirm something is to say or show that it is true.
2 If you confirm an arrangement or booking, you say it is definite.

Synonyms: (sense 1) prove, verify

confiscate confiscates confiscating confiscated
VERB To confiscate something is to take it away from someone as a punishment.
confiscation NOUN

conflict conflicts conflicting conflicted
Said "**con**-flict" NOUN **1** disagreement and argument.
2 a war or battle.
Said "con-**flict**" VERB **3** When two ideas or interests conflict, they are different and it seems impossible for them both to be true.

Synonyms: (sense 3) be incompatible, clash, disagree

conform conforms conforming conformed
VERB **1** to behave the way people expect you to.
2 If something conforms to a law or to someone's wishes, it is what is required or wanted.
conformist NOUN OR ADJECTIVE

a b c d e f g h i j k l m n o p q r s t u v w x y z

Duco means I lead in Latin. Which words on this page derive from it?

A B C D E F G H I J K L M N O P Q R S T U V W X Y Z

confront confronts confronting confronted
VERB **1** If you confront someone, you meet them face to face, especially when you are going to fight or argue with them.
2 If you are confronted with a problem or task, you have to deal with it.

confrontation confrontations
NOUN a serious dispute or fight between people or groups of people.

confuse confuses confusing confused
VERB **1** If you confuse two things, you mix them up and think one of them is the other.
2 To confuse someone means to make them uncertain about what is happening or what to do.
3 to make something more complicated.
confusing ADJECTIVE **confusion** NOUN

Synonyms: (sense 2) baffle, bewilder

congested
ADJECTIVE to be overcrowded and full.
congestion NOUN

congratulate congratulates congratulating congratulated
VERB to praise someone for something they have done.
congratulation NOUN

congregation congregations
NOUN the people attending a service in a church.
congregational ADJECTIVE

congress congresses
NOUN a large meeting held to discuss ideas or policies.

congruent
ADJECTIVE Two triangles are congruent if they are exactly the same shape and proportions.
congruence NOUN

conical
ADJECTIVE shaped like a cone.

conifer conifers
NOUN any type of evergreen tree that produces cones.
coniferous ADJECTIVE

conjunction conjunctions
NOUN In grammar, a conjunction is a word, such as "and", "but" and "while", that links two other words or two clauses. See **connective**.

conjurer conjurers
NOUN someone who entertains people by doing magic tricks.
conjuring NOUN

conker conkers
NOUN a hard, brown nut from a horse chestnut tree.

connect connects connecting connected
VERB **1** To connect two things is to join them together.
2 If one thing or person is connected with another, there is a link between them.

connection connections
NOUN **1** a link or relationship between things.
2 the point where two wires or pipes are joined together.
3 If you get a connection at a station or airport, you continue your journey by catching another train, bus or plane.
PLURAL NOUN **4** Someone's connections are the people they know.

connective connectives
NOUN a word which connects other clauses, phrases or individual words, often called a **conjunction**.

conquer conquers conquering conquered
VERB **1** to take control of a country by force.
2 to succeed in controlling something difficult or dangerous. *You must conquer your fear of water.*
conqueror NOUN

conquest conquests
NOUN **1** the conquering of a country or group of people.
2 Conquests are lands captured by conquest.

conscience consciences
NOUN the part of your mind that tells you what is right and wrong.

conscientious
Said "kon-shee-**en**-shus" ADJECTIVE careful, meticulous and thorough in doing your work.
conscientiously ADVERB
conscientiousness NOUN

conscious
ADJECTIVE **1** awake, not asleep or unconscious.
2 If you are conscious of something, you are aware of it.
3 A conscious action or effort is done deliberately.
consciously ADVERB **consciousness** NOUN

consecutive
ADJECTIVE happening one after the other, in a row. In mathematics, consecutive numbers are, for example, 5, 6, 7.
consecutively ADVERB

consent consents consenting consented
VERB **1** to agree that something will happen or give permission for it to happen.
NOUN **2** permission to do something.

consequence consequences
NOUN the result or effects of an action.
consequent ADJECTIVE **consequently** ADVERB

conservation
NOUN the preservation of the environment.
conservationist NOUN OR ADJECTIVE

► Chose, choose; lose, loose; nose, noose: why do these pairs of words confuse some people?

conservative
ADJECTIVE **1** In Britain, the Conservative Party is one of the main forces in politics.
2 A conservative person is one who is not willing to accept changes or new ideas.
3 A conservative estimate or guess is a cautious or moderate one.

conservatory **conservatories**
NOUN a room with glass walls and a glass roof in which plants are kept.

conserve **conserves conserving conserved**
VERB to keep or protect something from damage, decay or loss.

consider **considers considering considered**
VERB **1** to think about something carefully.
2 If you consider something to be the case, you think or judge it to be so.

Synonyms: (sense 1) contemplate, ponder, reflect

considerable
ADJECTIVE A considerable amount of something is a lot of it.
considerably ADVERB

considerate
ADJECTIVE Someone who is considerate pays attention to other people's needs and feelings.
considerately ADVERB

consideration **considerations**
NOUN **1** careful thought about something.
2 If you show consideration for someone you take account of their needs and feelings.
3 a factor that has to be considered.

considering
CONJUNCTION OR PREPOSITION You say considering to show that you are taking something into account. *He is a great little golfer considering he is only eight.*

consist **consists consisting consisted**
VERB Something that consists of particular things is formed from them.

consistency **consistencies**
NOUN **1** the quality of being consistent.
2 thickness.

consistent
ADJECTIVE If you are consistent, you keep doing something the same way.
consistently ADVERB

consolation **consolations**
NOUN **1** the act of making someone more cheerful.
2 A consolation prize is one that you receive for not winning, often for coming last.

console **consoles consoling consoled**
VERB To console someone who is unhappy is to make them more cheerful.

consonant **consonants**
NOUN All letters except the vowels are consonants. See **vowel**.

conspicuous
ADJECTIVE easily seen or noticed.
conspicuously ADVERB **conspicuousness** NOUN

conspiracy **conspiracies**
NOUN a secret plot to do something wrong or illegal, involving several people.
conspirator NOUN

conspire **conspires conspiring conspired**
VERB When people conspire, they plot together to do something illegal.

constable **constables**
NOUN a police officer of the lowest rank.
constabulary NOUN

constant
ADJECTIVE **1** happening all the time or always there.
2 staying the same.
constantly ADVERB **constancy** NOUN

constellation **constellations**
NOUN a group of stars.

constipated
ADJECTIVE finding it difficult or impossible to pass solid waste from your body.
constipation NOUN

constituency **constituencies**
NOUN a town or area represented by an MP.
constituent NOUN

constitute **constitutes constituting constituted**
VERB to constitute something is to make up something or form something. *Two bookable offences constitute a reason for being sent off.*

constitution **constitutions**
NOUN **1** The constitution of a country is the system of laws which formally states people's rights and duties.
2 Your constitution is your health.
constitutional ADJECTIVE **constitutionally** ADVERB

construct **constructs constructing constructed**
VERB to build or make.

construction **constructions**
NOUN **1** the act of building or making something.
2 something that has been built or made.

constructive
ADJECTIVE Constructive criticisms and comments are helpful.
constructively ADVERB

consul **consuls**
NOUN an official who lives in a foreign city and who looks after the interests of people there who are citizens of their own country.

consult **consults consulting consulted**
VERB **1** to ask someone for their opinion or advice.
2 If you consult a book or map, you look at it for information.
consultation NOUN

A B C D E F G H I J K L M N O P Q R S T U V W X Y Z

consultant consultants
NOUN **1** an experienced doctor who specializes in one type of medicine.
2 someone who gives expert advice.
consultancy NOUN

consume consumes consuming consumed
VERB **1** to eat or drink something.
2 To consume fuel or energy is to use it up.
consumable ADJECTIVE

consumer consumers
NOUN someone who buys things or uses services.

consumption
NOUN **1** the using of fuel or food or the amount used.
2 OLD-FASHIONED tuberculosis.

contact contacts contacting contacted
NOUN **1** If you are in contact with someone, you regularly communicate with them.
2 When things are in contact, they are touching each other.
3 someone you know in an organization or place who helps you or gives you information.
VERB **4** to get in touch with someone.

contact lens contact lenses
NOUN a small plastic lens that you put in your eye instead of wearing glasses to help you see better.

contagious
ADJECTIVE A contagious disease can be caught by touching people or things infected with it. See **infectious**.
contagion NOUN

contain contains containing contained
VERB **1** If a substance contains something, that thing is inside it.
2 FORMAL to stop something increasing or spreading. *Efforts to contain the Great Fire of London proved unsuccessful.*

container containers
NOUN **1** something which you keep things in, such as a box or a bottle.
2 a large sealable metal case of a standard size which can be transported by road, rail or sea.

contaminate contaminates contaminating contaminated
VERB If something is contaminated by dirt, chemicals or radiation, it is made impure and harmful.
contamination NOUN

contemplate contemplates contemplating contemplated
VERB to think carefully about something for a long time.
contemplation NOUN

contemporary contemporaries
ADJECTIVE **1** produced or happening now.
NOUN **2** Your contemporaries are the people of similar age to you, or who are alive at the same time.

contempt
NOUN If you treat someone or something with contempt, you show no respect for them.

contend contends contending contended
VERB **1** To contend with a difficulty is to deal with it.
2 When people contend for something, they compete for it.
contender NOUN

content contents
Said "**con**-tent" NOUN **1** The content of a piece of writing or a film is what is expressed in it.
PLURAL NOUN **2** The contents of something are the things inside it.
Said "con-**tent**" ADJECTIVE **3** happy or satisfied.

contented
ADJECTIVE happy and satisfied with your life.
contentedly ADVERB **contentment** NOUN

contest contests contesting contested
Said "**con**-test" NOUN **1** a competition or game.
2 a struggle for power: *a contest to see who would become president.*
Said "con-**test**" VERB **3** If you contest a decision or statement, you object to it formally.

contestant contestants
NOUN a competitor.

context contexts
NOUN The context of something is the surrounding circumstances or material which help to explain it: *the historical context in which Shakespeare wrote.*

continent continents
NOUN **1** a very large area of land, such as Africa or Asia.
2 In Britain, the mainland of Europe is sometimes called the Continent.

continental
ADJECTIVE relating to the mainland of Europe.

continual
ADJECTIVE happening again and again at close intervals, repeatedly. See **continuous**.
continually ADVERB

Synonyms: constant, incessant

continue continues continuing continued
VERB to keep on doing something.
continuation NOUN

Synonyms: carry on, go on, proceed

continuous
ADJECTIVE happening or existing without stopping.
✔ *Continuous* is distinct from *continual* in that something *continuous* never stops. Something which is *continual* may stop occasionally, but not for long.

 ► How many different words for eating and drinking can you think of?

contour **contours**
NOUN 1 The contours of something are its general shape.
2 On a map, a contour is a line joining points of equal height.

contra-
PREFIX against or opposite to.

contraception
NOUN methods of preventing pregnancy.

contraceptive **contraceptives**
NOUN a device or pill for preventing pregnancy.

contract **contracts contracting contracted**
Said "**con**-tract" **NOUN 1** a legal agreement about the sale of something or work done for money.
Said "con-**tract**" **VERB 2** to become smaller or shorter.

contraction **contractions**
NOUN the shortening of a material or body part such as a muscle.

Antonym: expansion

contradict **contradicts contradicting contradicted**
VERB If you contradict someone, you say that what they have just said is wrong.
contradiction NOUN **contradictory** ADJECTIVE

contraption **contraptions**
NOUN a strange-looking machine or piece of equipment.

contrary
ADJECTIVE 1 Contrary ideas or opinions are opposed to each other.
PHRASE 2 You say **on the contrary** when you are contradicting what someone has just said.

contrast **contrasts contrasting contrasted**
NOUN 1 a great difference between things.
VERB 2 to describe or emphasize the differences between things.
3 If one thing contrasts with another, it is very different.

contribute **contributes contributing contributed**
VERB 1 to contribute money is to help pay for something.
2 If you contribute to something, you help to make it successful.
contribution NOUN

Synonyms: (sense 1) donate, give

control **controls controlling controlled**
VERB 1 To control something is to have power over it.
2 If you control yourself, you make yourself behave calmly when you are angry or upset.
NOUN 3 the power over something.
4 The controls on a machine are the knobs or other devices used to work it.
PHRASE 5 If something is **out of control**, nobody has any power over it.
controller NOUN

controversial
ADJECTIVE Something that is controversial causes a lot of discussion and argument, because many people disapprove of it.
controversially ADVERB

controversy **controversies**
Said "**kon**-trov-er-see" *or* "kon-**trov**-er-see"
NOUN discussion and argument because there are strong feelings of disapproval.

conundrum **conundrums**
NOUN; FORMAL a puzzling problem.

convalescent
ADJECTIVE recovering from illness.

convection
NOUN the process by which heat travels through gases and liquids.
convector NOUN

convenient
ADJECTIVE If something is convenient, it is easy to use or do.
conveniently ADVERB **convenience** NOUN

Synonyms: handy, useful

convent **convents**
NOUN a building where nuns live, or a school run by nuns.

convention **conventions**
NOUN 1 an accepted way or behaving or doing something.
2 a large meeting of an organization or political group: *the Geneva Convention.*

conventional
ADJECTIVE thinking or behaving in an ordinary and usual way.
convention NOUN

converge **converges converging converged**
VERB to meet or join at a particular place.

conversation **conversations**
NOUN a talk between people.
conversational ADJECTIVE

conversion **conversions**
NOUN the act of turning one thing into another.

convert **converts converting converted**
Said "con-**vert**" **VERB 1** to change one thing into another. For example, in mathematics you can convert a fraction into a decimal: $\frac{1}{2} = 0{\cdot}5$.
2 If someone converts you, they persuade you to change your religious or political beliefs.
Said "**con**-vert" **NOUN 3** someone who has changed their religious or political beliefs.

convex
ADJECTIVE A convex surface bulges outwards.

Antonym: concave

a b c d e f g h i j k l m n o p q r s t u v w x y z

convey conveys conveying conveyed
VERB 1 FORMAL to carry someone or something to a place, to transport.
2 If you convey information to someone, you pass it on to them so that they absorb and understand it.

conveyor belt conveyor belts
NOUN a moving strip used in factories for transporting objects.

convict convicts convicting convicted
Said "con-**vict**" VERB 1 If someone is convicted of a crime, they are found guilty of it in a law court.
Said "**con**-vict" NOUN 2 someone serving a prison sentence.

conviction convictions
NOUN 1 If someone has a conviction, they have been found guilty in a court of law.
2 a strong belief or opinion.

convince convinces convincing convinced
VERB to persuade someone that what you say is true.

convoy convoys
NOUN a group of vehicles or ships travelling together.

cook cooks cooking cooked
VERB 1 to prepare food for eating.
NOUN 2 someone who prepares and cooks food.

cooker cookers
NOUN a device for cooking food.

cookery
NOUN the activity of preparing and cooking food.

cool cooler coolest; cools cooling cooled
ADJECTIVE 1 Something cool has a low temperature but is not cold.
2 If you are cool in a difficult situation, you stay calm.
3 INFORMAL trendy and acceptable.
VERB 4 to become less warm.
coolness NOUN

coop coops
NOUN a cage for chickens or rabbits.

cooperate cooperates cooperating cooperated
Said "koh-**op**-er-ate" VERB 1 When people cooperate, they work or act together.
2 to do what someone asks.
cooperative ADJECTIVE **cooperation** NOUN

coordinate coordinates coordinating coordinated
VERB to organize the people or things involved in an activity.
coordinator NOUN

coordinates
PLURAL NOUN On a map or grid, coordinates are a pair of numbers or letters which tell you where a point is on the map or grid.

coordination
NOUN 1 the act of organizing things to happen at the right time.
2 If you have good coordination you can make your brain and the different parts of your body work well together.
coordinated ADJECTIVE

cop cops
NOUN; INFORMAL a policeman.

cope copes coping coped
VERB to deal with a problem or task successfully.

copper
NOUN a reddish-brown metal.

copy copies copying copied
NOUN 1 something made to look like something else.
2 A copy of a book, newspaper, or record is one of many identical ones produced at the same time.
VERB 3 to mimic someone or something.
4 to make a copy of something.

Synonyms: (sense 4) duplicate, reproduce

copyright copyrights
NOUN If someone has the copyright on a piece of writing or music, it cannot be copied or performed without their permission.

coral corals
NOUN a hard substance that forms in tropical seas from the skeletons of tiny animals called corals.

cord cords
NOUN strong, thick string.

cordial cordials
NOUN 1 a sweet drink made from fruit juice.
ADJECTIVE 2 warm and friendly.
cordially ADVERB **cordiality** NOUN

corduroy
NOUN a thick, ridged cloth.

core cores
NOUN 1 the hard central part of a fruit such as an apple.
2 the central or most important part of something.

cork corks
NOUN 1 a soft, light substance which forms the bark of a cork oak tree.
2 a piece of cork pushed into the end of a bottle to close it.

corkscrew corkscrews
NOUN a device for pulling corks out of bottles.

corn
NOUN a general word for crops such as wheat and barley and their seeds.

corner corners cornering cornered
NOUN 1 a place where two sides or edges of something meet.
VERB 2 To corner a person or animal is to get them into a place they cannot escape from.

 ► Joke. Why was the farmer cross? Someone trod on his corn.

cornet cornets
NOUN a small brass instrument used in brass and military bands.

cornflour
NOUN a fine white flour made from maize and used in cooking to thicken sauces.

cornflower cornflowers
NOUN a small plant with bright flowers, usually blue.

corny cornier corniest
ADJECTIVE very obvious and not at all original: *corny old jokes.*

coronation coronations
NOUN the ceremony at which a king or queen is crowned.
[from Latin *corona* meaning crown]

coroner coroners
NOUN an official who investigates the deaths of people who have died in a violent or unusual way.

corporal corporals
NOUN a junior officer of low rank in the army or air force.

corporal punishment
NOUN the punishing of people by beating them.

corporation corporations
NOUN 1 a very large business or organization.
2 a group of people responsible for running a city.
corporate ADJECTIVE

corps
Said "**cor**" **NOUN 1** a part of the army with special duties: *the Army Cadet Corps.*
2 a small group of people who do a special job: *the press corps.*

corpse corpses
NOUN a dead body.

correct corrects correcting corrected
ADJECTIVE 1 If something is correct, there are no mistakes in it.
VERB 2 to put right something which is wrong.

Synonyms: (sense 2) amend, rectify

correspond corresponds corresponding corresponded
VERB 1 If one thing corresponds to another, they are either very similar or closely related. *The steering wheel of a car corresponds to the joystick of an aircraft.*
2 When people correspond, they write to each other.
corresponding ADJECTIVE

correspondence
NOUN 1 the writing of letters; also the letters written.
2 If there is a correspondence between two things, they are very similar or closely related.

correspondent correspondents
NOUN a newspaper, television or radio reporter.

corridor corridors
NOUN a passage in a building or train.

corrode corrodes corroding corroded
VERB when metal corrodes, it is gradually destroyed by a chemical or rust.
corrosion NOUN **corrosive** ADJECTIVE

corrugated
ADJECTIVE Corrugated metal or cardboard has parallel, curved ridges to make it stronger.
[from Latin *corrugare* meaning to wrinkle up]

corrupt corrupts corrupting corrupted
ADJECTIVE 1 Corrupt people act dishonestly or illegally in return for money or power.
VERB 2 To corrupt someone means to make them dishonest or immoral.

Synonyms: (sense 1) crooked, dishonest

corset corsets
NOUN Corsets are stiff underwear for the trunk of your body.

cosmetics
PLURAL NOUN substances such as lipstick or face powder.

cosmic
ADJECTIVE belonging or related to the universe.

cosmos
NOUN the universe.

cost costs costing cost
NOUN 1 the amount of money needed to buy, do or make something.
2 The cost of achieving something is the loss or injury involved in achieving it.
VERB 3 You use "cost" to talk about the amount of money you have to pay for something. *How much does it cost?*
4 to lose something as the result of a mistake or bad luck. *That careless mistake cost me twenty marks in the exam.*

costly costlier costliest
ADJECTIVE expensive.

costume costumes
NOUN 1 a set of clothes worn by an actor.
2 the clothing worn in a particular place or during a particular period: *people in 18th-century costume.*

cosy cosier cosiest; cosies
ADJECTIVE 1 warm and comfortable.
NOUN 2 A soft cover put over a teapot to keep the tea warm.

cot cots
NOUN a baby's bed with high rails around it.

cottage cottages
NOUN a small house in the country.

cottage cheese
NOUN a type of soft white lumpy cheese.

Corps is also French word; it comes from the Latin *corpus* meaning body. ◀

a b c d e f g h i j k l m n o p q r s t u v w x y z

A B C D E F G H I J K L M N O P Q R S T U V W X Y Z

cotton
NOUN 1 cloth made from the soft fibres of a particular plant.
2 thread used for sewing.

couch **couches**
NOUN a long, soft piece of furniture for sitting or lying on.

cough **coughs coughing coughed**
Said "**koff**" **VERB 1** When you cough, you force air out of your throat with a sudden harsh noise.
NOUN 2 an illness that makes you cough a lot.

could
VERB 1 You use "could" to say that you were able or allowed to do something. *I could see that something was wrong.*
2 You use "could" to say that something might happen or might be the case. *It could rain tomorrow.*
3 You use "could" when you are asking for something politely. *Could you tell me how to get to the station?*

couldn't
an abbreviated form of **could not**.

council **councils**
NOUN a group of people elected to look after the affairs of a town, city, district or county.

councillor **councillors**
NOUN an elected member of a local council.

counsel **counsels counselling counselled**
VERB To counsel people is to listen to their problems and help them towards a solution.
counselling NOUN **counsellor** NOUN

count **counts counting counted**
VERB 1 To say numbers in the right order.
2 If you count things, you add them up to see how many there are.
3 If something counts in a situation, it is important or valuable.
4 To count as something means to be regarded as that thing. *She was eighteen, but her parents still counted her as a child.*
5 To count on someone means to rely on them.
NOUN 6 a number reached by counting. *At the last count I had over 500 CDs.*
7 a European nobleman: *the notorious Count Dracula.*

Synonyms: (sense 2) calculate, reckon, tot up

countdown **countdowns**
NOUN the counting aloud of numbers in reverse order before something happens, especially before a rocket launch.

counter **counters**
NOUN 1 a surface over which goods are sold in a shop.
2 small object used in a board game.
3 a machine used to count things, for example, the number of people going into a building.

counterfeit **counterfeits counterfeiting counterfeited**
Said "**kown**-ter-fit" **ADJECTIVE 1** Something counterfeit is not genuine but has been made to look genuine to deceive people.
VERB 2 To counterfeit something is to make a false version of it.
counterfeiter NOUN

countess **countesses**
NOUN the wife of a count or earl, or a woman with the same rank as a count or earl.

countless
ADJECTIVE very many.

country **countries**
NOUN 1 one of the political areas the world is divided into.
2 land that is away from towns and cities.

countryside
NOUN land that is away from towns and cities.

county **counties**
NOUN a region with its own local government.

couple **couples coupling coupled**
NOUN 1 A couple of things or people means two of them.
2 two people who are married, or who live or go out together.
VERB 3 If one thing is coupled with another, the two things are combined.

couplet **couplets**
NOUN two lines of poetry together, especially two that rhyme.

coupon **coupons**
NOUN 1 a voucher which allows you to pay less than usual for something.
2 a form which you fill in to ask for information or to enter a competition.

courage
NOUN the quality shown by people who do things knowing they are dangerous or difficult.

courageous
ADJECTIVE brave, daring.
courageously ADVERB

courgette **courgettes**
Said "koor-**jet**" **NOUN** a type of small marrow with dark green skin. It is also called **zucchini**.

courier **couriers**
Said "**koo**-ree-er" **NOUN 1** someone employed by a travel company to look after people on holiday.
2 someone employed to deliver special letters quickly.

 ► The names of counties, such as Yorkshire, Argyll and Gwynedd, begin with capital letters.

course courses
NOUN **1** a series of lessons or lectures.
2 a piece of land where races take place or golf is played.
3 the route a ship or aircraft takes.
4 one of the parts of a meal.
5 a series of medical treatments: *a course of injections*.
PHRASE **6** **Of course** means certainly.

court courts
NOUN **1** a place where legal matters are decided by a judge and jury or a magistrate.
2 a place where a game such as tennis or badminton is played.

courteous
Said "**kur**-tee-uss" ADJECTIVE polite and considerate.
courteously ADVERB

courtyard courtyards
NOUN a flat area of ground surrounded by buildings or walls.

cousin cousins
NOUN Your cousin is the child of your uncle or aunt.

cove coves
NOUN a small bay.

cover covers covering covered
VERB **1** If you cover something, you put something else over it to protect it or hide it.
2 If something covers something else, it forms a layer over it. *Snow covered the hills.*
3 If you cover a particular distance, you travel that distance.
4 To cover a subject means to discuss it in a lecture, course, book, programme, etc.
NOUN **5** something put over an object to protect it or keep it warm.
cover up VERB If you cover up something you do not want people to know about, you hide it from them.

coverage
NOUN the amount of time given to a particular subject by the newspapers, television and radio.

cow cows
NOUN **1** a large, female domesticated mammal, kept for its milk or meat.
2 a mature female of various other mammals such as the elephant and whale.

coward cowards
NOUN someone who is easily frightened and avoids dangerous or difficult situations.
cowardly ADJECTIVE **cowardliness** NOUN

cowboy cowboys
NOUN **1** a man employed to look after cattle in America.
2 INFORMAL an unreliable contractor who does shoddy, over-priced work.

cower cowers cowering cowered
VERB to crouch or move backwards in fear.

Synonyms: cringe, shrink

cox coxes
NOUN a person who steers a boat.

coy coyer coyest
ADJECTIVE If someone is coy, they pretend to be shy and modest.
coyly ADVERB

crab crabs
NOUN a type of edible shellfish.

crack cracks cracking cracked
VERB **1** If something cracks it becomes damaged, with lines appearing on its surface.
2 If you crack a joke, you tell it.
3 If you crack a problem or code, you solve it.
NOUN **4** one of the lines appearing on something when it cracks.
PHRASE **5** If you **have a crack** at something, you try to do it.

Synonyms: (sense 4) break, fracture, gap

cracker crackers
NOUN **1** a thin, crisp biscuit that is often eaten with cheese.
2 a paper-covered tube that pulls apart with a bang and usually has a toy and paper hat inside.

crackle crackles crackling crackled
VERB to make a rapid series of short, harsh noises.

cradle cradles
NOUN a box-shaped bed for a baby.

craft crafts
NOUN **1** an activity such as weaving, carving or pottery.
2 a boat, plane or spacecraft.

craftsman craftsmen
NOUN a person who makes things skilfully with their hands.
craftsmanship NOUN **craftswoman** NOUN

crafty craftier craftiest
ADJECTIVE Someone who is crafty gets what they want by tricking people in a clever way.
craftily ADVERB **craftiness** NOUN

crag crags
NOUN a steep rugged rock or peak.

cram crams cramming crammed
VERB to fill something completely in a rough way.

Synonyms: pack, squeeze, stuff

cramp
NOUN a pain caused by a muscle contracting.

cramped
ADJECTIVE If a room or building is cramped, it is not big enough for the people or things in it.

Pun. Pat's only been in the army three weeks, and they've already made him a court martial!

A B C D E F G H I J K L M N O P Q R S T U V W X Y Z

crane cranes
NOUN 1 a machine that moves heavy things by lifting them in the air.
2 a large bird with a long neck and long legs.

crane-fly crane-flies
NOUN a daddy-long-legs.

crank cranks
NOUN 1 INFORMAL someone who has strange ideas or who behaves in an odd way.
2 a handle-like device you turn to make a machine move or operate.

cranny crannies
NOUN a very narrow opening in a wall or rock.

crash crashes crashing crashed
NOUN 1 an accident in which a moving vehicle hits something and is damaged.
2 a sudden loud noise.
VERB 3 When a vehicle crashes, it hits something and gets damaged.

crash helmet crash helmets
NOUN headgear worn by a motorcyclist to protect against injury.

crate crates
NOUN a large box used for transporting or storing things.

crater craters
NOUN a wide hole in the ground caused by something hitting it or by an explosion.

crave craves craving craved
VERB to want something very much.
craving NOUN

crawl crawls crawling crawled
VERB 1 to move forward on your hands and knees.
2 to move forward very slowly.

crayon crayons
NOUN a coloured pencil or a stick of coloured wax.

craze crazes
NOUN something that is very popular for a short time.

crazy crazier craziest
ADJECTIVE 1 INFORMAL very strange or foolish.
2 INFORMAL If you are crazy about something or someone, you like them very much.

creak creaks creaking creaked
VERB 1 If something creaks, it makes a harsh squeaking sound when it moves or when you stand on it.
NOUN 2 a harsh squeaking noise.
creaky ADJECTIVE

cream creams
NOUN 1 a thick, yellowish-white liquid taken from the top of milk.
2 a substance that you can rub into your skin to make it soft or protect it.
ADJECTIVE 3 yellowish-white.
creamy ADJECTIVE

crease creases creasing creased
NOUN 1 an irregular line that appears on cloth or paper when it is crumpled.
2 a straight line on something that has been pressed or folded neatly.
VERB 3 to make lines appear on something.

create creates creating created
VERB to cause something to happen or exist.
creator NOUN **creation** NOUN

creative
ADJECTIVE Creative people are good at inventing and developing new ideas.
creatively ADVERB **creativity** NOUN

creature creatures
NOUN any living thing that is not a plant.

crèche crèches
Said "**kresh**" NOUN a place where small children are looked after while their parents are working.

credible
ADJECTIVE If someone or something is credible, you can believe or trust them.
credibility NOUN

credit credits
NOUN 1 a system where you pay for goods after you have received them.
2 If you get the credit for something, people praise you for it.

credit card credit cards
NOUN a plastic card that allows you to receive goods before you pay for them.

creed creeds
NOUN a statement of what someone believes in, particularly religious beliefs.

creek creeks
NOUN a narrow inlet where the sea comes a long way into the land.

creep creeps creeping crept
VERB to move quietly and slowly.

creepy creepier creepiest
ADJECTIVE; INFORMAL strange and frightening.

cremate cremates cremating cremated
VERB If someone's dead body is cremated, it is burned after a funeral service.
cremation NOUN

crematorium crematoriums or crematoria
NOUN a building in which the bodies of dead people are cremated.

crepe
Said "**krayp**" NOUN 1 thin ridged fabric.
2 a type of rubber with a rough surface.

crept
the past tense of **creep**.

crescent crescents
NOUN a curved shape that is wider in its middle than at the ends, which are pointed.

► Creed, credible and incredible come from the Latin *credo* meaning I believe.

cress
NOUN a plant with small, strong-tasting leaves, used in salads.

crest crests
NOUN 1 The crest of a hill or wave is its highest part.
2 a tuft of feathers on top of a bird's head.
3 a small picture or design that is the emblem of a noble family, a town or an organization.

crevice crevices
NOUN a narrow crack or gap in rock.

crew crews
NOUN people with special technical skills who work together: *a film crew; an aircraft crew.*

crib cribs cribbing cribbed
VERB 1 INFORMAL to copy what someone else has written and pretend it is your own work.
NOUN 2 OLD-FASHIONED a baby's cot.

cricket crickets
NOUN 1 a team game played with bat, ball and wickets, usually outdoors.
2 a small jumping insect that produces sounds by rubbing its wings together.

cried
the past participle of **cry**.

cries
1 the plural form of the noun **cry**.
2 the third person singular of the verb **cry**.

crime crimes
NOUN an action for which you can be punished by law.

Synonyms: misdemeanour, offence

criminal criminals
NOUN 1 someone who has committed a crime.
ADJECTIVE 2 involving or related to crime: *criminal activities.*
criminally ADVERB

Synonyms: (sense 1) crook, lawbreaker, offender

crimson
NOUN OR ADJECTIVE dark purplish-red.

cringe cringes cringing cringed
VERB to back away from someone or something because you are afraid or embarrassed.

crinkle crinkles crinkling crinkled
VERB 1 If something crinkles, it becomes slightly creased or folded.
NOUN 2 small creases or folds.
crinkly ADJECTIVE

cripple cripples crippling crippled
NOUN 1 someone who cannot move their body properly because it is weak or affected by disease.
VERB 2 to injure someone so severely that they can never move properly again.
crippled ADJECTIVE **crippling** ADJECTIVE

crisis crises
*Said "***kry***-seez" in the plural* NOUN a very serious or dangerous situation.

crisp crisper crispest; crisps
ADJECTIVE 1 pleasantly fresh and firm.
NOUN 2 Crisps are thin slices of fried potato.
crispy ADJECTIVE **crispness** NOUN

critic critics
NOUN 1 someone who writes reviews of books, films, plays or musical performances.
2 someone who publicly criticizes a person or system.

critical
ADJECTIVE 1 A critical time or situation is a very important one.
2 If you are critical of something or someone, you criticize them.

criticism criticisms
NOUN 1 the action of expressing disapproval of someone or something.
2 a statement that expresses disapproval.
3 an assessment of something, noting its good and bad points: *theatre criticism.*

criticize criticizes criticizing criticized; also spelt **criticise**
VERB to say what you think is wrong with someone or something.

Synonyms: disparage, find fault with

croak croaks croaking croaked
VERB When animals and birds croak, they make harsh, low sounds.
croak NOUN **croaky** ADJECTIVE

crochet
*Said "***kroh-shay***"* NOUN a way of making material out of thread using a needle with a small hook at one end.

crockery
NOUN plates, cups, and saucers.

crocodile crocodiles
NOUN a large, scaly, meat-eating reptile which lives in tropical rivers.

crocus crocuses
NOUN Crocuses are yellow, purple or white flowers that grow in early spring.

croissant croissants
*Said "***krwus***-son"* NOUN a light, crescent-shaped roll eaten at breakfast.

crook crooks
NOUN 1 INFORMAL a criminal.
2 The crook of your elbow or knee is the soft, inside part where you bend your arm or leg.
3 A crook is the bent staff a shepherd holds to help guide his sheep, particularly in the past.

crooked
*Said "***kroo***-kid"* ADJECTIVE 1 bent or twisted.
2 dishonest.
crookedly ADVERB **crookedness** NOUN

Crochet is a French word meaning small hook.

a b c d e f g h i j k l m n o p q r s t u v w x y z

crop crops cropping cropped
NOUN **1** Crops are plants such as wheat and potatoes that are grown for food.
VERB **2** If something crops up, it occurs unexpectedly.

cross crosses crossing crossed; crosser crossest
VERB **1** If you cross somewhere you go from one side to the other.
2 Lines or roads that cross go across each other.
3 If a thought crosses your mind, you think of it.
4 If you cross your legs or your fingers, you put one on top of the other.
NOUN **5** a vertical bar or line crossed by a shorter horizontal bar or line, or anything shaped like this.
6 Something that is a cross between two things is a mixture of both things.
ADJECTIVE **7** angry, grumpy.
cross out VERB to draw a line through something because it is wrong.
crossly ADVERB

crossbow crossbows
NOUN a weapon consisting of a small bow fixed at the end of a piece of wood, held horizontally.

cross-country
NOUN **1** the sport of running in open countryside.
ADJECTIVE OR ADVERB **2** across country.

cross-eyed
ADJECTIVE A cross-eyed person has eyes that seem to look towards each other.

crossing crossings
NOUN **1** a place where you can cross a road or railway safely.
2 a journey by ship to a place at the other side of the sea.

cross-legged
ADJECTIVE If you sit cross-legged, your knees point outwards and your feet are tucked under them.

crossroads
NOUN a junction where two or more roads cross each other.

cross-section cross-sections
NOUN **1** A cross-section of a group of people is a fair sample of them.
2 a diagram of an object showing what you would see if you could cut it across the centre.

crossword crosswords
NOUN a word game in which you work out answers to clues and write them into a grid of squares.

crouch crouches crouching crouched
VERB to keep low, leaning forward with your legs bent.

crow crows crowing crowed
NOUN **1** a large black bird which makes a loud, harsh noise.
VERB **2** to utter a loud squawking sound.
3 to boast about what you have done.
PHRASE **4** The distance to a place **as the crow flies** is the distance measured in a straight line.

crowbar crowbars
NOUN a heavy iron bar used as a lever or for forcing things open.

crowd crowds crowding crowded
NOUN **1** a large group of people gathered together.
VERB **2** to gather closely together in a large group.

Synonyms: (sense 1) mass, mob, multitude

crown crowns crowning crowned
NOUN **1** the headdress of a king or queen.
2 the top of your head.
VERB **3** When a king or queen is crowned, a crown is put on their head and they are officially made king or queen.

crucial
Said "**kroo**-shl" ADJECTIVE very important.

Synonyms: critical, decisive, vital

crucifix crucifixes
NOUN a cross with a figure representing Jesus Christ being crucified on it.

crucify crucifies crucifying crucified
VERB to tie or nail someone to a cross and leave them there to die.
crucifixion NOUN

crude cruder crudest
ADJECTIVE **1** rough and simple.
2 rude, coarse and vulgar.
crudely ADVERB **crudeness** NOUN

Synonyms: (sense 1) makeshift, primitive

cruel crueller cruellest
ADJECTIVE Cruel people deliberately cause pain or distress.
cruelly ADVERB **cruelty** NOUN

Synonyms: brutal, heartless, callous

cruise cruises cruising cruised
NOUN **1** a holiday in which you tour round on a ship.
VERB **2** When a vehicle cruises, it moves at a steady comfortable speed.

cruiser cruisers
NOUN **1** a motor boat with a cabin you can sleep in.
2 a large fast warship.

crumb crumbs
NOUN a very small piece of bread or cake.

crumble crumbles crumbling crumbled
VERB to break into small pieces.
crumbly ADJECTIVE

 ► These words end "-mb": crumb, lamb, climb, limb, dumb. Can you add to the list?

crumpet crumpets
NOUN a round, flat bread-like cake which you eat toasted.

crumple crumples crumpling crumpled
VERB to squash something up so that it is full of creases and folds.

crunch crunches crunching crunched
VERB to crush something noisily, for example between your teeth or under your feet.

crusade crusades
NOUN a long and determined attempt to achieve something you believe in strongly.
crusader NOUN

crush crushes crushing crushed
VERB 1 to squeeze something hard, often so much that its shape is destroyed.
2 to defeat someone completely.

crust crusts
NOUN the hard outside part of a loaf.

crustacean crustaceans
Said "kruss-**tay**-shn" NOUN a creature with a shell and several pairs of legs. Crabs, lobsters, and shrimps are crustaceans.

crutch crutches
NOUN a stick used by injured people to support them.

cry cries crying cried
VERB 1 to weep.
2 to shout or yell.
NOUN 3 a shout or yell.

Synonyms: (sense 1) sob, whimper
(sense 2) bellow, bawl, boom

crypt crypts
NOUN an underground room beneath a church, usually a burial place.

crystal crystals
NOUN a piece of a mineral that has formed naturally into a regular shape.
crystalline ADJECTIVE

crystallize crystallizes crystallizing crystallized; also spelt **crystallise**
VERB If a substance crystallizes, it turns into crystals.

cub cubs
NOUN 1 Some young animals are called cubs.
2 The Cubs is an organization for young boys before they join the Scouts.

cube cubes
NOUN a solid shape with six equal square faces.

cubic
ADJECTIVE 1 used in measurements of volume: *cubic centimetres*.
2 cube-shaped.

cubicle cubicles
NOUN a small enclosed area, for example in a changing room, where you can dress and undress.

cuboid cuboids
NOUN OR ADJECTIVE a solid shape with six rectangular faces.

cuckoo cuckoos
NOUN a grey bird with a two-note call that lays its eggs in other birds' nests.

cucumber cucumbers
NOUN a long, thin, green vegetable which is eaten raw.

cud
NOUN When a cow chews the cud, it chews partly digested food which it brings back to the mouth from its stomach.

cuddle cuddles cuddling cuddled
VERB to hug.
cuddle NOUN

cuddly cuddlier cuddliest
ADJECTIVE Cuddly people, animals, or toys are soft or pleasing in some way so that you want to cuddle them.

cue cues
NOUN 1 something said or done by a performer that is a signal for another performer to begin.
2 a long stick used to hit the balls in snooker and pool.

cuff cuffs
NOUN 1 the end part of a sleeve.
PHRASE 2 If you are speaking **off the cuff**, you have not prepared what you are saying beforehand.

cul-de-sac cul-de-sacs
Said "**kul**-des-sak" NOUN a dead end.
[from French *cul* + *de* + *sac* meaning bottom of the bag]

culprit culprits
NOUN someone who has done something harmful or wrong.

cult cults
NOUN 1 a small religious group, especially one which is considered strange.
2 something or someone that is highly popular with a particular group of people.

cultivate cultivates cultivating cultivated
VERB To cultivate land is to grow crops on it.
cultivation NOUN

culture cultures
NOUN 1 Culture refers to the arts and to people's appreciation of them.
2 The culture of a particular society is its ideas, customs and art.
cultural ADJECTIVE **cultured** ADJECTIVE

cunning
ADJECTIVE A cunning person or plan achieves things in a clever way, often by deceiving people.
cunningly ADVERB

Synonyms: crafty, sly, wily

A B C D E F G H I J K L M N O P Q R S T U V W X Y Z

cup cups
NOUN a drinking container with a handle.

cupboard cupboards
NOUN a piece of furniture with doors and shelves.

curator curators
NOUN the person in a museum or art gallery who is in charge of the exhibits.

curb curbs curbing curbed
VERB To curb something is to keep it within limits.

curdle curdles curdling curdled
VERB When milk curdles, it turns sour.

curds
PLURAL NOUN the thick white substance formed when milk turns sour.

cure cures curing cured
VERB **1** to make a sick person well again.
NOUN **2** a healing remedy.

curfew curfews
NOUN If a curfew is imposed, people must stay indoors between set times at night.

curiosity curiosities
NOUN **1** the desire to know about things.
2 something which is unusual and interesting.

curious
ADJECTIVE **1** keen to know more about something.
2 unusual or difficult to understand. *A curious thing happened to me today.*

Synonyms: (sense 1) inquiring, inquisitive, nosy

curl curls curling curled
NOUN **1** Curls are pieces of hair shaped in tight curves and circles.
VERB **2** to move in a curve or spiral.
curly ADJECTIVE

currant currants
NOUN Currants are small dried grapes often used in cakes and puddings.

currency currencies
NOUN A country's currency is its coins and banknotes, or its money system generally.

current currents
NOUN **1** a steady continuous flowing movement of water or air.
2 a flow of electricity through a wire or circuit.
ADJECTIVE **3** happening, being done, or being used at the present time.

curriculum curriculums or curricula
Said "kur-**rik**-yoo-lum" NOUN the different courses taught at a school or university.
curricular ADJECTIVE

curry curries
NOUN an Indian dish made with hot spices.

curse curses cursing cursed
VERB **1** to swear because you are angry.
NOUN **2** an evil supernatural charm.
cursed ADJECTIVE

cursor cursors
NOUN a pointer on a computer screen which shows where the next letter or symbol is.

curtain curtains
NOUN pieces of material which can be pulled across a window.

curtsy curtsies curtsying curtsied; also spelt **curtsey**
VERB When a woman curtsies, she lowers her body briefly, bending her knees, to show respect.
curtsy or **curtsey** NOUN

curve curves curving curved
NOUN **1** a smooth, gradually bending line.
VERB **2** to move in a curve or have the shape of a curve.
curved ADJECTIVE

cushion cushions
NOUN a soft object which you put on a seat to make it more comfortable.

custard
NOUN a sweet yellow sauce made from milk and eggs, or milk and a powder.

custody
NOUN **1** To have custody of a child means to have the legal right to keep it and look after it.
PHRASE **2** Someone who is **in custody** is being kept in prison until they go to court.
custodial ADJECTIVE

custom customs
NOUN **1** a traditional activity.
2 something usually done at a particular time or in particular circumstances. *It was my custom to have breakfast in bed on Saturday mornings.*
customarily ADVERB

Synonyms: (sense 1) convention, tradition (sense 2) habit, practice

customary
ADJECTIVE usual, normal.
customarily ADVERB

customer customers
NOUN A shop's or firm's customers are the people who buy its goods.

customs
PLURAL NOUN Customs is the place at a border, airport or port where you have to declare any taxable goods you are bringing into a country.

► *Curriculum* is a Latin word meaning a racecourse or race chariot.

cut **cuts cutting cut**
VERB **1** If you cut something, you use a knife, scissors or some other sharp tool to slice into it or remove parts of it.
2 If you cut yourself, you injure yourself on a sharp object.
3 If you cut the amount of something, you reduce it.
NOUN **4** a mark made with a knife or other sharp tool.
5 an injury caused by a sharp object.

cute **cuter cutest**
ADJECTIVE pretty or attractive.

cutlass **cutlasses**
NOUN a curved sword that was used by sailors.

cutlery
NOUN knives, forks, and spoons.

cutlet **cutlets**
NOUN a small piece of meat which you fry or grill.

cutting **cuttings**
NOUN **1** something cut from a newspaper or magazine.
2 a part cut from a plant and used to grow a new plant.
ADJECTIVE **3** a cutting remark is unkind and likely to hurt someone.

cycle **cycles cycling cycled**
VERB **1** to ride a bicycle.
NOUN **2** a bicycle.
3 a series of events which is continually repeated: *the cycle of births and deaths.*
cyclist NOUN

cyclone **cyclones**
NOUN a violent tropical storm, a hurricane.
cyclonic ADJECTIVE

cygnet **cygnets**
Said "**sig**-net" NOUN a young swan.

cylinder **cylinders**
NOUN a three-dimensional shape with circular ends and curved parallel sides, such as a food can or the tube of a strip light.
cylindrical ADJECTIVE

cymbal **cymbals**
NOUN a circular brass plate used as a percussion instrument. Cymbals are clashed together or hit with a stick.

cynic **cynics**
Said "**sin**-ik" NOUN a critical person.

cynical
ADJECTIVE believing that people always behave selfishly or dishonestly.
cynically ADVERB **cynicism** NOUN

A B C D E F G H I J K L M N O P Q R S T U V W X Y Z

Dd

dab **dabs dabbing dabbed**
VERB **1** to touch with quick light strokes.
PHRASE **2** INFORMAL If you are a **dab hand** at something, you are very skilled at it.
dab NOUN

dabble **dabbles dabbling dabbled**
VERB If you dabble in something, you work or play at it without being seriously involved in it.
dabbler NOUN

dachshund **dachshunds**
Said "**daks**-hoond" NOUN a small dog with a long body and very short legs.
[a German word meaning badger-dog]

dad or **daddy** **dads** or **daddies**
NOUN; INFORMAL Your dad or daddy is your father.

daddy-long-legs
NOUN a harmless flying insect with very long legs.

Synonym: crane-fly

daffodil **daffodils**
NOUN a yellow early spring flowering plant, grown from a bulb.

daft **dafter daftest**
ADJECTIVE stupid, silly.

dagger **daggers**
NOUN **1** a weapon like a short knife.
PHRASE **2** If you **look daggers** at someone, you glare or scowl angrily at them.

daily
ADJECTIVE **1** occurring every day.
2 relating to a single day or to one day at a time: *the daily rate for the job.*

dainty **daintier daintiest**
ADJECTIVE very delicate and pretty.
daintily ADVERB **daintiness** NOUN

dairy **dairies**
NOUN **1** a shop or company that supplies milk and milk products.
2 A dairy farm is one which keeps cattle to produce milk.
ADJECTIVE **3** Dairy products are foods made from milk, such as butter, cheese, cream and yogurt.

daisy **daisies**
NOUN a small wild flower with a yellow centre and small white petals.

dale **dales**
NOUN a valley.

Dalmatian **Dalmatians**
NOUN a large dog with short smooth white hair and black or brown spots.

dam **dams**
NOUN a barrier built across a river to hold back water.

damage **damages damaging damaged**
VERB **1** to harm or spoil something.
NOUN **2** injury or harm done to something.
PLURAL NOUN **3** Damages is the money awarded by a court to compensate someone for loss or harm.

dame **dames**
NOUN **1** the title given to a woman who has been awarded a certain honour by the queen: *Dame Marian Bell.*
2 a comic woman in pantomime, normally played by a man.

damn **damns damning damned**
Said "**dam**" VERB **1** to curse or condemn someone.
INTERJECTION **2** "Damn" is a swearword.
damned ADJECTIVE

damp **damper dampest**
ADJECTIVE slightly wet.
dampness NOUN

dampen **dampens dampening dampened**
VERB to make something damp.

damson **damsons**
NOUN a small blue-black plum.

dance **dances dancing danced**
VERB **1** to move around in time to music.
NOUN **2** a series of rhythmic movements in time to music.
3 a social event where people dance.
dancer NOUN **dancing** NOUN

dandelion **dandelions**
NOUN a wild plant with yellow flowers.
[from Old French *dent de lion* meaning lion's tooth, referring to the shape of the leaves]

dandruff
NOUN small, loose scales of dead skin in someone's hair.

danger **dangers**
NOUN **1** the possibility that someone may be harmed or killed.
2 something or someone that can hurt or harm you.

Synonyms: (sense 1) hazard, peril, risk

dangerous
ADJECTIVE likely to hurt or harm you.
dangerously ADVERB

Synonyms: hazardous, perilous, unsafe

dangle **dangles dangling dangled**
VERB to swing or hang loosely.

dappled
ADJECTIVE marked with patches of a different or darker shade.

▶ The letter D is believed to have been developed from the picture of a door.

dare dares daring dared
VERB 1 to have the courage to do something.
2 to challenge someone to do something in order to prove their courage.
✔ When *dare* is used in a question or with a negative, it does not add an *s*: *Dare she come?; He dare not come.*

daredevil daredevils
NOUN a person who enjoys doing dangerous things.

daring
ADJECTIVE A daring person does bold and adventurous things without thinking of their own safety.

dark darker darkest
ADJECTIVE 1 not light enough to see properly.
2 black or a shade close to black.
NOUN 3 The dark is the lack of light in a place.
darkly ADVERB **darkness** NOUN

Synonyms: (sense 1) dim, gloomy, murky

darken darkens darkening darkened
VERB to make something dark or to become darker.

darling darlings
NOUN You call someone darling if you love them or like them very much.

darn darns darning darned
VERB to mend a hole in a garment with crossing stitches.

dart darts darting darted
NOUN 1 a small pointed arrow.
PLURAL NOUN 2 Darts is a game in which the players throw darts at a round board with numbered sections.
VERB 3 to move quickly and suddenly from one place to another.

dartboard dartboards
NOUN the target in the game of darts, a circular cork board with numbered sections and a bull's-eye at the centre.

dash dashes dashing dashed
VERB 1 to rush somewhere.
2 If your hopes or ambitions are dashed, they are ruined.
NOUN 3 a rush somewhere.
4 the punctuation mark (–).

WHAT DOES THE DASH DO?
The dash (–) marks an abrupt change in the flow of a sentence, either showing a sudden change of subject, or marking off extra information.
The dash can also show that a speech has been cut off suddenly:
"I'm not sure – what was the question again?"
"Go ahead and –" he broke off as Robbie seized his arm.

dashboard dashboards
NOUN the instrument panel in a motor vehicle.

data
NOUN information, usually in the form of facts or statistics.
✔ *Data* is really a plural word, but it is usually used as a singular.

database databases
NOUN a collection of information stored in a computer.

date dates dating dated
NOUN 1 a particular day or year.
2 an appointment to meet someone, especially a boyfriend or girlfriend.
VERB 3 If you date something, you find out when it began or was made.
4 If you date someone you have a romantic relationship with them.
5 If something dates from a particular time, that is when it happened or was made.
PHRASE 6 Something that is **out of date** is old-fashioned and no longer useful.

daughter daughters
NOUN Someone's daughter is their female child.

dawdle dawdles dawdling dawdled
VERB to walk slowly or lag behind.

dawn dawns dawning dawned
NOUN 1 the time in the morning when light first appears in the sky.
2 the very beginning of something.
VERB 3 When the day dawns, it begins.
4 If a fact or idea dawns on you, you become aware of it.

day days
NOUN 1 a period of 24 hours beginning and ending at midnight.
2 the period of time when it is light.

daybreak
NOUN the time in the morning when light first appears in the sky.

daydream daydreams daydreaming daydreamed
NOUN 1 a series of pleasant thoughts about things that you would like to happen.
VERB 2 to let your thoughts wander onto pleasant thoughts.

daylight
NOUN the light from the sun.

daytime
NOUN the time between dawn and dusk, that is, when it is light.

day-to-day
ADJECTIVE happening every day as part of ordinary routine life.

daze
PHRASE If you are **in a daze**, you are confused and bewildered.
dazed ADJECTIVE

Darken is the verb form of dark. What verbs match these adjectives: pure, clean, simple?

A B C D E F G H I J K L M N O P Q R S T U V W X Y Z

dazzle dazzles dazzling dazzled
VERB If a bright light dazzles you, it blinds you for a moment.
dazzling ADJECTIVE

de-
PREFIX from, away, out of. When de- is added to a noun or verb, it changes the meaning to its opposite, for example deconstruct and deforestation.

dead
ADJECTIVE **1** no longer alive.
2 no longer used or functioning. *The phone went dead.*
ADVERB **3** precisely or exactly. *The boat was dead ahead.*

deaden deadens deadening deadened
VERB to make something less intense. *The injection deadened the pain.*

dead end dead ends
NOUN a street that is closed off at one end, a cul-de-sac.

dead heat dead heats
NOUN If a race ends in a dead heat, two or more competitors reach the finish at the same time.

deadline deadlines
NOUN a time or date before which something must be done.

deadlock
NOUN a situation in which neither side in a dispute is willing to give in.

Synonyms: impasse, stalemate

deadly deadlier deadliest
ADJECTIVE **1** likely or able to cause death.
ADVERB **2** absolutely, very. *I am being deadly serious about this.*

deaf deafer deafest
ADJECTIVE unable to hear.

deafen deafens deafening deafened
VERB If you are deafened by a noise, it is so loud that you cannot hear anything else.
deafening ADJECTIVE **deafeningly** ADVERB

deal deals dealing dealt
NOUN **1** an agreement or arrangement, especially in business.
VERB **2** If you deal with a matter, you do what is necessary to sort it out.
3 to buy and sell.
4 to give out playing cards in a game.
PHRASE **5** A **good deal** or a **great deal** of something is a lot of it: *a great deal of money.*

dealer dealers
NOUN a person or firm whose business involves buying or selling things.

dean deans
NOUN **1** in a university or college, a dean is a person responsible for administration or for the welfare of the students.
2 In the Church of England, a dean is a clergyman who is responsible for administration.

dear dearer dearest
ADJECTIVE **1** much loved.
2 costing a lot.
dearly ADVERB

Synonyms: (sense 2) costly, expensive

death deaths
NOUN the end of life.

deathly
ADJECTIVE like death. *There was a deathly hush. She went deathly pale.*

debatable
ADJECTIVE If you say that something is debatable, you are not certain that it is true or correct.

Synonyms: doubtful, questionable

debate debates debating debated
NOUN **1** a discussion of opposing views, often formally organized.
VERB **2** to discuss opposing views in a formal manner.
3 If you are debating whether to do something, you are considering whether to do it.

debris
Said "**day**-bree" NOUN fragments or rubble left after something has been destroyed.

debt debts
Said "**det**" NOUN **1** a sum of money that you owe someone.
2 the state of owing money.
debtor NOUN

debut debuts
Said "**day**-byoo" NOUN a performer's first public appearance.

decade decades
NOUN a period of ten years.

decaffeinated
Said "dee-**kaf**-in-ate-ed" ADJECTIVE Decaffeinated coffee or tea has had most of the caffeine removed.

decathlon decathlons
Said "de-**cath**-lon" NOUN an athletics event involving ten different activities.

decay decays decaying decayed
VERB When things decay, they rot or go bad.
decay NOUN

deceased
NOUN; FORMAL The deceased is someone who has recently died.
deceased ADJECTIVE

deceit
NOUN behaviour intended to make people believe something that is not true.
deceitful ADJECTIVE **deceitfully** ADVERB

► What do these idioms mean: dead heat, dead weight, dead ringer, dead language?

deceive **deceives deceiving deceived**
VERB to make a person believe something that is not true.

December
NOUN the twelfth month of the year.

decent
ADJECTIVE **1** honest and respectable.
2 INFORMAL acceptable in standard or quality. *We had a decent meal at the restaurant.*
decency NOUN

deception **deceptions**
NOUN **1** something that is intended to trick or deceive someone.
2 the act of deceiving someone.

deceptive
ADJECTIVE likely to make people believe something that is not true.
deceptively ADVERB

Synonyms: false, misleading

decibel **decibels**
NOUN the unit used for measuring noise levels.

decide **decides deciding decided**
VERB **1** to make up your mind, to choose.
2 If something decides a situation, it makes a particular result certain.
decider NOUN

deciduous
ADJECTIVE Deciduous trees lose their leaves in the autumn every year.

decimal **decimals**
ADJECTIVE **1** A decimal system involves counting in units of ten.
2 If the answer to a sum is required to a certain decimal place, it means that you must have that number of figures to the right of the decimal point. For example, 0·23 has two decimal places.
3 A decimal point is the dot in a decimal number which separates whole numbers (on the left) from decimals (on the right).
NOUN **4** a decimal fraction in which a dot called a decimal point is followed by numbers representing tenths, hundredths and thousandths. For example, 0·1 represents one tenth [$\frac{1}{10}$].

decipher **deciphers deciphering deciphered**
VERB to work out the meaning of a code or of other types of writing that are not clear.

decision **decision**
NOUN a choice or judgement that is made about something.

decisive
Said "dis-**sigh**-siv" ADJECTIVE **1** having great influence on the result of something. *It was the decisive moment of the race.*
2 able to make decisions firmly and quickly.
decisively ADVERB **decisiveness** NOUN

deck **decks**
NOUN one of the levels on a ship or double-decker bus.

deckchair **deckchair**
NOUN a low folding chair with a fabric seat.

declaration **declarations**
NOUN a firm, forceful statement, often an official announcement.

declare **declares declaring declared**
VERB **1** to say something firmly and forcefully. *She declared that she would fight on.*
2 to announce something officially or formally. *War was declared between the two countries.*

decline **declines declining declined**
VERB **1** to become smaller or weaker.
2 If you decline something, you politely refuse to accept it or do it.
decline NOUN

decode **decodes decoding decoded**
VERB to convert a coded message into ordinary language.
decoder NOUN

decompose **decomposes decomposing decomposed**
VERB to decay through chemical or bacterial action, to rot.
decomposition NOUN

decorate **decorates decorating decorated**
VERB **1** to make something more attractive by adding attractive things to it.
2 to paint or wallpaper a room or building.
decorator NOUN

Synonyms: (sense 1) adorn, ornament

decoration **decorations**
NOUN **1** Decorations are features added to something to make it more attractive.
2 If someone receives a decoration, they are awarded a medal by the government for their achievement.
decorative ADJECTIVE **decoratively** ADVERB

decoy **decoys**
NOUN a person or object that is used to lead someone or something into danger.
decoy VERB

decrease **decreases decreasing decreased**
VERB **1** If something decreases or if you decrease it, it becomes less or smaller.
NOUN **2** a reduction in the amount or size of something.

decree **decrees decreeing decreed**
VERB **1** If a person in power decrees something, they state formally that it will happen.
NOUN **2** an official decision or order.

decrepit
ADJECTIVE broken or worn out by use or old age. [from Latin *crepare* meaning to creak or to crack]

a b c d e f g h i j k l m n o p q r s t u v w x y z

A B C D E F G H I J K L M N O P Q R S T U V W X Y Z

dedicate dedicates dedicating dedicated
VERB 1 to give your time and energy to something. *She dedicated her life to caring for others.*
2 If you dedicate a book or piece of music to someone, you say that it is written for them, as a sign of respect or affection.
dedication NOUN

Synonyms: (sense 1) commit, devote

deduce deduces deducing deduced
VERB to work something out from other facts that you know are true.

Synonyms: conclude, reason

deduct deducts deducting deducted
VERB to subtract, take away.

deduction deductions
NOUN 1 an amount which is taken away from a total.
2 a conclusion that you have reached because of other things that you know are true.

deed deeds
NOUN 1 something that is done: *a good deed.*
2 a legal document, especially one concerning the ownership of land or buildings.

deep deeper deepest
ADJECTIVE 1 extending a long way down from the surface.
2 great or intense.
3 A deep sound is a low one.
deeply ADVERB **depth** NOUN

deepen deepens deepening deepened
VERB to make something deeper or to become deeper.

deer
NOUN a large, hoofed mammal that lives wild in parts of Britain.
✔ The plural of *deer* is *deer.*

deface defaces defacing defaced
VERB If you deface a wall or notice, you spoil it by writing or drawing on it.

default defaults defaulting defaulted
NOUN 1 In computing, the default is what happens if you do not alter the settings yourself.
PHRASE 2 If something happens **by default**, it happens because something else which might have prevented it has failed to happen.
VERB 3 If someone defaults on something they have legally agreed to do, they fail to do it. *He defaulted on repayment of the loan.*

defeat defeats defeating defeated
VERB 1 to win a victory over someone or something, or cause them to fail.
NOUN 2 the state of being beaten or of failing.
3 A defeat is an occasion on which someone is beaten or fails to achieve something.

defect defects defecting defected
Said "**dee**-fect" NOUN 1 a fault or flaw in something.
Said "diff-**ect**" VERB 2 If someone defects, they leave their own country or organization and join a rival one.
defection NOUN **defector** NOUN

defective
ADJECTIVE faulty, not working properly.

defence defences
NOUN 1 action that is taken to protect someone or something from attack.
2 the case presented in a court of law for the person on trial.

defend defends defending defended
VERB 1 If you defend someone or something, you protect them from harm or danger.
2 to argue in support of a person or an idea.
defender NOUN

defendant defendants
NOUN a person who has been accused of a crime in a court of law, the accused.

defensive
ADJECTIVE 1 intended or designed for protection.
2 someone who is defensive feels unsure and threatened by other people's opinions and attitudes.
defensively ADVERB

defer defers deferring deferred
VERB to delay or postpone an action or event.

defiant
ADJECTIVE not willing to obey someone or behave in the expected way.
defiantly ADVERB **defiance** NOUN

deficiency deficiencies
NOUN a lack of something.
deficient ADJECTIVE

deficit deficits
Said "**def**-iss-it" NOUN the amount by which money received by an organization is less than money spent.

define defines defining defined
VERB to say what something is or what it means.

definite
ADJECTIVE 1 clear and unlikely to be changed.
2 true rather than being someone's guess or opinion.
definitely ADVERB

definite article
NOUN the word "the".

Antonym: indefinite article

definitely
ADVERB certainly, surely.

definition definitions
NOUN a statement explaining the meaning of a word or idea.
definitive ADJECTIVE

► Benjamin Disraeli, Prime Minister in 1868 and 1874–80, claimed to hate definitions.

deflate deflates deflating deflated
VERB If you deflate something such as a tyre or balloon, you let out all the air or gas in it.
deflation NOUN

deflect deflects deflecting deflected
VERB To deflect something means to turn it aside or make it change direction.
deflection NOUN

deforestation
NOUN the action of destroying many trees in an area.

deformed
ADJECTIVE disfigured or abnormally shaped.
deformity NOUN

defrost defrosts defrosting defrosted
VERB **1** to remove the ice from a freezer or refrigerator.
2 If you defrost frozen food, you let it thaw out.

deft defter deftest
ADJECTIVE quick and skilful in your movements.
deftly ADVERB **deftness** NOUN

defuse defuses defusing defused
VERB **1** To defuse a bomb means to remove its fuse or detonator so that it cannot explode.
2 To defuse a dangerous or tense situation means to make it less dangerous or tense.

defy defies defying defied
VERB **1** to refuse to obey a person, law or rule.
2 FORMAL If you defy someone to do something that you think is impossible, you challenge them to do it.
3 If something defies description or explanation, it is extremely difficult to describe or understand.

Synonyms: (sense 1) disregard, flout, resist

degenerate degenerates degenerating degenerated
VERB to become worse.
degeneration NOUN

degree degrees
NOUN **1** a unit of measurement for temperatures, angles and longitude and latitude; written as ° after a number.
2 an amount of a feeling or quality. *This sun cream will provide a high degree of protection.*
3 a university qualification gained after completing a course of study there.

dehydrated
ADJECTIVE If someone is dehydrated they are weak or ill because they have lost too much water from their body.

de-ice de-ices de-icing de-iced
VERB to remove the ice from something which is covered in it.

deity deities
NOUN a god or goddess.

dejected
ADJECTIVE miserable and unhappy.
dejectedly ADVERB **dejection** NOUN

delay delays delaying delayed
VERB **1** If you delay doing something, you do not do it until a later time.
2 If something delays you, it makes you late or slows you down.
delay NOUN

Synonyms: (sense 1) postpone, put off

delete deletes deleting deleted
VERB to cross out or remove something.
deletion NOUN

deliberate
ADJECTIVE intentional, done on purpose.
deliberately ADVERB

delicacy delicacies
NOUN **1** grace and attractiveness.
2 Something that is said or done with delicacy is said or done so that nobody is offended.
3 a rare or expensive food that is considered nice to eat.

delicate
ADJECTIVE **1** fine, graceful or subtle in character.
2 fragile and needing to be handled carefully.
3 precise or sensitive and able to notice very small changes: *a delicate instrument.*
delicately ADVERB

delicatessen delicatessens
NOUN a shop selling unusual or imported foods.

delicious
ADJECTIVE extremely tasty.
deliciously ADVERB

Synonyms: delectable, scrumptious

delight delights delighting delighted
NOUN **1** great pleasure or joy.
VERB **2** If something delights you or if you are delighted by it, it gives you a lot of pleasure.

delightful
ADJECTIVE very pleasant and attractive.
delightfully ADVERB

delinquent delinquents
NOUN a young person who commits minor crimes.
delinquency NOUN

delirious
ADJECTIVE **1** unable to speak or act in a rational way because of illness or fever.
2 wildly excited and happy.
deliriously ADVERB

deliver delivers delivering delivered
VERB **1** If you deliver something to someone, you take it and give it to them.
2 If someone delivers a baby, they help the woman who is giving birth.

Dejected comes from Latin, and literally means thrown down.

A B C D E F G H I J K L M N O P Q R S T U V W X Y Z

delta deltas
NOUN a broad, flat area where a river splits into several smaller streams before entering the sea.
[from the shape of the Greek letter *delta*]

deluge deluges deluging deluged
NOUN 1 a sudden, heavy downpour of rain.
VERB 2 To be deluged with things means to be overwhelmed by a great number of them.

delusion delusions
NOUN a mistaken or misleading belief or idea.
delude VERB

de luxe
Said "de **luks**" ADJECTIVE rich, luxurious or of superior quality.

demand demands demanding demanded
VERB 1 to ask for something forcefully.
2 If a situation demands a particular quality, it needs it.
NOUN 3 a forceful request.
4 If there is demand for something, a lot of people want to buy it or have it.
5 The demands of a job or activity are the efforts that are needed in order to do it.
demanding ADJECTIVE

demerara
Said "dem-er-**air**-a" NOUN light brown cane sugar.

democracy democracies
NOUN a system where the people of a country elect their government by free vote and have freedom of speech.

democrat democrats
NOUN a person who believes in democracy, personal freedom and equality.

democratic
ADJECTIVE 1 A democratic decision is one that is agreed on by a majority of people.
2 A democratic society is one that has freedom of speech and a government elected by the people.
democratically ADVERB

demolish demolishes demolishing demolished
VERB to pull down or break up a building.
demolition NOUN

demon demons
NOUN an evil spirit or devil.

demonstrate demonstrates demonstrating demonstrated
VERB 1 If you demonstrate something to somebody, you show them how to do it or how it works.
2 to show that something is true. *This demonstrates exactly what I mean.*
3 to march or gather together as a protest.
demonstrator NOUN

demonstration demonstrations
NOUN 1 a march or gathering in which people show their support for something or their opposition to it.
2 a talk or explanation that shows how to do something.
3 a clear proof of something.

demote demotes demoting demoted
VERB to put in a lower rank or position, often as a punishment.
demotion NOUN

den dens
NOUN 1 the home of some wild animals such as lions or foxes.
2 a secret place where people meet.

denial denials
NOUN 1 a statement that something is untrue.
2 The denial of a request is a refusal of it.

denim denims
NOUN 1 a strong cotton cloth, usually blue, used for making clothes.
PLURAL NOUN 2 Denims are jeans made from denim.
denim ADJECTIVE
[from French *serge de Nîmes* meaning serge (a type of cloth) from Nîmes (a city in France) where the cloth was first made]

denominator denominators
NOUN In mathematics, the denominator is the number which forms the bottom part of a fraction. See **common denominator**, **numerator**.

denote denotes denoting denoted
VERB If one thing denotes another, it is a sign of it or it represents it. *Owning a big house usually denotes wealth, but not always.*

dense denser densest
ADJECTIVE 1 thickly crowded or packed together.
2 difficult to see through.
3 INFORMAL If you say that someone is dense, you mean that they are very stupid.
densely ADVERB

density densities
NOUN 1 the degree to which something is filled or occupied. *Tokyo has a very high population density.*
2 The density of a substance is how compact it is, measured by the relation of its mass to its volume. For example, a kilogram of lead has a much higher density than a kilogram of cornflakes.

dent dents denting dented
VERB to make a hollow in a solid surface, often damaging it.
dent NOUN

dental
ADJECTIVE relating to the teeth.

► Delta is the fourth letter in the Greek alphabet. ►

dentist dentists
NOUN a person who is qualified to treat people's teeth.
dentistry NOUN

dentures
PLURAL NOUN false teeth.

deny denies denying denied
VERB 1 to say that something is not true, contradict.
2 If you deny someone something, you refuse to give it to them.
denial NOUN

deodorant deodorants
NOUN a substance or spray used to hide the smell of perspiration.
deodorant ADJECTIVE

depart departs departing departed
VERB to leave a place and go away.
departure NOUN

department departments
NOUN one of the sections into which an organization is divided.

department store department stores
NOUN a large shop which sells many different types of goods, each type in a separate department.

depend depends depending depended
VERB 1 If you depend on someone or something, you trust them and rely on them.
2 If one thing depends on another, it is very strongly influenced by it. *The cooking time depends on the size of the potato.*

dependable
ADJECTIVE reliable and trustworthy.
dependability NOUN

dependant dependants
NOUN someone who relies on another person for financial support. *His dependants were a wife, three children and his elderly mother.*

dependent
ADJECTIVE reliant on someone or something. *Babies are dependent on others for their survival.*

depict depicts depicting depicted
VERB to represent someone or something in painting, sculpture or other art form.
depiction NOUN

deplorable
ADJECTIVE shocking or regrettable.
deplorably ADVERB

deplore deplores deploring deplored
VERB to condemn something because you feel it is wrong.

deport deports deporting deported
VERB If a government deports a foreign person, it sends them out of the country because they have committed a crime or because they do not have the right to be there. See **exile**.
deportation NOUN

deposit deposits depositing deposited
VERB 1 If you deposit something, you put it down or leave it somewhere.
NOUN 2 a sum of money given as a first payment for goods or services.

depot depots
Said "**dep**-oh" NOUN a place where large supplies of materials or equipment may be stored.

depress depresses depressing depressed
VERB If something depresses you it makes you feel gloomy.
depressed ADJECTIVE

depression depressions
NOUN 1 a state of mind in which someone feels unhappy and has no energy or enthusiasm.
2 a weather system where the air pressure is low, usually bringing rain.

deprive deprives depriving deprived
VERB If you deprive someone of something, you take it away from them or prevent them from having it.
deprived ADJECTIVE **deprivation** NOUN

depth depths
NOUN 1 The depth of something is how deep it is; the measurement or distance between its top and bottom.
2 The depth of something such as an emotion is its intensity.

deputy deputies
NOUN Someone's deputy is a person who acts on their behalf when they are away.
deputize VERB

derail derails derailing derailed
VERB If a train is derailed, its wheels come off the track.

derby derbies
Said "**dar**-bee" NOUN A local derby is a sporting event between two teams from the same area.

derelict
ADJECTIVE abandoned and falling into ruins.

derivation derivations
NOUN The derivation of something is its origin or source. *Many of the words in this dictionary have their derivations explained.*

derive derives deriving derived
VERB 1 FORMAL to get from something. *She derived great pleasure from playing the recorder.*
2 If something derives from something else, it develops from it.

derrick derricks
NOUN a crane or framework used to help lift something.

descant descants
NOUN The descant to a tune is that tune played at the same time but at a higher pitch.

A B C D E F G H I J K L M N O P Q R S T U V W X Y Z

descend **descends descending descended**
VERB to move downwards.
descending ADJECTIVE **descent** NOUN

descendant **descendants**
NOUN A person's descendants are the people in later generations who are related to them. **ancestor**.

describe **describes describing described**
VERB to say what someone or something is like.

description **descriptions**
NOUN an account or picture of something in words.
descriptive ADJECTIVE

desert **deserts deserting deserted**
Said "**dez**-ert" NOUN **1** an area of land, usually in a hot region, which has almost no water, rain, trees or plants.
Said "diz-**ert**" VERB **2** If someone deserts you, they leave you and no longer help or support you.
✔ Do not confuse *desert* with *dessert*.

deserted
Said "diz-**ert**-ed" ADJECTIVE **1** If a place is deserted, there is no one there.
2 If a person has been deserted, they have been abandoned by others.

deserve **deserves deserving deserved**
VERB If you deserve something, you are worthy of it.
deserving ADJECTIVE

design **designs designing designed**
VERB **1** If you design something new, you plan what it should be like.
NOUN **2** a drawing from which something can be built or made.
3 a decorative pattern of lines or shapes.
designer NOUN

designate **designates designating designated**
Said "**dez**-ig-nate" VERB **1** to label or name something formally. *The room was designated a non-smoking area.*
2 If you designate someone to do something, you appoint them to do it.
designation NOUN

desirable
ADJECTIVE worth having or doing.
desirability NOUN

desire **desires desiring desired**
VERB **1** If you desire something, you want it.
NOUN **2** a strong feeling of wanting something.
desirable ADJECTIVE

Synonym: (sense 2) longing

desk **desks**
NOUN a table which you sit at to write or work.
[from Latin *desca* meaning table]

desktop **desktops**
ADJECTIVE **1** of a convenient size to be used on a desk or table.
NOUN **2** In some computer software, the desktop is the first screen that appears, showing the main functions available to use.

desolate
ADJECTIVE **1** deserted and bleak.
2 lonely and sad.
desolation NOUN

despair **despairs despairing despaired**
VERB If you despair, you lose all hope.
despair NOUN **despairing** ADJECTIVE
despairingly ADVERB

despatch
another spelling of **dispatch**.

desperate
ADJECTIVE If you are desperate, you are in such a bad situation that you will try anything to change it.
desperately ADVERB **desperation** NOUN

despicable
ADJECTIVE A despicable action is one that people think is mean, vile or utterly wrong in some similar way.
despicably ADVERB

despise **despises despising despised**
VERB If you despise someone or something, you dislike them very much.

Synonyms: hate, loathe

despite
PREPOSITION in spite of.

despondent
ADJECTIVE dejected and unhappy.
despondently ADVERB **despondency** NOUN

dessert **desserts**
Said "diz-**ert**" NOUN a sweet food that you eat at the end of a meal.
✔ Do not confuse *dessert* with *desert*.

destination **destinations**
NOUN the place you are going to.

destined
ADJECTIVE meant or intended to happen.

destiny **destinies**
NOUN **1** Your destiny is all the things that are going to happen to you in your future life.
2 Destiny is the force which some people believe controls your life.

destitute
ADJECTIVE without money or possessions and therefore in great need.
destitution NOUN

destroy **destroys destroying destroyed**
VERB to damage something so much that it is completely ruined.
destruction NOUN **destroyer** NOUN

Synonyms: demolish, ruin, wreck

► Do you know the difference between a desert and a dessert?

destructive
ADJECTIVE causing or able to cause great harm, damage or injury.
destructively ADVERB **destructiveness** NOUN

detach **detaches detaching detached**
VERB to remove or unfasten something, to separate.
detachable ADJECTIVE

detached
ADJECTIVE separate or standing apart.

detail **details**
NOUN 1 A detail of something is one of its individual facts or features.
PLURAL NOUN 2 If you ask for details about something, you want further information.
detailed ADJECTIVE

detain **detains detaining detained**
VERB to force someone to stay.

detect **detects detecting detected**
VERB to notice or find something.
detection NOUN **detectable** ADJECTIVE

detective **detectives**
NOUN a person who investigates mysteries or crimes.

detector **detectors**
NOUN an instrument which is used to detect the presence of something.

detention
NOUN 1 a form of school punishment in which a pupil is made to stay in school during a break or after the other children have gone home.
2 the arrest or imprisonment of someone.

deter **deters deterring deterred**
VERB To deter someone from doing something means to put them off wanting to do it.
deterrence NOUN

detergent **detergents**
NOUN a chemical substance used for washing or cleaning things.
[from Latin *detergens* meaning wiping off]

deteriorate **deteriorates deteriorating deteriorated**
VERB to get worse.
deterioration NOUN

determination
NOUN great firmness after you have made up your mind to do something.

determine **determines determining determined**
VERB 1 If something determines a situation, it causes or controls it.
2 To determine something is to decide or settle it firmly.
3 To determine something means to find out or calculate the facts about it. *He bit the coin to determine if it was real or a fake.*

Synonyms: (sense 3) ascertain, find out, verify

determined
ADJECTIVE If you are determined to do something, you will not let anything stop you from doing it.
determinedly ADVERB

Synonyms: intent on, resolute

determiner **determiners**
NOUN A determiner limits the meaning of a noun or noun phrase in some way. For example, the word "their" in the phrase "their black cat" is a determiner. Other determiners include "a", "the", "some" and "those".

deterrent **deterrents**
NOUN something which puts people off doing something: *the nuclear deterrent.*

detest **detests detesting detested**
VERB to dislike strongly.
detestation NOUN **detestable** ADJECTIVE

Synonyms: hate, loathe

detonate **detonates detonating detonated**
VERB to cause a bomb or mine to explode.
detonation NOUN **detonator** NOUN
[from Latin *detonare* meaning to thunder]

detour **detours**
NOUN If you make a detour on a journey, you go by a longer or less direct route.

deuce **deuces**
Said "**joos**" NOUN In tennis, deuce is the score of forty all.

devastate **devastates devastating devastated**
VERB 1 to damage severely or destroy.
2 to upset greatly.
devastated ADJECTIVE **devastating** ADJECTIVE
devastation NOUN

develop **develops developing developed**
VERB 1 When something develops or when you develop it, it grows or becomes more advanced.
2 To develop photographs or film means to produce a picture from the negative.

development **developments**
NOUN 1 gradual growth or progress.
2 a new stage in a series of events: *the latest developments in technology.*
3 a large building project.

device **devices**
NOUN a machine or tool used for a particular purpose.

devil **devils**
NOUN an evil spirit (in several religions, the most powerful evil spirit).

devious
ADJECTIVE insincere, dishonest and sly.
deviously ADVERB **deviousness** NOUN

a b c d e f g h i j k l m n o p q r s t u v w x y z

Device is often found in dictionary definitions, meaning a gadget or machine to do something.

A B C D E F G H I J K L M N O P Q R S T U V W X Y Z

devise devises devising devised
VERB to invent or design.

devolution
NOUN In Britain, the passing of certain central government powers to regional assemblies.

devote devotes devoting devoted
VERB If you devote yourself to something, you give all your time and energy to it.

devoted
ADJECTIVE very loving and loyal.
devotion NOUN **devotedly** ADVERB

devour devours devouring devoured
VERB to eat something hungrily or greedily.

devout
ADJECTIVE A devout person has strong religious beliefs and worships regularly.

dew
NOUN drops of moisture formed at night by condensation on the ground and other cool surfaces.
dewy ADJECTIVE

diabetes
Said "dy-a-**bee**-teez" NOUN an illness in which a person has too much sugar in their blood.
diabetic NOUN OR ADJECTIVE

diabolical
ADJECTIVE **1** extremely wicked and cruel.
2 INFORMAL dreadful and very annoying: *a diabolical mistake.*
diabolically ADVERB

diagnose diagnoses diagnosing diagnosed
VERB To diagnose an illness or problem means to identify what is wrong.
diagnosis NOUN **diagnostic** ADJECTIVE

diagonal
NOUN **1** a straight line that joins the corners of a shape.
ADJECTIVE **2** in a slanting direction.
diagonally ADVERB

diagram diagrams
NOUN a drawing that shows or explains something.
diagrammatic ADJECTIVE
diagrammatically ADVERB

dial dials dialling dialled
NOUN **1** The dial on a clock or meter is the part where the time or a measurement is shown.
VERB **2** If you dial a telephone number, you select the number you want.

dialect dialects
NOUN a form of a language spoken in a particular geographical area.

dialogue dialogues
NOUN **1** conversation in a novel, film or play.
2 communication between people or groups of people. *The company opened up dialogue with the unions over the wages deal.* See **narrative**.

diameter diameters
NOUN The diameter of a circle is the length of a straight line drawn across it through its centre.

diamond diamonds
NOUN **1** a precious stone made of pure carbon.
2 an upright parallelogram shape.
3 Diamonds are one of the four suits in a pack of playing cards.

diaphragm diaphragms
Said "**dy**-a-fram" NOUN In mammals, the diaphragm is the muscular wall which separates the lungs from the stomach.

diarrhoea
Said "dy-a-**ree**-a" NOUN a stomach illness in which the solid waste that you pass is more liquid than usual.

diary diaries
NOUN a book with daily spaces to record events of your life.

dice dices dicing diced
NOUN **1** a small cube with numbers on each side, used in games.
VERB **2** To dice food means to cut it into small cubes.
diced ADJECTIVE

dictate dictates dictating dictated
VERB **1** to say something aloud for someone else to write down.
2 to tell someone what they must do.
3 to cause or influence something. *What we wear is largely dictated by the weather.*
dictation NOUN

dictator dictators
NOUN a ruler who has complete power in a country.

dictionary dictionaries
NOUN a book such as this one in which words are listed alphabetically and explained or translated into another language.

did
the past participle of **do**.

didgeridoo didgeridoos
NOUN an Australian musical wind instrument made in the shape of a long tube.

didn't
abbreviated form of **did not**.

die dies dying died
VERB **1** to cease to be alive or to exist.
2 When something dies away or dies down, it becomes less intense and disappears.
3 INFORMAL If you are dying to do something, you are very keen to do it.
dying ADJECTIVE

Synonyms: (sense 1) expire, pass away, perish

diesel diesels
Said "**dee**-zel" NOUN a heavy fuel used in trains, buses, lorries and some cars.

 ► When writing dialogue, do not use the word "said" too often. Notice how authors avoid it.

diet diets
NOUN 1 Your daily diet is the usual food that you eat.
2 If people are on a diet, they eat only certain foods, often because they are trying to lose weight.
diet VERB

differ differs differing differed
VERB 1 If two or more things differ, they are unlike each other.
2 If people differ, they disagree about something.
differing ADJECTIVE

difference differences
NOUN 1 The difference between things is the way in which they are unlike each other.
2 To find the difference between two amounts you subtract the smaller amount from the bigger one.

Synonyms: (sense 1) disparity, dissimilarity, distinction

different
ADJECTIVE 1 unlike something else.
2 unusual and out of the ordinary. *That's a very different dress!*
3 distinct and separate, although of the same kind: *different charities.*
✔ Use *different from* rather than *different to. Different than* is American.

difficult
ADJECTIVE 1 not easy.
2 Someone who is difficult behaves in an unreasonable way.

Synonyms: (sense 1) demanding, hard, laborious

difficulty difficulties
NOUN 1 the fact or quality of being difficult.
2 a problem.

dig digs digging dug
VERB 1 to make a hole in the ground with a spade or shovel.
2 to press hard into something. *That rucksack frame digs into my back.*
PLURAL NOUN 3 If someone lives in digs, they are a lodger in someone else's house.

digest digests digesting digested
Said "dy-**jest**" VERB 1 To digest food means to break it down into very small pieces so that it can be easily absorbed and used by your body. Some of this process takes place in your stomach.
2 to understand and take in information.
Said "**dy**-jest" NOUN 3 a shortened version of a report, article or book.
digestion NOUN **digestible** ADJECTIVE

digestive
ADJECTIVE related to the body's system for digesting food.

digit digits
Said "**dij**-it" NOUN 1 FORMAL Your digits are your fingers or toes.
2 a written symbol for any of the numbers from 0 to 9: *18 is a two-digit number.*

digital
ADJECTIVE 1 displaying information, especially time, in numbers rather than by a pointer moving round a dial.
2 Digital systems record or transmit information as numbers in the form of thousands of very small signals.

digital television
NOUN television in which the pictures are transmitted in digital form and decoded at your television set.

dignified
ADJECTIVE a dignified person behaves in a serious, calm and controlled way.

dignity
NOUN behaviour which is serious, calm and controlled.

dilapidated
ADJECTIVE falling to pieces and generally in a bad condition.

dilemma dilemmas
NOUN a difficult situation in which you have to choose between two or more alternatives.

diligent
ADJECTIVE hard-working and showing care and perseverance.
diligently ADVERB **diligence** NOUN

dilute dilutes diluting diluted
VERB To dilute a liquid means to add water or another liquid to it to make it weaker.
dilution NOUN

dim dimmer dimmest; dims dimming dimmed
ADJECTIVE 1 not bright or not easy to see.
2 INFORMAL not very intelligent.
VERB 3 If lights dim or are dimmed, they become less bright.
dimly ADVERB

dimension dimensions
NOUN The dimensions of something are its measurements or its size.

diminish diminishes diminishing diminished
VERB to reduce in size or importance.

diminutive
ADJECTIVE very small.

dimple dimples
NOUN a small hollow in someone's cheek or chin.
dimpled ADJECTIVE

din dins
NOUN a loud and unpleasant noise.

Digit and digital from the Latin *digitus* meaning toe or finger.

A B C D E F G H I J K L M N O P Q R S T U V W X Y Z

dine dines dining dined
VERB; FORMAL to eat an evening meal.

dinghy dinghies
Said "**ding**-ee" NOUN a small boat which is sailed, rowed or powered by outboard motor.

dingo dingoes
NOUN a wild dog of Australia.

dingy dingier dingiest
Said "**din**-jee" ADJECTIVE shabby, dirty and lacking colour.

dinner dinners
NOUN **1** the main meal of the day, eaten either in the evening or at lunchtime.
2 a formal social occasion in the evening, at which a meal is served.

dinosaur dinosaurs
Said "**dy**-no-sor" NOUN a large reptile which lived in prehistoric times.
[from Greek *deinos* + *sauros* meaning terrible lizard]

dip dips dipping dipped
VERB **1** to put something briefly into a liquid.
2 to make a downward movement.
NOUN **3** a sauce that you eat by dipping savoury biscuits, raw vegetables or crisps into it.

diploma diplomas
NOUN a qualification awarded by a college or university.

diplomacy
NOUN **1** the managing of relationships between countries.
2 skill in dealing with people without offending or upsetting them.
diplomatic ADJECTIVE **diplomatically** ADVERB

diplomat diplomats
NOUN **1** an official who negotiates with another country on behalf of his or her own country.
2 INFORMAL someone who is very tactful and knows the right thing to say.

dire direr direst
ADJECTIVE disastrous, urgent or terrible.

direct directs directing directed
ADJECTIVE **1** going somewhere in a straight line or by the shortest route.
2 If someone's behaviour is direct, they are honest and say what they mean.
VERB **3** to aim or point one thing at another.
4 If you direct someone somewhere, you tell them how to get there.
5 Someone who directs a film or play organizes the way it is made and performed.

Synonyms: (sense 2) frank, open, straightforward

direction directions
NOUN **1** the general line that someone or something is moving or pointing in.
PLURAL NOUN **2** Directions are instructions that tell you how to do something or how to get somewhere.

directly
ADVERB **1** in a straight line.
2 straight away.

director directors
NOUN **1** The directors of a company are its senior managers.
2 The director of a film or play is the person who decides how it is made and performed.

directory directories
NOUN a book which gives lists of information such as people's names, addresses and telephone numbers.

direct speech
NOUN the reporting of what someone has said or written, by quoting their exact words, placed between inverted commas (quotation marks).

dirt
NOUN **1** any substance such as dust, mud or stains.
2 You can refer to the earth on the ground as the dirt.

dirty dirtier dirtiest
ADJECTIVE **1** marked or covered with dirt.
2 unfair or dishonest.
3 about sex in a way that many people find offensive, indecent.

Synonyms: (sense 1) filthy, grubby, mucky

dis-
PREFIX Dis- is added to the beginning of words to form a word that means the opposite: *disagree*.

disability disabilities
NOUN a physical or mental condition or illness that restricts someone's way of life.

disabled
ADJECTIVE Disabled people have an illness or injury that restricts their way of life.

disadvantage disadvantages
NOUN an unfavourable or harmful circumstance.
disadvantaged ADJECTIVE

Synonyms: drawback, handicap

disagree disagrees disagreeing disagreed
VERB **1** If you disagree with someone, you have a different opinion to theirs.
2 If you disagree with an action or proposal, you believe it is wrong.
3 If food or drink disagrees with you, it makes you feel unwell.
disagreement NOUN

disagreeable
ADJECTIVE unpleasant or unhelpful and unfriendly.
disagreeably ADVERB

 ► More words from French: disco (from *discothèque*), souvenir, battle, beef, pasteurize... ►

disappear **disappears disappearing disappeared**
VERB 1 If someone or something disappears, they go where they cannot be seen or found.
2 to stop existing or happening. *The pain suddenly disappeared.*
disappearance NOUN

Synonyms: (sense 2) fade away, vanish

disappoint **disappoints disappointing disappointed**
VERB If someone or something disappoints you, they are not as good as you had hoped or do not do what you had hoped.
disappointing ADJECTIVE **disappointment** NOUN
disappointingly ADVERB

disapprove **disapproves disapproving disapproved**
VERB To disapprove of something or someone means to believe they are wrong or bad.
disapproval NOUN **disapproving** ADJECTIVE
disapprovingly ADVERB

disaster **disasters**
NOUN 1 a very bad accidental event, such as an earthquake or a plane crash.
2 a complete failure.
disastrous ADJECTIVE **disastrously** ADVERB

Synonyms: calamity, catastrophe

disc **discs**; also spelt **disk**
NOUN a flat round object.

discard **discards discarding discarded**
VERB to get rid of something because you do not want it.

Synonyms: dump, throw away

discharge **discharges discharging discharged**
VERB 1 If something discharges or is discharged, it is given or sent out. *The tanker discharged oil into the sea.*
2 To discharge someone from hospital means to allow them to leave.
3 If someone is discharged from a job, they are dismissed from it.
4 FORMAL If you discharge your duties, you carry them out.
NOUN 5 a substance that is released from the inside of something: *a discharge from a boil.*
6 a dismissal or release from a job or an institution.

disciple **disciples**
Said "dis-**sigh**-pl" **NOUN** a follower of someone or something.

discipline **disciplines disciplining disciplined**
Said "**dis**-si-plin" **NOUN 1** making people obey rules and punishing them when they break them.
2 the ability to behave and work in a controlled way.
VERB 3 to punish someone.
disciplinary ADJECTIVE **disciplined** ADJECTIVE

disc jockey **disc jockeys**
NOUN someone who introduces and plays pop records on the radio, at a disco or in clubs.

disclose **discloses disclosing disclosed**
VERB to tell new or secret information to someone.
disclosure NOUN

disco **discos**
NOUN a club where people go to dance to pop music; also the equipment that plays the music.

discomfort **discomforts**
NOUN 1 distress or slight pain.
2 a feeling of worry or embarrassment.

disconnect **disconnects disconnecting disconnected**
VERB If someone disconnects your fuel supply or telephone, they cut you off.
disconnection NOUN

discontent
NOUN unhappiness or dissatisfaction with your current situation in life.
discontented ADJECTIVE

discontinue **discontinues discontinuing discontinued**
VERB To discontinue something means to stop doing it.
discontinuation NOUN

discount **discounts**
NOUN a reduction in the price of something.

discourage **discourages discouraging discouraged**
VERB 1 If something or someone discourages you, they make you lose your enthusiasm for something.
2 If you discourage someone from doing something or if you discourage it, you try to persuade them not to do it.
discouraging ADJECTIVE **discouragement** NOUN

Synonyms: (sense 1) demoralize, dishearten (sense 2) dissuade, put off

discover **discovers discovering discovered**
VERB to find or learn about something for the first time.
discovery NOUN **discoverer** NOUN

discreet
ADJECTIVE tactful, able to keep things private or secret.
discreetly ADVERB

discriminate **discriminates discriminating discriminated**
VERB 1 To discriminate between things means to recognize the differences between them.
2 To discriminate against a person or group means to treat them unfairly, usually because of their race, colour or sex.
discrimination NOUN

discus **discuses**
NOUN a disc with a heavy middle, thrown by athletes.

a b c d e f g h i j k l m n o p q r s t u v w x y z

discuss discusses discussing discussed
VERB to talk about something in detail.
discussion NOUN

disease diseases
NOUN an illness.
diseased ADJECTIVE

disembark disembarks disembarking disembarked
VERB to land or unload from a ship, aircraft or bus.
disembarkation NOUN

disgrace disgraces disgracing disgraced
NOUN 1 the state you are in when other people disapprove of what you have done.
2 If something is a disgrace, it is unacceptable.
3 someone whose behaviour makes other people feel ashamed.
VERB 4 If you disgrace yourself you cause other people to disapprove of you.

Synonyms: (senses 1 and 4) dishonour, shame

disgraceful
ADJECTIVE If something is disgraceful, people disapprove of it strongly and think that those who are responsible for it should be ashamed.
disgracefully ADVERB

Synonyms: scandalous, shameful, shocking

disgruntled
ADJECTIVE discontented or in a bad mood.

disguise disguises disguising disguised
VERB 1 to change your appearance so that people will not recognize you.
2 To disguise a feeling means to hide it or to pretend that it is something else.
disguise NOUN

disgust disgusts disgusting disgusted
NOUN 1 a strong feeling of dislike or disapproval.
VERB 2 To disgust someone is to make them feel a strong sense of dislike or disapproval.
disgusted ADJECTIVE disgusting ADJECTIVE

Synonyms: (sense 1) loathing, repugnance, revulsion
(sense 2) revolt, sicken

dish dishes
NOUN 1 a shallow container for cooking or serving food.
2 food of a particular kind or food cooked in a particular way: *a vegetarian dish.*

disheartened
ADJECTIVE disappointed.

dishevelled
Said "dish-**ev**-ld" ADJECTIVE having untidy clothes, hair, etc.

dishonest
ADJECTIVE not truthful or able to be trusted.
dishonestly ADVERB dishonesty NOUN

dishwasher dishwashers
NOUN a machine for washing dishes.

disinfect disinfects disinfecting disinfected
VERB to clean thoroughly with disinfectant in order to prevent the spread of germs.

disinfectant disinfectants
NOUN a chemical substance that kills germs.

disintegrate disintegrates disintegrating disintegrated
VERB to break into many pieces and so be destroyed.
disintegration NOUN

disinterested
ADJECTIVE If someone is disinterested, they are neutral in a situation and so can act fairly to both sides. *Judges, referees and umpires must always be disinterested.*
disinterestedly ADVERB
✔ To mean not interested, use *uninterested.*

disk
another spelling of **disc**.

dislike dislikes disliking disliked
VERB to think that someone or something is unpleasant.
dislike NOUN

dislocate dislocates dislocating dislocated
VERB to put a bone or joint out of place.

dislodge dislodges dislodging dislodged
VERB to move or force something out of place.

disloyal
ADJECTIVE Someone who is disloyal does not remain firm in their friendship or support for someone or something.
disloyally ADVERB disloyalty NOUN

dismal
Said "**diz**-mal" ADJECTIVE 1 rather gloomy and depressing.
2 INFORMAL depressingly bad.
dismally ADVERB

dismantle dismantles dismantling dismantled
VERB to take something to pieces.

dismay dismays dismaying dismayed
NOUN 1 a feeling of fear and worry.
VERB 2 If someone or something dismays you, it fills you with alarm and worry.

dismiss dismisses dismissing dismissed
VERB 1 to tell a person to leave their job, to sack.
2 to decide that something is not important enough to think about. *She dismissed the option.*
3 to tell someone to leave a place. *Miss Eastwood dismissed the rest of the class.*
dismissal NOUN

dismount dismounts dismounting dismounted
VERB To dismount from a horse or bicycle means to get off it.

 ► Disinterested means impartial, uninterested means bored. They are not the same.

disobey **disobeys disobeying disobeyed**
VERB to refuse deliberately to do what you are told.
disobedient ADJECTIVE **disobediently** ADVERB **disobedience** NOUN

disorder **disorders**
NOUN **1** a state of being untidy or badly organized.
2 a situation where people are being badly behaved or unruly; chaos; disruption.
3 A disorder is a physical or mental problem or illness.
disorderly ADJECTIVE **disorderliness** NOUN

disorganized or **disorganised**
ADJECTIVE confused and badly prepared or arranged.
disorganization NOUN

disown **disowns disowning disowned**
VERB To disown someone or something means to refuse to admit any connection with them.

dispatch **dispatches dispatching dispatched**; also spelt **despatch**
VERB to send someone or something to a particular place for a special reason.

dispensary **dispensaries**
NOUN a place where medicines are prepared and given out.

dispense **dispenses dispensing dispensed**
VERB **1** To dispense medicines means to prepare them and give them out.
2 To dispense with something means to do without it or do away with it. *As it's hot, you can dispense with your ties today.*

dispenser **dispensers**
NOUN a machine or container designed to issue things such as cash or paper towels.

dispersal **dispersals**
NOUN **1** the scattering of something over a wide area.
2 the action of things or people moving apart and going away in different directions.

disperse **disperses dispersing dispersed**
VERB to scatter over a wide area.

displace **displaces displacing displaced**
VERB **1** If one thing displaces another, it takes its place, often by force.
2 If people are displaced, they are forced to leave their home or country.
3 to move something from its correct position.

display **displays displaying displayed**
VERB **1** If you display something, you show it to people.
2 If you display an emotion, you behave in a way that shows you feel it.
NOUN **3** an arrangement of things designed to attract people's attention.

displease **displeases displeasing displeased**
VERB to make someone annoyed, dissatisfied or offended.
displeasing ADJECTIVE **displeasure** NOUN

disposable
ADJECTIVE designed to be thrown away after use.
disposability NOUN

disposal
NOUN **1** the act of getting rid of something that is no longer wanted or needed.
PHRASE **2** If someone or something is **at your disposal**, they are available for your use.

dispose **disposes disposing disposed**
VERB If you dispose of something, you get rid of it.

disprove **disproves disproving disproved**
VERB to show that something is not true.

dispute **disputes disputing disputed**
NOUN **1** an argument.
VERB **2** If you dispute a fact or theory, you say that it is incorrect or untrue.

disqualify **disqualifies disqualifying disqualified**
VERB If someone is disqualified from an activity they are officially stopped from taking part or doing it.

disregard **disregards disregarding disregarded**
VERB to pay little or no attention to something.
disregard NOUN

disrespect
NOUN contempt or lack of respect.
disrespectful ADJECTIVE **disrespectfully** ADVERB

disrupt **disrupts disrupting disrupted**
VERB To disrupt an event or system means to break it up or throw it into confusion.
disruption NOUN **disruptive** ADJECTIVE

dissatisfied
ADJECTIVE not pleased or not contented.
dissatisfaction NOUN

dissect **dissects dissecting dissected**
VERB To dissect a plant or a dead body means to cut it up so that it can be scientifically examined.
dissection NOUN

dissent **dissents dissenting dissented**
NOUN **1** a strongly different opinion.
VERB **2** to express a difference of opinion about something.
dissenter NOUN **dissenting** ADJECTIVE

dissolve **dissolves dissolving dissolved**
VERB If you dissolve something or if it dissolves in a liquid, it mixes in with the liquid.

dissuade **dissuades dissuading dissuaded**
Said "dis-**wade**" VERB to persuade someone not to do something.

The prefix "dis-" becomes "diss-" only when joined to a word beginning with s.

A B C D E F G H I J K L M N O P Q R S T U V W X Y Z

distance distances
NOUN 1 The distance between two points is the amount of space between them.
2 the fact of being far away.

distant
ADJECTIVE 1 far away in space or time.
2 A distant relative is someone to whom you are not closely related.
3 Someone who is distant is cold and unfriendly.

Synonyms: (sense 3) aloof, reserved, stand-offish

distil distils distilling distilled
VERB When a liquid is distilled, it is heated until it evaporates and then cooled to enable purified liquid to be collected.
distillation NOUN

distillery distilleries
NOUN a place where whisky or other strong alcoholic drink is made, using a process of distillation.

distinct
ADJECTIVE 1 If one thing is distinct from another, there is a clear and important difference between them.
2 If something is distinct, you can hear, smell, see or sense it clearly.
distinctly ADVERB

distinction distinctions
NOUN 1 a difference between two things.
2 a special honour or claim. *It had the distinction of being the largest square in Europe.*
3 a quality of excellence and superiority. *We supply furniture of distinction.*
4 the highest level of achievement in an examination.

distinctive
ADJECTIVE Something that is distinctive has a special quality which makes it easy to recognize.
distinctively ADVERB **distinctiveness** NOUN

distinguish distinguishes distinguishing distinguished
VERB to be able to tell the difference between one thing and another.

distinguished
ADJECTIVE 1 dignified in appearance or behaviour.
2 having a very high reputation.

distort distorts distorting distorted
VERB 1 If something is distorted, it is changed so that it seems strange or unclear.
2 If you distort a statement or an argument, you change it so that it is untrue.

distract distracts distracting distracted
VERB to stop someone from concentrating.
distraction NOUN **distracting** ADJECTIVE

Synonyms: divert, sidetrack

distress distresses distressing distressed
NOUN 1 suffering caused by pain or sorrow.
VERB 2 If something distresses you, it causes you to be upset or worried.
PHRASE 3 If someone or something is **in distress**, they are in danger and need help.

distribute distributes distributing distributed
VERB 1 to deliver things.
2 to share out.
distribution NOUN

district districts
NOUN an area of a town or country.

distrust distrusts distrusting distrusted
VERB 1 If you distrust someone, you are suspicious of them because you are not sure whether they are honest.
NOUN 2 suspicion.
distrustful ADJECTIVE **distrustfully** ADVERB

disturb disturbs disturbing disturbed
VERB 1 If you disturb someone, you interrupt their peace or privacy.
2 If something disturbs you, it makes you feel upset or worried.

disturbance disturbances
NOUN 1 the state of being disturbed.
2 an incident in which people behave violently in public.

disused
ADJECTIVE neglected and no longer used.

ditch ditches
NOUN a channel cut into the ground at the side of a road or field.

dither dithers dithering dithered
VERB to be unsure and hesitant.

ditto
NOUN the same again. In written lists, ditto is represented by the mark („) to avoid repetition.

divan divan
NOUN a low bed, or a couch without a back or arms.

dive dives diving dived
VERB 1 to jump head-first into water with your arms above your head.
2 to go under the surface of a sea or lake using breathing equipment.
3 to move quickly downwards.

diver divers
NOUN a person who works or explores underwater.

diverse
ADJECTIVE very different, varied.
diversity NOUN

diversion diversions
NOUN 1 a special route arranged for traffic when the usual route is closed.
2 something that takes your attention away from what you should be concentrating on.

 ► Can you distinguish between these words: morning mourning; dying dyeing; singing singeing?

divert **diverts diverting diverted**
VERB to change the course or direction of something.

divide **divides dividing divided**
VERB **1** to separate into two or more parts.
2 In mathematics, to divide a larger number by a smaller number means to calculate how many times the larger number contains the smaller number.

divine
ADJECTIVE having the qualities of a god or goddess.
divinely ADVERB

divisible
ADJECTIVE able to be divided. *Ten is exactly divisible by five.*
divisibility NOUN

division **divisions**
NOUN **1** Division is the act of separating something into two or more parts.
2 any one of the parts into which something is divided. *Division One of the league.*

divisor **divisors**
NOUN a number by which another number is divided.

divorce **divorces divorcing divorced**
VERB When a married couple divorce, they legally end their marriage.
divorce NOUN

Diwali or **Divali**
NOUN a Hindu festival held in October or November celebrating Lakshmi, goddess of wealth, and marked by lights, feasting and gifts.

DIY
NOUN the activity of making or repairing things yourself. DIY is an abbreviation for do-it-yourself.

dizzy **dizzier dizziest**
ADJECTIVE feeling that you are losing your balance and are about to fall.
dizzily ADVERB **dizziness** NOUN

DJ **DJs**; also spelt **dj**
NOUN a disc jockey. See **disc jockey**.

do **does doing did done; dos**
VERB **1** to perform a task or activity.
2 If something will do, it is satisfactory.
3 an auxiliary verb used to form questions, negatives and to give emphasis to the main verb of a sentence. *What do you think? I don't know. That does look nice.*
NOUN **4** INFORMAL a party or other social event. *We're having a little do on Saturday.*
PHRASE **5** If one thing has **something to do with** another, the two things are connected.
do up VERB **1** to fasten.
2 to repair and decorate a place.

docile
ADJECTIVE quiet, calm and easily controlled.

dock **docks docking docked**
NOUN **1** an enclosed area in a port where ships are loaded, unloaded or repaired.
2 the place where the accused person stands in a court of law.
3 a weed with broad leaves, commonly used to relieve nettle stings.
VERB **4** When a ship docks, it is brought into a dock.
5 When one spacecraft docks with another, it joins up with it.

docker **dockers**
NOUN a person who whose job it is to load and unload ships at the docks.

doctor **doctors**
NOUN **1** a person who is qualified in medicine and treats people who are ill.
2 the title given to someone who has been awarded the highest academic degree by a university. *She is a doctor of philosophy.*
[from Latin *doctor* meaning teacher]

document **documents documenting documented**
NOUN **1** a piece of paper which provides an official record of something.
VERB **2** to make a detailed record of something.

documentary **documentaries**
NOUN a radio or television programme giving information about real people and events.

dodge **dodges dodging dodged**
VERB **1** to avoid by quickly moving aside.
2 Someone who dodges tax avoids paying it.

dodgem **dodgems**
NOUN; TRADEMARK Dodgems are electric bumper cars at a fairground.

dodgy
ADJECTIVE; INFORMAL **1** dangerous, risky or unreliable.
2 suspected of being illegal or untrustworthy.

doe **does**
NOUN a female deer, rabbit or hare.

does
the third person singular of the present tense of **do**.

doesn't
contraction of **does not**.

dog **dogs**
NOUN a four-legged canine mammal often kept as a pet.

dogged
ADJECTIVE
Said "**dog**-ged" showing determination to continue with something, even if it is very difficult.
doggedly ADVERB

do-it-yourself
NOUN the activity of decorating, repairing and improving your own home.

A B C D E F G H I J K L M N O P Q R S T U V W X Y Z

doldrums
PHRASE; INFORMAL If you are **in the doldrums**, you are feeling miserable or bored.

dole doles doling doled
NOUN 1 In Britain dole is a common informal name for money given regularly by the government to people who are unemployed.
VERB 2 If you dole something out, you give a certain amount of it to each individual in a group.

doll dolls
NOUN a child's toy which looks like a small person or baby.

dollar dollars
NOUN a unit of money in the USA, Canada and some other countries. A dollar is worth 100 cents and is represented by the symbol $.

dolphin dolphins
NOUN an intelligent sea mammal with fins and a pointed nose.

domain domains
NOUN 1 a particular area of activity or interest.
2 an area over which someone has control or interest.

dome domes
NOUN a rounded roof.

domestic
ADJECTIVE 1 involving or concerned with the home and family.
2 happening or existing within a country. *Domestic flights leave at a different terminal from international flights.*

domesticated
ADJECTIVE If a wild animal has been domesticated, it has been controlled.

dominant
ADJECTIVE having the main control or influence over something; dominating.
domination NOUN

dominate dominates dominating dominated
VERB To dominate someone or something means to have power over them or it; to be the most powerful or important.

domino dominoes
NOUN Dominoes are small rectangular blocks marked with spots, used for playing a game.

donate donates donating donated
VERB to give in order to help someone or something.
donation NOUN

done
the past participle of **do**.

donkey donkeys
NOUN a horse-like animal.

donor donors
NOUN someone who gives some of their blood or a part of their body to help a person who is ill.

don't
abbreviated form of **do not**.

doodle doodles
NOUN a drawing done when you are thinking about something else or when you are bored.
doodle VERB

doom
NOUN a terrible fate or event in the future which you can do nothing to prevent.

doomed
ADJECTIVE Someone or something that is doomed is certain to fail.

door doors
NOUN a swinging or sliding panel for opening and closing the entrance to something; also the entrance itself.

doorway doorways
NOUN an opening in a wall for a door.

dope dopes doping doped
VERB 1 If someone dopes you, they put a drug into your food or drink.
NOUN 2 INFORMAL an illegal drug.
3 If you say someone is a dope you think they are stupid or slow to understand.

dormant
ADJECTIVE Something that is dormant is not active, growing or being used.

dormitory dormitories
NOUN a large bedroom where several people sleep.

dormouse dormice
NOUN a mammal like a large mouse, with a furry tail.

dose doses
NOUN a measured amount of a medicine or drug.

dot dots
NOUN a very small, round mark.

double doubles doubling doubled
ADJECTIVE 1 twice the usual size.
2 consisting of two parts.
3 A double room is a room for two people.
VERB 4 If something doubles or if you double it, it becomes twice as large.
5 to multiply by 2.
6 To double as something means to have a second use as well as the main one. *Their home doubles as an office.*
NOUN 7 Your double is someone who looks exactly like you.
8 Doubles is a game of tennis or badminton in which two people play against two other people.

double bass double basses
NOUN a musical instrument like a very large violin, which you play standing up.

► Learn these words, all of which contain double consonants: occasional, paraffin, parallel... ►

double-cross **double-crosses double-crossing double-crossed**
VERB If someone double-crosses you, they cheat you by pretending to do what you both planned, when in fact they do the opposite.

double-decker **double-deckers**
ADJECTIVE **1** having two tiers or layers.
NOUN **2** a bus with two floors.

doubly
ADVERB twice as much. *The guard checked the gate again to be doubly sure no one had got in.*

doubt **doubts doubting doubted**
NOUN **1** uncertainty as to whether something is true or possible.
VERB **2** If you doubt something, you think that it is probably not true or possible.

Synonyms: (sense 1) misgiving, qualm, uncertainty

doubtful
ADJECTIVE unlikely or uncertain.
doubtfully ADVERB

doubtless
ADVERB certainly, without doubt.

dough
*Rhymes with "**go**"* NOUN **1** a mixture of flour and water and sometimes other ingredients, used to make bread, pastry or biscuits.
2 INFORMAL money.
doughy ADJECTIVE

doughnut **doughnuts**
NOUN a ring of sweet dough cooked in hot fat.

douse **douses dousing doused**; also spelt **dowse**
VERB If you douse a fire, you stop it burning by throwing water over it.

dove **doves**
NOUN a bird like a small pigeon.

dowdy
ADJECTIVE wearing dull and unfashionable clothes.

down
PREPOSITION OR ADVERB **1** towards the ground, towards a lower level or in a lower place.
PREPOSITION **2** If you go down somewhere, you go along it.
ADVERB **3** If you put something down, you place it on a surface.
4 If an amount of something goes down, it decreases.
ADJECTIVE **5** to be down is to be depressed.

Antonym: up

downcast
ADJECTIVE feeling sad and dejected.

downfall
NOUN **1** the failure of a person or institution that has previously been successful or powerful.
2 the thing that causes someone's failure.

downhill
ADVERB **1** moving down a slope.
2 worse. *The business has gone downhill recently.*

Antonym: uphill

download **downloads downloading downloaded**
VERB to copy or transfer data or programs from one computer to another.

downpour **downpours**
NOUN a heavy fall of rain.

downright
ADJECTIVE OR ADVERB You use "downright" to emphasize that something is extremely unpleasant or bad. *The staff are often unhelpful and sometimes downright rude.*

downstairs
ADJECTIVE OR ADVERB on a lower floor or on the ground floor.

Antonym: upstairs

downstream
ADJECTIVE OR ADVERB moving in the direction of the current of a river.

Antonym: upstream

downwards or **downward**
ADVERB OR ADJECTIVE **1** towards the ground or towards a lower level.
2 If an amount or rate moves downwards, it decreases.

Antonym: upwards

doze **dozes dozing dozed**
VERB to sleep lightly for a short period.
doze NOUN

dozen **dozens**
NOUN A dozen things is twelve of them.

Dr
abbreviation for **doctor** or **Drive**.

drab **drabber drabbest**
ADJECTIVE dreary, dull and unattractive.
drabness NOUN **drably** ADVERB

draft **drafts drafting drafted**
NOUN **1** an early version of a piece of writing.
VERB **2** When you draft a piece of writing, you write the first version of it.

drag **drags dragging dragged**
VERB to pull something slowly and with difficulty.

dragon **dragons**
NOUN In stories and legends, a dragon is a fierce animal like a large lizard with wings and claws that breathes fire.

dragonfly **dragonflies**
NOUN a colourful insect which is often found near water.

a b c d e f g h i j k l m n o p q r s t u v w x y z

A B C D E F G H I J K L M N O P Q R S T U V W X Y Z

drain drains draining drained
VERB **1** If you drain something or if it drains, liquid flows out of it or off it.
2 If something drains your strength or resources, it uses them up.
NOUN **3** a pipe that carries water or sewage away from a place, or an opening in a surface that leads to the pipe.

drake drakes
NOUN a male duck.

drama dramas
NOUN **1** a serious play for the theatre, television or radio.
2 a general name for plays and the theatre.
3 the exciting aspects of a real-life situation. *There was drama in the courtroom when the judge collapsed.*

dramatic
ADJECTIVE **1** related to plays and the theatre.
2 A dramatic change or event happens suddenly and is very noticeable.
dramatically ADVERB

dramatist dramatists
NOUN someone who writes plays; a playwright.

dramatize dramatizes dramatizing dramatized
VERB **1** to write a story in the form of a play.
2 to behave in an exaggerated and over-dramatic way.
dramatization NOUN

drank
past tense of **drink**.

drape drapes draping draped
VERB to arrange a piece of cloth in loose folds.

drastic
ADJECTIVE A drastic course of action is extreme and is usually taken urgently.

draught draughts
Said "**draft**" NOUN **1** a current of cold air.
2 Draughts is a game for two people played with round pieces on a chessboard.
draughty ADJECTIVE

draw draws drawing drew drawn
VERB **1** to use a pen or pencil to make a picture of something.
2 to move somewhere. *The taxi slowly drew away.*
3 If you draw money out of a bank account, you take it out.
4 to pull. *Please draw the curtains. Vacuum cleaners draw dust from the carpet into the bag.*
NOUN **5** the result of a game or competition in which nobody wins.
draw up VERB to prepare and write a plan, document, list, etc.

drawback drawbacks
NOUN a fault or problem with something.

drawbridge drawbridges
NOUN a bridge that can be pulled up or lowered, especially in a castle.

drawer drawers
NOUN a part of a desk, table etc. to contain things, which slides in and out.

drawing drawings
NOUN a picture made with a pen or pencil.

drawing pin drawing pins
NOUN a short nail with a broad, flat top.

drawing room drawing rooms
NOUN; FORMAL a room in a house where people relax or entertain guests.

drawl drawls drawling drawled
VERB to speak slowly with long vowel sounds.

drawn
past participle of **draw**.

dread dreads dreading dreaded
VERB to feel very worried and frightened about something which is going to happen.
dread NOUN **dreaded** ADJECTIVE

dreadful
ADJECTIVE very bad or unpleasant.
dreadfully ADVERB

Synonyms: atrocious, awful, terrible

dreadlocks
PLURAL NOUN hair worn in long matted or tightly curled strands.

dream dreams dreaming dreamed or dreamt
NOUN **1** thoughts while you sleep.
2 a situation or event you would very much like to happen.
VERB **3** to see events in your mind while you are asleep.
4 to think about something you would very much like to happen.
5 If you say you would not dream of doing something, you are emphasizing that you would not do it.
dreamer NOUN

dreary drearier dreariest
ADJECTIVE dull or boring.
dreariness NOUN **drearily** ADVERB

dredge dredges dredging dredged
VERB To dredge a harbour or river means to clear a channel for boats by removing sand or mud from the bed.
dredger NOUN

drenched
ADJECTIVE soaking wet.

dress dresses dressing dressed
NOUN **1** a piece of clothing worn by a woman or girl.
2 any clothing worn by men or women. *All the men were in evening dress.*
VERB **3** When you dress or get dressed, you put clothes on.

dresser dressers
NOUN a piece of kitchen or dining room furniture with cupboards or drawers in the lower part and open shelves in the top part.

 ► Drama is a word from the Greek meaning something performed.

dressing **dressings**
NOUN 1 a sauce for food, especially salad.
2 a covering put on a wound to protect it while it heals.

dressing gown **dressing gowns**
NOUN a loose robe worn around the house, usually before getting dressed.

dress rehearsal **dress rehearsals**
NOUN the final rehearsal of a play before its performance.

drew
past participle of **draw**.

dribble **dribbles dribbling dribbled**
VERB 1 If someone dribbles, saliva trickles from their mouth.
2 In sport, to dribble means to move a ball along by repeatedly tapping it with your feet or a stick.
dribble NOUN

dried
past tense and past participle of **dry**.

drier
alternative form of **dryer**. See **dry**.

drift **drifts drifting drifted**
VERB 1 When something drifts, it is carried along by the wind or by water.
2 When people drift somewhere, they move there slowly or without a plan.

driftwood
NOUN wood that is washed up on a beach.

drill **drills drilling drilled**
NOUN 1 a tool for making holes.
2 a routine procedure or routine training: *a fire drill.*
VERB 3 to use a drill.

drink **drinks drinking drank drunk**
VERB 1 to take liquid into your mouth and swallow it.
2 to drink alcohol.
NOUN 3 a liquid you drink.
4 an alcoholic drink.

Synonyms: (sense 1) imbibe, sip, swallow
(sense 4) booze, tipple

drip **drips dripping dripped**
VERB 1 When liquid drips, it falls in small drops.
2 When an object drips, drops of liquid fall from it.
drip NOUN

drive **drives driving drove driven**
VERB 1 to operate a vehicle and control its movements.
2 to supply the power that makes a machine work. *The mill wheel is driven by water.*
3 If something or someone drives you to do something, they cause you to do it. *Jealousy sometimes drives people to murder.*
NOUN 4 a journey in a vehicle.
5 a private road that leads from a public road to a person's house.

drizzle
NOUN light rain.
drizzle VERB

drone **drones droning droned**
VERB 1 to make a low, continuous humming noise.
2 If someone drones on, they keep talking or reading aloud in a boring way.
NOUN 3 a continuous low dull sound.
4 a male bee.

drool **drools drooling drooled**
VERB If someone drools, saliva dribbles from their mouth without them being able to stop it.

droop **droops drooping drooped**
VERB to hang or sag downwards with no strength or firmness.
[from Old Norse *drupa* meaning to hang one's head in sorrow]

drop **drops dropping dropped**
VERB 1 to allow something to fall.
2 to become less. *The temperature drops quickly at night.*
3 If your voice drops or if you drop your voice, you speak more quietly.
4 If you drop something or someone at a place, you take them there.
5 If you drop in to someone's house, you call there briefly.
NOUN 6 a very small quantity of a liquid.
7 a decrease. *After the Christmas rush, the store reported a drop in sales.*

drought **droughts**
*Rhymes with "***shout***"* NOUN a long period during which there is no rain.

drove
past tense of **drive**.

drown **drowns drowning drowned**
VERB When someone drowns or is drowned, they die because they have gone under water and cannot breathe.

drowsy **drowsier drowsiest**
ADJECTIVE feeling sleepy.

drudgery
NOUN hard, uninteresting work.

drug **drugs drugging drugged**
NOUN 1 a chemical given to people to treat illness or disease.
2 Drugs are substances that some people smoke, swallow or inject because of their stimulating or calming effects. Drugs can be harmful to health and may be illegal.
VERB 3 To drug someone means to give them a drug in order to make them unconscious.
drugged ADJECTIVE

druid **druids**
*Said "***droo***-id"* NOUN a priest of an ancient religion in northern Europe.

drum drums drumming drummed
NOUN **1** a musical instrument consisting of a skin stretched tightly over a round frame.
2 an object or container shaped like a drum: *an oil drum.*
VERB **3** to play the drums.
4 to hit regularly, making a continuous beating sound. *Rain drummed on the roof.*
drummer NOUN

drumstick drumsticks
NOUN **1** a stick used for beating a drum.
2 the lower part of the leg of a chicken, which is cooked and eaten.

drunk drunks
1 the past participle of **drink**.
ADJECTIVE **2** If someone is drunk, they have consumed too much alcohol.
NOUN **3** A drunk is someone who is drunk or who often gets drunk.

dry drier or dryer driest; dries drying dried
ADJECTIVE **1** containing no water or liquid.
2 Dry sherry or wine does not taste sweet.
VERB **3** When you dry something or when it dries, liquid is removed from it.
dry up VERB **1** If a supply dries up, it ceases.
2 INFORMAL to forget what you were going to say.

dry-clean dry-cleans dry-cleaning dry-cleaned
VERB to clean clothes with a liquid chemical rather than with water.
dry-cleaner NOUN

dryer dryers; also spelt **drier**
NOUN a device for removing moisture from something using heat.

dual
ADJECTIVE having two parts, functions or aspects.
[from Latin *duo* meaning two]

dual carriageway dual carriageways
NOUN a wide road on which traffic travelling in opposite directions is separated by grass, a barrier, etc.

dub dubs dubbing dubbed
VERB **1** If a film is dubbed, the voices on the soundtrack are not those of the actors, but those of other actors speaking in a different language.
2 If something is dubbed a particular name, it is given that name. *Elvis Presley was dubbed "the King".*

dubious
ADJECTIVE **1** not entirely honest, safe or reliable.
2 doubtful.
dubiously ADVERB

Synonyms: (sense 1) questionable, suspect

duchess duchesses
NOUN a woman who has the same rank as a duke or who is a duke's wife or widow. See **duke**.

duck ducks ducking ducked
NOUN **1** a bird that lives in water and has webbed feet and a large flat beak.
VERB **2** to move your head quickly downwards in order to avoid being hit or seen.

duckling ducklings
NOUN a young duck.

duct ducts
NOUN a pipe or channel through which liquid or gas flows.

dud duds
NOUN something which does not function properly.

due
ADJECTIVE **1** expected to happen or arrive.
PHRASE **2** **Due to** means because of.
duly ADVERB

duel duels
NOUN **1** a fight arranged between two people using deadly weapons, to settle a quarrel.
2 any contest or conflict between two people.

duet duets
NOUN a piece of music sung or played by two people.

dug
past tense of **dig**.

dugout dugouts
NOUN **1** a shelter dug in the ground for protection.
2 a canoe made by hollowing out a log.

duke dukes
NOUN a nobleman with a rank just below that of a prince. See **duchess**.

dull duller dullest
ADJECTIVE **1** not interesting.
2 not bright, sharp or clear.
3 A dull day is cloudy and overcast.
dully ADVERB **dullness** NOUN

dumb dumber dumbest
ADJECTIVE **1** unable to speak.
2 INFORMAL stupid.

dumbfounded
ADJECTIVE speechless with amazement.

dummy dummies
NOUN **1** a piece of flexible rubber or plastic which a baby sucks on.
2 an imitation or model of something which is used for display.

dump dumps dumping dumped
VERB **1** If something is dumped somewhere, it is put there because it is no longer wanted.
2 to put something in a place in a careless way.
NOUN **3** a place where rubbish is left.
4 INFORMAL an unattractive and unpleasant place to live in.

dumpling dumplings
NOUN a small lump of dough that is cooked and eaten with meat and vegetables.

 ► Which proverb fits you? Too much bed makes a dull head. All work and no play makes Jack a dull boy.

dune dunes
NOUN A hill of sand near the sea or in the desert.

dung
NOUN the solid waste from large animals, sometimes called manure.

dungarees
PLURAL NOUN trousers which have a bib covering the chest and straps over the shoulders.

dungeon dungeons
Said "**dun**-jun" NOUN an underground prison.

dunk dunks dunking dunked
VERB to dip something briefly into a liquid.

duo duos
NOUN 1 a pair of musical performers.
2 Any two people doing something together can be referred to as a duo.

dupe dupes duping duped
VERB to trick someone.

duplicate duplicates duplicating duplicated
VERB 1 to make an exact copy of something.
NOUN 2 something that is identical to something else.
ADJECTIVE 3 identical to or an exact copy of.
duplication NOUN

durable
ADJECTIVE strong and lasting for a long time.
durability NOUN

duration
NOUN the length of time over which something happens.

during
PREPOSITION happening throughout a particular time or at a particular point within a period of time.

dusk
NOUN the time as night is falling when it is not completely dark.

dust dusts dusting dusted
NOUN 1 very small dry particles of earth, sand or dirt.
VERB 2 to remove dust from furniture or other objects.

dustbin dustbins
NOUN a large container for rubbish.

duster dusters
NOUN a cloth for dusting with.

dustman dustmen
NOUN someone whose job is to collect the rubbish from people's houses.

dustpan dustpans
NOUN an open container with a handle into which you sweep dust.

dusty dustier dustiest
ADJECTIVE covered with dust.

duty duties
NOUN 1 If something is your duty, you believe that you ought to do it because it is your responsibility.
2 Your duties are the tasks which you do as part of your job.
NOUN 3 tax paid to the government on goods that you buy.
PHRASE 4 If someone such as a policeman or a nurse is **on duty**, they are working. If they are **off duty**, they are not working.
dutiful ADJECTIVE dutifully ADVERB

duvet duvets
Said "**doo**-vay" NOUN a large cover filled with feathers or similar material, which you use on a bed instead of sheets and blankets.

DVD
NOUN an abbreviation for digital video disk.

dwarf dwarfs dwarfing dwarfed
NOUN 1 a person who is much smaller than average size.
VERB 2 If one thing dwarfs another, it is so much bigger that it makes it look very small.
dwarf ADJECTIVE

dwell dwells dwelling dwelled or dwelt
VERB; LITERARY To dwell somewhere means to live there.

dwelling dwellings
NOUN; FORMAL Someone's dwelling is the house or other place where they live.

dwindle dwindles dwindling dwindled
VERB to become smaller or weaker.

dye dyes dyeing dyed
VERB to change the colour of something by soaking it in a special liquid.
dye NOUN

dying
1 the present participle of **die**.
ADJECTIVE 2 relating to the moment of death: *a dying wish.*

dyke dykes; also spelt **dike**
NOUN 1 a drainage ditch, usually in low-lying countryside.
2 a thick wall that prevents the sea or a river from flooding onto land.

dynamic
ADJECTIVE full of energy, ambition and new ideas.
dynamism NOUN

dynamite
NOUN a kind of explosive.

dynamo dynamos
NOUN a device that converts mechanical energy into electricity.

dynasty dynasties
NOUN a series of rulers of a country, all belonging to the same family.

DVD can also mean digital versatile disk. What does "versatile" mean?

dyslexia

Said "dis-**lek**-see-a" **NOUN** difficulty with reading and writing caused by a slight disorder of the brain.

dyslexic ADJECTIVE AND NOUN

dystrophy

NOUN a disorder of the body which causes muscles or other tissues to stop working and waste away.

 ► Continue this word chain: dystrophy, hyena, national, allocate, terror... Can you do eight more?

Ee

each
ADJECTIVE OR PRONOUN **1** every one of a group, considered as single things: *each child.*
PHRASE **2** If people do something to **each other**, each person does it to the other person or persons. *She and Chris smiled at each other.*
✔ Wherever you use *each other* you could also use *one another.*

eager
ADJECTIVE wanting very much to do or have something, keen, enthusiastic.
eagerly ADVERB **eagerness** NOUN

eagle eagles
NOUN a large bird of prey.

ear ears
NOUN Your ears are the external parts of your body through which sound is funnelled.

earache earaches
NOUN pain in the ear.

eardrum eardrums
NOUN Your eardrums are thin pieces of tightly stretched skin inside your ears which vibrate so that you can hear sounds.

earl earls
NOUN a British nobleman.

early earlier earliest
ADJECTIVE OR ADVERB **1** before the arranged or expected time.
2 near the beginning of a day, evening or other period of time.

Synonyms: (sense 1) premature, untimely

earn earns earning earned
VERB **1** to receive money in return for work that you do.
2 If you earn praise, respect, etc., you receive it because you deserve it.

earnest
ADJECTIVE **1** sincere in what you say or do.
PHRASE **2** If something begins **in earnest** it happens to a greater or more serious extent than before.
3 If you are **in earnest** about something, you are serious about it.
earnestly ADVERB **earnestness** NOUN

earnings
NOUN the money that you earn.

earphones
PLURAL NOUN very small speakers worn in your ears to listen to a radio or disc player.

earring earrings
NOUN pieces of jewellery which you attach to your ears.

earth
NOUN **1** The earth is the planet on which we live.
2 the dry land on the surface of the earth, especially the soil in which things grow.

earthly
ADJECTIVE concerned with life on earth, rather than heaven or life after death.

earthquake earthquakes
NOUN a shaking of the ground caused by movement of the earth's crust.

earthworm earthworms
NOUN a worm that lives in soil.

earthy earthier earthiest
ADJECTIVE **1** looking or smelling like earth.
2 An earthy person is open and direct, often in a crude way.

earwig earwigs
NOUN a small, thin, brown insect which has a pair of pincers at the end of its body.
[from Old English *earwicga* meaning ear insect; it was believed to creep into people's ears]

ease eases easing eased
NOUN **1** If you do something with ease, you do it without difficulty or effort.
VERB **2** When something eases, or when you ease it, it becomes less intense.
3 To move slowly carefully and smoothly.

easel easels
NOUN an upright frame on legs that supports a picture, blackboard, etc.

easily
ADVERB **1** without difficulty.
2 without a doubt. *She was easily the best runner in the race.*

east
NOUN **1** the direction in which you look to see the sun rise.
2 The east of a place is the part which is farthest towards the east.
ADJECTIVE OR ADVERB **3** in, towards or from the east.

Easter
NOUN a Christian religious festival celebrating the resurrection of Christ.
[from Old English *Eastre*, a pre-Christian Germanic goddess with a festival in spring]

easterly
ADJECTIVE OR ADVERB **1** to or towards the east.
2 An easterly wind blows from the east.

eastern
ADJECTIVE in or from the east.

eastward or **eastwards**
ADVERB towards the east.

easy easier easiest
ADJECTIVE **1** done without difficulty.
2 comfortable and without problems.
✔ Although *easy* is an adjective, it can be used as an adverb in phrases like *take it easy.*

The letter E may have begun as a picture of a man holding his hands up in a gesture of joy.

A B C D E F G H I J K L M N O P Q R S T U V W X Y Z

eat **eats eating ate eaten**
VERB 1 to chew food and swallow it.
2 to have a meal.
eat away VERB to destroy something slowly, to erode. *The sea had eaten away the cliffs.*

Synonyms: (sense 1) devour, scoff, nibble

eaves
PLURAL NOUN The eaves of a roof are the lower edges which jut out over the walls.

eavesdrop **eavesdrops eavesdropping eavesdropped**
VERB to listen secretly to what other people are saying.
eavesdropper NOUN

ebb **ebbs ebbing ebbed**
VERB 1 When the sea or the tide ebbs, it flows back out.
2 If a person's feeling or strength ebbs, it gets weaker.
PHRASE 3 If someone or something is **at a low ebb**, they are very weak.

ebony
NOUN 1 a hard, dark-coloured wood, used for making furniture.
NOUN OR ADJECTIVE 2 very deep black.

eccentric **eccentrics**
Said "ik-**sen**-trik" **ADJECTIVE 1** having habits or opinions which other people think are odd or peculiar.
NOUN 2 someone who is eccentric.
eccentricity NOUN **eccentrically** ADVERB

echo **echoes echoing echoed**
VERB 1 If a sound echoes, it is reflected off a surface so you hear it again after the original sound has stopped.
NOUN 2 a sound which is caused by sound waves reflecting off a surface.
3 a repetition, imitation, or reminder of something. *Echoes of the past are everywhere.*

eclipse **eclipses**
NOUN An eclipse occurs when one object in space passes in front of another and hides it from view for a short time. For example, an eclipse of the sun occurs when the moon passes between the sun and the earth.

ecology
NOUN the relationship between living things and their environment; also the study of this relationship.
ecological ADJECTIVE **ecologically** ADVERB
ecologist NOUN

economical
ADJECTIVE 1 cheap to use or operate.
2 Someone who is economical spends money carefully and sensibly.
economically ADVERB

economics
NOUN the study of the way in which money, industry and trade are organized in a country.
economist NOUN

economy **economies**
NOUN 1 the system by which money, industry and trade are organized.
ADJECTIVE 2 Economy goods or services are cheaper than usual.

ecosystem **ecosystems**
NOUN the relationship between plants and animals and their environment.

ecstasy **ecstasies**
NOUN 1 a feeling of extreme happiness.
2 INFORMAL Ecstasy is a strong illegal drug that can cause hallucinations.
ecstatic ADJECTIVE **ecstatically** ADVERB

eczema
Said "**ek**-sim-ma" **NOUN** an itchy skin disease.

edge **edges edging edged**
NOUN 1 The edge of something is a border or line where it ends or meets something else.
2 The edge of a blade is its thin, sharp side.
VERB 3 If you edge something, you make a border for it. *The veil was edged with lace.*
4 If you edge somewhere, you move there very gradually. *The ferry edged into the jetty.*
PHRASE 5 If you **have the edge** over someone, you have a slight advantage over them.

Synonyms: (sense 1) border, brink, margin

edgy **edgier edgiest**
ADJECTIVE anxious and irritable.
edgily ADVERB **edginess** NOUN

edible
ADJECTIVE safe and pleasant to eat.

edit **edits editing edited**
VERB 1 If you edit a piece of writing, you correct and cut it to produce a finished version.
2 To edit a book means to collect pieces of writing by different authors and prepare them for publication.
3 To edit a newspaper means to have overall charge of it, and be responsible for what is printed.
4 To edit a film or television programme means to select pieces from everything which was shot and arrange them in a particular order.

edition **editions**
NOUN 1 An edition of a book or magazine is a particular version of it that is printed at one time.
2 An edition of a television or radio programme is a single programme that is one of a series.

editor **editors**
NOUN 1 a person who is responsible for the content of a newspaper or magazine.
2 a person who checks material for books and makes corrections to it before it is published.
3 a person who selects material shot for a film or television programme and puts it together as a final version.

 ► What does an animal eat if it is a herbivore, a carnivore, an omnivore? Use an adult dictionary to find nucivore.

editorial editorials
ADJECTIVE 1 editorial work is work involved in preparing a newspaper, book or magazine for publication.
NOUN 2 an article in a newspaper expressing the views of the editor or the publisher on an issue of current importance.

educate educates educating educated
VERB 1 When someone is educated, they are taught at a school or college.
2 To educate people means to improve their understanding of a particular subject.

education
NOUN learning and teaching.
educational ADJECTIVE **educationally** ADVERB

eel eels
NOUN a long, thin, snake-like fish.

eerie eerier eeriest
ADJECTIVE strange and frightening.
eerily ADVERB

effect effects
NOUN 1 the change or reaction that something causes. *Smoking cigarettes can have a bad effect on your health.*
2 the overall impression that someone or something creates. *The flowing fabric created the effect of a river.*
PHRASE 3 When something **takes effect**, it starts to happen or starts to have results at that time. *The law will take effect next year.*
✔ Do not confuse *effect* with *affect*. Their meanings are connected, but you should use each word in a different context.

effective
ADJECTIVE achieving the intended results.
effectively ADVERB **effectiveness** NOUN

efficient
ADJECTIVE capable of doing something well, without wasting time or energy.
efficiently ADVERB **efficiency** NOUN

Synonyms: capable, competent, proficient

effort efforts
NOUN 1 the physical or mental energy needed to do something.
2 an attempt to do something.

Synonyms: (sense 1) exertion, trouble, work

effortless
ADJECTIVE done easily.
effortlessly ADVERB

eg or **e.g.**
for example.
[from the Latin *exempli gratia*]

egg eggs
NOUN 1 a rounded object produced by female birds, reptiles, fish and insects, from which a young bird, reptile, etc. later emerges.
2 a hen's egg that is eaten as food.

Eid
Said "**eed**" NOUN a festival at the end of the Muslim fast of Ramadan.

eiderdown eiderdowns
NOUN a thick bed covering, usually filled with feathers.

eight eights
the number 8.
eighth

eighteen
the number 18.
eighteenth

eighty eighties
the number 80.
eightieth

either
ADJECTIVE, PRONOUN OR CONJUNCTION 1 You use "either" to refer to each of two possible alternatives: *either go or stay.*
ADJECTIVE 2 You use "either" to refer to both of two things: *on either side.*
✔ *either* can be followed by *is* or *are*: *either of these books is useful; either of these books are useful.*

eject ejects ejecting ejected
VERB 1 to push or send someone or something out forcefully.
2 to bale out of a plane in an emergency using an ejector seat.
ejection NOUN

elaborate elaborates elaborating elaborated
Said "el-**ab**-or-ut" ADJECTIVE 1 having many different parts: *an elaborate system of roads.*
2 carefully planned, detailed and exact: *elaborate plans.*
3 highly decorated or complicated: *elaborate designs.*
Said "el-**ab**-or-ate" VERB 4 If you elaborate on something, you add more information or detail about it.
elaborately ADVERB **elaboration** NOUN

Synonyms: (sense 3) fancy, ornate

elastic
NOUN 1 rubber material which stretches when you pull it and returns to its original shape when you let it go.
ADJECTIVE 2 able to stretch easily.

elation
NOUN a feeling of great happiness.
elated ADJECTIVE

elbow elbows
NOUN the joint where your arm bends in the middle.

elder eldest
ADJECTIVE The elder of two people is the one who was born first; older.
✔ Use *elder* and *eldest* only when talking about people within families. Use *older* and *oldest* for other people or things.

A B C D E F G H I J K L M N O P Q R S T U V W X Y Z

elderly
ADJECTIVE Someone who is elderly is old.

eldest
ADJECTIVE The eldest of three or more people is the one who was born first; older. See **elder**.

elect elects electing elected
VERB to vote for a person to represent you.

election elections
NOUN the process of voting for someone to represent you.
electoral ADJECTIVE

electric
ADJECTIVE 1 powered or produced by electricity.
PHRASE 2 An **electric shock** is a sudden violent jolt to the body caused by an **electric current** travelling through it. It can kill.
electrify VERB
✔ The word *electric* is an adjective and should not be used as a noun.

electrical
ADJECTIVE using or producing electricity.
electrically ADVERB

electrician electricians
NOUN a person whose job it is to repair and install electrical equipment.

electricity
NOUN a form of energy that provides power for heating, lighting and machines.

electrocute electrocutes electrocuting electrocuted
VERB to kill someone as a result of electric shock.
electrocution NOUN

electromagnet electromagnets
NOUN a magnet made up of an iron or steel core with a coil of wire round it, through which an electric current is passed.
electromagnetic ADJECTIVE

electronic
ADJECTIVE An electronic device has transistors or silicon chips which control an electric current.
electronically ADVERB

electronics
NOUN Electronics is the technology of electronic devices such as televisions and computers; also the study of how these devices work.

elegant
ADJECTIVE attractive and graceful.
elegantly ADVERB elegance NOUN

element elements
NOUN 1 a part of something which combines with others to make a whole.
2 In chemistry, an element is one of the 105 known basic substances which are made up of only one type of atom.
PLURAL NOUN 3 The elements are the weather conditions.

elementary
ADJECTIVE simple, basic and straightforward.

elephant elephants
NOUN a very large mammal with a long trunk, large ears and ivory tusks.

elevate elevates elevating elevated
VERB 1 to raise something up: *elevate your broken leg.*
2 To elevate someone to a higher position means to give them greater importance.

elevator elevators
NOUN In American English, an elevator is a lift.

eleven elevens
the number 11.
eleventh

elf elves
NOUN a mischievous fairy.

eligible
Said "**el**-lij-i-bl" ADJECTIVE 1 suitable or having the right qualifications for something.
2 An eligible bachelor is a man whom many women might like to marry.
eligibility NOUN

eliminate eliminates eliminating eliminated
VERB 1 to remove something or someone completely.
2 If a team or a person is eliminated from a competition, they are defeated and take no further part.
elimination NOUN

elite elites; also spelt **élite**
Said "ill-**eet**" ADJECTIVE 1 the best of its kind.
NOUN 2 a group of the most powerful, rich or talented people in a society.

elk elks
NOUN a large kind of deer.

ellipse ellipses
NOUN a regular oval shape, like a circle seen from an angle.

ellipsis ellipses
NOUN 1 the omission of parts of a sentence when the sentence can be understood without these parts. An example is "You coming too?", instead of "Are you coming too?".
2 the punctuation mark (...) inserted where words have been omitted from a sentence.

elm elms
NOUN a tall tree with broad leaves.

elocution
NOUN the art or study of speaking clearly or well in public.

elongated
ADJECTIVE long and thin.
elongate VERB elongation NOUN

eloquent
ADJECTIVE able to speak or write skilfully and with ease.
eloquently ADVERB eloquence NOUN

else
ADVERB **1** other than this; more than this. *Let's go somewhere else. What else did you buy?*
PHRASE **2** You say **or else** to introduce a possibility or alternative. *He's either a genius or else he's mad. Do what I say – or else.*

elsewhere
ADVERB in or to another place.

elude eludes eluding eluded
Said "ill-**ood**" VERB **1** to avoid or escape from someone.
2 If a fact or an idea eludes you, you cannot remember it or understand it.

elusive
ADJECTIVE difficult to find, achieve, describe or remember.

elves
the plural of **elf**.

e-mail or **email**
NOUN **1** the sending of messages by the Internet. E-mail is short for electronic mail.
2 mail sent by the Internet.
e-mail VERB

embankment embankments
NOUN a man-made ridge built to support a road or railway or to prevent water from overflowing.

embark embarks embarking embarked
VERB **1** to go onto a ship at the start of a journey.
2 If you embark on something, you start it. *She's embarking on a new career.*
embarkation NOUN

embarrass embarrasses embarrassing embarrassed
VERB to make someone feel ashamed or awkward.
embarrassing ADJECTIVE **embarrassment** NOUN

embassy embassies
NOUN the building in a foreign country in which an ambassador and their staff work.

embedded
ADJECTIVE **1** fixed firmly and deeply.
2 In computing, an embedded command is a process which happens automatically when a program is run.

embers embers
NOUN Embers are glowing pieces of coal or wood from a dying fire.

emblem emblems
NOUN an object or a design representing a country, an organization or an idea.

embrace embraces embracing embraced
VERB to hug or kiss someone to show affection or as a greeting.
embrace NOUN

embroider embroiders embroidering embroidered
VERB to sew a decorative design onto fabric.
embroidery NOUN

embryo embryos
Said "**em**-bree-oh" NOUN a human being or other animal in the very early stages of development in the womb.
embryonic ADJECTIVE

emerald emeralds
NOUN **1** a bright green precious stone.
NOUN OR ADJECTIVE **2** bright green.

emerge emerges emerging emerged
VERB **1** to come out from somewhere.
2 to become known: *the truth finally emerged.*
emergence NOUN

emergency emergencies
NOUN an unexpected and serious situation which must be dealt with quickly.

Synonym: crisis

emigrate emigrates emigrating emigrated
VERB to go to live permanently in another country. See **immigrate**.
emigration NOUN **emigrant** NOUN

eminent
ADJECTIVE well-known and respected for what you do.
eminently ADVERB

emission emissions
NOUN; FORMAL the release of something such as gas or radiation into the atmosphere.

emit emits emitting emitted
VERB To emit something means to give it out or release it. *She emitted a long, low whistle.*

emotion emotions
NOUN a strong feeling, such as love or fear.

emotional
ADJECTIVE **1** If someone is emotional, they show their feelings openly.
2 relating to feelings and emotions.
emotionally ADVERB

empathize empathizes empathizing empathized; also spelt **empathise**
VERB If you empathize with someone, you understand how they are feeling.
empathy NOUN

emperor emperors
NOUN a male ruler of an empire. See **empress**.

emphasis emphases
NOUN special importance or extra stress that is given to something. *When we say "English", we put the emphasis on the first syllable.*

emphasize emphasizes emphasizing emphasized; also spelt **emphasise**
VERB **1** to stress the importance of something.
2 If you emphasize a word when you are reading aloud, you say it more strongly than the words around it.

Consider how a change of emphasis alters the meaning of: convict, present, subject, suspect.

empire empires
NOUN **1** a group of countries controlled by one country.
2 A business empire is a large group of companies controlled by a single person or company.

employ employs employing employed
VERB **1** If you employ someone, you pay them to work for you.
2 to use something for a particular purpose. *Advertisers employ cunning methods.*

Synonyms: (sense 1) engage, hire, take on

employee employees
NOUN a person who is paid to work for a company or organization.

employer employers
NOUN a person or organization that people work for.

employment
NOUN paid work.

Antonym: unemployment

empress empresses
NOUN a woman who rules an empire, or the wife of an emperor. See **emperor**.

empty emptier emptiest; empties emptying emptied
ADJECTIVE **1** having nothing or nobody inside.
2 without purpose, value or meaning.
VERB **3** If you empty something, or if you empty its contents, you remove the contents.
emptiness NOUN

Synonyms: (sense 3) clear, evacuate

emu emus
Said "**ee**-myoo" NOUN a large Australian bird which can run fast but which cannot fly.

enable enables enabling enabled
VERB to make something possible.

enamel enamels
NOUN **1** a substance like glass, used to decorate or protect metal or china.
2 The enamel on your teeth is the hard, white substance that forms the outer part.

enchanted
ADJECTIVE fascinated or charmed by someone or something.

enchanting
ADJECTIVE attractive, delightful or charming.
enchantingly ADVERB **enchanted** ADJECTIVE **enchantment** NOUN

encircle encircles encircling encircled
VERB to surround.

enclose encloses enclosing enclosed
VERB **1** to surround an object or area with something solid.
2 If you enclose something with a letter, you put it in the same envelope.
enclosed ADJECTIVE

enclosure enclosures
NOUN an area of land surrounded by a fence or wall and used for a particular purpose.

encore encores
Said "**ong**-kor" NOUN a short extra performance given by an entertainer because the audience asks for it.

encounter encounters encountering encountered
VERB **1** to meet something or be faced with it.
NOUN **2** a meeting, especially when it is difficult or unexpected.

encourage encourages encouraging encouraged
VERB **1** to give someone the courage and confidence to do something.
2 to persuade. *We want to encourage people to visit the Highlands.*
encouraging ADJECTIVE **encouragement** NOUN

Synonyms: (sense 1) hearten, inspire

encyclopedia encyclopedias; also spelt **encyclopaedia**
Said "en-sigh-klop-**ee**-dee-a" NOUN a book or set of books giving information about many different subjects.

end ends ending ended
NOUN **1** the last or farthest part of something.
VERB **2** If something ends, or if you end it, it finishes.

endanger endangers endangering endangered
VERB to cause something to be in a dangerous and harmful situation.
endangered ADJECTIVE

Synonyms: jeopardize, put at risk

endeavour endeavours endeavouring endeavoured
Said "en-**dev**-er" VERB **1** FORMAL to try very hard.
NOUN **2** FORMAL an effort to do or achieve something.

ending endings
NOUN the last part of something, such as a film or a story.

endless
ADJECTIVE having, or seeming to have, no end.
endlessly ADVERB

endure endures enduring endured
VERB **1** If you endure a difficult situation, you put up with it calmly and patiently.
2 If something endures, it lasts or continues to exist.
enduring ADJECTIVE **endurance** NOUN

enemy enemies
NOUN someone who is opposed to you, especially someone who intends to harm you.
enmity NOUN

Synonyms: adversary, foe

 ► Use a large dictionary to find out what the meanings of employee, payee and interviewee have in common.

energetic
ADJECTIVE having or showing energy or enthusiasm.
energetically ADVERB

Synonyms: active, lively, vigorous

energy **energies**
NOUN **1** the physical strength needed to do active things.
2 the power that makes machines work, makes things move, light up, make a sound or get hotter.
energize VERB

Synonyms: (sense 1) drive, stamina, vigour

enforce **enforces enforcing enforced**
VERB If you enforce a law or a rule, you make sure that it is obeyed.
enforceable ADJECTIVE **enforcement** NOUN

engage **engages engaging engaged**
VERB **1** If you engage in an activity you take part in it.
2 If you engage someone or their attention, you involve them.

engaged
ADJECTIVE **1** When two people are engaged, they have agreed to marry each other.
2 If someone or something is engaged, they are occupied or busy.
3 If a telephone line is engaged, it is already being used by the person you are trying to phone.

engagement **engagements**
NOUN **1** an appointment that you have with someone.
2 an agreement that two people have made with each other to get married.

engine **engines**
NOUN **1** the part of a vehicle that produces the power to make it move.
2 the large vehicle that pulls a railway train.

engineer **engineers**
NOUN **1** a person trained in designing and building machinery and electrical devices, or roads and bridges.
2 a person trained to service and repair machinery.
engineering NOUN

engrave **engraves engraving engraved**
VERB **1** to cut letters or designs into a hard surface with a tool.
2 If something is engraved on your mind, memory or heart, it is fixed there permanently so that you feel that you will never forget it.

engraving **engravings**
NOUN a picture or design that has been cut into a hard surface.
engraver NOUN

engrossed
ADJECTIVE If you are engrossed in something, it holds all your attention.

engulf **engulfs engulfing engulfed**
VERB to completely cover or surround. *When the dam wall broke, the villages below were engulfed by water.*

enhance **enhances enhancing enhanced**
VERB To enhance something means to improve, increase or strengthen it or to make it more valuable or attractive.
enhancement NOUN

enjoy **enjoys enjoying enjoyed**
VERB **1** If you enjoy something, it gives you pleasure.
PHRASE **2** If you **enjoy yourself**, you are happy and have fun.
enjoyable ADJECTIVE **enjoyment** NOUN

enlarge **enlarges enlarging enlarged**
VERB to make something bigger.
enlargement NOUN

enlist **enlists enlisting enlisted**
VERB **1** to join the army, navy or air force.
2 If you enlist someone's help, you persuade them to help you in something you are doing.

enormous
ADJECTIVE very large in size or amount.
enormously ADVERB

Synonyms: colossal, huge, massive

enough
ADJECTIVE, ADVERB OR PRONOUN **1** sufficient.
ADVERB **2** very or fairly. *The rest of the evening passed pleasantly enough.*

enquire **enquires enquiring enquired**; also spelt **inquire**
VERB to ask for particular information.
enquiry NOUN

enrage **enrages enraging enraged**
VERB to make someone very angry.
enraged ADJECTIVE

enrich **enriches enriching enriched**
VERB to improve the quality or value of something.
enrichment NOUN

enrol **enrols enrolling enrolled**
VERB to register to join or become a member of a college, course, etc.
enrolment NOUN

ensure **ensures ensuring ensured**
VERB to make certain.

entangle **entangles entangling entangled**
VERB If something is entangled in something else, it is caught or tangled up in it.
entanglement NOUN

enter **enters entering entered**
VERB **1** to go in.
2 to become a member of something. *He entered the school in 1997.*
3 If you enter a competition, you take part in it.
4 If you enter something in a diary or a list, you write it down.

The "en-" prefix generally means to put something in a particular condition.

A B C D E F G H I J K L M N O P Q R S T U V W X Y Z

enterprise **enterprises**
NOUN 1 the quality of imagination and initiative, especially in thinking of ideas to make money.
2 a business or company.
3 a project or task, especially one that involves risk or difficulty.

enterprising
ADJECTIVE full of boldness and new ideas, and ready to start new projects and tasks.

entertain **entertains entertaining entertained**
VERB 1 to keep people amused or interested.
2 If you entertain guests, you invite them to your home and give them food.
entertainer NOUN **entertainment** NOUN

enthusiasm **enthusiasms**
NOUN interest, eagerness or delight in something.

Synonyms: keenness, passion, zeal

enthusiastic
ADJECTIVE showing great excitement, eagerness or approval for something.
enthusiastically ADVERB

entice **entices enticing enticed**
VERB to tempt someone to do something.
enticement NOUN

entire
ADJECTIVE all of something, whole.

entirely
ADVERB wholly and completely, fully.

entitle **entitles entitling entitled**
VERB 1 If you are entitled to something, you have the right to have it or do it.
2 If a book, film, etc. is entitled something, that is its name.
entitlement NOUN

entrance **entrances entrancing entranced**
Said "**en**-trunss" **NOUN 1** the doorway, gate or other opening to a place.
2 a person's arrival in a place, or the way in which they arrive. *Sharon made a dramatic entrance by falling down the stairs.*
Said "en-**transs**" **VERB 3** If something entrances you, it gives you a feeling of wonder and delight.
entrancing ADJECTIVE

entrant **entrants**
NOUN a person who officially enters a competition or an organization.

entrust **entrusts entrusting entrusted**
VERB If you entrust something to someone, you give them the care and protection of it.

entry **entries**
NOUN 1 the act of entering a place.
2 a place through which you enter somewhere.
3 something which you write in order to take part in a competition.
4 something written in a diary or list.

Synonyms: (sense 2) entrance, way in

envelope **envelopes**
NOUN the paper cover in which you send a letter through the post.

envious
ADJECTIVE full of envy.
enviously ADVERB

environment **environments**
NOUN 1 Your environment is your surroundings, especially the conditions in which you live or work.
2 The environment is the natural world around us.
environmental ADJECTIVE
environmentally ADVERB
✔ There is an *n* before the *m* in *environment.*

environmentalist **environmentalists**
NOUN a person who is concerned with the problems of the natural environment, such as pollution.
✔ There is an *n* before the *m* in *environmentalist.*

envy **envies envying envied**
VERB 1 If you envy someone, you wish that you had what they have.
NOUN 2 the feeling of wanting what someone else has.

epic **epics**
NOUN 1 a long story of heroic events and actions.
ADJECTIVE 2 very impressive or ambitious: *epic adventures with a rowing boat in the Pacific.*

epidemic **epidemics**
NOUN 1 an occurrence of a disease in one area, spreading quickly and affecting many people.
2 a rapid development or spread of something: *an epidemic of crime.*

epilepsy
NOUN a condition of the brain which causes fits and periods of unconsciousness.
epileptic NOUN OR ADJECTIVE

epilogue **epilogues**
Said "**ep**-ill-og" **NOUN** a passage added to the end of a book or play as a conclusion.

episode **episodes**
NOUN 1 one of the programmes in a serial on television or radio.
2 an event or period of time, especially one that is important or unusual.

epistle **epistles**
Said "ip-**piss**-sl" **NOUN 1 FORMAL** a letter.
2 The Epistles are the books in the New Testament originally written as letters.

epitaph **epitaphs**
Said "**ep**-it-ahf" **NOUN** words on a tomb or memorial about the person who has died.

 ► The "epi-" prefix is from a Greek word meaning upon or above.

eponymous
Said "ip-**on**-im-uss" ADJECTIVE; FORMAL The eponymous hero or heroine of a play or book is the person whose name forms its title: *Hamlet, the eponymous hero of Shakespeare's play.*

equal **equals equalling equalled**
ADJECTIVE **1** having the same in size, amount or value.
VERB **2** To equal a score or record means to be as good as it is.
equality NOUN

equalize **equalizes equalizing equalized**
VERB to make the score in a match level by scoring a goal, a try, etc.

equally
ADVERB in the same proportion; to the same degree. *I would have been equally happy with a trip to the seaside or to the city.*

equation **equations**
NOUN a mathematical formula stating that two amounts or values are the same.

equator
Said "ik-**way**-tor" NOUN an imaginary line drawn round the middle of the earth, lying halfway between the North and South poles.
equatorial ADJECTIVE

equestrian
Said "ik-**west**-ree-an" ADJECTIVE relating to or involving horses.

equilateral
ADJECTIVE An equilateral triangle has sides that are all the same length.

equinox **equinoxes**
NOUN a day in September and a day in March, when the day and night are of equal length.

equip **equips equipping equipped**
VERB If a person or thing is equipped with something, they have it or are provided with it. *The boat was equipped with all the latest technology.*

Synonyms: provide, supply

equipment
NOUN all the things such as tools or machines that are used for a particular purpose.

Synonyms: apparatus, gear, tools

equivalent **equivalents**
ADJECTIVE **1** equal in use, size, value or effect. *In mathematics* $\frac{1}{2}$ *and* $\frac{5}{10}$ *are equivalent fractions.*
NOUN **2** something that has the same use, value or effect as something else. *In energy terms, riding a bike for half a mile is the equivalent of running 100 metres.*
equivalence NOUN

era **eras**
Said "**ear**-a" NOUN a period of time distinguished by a particular feature: *the Victorian era.*

erase **erases erasing erased**
VERB to rub out, to remove all traces of something.

erect **erects erecting erected**
VERB **1** to build or assemble something.
ADJECTIVE **2** straight and upright.
erectly ADVERB **erection** NOUN

erode **erodes eroding eroded**
VERB If something erodes or is eroded, it is gradually worn or eaten away and destroyed.

erosion
NOUN erosion is the gradual wearing away and destruction of something: *soil erosion.*

errand **errands**
NOUN a short trip you make in order to do a job for someone.

erratic
ADJECTIVE not following a regular pattern or a fixed course; unpredictable. *The drunk's erratic driving gave him away.*
erratically ADVERB

error **errors**
NOUN a mistake or something you have done wrong.
err VERB

erupt **erupts erupting erupted**
VERB **1** When a volcano erupts, it throws out a lot of hot lava and ash.
2 When a situation erupts, it begins suddenly and violently.
eruption NOUN

escalate **escalates escalating escalated**
VERB If a situation escalates, it becomes greater in size, seriousness, or intensity.
escalation NOUN

escalator **escalators**
NOUN a mechanical moving staircase.

escape **escapes escaping escaped**
VERB **1** to get free of someone or something.
2 to succeed in avoiding something unpleasant. *She escaped serious injury.*
NOUN **3** the act of escaping from a particular place or situation.
4 a situation or activity which distracts you from something less pleasant. *Sport provides an escape for many people.*

escort **escorts escorting escorted**
NOUN **1** a person or vehicle that travels with another in order to protect or guide them.
2 a person who accompanies another person of the opposite sex to a social event.
VERB **3** If you escort someone, you go with them somewhere, especially in order to protect or guide them.

Eskimo **Eskimos**
NOUN a member of a group of people who live in Northern Canada, Greenland, Alaska and Eastern Siberia. Eskimos who come from North America or parts of Greenland are called Inuits.

Some words from Inuit, the Eskimo language: igloo, anorak, kayak.

A B C D E F G H I J K L M N O P Q R S T U V W X Y Z

especially
ADVERB specially or particularly.

espionage
Said "**ess**-pee-on-ahj" NOUN the act of spying.

essay essays
NOUN a short piece of writing on a particular subject, especially one written as an exercise by a student.
[from French *essai* meaning attempt]

essence essences
NOUN 1 the most basic and important part of something: *the essence of the matter.*
2 a concentrated liquid, used for flavouring food.

essential essentials
ADJECTIVE 1 absolutely necessary.
NOUN 2 The essentials are things that are absolutely necessary.

establish establishes establishing established
VERB 1 to found or create an organization or system.
2 to find out for certain; to prove something is correct. *We must establish how she did it!*

establishment establishments
NOUN 1 the act of setting up an organization or system.
2 a shop, business or other sort of organization or institution.

estate estates
NOUN 1 a large area of land in the country owned by one person or organization.
2 a specific area used for housing or industry.

estate agent estate agents
NOUN a person or business that sells houses and land.

esteem
NOUN If you hold someone in high esteem, you respect and admire them.
esteemed ADJECTIVE

estimate estimates estimating estimated
VERB 1 If you estimate an amount or quantity, you calculate it approximately.
NOUN 2 an approximate calculation of an amount or quantity.
estimation NOUN

estuary estuaries
Said "**est**-yoo-ree" NOUN the wide part of a river near where it joins the sea and where fresh water mixes with salt water.

etc.
a written abbreviation for **et cetera**.

et cetera
Said "et-**set**-ra" "Et cetera" is used at the end of a list to indicate that there are other similar things that you could have mentioned if time or space allowed. It is abbreviated as "etc.".
✔ *Et cetera* is often wrongly pronounced. Note that the second letter is *t* not *c*.

etch etches etching etched
VERB 1 If you etch a design or pattern on a surface, you cut it into the surface by using acid or a sharp tool.
2 If a vivid experience is etched on your mind, you will never forget it.

eternal
ADJECTIVE lasting forever, or seeming to last forever.
eternally ADVERB **eternity** NOUN

Synonyms: endless, everlasting, perpetual

ethnic
ADJECTIVE relating to different racial groups of people.

etiquette
Said "**et**-ik-ket" NOUN a set of rules for behaviour in a particular social situation: *wedding etiquette.*

etymology
Said "et-tim-**ol**-loj-ee" NOUN 1 the study of the origin of words and how they have changed through time.
2 the origin and development of a particular word.
etymological ADJECTIVE **etymologically** ADVERB

EU
NOUN an abbreviation for European Union, a group of European countries that have joined together for economic and trade purposes.

eucalyptus eucalyptuses; also spelt **eucalypt**
NOUN an evergreen tree originally from Australasia.

euphemism euphemisms
NOUN a polite word or expression that you can use instead of one that might offend or upset people: *"To pass away" is a euphemism for "to die".*
euphemistic ADJECTIVE **euphemistically** ADVERB

euro euros
NOUN the common unit of currency used in countries which are members of the European Monetary Union.

euthanasia
Said "yooth-a-**nay**-zee-a" NOUN the act of painlessly killing a dying person in order to stop their suffering.

evacuate evacuates evacuating evacuated
VERB 1 If someone is evacuated, they are removed from a place of danger to a place of safety.
2 If you evacuate a place, you move out of it for a period of time, usually because it is dangerous.
evacuation NOUN

evacuee evacuees
NOUN a person who in wartime is sent to live somewhere else for their safety.

 ► Etymology. What links these words: decimal, decade, December, decimetre, decimate?

evade evades evading evaded
VERB **1** If you evade something or someone, you keep moving in order to keep out of their way.
2 If you evade a problem or question, you avoid dealing with it.

evaluate evaluates evaluating evaluated
VERB to assess the quality, value or significance of something.
evaluation NOUN

evaporate evaporates evaporating evaporated
VERB When a liquid evaporates, it changes from its liquid state into a gas or vapour.
evaporation NOUN

evasion evasions
NOUN deliberately avoiding doing something in a cunning or devious way.

evasive
ADJECTIVE A person giving an evasive answer to a question is trying to to avoid telling the full truth.

eve eves
NOUN the evening or day before an event or occasion.

even
ADJECTIVE **1** smooth and flat.
2 An even measurement or rate stays at about the same level.
3 An even number is one that can be divided exactly by two, such as 2, 4 and 6.
ADVERB **4** "Even" is used to suggest that something is unexpected or surprising. *He hadn't even washed!*
5 "Even" is used to say that something is greater in degree. *Our teacher was even more angry than usual.*
PHRASE **6** **Even if** or **even though** are used to introduce something that is surprising in relation to the rest of the sentence. *Even if it rains, we'll still go. I was happy, even though I was exhausted.*
evenly ADVERB **evenness** NOUN

Antonym: (sense 1) uneven
(sense 3) odd

evening evenings
NOUN the part of the day between the end of the afternoon and bedtime.

event events
NOUN **1** something that happens, especially when it is unusual or important: *passing my exam was the most important event in my life.*
2 an organized activity, such as a sports match.

Synonyms: (sense 1) happening, incidence, occurrence

eventful
ADJECTIVE full of things happening: *an eventful day.*

eventually
ADVERB in the end, especially after a lot of delays or problems.

ever
ADVERB **1** at any time.
PHRASE **2** You use **ever since** to emphasize that something has been true since the time mentioned, and is still true. *He has loved trains ever since he was a child.*
3 INFORMAL **Ever so** means very. *Ooh, thank you ever so much.*

evergreen evergreens
NOUN a tree or bush which has green leaves all the year round.

everlasting
ADJECTIVE never coming to an end.

every
ADJECTIVE **1** "Every" is used to refer to all the members of a group or all the parts of something.
2 "Every" is also used to indicate that something happens at regular intervals: *every 30 seconds.*
3 "Every" is used before some nouns to emphasize what you are saying: *every chance of success.*
PHRASE **4** If something happens **every other** day, it happens on alternate days.

everybody
PRONOUN **1** all the people in a group.
2 all the people in the world.
✔ *Everybody* and *everyone* mean the same.

everyday
ADJECTIVE usual or ordinary. *Housework is an everyday occupation.*

everyone
PRONOUN **1** all the people in a group.
2 all the people in the world.
✔ *Everyone* and *everybody* mean the same.

everything
PRONOUN all the parts of something or the whole of something.

everywhere
ADVERB in or to all places.

evict evicts evicting evicted
VERB to force someone officially to leave the house they are living in.
eviction NOUN

evidence
NOUN **1** anything that you see, read or are told which gives you reason to believe something. *Her excellent exam results were evidence of her intelligence.*
2 the information used in a court of law to try to prove something.

evident
ADJECTIVE easily noticed or understood. *It was evident from Rover's muddy paws that he had been in the stream.*
evidently ADVERB

a b c d e f g h i j k l m n o p q r s t u v w x y z

Pun. At what time of day was Adam born? A little before Eve.

A B C D E F G H I J K L M N O P Q R S T U V W X Y Z

evil evils
ADJECTIVE **1** very wrong or bad and causing harm to people.
NOUN **2** all the wicked or bad things that happen in the world: *good and evil.*
evilly ADVERB

evolution
Said "ee-vol-**oo**-shn" NOUN **1** the process of gradual change taking place over many thousands of years, during which time living things slowly change as they adapt to different environments.
2 any process of gradual change and development over a period of time.
evolutionary ADJECTIVE

evolve evolves evolving evolved
VERB When living things evolve, they gradually change and develop into different forms.

ewe ewes
Said "**yoo**" NOUN a female sheep.

ex-
PREFIX **1** former. *The doorman was an ex-boxer.*
2 out of, outside of.

exact
ADJECTIVE **1** correct and complete in every detail.
2 precise, particular. *I don't remember her exact words.*
exactly ADVERB

exaggerate exaggerates exaggerating exaggerated
VERB to make something seem better, worse, bigger or more important than it really is.
exaggerated ADJECTIVE **exaggeration** NOUN

exam exams
NOUN an official test that aims to find out your knowledge or skill in a subject.

examination examinations
NOUN **1** an exam.
2 a close inspection of something.
3 A medical examination is a check by a doctor to find out the state of your health.
examiner NOUN

examine examines examining examined
VERB **1** to inspect something carefully.
2 If a doctor examines you, he or she checks your body to find out how healthy you are.

example examples
NOUN **1** something which represents or is typical of a particular group of things. *Pacman and Space Invaders are examples of early computer games.*
2 If you say someone is an example to people, you mean that they behave in a good way which people should copy.
PHRASE **3** You use **for example** to give an example of something you are talking about.

Synonyms: (sense 1) sample, specimen

exasperate exasperates exasperating exasperated
VERB If someone or something exasperates you, they irritate you and make you angry.
exasperating ADJECTIVE **exasperation** NOUN

excavate excavates excavating excavated
VERB **1** to remove earth from the ground by digging.
2 When archaeologists excavate objects, they carefully dig them up from the ground to discover information about the past.
excavation NOUN **excavator** NOUN

exceed exceeds exceeding exceeded
VERB If something exceeds a particular amount, it is greater than that amount.

exceedingly
ADVERB extremely, very much.

excel excels excelling excelled
VERB If you excel at something, you are very good at it.

excellent
ADJECTIVE very good indeed.

Synonyms: first-rate, outstanding, superb

except
PREPOSITION You use "except" or "except for" to introduce the only thing or person that a statement does not apply to. *I like all liquorice allsorts except the brown ones.*

exception exceptions
NOUN somebody or something that is not included in a general statement. *All the class like PE, with the exception of Ali.*

exceptional
ADJECTIVE **1** unusually talented or clever.
2 unusual and likely to happen very rarely: *in exceptional circumstances.*
exceptionally ADVERB

excerpt excerpts
NOUN a short piece of writing or music which is taken from a larger piece.

excess
ADJECTIVE **1** more than is needed or allowed. *The airline would not allow any excess baggage on the flight.*
PHRASE **2 In excess of** a particular amount means more than that amount.

excessive
ADJECTIVE too great in amount or degree.

exchange exchanges exchanging exchanged
VERB to swap.
exchange NOUN

excite excites exciting excited
VERB If something excites you, it makes you feel very happy and enthusiastic.
excitement NOUN

Synonyms: arouse, thrill

 ► Language evolves. These words have changed their spellings: newt, nickname, alright, program.

exciting
ADJECTIVE causing you to feel happy and enthusiastic, stimulating.

exclaim exclaims exclaiming exclaimed
VERB to cry out suddenly or loudly because you are excited or shocked.

exclamation exclamations
NOUN a word or phrase spoken suddenly to express a strong feeling.

exclamation mark exclamation marks
NOUN the punctuation mark (!).

WHAT DOES THE EXCLAMATION MARK DO?
The exclamation mark (!) is used to express strong feeling:
I don't believe it!
The exclamation mark can lose its effect if used too much. After a sentence expressing mild excitement or humour it is better to use a full stop:
It is a beautiful day.

exclude excludes excluding excluded
VERB **1** If you exclude something you choose not to include or consider it.
2 to prevent someone from entering somewhere or taking part in something.
exclusion NOUN

exclusive
ADJECTIVE **1** available only to a small group of rich or privileged people: *an exclusive club.*
2 belonging to a particular person or group only. *Our school will have exclusive use of the field centre.*

excrete excretes excreting excreted
VERB When you excrete waste matter from your body you get rid of it; for example, you excrete dissolved waste in sweat and urine.

excruciating
Said "iks-**kroo**-shee-ate-ing" ADJECTIVE extremely painful.

excursion excursions
NOUN a short journey or outing.

excuse excuses excusing excused
Said "ex-**kyooss**" NOUN **1** a reason which you give for not doing something, or for doing something wrong.
Said "ex-**kyooze**" VERB **2** If you excuse someone's behaviour, you give reasons for why they behaved in that way.
3 If you excuse somebody for something wrong they have done, you forgive them for it.
4 If someone is excused from a duty or responsibility, they are allowed not to do it.
PHRASE **5** You say **excuse me** to try to catch somebody's attention, or to apologize for an interruption or for rude behaviour.

execute executes executing executed
VERB **1** to kill someone as a punishment for a crime.
2 If you execute a plan, you carry it out or perform it.
execution NOUN **executioner** NOUN

executive executives
NOUN a person who is employed by a company at a senior level.

exempt exempts exempting exempted
ADJECTIVE If you are exempt from a rule or a tax, you are excused from it.
exempt VERB **exemption** NOUN

exercise exercises exercising exercised
NOUN **1** any activity which you do in order to get fit or stay healthy.
2 Exercises are a series of movements which you do in order to get fit or stay healthy.
3 Exercises are activities which you do in order to practise a particular skill. *Playing scales is a good piano exercise.*
VERB **4** to do activities which help you to get fit and stay healthy; to train.

exert exerts exerting exerted
VERB **1** To exert pressure means to apply it.
2 If you exert yourself you make a physical or mental effort.

exhale exhales exhaling exhaled
VERB to breathe out.
exhalation NOUN

exhaust exhausts exhausting exhausted
VERB **1** If something exhausts you, it makes you very tired. *Several lengths of the swimming pool left her exhausted.*
2 If you exhaust a supply of something, such as money or food, you use it up completely.
NOUN **3** the pipe which carries the gas out of a vehicle engine.
exhausting ADJECTIVE

Synonyms: (sense 1) fatigue, tire out, wear out

exhausted
ADJECTIVE extremely tired.
exhaustion NOUN

exhibit exhibits exhibiting exhibited
VERB **1** to put something on public display or into a show.
2 to show. *He exhibited all the symptoms of measles.*
NOUN **3** anything which is put on display in an exhibition, museum, gallery, etc.

exhibition exhibitions
NOUN an event at which objects of interest are displayed to the public.

exile exiles exiling exiled
NOUN **1** If somebody lives in exile, they live in a foreign country because they are not allowed to live in their own country, usually for political reasons.
2 a person who lives in exile.
VERB **3** to send someone away from their own country to live abroad. See **deport**.

Excruciating takes its meaning from crucifixion, being put to death on a cross.

exist **exists existing existed**
VERB If something exists, it is present in the world as a real or living thing. *She tried to pretend her problems didn't exist.*
existing ADJECTIVE **existence** NOUN

exit **exits**
NOUN **1** a doorway through which you can leave a public place.
2 If you make an exit, you leave a place.

exotic
ADJECTIVE **1** attractive or interesting through being unusual.
2 coming from a foreign country, especially a distant one.
exotically ADVERB

expand **expands expanding expanded**
VERB to become larger or to make something larger.
expanding ADJECTIVE **expansion** NOUN

expanse **expanses**
NOUN a very large or widespread area.
expansive ADJECTIVE

expect **expects expecting expected**
VERB **1** to believe that something will happen.
2 to believe that someone or something is going to arrive.
3 to believe that you have a right to get or have something. *I expect the best service in this hotel.*
4 If you say a woman is expecting, she is expecting a baby.

Synonyms: (sense 1) look forward to, anticipate

expectant
ADJECTIVE **1** believing that something is about to happen, especially something exciting.
2 An expectant mother or father is someone whose baby is going to be born soon.
expectantly ADVERB **expectancy** NOUN

expectation **expectations**
NOUN a strong belief or hope that something will happen.

expedition **expeditions**
NOUN **1** an organized journey made for a special purpose, such as to explore.
2 a short journey or outing: *a fishing expedition.*

expel **expels expelling expelled**
VERB **1** If someone is expelled from a school or club, they are officially told to leave because they have behaved badly. See **expulsion**.
2 If a gas or liquid is expelled from a place, it is forced out of it.

expense **expenses**
NOUN **1** the money that something costs. *We went to great expense to buy that bike.*
2 Expenses are the money somebody spends in connection with their work, which is paid back to them by their employer.

Synonyms: (sense 1) cost, expenditure, outlay

expensive
ADJECTIVE If something is expensive, it costs a lot of money.
expensively ADVERB

experience **experiences experiencing experienced**
NOUN **1** a general word for all the things that you have done or that have happened to you.
2 An experience is something that you do or something that happens to you, especially something new or unusual.
3 knowledge or skill in a particular job or activity, which you have gained from doing that job or activity. *He got the job because he had two years' experience.*
VERB **4** If you experience something, it happens to you or you are affected by it: *to experience good luck.*

Synonyms: (sense 4) go through, undergo

experienced
ADJECTIVE An experienced person has been doing a particular job or activity for a long time and knows a lot about it.

experiment **experiments experimenting experimented**
NOUN **1** a scientific test which aims to prove or discover something.
VERB **2** to carry out an experiment.
experimental ADJECTIVE **experimentally** ADVERB

expert **experts**
NOUN a person who is very skilled at something or who knows a lot about a particular subject.
expert ADJECTIVE **expertly** ADVERB

Synonyms: authority, master, specialist

expertise
Said "eks-per-**teez**" NOUN special skill or knowledge.

expire **expires expiring expired**
VERB **1** When something expires, it reaches the end of the period of time for which it is valid. *My library ticket expired.*
2 LITERARY When someone expires, they die.
expiry NOUN

explain **explains explaining explained**
VERB to give information about something or reasons for it so that it can be understood.
explanatory ADJECTIVE

Synonyms: clarify, elucidate, make clear

explanation **explanations**
NOUN a statement giving reasons for why something has happened.

explode **explodes exploding exploded**
VERB **1** to burst with great force.
2 to express strong feelings suddenly or violently: *he exploded in anger.*

 ► Some words from Latin: exit, stamina, appendix, formula, index, radius, alibi.

exploit **exploits exploiting exploited**
Said "ex-**ploit**" **VERB 1** to take advantage of a person or a situation for your own gain.
2 to make the best use of something, often for profit. *We ought to exploit the power of computers.*
Said "**ex**-ploit" **NOUN 3** something daring or interesting that somebody has done. *His exploits were legendary.*
exploitation NOUN

explore **explores exploring explored**
VERB to travel around a place to discover what it is like.
explorer NOUN **exploration** NOUN

explosion **explosions**
NOUN a sudden violent burst of energy, for example one caused by a bomb.

explosive **explosives**
NOUN 1 a substance or device that is designed to explode.
ADJECTIVE 2 capable of exploding or likely to explode.
3 happening suddenly and making a loud noise.
4 An explosive situation is one which is likely to have serious or dangerous effects.

export **exports exporting exported**
VERB 1 to sell goods to other countries.
NOUN 2 Exports are goods which are sold to other countries.

expose **exposes exposing exposed**
VERB 1 to uncover something and make it visible.
2 To expose a person to something dangerous means to put them in a situation in which it might harm them.

exposure **exposures**
NOUN 1 the exposing of something.
2 the harmful effect on the body caused by bad weather, especially cold.

express **expresses expressing expressed**
VERB 1 to show what you think or feel by saying or doing something.
ADJECTIVE 2 very fast: *an express train.*

expression **expressions**
NOUN 1 the act of showing ideas, feelings etc. through words, actions, art, etc.
2 the look on someone's face which shows what they are thinking or feeling.
3 a word or phrase. *"Daft as a brush" is an old Lancashire expression.*

expressive
ADJECTIVE 1 showing feelings clearly.
2 full of expression.
expressively ADVERB **expressiveness** NOUN

expulsion **expulsions**
NOUN the act of officially banning someone from a place or institution. See **expel**.

exquisite
ADJECTIVE extremely beautiful and pleasing.
exquisitely ADVERB

extend **extends extending extended**
VERB 1 to make something larger or longer. *We're going to extend our house.*
2 to stretch for a certain distance. *The caves extend for 18 km.*
3 to last for a certain time. *Her career extended from 1894 to 1920.*
4 If something extends from a place, it sticks out from it. *A ruler extended from his pocket.*

extension **extensions**
NOUN 1 a room or building which is added to an existing building.
2 an extra period of time for which something continues to exist or to be valid.

extensive
ADJECTIVE 1 covering a large area.
2 very great in effect: *extensive repairs.*
extensively ADVERB

extent
NOUN The extent of a situation is how great, important or serious it is.

exterior **exteriors**
NOUN The exterior of something is its outside.

Antonym: interior

exterminate **exterminates exterminating exterminated**
VERB When animals or people are exterminated, they are deliberately killed, often in large numbers.
extermination NOUN

external
ADJECTIVE existing or happening on the outside of something.
externally ADVERB

Antonym: internal

extinct
ADJECTIVE 1 no longer in existence.
2 An extinct volcano is no longer likely to erupt.
extinction NOUN

extinguish **extinguishes extinguishing extinguished**
VERB To extinguish a light or fire means to put it out.
extinguisher NOUN

extra
ADJECTIVE OR ADVERB more than is usual, necessary or expected.

extract **extracts extracting extracted**
Said "ex-**tract**" **VERB 1** To extract something from a place means to get it out, often by force.
Said "**ex**-tract" **NOUN 2** a small section taken from a book or piece of music.
extraction NOUN

The prefix "ex-" is a Latin word meaning out of.

A B C D E F G H I J K L M N O P Q R S T U V W X Y Z

extraordinary
ADJECTIVE very unusual or surprising.
extraordinarily ADVERB

Synonyms: exceptional, remarkable

extraterrestrial
ADJECTIVE happening or existing beyond the earth's atmosphere.

extravagant
ADJECTIVE spending or costing more money than is reasonable or affordable.
extravagantly ADVERB **extravagance** NOUN

extreme
ADJECTIVE **1** very great in degree or intensity.
2 at the furthest point or edge of something.

extremely
ADVERB very, greatly.

exuberant
ADJECTIVE full of energy and cheerfulness.
exuberantly ADVERB **exuberance** NOUN

eye **eyes eyeing** or **eying eyed**
NOUN **1** Your eyes are the parts of your body with which you see.
2 The eye of a needle is the tiny hole through which you pass the thread.
VERB **3** to look at something carefully and suspiciously.

eyeball **eyeballs**
NOUN the whole of the ball-shaped part of the eye.

eyebrow **eyebrows**
NOUN the line of hair growing on the bone above each eye.

eyelash **eyelashes**
NOUN Your eyelashes are hairs that grow on the edges of your eyelids.

eyelid **eyelids**
NOUN Your eyelids are the folds of skin which cover your eyes when they are closed.

eyesight
NOUN the ability to see.

eyesore **eyesores**
NOUN Something that is an eyesore is extremely ugly.

eyewitness **eyewitnesses**
NOUN a person who has seen an event and can describe what happened.

 ► There is a silent "a" in extraordinary, aisle and parliament.

Ff

fable **fables**
NOUN a story intended to teach a moral lesson.

fabric **fabrics**
NOUN cloth, material.

fabricate **fabricates fabricating fabricated**
VERB 1 to make up a story or an explanation in order to deceive people.
2 to fabricate something is to make or manufacture it.
fabrication NOUN

fabulous
ADJECTIVE wonderful or very impressive.
fabulously ADVERB

face **faces facing faced**
NOUN 1 the front part of your head from your chin to your forehead.
2 the expression on your face: *a happy face.*
3 a surface or side of something. *A cube has six faces.*
VERB 4 To face something or someone means to be opposite them, looking in their direction.
5 If you are faced with something difficult or unpleasant, you have to deal with it.

Synonyms: (sense 1) countenance, visage

facetious
Said "fas-**see**-shuss" **ADJECTIVE** witty or amusing but in a rather silly or inappropriate way.
facetiously ADVERB **facetiousness** NOUN

facilitate **facilitates facilitating facilitated**
VERB to make something easier to happen. *Her donation facilitated the building of a new ward at the hospital.*
facilitation NOUN

facility **facilities**
NOUN Facilities are buildings, equipment or services that are provided for a particular purpose.

fact **facts**
NOUN 1 a piece of information that is true, or something that has actually happened.
PHRASE 2 In fact and **as a matter of fact** mean actually or really, and are used for emphasis. *This was, in fact, what happened.*

factor **factors**
NOUN 1 something that can affect a result. *House dust mites are a major factor in asthma.*
2 In mathematics, a factor is a whole number which will divide exactly into another whole number. For example, 1, 2, 3, 4 and 6 are all factors of 12.

factory **factories**
NOUN a building or group of buildings where goods are made in large quantities.

factual
ADJECTIVE relating to the facts of something.

fad **fads**
NOUN a temporary fashion or craze.

fade **fades fading faded**
VERB to slowly become less bright or less loud.

fag **fags**
NOUN 1 INFORMAL a cigarette.
2 OLD-FASHIONED If you describe something as a fag, you mean that it is boring or tiring.

Fahrenheit
Said "**far**-ren-hite" **NOUN** a scale of temperature in which the freezing point of water is 32 °F and the boiling point is 212 °F.

fail **fails failing failed**
VERB 1 If you fail, you do not succeed.
2 If you fail an exam, you do not pass.
3 If something fails, it becomes less effective or doesn't work. *The new video failed to record.*
PHRASE 4 Without fail means definitely or regularly

failing **failings**
NOUN 1 a fault in something or someone.
PHRASE 2 Failing that is used to introduce an alternative. *You could go by train or, failing that, get a bus.*

failure **failures**
NOUN 1 a lack of success.
2 an unsuccessful person, thing or action. *The project was a failure.*
3 Your failure to do something is not doing it when you were supposed to. *He tried to explain his failure to turn up.*

faint **fainter faintest; faints fainting fainted**
ADJECTIVE 1 not strong or intense. *The colour was faint.*
2 feeling dizzy and unsteady.
VERB 3 to lose consciousness for a short time.
faintly ADVERB

Synonyms: (sense 3) black out, pass out, swoon

fair **fairer fairest; fairs**
ADJECTIVE 1 reasonable and just: *fair wages.*
2 quite large. *The building was a fair size.*
3 light or pale: *fair hair; fair skin.*
4 When the weather is fair, it is not cloudy or rainy.
NOUN 5 a form of outdoor entertainment with games and rides.
6 an event at which people display or sell goods: *a craft fair.*
fairness NOUN

fairground **fairgrounds**
NOUN a place where a fair is held, involving rides, competitions and sideshows.

fairly
ADVERB 1 quite: *fairly sunny.*
2 in a fair and reasonable manner.

The letter F seems to have been made from the picture of a long, hooked implement.

fairy fairies
NOUN In stories, fairies are small, supernatural creatures with magical powers.

fairy tale fairy tales
NOUN a story of magical events.

faith faiths
NOUN 1 a feeling of confidence or trust in something.
2 a particular religion.

faithful
ADJECTIVE 1 loyal to someone or something and continuing to support them.
2 accurate and truthful: *a faithful copy.*
faithfully ADVERB **faithfulness** NOUN
✔ Finish a letter *Yours faithfully* if you don't know the name of the person you are writing to. If you know the person's name, finish the letter *Yours sincerely* (unless it is someone you know really well).

fake fakes faking faked
NOUN 1 an imitation of something made to trick people into thinking that it is genuine.
ADJECTIVE 2 imitation and not genuine.
VERB 3 to pretend something. *They faked the burglary.*

Synonyms: (sense 1) copy, imitation, sham
(sense 2) artificial, phoney
(sense 3) feign, pretend, simulate

falcon falcons
NOUN a bird of prey that can be trained to hunt small animals, including other birds.

fall falls falling fell fallen
VERB 1 to drop towards the ground.
2 to move quickly downwards. *Her weight fell to under 45 kilograms.*
3 If you fall ill, fall asleep, or fall in love, you change quite quickly to that new state.
4 If something falls in a particular position it happens there. *The spotlight fell on her. 27 July falls on a Monday.*
5 If you fall for a trick or a lie, you are deceived by it.
NOUN 6 If you have a fall, you fall over.
7 a fall is a reduction in something: *a fall in the number of pupils.*
8 In America, the autumn is called the fall.
fall out VERB If people fall out, they disagree and quarrel.
fall through VERB If an arrangement falls through, it fails to happen.

fallout
NOUN radioactive particles that fall to the earth after a nuclear explosion.

false
ADJECTIVE 1 untrue or incorrect.
2 not real or genuine but intended to seem real: *false teeth.*
falsely ADVERB **falseness** NOUN

falter falters faltering faltered
VERB to hesitate or become unsure or unsteady.

fame
NOUN the state of being very well-known.

Synonyms: prominence, renown, repute

familiar
ADJECTIVE 1 well-known or easy to recognize: *familiar faces; familiar stories.*
2 If someone is too familiar with you, they treat you as a close friend when this is not appropriate or acceptable.
familiarly ADVERB **familiarity** NOUN

family families
NOUN a group of people who are related to each other, especially parents and their children.

family planning
NOUN the practice of controlling the number of children you have, usually by contraception.

family tree family trees
NOUN a chart showing your present family and the way it is descended from your ancestors.

famine famines
NOUN a serious shortage of food which may cause many deaths.

famished
ADJECTIVE; INFORMAL very hungry.

famous
ADJECTIVE very well-known.
famously ADVERB

Synonyms: prominent, well-known, renowned

fan fans
NOUN 1 an enthusiastic admirer of someone or something; short for **fanatic**.
2 a device that keeps a room or machine cool by creating a draught of air.
VERB 3 to create a current of cool air by moving a flat object up and down fast.

fanatic fanatics
NOUN a person who is very extreme in their support for a cause or in their enthusiasm for a particular activity.
fanatical ADJECTIVE **fanatically** ADVERB
fanaticism NOUN

fanciful
ADJECTIVE imaginary, not based on fact.

fancy fancies fancying fancied; fancier fanciest
VERB 1 If you fancy something, you want to have it or do it. *Do you fancy a cup of tea?*
ADJECTIVE 2 special and elaborate: *fancy furniture.*

Synonym: (sense 2) ornate

fancy dress
NOUN a costume that makes you look like a character or an animal, which you wear to a party or carnival.

 ► Some people have become famous for their inventions: Rudolf Diesel, William Hoover, Laszlo Biro.

fanfare fanfares
NOUN a short, loud, musical introduction to a special event, usually played on trumpets.

fang fangs
NOUN long, pointed teeth.

fantastic
ADJECTIVE **1** wonderful and very pleasing.
2 extremely large in degree or amount: *a fantastic salary.*
3 strange and difficult to believe in: *the fantastic creatures of mythology.*
fantastically ADVERB

Synonyms: (sense 1) marvellous, terrific, splendid

fantasy fantasies
NOUN a story or situation created in someone's imagination.

Antonym: reality

far farther farthest; further furthest
ADVERB **1** a long distance or time away: *far from here.*
2 very much or to a great extent: *far more important.*
ADJECTIVE **3** very distant or the more distant of two things: *a far corner.*
4 If a change is far-reaching, it affects a great many people and places.
PHRASE **5** **So far** means until the present moment.
6 **as far as I know** or **so far as I recall** indicates that you are not sure of something.
✔ It's preferable to use *farther* and *farthest* for a physical distance. Use *further* and *furthest* for extra effort or time.

farce farces
NOUN **1** a humorous play in which ridiculous and unlikely situations occur.
2 a disorganized and ridiculous situation. *As rain flooded the pitch, the football match became a farce.*
farcical ADJECTIVE

fare fares faring fared
NOUN **1** the money that you pay for a journey on a bus, train, taxi, boat or plane.
VERB **2** How someone fares in a particular situation is how successful they are.

farewell
INTERJECTION goodbye.

far-fetched
ADJECTIVE unlikely to be true.

farm farms
NOUN land and buildings used for growing crops and raising animals.
farming NOUN

farmer farmers
NOUN a person who operates or manages a farm.

farmhouse farmhouses
NOUN the main house on a farm.

farmyard farmyards
NOUN an area surrounded by or adjacent to farm buildings.

fascinate fascinates fascinating fascinated
VERB If something fascinates you, it interests you so much that you think about it and nothing else.
fascinating ADJECTIVE **fascination** NOUN

Synonyms: absorb, enthrall, intrigue

fashion fashions fashioning fashioned
NOUN **1** a style of dress or a way of behaving that is popular at a particular time.
2 the way in which something is done: *in a brisk fashion.*
VERB **3** If you fashion something, you make or shape it.
fashionable ADJECTIVE **fashionably** ADVERB

fast faster fastest; fasts fasting fasted
ADJECTIVE OR ADVERB **1** quick.
2 If a clock is fast, it shows a time that is later than the real time.
ADVERB **3** firmly fixed: *stuck fast.*
PHRASE **4** If you are **fast asleep**, you are in a deep sleep.
VERB **5** to eat no food for a period of time, usually for religious reasons.
NOUN **6** a period of time during which someone does not eat food.

Synonyms: (sense 1) rapid, speedy, swift

fasten fastens fastening fastened
VERB to attach something firmly to something else.
fastener NOUN **fastening** NOUN

fast food
NOUN hot food that is prepared and served very quickly after you have ordered it.

fat fatter fattest; fats
ADJECTIVE **1** Someone who is fat has too much fat on their body.
2 very thick or wide: *a fat pile of letters.*
NOUN **3** the flesh that animals, including humans, have under their skin, used for energy to do things and warmth.
4 a substance obtained from animals and plants and used in cooking.
fatness NOUN

Synonyms: (sense 1) overweight, plump, podgy

fatal
ADJECTIVE **1** A fatal accident or illness causes someone's death.
2 A fatal action has bad results: *a fatal mistake that lost the match.*

fatality fatalities
NOUN a death caused by accident or violence.

a b c d e f g h i j k l m n o p q r s t u v w x y z

Joke. How can you make a slow horse fast? Tie it up.

A B C D E F G H I J K L M N O P Q R S T U V W X Y Z

fate fates
NOUN **1** Some people believe that fate is a power which controls everything which happens.
2 Someone's fate is what happens to them. *The exact fate of the Titanic wasn't known until the 1980s.*

Synonyms: (sense 1) destiny, providence

father fathers
NOUN **1** a male parent.
2 "Father" is used to address a priest in some Christian churches.
fatherly ADJECTIVE

father-in-law fathers-in-law
NOUN A person's father-in-law is the father of their husband or wife.

fathom fathoms fathoming fathomed
NOUN **1** a unit for measuring the depth of water. It is equal to about 1·83 metres.
VERB **2** to understand something after careful thought. *Fiona fathomed out the code.*

fatigue fatigues fatiguing fatigued
Said "fat-**eeg**" NOUN **1** extreme tiredness.
VERB **2** If you are fatigued by something, it makes you extremely tired.

fatten fattens fattening fattened
VERB If you fatten animals, you feed them so that they put on weight.

fatty
ADJECTIVE Fatty foods contain a high proportion of fat.

fault faults faulting faulted
NOUN **1** If something which has gone wrong is your fault, you are to blame for it.
2 a weakness or imperfection in someone or something.
VERB **3** If you cannot fault someone or something, you cannot find any reason to criticize them.

faulty
ADJECTIVE not working properly.

Antonym: faultless

favour favours favouring favoured
NOUN **1** If you do someone a favour, you do something which helps them.
2 If you regard someone with favour, you like or support them.
PHRASE **3** If you are **in favour** of something, you agree with it and think it should happen.
4 Something that is **in your favour** is a help or advantage to you.
VERB **5** to prefer. *Some people favour white bread, others brown.*

favourable
ADJECTIVE Something which is favourable helps or benefits you in some way.
favourably ADVERB

favourite favourites
NOUN **1** the person or thing you like best.
2 the animal or person expected to win in a race or contest.
favourite ADJECTIVE

favouritism
NOUN behaviour in which you are unfairly more helpful or more generous to one person than to other people.

fawn fawns
NOUN OR ADJECTIVE **1** pale yellowish-brown.
NOUN **2** a very young deer.

fax faxes faxing faxed
NOUN **1** a machine that sends and receives documents electronically along a telephone line.
2 a copy of a document sent electronically along a telephone line.
VERB **3** to send a document electronically along a telephone line.

fear fears fearing feared
NOUN **1** a feeling of being afraid.
VERB **2** to be afraid of someone or something.
3 If you fear something bad will happen, you are worried that it will happen.

Synonyms: (sense 1) dread, fright, terror

fearful
ADJECTIVE **1** afraid and full of fear.
2 extremely unpleasant or worrying: *a fearful mess*.
fearfully ADVERB

fearless
ADJECTIVE brave and showing no fear.
fearlessly ADVERB

fearsome
ADJECTIVE terrible or frightening.

feasible
ADJECTIVE If something is feasible, it can be done.
feasibility NOUN

feast feasts
NOUN a large and special meal for many people.

feat feats
NOUN an impressive and difficult achievement.

feather feathers
NOUN A bird's feathers are the light soft things covering its body.

feature features featuring featured
NOUN **1** a specially interesting or important part of something.
2 Your features are your eyes, nose, mouth and other parts of your face.
3 an article in a magazine or television programme on a particular subject.
VERB **4** to include, emphasize or show. *The new series features top stars.*

 ► Finish these proverbs. Birds of a feather flock...? The early bird catches...? A bird in the hand...?

February
NOUN the second month of the year.
[from *Februa*, a Roman festival of purification]

fed
the past tense of **feed**.

federal
ADJECTIVE relating to a system of government in which a group of states is controlled by a central government, but each state has its own local powers. *The United States of America is a federal country.*

fed up
ADJECTIVE; INFORMAL unhappy or bored.

fee fees
NOUN a charge or payment for a job, service or activity.

feeble feebler feeblest
ADJECTIVE weak or lacking in power or influence.
feebly ADVERB **feebleness** NOUN

feed feeds feeding fed
VERB **1** to give food to a human or other animal.
2 When a human baby or other animal feeds, it eats.
3 If you feed something into a container or machine, you put it there in a slow, careful way.
NOUN **4** Feed is food for animals other than humans.

feedback
NOUN comments and information about the quality or success of something.

feel feels feeling felt
VERB **1** to experience an emotion or sensation.
2 to touch something carefully.
3 If you talk about how something feels, you are describing the emotions and sensations connected with it.
4 to think. *I feel we should go.*
NOUN **5** The feel of something is how it feels to you when you touch it.
PHRASE **6** If you **feel like** doing something, you want to do it.

feeler feelers
NOUN an insect's antennae.

feeling feelings
NOUN **1** an emotion.
2 a physical sensation.
3 Your feelings about something are your general attitudes or thoughts about it.

feet
the plural of **foot**.

feline
Said "**fee**-line" ADJECTIVE belonging or relating to the cat family.

fell fells felling felled
1 the past tense of **fall**.
VERB **2** To fell a tree is to cut it down.

fellow fellows
NOUN **1** OLD-FASHIONED a man.
ADJECTIVE **2** You use "fellow" to describe people who have something in common with you. *He needed the help of his fellow teachers.*

felt
1 the past tense and past participle of **feel**.
NOUN **2** a thick cloth made by pressing short threads together.

female females
NOUN **1** an animal, including a human, that belongs to the sex that can have babies or young.
ADJECTIVE **2** concerning or relating to females.

Antonym: male

feminine
ADJECTIVE **1** relating to women.
2 considered to be typical of women.
ADJECTIVE OR NOUN **3** in the grammar of some languages, a gender of nouns associated with the female sex.
femininity NOUN

Antonym: masculine

WHAT IS THE FEMININE?
Feminine nouns denote female humans and other animals:
The girl put on her coat – girl is feminine.
It is customary to refer to countries and vehicles as if they were feminine:
The ship came into view, her sails swelling in the breeze.
Also look at the grammar boxes at gender, masculine and neuter.

feminism
NOUN the belief that women should have the same rights and opportunities as men.
feminist NOUN

fen fens
NOUN an area of low, flat marshy land.

fence fences fencing fenced
NOUN **1** a wooden or wire barrier between two areas of land.
VERB **2** When two people fence, they fight each other as a sport using special non-harmful swords.
fencing NOUN

fend fends fending fended
VERB **1** If you fend off an attack or unwelcome questions or attention, you defend and protect yourself.
PHRASE **2** If you have to **fend for yourself**, you have to look after yourself.

a b c d e f g h i j k l m n o p q r s t u v w x y z

The word "February" is often misspelt. What mistake do you think people usually make?

ferment **ferments fermenting fermented**
VERB When wine, beer or fruit ferments, a chemical change takes place in it, often producing alcohol.
fermentation NOUN

fern **ferns**
NOUN a plant with long feathery leaves and no flowers.

ferocious
ADJECTIVE violent and fierce: *ferocious dogs; ferocious storms.*
ferociously ADVERB **ferocity** NOUN
[from Latin *ferox* meaning like a wild animal]

ferret **ferrets**
NOUN a small fierce animal related to the weasel.

ferry **ferries ferrying ferried**
NOUN **1** a boat that carries people and vehicles across short stretches of water.
VERB **2** To ferry people or goods somewhere is to transport them back and forth on a short journey.

fertile
ADJECTIVE **1** Fertile land is capable of producing strong, healthy plants.
2 creative: *a fertile imagination.*
3 able to have babies.
fertility NOUN

fertilize **fertilizes fertilizing fertilized**; also spelt **fertilise**
VERB **1** When a female animal or an egg is fertilized, the male sperm joins with the female egg. In plants, the male pollen fertilizes the female part of the plant.
2 To fertilize land is to put manure or chemicals onto it to feed the plants growing there.
fertilization NOUN

fertilizer **fertilizers**; also spelt **fertiliser**
NOUN a substance put onto soil to improve plant growth.

fervent
ADJECTIVE showing strong, sincere and enthusiastic feeling.
fervently ADVERB

festival **festivals**
NOUN **1** an organized series of events and performances.
2 a day or period of religious celebration.

festive
ADJECTIVE full of happiness and celebration.
festivity NOUN

fetch **fetches fetching fetched**
VERB **1** to go to where something is and bring it back.
2 If something fetches a particular sum of money, it is sold for that amount.

fete **fetes**
*Rhymes with "***date***"* NOUN an outdoor event with competitions, displays and goods for sale.

feud **feuds feuding feuded**
Said "**fyood**" NOUN **1** a long-term and very bitter quarrel, especially between families.
VERB **2** to take part in a feud.

feudal
ADJECTIVE relating to the social and political system that existed in Europe in the Middle Ages, when lords ruled over the ordinary people who lived and worked on their land.
feudalism NOUN

fever **fevers**
NOUN **1** a high body temperature due to illness.
2 a fever is a state of extreme agitation: *a fever of excitement.*

feverish
ADJECTIVE **1** in a state of extreme excitement or agitation.
2 suffering from a high body temperature.
feverishly ADVERB

few **fewer fewest**
ADJECTIVE OR NOUN **1** Few is used to refer to a small number of things or people: *a few moments ago. Sara had few friends.*
PHRASE **2** **Quite a few** or **a good few** means quite a large number of things or people.
✔ Use *fewer* for amounts that can be counted, such as: *fewer than five visits.* For amounts that can't be counted, use *less.*

fiancé **fiancés**
Said "fee-**on**-say" NOUN The man to whom a woman is engaged.

fiancée **fiancées**
NOUN The woman to whom a man is engaged.

fiasco **fiascos**
Said "fee-**ass**-koh" NOUN If an event is a fiasco, it goes disastrously wrong, especially in a ludicrous, disorganized way.

fib **fibs fibbing fibbed**
NOUN **1** a small, insignificant lie.
VERB **2** to tell a small lie.
fibber NOUN

fibre **fibres**
NOUN **1** a thin thread of a substance used to make cloth.
2 the part of plants that can be eaten but not digested; it helps food pass quickly through the body.
fibrous ADJECTIVE

fickle
ADJECTIVE A fickle person keeps changing their mind about who or what they like or want.

fiction
NOUN Fiction is stories about imaginary people and events.
fictional ADJECTIVE

Antonym: non-fiction

 ► Ancient proverb: few words are best.

fiddle **fiddles fiddling fiddled**
VERB **1** If you fiddle with something, you keep moving it or touching it restlessly.
2 INFORMAL to swindle, or change something dishonestly for your own profit.
NOUN **3** INFORMAL a dishonest action or scheme to get money.
4 a violin.
fiddler NOUN

fiddly **fiddlier fiddliest**
ADJECTIVE small and difficult to do or use.

fidelity
NOUN being faithful.

fidget **fidgets fidgeting fidgeted**
VERB **1** to keep changing your position because of nervousness or boredom.
NOUN **2** someone who fidgets.
fidgety ADJECTIVE

field **fields fielding fielded**
NOUN **1** an area of land where crops are grown or animals are kept.
2 an area of land where sports are played.
3 an area where particular rocks or minerals are to be found.
4 a particular subject or area of interest: *the field of 16th-century pottery.*
VERB **5** To field in cricket is to stop and return the ball after the batsman has hit it.
6 To field questions is to deal with them quickly and skilfully.
fielder NOUN

fiend **fiends**
*Said "***feend***"* NOUN **1** a devil or evil spirit.
2 a very wicked or cruel person.

fierce **fiercer fiercest**
ADJECTIVE **1** very aggressive: *a fierce lion.*
2 strong or intense: *a fierce pain.*

fiery
ADJECTIVE **1** involving fire or seeming like fire: *a fiery colour.*
2 showing great anger, energy or passion: *a fiery debate.*

fifteen
the number 15.
fifteenth

fifth **fifths**
1 The fifth item in a series is the one counted as number five.
2 A fifth is one of five equal parts.

fifty **fifties**
the number 50.
fiftieth

fifty-fifty
ADVERB **1** divided equally into two portions.
ADJECTIVE **2** If something has a fifty-fifty chance of happening, it is just as likely not to happen as to happen.

fig **figs**
NOUN a soft, sweet fruit full of tiny seeds which is often eaten dried.

fight **fights fighting fought**
VERB **1** to take part in a battle or a boxing match, or in some other attempt to hurt or kill someone.
2 to try in a determined way to prevent something or to achieve something: *a fight for freedom.*
NOUN **3** a situation in which people hit or try to hurt each other.
4 a determined attempt to prevent or achieve something.

Synonyms: battle, struggle

figurative
ADJECTIVE If you use a word or expression in a figurative sense, you use it with a more abstract or imaginative meaning than its ordinary one. *He was built like a house.*
figuratively ADVERB

figure **figures figuring figured**
NOUN **1** a written number or the amount a number stands for.
2 the shape of a person.
3 a person. *He was a major figure in the trial.*
VERB **4** To figure in something is to appear in it or be included in it. *Sammy figured in the painting.*
5 INFORMAL If you figure something is the case, you guess that it is so. *I figured she really liked me.*

figure of speech **figures of speech**
NOUN an expression such as a simile or idiom in which the words are not used in their literal sense. *It's raining cats and dogs.*

filament **filaments**
NOUN on a flower, the slender part of a stamen that supports the anther.

file **files filing filed**
NOUN **1** a box or folder in which documents are kept; also used of the information kept in the file.
2 In computing, a file is a set of related data with its own name.
3 a tool with rough surfaces, used for smoothing and shaping hard materials.
VERB **4** to put a document or computer data in its correct place with similar documents.
5 to file, or to go in single file, is to walk one behind the other in a line.
6 to smooth or shape something with a file.

fill **fills filling filled**
VERB **1** If you fill something or if it fills up, it becomes full and no more can fit in.
2 If something fills a need, it satisfies that need.
NOUN **3** If you have had your fill of something, you don't want any more of it.
fill in VERB **1** to write information in the spaces of a form, coupon, etc.
2 If you fill someone in, you bring them up to date with the latest information.

a b c d e f g h i j k l m n o p q r s t u v w x y z

Notice the spelling of these ordinal numbers: fifth, eighth, ninth, twelfth, twentieth, hundredth.

fillet fillets filleting filleted
NOUN **1** a strip of tender meat or fish without any bones.
VERB **2** to prepare meat or fish by cutting out the bones.

filling fillings
NOUN **1** a small amount of metal or plastic put into a hole in a tooth by a dentist.
2 the soft food mixture inside a sandwich, cake or pie.

film films filming filmed
NOUN **1** a series of moving pictures usually shown in a cinema, on television or on video.
2 a strip of specially treated thin plastic used in a camera to take photographs.
3 a very thin layer of powder or liquid.
VERB **4** to use a film or video camera.

filter filters filtering filtered
NOUN **1** a device that allows some substances, lights or sounds to pass through it, but not others.
VERB **2** to pass a substance through a filter.
3 If something filters somewhere, it gets there slowly or faintly. *Traffic filtered into the city. Light filtered through the curtains.*
filtration NOUN

filth
ADJECTIVE disgusting dirt and muck.
filthy ADJECTIVE

fin fins
NOUN a thin, flat structure on the body of a fish, used to help guide it through the water.

final
ADJECTIVE **1** last.
2 A decision that is final cannot be changed or questioned.
NOUN **3** the last game or contest in a series, which decides the overall winner.

finale finales
Said "fin-**ah**-lay" NOUN the last act of a piece of music or show.

finalist finalists
NOUN a person taking part in the final of a competition.

finally
ADVERB **1** If something finally happens, it happens after a long delay.
2 You use "finally" to introduce a final point or topic.

Synonyms: (sense 1) at last, eventually
(sense 2) in conclusion, lastly

finance finances financing financed
VERB **1** To finance a project or purchase is to provide the money to pay for it.
NOUN **2** money or loans used to pay for something.
3 the management of money, loans and investments.
financial ADJECTIVE

find finds finding found
VERB **1** to discover, either after a deliberate search or by accident.
2 to obtain something. *I must find a pen.*
3 to become aware of a situation. *She found he had gone.*
4 to think or feel about something in a certain way. *I found the book very interesting.*
5 to live or exist in a certain place. *Elephants are found in Africa.*
6 to form an opinion about someone. *I found him very funny.*
find out VERB to learn or discover something.
finder NOUN

fine finer finest; fines fining fined
ADJECTIVE **1** very good: *a fine theatre.*
2 satisfactory or acceptable. *Your exam grade was fine.*
3 feeling well and quite happy. *I'm fine.*
4 sunny and not raining.
5 very delicate, narrow or small: *a fine strand of hair.*
NOUN **6** a sum of money paid as a punishment.
VERB **7** Someone who is fined has to pay a sum of money as a punishment.
finely ADVERB

finger fingers fingering fingered
NOUN **1** Your fingers are the four long jointed parts at the end of your hands.
VERB **2** to finger something is to feel it with your fingers.

fingernail fingernails
NOUN one of the hard coverings at the ends of your fingers.

fingerprint fingerprints
NOUN Your fingerprints are the unique marks made by the tip of your fingers when you touch something.

finish finishes finishing finished
VERB **1** to finish something is to complete it.
2 if an event finishes, it ends.
NOUN **3** the last part of something. *The match had an exciting finish.*

fir firs
NOUN a tall, pointed, evergreen tree that has thin needle-like leaves and produces cones.

fire fires firing fired
NOUN **1** the flames produced when something burns.
2 a mass of burning material.
3 a device that uses electricity or gas to heat a room.
VERB **4** to operate a gun so that a bullet is released.
5 INFORMAL to dismiss or sack someone from a job.
PHRASE **6** If something is **on fire**, it is burning.
7 If you **set fire** to something, you start it burning.
8 If someone **opens fire**, they start shooting.

 ► Film words: camera, action, pan, zoom, credits, cut, editing, rushes, shot, sequence.

firearm firearms
NOUN a gun.

fire brigade fire brigades
NOUN an organization which has the job of putting out fires.

fire drill fire drills
NOUN a practice of what to do if there is a fire in the building.

fire engine fire engines
NOUN a large vehicle that carries equipment for putting out fires.

fire escape fire escapes
NOUN an emergency exit or staircase for use if there is a fire.

fire extinguisher fire extinguishers
NOUN a metal cylinder containing water or foam for spraying onto a fire.

firefighter firefighters
NOUN a person whose job is to put out fires.

fireplace fireplaces
NOUN the opening beneath a chimney where a fire can be lit.

fireproof
ADJECTIVE resistant to fire.

fire station fire stations
NOUN a building where fire engines are kept and where firefighters wait to be called out.

firework fireworks
NOUN an object which produces coloured sparks, smoke or loud bangs when lit.

firm firmer firmest; firms
ADJECTIVE **1** Something that is firm is fairly hard and does not change shape very much when it is pressed.
2 A firm grasp or push is one which is strong or controlled.
3 Someone who is firm behaves in a fairly strict way and will not change their mind.
NOUN **4** a business that sells or produces something.
firmly ADVERB **firmness** NOUN

first
ADJECTIVE OR ADVERB **1** before all others: *first in line.*
ADJECTIVE **2** more important than anything else: *first prize.*
ADVERB **3** for the first time. *The couple first met in 1996.*
PHRASE **4** **At first** refers to what happens at the beginning of something.
firstly ADVERB

Antonym: (sense 1) last

first aid
NOUN emergency medical treatment given to an injured person.
first aider NOUN

first class
ADJECTIVE of the highest quality or standard.

first person
NOUN In English grammar, the first person is the form of the pronoun or the verb that goes with "I" or "we".

THE FIRST PERSON
If a book or account is written in the first person, it is written as though the author is speaking directly to the reader:
I did this...
I said that...

fish fishes fishing fished
NOUN **1** a creature with a tail and fins that lives in water.
2 the flesh of a fish eaten as food.
VERB **3** to try to catch fish.
✔ The plural of *fish* is usually *fish*, but *fishes* is also acceptable.
fishing NOUN

fisherman fishermen
NOUN a person whose job is to catch fish, or who catches fish for sport.

fishmonger fishmongers
NOUN a shopkeeper who sells fish; also the shop itself.

fishy fishier fishiest
ADJECTIVE **1** smelling of fish.
2 INFORMAL suspicious or doubtful. *Something fishy was going on.*

fist fists
NOUN a hand with the fingers curled tightly towards the palm.

fit fits fitting fitted; fitter fittest
VERB **1** If something fits, it is the right shape or size for a particular person or position.
2 If you fit something somewhere, you put it in position there.
NOUN **3** If someone has a fit, they lose consciousness and their body makes uncontrollable movements.
4 a sudden uncontrolled outburst of laughter, coughing, rage, panic, etc.
ADJECTIVE **5** good enough or suitable. *She was fit for the job.*
6 healthy and physically strong.

Synonyms: (sense 1) match, suit
(sense 3) convulsion, seizure

fitness
NOUN the state of being fit.

fitting fittings
ADJECTIVE **1** right or suitable: *a fitting reward.*
NOUN **2** a small part that is attached to a piece of equipment or furniture. *Where's the fitting for the bicycle pump?*
3 If you have a fitting, you try on a garment that is being made to see if it fits you properly.

five fives
the number 5.

a b c d e f g h i j k l m n o p q r s t u v w x y z

First person: I/we said...; second person: you said...; third person: he/she/it/they said...

A B C D E F G H I J K L M N O P Q R S T U V W X Y Z

fix fixes fixing fixed
VERB **1** to attach something securely to something else.
2 to repair something that is broken.
3 to decide on something and arrange it. *We fixed a date for the wedding.*
4 INFORMAL To fix something is to arrange the outcome unfairly or dishonestly. *The match was fixed.*
PHRASE **5** If you are **in a fix** you are in a difficult situation.

Synonyms: (sense 2) mend, repair

fixture fixtures
NOUN a sports event due to take place on a particular date.

fizz fizzes fizzing fizzed
VERB Something that fizzes makes a hissing sound, often accompanied by bubbles.

fizzle fizzles fizzling fizzled
VERB Something that fizzles makes a weak hissing or spitting sound.

fizzy fizzier fizziest
ADJECTIVE Fizzy drinks have bubbles containing carbon dioxide in them.

flabbergasted
ADJECTIVE extremely surprised.

flabby flabbier flabbiest
ADJECTIVE Someone who is flabby is rather fat and unfit, with loose flesh around the body.
flab NOUN **flabbiness** NOUN

flag flags
NOUN a piece of coloured cloth, used as the symbol of a country or as a signal.

flake flakes
NOUN a tiny, thin bit of something.

flame flames
NOUN a hot bright stream of burning gas that comes from something which is very hot.

flamingo flamingos or flamingoes
NOUN a long-legged wading bird with pink feathers and a long neck.

flammable
ADJECTIVE likely to catch fire and burn easily.
✔ *Inflammable* has the same meaning, but *flammable* is used more often.

Antonym: non-flammable

flan flans
NOUN an open sweet or savoury tart with a pastry or cake base.

flank flanks
NOUN the side of an animal between the ribs and the hip.

flannel flannels
NOUN **1** a lightweight woollen fabric.
2 a small square of towelling, used for washing yourself.
3 INFORMAL Flannel is also long-winded or evasive talk.

flap flaps flapping flapped
VERB **1** to move quickly up and down or from side to side, as a bird moves its wings.
2 to become agitated or flustered. *The chef burnt the beef and started to flap.*
NOUN **3** a loose piece of something such as cloth or paper that is attached at one edge.

flare flares flaring flared
NOUN **1** a device that produces a brightly coloured flame, used especially as an emergency signal.
VERB **2** If a fire flares, it suddenly burns much more vigorously.
3 If violence or a conflict flares or flares up, it suddenly starts or becomes more serious.

flash flashes flashing flashed
NOUN **1** a sudden short burst of light.
VERB **2** to shine suddenly and briefly.
3 If something flashes past, it moves or happens very quickly.
4 to show something briefly. *He flashed his identity card at the doorman.*

flashback flashbacks
NOUN a scene in a film, play, or book that returns to events in the past.

flashlight flashlights
NOUN a large, powerful torch.

flashy flashier flashiest
ADJECTIVE expensive and fashionable in appearance, in a vulgar way.

flask flasks
NOUN **1** an insulated bottle used for carrying hot or cold drinks around with you.
2 a long-necked glass bottle with a bowl-shaped base, used in laboratories.

flat flatter flattest; flats
ADJECTIVE **1** level and smooth, and usually not very tall or deep.
2 A flat tyre or ball has not got enough air in it.
3 A flat battery has lost its power.
NOUN **4** a set of rooms for living in, on a single floor of a larger building.
ADVERB **5** a time such as "five minutes flat" means exactly five minutes.

Synonyms: (sense 1) even, level

flatten flattens flattening flattened
VERB to make or become flat or flatter.

flatter flatters flattering flattered
VERB **1** to praise someone in an exaggerated way, either to please them or to persuade them to do something.
2 If you flatter yourself, you believe, perhaps mistakenly, something good about yourself or your abilities.
3 Something that flatters you makes you appear more attractive.
flattery NOUN **flatterer** NOUN
flattering ADJECTIVE

Synonyms: (sense 1) butter up, praise

 ► A prefix is added at the start of a root word, and a suffix at the end.

flaunt **flaunts flaunting flaunted**
VERB If you flaunt your possessions or talents, you display them too obviously or proudly.

flavour **flavours flavouring flavoured**
NOUN **1** the taste of food.
2 the flavour of something is its distinctive characteristic or quality. *The day out had a real flavour of excitement.*
VERB **3** to add something to food in order to give it a particular taste.
flavoured ADJECTIVE **flavouring** NOUN

flaw **flaws**
NOUN a fault, error or weakness lying deep within something. *The pattern on the cup had a flaw. The flaw in John's character was selfishness.*
flawed ADJECTIVE **flawless** ADJECTIVE

flax
NOUN Flax is a plant used for making rope and cloth.

flea **fleas**
NOUN a small, wingless, jumping insect which feeds on blood.

fledgling **fledglings**
NOUN a young bird that is learning to fly.

flee **flees fleeing fled**
VERB to run away from a place or from danger.

Synonym: escape

fleece **fleeces fleecing fleeced**
NOUN **1** a sheep's coat of wool.
VERB **2** INFORMAL To fleece someone is to overcharge or swindle them.
fleecy ADJECTIVE

fleet **fleets**
NOUN a group of ships or vehicles owned by the same organization or travelling together.

fleeting
ADJECTIVE lasting for a very short time: *a fleeting glimpse.*

flesh
NOUN the soft part of your body between the bones and the skin.
fleshy ADJECTIVE

flew
the past tense of **fly**.

flex **flexes flexing flexed**
NOUN **1** a length of covered wire which carries electricity to an appliance.
VERB **2** If you flex your muscles, you bend and stretch them.

flexible
ADJECTIVE **1** able to be bent easily without breaking.
2 able to adapt easily to changing circumstances.
flexibility NOUN

flick **flicks flicking flicked**
VERB **1** If you flick something, you move it sharply with your finger.
NOUN **2** a sudden quick movement: *a flick of the head.*

flicker **flickers flickering flickered**
VERB **1** If a light or a flame flickers, it shines and moves unsteadily.
NOUN **2** a short unsteady light or movement of light.
3 A flicker of a feeling is a very brief experience of it.

flies
the plural of **fly**.

flight **flights**
NOUN **1** the action of flying or the ability to fly.
2 a journey made by aeroplane.
3 the act of running away.
4 A flight of stairs or steps is a row of them.

flight attendant **flight attendants**
NOUN a person who looks after passengers on an aircraft.

flimsy **flimsier flimsiest**
ADJECTIVE **1** made of something very thin or weak and not providing much protection.
2 Flimsy evidence is not very convincing.

flinch **flinches flinching flinched**
VERB to make a sudden small movement in fear or pain.

fling **flings flinging flung**
VERB to throw something using a lot of force.

flint **flints**
NOUN a hard greyish-black mineral found in some rocks, which produces a spark when struck against steel.

flip **flips flipping flipped**
VERB **1** to turn something over quickly and sharply.
2 to hit something sharply with your finger or thumb.
3 INFORMAL If someone flips, they suddenly become very angry or upset.

flippant
ADJECTIVE showing an inappropriate lack of seriousness.
flippantly ADVERB **flippancy** NOUN

flipper **flippers**
NOUN **1** one of the broad, flat limbs of sea animals, for example seals or penguins, used for swimming.
2 Flippers are broad, flat pieces of rubber which divers attach to their feet to help them swim.

flirt **flirts flirting flirted**
VERB **1** If you flirt with someone, you behave as if you are sexually attracted to them, but without serious intentions.
2 If you flirt with an idea, you consider it without seriously intending to do anything about it.
3 If you flirt with danger, you run a risk.
NOUN **4** someone who often flirts with people.
flirtation NOUN **flirtatious** ADJECTIVE

a b c d e f g h i j k l m n o p q r s t u v w x y z

Find words to complete these phrases: a fleet of...; a litter of...; a shoal of...?

A B C D E F G H I J K L M N O P Q R S T U V W X Y Z

flit **flits flitting flitted**
VERB to fly or move somewhere with quick light movements.

float **floats floating floated**
VERB **1** to lie on or just below the surface of a liquid.
2 to hang in the air or move slowly through it.
NOUN **3** a light object that helps something or someone to float in water.

flock **flocks flocking flocked**
NOUN **1** a group of birds, sheep or goats.
VERB **2** If people flock somewhere, they go there in large numbers.

flog **flogs flogging flogged**
VERB **1** to beat someone with a whip or stick.
2 INFORMAL to sell something.
flogging NOUN

flood **floods flooding flooded**
NOUN **1** If there is a flood, a large amount of water covers an area that is usually dry.
2 A flood of something is a large amount of it occurring suddenly. *The television programme generated a flood of complaints.*
VERB **3** to cover or to be covered with water. *The river burst its banks and flooded the town centre.*
4 to move somewhere in large uncontrolled groups. *Pop fans flooded to the concert.*

Synonyms: (sense 1) deluge, torrent
(sense 2) stream, torrent

floodlight **floodlights**
NOUN a very powerful outdoor lamp used to light up public buildings and sports grounds.
floodlit ADJECTIVE

floor **floors**
NOUN **1** the part of a room that you walk on.
2 one of the levels in a building.
3 the ground at the bottom of a valley or ocean.

floorboard **floorboards**
NOUN one of the long planks of wood from which a floor is made.

flop **flops flopping flopped**
VERB **1** to fall loosely and rather heavily.
2 INFORMAL to fail. *The show was a flop.*
NOUN **3** INFORMAL a flop is something that is completely unsuccessful.

floppy **floppier floppiest**
ADJECTIVE tending to hang downwards in a rather loose way.

floppy disk **floppy disks**
NOUN a small disk of magnetic material on which computer data is stored.

floral
ADJECTIVE made from flowers or patterned with flowers.

florist **florists**
NOUN a shopkeeper who sells flowers; also the shop itself.

floss
NOUN Dental floss is soft, silky threads or fibre which you use to clean between your teeth.
floss VERB

flounder **flounders floundering floundered**
VERB **1** to struggle to move or stay upright, for example in water or mud.
2 If you flounder in a conversation or situation, you find it difficult to decide what to say or do.

flour
NOUN a white or brown powder made by grinding grain, and used in bread, cakes and pastry.

flourish **flourishes flourishing flourished**
VERB **1** to develop or function successfully or healthily.
2 to wave or display something so that people notice it. *To stop the taxi she flourished her umbrella.*
NOUN **3** a bold sweeping or waving movement.

flow **flows flowing flowed**
VERB **1** to move in a steady and continuous manner.
NOUN **2** a steady continuous movement: *a flow of water; a flow of traffic.*

flow chart **flow charts**
NOUN a diagram showing how certain steps and choices lead to various results and actions.

flower **flowers flowering flowered**
NOUN **1** the blossoms or blossoms on a plant. Some flowers are brightly coloured or perfumed.
2 the part of a plant found at the end of the stem that contains stamens and carpels, the male and female parts of the plant.
VERB **3** When a plant flowers, it produces flowers.

flown
the past participle of **fly**.

flu
NOUN an illness similar to a bad cold, but more serious. Flu is short for influenza.

fluctuate **fluctuates fluctuating fluctuated**
VERB to change constantly and unpredictably.
fluctuation NOUN

flue **flues**
NOUN a pipe which takes fumes and smoke away from a stove or boiler.

fluent
ADJECTIVE Someone who is fluent in a foreign language can speak it correctly and without hesitation.
fluency NOUN

 ► Pun. Why did a mother advise her boys to call their cattle ranch *Focus*? ►

fluff **fluffs fluffing fluffed**
NOUN 1 soft, light, woolly threads or fibres bunched together.
VERB 2 If you fluff something up or out, you brush or shake it to make it seem larger and lighter.
3 INFORMAL If you fluff your words while acting in a play, you forget them or get them wrong.

fluffy **fluffier fluffiest**
ADJECTIVE 1 covered with fluff.
2 soft and light.

fluid **fluids**
NOUN 1 a liquid.
ADJECTIVE 2 smooth and flowing.
fluidity NOUN

fluke **flukes**
NOUN an accidental success or piece of good luck.
fluky ADJECTIVE

flung
the past tense of **fling**.

fluorescent
Said "floo-er-**ess**-nt" **ADJECTIVE 1** A fluorescent colour or object appears to be brighter when another light is shone onto it, because it gives out its own light.
2 A fluorescent light is in the form of a tube and shines with a hard bright light.
fluorescence NOUN

fluoride
NOUN a chemical compound containing fluorine often added to toothpaste and water supplies to help prevent tooth decay.

flush **flushes flushing flushed**
VERB 1 If you flush, your face goes red.
2 If you flush a toilet, you force water through it to clean it.
NOUN 3 In cards, a flush is a hand all of one suit.
ADJECTIVE 4 Something that is flush with a surface is level with it or flat against it.
5 INFORMAL Someone who is flush has plenty of money.

flustered
ADJECTIVE confused, nervous and rushed.

flute **flutes**
NOUN a musical wind instrument which you hold sideways to your mouth.
flautist NOUN

flutter **flutters fluttering fluttered**
VERB 1 to flap or wave with small, quick movements.
NOUN 2 If you are in a flutter, you are excited and nervous.
3 INFORMAL If you have a flutter, you have a small bet.

fly **flies flying flew flown**
NOUN 1 an insect with two wings.
2 The front opening on a pair of trousers is called the fly or the flies.
VERB 3 When a bird, insect or aircraft flies, it moves through the air.
4 to travel in or control an aircraft.
5 to move very quickly. *She flew downstairs and opened the door.*
flying ADJECTIVE OR NOUN **flyer** NOUN

flying saucer **flying saucers**
NOUN a large disc-shaped spacecraft which some people claim to have seen, a UFO.

flyover **flyovers**
NOUN a structure carrying one road over another at a junction or intersection.

foal **foals foaling foaled**
NOUN 1 a young horse.
VERB 2 When a female horse foals, she gives birth.

foam **foams foaming foamed**
NOUN 1 a mass of tiny bubbles.
2 light spongy material used, for example, in furniture or packaging.
VERB 3 When something foams, it forms a mass of small bubbles.

focus **focuses** or **focusses focusing** or **focussing focused** or **focussed; focuses**
VERB 1 to adjust your eyes or a camera so that an image is clear.
2 to concentrate on something.
NOUN 3 a point upon which attention or an activity is directed: *the focus of the conversation.*
PHRASE 4 If an image is **in focus**, the edges of the image are clear and sharp. If it is **out of focus**, the edges are blurred.
[from Latin *focus* meaning hearth. The hearth was seen as the centre of a Roman home]

fodder
NOUN food for farm animals or horses.

foe **foes**
NOUN an enemy.

foetus **foetuses**; also spelt **fetus**
Said "**fee**-tus" **NOUN** an unborn child or animal in the womb.

fog
NOUN a thick mist caused by tiny drops of water in the air.
foggy ADJECTIVE

foil **foils foiling foiled**
VERB 1 If you foil someone's attempt at something, you prevent it from succeeding.
NOUN 2 thin, paper-like sheets of metal used to wrap food.

fold **folds folding folded**
VERB 1 If you fold something such as paper, you bend it so that one part lies over another.
NOUN 2 a crease or bend in paper or cloth.

folder **folders**
NOUN 1 a thin piece of folded cardboard used for keeping papers together.
2 in some computer software, folders are directories or sub-directories where individual data files are stored.

A B C D E F G H I J K L M N O P Q R S T U V W X Y Z

foliage
NOUN a general word for leaves and plants.

folk folks
NOUN 1 people.
ADJECTIVE 2 Folk music and folk art are traditional or typical of a particular people.

folklore
NOUN the traditional stories and beliefs of a community.

follow follows following followed
VERB 1 to move along behind someone or something.
2 to do what instructions, directions or advice say. *She followed the signpost.*
3 to happen afterwards: *in the days following his birthday.*
4 If something follows from something else, it is true as a result of it. *If she's got good marks, it follows that she must be fairly bright.*
5 to understand a story, conversation, etc. *Can you follow what the teacher's saying?*
6 to support a particular team, campaign, etc. *She follows the royal family with devotion.*

follower followers
NOUN The followers of a person or belief are the people that support them.

following
ADJECTIVE 1 coming afterwards or later.
NOUN 2 If a person or organization has a following, they have a group of supporters.

folly follies
NOUN a foolish act or foolish behaviour.

fond fonder fondest
ADJECTIVE If you are fond of someone or something, you like them.
fondly ADVERB

fondle fondles fondling fondled
VERB to stroke something affectionately.

font fonts
NOUN 1 one of the different styles of lettering available when you print out a document on a word processor.
2 a large stone bowl in a church that holds the water for baptisms.

food foods
NOUN Food is what humans and other animals eat.

food chain food chains
NOUN a series of organisms which feed on each other in turn: a mouse eats a berry and a fox eats a mouse.

fool fools fooling fooled
NOUN 1 someone who is not sensible and shows poor judgement.
VERB 2 If you fool someone, you deceive or trick them.

foolish
ADJECTIVE not sensible and showing poor judgement.
foolishly ADVERB **foolishness** NOUN

foolproof
ADJECTIVE so well designed or simple to use that it cannot fail.

foot feet
NOUN 1 the part of your body at the end of your leg.
2 the part of something that is farthest from the top: *the foot of the mountain.*
3 a unit of length equal to 12 inches or about 30·5 centimetres.
4 In poetry, a foot is the basic unit of rhythm containing two or three syllables.

football footballs
NOUN 1 any game in which the ball can be kicked, such as soccer, American football and Australian Rules.
2 a ball used in any of these games.
footballer NOUN

foothills
PLURAL NOUN hills at the base of a mountain.

foothold footholds
NOUN a place where you can put your foot when climbing. *His first job was a foothold on the ladder to success.*

footing footings
NOUN a secure grip by and for your feet.

footlights
PLURAL NOUN the lights pointing upwards from the front of a stage.

footnote footnotes
NOUN a note at the bottom of a page or an additional comment giving extra information.

footpath footpaths
NOUN a path for people to walk on.

footprint footprints
NOUN a mark left by a foot or shoe.

footstep footsteps
NOUN the sound made by someone's feet when they are walking.

for
PREPOSITION 1 meant to be given to or used by a particular person: *a table for two.*
2 "For" is used when explaining the reason, cause, or purpose of something. *This is my excuse for going to Italy.*
3 You use "for" to express a quantity, time or distance. *We talked for a couple of minutes.*
4 If you are for something, you support it or approve of it. *I'm all for it!*

forbid forbids forbidding forbade forbidden
VERB to give an order that something must not be done, to prohibit.
✔ *Forbade* is usually pronounced "for-**bad**".

 ► Punctuate this: the boy said the teacher is a fool. Can you do it to make it mean the opposite?

force forces forcing forced
VERB **1** to make someone do something against their will.
2 to use a lot of strength to move or open something.
NOUN **3** violence or great strength.
4 an organized group of people, especially soldiers, airmen or police.
5 Forces of a particular kind are processes or events that seem to be outside human control: *the forces of nature.*
6 Forces are pushes or pulls that make things start or stop moving, move faster or slower, change shape or direction.

Synonyms: (sense 1) compel, drive, make

forceps
PLURAL NOUN a pair of long tongs or tweezers.

forcible
ADJECTIVE using force.
forcibly ADVERB

ford fords fording forded
NOUN **1** a shallow place in a river where it is possible to cross on foot or in a vehicle.
VERB **2** To ford a river is to cross it on foot or in a vehicle.

forecast forecasts forecasting forecast or forecasted
NOUN **1** a prediction of what will happen.
VERB **2** to predict what will happen.

forefinger forefingers
NOUN the finger next to the thumb, also called the index finger.

foreground
NOUN In a picture, the foreground is the part that seems nearest to you.

forehead foreheads
NOUN the flat area at the front of your head above your eyes.

foreign
ADJECTIVE **1** belonging to or involving a country that is not your own.
2 unfamiliar or uncharacteristic. *A lot of our school work is completely foreign to my parents.*

foreigner foreigners
NOUN a person from another country.

foreman foremen
NOUN a person in charge of a group of workers, for example on a building site.

foremost
ADJECTIVE The foremost of a group of things is the most important or the best one.

forename forenames
NOUN a person's first name, sometimes called Christian name.

foresee foresees foreseeing foresaw foreseen
VERB to predict or expect that something will happen.
foreseeable ADJECTIVE

forest forests
NOUN a large area of trees growing close together.

forestry
NOUN the study and work of growing, maintaining and harvesting forests.

foretell foretells foretelling foretold
VERB to predict what will happen.

forever
ADVERB permanently or continually.

foreword forewords
NOUN an introduction in a book.

forfeit forfeits forfeiting forfeited
VERB If you forfeit something, you have to give it up as a penalty.
forfeit NOUN

forgave
the past tense of **forgive**.

forge forges forging forged
NOUN **1** a place where a blacksmith works making metal goods by hand.
VERB **2** Someone who forges money, documents or paintings makes illegal copies of them.
3 To forge metal is to hammer and bend it into shape while hot.
4 To forge a relationship is to create a strong and lasting relationship.
5 To forge ahead is to progress quickly.

forgery forgeries
NOUN the crime of forging money, documents or paintings; also something that has been forged.
forger NOUN

forget forgets forgetting forgot forgotten
VERB to fail to remember something.

forgetful
ADJECTIVE A forgetful person often forgets things.
forgetfully ADVERB **forgetfulness** NOUN

forgive forgives forgiving forgave forgiven
VERB If you forgive someone who has done something wrong, you stop being angry with them.

fork forks
NOUN **1** an implement with points used for eating food.
2 a tool with points used for gardening.
3 the place where a road divides into two roads forming a "Y" shape.

forlorn
ADJECTIVE **1** lonely, unhappy and uncared for.
2 desperate and without any expectation of success: *a forlorn attempt.*
forlornly ADVERB

Your surname is your family name, such as Smith; your forename is your personal name, such as John.

A B C D E F G H I J K L M N O P Q R S T U V W X Y Z

form **forms forming formed**
NOUN **1** The form of something is its shape.
2 a type or kind of something: *a new form of greeting.*
3 a sheet of paper with questions and spaces for you to fill in the answers.
4 In sport, a person's form refers to their ability or success over a period of time.
5 In school, a form is a class of pupils.
VERB **6** to make a particular shape.
7 The things that form something are the things it consists of. *Real events form the basis of the novel.*
8 to create, organize or start something.

formal
ADJECTIVE **1** Formal language or behaviour is correct and serious, rather than relaxed and friendly.
2 A formal action or event is an official one.
formally ADVERB

formality **formalities**
NOUN an action or process that is carried out as part of an official procedure.

format **formats formatting formatted**
NOUN **1** the way something is arranged and presented: *the format of the TV programme.*
VERB **2** to prepare a floppy disk for use, which erases all previous files.

formation **formations**
NOUN **1** the pattern or shape of something.
2 the start or creation of something.
formative ADJECTIVE

former
ADJECTIVE **1** Former is used to indicate what someone or something used to be, but no longer is. *She is a former tennis champion.*
NOUN **2** You use "the former" to refer to the first of two things that you have just mentioned. *If I had to choose between happiness and money, I would choose the former.*
formerly ADVERB

Antonym: (sense 2) latter

formidable
ADJECTIVE very difficult to deal with or overcome, and therefore rather frightening or impressive: *a formidable opponent.*
formidably ADVERB

formula **formulae** or **formulas**
NOUN **1** a group of letters, numbers or symbols which stand for a mathematical or scientific rule.
2 a list of quantities of substances that, when mixed, make another substance, for example in chemistry.
3 a plan for dealing with a particular problem: *a formula for success.*

forsake **forsakes forsaking forsook forsaken**
VERB To forsake someone or something is to give up or abandon them.

fort **forts**
NOUN **1** a strong building built for defence.
PHRASE **2** If you **hold the fort** for someone, you manage their affairs while they are away.

forth
ADVERB **1** FORMAL To go forth from a place means to leave it.
2 To bring something forth means to make it visible.

fortification **fortifications**
NOUN Fortifications are buildings, walls, and ditches used to protect a place.

fortify **fortifies fortifying fortified**
VERB **1** to strengthen somewhere against attack.
2 to make someone feel stronger, more determined or better prepared.

fortnight **fortnights**
NOUN a period of two weeks.

fortress **fortresses**
NOUN a castle or well-protected town built for defence.

fortunate
ADJECTIVE lucky.
fortunately ADVERB

fortune **fortunes**
NOUN **1** Fortune or good fortune is good luck.
2 a large amount of money. *The holiday cost them a fortune.*
3 The fortunes of someone are the extent to which they are successful or unsuccessful. *The film follows the fortunes of a boy and his dog.*
4 A fortune-teller is someone who predicts the future for people.

forty **forties**
the number 40.
fortieth

forward **forwards forwarding forwarded**
ADVERB OR ADJECTIVE **1** in the front or towards the front.
2 towards a future time.
VERB **3** If a letter is forwarded to someone, it is sent to them at their new address.
NOUN **4** In a game such as football or hockey, a forward is a player in an attacking position.

fossil **fossils**
NOUN **1** the remains or impression of an animal or plant from a previous age, preserved in rock.
2 Fossil fuels are fuels such as coal, oil and natural gas which have been formed from rotting animals and plants over millions of years.
fossilize VERB

foster **fosters fostering fostered**
VERB **1** If someone fosters a child, they look after the child for a period in their home, but do not become its legal parent.
ADJECTIVE **2** Foster parents are people who foster a child.
foster home NOUN

 ► Find out which creatures live in a: form, lodge, earth, holt, drey, byre, lair, burrow, eyrie?

fought
the past tense and past participle of **fight**.

foul **fouler foulest; fouls fouling fouled**
ADJECTIVE **1** very unpleasant.
VERB **2** To foul something is to make it dirty.
3 In sport, if a player fouls another player, they touch them in a way that breaks the rules.
NOUN **4** an action in sport that breaks the rules.

found **founds founding founded**
1 the past tense and past participle of **find**.
VERB **2** to create an organization or company.

foundation **foundations**
NOUN **1** the layer of solid material, such as concrete, below the ground on which a building is constructed.
2 the basis on which something is founded.

founder **founders foundering foundered**
NOUN **1** the person who sets up an institution or organization.
VERB **2** If a ship founders, it sinks.

foundry **foundries**
NOUN a factory where metal is melted and made into shapes.

fountain **fountains**
NOUN a jet of water forced into the air by a pump.

fountain pen **fountain pens**
NOUN a refillable pen with a nib supplied with ink from a container inside the pen.

four **fours**
1 the number 4.
PHRASE **2** If you are **on all fours**, you are on your hands and knees.

fourteen
the number 14.
fourteenth

fourth **fourths**
1 The fourth item in a series is the one counted as number four.
2 one of four equal parts, a quarter.
fourthly

fowl **fowls**
NOUN a bird such as chicken or duck that is kept or hunted for its meat or eggs.

fox **foxes foxing foxed**
NOUN **1** a wild animal similar to a dog, with reddish-brown fur and a thick tail.
VERB **2** If something foxes you, it puzzles or baffles you.

foyer **foyers**
Said "**foy**-ay" NOUN a large open area just inside the main doors of a cinema, hotel or public building.

fraction **fractions**
NOUN **1** In arithmetic, a fraction is a part of a whole number.
2 a tiny proportion or amount of something. *She hesitated for a fraction of a second.*
fractional ADJECTIVE **fractionally** ADVERB

fracture **fractures fracturing fractured**
VERB to crack or break something, especially a bone.
fracture NOUN

fragile
ADJECTIVE easily broken or damaged.
fragility NOUN

fragment **fragments**
NOUN a small piece or part of something.
fragment VERB

fragrant
ADJECTIVE smelling sweet or pleasant.

frail **frailer frailest**
ADJECTIVE **1** not strong or healthy.
2 easily broken or damaged.
frailty NOUN

frame **frames framing framed**
NOUN **1** the structure surrounding a door, window or picture.
2 an arrangement of connected bars: *a climbing frame.*
3 Your frame is your body.
VERB **4** to put a picture, poster or photograph into a frame.

framework **frameworks**
NOUN **1** a structure that forms a support or frame for something.
2 a set of rules or ideas which you use to decide what to do: *a new framework for the teaching of English.*

frank **franker frankest**
ADJECTIVE speaking or behaving openly and honestly.
frankly ADVERB **frankness** NOUN

frantic
ADJECTIVE behaving in a wild, desperate way because of anxiety or fear.
frantically ADVERB

fraud **frauds**
NOUN **1** the crime of getting money by deceit.
2 someone or something that deceives people.

frayed
ADJECTIVE If a rope is frayed, it has loose threads hanging from it.

freak **freaks**
NOUN **1** someone whose appearance or behaviour is very unusual.
ADJECTIVE **2** A freak event is very unusual: *a freak frost in July.*
freakish ADJECTIVE

freckle **freckles**
NOUN Freckles are small, light brown spots on someone's skin.
freckled ADJECTIVE

a b c d e f g h i j k l m n o p q r s t u v w x y z

free freer freest; frees freeing freed
ADJECTIVE **1** If something is free, you can have it without paying for it.
2 not controlled or limited.
3 To be free of something unpleasant means not to be affected by it.
4 not busy or not being used.
5 If a structure is free-standing, it can stand on its own without support.
VERB **6** to release.

freedom
NOUN **1** being free to do what you want.
2 a state of being free from something unpleasant: *freedom from hunger.*

Synonym: (sense 1) liberty

freehand
ADJECTIVE OR ADVERB A freehand drawing is done without instruments such as a ruler or compasses.

freelance
ADJECTIVE OR ADVERB A freelance worker is not employed by one organization, but is paid for each job they do.
[In medieval times, a *free lance* was a mercenary soldier who would fight on behalf of anybody who would pay him]

free-range
ADJECTIVE Free-range eggs are laid by hens that can move and feed freely on an area of open ground.

free verse
NOUN poetry which does not have a strict rhyme or metre.

freeway freeways
NOUN a motorway in the USA and other countries.

freeze freezes freezing froze frozen
VERB **1** When a liquid freezes, or when something freezes it, it becomes solid because it is very cold.
2 to put food in a freezer to preserve it.
3 to stop moving suddenly because there is danger.

freezer freezers
NOUN a refrigerator which freezes and stores food at very low temperatures for a long time.

freezing
ADJECTIVE; INFORMAL very cold.

freezing point
NOUN The freezing point of a liquid or gas is the temperature at which it freezes and changes into a solid.

freight
NOUN goods moved by lorries, ships or other transport; also the moving of these goods.

French fries
PLURAL NOUN another name for chips.

French horn French horns
NOUN a musical wind instrument consisting of a brass tube wound in a circle.

french window french windows
NOUN French windows are glass double doors that lead into a garden or onto a balcony.

frenzy frenzies
NOUN If someone is in a frenzy, their behaviour is wild and uncontrolled.
frenzied ADJECTIVE

frequency frequencies
NOUN **1** The frequency of an event is how often it happens.
2 A radio frequency is the exact location of a radio station on the dial.
3 A frequency table is a chart that records how often something happens.

frequent
ADJECTIVE happening often, habitual.
frequently ADVERB

fresh fresher freshest
ADJECTIVE **1** Fresh food has been obtained or prepared recently, and is not tinned, frozen or preserved in any way.
2 A fresh thing replaces a previous one or is added to it. *Fresh snow had fallen.*
3 Fresh water, such as the water in a river or lake, is not salty.
4 If you are fresh from something, you have experienced it recently.
freshly ADVERB **freshness** NOUN

freshwater
ADJECTIVE A freshwater lake or pool is not salty.

fret frets fretting fretted
VERB **1** to worry.
NOUN **2** The frets on a stringed instrument, such as a guitar, are the metal ridges across its neck.
fretful ADJECTIVE **fretfully** ADVERB
[from Old English *fretan* meaning to eat]

friar friars
NOUN a type of monk.

friction
NOUN **1** the force that stops things from moving freely when they rub against each other.
2 disagreement and quarrels between people.
frictional ADJECTIVE

Friday Fridays
NOUN the day between Thursday and Saturday.

fridge fridges
NOUN another word for a **refrigerator**.

friend friends
NOUN someone you know well and like, but who is not related to you.
friendship NOUN

Synonyms: companion, mate, pal

 ► These Old French words come from the 1066 Norman invasion: beef, pork, veal, charity, humour.

friendly **friendlier friendliest**
ADJECTIVE **1** behaving in a kind and pleasant way to other people.
2 If you are friendly with someone, you like each other and enjoy spending time together.
friendliness NOUN

friendship **friendships**
NOUN a friendly relationship between people.

frieze **friezes**
NOUN a strip of decoration along the top of a wall.

frigate **frigates**
NOUN a small, fast warship.

fright
NOUN a sudden feeling of fear.

frighten **frightens frightening frightened**
VERB to make someone afraid.
frightened ADJECTIVE **frightening** ADJECTIVE

frightful
ADJECTIVE very bad or unpleasant.
frightfully ADVERB

frill **frills**
NOUN **1** a strip of cloth with many folds, attached to something as a decoration.
2 INFORMAL If something has no frills it is very plain and simple.
frilly ADJECTIVE

fringe **fringes**
NOUN **1** the hair that hangs over a person's forehead.
2 a decoration on clothes and other objects, consisting of a row of hanging threads.
3 The fringes of a place are the parts farthest from its centre; the outer edges.

frisk **frisks frisking frisked**
VERB **1** When animals frisk, they run around in a happy, energetic way.
2 INFORMAL to search someone quickly with the hands to see if they are hiding a weapon.

frisky **friskier friskiest**
ADJECTIVE energetic and wanting to have fun.
friskily ADVERB **friskiness** NOUN

fritter **fritters frittering frittered**
VERB **1** If you fritter away your time or money, you waste it.
NOUN **2** Fritters consist of food dipped in batter and fried.

frivolous
ADJECTIVE inappropriately silly or light-hearted.
frivolously ADVERB **frivolity** NOUN

frizzy
ADJECTIVE Frizzy hair has stiff, wiry curls.

frock **frocks**
NOUN; OLD-FASHIONED a dress.

frog **frogs**
NOUN a small, amphibious, leaping creature with big eyes.

frolic **frolics frolicking frolicked**
VERB to run around and play in a lively way.
frolicsome ADJECTIVE
[from Dutch *vrolijk* meaning joyful]

from
PREPOSITION **1** You use "from" to say what the source, origin or starting point of something is. *I come from Manchester.*
2 You use "from" when stating the range of something. *From 1972 to 1974 he lived abroad.*
3 In mathematics, "from" can be used as a subtraction: *take 3 from 5.*

front **fronts**
NOUN **1** the part of something that faces forward.
2 In a war, the front is the place where two armies are fighting.
3 a front is a false outward appearance that you put on: *a brave front.*
ADJECTIVE **4** at the opposite end or side to the back: *the front seat of the car.*

frontier **frontiers**
NOUN a border between two countries.

frost **frosts**
NOUN When there is a frost, the temperature outside falls below freezing.

frostbite
NOUN damage to the fingers, toes or ears caused by extreme cold.
frostbitten ADJECTIVE

frosty **frostier frostiest**
ADJECTIVE If it is frosty, the temperature is below freezing point.

froth **froths frothing frothed**
NOUN **1** a mass of small bubbles on the surface of a liquid.
VERB **2** If a liquid froths, small bubbles appear on its surface.
frothy ADJECTIVE

frown **frowns frowning frowned**
VERB to move your eyebrows closer together, because you are annoyed, worried or puzzled.
frown NOUN

froze
the past tense of **freeze**.

frozen
the past participle of **freeze**.

fruit **fruits**
NOUN the part of a plant that contains or supports the seeds. Apples, tomatoes and strawberries are fruits.

fruitful
ADJECTIVE having good and useful results: *a very fruitful meeting.*
fruitfully ADVERB **fruitfulness** NOUN

fruitless
ADJECTIVE not achieving anything.
fruitlessly ADVERB **fruitlessness** NOUN

Adverbial pun. "Who ate my apple?" said John fruitlessly.

A B C D E F G H I J K L M N O P Q R S T U V W X Y Z

fruity
ADJECTIVE tasting or smelling of fruit.

frustrate **frustrates frustrating frustrated**
VERB **1** If something frustrates you, it prevents you doing what you want and makes you upset.
2 to prevent something happening. *We were frustrated by the weather from going to the beach.*
frustrating ADJECTIVE **frustrated** ADJECTIVE
frustration NOUN

Synonyms: (sense 2) to foil, to thwart

fry **fries frying fried**
VERB to cook food in a pan containing hot fat.
fried ADJECTIVE

fudge
NOUN a soft brown sweet made from butter, milk and sugar.

fuel **fuels fuelling fuelled**
NOUN **1** a substance such as coal or petrol which is burned to provide heat or power.
VERB **2** to provide power through fuel.

fugitive **fugitives**
Said "**fyoo**-jit-tiv" NOUN someone who is running away or hiding, especially from the police.

fulfil **fulfils fulfilling fulfilled**
VERB If you fulfil a promise, hope or duty, you carry it out or achieve it.
fulfilment NOUN

full **fuller fullest**
ADJECTIVE **1** containing as much as it is possible to hold.
2 containing a lot of things.
3 to the greatest possible extent: *full volume.*
4 complete or whole: *full details.*
ADVERB **5** completely or wholly. *Turn the taps full on.*
fully ADVERB **fullness** NOUN

Synonyms: (sense 1) chock-a-block, crammed, packed

full moon **full moons**
NOUN the moon when it appears as a complete circle in the sky.

full stop **full stops**
NOUN the punctuation mark (.) used at the end of a sentence and after an abbreviation or initial.

THE FULL STOP
The full stop (.) marks the end of any sentence which is not a question or an exclamation:
The rain is falling.
It is used after initials:
Theophilus T. Wildebeeste, W. B. Yeats
It is used in some abbreviations:
etc., e.g., m.p.h.
Many abbreviations used to take a full stop but commonly do not have one now, such as:
Mr, Mrs, Dr, St John, Revd

full-time
ADJECTIVE OR ADVERB If you work full-time, you work for the whole of each normal working week.

fumble **fumbles fumbling fumbled**
VERB to feel or handle something clumsily.

fume **fumes fuming fumed**
NOUN **1** Fumes are unpleasant-smelling gases and smoke, often toxic.
VERB **2** If you are fuming, you are very angry.

fun
NOUN **1** pleasant, enjoyable and light-hearted activity.
PHRASE **2** If you **make fun of** someone, you tease them or make jokes about them.

function **functions functioning functioned**
NOUN **1** the purpose or job something was designed for.
VERB **2** to operate or work.
functional ADJECTIVE

fund **funds funding funded**
NOUN **1** an amount of money collected for a particular purpose.
VERB **2** To fund something means to provide money for it.

fundamental
ADJECTIVE basic and essential.

funeral **funerals**
Said "**fyoo**-ner-al" NOUN a ceremony for the burial or cremation of someone who has died.

fungus **fungi** or **funguses**
NOUN an organism such as a mushroom or mould, without flowers or leaves, that obtains food by growing on other organisms, either dead or alive.
fungal ADJECTIVE

funnel **funnels funnelling funnelled**
NOUN **1** an open cone narrowing to a tube, used to pour substances into containers.
2 a metal chimney on a ship or steam engine.
VERB **3** If something is funnelled somewhere, it is directed through a narrow space.

funny **funnier funniest**
ADJECTIVE **1** causing amusement or laughter.
2 strange or puzzling.
funnily ADVERB

Synonyms: (sense 1) amusing, comical, humorous
(sense 2) odd, peculiar, weird

funny bone **funny bones**
NOUN a sensitive area near your elbow which can give you a tingling sensation if you hit it accidentally.

fur
NOUN the thick hair that grows on the bodies of many animals.
furry ADJECTIVE

 ▶ Adverbial pun. "Is that where they bury people?" she asked gravely.

furious
ADJECTIVE **1** extremely angry.
2 involving great energy or effort: *furious activity.*
furiously ADVERB

furnace **furnaces**
NOUN a container for a very large, hot fire, such as used in industry for melting metals.

furnish **furnishes furnishing furnished**
VERB to put furniture into a room, house, etc.

furniture
NOUN movable objects such as tables, chairs and wardrobes.

furrow **furrows**
NOUN a long, shallow trench made by a plough.

further
ADVERB **1** a comparative form of **far**.
ADJECTIVE **2** additional or more.
✔ For extra effort or time, use *further* and *furthest*: *a further delay is likely*. For physical distance, use *farther* and *farthest*.

furthermore
ADVERB; FORMAL in addition, moreover.

furthest
ADVERB the superlative form of **far**.

furtive
ADJECTIVE secretive, sly and cautious: *a furtive smile.*
furtively ADVERB

fury
NOUN violent or extreme anger.

fuse **fuses fusing fused**
NOUN **1** a safety device in a plug or electrical appliance consisting of a wire which melts if a fault occurs, cutting off the electricity.
2 a long cord attached to some types of simple bomb which is lit to detonate.
VERB **3** When an electrical appliance fuses, it stops working because the fuse has melted to protect it.
4 If two things fuse together, they melt under heat and then cannot be separated when they cool down.

fuselage **fuselages**
Said "**fyoo**-zil-ahj" NOUN the main body of an aircraft.

fuss **fusses fussing fussed**
VERB **1** to behave with unnecessary anxiety and concern for unimportant things.
NOUN **2** unnecessarily anxious or excited behaviour.

fussy **fussier fussiest**
ADJECTIVE **1** likely to fuss a lot.
2 having too much elaborate detail.
fussily ADVERB

futile
ADJECTIVE having no chance of success.
futility NOUN

future
NOUN **1** the period of time after the present.
ADJECTIVE **2** relating to or occurring after the present. *He is the future king.*
PHRASE **3** **In future** means from now on.

fuzzy **fuzzier fuzziest**
ADJECTIVE unclear, blurred.

Continue this word chain: furious, usual, alive, vest, stable... Can you do eight more?

A B C D E F G H I J K L M N O P Q R S T U V W X Y Z

Gg

gabble **gabbles gabbling gabbled**
VERB to talk so fast that it is difficult for people to understand.
gabble NOUN

gadget **gadgets**
NOUN a small machine or tool.

Synonyms: contraption, device

Gaelic
Said "**gal**-lik" (Scotland) or "**gay**-lik" (Ireland)
NOUN a language spoken in some parts of Scotland and Ireland.

gag **gags gagging gagged**
NOUN 1 a strip of cloth which is tied round someone's mouth to stop them speaking.
2 INFORMAL a joke told by a comedian.
VERB 3 To gag someone means to put a gag round their mouth.
4 If you gag, you choke and nearly vomit.

gain **gains gaining gained**
VERB 1 to acquire or obtain something gradually. *I gained 20 Brownie badges.*
NOUN 2 an increase: *a gain of 15%.*

gala **galas**
NOUN a special public celebration, performance or sporting event.

galaxy **galaxies**
NOUN a huge group of stars that extends over millions of miles.
galactic ADJECTIVE

gale **gales**
NOUN an extremely strong wind.

gallant
ADJECTIVE brave and honourable.
gallantly ADVERB **gallantry** NOUN

galleon **galleons**
NOUN a large sailing ship used in the sixteenth and seventeenth centuries.

gallery **galleries**
NOUN 1 a building or room where works of art are shown.
2 In a theatre or large hall, the gallery is a raised area at the back or sides.

galley **galleys**
NOUN 1 a kitchen in a ship or aircraft.
2 a ship, rowed with oars, used in ancient and medieval times.

gallon **gallons**
NOUN a unit of measurement for liquids equal to eight pints or about 4·56 litres.

gallop **gallops galloping galloped**
VERB When a horse gallops, it runs very fast, so that during each stride all four feet are off the ground at the same time.

gallows
NOUN a frame on which criminals used to be hanged.

galore
ADJECTIVE in very large numbers. *There were cakes galore at the party.*

gamble **gambles gambling gambled**
VERB 1 to bet money on the result of a contest or race.
2 If you gamble something, you risk losing it in the hope of gaining an advantage.
gamble NOUN **gambler** NOUN

game **games**
NOUN 1 an enjoyable activity with a set of rules which is played by individuals or teams against each other.
2 an imaginative activity played by small children: *a game of cowboys and Indians.*
3 Game is wild animals, such as deer, pheasant and grouse, that are hunted for food.
ADJECTIVE 4 Someone who is game is willing to try something unusual or difficult: *game for a laugh.*
gamely ADVERB

gamekeeper **gamekeepers**
NOUN a person employed to look after game animals on a country estate.

gammon
NOUN cured meat from a pig, similar to bacon.

gander **ganders**
NOUN a male goose.

gang **gangs ganging ganged**
NOUN 1 a group of people who join together for some purpose, such as to commit a crime.
VERB 2 INFORMAL If people gang up on you, they join together to oppose you.

gangplank **gangplanks**
NOUN a plank used for boarding and leaving a ship or boat.

gangster **gangsters**
NOUN a violent criminal who is a member of a gang.

gangway **gangways**
NOUN 1 a space between rows of seats for people to walk down, for example, in a cinema or theatre.
2 A ship's gangway is a gangplank.

gaol
another spelling of **jail**.

gap **gaps**
NOUN a space between two things or a hole in something solid.

Synonyms: hole, opening, space

gape **gapes gaping gaped**
VERB 1 to stare with your mouth open in surprise.
2 to be wide open: *gaping holes.*

 ► Like the letter C, the letter G developed from the idea of a weapon.

garage garages
NOUN 1 a building in which you can keep a car.
2 a place where cars are repaired or where petrol is sold.

garbage
NOUN 1 In American English, garbage is rubbish, especially waste from a kitchen.
2 INFORMAL something that is worthless or useless, especially speech or writing. *Don't talk garbage.*

garbled
ADJECTIVE Garbled messages are jumbled and the details may be wrong.

garden gardens gardening gardened
NOUN 1 an area of land next to a house, with plants, trees and grass.
VERB 2 to work on your garden.
gardening NOUN

gardener gardeners
NOUN a person who looks after a garden as a job or as a hobby.

gargle gargles gargling gargled
VERB to rinse the back of your throat by putting some liquid in your mouth and making a bubbling sound without swallowing the liquid.

gargoyle gargoyles
NOUN a stone carving below the roof of an old building, in the shape of an ugly or comical person or animal.

garland garlands
NOUN a circle of flowers and leaves which is worn around the neck or head.

garlic
NOUN a small, white, onion-like edible bulb.

garment garments
NOUN a piece of clothing.

garnish garnishes garnishing garnished
NOUN 1 something used for decoration in cooking, such as a sprig of parsley.
VERB 2 to decorate food with a garnish.

garrison garrisons
NOUN a group of soldiers stationed in a town in order to guard it; also the buildings in which these soldiers live.

garter garters
NOUN a piece of elastic worn round the top of a stocking or sock to stop it slipping.

gas gases; gasses gassing gassed
NOUN 1 any substance that is not liquid or solid, such as oxygen or the fuel known as gas that is used for heating and cooking.
2 In American English, gas is petrol.
VERB 3 To gas people or other animals means to kill them with poisonous gas.
✔ The plural of the noun *gas* is *gases*. The verb forms of *gas* are spelt with a double *s*.

gash gashes gashing gashed
VERB to make a long, deep cut.
gash NOUN

gasoline
NOUN In American English, gasoline is petrol.

gasp gasps gasping gasped
VERB to take a short, quick breath because you are surprised or in pain.
gasp NOUN

gastric
ADJECTIVE occurring in the stomach or involving the stomach.

gate gates
NOUN a barrier which is used at the entrance to a garden or field.

gateau gateaux
Said "**gat**-toe" NOUN a rich layered cake with cream in it.

gateway gateways
NOUN an entrance through a wall or fence where there is a gate.

gather gathers gathering gathered
VERB 1 to come together in a group. *Children, gather round!*
2 to bring things together in one place. *I gathered some flowers.*
3 If something gathers speed or strength, it gradually becomes faster or stronger.
4 If you gather something, you learn it, often from what someone says. *I gather he lives abroad.*

Synonyms: (sense 1) assemble, congregate
(sense 2) amass, assemble, collect

gathering gatherings
NOUN a meeting of people who have come together for a particular purpose.

gaudy gaudier gaudiest
Said "**gaw**-dee" ADJECTIVE very colourful in a vulgar way.
gaudily ADVERB gaudiness NOUN

gauge gauges gauging gauged
Said "**gayj**" NOUN 1 a piece of equipment that measures the amount of something: *a rainfall gauge.*
VERB 2 to estimate or calculate something. *He gauged the wind at over 30 knots.*

gauze
NOUN 1 very fine cloth with lots of tiny holes in it which is often used in bandages.
2 very fine metal mesh.

gave
the past tense of **give**.

gay gays
ADJECTIVE 1 homosexual.
NOUN 2 a homosexual person, especially a homosexual man.
✔ *Gay* also has an old-fashioned meaning of "lively and full of fun". The noun *gaiety* is related to this older meaning.

a b c d e f g h i j k l m n o p q r s t u v w x y z

Garden words: organic, compost, fertilizer, shrub, lawnmower, annual, border. ◀

A B C D E F G H I J K L M N O P Q R S T U V W X Y Z

gaze gazes gazing gazed
VERB **1** to look steadily at something for a long time.
NOUN **2** a long steady look at something.

Synonym: stare

gazelle gazelles
NOUN a small antelope found in Africa and Asia.

gazette gazettes
NOUN a newspaper or a journal.

gear gears
NOUN **1** a piece of machinery, especially in a car or on a bicycle, which controls the rate at which energy is converted into movement.
2 clothes or equipment you need for a particular activity.

geese
the plural of **goose**.

gel gels
Said "**jel**" NOUN a smooth, soft, jelly-like substance.

gem gems
NOUN **1** a jewel or precious stone.
2 You can describe something that is extremely rare, good or beautiful as a gem. *A gem of a novel.*

gender genders
NOUN Gender is the sex of a person or other animal.

WHAT IS GENDER?
When we talk about the gender of a noun, we mean whether the noun is referred to as he, she or it. There are three genders: masculine, feminine and neuter.
Masculine nouns refer to male people and animals:
The boy put on his coat – boy is masculine.
Feminine nouns refer to female people and animals:
The girl put on her coat – girl is feminine.
Neuter nouns refer to objects and abstract ideas:
The kettle will switch itself off – kettle is neuter.

gene genes
Said "**jeen**" NOUN one of the tiny parts of a living cell which controls a living thing's characteristics and which is passed on to the next generation.

general generals
ADJECTIVE **1** relating to the whole of something or to most things in a group. *The teacher's general appearance was very smart.*
2 true, suitable or relevant in most situations: *a general rule.*
3 including or involving a range of different things; not specialized: *a general hospital.*
NOUN **4** an army officer of very high rank.
PHRASE **5 In general** is used to indicate that a statement is true in most cases or that it applies to most people or things. *In general, children like video games.*

Synonym: (sense 1) overall
(sense 2) common, universal, widespread

general election general elections
NOUN an election for a new government, which all the people of a country may vote in. See **by-election**.

generalize generalizes generalizing generalized; also spelt **generalise**
VERB **1** to make general statements based on detailed facts or experience.
2 to speak unfairly or incorrectly about a whole category or people based on experience of just a small sample of this category.
3 In mathematics or science, to identify and extract a general rule from detailed facts.
generalization NOUN

generally
ADVERB usually, normally.

general practitioner general practitioners
NOUN a doctor who works in the community and does not specialize. Often known as a GP.

generate generates generating generated
VERB to create or produce something. *Wind power can generate electricity.*

generation generations
NOUN **1** all the people of a similar age.
2 the period of time that it takes for children to grow up and have children of their own, normally taken to be 25–30 years.
3 the production of electricity.

generator generators
NOUN a machine which produces electricity from another form of energy such as fuel oil, gas, wind or water.

generous
ADJECTIVE **1** A generous person gives more of something, especially money, than is usual or expected.
2 larger than usual or expected: *a generous portion.*
generously ADVERB **generosity** NOUN

genetic
ADJECTIVE **1** If someone has a genetic characteristic, it has been passed down to them through their parents' genes.
NOUN **2** Genetics is the science of studying genes.

genial
ADJECTIVE cheerful, friendly and kind.
genially ADVERB **geniality** NOUN

genie genies
Said "**jee**-nee" NOUN a magical being that obeys the wishes of the person who controls it.
[from Arabic *jinni* meaning demon]

genitals
PLURAL NOUN the reproductive organs of males and females.
genital ADJECTIVE

 ► Some collective nouns: a gaggle of geese, a building of rooks, a leap of leopards.

genius **geniuses**
NOUN 1 a highly intelligent, creative or talented person.
2 very great ability or skill in something.

genre **genres**
Said "**jahn**-ra" **NOUN**; **FORMAL** a particular style in literature and art: *the genre of horror stories.*

gentle **gentler gentlest**
ADJECTIVE mild and calm.
gently ADVERB **gentleness** NOUN

Antonyms: rough, violent

gentleman **gentlemen**
NOUN a man who is polite and well-educated; also a polite way of referring to any man.

genuine
Said "**jen**-yoo-in" **ADJECTIVE** real and exactly what it appears to be. *The signature was genuine.*
genuinely ADVERB **genuineness** NOUN

genus **genera**
Said "**jee**-nuss" **NOUN** In biology, a genus is a class of animals or closely related plants.

geography
NOUN the study of the natural features of the earth including landscape, climate, soil, vegetation, etc. and human response to them.
geographical ADJECTIVE **geographically** ADVERB **geographer** NOUN

geology
NOUN the study of the earth's structure, especially the layers of rock and soil that make up the surface of the earth.
geological ADJECTIVE **geologist** NOUN

geometry
NOUN the branch of mathematics that deals with lines, angles, curves and spaces.
geometrical ADJECTIVE **geometrically** ADVERB
[from Greek *geometrein* meaning to measure the land]

geranium **geraniums**
NOUN a garden plant with red, pink or white flowers.

gerbil **gerbils**
Said "**jer**-bil" **NOUN** a small rodent with long back legs, often kept as a pet.

germ **germs**
NOUN a very small organism that causes disease.

germinate **germinates germinating germinated**
VERB When a seed germinates, it starts to grow.
germination NOUN

gesticulate **gesticulates gesticulating gesticulated**
Said "jes-**stik**-yoo-late" **VERB** to move your hands and arms around while you are talking.
gesticulation NOUN

gesture **gestures gesturing gestured**
NOUN 1 a movement of your hands or head that conveys a message or feeling.
2 an action that expresses your attitudes or intentions. *We sent a bunch of flowers as a gesture of thanks.*
VERB 3 to move your hands or head in order to communicate a message or feeling.

get **gets getting got**
VERB 1 become. *It was beginning to get dark.*
2 to fetch something or be given something. *I'll get a cup of coffee. I got your message.*
3 If you get into a particular situation, you put yourself in that situation. *You might get into trouble.*
4 If you get somewhere, you go there. *It was late when she got home.*
5 If you get a train, bus or plane, you travel on it. *You can get a bus there.*
6 If you get a joke or get the point of something, you understand it.
get at **VERB 1** If someone is getting at you, they are criticizing you in an unkind way.
2 If you ask someone what they are getting at, you are asking them to explain what they mean.
get on **VERB 1** If you get on with a task, you start doing it or continue doing it.
2 If you get on with someone, you have a friendly relationship with them.
3 If you are getting on well, you are making good progress.
get over **VERB** to recover from something unpleasant.
get through **VERB 1** to complete something difficult.
2 If you get through to someone, you make them understand what you are saying.
3 If you get through to someone on the telephone, you succeed in talking to them.

Synonyms: (get, sense 3) land, find yourself
(sense 4) arrive, return, come
(sense 5) catch, board

getaway **getaways**
NOUN an escape.

geyser **geysers**
Said "**gee**-zer" **NOUN** a spring through which hot water and steam gush up in spurts.

ghastly **ghastlier ghastliest**
ADJECTIVE extremely horrible and unpleasant.

ghetto **ghettoes** or **ghettos**
NOUN a part of a city where many poor people of a particular race live.

ghost **ghosts**
NOUN the spirit of a dead person.
ghostly ADJECTIVE

Synonyms: phantom, spectre, spirit

ghoulish
Said "**goo**-lish" **ADJECTIVE** very interested in unpleasant things such as death and murder.

These words have a hard "g" and a silent "h": aghast, ghastly, gherkin, ghetto, ghoulish.

a b c d e f g h i j k l m n o p q r s t u v w x y z

A B C D E F G H I J K L M N O P Q R S T U V W X Y Z

giant giants
NOUN 1 a huge person in a myth or legend.
ADJECTIVE 2 much larger than other similar things.

gibberish
NOUN speech that makes no sense at all.

giddy giddier giddiest
ADJECTIVE feeling unsteady on your feet.
giddily ADVERB **giddiness** NOUN

gift gifts
NOUN 1 a present.
2 a natural skill or ability. *Clare had a gift for making things.*

gifted
ADJECTIVE having a special ability: *gifted writers.*

gigantic
ADJECTIVE extremely large.

giggle giggles giggling giggled
VERB to laugh in a child-like, high-pitched helpless way.
giggle NOUN

gilded
ADJECTIVE covered with a thin layer of gold.

gill gills
NOUN the organ for breathing used by animals that need to take oxygen from the water they live in. A fish has gills on the side of its head.

gimmick gimmicks
NOUN a device that is not really necessary but is used to attract interest or sales.
gimmicky ADJECTIVE

gin
NOUN a strong, colourless alcoholic drink.

ginger
NOUN 1 a plant root with a hot, spicy flavour, used in cooking and drinks.
ADJECTIVE 2 bright orangey-brown.

gingerbread
NOUN a sweet, ginger-flavoured cake.

gingerly
ADVERB OR ADJECTIVE cautiously and carefully.

Gipsy
another spelling of **Gypsy**.

giraffe giraffes
NOUN a tall, four-legged African mammal with a very long neck.

girder girders
NOUN a large metal beam used in building.

girl girls
NOUN a female child or young woman.

girlfriend girlfriends
NOUN a woman or girl with whom someone is having a romantic relationship.

giro giros
Said "**jie**-roh" **NOUN** In Britain, a regular cheque from the government for unemployed or sick people.

girth
NOUN the measurement all the way round something or someone.

gist
Said "**jist**" **NOUN** the general meaning or most important points in a piece of writing or speech.

give gives giving gave given
VERB 1 to hand or provide someone with something. *I gave her the money.*
2 "Give" is also used to express physical actions and speech. *She gave him a nudge.*
3 If you give a party or meal, you are the host of it.
give in VERB If you give in, you admit that you are defeated.
give up VERB 1 to stop doing something.
2 to admit that you cannot do something.

Synonyms: (give, sense 1) grant, present, donate

given
the past participle of **give**.

glacier glaciers
Said "**glass**-yer" **NOUN** a huge frozen mass of very slow-moving ice.

glad gladder gladdest
ADJECTIVE happy and pleased.
gladly ADVERB **gladness** NOUN

Synonyms: delighted, thrilled, content

glade glades
NOUN a grassy space in a forest.

gladiator gladiators
NOUN In ancient Rome, gladiators were slaves trained to fight in arenas to provide entertainment.

glamour
NOUN the charm and excitement of a fashionable or attractive person or place.
glamorous ADJECTIVE

glance glances glancing glanced
VERB 1 to look at something quickly.
2 If one object glances off another, it hits it at an angle and bounces away.
NOUN 3 a quick look.

gland glands
NOUN Glands are organs in your body, such as the thyroid gland and the sweat glands, which either produce chemical substances for your body to use, or which help to get rid of waste products from your body.
glandular ADJECTIVE

glare glares glaring glared
VERB 1 to look angrily at someone.
NOUN 2 a hard, angry look.
3 extremely bright light.

glaring
ADJECTIVE very obvious: *a glaring mistake.*

 ► Find a word on this page associated with: Antarctic, error, pupil, arena.

glass glasses
NOUN 1 the hard transparent or translucent substance that windows and bottles are made from.
2 a container for drinking out of, made of glass.

glasses
PLURAL NOUN two lenses in a frame which some people wear over their eyes to improve their eyesight.

Synonym: spectacles

glassy
ADJECTIVE 1 smooth and shiny like glass.
2 A glassy look has no expression.

glaze glazes glazing glazed
NOUN 1 a smooth shiny surface on pottery.
VERB 2 To glaze pottery means to cover it with a glaze.
3 To glaze a window means to fit a sheet of glass into it.
glaze over VERB If your eyes glaze over, they lose all expression, usually because you are bored.

gleam gleams gleaming gleamed
VERB 1 to shine and reflect light.
NOUN 2 a pale shining light.
gleaming ADJECTIVE

glee
NOUN great joy, delight.

glen glens
NOUN a deep, narrow valley, especially in Scotland or Ireland.

glide glides gliding glided
VERB 1 to move smoothly.
2 When birds or aeroplanes glide, they float on air currents.

glider gliders
NOUN an aeroplane without an engine, which flies by floating on air currents.

glimmer glimmers glimmering glimmered
NOUN 1 a faint, unsteady light.
2 A glimmer of a feeling or quality is a faint sign of it.
VERB 3 to produce a faint, unsteady light.

glimpse glimpses glimpsing glimpsed
VERB to see something very briefly.
glimpse NOUN

glint glints glinting glinted
VERB 1 to reflect quick flashes of light.
NOUN 2 a quick flash of light.
3 A glint in someone's eye is a brightness expressing some emotion.

glisten glistens glistening glistened
Said "**gliss**-sn" VERB to shine or sparkle.

glitter glitters glittering glittered
VERB 1 to shine in a sparkling way.
NOUN 2 sparkling light.

gloat gloats gloating gloated
VERB to show your pleasure cruelly about your own success or someone else's failure. *He gloated over his victory, taunting his rivals.*

global
ADJECTIVE 1 concerning the whole world.
2 In computing, a global command is one that applies to a great number of files, directories, etc.

global warming
PHRASE an increase in the world's overall temperature believed to be caused by the greenhouse effect.

globe globes
NOUN 1 a ball-shaped object especially one with a map of the earth on it.
2 the world.

gloom
NOUN 1 darkness or dimness.
2 a feeling of unhappiness or despair.

gloomy gloomier gloomiest
ADJECTIVE feeling unhappy or pessimistic.
gloomily ADVERB

glorious
ADJECTIVE 1 beautiful and impressive to look at: *glorious weather.*
2 involving great fame or success: *a glorious victory.*
gloriously ADVERB

glory glories
NOUN 1 fame and admiration for an achievement. *The scientists won glory for their discovery.*
2 something considered splendid or admirable: *the glories of the Alps.*

gloss glosses glossing glossed
NOUN 1 a bright shine on a surface.
VERB 2 If you **gloss over** a problem or fault you try to ignore it or deal with it very quickly.

glossary glossaries
NOUN a list of explanations of specialist words, usually found at the back of a book.

glossy glossier glossiest
ADJECTIVE 1 smooth and shiny.
2 Glossy magazines are printed on expensive, shiny paper.

glove gloves
NOUN clothing for your hands.

glow glows glowing glowed
VERB 1 to shine with a dull, steady light.
2 to look happy and healthy.
NOUN 3 a dull, steady light.
4 a strong feeling of happiness.
glowing ADJECTIVE

glower glowers glowering glowered
Rhymes with "**shower**" VERB to stare angrily.

a b c d e f g h i j k l m n o p q r s t u v w x y z

Many surnames derive from jobs. The ancestors of people called Glover made gloves for a living.

A B C D E F G H I J K L M N O P Q R S T U V W X Y Z

glucose
NOUN a substance found in all animals and plants that provides them with energy. It is sometimes used to sweeten food and drinks. Plants produce glucose during photosynthesis.

glue glues gluing or glueing glued
NOUN **1** a substance used for sticking things together.
VERB **2** to stick one object to another using glue.

glum glummer glummest
ADJECTIVE miserable and depressed.
glumly ADVERB **glumness** NOUN

glutton gluttons
NOUN **1** a person who eats too much.
2 If you are a glutton for punishment or hard work, you seem very eager for it.
gluttonous ADJECTIVE **gluttony** NOUN
[from Latin *gluttus* meaning greedy]

gnarled
Said "**narld**" ADJECTIVE old, twisted and rough.

gnash gnashes gnashing gnashed
Said "**nash**" VERB If you gnash your teeth, you grind them together because you are angry or in pain.

gnat gnats
Said "**nat**" NOUN a tiny flying insect which bites.

gnaw gnaws gnawing gnawed
Said "**naw**" VERB **1** to bite and chew at something repeatedly.
2 If a feeling gnaws at you, it keeps worrying you.

gnome gnomes
Said "**nome**" NOUN a tiny, old man in fairy stories.

go goes going went gone
NOUN **1** an attempt at doing something; a try.
VERB **2** to move or travel somewhere.
3 to become. *She felt she was going mad.*
4 If you are going to do something, you intend to do it.
5 to attend regularly. *I go to primary school.*
6 to lead or pass through somewhere. *Does this road go to the station?*
7 to spend time doing something. *Shall we go swimming?*
8 to progress or proceed. *The party is going really well.*
9 to function or work. *Is the clock still going?*
10 If one number goes into another, it can be divided into it.
go off VERB **1** to explode or fire.
2 to stop liking someone or something.
3 If food goes off, it starts to decay and tastes unpleasant.
go on VERB **1** to continue.
2 to happen. *What on earth is going on?*
go out VERB **1** If you go out with someone, you have a romantic relationship with them.
2 If a light or flame goes out, it stops shining or burning.
go through VERB If you go through an unpleasant time, you experience it.
go with VERB If something goes with something, it accompanies it. *White wine goes well with fish.*

goal goals
NOUN **1** In certain games, the goal is the space which is the target for scoring.
2 the name for the point scored when a player puts the ball into the goal.
3 Your goal is something that you hope to achieve. *Our goal is to raise money.*

goalkeeper goalkeepers
NOUN a player whose job is to guard the goal.

goalpost goalposts
NOUN **1** one of the two upright posts of a goal.
PHRASE **2** If someone is said to have **moved the goalposts** they have unfairly changed the rules and conditions of a situation after it has already started.

goat goats
NOUN an animal similar to a sheep, with shaggy hair, a beard and horns.

gobble gobbles gobbling gobbled
VERB **1** to eat food very quickly.
2 When a turkey gobbles, it makes a loud gurgling sound.

gobbledygook or **gobbledegook**
NOUN language that is impossible to understand because it is so formal or complicated.

goblet goblets
NOUN a glass or metal drinking container with a long stem.

goblin goblins
NOUN an ugly, mischievous creature in fairy stories.

god gods
NOUN **1** The name God is given to the being who is worshipped by Christians, Jews and Muslims as the creator and ruler of the world.
2 a being in any religion who is believed to have power over an aspect of life or a part of the world. *Mars, the Roman god of war.*

godchild godchildren
NOUN At a child's baptism in a Christian church, if you agree to be responsible for the child's religious upbringing, that child becomes your godchild.
goddaughter NOUN **godson** NOUN

goddess goddesses
NOUN a female god.

godparent godparents
NOUN someone who agrees to be responsible for a child's religious upbringing when that child is baptized in a Christian church.
godfather NOUN **godmother** NOUN

 ▶ Words used for God, Jesus and other religious figures usually begin with a capital letter.

goggles
PLURAL NOUN Goggles are special glasses that fit closely round the eyes to protect them.

go-kart go-karts
NOUN a very small, low motor vehicle with four wheels, used for racing.

gold
NOUN 1 a valuable yellow-coloured metal, used for making jewellery and as an international currency.
ADJECTIVE 2 made of gold.
3 a deep yellow colour.

golden
ADJECTIVE 1 made of gold or the colour of gold.
2 excellent or ideal: *a golden opportunity*.

goldfish
NOUN a small orange-coloured fish, often kept in ponds or bowls.

golf
NOUN a game in which players use special clubs to hit a ball into holes that are spread out over a large area of grassy land.
golfer NOUN **golfing** NOUN

gondola gondolas
Said "**gon**-dol-la" NOUN a long narrow boat, propelled with a long pole, used in Venice.

gone
the past participle of **go**.

gong gongs
NOUN a flat, circular piece of metal that is hit with a hammer to make a loud sound, often as a signal for something.

good better best
ADJECTIVE 1 pleasant or enjoyable.
2 of a high quality.
3 sensible or valid: *a good reason*.
4 kind and thoughtful. *That's very good of you.*
5 well-behaved.
6 "Good" can be used to emphasize something. *I waited a good hour.*
NOUN 7 the things that are considered to be morally right: *the forces of good and evil.*
8 anything which is desirable or beneficial. *The break has done me good.*
PHRASE 9 **For good** means for ever.
10 **As good as** means almost. *The job is as good as done.*
✔ You should say that *a person did well* not *did good*.

Antonyms: (sense 1) bad
(sense 2) bad, poor, shoddy
(sense 3) bad
(sense 7) evil, wickedness

goodbye
INTERJECTION You say goodbye when you are leaving someone or ending a phone conversation.

Good Friday
NOUN the Friday before Easter Sunday, when Christians remember the crucifixion of Christ.

good-natured
ADJECTIVE friendly, pleasant and even-tempered.

goodness
NOUN 1 the quality of being kind.
INTERJECTION 2 People say "Goodness!" or "My goodness!" when they are surprised.

good night
INTERJECTION an expression used when leaving someone at night, especially when going to bed.

goods
PLURAL NOUN things for sale.

goose geese
NOUN a fairly large bird with webbed feet and a long neck.

gooseberry gooseberries
NOUN a round, green berry that grows on a bush and has a sharp taste.

goose pimples
NOUN the tiny lumps that appear on your skin when you are cold or afraid.

gore gores goring gored
VERB 1 If an animal gores somebody, it wounds them badly with its horns or tusks.
NOUN 2 OLD-FASHIONED blood.

gorge gorges gorging gorged
NOUN 1 a deep, narrow, rocky valley.
VERB 2 If you gorge yourself, you eat a lot of food greedily.

gorgeous
ADJECTIVE extremely pleasant or attractive.

gorilla gorillas
NOUN a very large ape.
[from *Gorillai*, the Greek name for an African tribe with hairy bodies]

gorse
NOUN a dark green, wild shrub that has small yellow flowers and sharp prickles.

gory gorier goriest
ADJECTIVE with a lot of blood or bloodshed.

gosling goslings
Said "**goz**-ling" NOUN a young goose.

gospel gospels
NOUN 1 The Gospels are the four books in the New Testament which describe the life and teachings of Jesus Christ.
PHRASE 2 If you take something **as gospel** or **gospel truth**, you believe that it is true.
[from Old English *god* + *spel* meaning good message]

gossip gossips gossiping gossiped
NOUN 1 informal conversation, often about other people's private affairs.
VERB 2 to talk informally with someone, especially about other people.

got
the past participle of **get**.

a b c d e f g h i j k l m n o p q r s t u v w x y z

Goodbye is a shortened form of "God be with you".

gouge gouges gouging gouged
Said "**gowj**" VERB 1 to make a hole in something with a pointed object.
2 If you gouge something out, you force it out of position with your fingers or a sharp tool.

govern governs governing governed
VERB 1 To govern a country means to control it officially.
2 to influence or control. *Our lives are governed by habit.*

government governments
NOUN the group of people who govern a country.
✔ Note that there is an *n* in the middle of *government.*

governor governors
NOUN a person who controls or organizes a state or institution.

gown gowns
NOUN 1 a long, formal dress.
2 a long black cloak worn by people such as judges and lawyers.

grab grabs grabbing grabbed
VERB 1 to take or pick something up roughly.
2 If you grab an opportunity, you take advantage of it eagerly.
[from German *grabben* meaning to seize or to scramble for]

grace graces
NOUN 1 an elegant way of moving.
2 a pleasant, kind way of behaving.
3 a short prayer of thanks said before a meal.
PHRASE 4 If you do something **with good grace**, you do it cheerfully and without complaining.

graceful
ADJECTIVE able to move or do things smoothly and elegantly.
gracefully ADVERB

gracious
ADJECTIVE 1 kind, polite, and pleasant.
2 "Good gracious" is an exclamation of surprise.
graciously ADVERB

grade grades grading graded
NOUN 1 the quality of something relative to other similar things: *different grades of paper.*
2 the mark which you get in an exam.
3 In schools in the United States, a grade is a group of classes for children of a similar age. *She's in the sixth grade.*
VERB 4 To grade things means to judge them according to their quality or size.

gradient gradients
NOUN a slope or the steepness of a slope.

gradual
ADJECTIVE happening slowly over a long period of time.
gradually ADVERB

graduate graduates graduating graduated
Said "**grad**-yoo-ut" NOUN 1 a person who has completed a first degree at a university.
Said "grad-you-**ate**" VERB 2 to graduate from one thing to another means to progress gradually towards the second thing. *The rider graduated from learning to trot to learning to canter.*
3 to complete a first degree at a university.

graffiti
Said "graf-**fee**-tee" NOUN slogans or drawings scribbled, sprayed or painted on walls.
[from Italian *graffiare* meaning to scratch a surface]
✔ Although *graffiti* is a plural in Italian, the language it comes from, in English it can be used as a singular noun or a plural noun.

grain grains
NOUN 1 a cereal plant such as wheat, or a single grain of that plant.
2 a tiny piece of sand, salt, etc.

gram grams
NOUN a unit of weight equal to one thousandth of a kilogram, abbreviated "g".
[from Greek *gramma* meaning small weight]

grammar
NOUN 1 the rules of a language that state how words can be combined to form sentences.
2 In Britain, a grammar school is a secondary school for pupils of high ability.

grammatical
ADJECTIVE 1 relating to grammar.
2 following the rules of grammar correctly.
grammatically ADVERB

granary granaries
NOUN 1 a building for storing grain.
ADJECTIVE 2 TRADEMARK Granary bread contains whole grains of wheat.

grand grander grandest
ADJECTIVE 1 splendid or impressive.
2 very important or ambitious.
NOUN 3 INFORMAL a thousand pounds or a thousand dollars. *This car cost twenty grand.*
grandly ADVERB

Synonyms: (sense 1) imposing, magnificent

WORD FAMILY: grand
gran, grandma, grandmother **NOUN**
granny, grannies **NOUN**
nan, nanny, nannies **NOUN**
grandchild, grandchildren **NOUN**
grandad, grandads, grandfather **NOUN**
grandpa, grandpas **NOUN**
granddaughter, granddaughters **NOUN**
grandparent, grandparents **NOUN**
grandson, grandsons **NOUN**

grandchild grandchildren
NOUN Someone's grandchildren are the children of their son or daughter.

 ► Political words: parliament, government, legislation, taxation, prime minister, chancellor.

grandfather clock grandfather clocks
NOUN a clock in a tall wooden case that stands on the floor.

grandparent grandparents
NOUN Your grandparents are the parents of your father or mother.

grand piano grand pianos
NOUN a large flat piano with horizontal strings.

grandstand grandstands
NOUN a structure with a roof and seats for spectators at a sports ground.

granite
Said "**gran**-nit" NOUN a very hard rock used in building and road making.

grant grants granting granted
NOUN 1 an amount of money that the government or other organization gives to someone for a particular purpose.
VERB 2 If you grant something to someone, you allow them to have it.
PHRASE 3 If you **take something for granted**, you believe it without thinking about it.
4 If you **take someone for granted** you expect their help but fail to show that you are grateful for it.

grape grapes
NOUN a small green or purple vine fruit, eaten raw, dried to make raisins, currants and sultanas or used to make wine.

grapefruit grapefruits
NOUN a large, round, yellow or pink citrus fruit.

grapevine grapevines
NOUN 1 a climbing plant which grapes grow on.
PHRASE 2 If you hear some news **on the grapevine**, it has been passed on from person to person, usually unofficially or secretly.

graph graphs
NOUN a chart or diagram showing number information in a visual way. Most graphs have a horizontal and vertical axis, each representing a different set of information.

graphic graphics
ADJECTIVE 1 A graphic description of something unpleasant is very detailed and realistic.
NOUN 2 Graphics are drawings and pictures composed of simple lines and strong colours.
[from Greek *graphein* meaning to write]

grapple grapples grappling grappled
VERB 1 to struggle with someone while fighting.
2 If you grapple with a problem, you try hard to solve it.

grasp grasps grasping grasped
VERB 1 to hold something firmly.
2 If you grasp an idea, you understand it.
NOUN 3 a firm hold.
4 an understanding. *Jamal has a good grasp of maths.*

grass grasses
NOUN the common green plant that grows in fields on lawns and in parks.
grassy ADJECTIVE

grasshopper grasshoppers
NOUN an insect with long back legs which it uses for jumping and making a high-pitched sound.

grate grates grating grated
NOUN 1 a framework of metal bars in a fireplace.
VERB 2 to shred food into small pieces by rubbing it against a tool called a grater.

grateful
ADJECTIVE pleased and thankful, appreciative.
gratefully ADVERB

grating gratings
NOUN 1 a secure metal frame of crossed bars filling a gap in a wall or floor.
ADJECTIVE 2 A grating sound is harsh and unpleasant.

gratitude
NOUN the feeling of being grateful.

grave graves; graver gravest
NOUN 1 a place where a dead person is buried.
ADJECTIVE 2 FORMAL serious.
gravely ADVERB

gravel
NOUN small stones used for making roads and paths.

gravestone gravestones
NOUN a large stone placed over someone's grave, with their name on it.

Synonym: tombstone

graveyard graveyards
NOUN an area of land where dead people are buried.

gravity
NOUN 1 a force of attraction, such as the force that pulls things towards the earth. Gravity makes things fall to the ground when you drop them.
2 FORMAL extreme seriousness.

gravy
NOUN a brown sauce made from meat juices.

graze grazes grazing grazed
VERB 1 When animals graze, they eat grass.
2 If something grazes a part of your body, it scrapes against it, injuring you slightly.
graze NOUN

grease greases greasing greased
NOUN 1 a thick substance used for oiling machines.
2 an oily substance produced by your skin.
VERB 3 to put grease on something.
greasy ADJECTIVE

a b c d e f g h i j k l m n o p q r s t u v w x y z

A B C D E F G H I J K L M N O P Q R S T U V W X Y Z

great **greater greatest**
ADJECTIVE **1** very large in size, amount or degree.
2 very important.
3 very good.
greatly ADVERB **greatness** NOUN

greedy **greedier greediest**
ADJECTIVE wanting more of something than is necessary or fair.
greed NOUN **greedily** ADVERB

green **greener greenest**
ADJECTIVE OR NOUN **1** the colour of grass.
2 a smooth flat area of grass.
ADJECTIVE **3** INFORMAL related to environmental issues.

greenery
NOUN a lot of trees, bushes or other green plants together in one place.

greengrocer **greengrocers**
NOUN a shopkeeper who sells vegetables and fruit.

greenhouse **greenhouses**
NOUN a glass building in which people grow plants that need to be kept warm.

greenhouse effect
NOUN the gradual rise in temperature in the earth's atmosphere due to heat being absorbed by the sun and being trapped by gases such as carbon dioxide in the air around the earth.

greet **greets greeting greeted**
VERB **1** If you greet someone, you say something friendly like "hello" when you meet them.
2 If you greet something in a particular way, you react to it in that way. *We greeted the news with suspicion.*

Synonyms: (sense 1) hail, salute

greeting **greetings**
NOUN **1** something friendly that you say to someone when you meet them.
2 a friendly message that you write or send to someone.

grenade **grenades**
NOUN a small bomb, containing explosive or tear gas, which can be thrown.
[from Spanish *granada* meaning pomegranate]

grew
the past tense of **grow**.

grey **greyer greyest; greys**
ADJECTIVE OR NOUN the colour of ashes or of clouds on a rainy day.

greyhound **greyhounds**
NOUN a thin dog with long legs that can run very fast.

grid **grids**
NOUN **1** a pattern of lines crossing each other to form squares.
2 the network of wires and cables by which electricity is distributed throughout a country.

grief
NOUN **1** extreme sadness.
PHRASE **2** If someone is **grief-stricken**, they are full of sadness.
3 If someone or something **comes to grief**, they fail or are injured.

grievance **grievances**
NOUN a reason for complaining.

grieve **grieves grieving grieved**
VERB to be extremely sad, usually because someone has died.
grieving ADJECTIVE

Synonyms: lament, mourn

grill **grills grilling grilled**
NOUN **1** a part on a cooker where food is cooked by heat from above.
VERB **2** to cook food under a grill.
3 INFORMAL to question very thoroughly, to interrogate.

grim **grimmer grimmest**
ADJECTIVE **1** If a situation or piece of news is grim, it is very unpleasant and worrying.
2 Grim places are unattractive and depressing.
3 very serious or stern. *The members of the jury looked grim.*
grimly ADVERB

grimace **grimaces**
Said "grim-**mace**" NOUN a twisted expression of the face indicating disgust or pain.
grimace VERB

grime
NOUN thick dirt which gathers on the surface of something.
grimy ADJECTIVE

grin **grins grinning grinned**
VERB to smile broadly.
grin NOUN

grind **grinds grinding ground**
VERB **1** to crush something into a powder.
2 If you grind your teeth, you rub your upper and lower teeth together.
NOUN **3** The **daily grind** is your boring and tiresome daily routine.
PHRASE **4** If something **grinds to a halt**, it slows down and stops.

Synonyms: (sense 1) crush, powder, pulverize

grip **grips gripping gripped**
VERB **1** to hold something firmly, to grasp.
2 If something grips you, you give all your attention to it.
NOUN **3** a firm hold; grasp.
4 Your grip on a situation is your control over it.
gripping ADJECTIVE

 ► Words ending in "-ance" and "-ant" generally come from Old French.

grisly grislier grisliest
ADJECTIVE very nasty and horrible: *a grisly murder scene.*

gristle
Said "**gris**-sl" NOUN a tough, rubbery substance found in some meat.
gristly ADJECTIVE

grit grits gritting gritted
NOUN **1** very small stones, put on surfaces to make them less slippery.
2 determination in doing something difficult or unpleasant: *the youngster showed real grit.*
VERB **3** to put grit on an icy surface.
PHRASE **4** To **grit your teeth** means to decide to carry on in a difficult situation.
gritty ADJECTIVE

grizzly bear grizzly bears
NOUN a large greyish-brown bear from North America.

groan groans groaning groaned
VERB to make a long, low sound of pain, unhappiness, or disapproval.
groan NOUN

grocer grocers
NOUN a shopkeeper who sells many kinds of food.

grocery groceries
NOUN a grocer's shop.
PLURAL NOUN Groceries are food and other daily household supplies.

groin groins
NOUN the area where your legs join the main part of your body at the front.

groom grooms grooming groomed
NOUN **1** someone who looks after horses in a stable.
2 At a wedding, the groom is the bridegroom.
VERB **3** To groom an animal means to clean its fur.

groove grooves
NOUN a deep line cut into a surface.
grooved ADJECTIVE

grope gropes groping groped
VERB **1** to search blindly for something with your hands.
2 If you grope for something such as the solution to a problem, you try to think of it.

gross grosser grossest
ADJECTIVE **1** very bad: *gross rudeness.*
2 A gross amount is the total amount before any deductions are made.
grossly ADVERB

Antonym: (sense 2) net

grotesque
Said "groh-**tesk**" ADJECTIVE very strange and ugly.
grotesquely ADVERB

grotto grottoes or grottos
NOUN a small cave that people visit because it is attractive.

grotty grottier grottiest
ADJECTIVE; INFORMAL unattractive or of poor quality.

ground grounds grounding grounded
1 the past tense and past participle of **grind**.
NOUN **2** the surface of the earth.
3 land, especially land that is used for a particular purpose: *training ground; burial grounds; football ground.*
4 The ground dealt with by a book or course is the range of subjects it covers.
VERB **5** If an aircraft is grounded, it is not allowed to fly.
6 INFORMAL If a young person is grounded, they are not allowed to go out.
PHRASE **7** "Ground" is used in expressions such as **gain ground** and **new ground** to refer to the progress that someone or something makes. *The Internet is rapidly gaining ground in its popularity. These novels are breaking new ground.*

ground floor
NOUN the floor of a building that is approximately level with the ground.

grounds
PLURAL NOUN **1** The grounds of a large building are the garden or area of land which surrounds it.
2 The grounds for something are the reasons for it. *After receiving poor service, they had good grounds for complaint.*

groundsheet groundsheets
NOUN a large piece of waterproof material placed on the ground to sleep on when camping.

group groups grouping grouped
NOUN **1** a number of things or people that are linked in some way.
2 a number of musicians who perform pop music together.
VERB **3** When things or people are grouped together, they are linked in some way.

Synonyms: (sense 1) band, bunch, set

grouse grouses grousing groused
VERB **1** to grumble.
NOUN **2** a fat brown or grey moorland bird often shot for sport.

grove groves
NOUN; LITERARY a group of trees growing closely together.

grovel grovels grovelling grovelled
VERB to behave in an unpleasantly humble way towards someone you regard as important.
[from Middle English *on grufe* meaning lying on your belly]

The "t" is silent in: gristle, christen, bristle, bustle, glisten, jostle, moisten.

A B C D E F G H I J K L M N O P Q R S T U V W X Y Z

grow grows growing grew grown
VERB **1** to get bigger or increase.
2 If a tree or plant grows somewhere, it is alive there.
3 When people grow plants, they plant them and look after them.
4 to develop or change in a certain way. *He's growing old.*
5 INFORMAL If something grows on you, you gradually get to like it.
grow up VERB to become an adult.

Synonym: (sense 1) expand

growl growls growling growled
VERB **1** a low rumbling sound an angry animal makes.
2 to speak in a low, rough, rather angry voice.
growl NOUN

grown-up grown-ups
NOUN; INFORMAL an adult.
grown-up ADJECTIVE

growth growths
NOUN **1** the process by which something gets bigger, or develops to its full size.
2 an abnormal lump that grows inside or on a person, animal or plant.

grub grubs
NOUN **1** a wormlike insect that has just hatched from its egg.
2 INFORMAL food.

grubby grubbier grubbiest
ADJECTIVE rather dirty.
grubbiness NOUN

grudge grudges grudging grudged
NOUN **1** If you have a grudge against someone, you resent them because they have harmed you in the past.
VERB **2** If you grudge someone something, you give it to them unwillingly, or are not pleased that they have it.
grudging ADJECTIVE **grudgingly** ADVERB

gruelling
ADJECTIVE difficult and tiring.

gruesome
ADJECTIVE shocking and horrible: *a gruesome murder.*

gruff gruffer gruffest
ADJECTIVE If someone's voice is gruff, it sounds rough and unfriendly.
gruffly ADVERB

grumble grumbles grumbling grumbled
VERB **1** to complain in a bad-tempered way.
NOUN **2** a bad-tempered complaint.
grumbler NOUN

grumpy grumpier grumpiest
ADJECTIVE bad-tempered and fed-up.
grumpily ADVERB **grumpiness** NOUN

Synonyms: ill-tempered, irritable

grunt grunts grunting grunted
VERB a short, low, gruff sound like a pig makes.
grunt NOUN

guarantee guarantees guaranteeing guaranteed
NOUN **1** a written promise by a company that if a product develops a fault it will be replaced or repaired free of charge.
2 If something is a guarantee of something else, it makes it certain that it will happen.
VERB **3** If something or someone guarantees something, they make certain that it will happen.

Synonyms: (sense 1) assurance, pledge
(sense 3) ensure, promise, vow

guard guards guarding guarded
VERB **1** to watch someone or something carefully, either to protect them or to stop them from escaping.
NOUN **2** a person whose job is to guard a person, object or place.
3 a railway official in charge of a train.

Synonyms: (sense 1) defend, protect
(sense 2) protector, sentry, watchman

guardian guardians
NOUN someone who has been legally appointed to look after a child.
guardianship NOUN

guerrilla guerrillas; also spelt **guerilla**
Said "ger-**ril**-la" NOUN a member of a small unofficial army.

guess guesses guessing guessed
VERB to form an opinion about something without knowing all the relevant facts.
guess NOUN

Synonyms: estimate, suppose, speculate

guest guests
NOUN **1** someone who has been invited to stay at your home or attend an event.
2 The guests in a hotel are the people staying there.

guidance
NOUN help and advice.

guide guides guiding guided
NOUN **1** someone who shows you round places, or leads the way through difficult country.
2 a book which gives information about a particular place or subject.
3 A Guide is a girl who is a member of an organization equivalent to the Scouts which encourages discipline and practical skills.
VERB **4** to lead the way for someone.
5 If you are guided by something, it influences your actions or decisions.

guidebook guidebooks
NOUN a book which gives information about a place.

 ► Find words on this page to go with: warfare, race, unconditional, security.

guide dog guide dogs
NOUN a dog that has been trained to lead a blind person.

guideline guidelines
NOUN a piece of official advice about how something should be done.

guillotine guillotines
Said "**gil**-lot-teen" NOUN **1** a machine once used for beheading people, especially in France.
2 a piece of equipment with a long sharp blade, used for cutting paper.
guillotine VERB

guilt
NOUN **1** an unhappy feeling of having done something wrong.
2 Someone's guilt is the fact that they have done something wrong. *I'm convinced of Frank's guilt.*

guilty guiltier guiltiest
ADJECTIVE **1** If someone is guilty of doing something illegal or wrong, they did it.
2 If you feel guilty, you are unhappy because you think you have done something wrong.
guiltily ADVERB

guinea pig guinea pigs
NOUN **1** a small furry animal without a tail, often kept as a pet.
2 a person on which something new is tried out. *I was a guinea pig for a new type of margarine.*

guitar guitars
NOUN a musical instrument, usually with six strings and a long neck.

gulf gulfs
NOUN **1** a very large bay.
2 a large difference between two things or people.

gull gulls
NOUN a sea bird with long wings, white and grey or black feathers, and webbed feet.

gullet gullets
NOUN the tube that goes from your mouth to your stomach.

gullible
ADJECTIVE easily tricked.
gullibility NOUN

Synonym: naive

gully gullies
NOUN a channel or small valley.

gulp gulps gulping gulped
VERB **1** to swallow large quantities of drink or food.
2 to swallow air because you are nervous.
NOUN **3** a large quantity of drink or food swallowed at one time.

gum gums
NOUN **1** a flavoured substance that people chew but do not swallow.
2 glue for sticking paper.
3 Your gums are the firm flesh in which your teeth are set.

gumboots
PLURAL NOUN wellington boots.

gumtree gumtrees
NOUN a eucalyptus or other tree which produces gum.

gun guns
NOUN a weapon which fires bullets or shells.

gunfire
NOUN the repeated firing of guns.

gunpowder
NOUN an explosive powder made from a mixture of potassium nitrate and other substances.

gunshot gunshots
NOUN the sound of a gun being fired.

gurdwara
NOUN a Sikh place of worship.

gurgle gurgles gurgling gurgled
VERB to make a bubbling sound.
gurgle NOUN

guru gurus
Said "**goo**-rooh" NOUN a spiritual leader and teacher, especially in India.

gush gushes gushing gushed
VERB to flow out in large quantities.

Synonyms: pour, spurt, stream

gust gusts
NOUN a sudden rush of wind.
gust VERB

gut guts gutting gutted
PLURAL NOUN **1** Your guts are your internal organs, especially your intestines.
2 INFORMAL Guts is courage.
VERB **3** To gut a dead fish means to remove its internal organs.
4 If a building is gutted, the inside of it is destroyed, especially by fire.

Synonyms: (sense 1) entrails, innards, intestines

gutter gutters
NOUN the edge of a road, or a channel fixed to a roof, in which rain collects and flows away.
guttering NOUN

guy guys
NOUN **1** INFORMAL a man or boy.
2 a model of Guy Fawkes that is burnt on a bonfire on Guy Fawkes Day (5 November).

guzzle guzzles guzzling guzzled
VERB to drink or eat something quickly and greedily.

A B C D E F G H I J K L M N O P Q R S T U V W X Y Z

gym **gyms**
NOUN **1** gym is **gymnastics**.
2 a large room with special equipment for physical exercises; a gymnasium.

gymkhana **gymkhanas**
Said "jim-**kah**-na" NOUN an event in which people take part in horse-riding contests.

gymnasium **gymnasiums**
NOUN a room with special equipment for physical exercises; a gym.
[from Greek *gumnazein* meaning to exercise naked, because Greek athletes were naked when training]

gymnast **gymnasts**
NOUN someone who is trained in gymnastics.

gymnastics
NOUN precise, specific physical exercises, especially ones using equipment such as bars and ropes.

Gypsy **Gypsies**
NOUN a member of an ethnic group scattered across Europe, the Middle East and the Americas. Gypsies have a nomadic lifestyle, but some are settled on sites and in houses.
[from *Egyptian*, because people used to think gypsies came from Egypt]

 ► Every English word has a vowel sound. Note that "y" can make a vowel sound, as in cry, hymn, crypt, Gypsy.

Hh

habit **habits**
NOUN something that you do often or regularly.
habitual ADJECTIVE **habitually** ADVERB
[from Latin *habitus* meaning custom]

habitat **habitats**
NOUN the natural home of a plant or animal.
[from Latin *habitare* meaning to live or to inhabit]

hack **hacks hacking hacked**
VERB 1 to cut at something using rough strokes.
PHRASE 2 A **hacking cough** is a dry, painful cough with a harsh, unpleasant sound.

hacker **hackers**
NOUN; INFORMAL someone who uses a computer to break into the computer system of a company or government.

hacksaw **hacksaws**
NOUN a small saw with a narrow blade set in a frame.

had
the past tense of **have**.

haddock
NOUN an edible sea fish.

hag **hags**
NOUN; OFFENSIVE an ugly old woman.

haggard
ADJECTIVE looking very tired and ill.

haggis
NOUN a Scottish dish made from the internal organs of the sheep with oatmeal and spices.

haggle **haggles haggling haggled**
VERB to argue with someone, usually about the price of something.

haiku **haiku**
NOUN a form of concisely written poem arranged in three lines of five, seven and five syllables.
[a Japanese word, *hai* meaning amusement + *ku* meaning verse]

hail **hails hailing hailed**
NOUN 1 frozen rain.
2 A hail of things is a lot of them coming at you together: *a hail of bullets.*
VERB 3 When it is hailing, frozen rain is falling.
4 to call out or signal to attract attention. *She hailed a taxi.*

hailstone **hailstones**
NOUN a pellet of hail.

hair **hairs**
NOUN the fine, thread-like strands that grow on your head and body, and the bodies of some other animals.

WORD FAMILY: hair
hairbrush, hairbrushes **NOUN**
haircut, haircuts, hairstyle, hairstyles **NOUN**
hairdresser, hairdressers **NOUN**

hairpin **hairpins**
NOUN 1 a U-shaped wire used to hold hair in position.
ADJECTIVE 2 A hairpin bend is a U-shaped bend in the road.

hair-raising
ADJECTIVE very frightening or exciting.

hairy **hairier hairiest**
ADJECTIVE covered in hair.
hairiness NOUN

hajj **hajjes**; also spelt **hadj**
*Rhymes with "***badge***"* **NOUN** a pilgrimage to Mecca that every Muslim is supposed to make at least once in their lives.

halal or **hallal**
NOUN meat from animals that have been killed according to Muslim law.
halal ADJECTIVE

half **halves**
NOUN, ADJECTIVE OR ADVERB 1 one of two equal parts that make up a whole.
ADVERB 2 You can use "half" to say that something is only partly true. *I half expected him to hit me.*
PREPOSITION 3 **Half past** refers to a time that is thirty minutes after a particular hour.

half-baked
ADJECTIVE; INFORMAL Half-baked ideas or plans have not been properly thought out.

half-hearted
ADJECTIVE showing no real effort or enthusiasm.
half-heartedly ADVERB **half-heartedness** NOUN

half-mast
NOUN A flag at half-mast is flying halfway down the pole, usually as a signal of mourning.

half term
NOUN a short holiday midway through a school term.

half-time
NOUN a short break between two parts of a game when the players have a rest.

halfway
ADVERB OR ADJECTIVE at the middle of two points in place or time.

hall **halls**
NOUN 1 the room just inside the front entrance of a house which leads into other rooms.
2 a large room or building used for public events.
3 the great house of an estate: *Aston Hall.*

a b c d e f g h i j k l m n o p q r s t u v w x y z

A B C D E F G H I J K L M N O P Q R S T U V W X Y Z

hallowed
Said "**hal**-lode" ADJECTIVE respected as being holy: *hallowed ground.*

Halloween or **Hallowe'en**
NOUN October 31 (the eve of All Saints' Day), celebrated by children dressing up, often as ghosts and witches.

hallucinate **hallucinates hallucinating hallucinated**
Said "hal-**loo**-sin-ate" VERB to see strange things in your mind because of illness or drugs.
hallucination NOUN

halo **haloes** or **halos**
NOUN a circle of light around the head of a holy figure.

halt **halts halting halted**
VERB **1** to stop.
NOUN **2** a short standstill.

halter **halters**
NOUN a strap fastened round a horse's head so that it can be led easily.

halve **halves halving halved**
Said "**hahv**" VERB **1** to divide something into two equal parts.
2 to reduce the size or amount of something by half.

halves
the plural of **half**.

ham
NOUN **1** meat from the back leg of a pig, usually eaten cold, having been salted and dried or smoked.
ADJECTIVE **2** Ham acting is very amateurish, unsubtle acting.

hamburger **hamburgers**
NOUN a flat disc of minced meat, fried and eaten in a bread roll.

Synonym: beefburger

hammer **hammers hammering hammered**
NOUN **1** a tool used for hitting nails into things.
VERB **2** to hit something repeatedly with a hammer.

hammock **hammocks**
NOUN a piece of net or canvas hung between two supports and used as a bed.

hamper **hampers hampering hampered**
NOUN **1** a large basket with a lid, often used for carrying food to a picnic.
VERB **2** If something hampers you, it makes it difficult for you to do what you are trying to do.

Synonyms: (sense 2) handicap, hinder, impede

hamster **hamsters**
NOUN a small furry rodent which is often kept as a pet.
✔ There is no *p* in *hamster.*

hand **hands handing handed**
NOUN **1** Your hands are the parts of your body at the ends of your arms, below the wrist.
2 The hands of a clock or watch are the pointers that indicate what time it is.
VERB **3** to give something to someone.
PHRASE **4** Something that is **at hand**, **to hand**, or **on hand** is available, close by, and ready for use.
5 You use **on the one hand** and **on the other hand** to introduce the two parts of an argument or discussion that has two different points of view. *On the one hand, I like ice cream best, on the other hand, biscuits are nice too.*
6 If you do something **by hand**, you do it using your hands rather than a machine.
7 If someone **has a hand in** something, they are involved in doing it or creating it. *She had a hand in its design.*
8 If you **give** or **lend someone a hand**, you help them to do something.

handbag **handbags**
NOUN a small bag used mainly by women to carry money and personal items.

handbook **handbooks**
NOUN a book giving information and instructions about something.

handcuffs
PLURAL NOUN a pair of lockable metal clamps used to prevent prisoners from escaping by attaching them to something or someone.
handcuff VERB

handful **handfuls**
NOUN **1** A handful of something is the amount of it that you can hold in your hand.
2 A handful of people or things is a small number of them.

handicap **handicaps handicapping handicapped**
NOUN **1** a physical or mental disability.
2 something that makes it difficult for you to achieve something. *Jack found his lack of education a handicap when finding a job.*
3 In sport, a handicap is a disadvantage or advantage given to competitors according to their skill, in order to give all of them an equal chance of winning.
VERB **4** to make it difficult for someone to achieve something.
handicapped ADJECTIVE

handicraft **handicrafts**
NOUN an activity such as embroidery or pottery which involves making things with your hands; also the items produced.

handiwork
NOUN something that you have done or made yourself.

handkerchief **handkerchiefs**
NOUN a small square of fabric used for blowing your nose. Often shortened to **hanky**.

 ► Idioms. What does it mean to be an old hand, to have the upper hand, to have a free hand?

handle handles handling handled
NOUN **1** the part of a tool, bag or cup that you hold in order to pick it up or use it.
2 a knob or lever that is attached to a door and used to open and close it.
VERB **3** If you handle an object, you hold it or touch it with your hands.
4 If you handle something, you deal with it successfully.

handlebar handlebars
NOUN Handlebars are the bar and handles at the front of a bicycle, used for steering.

handshake handshakes
NOUN the grasping and shaking of a person's hand, as a greeting or a sign of agreement.

handsome
ADJECTIVE **1** attractive in a masculine way.
2 large and generous: *a handsome donation.*
handsomely ADVERB

Synonym: (sense 1) good-looking

handstand handstands
NOUN an upside down balance on your hands with your body and legs up in the air.

handwriting
NOUN your style of writing with a pen or pencil.

handy handier handiest
ADJECTIVE **1** useful, capable, skilful. *Your advice in came in very handy. She's handy with a paintbrush.*
2 convenient and nearby. *The corner shop was very handy.*

hang hangs hanging hung
VERB **1** Something that hangs is attached in a high place so that it does not touch the ground.
2 To hang someone means to kill them by suspending them by a rope around the neck.
hang about or **hang around** VERB; INFORMAL to stay or wait somewhere.
hang on VERB **1** to hold tightly to something.
2 INFORMAL to wait. *Hang on, I'll be with you in a minute.*
hang up VERB to put down a telephone receiver at the end of a call.
✔ For sense 2 of *hang*, the past tense and past participle are *hanged*.

hangar hangars
NOUN a large building where aircraft are kept.

hanger hangers
NOUN a coat hanger.

hang-glider hang-gliders
NOUN an unpowered aircraft consisting of a large frame covered in fabric, from which the pilot hangs in a harness.

hanker hankers hankering hankered
VERB If you hanker after something, you continually want it.

hanky hankies
NOUN a handkerchief.

Hanukkah or **Chanukah**
NOUN an eight-day Jewish festival of lights.

haphazard
Said "hap-**haz**-ard" ADJECTIVE not organized or planned.
haphazardly ADVERB

happen happens happening happened
VERB **1** to occur, come about or take place.
2 If you happen to do something, you do it by chance.
happening NOUN
✔ For planned events, do not use *happen* or *occur*; use, for example, *took place* instead. *The wedding took place on Saturday.* Only something unexpected *happens* or *occurs*.

happiness
NOUN a feeling of great contentment or pleasure.

happy happier happiest
ADJECTIVE **1** full of contentment or joy: *a happy smile.*
2 satisfied with something. *I'm happy with your work.*
3 willing to do something. *I'm happy to help.*

Synonyms: (sense 1) blissful, ecstatic, glad

harass harasses harassing harassed
Said "**har**-rass" VERB to trouble or annoy someone continually.
harassed ADJECTIVE **harassing** ADJECTIVE
harassment NOUN
[from Old French *harer* meaning to set a dog on]
✔ The American pronunciation har-**rass** is often used now in Britain.

harbour harbours
NOUN a sheltered area of water where boats can be moored.

hard harder hardest
ADJECTIVE OR ADVERB **1** requiring a lot of effort.
2 with a lot of force.
ADJECTIVE **3** firm and difficult to mark or scratch.
4 not easily bent or broken.
5 difficult.
6 showing no kindness or pity.
7 Hard drugs are very strong illegal drugs.

Synonyms: (sense 1) arduous, laborious, tough
(sense 4) inflexible, rigid, unyielding
(sense 5) baffling, complicated, puzzling

hardback hardbacks
NOUN OR ADJECTIVE a book with a stiff cover.

hard-boiled
ADJECTIVE A hard-boiled egg is one that has been boiled until it is solid throughout.

Idioms. What do we mean by hard up, hard cheese, hard hearted, hard luck, hard times?

hard disk hard disks
NOUN a magnetic disk within a computer on which computer data is stored.

harden hardens hardening hardened
VERB to make harder or to become harder.

hardly
ADVERB **1** almost not or not quite. *We were hardly ever there.*
2 certainly not. *It's hardly a secret.*
✔ Do not use *hardly* with a negative word like *not* or *no*: *he could hardly hear her* not *he could not hardly hear her.*

hardship hardships
NOUN a time or situation of suffering and difficulty.

hardware
NOUN **1** tools and equipment for use in the home and garden.
2 computer equipment. See **software**.

hard-wearing
ADJECTIVE strong, well-made and long-lasting.

hardwood hardwoods
NOUN strong, hard wood from a tree such as an oak; also the tree itself.

hardy hardier hardiest
ADJECTIVE tough and able to endure very difficult or cold conditions.
hardiness NOUN

hare hares haring hared
NOUN **1** an animal like a large rabbit, but with longer ears and legs.
VERB **2** to run very fast. *He hared off down the corridor.*

harm harms harming harmed
VERB **1** to injure or damage someone or something.
NOUN **2** injury or damage.

Synonym: (sense 1) hurt

harmful
ADJECTIVE having a bad effect on something. *Cigarettes are harmful to the body.*
harmfully ADVERB **harmfulness** NOUN

harmless
ADJECTIVE having no bad effects.
harmlessly ADVERB **harmlessness** NOUN

harmonica harmonicas
NOUN a small musical instrument like a mouth organ, which has a button you can press to raise the pitch of notes played.

harmony harmonies
NOUN **1** In music, harmony is a pleasant combination of musical notes.
2 a state of peaceful agreement and cooperation.
harmonious ADJECTIVE

harness harnesses harnessing harnessed
NOUN **1** a set of straps and fittings fastened round a horse so that it can pull a vehicle, or fastened round someone's body to attach something.
VERB **2** If you harness something, you bring it under control to use it. *We can harness water power to produce electricity.*

harp harps harping harped
NOUN **1** a musical instrument consisting of a triangular frame with vertical strings which you pluck with your fingers.
VERB **2** If someone harps on about something, they keep talking about it, especially in a boring way.
harpist NOUN

harpoon harpoons harpooning harpooned
NOUN **1** a spear attached to a rope, thrown or fired from a gun and used for catching whales or large fish.
VERB **2** to catch using a harpoon.

harpsichord harpsichords
NOUN a musical instrument like a small piano.

harsh harsher harshest
ADJECTIVE **1** hard, severe or tough: *harsh weather conditions.*
2 unkind and showing no sympathy: *a harsh decision.*
harshly ADVERB **harshness** NOUN

harvest harvests
NOUN **1** the act of gathering a crop, or the time when this is done.
2 a crop that has been gathered.
harvest VERB

has
the third person singular of **have**.

hash
PHRASE **1** If you **make a hash** of a job, you do it badly.
NOUN **2** a dish made of small pieces of meat and vegetables cooked together.

hasn't
contraction of **has not**.

hassle hassles hassling hassled
NOUN **1** INFORMAL something that is difficult or causes trouble.
VERB **2** to annoy someone by repeatedly asking them to do something.

haste
NOUN doing something quickly, especially too quickly.

hasten hastens hastening hastened
VERB To hasten means to move quickly or do something quickly.

hasty hastier hastiest
ADJECTIVE happening or acting quickly and without preparation.
hastily ADVERB

 ► What is a "hard copy" of something you have written? What is a "soft copy"?

hat hats
NOUN a covering for the head.

hatch hatches hatching hatched
VERB **1** When an egg hatches, the egg breaks open and the young bird or reptile emerges. Insects and fish also hatch from eggs.
2 To hatch a plot means to plan it.
NOUN **3** a small covered opening in a floor or wall.

hatchback hatchbacks
NOUN a car with a door at the back which opens upwards.

hatchet hatchets
NOUN **1** a small axe.
PHRASE **2** To **bury the hatchet** means to resolve a disagreement and become friends again.

hate hates hating hated
VERB **1** to dislike very much.
NOUN **2** a very strong feeling of dislike.
hateful ADJECTIVE

Synonyms: (sense 1) detest, loathe

hateful
ADJECTIVE extremely unpleasant.
hatefully ADVERB **hatefulness** NOUN

hatred
Said "**hay**-trid" NOUN an extremely strong feeling of dislike.

hat trick hat tricks
NOUN the same player scoring three goals in one football match, or taking three wickets with successive balls in a cricket match.

haughty haughtier haughtiest
Rhymes with "**naughty**" ADJECTIVE showing excessive pride; acting in a superior way.
haughtily ADVERB **haughtiness** NOUN

Synonyms: disdainful, proud, supercilious

haul hauls hauling hauled
VERB **1** to pull something with great effort.
NOUN **2** a quantity of something obtained: *a thief's haul.*
PHRASE **3** Something that is **a long haul** takes a lot of time and effort to achieve.

haunt haunts haunting haunted
VERB **1** If a ghost haunts a place, it is seen or heard there regularly.
2 If a memory or fear haunts you, it continually worries you.
haunting ADJECTIVE

haunted
ADJECTIVE **1** A haunted place is said to be regularly visited by a ghost.
2 If a person is haunted by something, they have a worry which they cannot get rid of.

have has having had
VERB **1** an auxiliary verb, used to form the past tense or to express completed actions. *They have never met. I have lost my watch.*
2 to own or possess something.
3 If you have something, you experience it, it happens to you, or you are affected by it. *I have an idea!*
4 to give birth to. *When is she having the baby?*
PHRASE **5** If you **have to** do something, you must do it.
6 If you **had better** do something, you ought to do it.

haven havens
Said "**hay**-ven" NOUN a safe place.

haven't
contraction of **have not**.

hawk hawks
NOUN a bird of prey with short rounded wings and a long tail.

hay
NOUN grass which has been cut and dried and is used as animal feed.

hay fever
NOUN an allergy to pollen and grass, causing sneezing and watering eyes.

haystack haystacks
NOUN a large, firmly built pile of hay.

hazard hazards
NOUN something which could be dangerous to you.
hazardous ADJECTIVE **hazardously** ADVERB

haze
NOUN If there is a haze, you cannot see clearly because there is moisture or smoke in the air.
hazy ADJECTIVE

hazel hazels
NOUN a variety of tree.

hazy
ADJECTIVE dim or vague: *a hazy memory. The air was hazy over the city.*

he
PRONOUN "He" is used to refer to a man, boy or male animal.

head heads heading headed
NOUN **1** the part of your body which has your eyes, brain and mouth in it.
2 your mind. *I can't get that song out of my head.*
3 the top or front of something or the most important end of it: *the head of the queue.*
4 the person in charge of a group or organization.
VERB **5** to be at the top of a list, organization, etc.
6 to move towards a particular place or outcome. *The bandits headed for the border.*
7 to hit a ball with your head.
ADJECTIVE OR ADVERB **8** The heads side of a coin is the side which has a person's head on it.

headache headaches
NOUN **1** a pain in the head.
2 If something is a headache, it causes a lot of difficulty and worry. *Finding somewhere to stay was a real headache.*

a b c d e f g h i j k l m n o p q r s t u v w x y z

header headers
NOUN A header in soccer is hitting the ball with your head.

heading headings
NOUN a piece of writing that is written or printed at the top of a page.

headlight headlights
NOUN A vehicle's headlights are the large bright lights at the front.

headline headlines
NOUN 1 A headline is the title of a newspaper story, printed in large letters at the top of it.
2 The headlines are the main points of the radio or television news.

headlong
ADVERB If you fall headlong, you fall with your head first.

head-on
ADJECTIVE If two vehicles have a head-on collision, the front of one meets the front of the other.
head-on ADVERB

headphones
PLURAL NOUN a pair of small speakers which you wear over your ears to listen to a CD, radio, etc. without other people hearing.

headquarters
NOUN the main office of an organization, often abbreviated to HQ.

head start
NOUN an advantage (either intentional or non-intentional) at the beginning of a race or other competition. *The boxer had a head start because he was taller.*

headstrong
ADJECTIVE determined to do something your own way and ignoring other people's advice.

head teacher head teachers
NOUN the person in charge of a school.

Synonyms: headmaster, headmistress

heal heals healing healed
VERB to become healthy again from injury: *the nasty wound healed.*
healing NOUN **healer** NOUN

health
NOUN 1 the condition of your body. *Smoking is bad for your health.*
2 a state in which you are fit and well. *They nursed the injured police officer back to health.*

Synonyms: (sense 2) fitness, wellbeing

healthy healthier healthiest
ADJECTIVE 1 fit, well and not ill.
2 good for you: *a healthy diet.*
healthily ADVERB

heap heaps heaping heaped
NOUN 1 a pile or mound of something.
VERB 2 to arrange things in a pile.

hear hears hearing heard
VERB 1 to receive sounds with your ears.
2 When you hear from someone, they write to you or phone you.
3 to receive information. *I heard that the school was to close.*
PHRASE 4 If you say that you **won't hear of** something, you refuse to allow it.

hearing hearings
NOUN 1 Your sense of hearing makes it possible for you to hear sounds.
2 A court trial or official meeting.

hearing aid hearing aids
NOUN a device to assist hearing, worn in or behind the ear.

hearse hearses
Said "**hurss**" NOUN a vehicle for carrying a dead person to their funeral.

heart hearts
NOUN 1 the organ in your chest that pumps the blood around your body.
2 Your heart is thought of as the centre of your emotions, especially of love.
3 the most central or important part of something: *the heart of the city.*
4 courage, determination or enthusiasm. *Don't lose heart, we're nearly home.*

heart attack heart attacks
NOUN a serious medical condition in which the heart beats irregularly or stops completely.

heartbroken
ADJECTIVE very sad and emotionally upset.

hearth hearths
Said "**harth**" NOUN the floor of a fireplace.

heartless
ADJECTIVE cruel and unkind.
heartlessly ADVERB **heartlessness** NOUN

hearty heartier heartiest
ADJECTIVE 1 cheerful and enthusiastic: *a hearty welcome.*
2 strongly felt: *a hearty dislike.*
3 A hearty meal is large and satisfying.
heartily ADVERB

heat heats heating heated
NOUN 1 warmth or the quality of being hot.
2 temperature. *Adjust the heat of the cooker.*
3 a preliminary competition which decides who will compete in the final. *Our team were eliminated in the heats.*
VERB 4 to raise the temperature of something.
heating NOUN

heater heaters
NOUN a device for supplying heat.

heath heaths
NOUN an area of open land covered with rough grass or heather.

heather
NOUN a wild plant with small purple or white flowers.

 ► Newspaper words: headline, editor, column, byline, feature, editorial, advertisement.

heatwave heatwaves
NOUN a period of exceptionally hot weather.

heave heaves heaving heaved
VERB 1 to move or throw something with a lot of effort.
2 If your stomach heaves, you vomit or suddenly feel sick.
3 If you heave a sigh, you sigh loudly.
heave to VERB When a ship **heaves to**, it stops moving.
heave NOUN
[from Old German *heffen* meaning to raise]

heaven
NOUN In some religions, heaven is a place of happiness where God is believed to live and where good people are believed to go when they die.

Antonym: hell

heavenly
ADJECTIVE 1 relating to heaven.
2 INFORMAL wonderful. *This cake tastes heavenly.*

heavy heavier heaviest
ADJECTIVE 1 Something that is heavy weighs a lot.
2 great in degree or amount: *a heavy downpour of rain.*
3 involving a lot of force: *a heavy blow.*
heavily ADVERB **heaviness** NOUN

heavy-duty
ADJECTIVE strong and hard-wearing: *heavy-duty boots.*

heavyweight heavyweights
NOUN a boxer in the heaviest weight group.

Hebrew Hebrews
Said "**hee**-broo" NOUN the name of the language spoken by Jewish people, also another name for Jews themselves.

hectare hectares
NOUN a unit of area equivalent to 10 000 square metres.

hectic
ADJECTIVE involving a lot of rushed activity: *a hectic schedule.*
hectically ADVERB

he'd
1 contraction of **he would**.
2 contraction of **he had**.

hedge hedges
NOUN a row of bushes along the edge of a garden, field or road.

hedgehog hedgehogs
NOUN a small, brown animal with sharp spikes covering its back.

heed heeds heeding heeded
VERB 1 to pay attention to what someone says.
NOUN 2 careful attention.

Synonyms: (sense 1) listen to, mind

heel heels
NOUN 1 the back part of your foot, below the ankle.
2 the raised part on the back of a shoe.

hefty heftier heftiest
ADJECTIVE of great size, force or weight: *a hefty blow.*

heifer heifers
Said "**hef**-fer" NOUN a young female cow that has not yet had a calf.

height heights
NOUN 1 the measurement of a person or object from bottom to top.
2 a high position or place.
3 The height of something is when it is at its most successful or intense: *the height of fame.*

heighten heightens heightening heightened
VERB 1 to make something taller.
2 to increase in intensity: *the excitement heightened.*

heir heirs
Said "**air**" NOUN A person's heir is the person who will inherit their property or title when they die.

heirloom heirlooms
Said "**air**-loom" NOUN a family possession passed from one generation to another.

held
the past tense of **hold**.

helicopter helicopters
NOUN an aircraft with rotating blades instead of wings, which enable it to take off vertically.

helium
Said "**hee**-lee-um" NOUN a gas that is lighter than air. Helium can be used to fill balloons.

hell
NOUN 1 In some religions, hell is the place where the souls of evil people are believed to go to be punished after death.
2 INFORMAL If you say that something is hell, you mean it is very unpleasant.

Antonym: heaven

he'll
contraction of **he will**.

hello
INTERJECTION a word used in greeting or when you answer the phone.

helm helms
NOUN 1 the position from which a boat is steered by wheel or tiller.
PHRASE 2 If someone is **at the helm**, they are in charge.

helmet helmets
NOUN a hard, protective hat.

"ha" is short for hectare. What abbreviations are used for centimetre, kilogram, millilitre, ounce?

A B C D E F G H I J K L M N O P Q R S T U V W X Y Z

help helps helping helped
VERB **1** to assist.
NOUN **2** assistance.
PHRASE **3** If you **help yourself** to something, you take it for yourself.
4 If you **can't help** something, you cannot control it or stop it happening.
helper NOUN

helpful
ADJECTIVE **1** If someone is helpful they help you in some way.
2 Something that is helpful makes a situation easier or better.
helpfully ADVERB **helpfulness** NOUN

Synonyms: (sense 1) cooperative, supportive (sense 2) beneficial, useful

helping helpings
NOUN an amount of food that you get in a single serving.

helpless
ADJECTIVE If you are helpless, you are unable to protect yourself or to do anything useful.
helplessly ADVERB **helplessness** NOUN

helter-skelter helter-skelters
NOUN a tall spiral-shaped slide, usually in a fairground.

hem hems hemming hemmed
NOUN **1** The hem of a garment is an edge which has been turned over and sewn in place.
VERB **2** To hem something means to sew a hem on it.
hem in VERB If someone is **hemmed in**, they are surrounded and prevented from moving.

hemisphere hemispheres
Said "**hem**-iss-feer" NOUN one half of the earth or of a sphere.

hen hens
NOUN a female chicken.

hence
ADVERB; FORMAL for this reason. *I'm going out now, hence I won't be able to help you.*

heptagon heptagons
NOUN a shape with seven straight sides.
heptagonal ADJECTIVE
[from Greek *heptagonos* meaning seven-angled]

her
PRONOUN OR ADJECTIVE "Her" is used to refer to a woman, girl or other female animal.

herald heralds heralding heralded
NOUN **1** a formal messenger.
VERB **2** Something that heralds a future event is a sign of that event.

heraldry
NOUN the study of coats of arms and the histories of families.
heraldic ADJECTIVE

herb herbs
NOUN a plant whose leaves are used as a medicine or to flavour food.

herbivore herbivores
NOUN an animal that eats only plants.
herbivorous ADJECTIVE

herd herds herding herded
NOUN **1** a large group of animals.
VERB **2** to make animals, including humans, move somewhere as a group.

here
ADVERB **1** in or to the place where you are. *Come here, Jim!*
2 in the place mentioned or indicated: *if you'll just sign here.*
3 Here refers to a time or situation that is happening now: *here's your chance.*
PHRASE **4** **Here and there** means in several different places. *She could only understand a few words here and there.*

hereditary
ADJECTIVE passed on to a child from a parent: *a hereditary disease.*

heredity
NOUN the process by which characteristics are passed down from parents to their children through the genes.

heritage
NOUN all the traditions and possessions of a family, country, etc. that have continued over many years.

hermit hermits
NOUN a person who lives alone with a simple way of life, especially for religious reasons.

hero heroes
NOUN **1** the main male character in a book, film or play.
2 a person who has done something brave or good.

heroic
ADJECTIVE brave, courageous.
heroically ADVERB

heroin
Said "**herr**-oh-in" NOUN a powerful drug used to prevent pain and taken illegally by some people for pleasure.

heroine heroines
Said "**herr**-oh-in" NOUN **1** the main female character in a book, film or play.
2 a woman who has done something brave or good.

heron herons
NOUN a wading bird with very long legs and a long beak and neck.

herring herrings
NOUN a silvery fish that lives in large shoals in northern seas.

 ► Homophones sound alike but are spelt differently. Examples include here/hear, there/their, aloud/allowed.

hers
PRONOUN "Hers" refers to something that belongs to or relates to a woman, girl or other female animal. *I'm a great friend of hers.*

herself
PRONOUN 1 "Herself" refers to the same woman, girl or other female animal that has already been mentioned. *Aya pulled herself out of the water.*
2 "Herself" is used to emphasize the female subject or object of a clause. *When I rang to complain, I spoke to the boss herself.*

he's
contraction of **he is**.

hesitant
ADJECTIVE If you are hesitant, you do not do something immediately because you are uncertain or worried.
hesitantly ADVERB **hesitancy** NOUN

Synonyms: irresolute, uncertain, unsure

hesitate **hesitates hesitating hesitated**
VERB to pause or show uncertainty.
hesitation NOUN

heterosexual
ADJECTIVE OR NOUN attracted to people of the opposite sex.

hexagon **hexagons**
NOUN a shape with six straight sides.

hibernate **hibernates hibernating hibernated**
VERB Animals that hibernate spend the winter in a state like deep sleep.
hibernation NOUN

hiccup **hiccups**; also spelt **hiccough**
Said "**hik**-kup" **NOUN** Hiccups are short, uncontrolled sounds in your throat, often caused by eating or drinking something too quickly.
hiccup VERB

hide **hides hiding hid hidden**
VERB 1 to put something where it cannot be seen, or prevent something from being discovered.
2 to go somewhere where you cannot easily be seen or found.
NOUN 3 the skin of a large animal.
hidden ADJECTIVE

Synonyms: (sense 1) conceal, disguise, mask

hide-and-seek
NOUN a game where people hide and others have to find them.

hideous
Said "**hid**-ee-uss" **ADJECTIVE** extremely ugly or unpleasant.
hideously ADVERB **hideousness** NOUN

hideout **hideouts**
NOUN a hiding place.

hieroglyphics
NOUN writing in the form of picture symbols, particularly that of ancient Egypt.
hieroglyphic ADJECTIVE

hi-fi **hi-fis**
NOUN stereo equipment on which you can play CDs and tapes.
hi-fi ADJECTIVE

higgledy-piggledy
ADJECTIVE OR ADVERB; INFORMAL in a great muddle or disorder.

high **higher highest; highs**
ADJECTIVE OR ADVERB 1 tall or a long way above the ground.
2 great in degree, quantity or intensity: *high winds.*
ADJECTIVE 3 towards the top of a scale of importance or quality: *high marks.*
NOUN 4 a high point or level. *Enthusiasm reached a new high.*

Synonyms: (sense 1) lofty, huge, towering

higher education
NOUN education at universities and colleges.

high jump
NOUN 1 an athletics event involving jumping over a high bar.
PHRASE 2 INFORMAL If you are **for the high jump**, you are going to be in trouble.

highlands
PLURAL NOUN mountainous or very hilly areas of land.

highlight **highlights highlighting highlighted**
VERB 1 to draw attention to a point or problem.
2 to mark text using a pen with pale fluorescent ink.
NOUN 3 the most exciting or interesting part of something.
highlighter NOUN

highly
ADVERB very, extremely: *highly delighted.*

Highness
NOUN Highness is used to address members of the royal family other than a king or queen.

high-pitched
ADJECTIVE A high-pitched sound is high and often rather shrill.

high-rise
ADJECTIVE High-rise buildings are very tall.

high school **high schools**
NOUN a secondary school.

high tide
NOUN the time, usually twice a day, when the sea is at its highest level at a certain part of coast.

highway **highways**
NOUN a road along which vehicles have a right to pass.

A B C D E F G H I J K L M N O P Q R S T U V W X Y Z

highwayman highwaymen
NOUN In the past, highwaymen were robbers on horseback who used to rob travellers.

hijack hijacks hijacking hijacked
VERB to take control illegally of a plane, train or road vehicle during a journey.
hijacker NOUN **hijacking** NOUN

hike hikes
NOUN a long country walk.
hike VERB **hiker** NOUN **hiking** NOUN

hilarious
ADJECTIVE very funny.
hilariously ADVERB **hilarity** NOUN

Synonyms: funny, humorous, uproarious

hill hills
NOUN a rounded area of high land.
hilly ADJECTIVE

hilt hilts
NOUN the handle of a sword or knife.

him
PRONOUN "Him" is used to refer to a man, boy or other male animal.

himself
PRONOUN **1** "Himself" refers to the same man, boy or other male animal that has already been mentioned. *He dried himself with a towel.*
2 "Himself" is used to emphasize the male subject or object of a clause. *The judge told me so himself.*

hind hinds
*Rhymes with "**blind**"* ADJECTIVE **1** used to refer to the back part of an animal: *the hind legs.*
NOUN **2** a female deer.

hinder hinders hindering hindered
*Said "**hin**-der"* VERB to get in someone's way and make something difficult for them.

Hindu Hindus
*Said "**hin**-doo"* NOUN **1** a person who believes in Hinduism, an Indian religion which has many gods and believes that people have another life on earth after death.
ADJECTIVE **2** belonging or relating to Hinduism.
Hinduism NOUN

hinge hinges hinging hinged
NOUN **1** the movable joint which attaches a door or window to its frame.
VERB **2** to depend entirely on something. *Arriving on time hinged on catching the early bus.*

hint hints hinting hinted
NOUN **1** an indirect suggestion. *She gave a hint about what would be in the test.*
2 a helpful piece of advice. *The book offers handy hints on looking after indoor plants.*
VERB **3** to suggest something indirectly.

Synonyms: (sense 1) clue, indication, suggestion
(sense 3) imply, insinuate, suggest

hip hips
NOUN Your hips are the two areas at the sides of your body between your waist and the tops of your legs; also the joints between your legs and pelvis.

hippo hippos
NOUN; INFORMAL a hippopotamus.

hippopotamus hippopotamuses or hippopotami
NOUN a large African animal with thick wrinkled skin and short legs that lives near rivers.
[from Greek *hippo* meaning horse + *potamos* meaning river]

hire hires hiring hired
VERB **1** to pay money to use something for a period of time.
2 If you hire someone, you pay them to do a job for you.

his
ADJECTIVE OR PRONOUN "His" refers to something that belongs or relates to a man, boy or other male animal. *I'm a good friend of his.*

hiss hisses hissing hissed
VERB to make a long "s" sound, especially to show disapproval or aggression.
hiss NOUN

histogram histograms
NOUN a graph consisting of rectangles of varying heights and widths that shows the frequency of values of a quantity. See **bar graph**.

historian historians
NOUN a person who studies and writes about history.

historic
ADJECTIVE important in the past or likely to be seen as important in the future. *The first moonwalk was a historic event.*

historical
ADJECTIVE occurring in or related to the past.
historically ADVERB

history histories
NOUN **1** the study of the past.
2 The history of a person, place or subject is the set of facts that are known about their past.

hit hits hitting hit
VERB **1** to strike with a lot of force.
2 INFORMAL If something hits you, it affects you. *Indira was badly hit by the sad news.*
3 If you hit on an idea or solution, you suddenly think of it.
NOUN **4** a record, play or film that is very popular and successful.
PHRASE **5** INFORMAL If you **hit it off** with someone, you become friendly with someone as soon as you meet them.

 ► Tongue twister: I like to hike from early to late, whatever the weather may be.

hitch hitches hitching hitched
NOUN **1** a slight problem or difficulty: *an administrative hitch.*
VERB **2** INFORMAL to hitchhike.
3 to hook something up or fasten it. *Each wagon was hitched onto the one in front.*

hitchhiking
NOUN travelling by getting free lifts from passing vehicles.
hitchhike VERB **hitchhiker** NOUN

hi tech or **high tech**
ADJECTIVE designed for or using advanced technology.

hither
ADVERB; OLD-FASHIONED to here. *Come hither, sire, and drink thy wine.*

HIV
NOUN the virus associated with the disease AIDS. HIV is an abbreviation for human immunodeficiency virus.

hive hives
NOUN **1** a structure in which bees that are kept by humans live.
PHRASE **2** a place which is a **hive of activity** is very busy with many people working hard.

hoard hoards hoarding hoarded
VERB **1** to save things even though they may no longer be useful.
NOUN **2** a store of things that has been saved or hidden.
hoarder NOUN
✔ Do not confuse *hoard* with *horde.*

Synonyms: (sense 1) save, stockpile, store
(sense 2) cache, stash, store

hoarding hoardings
NOUN a large advertising board by the side of a road.
✔ In the United States and Canada, a *hoarding* is known as a *billboard.*

hoarse hoarser hoarsest
ADJECTIVE A hoarse voice sounds rough and unclear.
hoarsely ADVERB **hoarseness** NOUN

hoax hoaxes
NOUN a trick or an attempt to deceive someone.
hoax VERB **hoaxer** NOUN

hobble hobbles hobbling hobbled
VERB to walk awkwardly because of pain or injury.

hobby hobbies
NOUN something that you do for enjoyment in your spare time.

hockey
NOUN a team game in which players use long sticks with curved ends to try to hit a small ball into the other team's goal.

hoe hoes hoeing hoed
NOUN **1** a long-handled gardening tool with a small square blade, used to remove weeds and break up the soil.
VERB **2** To hoe the ground means to use a hoe on it.

hog hogs hogging hogged
NOUN **1** a neutered male pig.
VERB **2** INFORMAL If you hog something, you take more than your share of it, or keep it for too long.
PHRASE **3** INFORMAL If you **go the whole hog**, you do something completely or thoroughly in a bold or extravagant way.

Hogmanay
NOUN the Scots name for New Year.

hoist hoists hoisting hoisted
VERB **1** to lift something, especially using a crane or other machinery.
NOUN **2** a machine for lifting heavy things.

hold holds holding held
VERB **1** to carry or support something, using your hands or arms.
2 to keep something in a particular position. *She held the door open.*
3 to contain. *The case holds up to forty cassettes.*
4 "Hold" often means the same as "have". *The girls plan to hold a party.*
5 If you hold someone responsible for something, you consider that they are responsible for it.
6 to wait for a short time. *The line is engaged. Will you hold?*
7 to keep someone as a prisoner. *I was held overnight in a cell.*
NOUN **8** the fact that you are holding something. *I released my hold on the bag.*
9 power or influence over someone. *Her boyfriend seemed to have a hold over her.*
10 the place where cargo or luggage is stored in a plane or a ship.
PHRASE **11** If you **grab hold of** something or **catch hold of** it, you close your hand tightly around it.
12 If you **get hold of** someone or something, you manage to get them or find them. *I couldn't get hold of any glitter pens.*
hold on VERB **1** to keep your hand firmly round something.
2 to keep something and prevent other people from getting it. *I'm going to hold on to this gadget – it's great!*

holdall holdalls
NOUN a large, soft bag for carrying clothing.

hold-up hold-ups
NOUN **1** a delay. *We were caught in a traffic hold-up for 20 minutes.*
2 A hold-up is a situation in which someone threatens people with a weapon in order to obtain money or valuables.

A B C D E F G H I J K L M N O P Q R S T U V W X Y Z

hole holes
NOUN an opening or hollow space in something.

Synonyms: aperture, gap, opening

Holi
NOUN a Hindu festival celebrated in the spring.

holiday holidays
NOUN 1 a period of time spent away from home for enjoyment.
2 a day when people do not go to work or school because of a national festival.
holiday VERB **holidaymaker** NOUN
[from Old English *haligdaeg* meaning holy day]

Synonym: (sense 1) vacation

hollow
ADJECTIVE 1 having a hole or space inside it.
2 A hollow statement has no real value or worth.

holly
NOUN an evergreen tree or shrub with spiky leaves which often has red berries in winter.

holocaust holocausts
Said "**hol**-o-kawst" NOUN 1 a large scale destruction or loss of life, especially as a result of war: *a nuclear holocaust.*
2 The Holocaust was the mass murder of Jews in Europe by the Nazis during World War II.

hologram holograms
NOUN a three-dimensional photographic image created by laser beams.

holster holsters
NOUN a holder for a hand gun, worn at the side of the body or under the arm.

holy holier holiest
ADJECTIVE 1 relating to God or to a particular religion.
2 Someone who is holy is religious and leads a pure and good life.
holiness NOUN

Synonyms: (sense 1) sacred, hallowed
(sense 2) devout, pious

home homes
NOUN 1 Your home is the house or flat where you live.
2 the place or country where you live or feel that you belong.
3 a building in which elderly or ill people live and receive care.

Synonyms: (sense 1) abode, dwelling, residence

homeless
ADJECTIVE having nowhere to live.
homelessness NOUN

homely
ADJECTIVE simple, ordinary and comfortable. *The holiday cottage was small and homely.*

home-made
ADJECTIVE made at home, rather than bought from a shop.

home page home pages
NOUN the page which comes up first when you log on to the Internet.

homesick
ADJECTIVE a feeling of unhappiness because you are away from home and miss your family and friends.
homesickness NOUN

homeward or **homewards**
ADJECTIVE OR ADVERB towards home.

homework
NOUN school work given to pupils to do at home.

homing
ADJECTIVE A homing device is able to guide itself to a target. An animal with a homing instinct is able to guide itself home.

homograph homographs
NOUN a word that is spelt the same as another word, but has a different meaning. For example the word "stalk" meaning a plant stem and "stalk" meaning to follow. See **homonym, homophone**.

homonym homonyms
NOUN one of a group of words that is pronounced or spelt in the same way but having different meanings. The two types of homonym are the homograph and the homophone. See **homograph, homophone**.

homophone homophones
NOUN a word that is pronounced the same way as another word but is spelt differently. For example to, two, and too are homophones. See **homograph, homonym**.

homosexual homosexuals
NOUN OR ADJECTIVE a person who is sexually attracted to people of the same sex. See **gay**.
homosexuality NOUN

honest
ADJECTIVE truthful and trustworthy.
honestly ADVERB

honesty
NOUN the quality of being truthful and trustworthy.

Synonyms: honour, integrity, truthfulness

honey
NOUN a sweet, edible, sticky substance made by bees.

honeycomb honeycombs
NOUN a wax structure consisting of rows of six-sided cells made by bees for storage of honey and the eggs.

honeymoon honeymoons
NOUN a holiday taken by a couple who have just got married.

 ► Homographs are spelt the same but sound different: minute, refuse, sow, entrance. ►

honeysuckle
NOUN a climbing plant with scented pink or cream flowers.

honk honks honking honked
VERB to make a short, loud sound like a goose, for example with a car horn.
honk NOUN

honour honours honouring honoured
NOUN 1 Your honour is your good reputation and the respect that other people have for you.
2 an award given to someone for something they have done.
3 something that you feel privileged to do. *It's an honour to meet you.*
VERB 4 to give someone special praise or attention, or an award.
5 to be honoured is to feel privileged to do something.
6 If you honour an agreement or promise, you keep it faithfully. *The business had enough money to honour its commitments.*
PHRASE 7 If something is done **in honour of** someone, it is done out of respect for them.

hood hoods
NOUN 1 a loose covering for the head, usually part of a coat or jacket.
2 In American English, the hood of a car is the bonnet.

hoof hooves or hoofs
NOUN the hard bony part of certain animals' feet.

hook hooks hooking hooked
NOUN 1 a curved piece of metal or plastic that is used for catching or holding things.
VERB 2 to attach something using a hook.

hooked
ADJECTIVE addicted to, or obsessed by, something: *hooked on soap-operas.*

hooligan hooligans
NOUN a destructive and violent young person.
hooliganism NOUN

Synonyms: delinquent, ruffian, yob

hoop hoops
NOUN a large ring, often used as a toy.

hooray
another spelling of **hurray**.

hoot hoots hooting hooted
VERB 1 to make a long "oo" sound like an owl.
2 If a car horn hoots, it makes a loud honking noise.
hoot NOUN

hoover hoovers hoovering hoovered
NOUN 1 TRADEMARK a vacuum cleaner.
VERB 2 to use a vacuum cleaner.

hooves
the plural of **hoof**.

hop hops hopping hopped
VERB 1 to jump on one foot.
2 When animals or birds hop, they jump with two feet together.
3 INFORMAL If you hop into or out of somewhere, you move there quickly and easily: *hop up onto the chair.*
NOUN 4 Hops are flowers of the hop plant, used for brewing beer.

hope hopes hoping hoped
VERB 1 If you hope that something will happen, you want or expect it to happen.
NOUN 2 the wish or expectation that things will go well in the future.

hopeful
ADJECTIVE having or giving hope. *Our players are hopeful of victory.*

hopefully
ADVERB 1 having hope. *Scott set out hopefully for the South Pole.*
2 with luck. *Hopefully, our team will win.*
✔ The use of *hopefully* to mean *with luck* is technically not grammatical, and should be avoided in formal written work.

hopeless
ADJECTIVE 1 having no hope.
2 certain to be unsuccessful: *a hopeless situation.*
3 very poor; lacking in ability.

hopscotch
NOUN a children's hopping game.

horde hordes
Rhymes with "**bored**" NOUN a large group or number of people or animals.
✔ Do not confuse *horde* with *hoard.*

horizon horizons
Said "hor-**eye**-zn" NOUN 1 the distant line where the sky seems to touch the land or sea.
2 Your horizons are the limits of what you want to do or are interested in. *Travel broadens your horizons.*
PHRASE 3 If something is **on the horizon**, it is almost certainly going to happen or be done in the future.

horizontal
Said "hor-riz-**zon**-tl" ADJECTIVE flat and level with the ground or with a line considered as a base.
horizontally ADVERB

Antonym: vertical

hormone hormones
NOUN a chemical made by one part of your body that stimulates or has a specific effect on another part of your body.

horn horns
NOUN 1 a warning device on a vehicle.
2 On a cow or goat, the horns are the hard points that grow from its head.

hornet hornets
NOUN a type of very large wasp.

a b c d e f g h i j k l m n o p q r s t u v w x y z

horoscope horoscopes
Said "**hor**-ros-kope" NOUN a prediction about what is going to happen to someone, based on the position of the sun, moon and stars. See **astrology**.

horrible
ADJECTIVE very unpleasant.
horribly ADVERB

Synonyms: dreadful, ghastly, nasty

horrid
ADJECTIVE very unpleasant indeed.
horridly ADVERB **horridness** NOUN

horrific
ADJECTIVE so bad or unpleasant that people are horrified.
horrifically ADVERB

horrify horrifies horrifying horrified
VERB If something horrifies you, it makes you feel dismay and disgust.
horrifying ADJECTIVE **horrifyingly** ADVERB

horror horrors
NOUN a strong feeling of alarm caused by something very unpleasant.
horrific ADJECTIVE **horrifically** ADVERB

horse horses
NOUN a large animal with a mane and tail, which people can ride.

horseback
PHRASE If you are **on horseback**, you are riding a horse.

horse chestnut horse chestnuts
NOUN a variety of tree whose nuts are conkers.

horsepower
NOUN a unit used for measuring how powerful an engine is.

horseshoe horseshoes
NOUN a U-shaped piece of iron nailed to a horse's hoofs to protect them.

horticulture
NOUN the study and practice of growing flowers, fruit and vegetables.
horticultural ADJECTIVE

hose hoses hosing hosed
NOUN **1** a long, flexible tube through which liquid or gas can be passed.
2 an old-fashioned men's garment looking like tight trousers.
3 another name for hosiery, an old-fashioned word for tights, socks and other underwear.
VERB **4** to wash or water something by using a hose.

hospice hospices
Said "**hoss**-piss" NOUN a hospital which provides care for people who are dying.

hospitable
ADJECTIVE friendly, generous and welcoming to guests or strangers.
hospitably ADVERB

hospital hospitals
NOUN a place where sick people are treated and looked after by doctors and nurses.

hospitality
NOUN showing a warm welcome to visitors or guests, often by offering them food and drink.

host hosts hosting hosted
NOUN **1** The host of a party is the person who gives it.
2 a large number of things: *a host of golden daffodils.*
VERB **3** To host an event means to give it. *I shall host a party.*
hostess NOUN

hostage hostages
NOUN a person who is illegally held prisoner by captors who make demands (such as for money) on the threat of injuring or killing them.

hostel hostels
NOUN a large house where people can stay cheaply for a short time.

hostile
ADJECTIVE aggressive.
hostility NOUN

hot hotter hottest
ADJECTIVE **1** having a high temperature.
2 Hot food, such as curry, is very spicy.
PHRASE **3** If you are **in hot pursuit** of someone, you are chasing them closely and very fast.
hotly ADVERB

hot dog hot dogs
NOUN a snack consisting of a frankfurter sausage in a bread roll.

hotel hotels
NOUN a building for paying guests.

hothouse hothouses
NOUN a greenhouse with heating.

hotpot hotpots
NOUN a meat or fish stew or casserole, with a top layer of sliced potatoes.

hound hounds hounding hounded
NOUN **1** a dog, especially one used for hunting or racing.
VERB **2** If someone hounds you, they constantly pursue or trouble you.

hour hours
NOUN **1** a period of 60 minutes.
2 The hours during which something happens is the period of time during which it happens.
[from Greek *hora* meaning season or time of day]

hourglass hourglasses
NOUN an ancient device that uses a trickle of sand to measure time.

hourly
ADVERB every hour.

 ► Horse chestnuts are called "conkers", which is perhaps derived from the French *conque* meaning shell.

A B C D E F G H I J K L M N O P Q R S T U V W X Y Z

house houses housing housed
Said "**howss**" **NOUN 1** a building where people live.
2 a particular type of building or company: *a publishing house.*
Said "**howz**" **VERB 3** to keep something within a building. *The gallery houses a fine art collection.*

houseboat houseboats
NOUN a boat which is moored permanently as someone's home.

household households
NOUN 1 all the people who live as a group in a house or flat.
PHRASE 2 Someone who is **a household name** is very well-known.
householder NOUN

housekeeper housekeepers
NOUN a person who is employed to do the cooking and cleaning in a house.

housekeeping
NOUN the cooking and cleaning in a house.

housewife housewives
NOUN a woman who does not have a paid job, but instead looks after her home and children.

housework
NOUN the daily chores around the house, such as washing and cleaning.

housing
NOUN a general word for the buildings that people live in.

hover hovers hovering hovered
VERB 1 When a bird, insect or aircraft hovers, it stays in the same position in the air.
2 to stand in an uncertain manner. *She hovered near the entrance.*

hovercraft hovercraft or hovercrafts
NOUN a vehicle which can travel fast over water or land supported by a cushion of air.

how
ADVERB 1 "How" is used to ask about, explain, or refer to the way in which something is done, known or experienced. *How did this happen?*
2 "How" is used to ask about or refer to a measurement or quantity. *How much does it cost?*
3 "How" is used to emphasize the following word or statement. *How strange!*

however
ADVERB 1 You use "however" when you are adding a comment which contrasts with what has just been said. *The house is old – however, it is in excellent condition.*
2 You use "however" to say that something makes no difference to a situation. *However hard we tried, we couldn't shift the rock.*

howl howls howling howled
VERB to make a long, loud wailing noise.
howl NOUN

hub hubs
NOUN 1 the centre part of a wheel.
2 the most important or active part of a place or organization. *The kitchen is the hub of most households.*

hubbub
NOUN great noise or confusion.

huddle huddles huddling huddled
VERB 1 If you huddle up, you curl up with your arms and legs close to your body.
2 If people huddle, they sit or stand close to one another, often for warmth.
NOUN 3 a small group of people, often discussing something.

hue hues FORMAL
NOUN colour: *the rosy hue of sunset.*

huff
PHRASE If you are **in a huff**, you are sulking or offended about something.
huffy ADJECTIVE **huffily** ADVERB

hug hugs hugging hugged
VERB to put your arms round someone and hold them close to you.
hug NOUN

Synonyms: cuddle, embrace

huge huger hugest
ADJECTIVE extremely large in amount, size or degree.
hugely ADVERB **hugeness** NOUN

Synonyms: enormous, gigantic, vast

hulk hulks
NOUN 1 a large, heavy person or thing.
2 the body of a ship that has been wrecked or abandoned.

hull hulls
NOUN the main part of a ship's body, which sits in the water.

hum hums humming hummed
VERB 1 to make a tune with your lips closed.
NOUN 2 a continuous low noise.

human humans
ADJECTIVE 1 relating to or concerning people.
NOUN 2 a person.
humanly ADVERB
[from Latin *humanus*, which is from *homo* meaning man]

human being human beings
NOUN a person.

humane
ADJECTIVE showing kindness and sympathy towards others.
humaneness NOUN **humanely** ADVERB

humanity
NOUN 1 people in general.
2 Someone who has humanity shows kindness and sympathy.

Joke. What kind of animal can jump higher than a house? All kinds; houses can't jump.

A B C D E F G H I J K L M N O P Q R S T U V W X Y Z

humble humbler humblest; humbles humbling humbled
ADJECTIVE 1 A humble person is modest and thinks that he or she has very little value.
2 small or not very important: *our humble home.*
VERB 3 To humble someone means to make them feel humiliated.
PHRASE 4 To **eat humble pie** means to behave humbly and admit that you are wrong.
humbly ADVERB **humbled** ADJECTIVE

Synonyms: (sense 1) modest, unassuming

humid
ADJECTIVE If the weather is humid, the air feels damp, heavy, and warm.
humidity NOUN **humidify** VERB

humiliate humiliates humiliating humiliated
VERB to make someone feel ashamed or appear stupid to other people.
humiliation NOUN **humiliating** ADJECTIVE

Synonyms: embarrass, mortify, shame

humility
NOUN the quality of being modest and humble.

hummingbird hummingbirds
NOUN a small bird with powerful wings that make a humming noise as they beat.

humour humours humouring humoured
NOUN 1 the quality of being funny.
2 the ability to be amused by certain things.
VERB 3 If you humour someone, you try to please them, so that they will not become upset.
humorous ADJECTIVE

Synonyms: (sense 1) comedy, funniness, wit

hump humps humping humped
NOUN 1 a small, rounded lump or mound.
VERB 2 INFORMAL If you hump something heavy, you carry or move it with difficulty.

hunch hunches hunching hunched
NOUN 1 a feeling or suspicion about something, not based on facts or evidence.
VERB 2 If you hunch your shoulders, you raise your shoulders and lean forwards.

hunchback hunchbacks
NOUN; OLD-FASHIONED someone who has a large hump on their back.

hundred hundreds
the number 100.
hundredth

hung
the past tense and past participle of **hang**.

hunger
NOUN the need or desire to eat.

hungry hungrier hungriest
ADJECTIVE wanting or needing food.
hungrily ADVERB

hunk hunks
NOUN 1 a large piece of something.
2 INFORMAL an attractive man.

hunt hunts hunting hunted
VERB 1 to chase and kill wild animals for food or sport.
2 to search for something.
NOUN 3 the act of searching for something or pursuing something.
hunter NOUN **hunting** NOUN OR ADJECTIVE

hurdle hurdles
NOUN 1 a frame or barrier that you jump over in certain athletics races.
2 a problem or difficulty, an obstacle.
hurdle VERB

hurl hurls hurling hurled
VERB to throw something with great force.

hurray or **hurrah** or **hooray**
INTERJECTION an exclamation of excitement or approval.

hurricane hurricanes
NOUN a very violent storm with strong winds.

hurry hurries hurrying hurried
VERB 1 to go quickly or to act quickly.
NOUN 2 Hurry is the speed with which you do something quickly. *He was in a hurry to leave.*
PHRASE 3 If you are **in a hurry** you either do or want to do something quickly.
hurry up VERB If you tell someone to hurry up, you want them to do something more quickly.

Synonyms: (sense 1) dash, fly, rush
(sense 2) haste, rush

hurt hurts hurting hurt
VERB 1 to cause physical pain to yourself or someone else.
2 If a part of your body hurts, you feel pain there.
3 to upset someone by being unkind.
ADJECTIVE 4 injured.
5 upset by other people's unkindness.
hurtful ADJECTIVE **hurtfully** NOUN

Synonyms: (sense 1) harm, injure

hurtle hurtles hurtling hurtled
VERB to move or travel very fast indeed, especially in an uncontrolled way.

husband husbands
NOUN A woman's husband is the man she is married to.

hush hushes hushing hushed
VERB 1 If you tell someone to hush, you are telling them to be quiet.
2 To hush something up means to keep it secret, especially something dishonest involving important people.
NOUN 3 If there is a hush, everything goes quiet.
hushed ADJECTIVE

 ► Find the connection between your "funny bone" and a word on this page.

husk husks
NOUN Husks are the dry outer covering of grain or seed.

husky huskier huskiest; huskies
ADJECTIVE 1 A husky voice is rough or hoarse.
NOUN 2 a large, strong dog with a thick coat, often used to pull sledges across snow.
huskily ADVERB

hustle hustles hustling hustled
VERB to make someone move by pushing and jostling them.

hut huts
NOUN a small simple building with one or two rooms.

hutch hutches
NOUN a wooden box with wire mesh at one side, in which small pets can be kept.

hyacinth hyacinths
Said "**high**-as-sinth" NOUN a sweet-smelling spring flower with many small, bell-shaped flowers.

hybrid hybrids
NOUN 1 a plant or animal that has been bred from two different types of plant or animal.
2 anything that is a mixture of two different things.

hydrant hydrants
NOUN a large water tap or valve in a road or street for emergencies.

hydraulic
Said "high-**drol**-lik" ADJECTIVE operated by water or other fluid under pressure.
hydraulics NOUN

hydroelectric
ADJECTIVE Hydroelectric power is electricity produced by flowing water dropping onto a turbine.
hydroelectricity NOUN

hydrogen
NOUN the lightest gas and the simplest chemical element. It is colourless, odourless and flammable.

hyena hyenas; also spelt **hyaena**
Said "high-**ee**-na" NOUN a wild animal like a dog, of Africa and Asia, that hunts in packs.

hygiene
Said "**high**-jeen" NOUN the practice of keeping yourself and your surroundings clean, especially to stop the spread of disease.
hygienic ADJECTIVE **hygienically** ADVERB

hymn hymns
NOUN a Christian song in praise of God.

hyperactive
ADJECTIVE A hyperactive person is unable to relax and is always in a state of restless activity.
hyperactivity NOUN

hypermarket hypermarkets
NOUN a very large supermarket.

hyphen hyphens
NOUN the punctuation mark (-).
hyphenate VERB **hyphenation** NOUN

HYPHEN
The hyphen (-) separates the different parts of certain words, particularly adjectives which combine two words:
left-handed

hypnosis
Said "hip-**noh**-sis" NOUN an artificial state of relaxation, in which the mind is extremely receptive to suggestions.
[from Greek *hupnos* meaning sleep]

hypnotize hypnotizes hypnotizing hypnotized; also spelt **hypnotise**
VERB to put someone into a state in which they seem to be asleep but can respond to questions and suggestions. See **trance**.
hypnotic ADJECTIVE **hypnotism** NOUN
hypnotist NOUN

hypocrite hypocrite
NOUN a person who tells people they should behave in a certain way, yet who does not behave in that way themselves.
hypocritical ADJECTIVE **hypocritically** ADVERB
hypocrisy NOUN

hypotenuse hypotenuses
Said "high-**pot**-tin-yooz" NOUN In a right-angled triangle, the hypotenuse is the longest side and is opposite the right angle.

hypothermia
NOUN a condition in which a person is very ill because they have been too cold for a long time.
[from Greek *hupo* meaning under + *therme* meaning heat]

hypothesis hypotheses
Said "high-**poth**-iss-iss" NOUN an idea or theory which you put forward in order to explain a group of facts.

hypothetical
ADJECTIVE based on assumption rather than fact or reality. *My ideas were purely hypothetical.*

hysteria
Said "hiss-**teer**-ee-a" NOUN a state of uncontrolled excitement or panic.

hysterical
ADJECTIVE 1 Someone who is hysterical is in a state of uncontrolled excitement or panic.
2 INFORMAL extremely funny.
hysterically ADVERB **hysterics** NOUN

Synonyms: (sense 1) frantic, frenzied

a b c d e f g h i j k l m n o p q r s t u v w x y z

Ii

I
PRONOUN A word you use to refer to yourself. *I am happy.*

ice
NOUN water in its frozen state.

iceberg icebergs
NOUN a large mass of ice floating in the sea. [from Dutch *ijsberg* meaning ice mountain]

icecap icecaps
NOUN a layer of ice and snow that permanently covers the North and South Poles.

ice cream ice creams
NOUN a very cold sweet usually made from a milk or custard base.

ice hockey
NOUN a team game played on ice in which players use long sticks with broad horizontal ends to try to hit a small ball into the other team's goal.

ice skate ice skates; ice-skates ice-skating ice-skated
NOUN 1 a boot with a metal blade along the bottom which you wear when skating on ice.
VERB 2 To ice-skate is to move about on ice wearing ice skates.

icicle icicles
Said "**eye**-sik-kl" **NOUN** a pointed piece of frozen water which hangs down from a surface.

icing
NOUN a mixture of powdered sugar and water or egg whites, used to decorate cakes.

icon icons
NOUN 1 a small picture on a computer screen which represents a program, which is activated if you click on the icon with the mouse.
2 a holy picture of Christ, the Virgin Mary, or a saint.

ICT
abbreviation for information and communications technology.

icy
ADJECTIVE 1 very cold.
2 An icy road or path has ice on it.
icily ADVERB

I'd
1 contraction for **I would**.
2 contraction for **I had**.

idea ideas
NOUN 1 a plan or possible course of action. *Have you an idea what to do?*
2 an opinion or belief. *She has some strange ideas.*
3 a general, but not detailed, knowledge of something. *Could you give me an idea of the cost?*

Synonyms: (sense 1) thought, theory, scheme (sense 2) notion, view

ideal
ADJECTIVE 1 the best possible person or thing for a particular purpose: *an ideal teacher; an ideal shot.*
NOUN 2 a principle or idea that you try to achieve because it seems perfect. *Perhaps the most important ideal of all is world peace.*
ideally ADVERB

identical
ADJECTIVE exactly the same.
identically ADVERB

identification
NOUN 1 a document such as a driving licence or passport which proves who someone is.
2 the act of identifying someone.

identify identifies identifying identified
VERB 1 to recognize or name someone or something. *Can you identify who is in this photo?*
2 If you identify yourself and show identification, you say who you are and prove it.
3 If you identify with someone, you understand their feelings and ideas.
identifiable ADJECTIVE

identity identities
NOUN Your identity is who you are.

idiom idioms
NOUN a group of words with a meaning that is not literal. *It is raining cats and dogs.*

idiot idiots
NOUN someone who is stupid or foolish.

Synonyms: fool, halfwit, moron

idiotic
ADJECTIVE extremely foolish or silly.
idiotically ADVERB

idle
ADJECTIVE 1 lazy.
2 doing nothing: *the machines lay idle.*
idleness NOUN **idly** ADVERB

idol idols
Said "**eye**-doll" **NOUN 1** a picture or statue which is worshipped as if it were a god.
2 a famous person who is loved and admired by fans.

idolize idolizes idolizing idolized; also spelt idolise
VERB If you idolize someone, you admire or love them very much.

i.e.
"i.e." means that is, and is used before explaining something more fully. It is an abbreviation for the Latin expression "id est".

 The letter I was probably made from a picture of a reaching hand.

if
CONJUNCTION **1** on the condition that. *I'll stay if Mum will let me.*
2 whether. *I asked Nell if she wanted to come shopping.*

igloo **igloos**
NOUN a dome-shaped house built out of blocks of snow by the Inuit, or Eskimo, people.

igneous
Said "**ig**-nee-us" ADJECTIVE Igneous rocks are formed by hot liquid rock cooling and becoming solid.

ignite **ignites igniting ignited**
VERB If you ignite something, or if it ignites, it starts burning.

ignition **ignitions**
NOUN **1** the part of an engine where the fuel is ignited.
2 the starting of an engine.

ignorant
ADJECTIVE **1** not knowing about something: *ignorant of the rules.*
2 not knowing about things in general. *Without education, we would all be ignorant.*
ignorantly ADVERB **ignorance** NOUN

Synonyms: (sense 1) unaware, unconscious, uninformed

ignore **ignores ignoring ignored**
VERB to deliberately take no notice of someone or something.

iguana **iguanas**
Said "ig-**wah**-na" NOUN a large tropical lizard.

il-
PREFIX used to give the opposite form of adjectives beginning with "l". For example, the opposite of "logical" is "illogical", the opposite of "legible" is "illegible".

ill
ADJECTIVE **1** not well, sick.
2 harmful or unpleasant: *ill effects.*

Synonyms: (sense 1) unhealthy, unwell

I'll
contraction of **I will**.

illegal
ADJECTIVE forbidden by the law.
illegally ADVERB

Synonyms: criminal, illicit, unlawful

illegible
Said "il-**lej**-i-bl" ADJECTIVE Writing which is illegible is unclear and very difficult to read.
illegibly ADVERB **illegibility** NOUN

illegitimate
Said "il-lij-**it**-tim-it" ADJECTIVE A person who is illegitimate was born to parents who were not married at the time.

illiterate
ADJECTIVE unable to read or write.
illiteracy NOUN **illiterately** ADVERB

illness **illnesses**
NOUN **1** the state of being ill.
2 a particular disease: *a cough is a common illness.*

Synonyms: (sense 2) ailment, malady, sickness

illogical
ADJECTIVE not reasonable, sensible or logical.
illogically ADVERB **illogicality** NOUN

ill-treat **ill-treats ill-treating ill-treated**
VERB to hurt or damage someone or something, or treat them cruelly.
ill-treatment NOUN

illuminate **illuminates illuminating illuminated**
VERB **1** to shine light on something to make it easier to see.
2 to make something easier to understand, for instance by giving examples.
3 In medieval times, when monks illuminated books, they decorated them with small brightly coloured pictures and designs.

illumination **illuminations**
NOUN **1** lighting.
2 Illuminations are the coloured lights put up to decorate a town, especially at Christmas.

illusion **illusions**
NOUN **1** something which you think you see clearly but does not really exist. *The magician performed the illusion of cutting a woman in half.*
2 a false belief which you think is true. *Their hopes proved to be an illusion.*
illusory ADJECTIVE

illustrate **illustrates illustrating illustrated**
VERB **1** to put pictures with a text that help to explain it.
2 If you illustrate a point when you are speaking, you make its meaning clearer, often by giving examples.
3 to show that something is true. *The picture illustrates the artist's brilliance.*

illustration **illustrations**
NOUN **1** a picture in a book or with other writing.
2 an example or a story which is used to make a point clear.

illustrator **illustrators**
NOUN a person who creates the pictures to illustrate a book.

I'm
contraction of **I am**.

im-
PREFIX **1** used to give the opposite form of adjectives. For example, "mature" and "possible" become "immature" and "impossible".
2 used to add to a root word the sense of going in. For example, "migrate" becomes "immigrate".

image images
NOUN **1** a mental picture: *an image of how it would be.*
2 any picture or photograph: *an image on the TV screen.*
3 the appearance which a person or organization presents to the public. *The tobacco industry has been trying to improve its image.*

imagery
NOUN The imagery of a poem or book is the descriptive language used.

imaginary
ADJECTIVE existing only in someone's mind, not in reality.

imagination imaginations
NOUN the ability to form new and exciting ideas.

imaginative
ADJECTIVE easily able to form new or exciting ideas; creative.
imaginatively ADVERB

imagine imagines imagining imagined
VERB **1** to form a picture or idea of something in your mind.
2 to think, believe or suppose. *I must have imagined the whole thing.*
imaginable ADVERB

Synonyms: (sense 1) conceive, picture, visualize

imam imams
Said "im-**am**" NOUN a person who leads prayer in a mosque.

imbecile imbeciles
Said "**im**-bis-seel" NOUN a stupid person.

Synonyms: fool, idiot

imitate imitates imitating imitated
VERB to copy someone or something.
imitator NOUN

Synonyms: copy, mimic

imitation imitations
NOUN a copy of something else.

immaculate
Said "im-**mak**-yoo-lit" ADJECTIVE **1** completely clean and tidy, spotless.
2 without any mistakes at all.
immaculately ADVERB

immature
ADJECTIVE **1** Something that is immature has not finished growing or developing.
2 not behaving in a sensible adult way.
immaturely ADVERB **immaturity** NOUN

immediate
ADJECTIVE **1** happening or being done without delay.
2 very close in time, space or relationship. *She's in my immediate circle of friends.*

immediately
ADVERB **1** without any delay.
2 very close in time or space.

Synonym: (sense 1) straight away

immense
ADJECTIVE very large in size or amount, huge.
immensely ADVERB **immensity** NOUN

Synonyms: gigantic, massive, vast

immerse immerses immersing immersed
VERB **1** to put something into a liquid so that it is completely covered.
2 If you are immersed in an activity you are completely involved in it.
immersion NOUN

immigrant immigrants
NOUN someone who has come to live in a country from another country.

immigrate immigrates immigrating immigrate
VERB to move permanently to another country.
immigration NOUN

imminent
ADJECTIVE going to happen very soon.
imminently ADVERB **imminence** NOUN

Synonyms: coming, impending, near

immobile
ADJECTIVE not moving or unable to move.

immobilize immobilizes immobilizing immobilized
VERB If you immobilize a vehicle, you make it unable to move.

immoral
ADJECTIVE Immoral behaviour does not fit in with most people's idea of what is right and proper.
immorality NOUN

immortal
ADJECTIVE **1** In stories, someone who is immortal will never die.
2 Something that is immortal is famous and will be remembered for a long time.
immortality NOUN

immune
Said "im-**yoon**" ADJECTIVE If you are immune to a disease, you are protected against it.
immunity NOUN

 ► Immaculate comes from the Latin *macula* meaning a spot or stain.

immunize **immunizes immunizing immunized**
VERB to inoculate someone against a particular disease so that they are protected against it.
immunization NOUN

Synonym: vaccinate

imp **imps**
NOUN a small mischievous creature in fairy stories.
impish ADJECTIVE

impact **impacts**
NOUN **1** the action of one object hitting another: *it exploded on impact.*
2 a strong effect on a situation or person. *We want these adverts to have maximum impact.*
impact VERB

impair **impairs impairing impaired**
VERB to damage something so that it stops working properly.

impale **impales impaling impaled**
VERB to pierce something with a sharp instrument. *I impaled the potato on my fork.*

impartial
ADJECTIVE having a fair and unbiased view of something; neutral.
impartially ADVERB **impartiality** NOUN

Synonyms: fair, neutral, objective

impatient
ADJECTIVE annoyed because you do not want to wait for something.
impatiently ADVERB **impatience** NOUN

impede **impedes impeding impeded**
VERB to make someone's progress difficult. *Protesters impeded the building of the motorway.*

imperative
ADJECTIVE **1** extremely urgent or important.
NOUN **2** In grammar, an imperative is the form of a verb that is used for giving orders, warnings or instructions. *Help me! Mind your head.*

imperfect
ADJECTIVE **1** not perfect.
NOUN **2** In grammar, the imperfect is a tense used to describe continuous or repeated actions which happened in the past. *I was swimming.*
imperfectly ADVERB **imperfection** NOUN

Synonyms: (sense 1) faulty, flawed

imperial
ADJECTIVE **1** relating to an empire or an emperor or empress.
2 The imperial system of measurement is the measuring system which uses inches, feet and yards, ounces and pounds, pints and gallons.

Antonym: (sense 2) metric

impersonal
ADJECTIVE Something that is impersonal makes you feel that individuals and their feelings do not matter. *The room was cold and impersonal.*

Synonyms: detached, dispassionate, inhuman

impersonate **impersonates impersonating impersonated**
VERB to pretend to be someone else.
impersonation NOUN **impersonator** NOUN

Synonym: mimic

impertinent
ADJECTIVE disrespectful and rude.
impertinently ADVERB **impertinence** NOUN

Synonyms: bold, cheeky, impudent

impetuous
ADJECTIVE If you are impetuous, you act quickly without thinking.
impetuously ADVERB **impetuosity** NOUN

implement **implements implementing implemented**
NOUN **1** a tool.
VERB **2** to carry out a plan, instructions etc., to put into action.
implementation NOUN

implore **implores imploring implored**
VERB to beg someone to do something.
imploring ADJECTIVE **imploringly** ADVERB

imply **implies implying implied**
VERB to suggest in an indirect way. *When you sigh like that, are you implying that you're bored?*

impolite
ADJECTIVE rude, ill-mannered.

import **imports importing imported**
VERB **1** to bring goods in from another country for use in your own country.
NOUN **2** products brought in from another country.

Antonym: export

important
ADJECTIVE **1** very necessary and significant.
2 having a lot of influence or power.
importance NOUN **importantly** ADVERB

Synonym: (sense 1) momentous

impose **imposes imposing imposed**
VERB **1** If you impose something on people, you force it on them.
2 If someone imposes on you, they expect you to do something for them which you do not want to do.
imposition NOUN

imposing
ADJECTIVE having an impressive appearance or manner.

A B C D E F G H I J K L M N O P Q R S T U V W X Y Z

impossible
ADJECTIVE not able to happen or be done.
impossibly ADVERB **impossibility** NOUN

imposter **imposters**
NOUN a person who pretends to be someone else, in order to get things they want.

impractical
ADJECTIVE not practical, sensible or realistic.
impracticality NOUN

impress **impresses impressing impressed**
VERB **1** If someone or something impresses you, it causes you to admire them.
2 If you impress something on someone, you make them understand the importance of it.

impression **impressions**
NOUN **1** the way someone or something looks or seems to you. *What were your first impressions of your school?*
2 If you **make an impression**, you have a strong effect on people you meet.
3 a mark made by pressing something hard on to a soft surface.

impressive
ADJECTIVE If something is impressive, you admire it.
impressively ADVERB **impressiveness** NOUN

imprint **imprints**
NOUN **1** the mark left by the pressure of one object on another.
2 If something leaves an imprint on your mind, it has a strong and lasting effect.
imprint VERB

imprison **imprisons imprisoning imprisoned**
VERB to lock someone up as a prisoner.
imprisonment NOUN

improbable
ADJECTIVE not probable or likely to happen.
improbably ADVERB **improbability** NOUN

Synonyms: doubtful, unlikely

improper
ADJECTIVE **1** illegal or dishonest: *improper dealings.*
2 not suitable or correct: *improper behaviour.*
3 An improper fraction is one in which the numerator is larger than the denominator, for example $\frac{3}{4}$ or $\frac{7}{4}$. They are sometimes called top-heavy fractions.
improperly ADVERB

improve **improves improving improved**
VERB If something improves or if you improve it, it gets better.
improvement NOUN

Synonyms: better, enhance

improvise **improvises improvising improvised**
VERB **1** to make or do something without planning in advance, and using only whatever materials are available.
2 When musicians or actors improvise, they make up the music or words as they go along.
improvised ADJECTIVE **improvisation** NOUN

impudent
ADJECTIVE behaving or speaking disrespectfully.
impudently ADVERB **impudence** NOUN

Synonyms: bold, cheeky, impertinent

impulse **impulses**
NOUN a strong urge to do something.

impulsive
ADJECTIVE tending to do things suddenly, without thinking about them carefully.
impulsively ADVERB **impulsiveness** NOUN

in
PREPOSITION OR ADVERB "In" is used to indicate position, direction, time and manner. *Put it in the pot. She was acting in a silly way.*

Antonym: out

in-
PREFIX **1** in, into: *incoming.*
2 "in-" is often added to words to form opposites. For example, "appropriate" becomes "inappropriate".

inability
NOUN a lack of ability to do something.
unable ADJECTIVE

inaccessible
ADJECTIVE impossible or very difficult to reach.
inaccessibly ADVERB **inaccessibility** NOUN

inaccurate
ADJECTIVE not accurate or correct.
inaccurately ADVERB **inaccuracy** NOUN

Synonyms: incorrect, wrong

inactive
ADJECTIVE not doing anything.
inactivity NOUN

Antonym: active

inadequate
ADJECTIVE **1** If something is inadequate, there is not enough of it, or it is not good enough in quality for a particular purpose.
2 If someone feels inadequate, they feel they do not possess the skills necessary to do a particular job or to cope with life in general.
inadequately ADVERB **inadequacy** NOUN

Synonyms: (sense 1) insufficient, meagre

inanimate
ADJECTIVE not alive: *an inanimate object.*

inappropriate
ADJECTIVE not suitable. *His clothes were inappropriate for the event.*
inappropriately ADVERB
inappropriateness NOUN

Synonyms: out of place, unfitting, unsuitable

 ► What is improper about an improper fraction?

inattentive
ADJECTIVE not paying attention.

inaudible
ADJECTIVE not loud enough to be heard.
inaudibly ADVERB

incapable
ADJECTIVE **1** not able to do something.
2 An incapable person is weak and helpless.
incapability NOUN

incendiary
ADJECTIVE An incendiary bomb is one designed to cause a fire.

incense **incenses incensing incensed**
NOUN **1** a spicy substance which is burned to create a sweet smell, especially during religious services.
VERB **2** If you are incensed by something, it makes you extremely angry.

incentive **incentives**
NOUN something that encourages you to do something. *Mum offered me a new bike as an incentive to work hard.*

incessant
ADJECTIVE continuing without stopping.
incessantly ADVERB

inch **inches**
NOUN a unit of length equal to about 2·54 centimetres.

incident **incidents**
NOUN an event, often one that involves something unpleasant: *a dramatic shooting incident.*

incidental
ADJECTIVE occurring as a minor part of something. *Incidental music is only heard in the background.*

incidentally
ADVERB by the way.

incinerator **incinerators**
NOUN a furnace for burning rubbish.
incinerate VERB **incineration** NOUN

incisor **incisors**
NOUN Your incisors are the square-ended teeth at the front of your mouth. See **canine**, **molar**.

inclination **inclinations**
NOUN If you have an inclination to do something, you think that you want to do it.

include **includes including included**
VERB If one thing includes another, the second thing is part of the first thing. *The book included a chapter on teachers.*

Synonyms: contain, incorporate

inclusive
ADJECTIVE An inclusive price includes all the goods and services that are being offered, with no extra charge for any of them.

incognito
Said "in-kog-**nee**-toe" ADVERB in disguise.

income **incomes**
NOUN the money a person earns.

income tax
NOUN a part of someone's income that they have to pay regularly to the government.

incompatible
ADJECTIVE Two things or people are incompatible if they are unable to live or exist together because they are completely different.
incompatibly ADVERB **incompatibility** NOUN

incompetent
ADJECTIVE not having the ability to do something properly.
incompetently ADVERB **incompetence** NOUN

incomplete
ADJECTIVE not complete or finished.
incompletely ADVERB

incomprehensible
ADJECTIVE not able to be understood.

incongruous
ADJECTIVE Something that is incongruous seems strange because it does not fit in to a place or situation.
incongruously ADVERB **incongruity** NOUN

inconsiderate
ADJECTIVE not considering other people's feelings.
inconsiderately ADVERB
inconsiderateness NOUN **inconsideration** NOUN

Synonyms: unkind, unthoughtful

inconsistent
ADJECTIVE unpredictable, and behaving differently in similar situations.
inconsistently ADVERB **inconsistency** NOUN

inconspicuous
ADJECTIVE not easily seen, not obvious.
inconspicuously ADVERB

inconvenience **inconveniences inconveniencing inconvenienced**
NOUN **1** If something causes inconvenience, it causes minor difficulty or problems for someone.
VERB **2** To inconvenience someone is to cause them minor difficulty or problems.
inconvenient ADJECTIVE **inconveniently** ADVERB

incorporate **incorporates incorporating incorporated**
VERB If something is incorporated into another thing, it becomes part of that thing.
incorporation NOUN

incorrect
ADJECTIVE wrong, untrue, inaccurate.
incorrectly ADVERB

A B C D E F G H I J K L M N O P Q R S T U V W X Y Z

increase increases increasing increased
VERB If something increases, or if you increase it, it becomes larger in number, level or amount.
increase NOUN

incredible
ADJECTIVE **1** difficult to believe.
2 INFORMAL wonderful.

Synonym: (sense 1) unbelievable
(sense 2) amazing

incredulous
ADJECTIVE unable to believe something, because it is very surprising or shocking.
incredulously ADVERB **incredulity** NOUN

incriminate incriminates incriminating incriminated
VERB If something incriminates you, it suggests that you are involved in a crime.

incubate incubates incubating incubated
Said "**in**-kyoo-bate" VERB When eggs are incubated, they are kept warm until they are ready to hatch.
incubation NOUN

incubator incubators
NOUN a piece of hospital equipment in which sick or weak newborn babies are kept warm.

incurable
ADJECTIVE cannot be cured or stopped: *an incurable disease; an incurable habit.*
incurably ADVERB

indebted
ADJECTIVE If you are indebted to someone, you are grateful to them.

indecent
ADJECTIVE Something that is indecent is shocking or rude, usually because it concerns nakedness or sex.
indecently ADVERB **indecency** NOUN

indecisive
ADJECTIVE someone who is indecisive finds it hard to make up their mind.

indeed
ADVERB You use "indeed" to emphasize a point that you are making. *The pudding was very good indeed.*

indefinite
ADJECTIVE **1** If something is indefinite, no time to finish has been decided. *No one can tell when an indefinite strike will end.*
2 vague or not exact: *indefinite memories.*

indefinite article indefinite articles
NOUN the grammatical term for **a** and **an**.

Antonym: definite article

indefinitely
ADVERB for an indefinite or unlimited time.

indelible
ADJECTIVE unable to be removed: *indelible ink.*
indelibly ADVERB

indent indents indenting indented
VERB If you indent a line of text, you leave an extra space in from the margin, for example, at the start of a new paragraph.

independent
ADJECTIVE **1** Someone who is independent does not need other people's help, or is very reluctant to ask for it.
2 separate from other people or things, so that it is not controlled or affected by them.
independently ADVERB **independence** NOUN

Synonyms: (sense 2) autonomous, self-governing

indestructible
ADJECTIVE unable to be destroyed.

index indexes
NOUN an alphabetical list at the back of a book, referring to items in the book.

index finger index fingers
NOUN your first finger, next to your thumb; your forefinger.

indicate indicates indicating indicated
VERB **1** If something indicates something, it shows that it is true.
2 to denote or signify.
3 to point to something.
4 to mention. *He has indicated that he may leave.*
5 If drivers indicate, they show which way they are going to turn, usually by operating flashing lights.

indication indications
NOUN a sign of what someone feels or is likely to happen.

indicative
ADJECTIVE **1** If something is indicative of something else, it is a sign of that thing. *A cold nose is often indicative of a healthy dog.*
NOUN **2** Verbs in the indicative mood are in the form used for making statements and questions about facts. *You aren't clean. Is Fred in?*

indicator indicators
NOUN **1** something which tells you what something is like or what is happening. *His yawning was an indicator that he was bored.*
2 A car's indicators are the lights at the front and back which are used to show when it is turning left or right.
3 a substance used in chemistry that shows if another substance is an acid or alkali by changing colour when it comes into contact with it.

indifferent
ADJECTIVE **1** If you are indifferent to something, you have no interest in it.
2 If something is indifferent, it is of a poor quality or low standard: *a pair of rather indifferent paintings.*
indifferently ADVERB **indifference** NOUN

 ► Funny saying. I used to be indecisive but now I'm not so sure.

indigestion
NOUN a pain you get when you find it difficult to digest food.

indignant
ADJECTIVE feeling angry about something that you think is unfair.
indignantly ADVERB

indigo
NOUN OR ADJECTIVE dark violet-blue.

indirect
ADJECTIVE **1** not coming by the straight course or route. *The road was indirect, but had lovely views.*
2 not coming as a direct effect or consequence of something. *I found out in an indirect way that my enquiries had failed.*
NOUN **3** In grammar, the indirect object is a noun or pronoun which receives or benefits from the action of verb and its direct object. For example, in the sentence "Dave threw the ball to the dog", "the ball" is the object and "the dog" is the indirect object.
indirectly ADVERB

indispensable
ADJECTIVE If something is indispensable, you cannot do without it.

indistinct
ADJECTIVE unclear, vague.

individual **individuals**
ADJECTIVE **1** relating to one particular person or thing.
NOUN **2** a person. *Jake was a nice individual.*
individually ADVERB **individuality** NOUN

indoor
ADJECTIVE situated or happening inside a building.

indoors
ADVERB If something happens indoors, it takes place inside a building.

induce **induces inducing induced**
VERB **1** To induce a state is to cause it. *Yoga induces a sense of calm and relaxation.*
2 If you induce someone to do something, you persuade them to do it. *She induced her friend to stay out far too late.*

indulge **indulges indulging indulged**
VERB If you indulge in something, you allow yourself to do something that you enjoy.
indulgence NOUN

indulgent
ADJECTIVE If you are indulgent, you treat someone with special kindness: *an indulgent father.*
indulgently ADJECTIVE

industrial
ADJECTIVE relating to industry.

industrial action
NOUN action taken by workers, such as striking, in protest over pay or working conditions.

industrious
ADJECTIVE An industrious person works very hard.

industry **industries**
NOUN **1** the work and processes involved in making things in factories.
2 all the people and processes involved in manufacturing a particular thing: *the film industry.*

inedible
ADJECTIVE too nasty or poisonous to eat.

ineffective
ADJECTIVE having little or no effect.

inefficient
ADJECTIVE badly organized, wasteful and slow.
inefficiently ADVERB **inefficiency** NOUN

inequality **inequalities**
NOUN a difference in size, status, wealth or position between different things, groups or people.

inert
ADJECTIVE **1** not moving and apparently lifeless.
2 In chemistry, an inert substance does not easily take part in a chemical reaction.

inertia
Said "in-**ner**-sha" NOUN **1** a feeling of laziness and unwillingness to do anything.
2 In science, inertia is the property of anything to continue exactly what it is doing (either standing still or moving) unless a force acts upon it.

inevitable
ADJECTIVE certain to happen, definite.
inevitably ADVERB **inevitability** NOUN

inexhaustible
ADJECTIVE An inexhaustible supply of something will never run out.

inexpensive
ADJECTIVE not costing much, cheap.
inexpensively ADVERB **inexpensiveness** NOUN

inexperienced
ADJECTIVE lacking experience of a situation or activity.
inexperience NOUN

Synonyms: new, raw, unpractised

inexplicable
ADJECTIVE not able to be explained.
inexplicably ADVERB

infallible
ADJECTIVE never wrong or making a mistake.
infallibility NOUN

infamous
Said "**in**-fe-muss" ADJECTIVE well-known because of something bad or evil.

infant **infants**
NOUN a baby or very young child.
[from Latin *infans* meaning unable to speak]

Find out the place names from which are these words are derived: indigo, attic, bayonet, canter, jersey.

A B C D E F G H I J K L M N O P Q R S T U V W X Y Z

infantile
ADJECTIVE Infantile behaviour is very silly and childish.

infantry
NOUN soldiers who fight on foot rather than in tanks or on horses.

infatuated
ADJECTIVE to have such strong feelings of love or passion for someone that you cannot think sensibly.
infatuation NOUN

infect **infects infecting infected**
VERB to cause disease in someone or something.

infection **infections**
NOUN **1** a disease caused by tiny organisms such as bacteria or viruses.
2 the state of being infected.

infectious
ADJECTIVE spreading from one person to another.
infectiously ADVERB **infect** VERB

Synonyms: catching, contagious

infer **infers inferring inferred**
VERB to work out that something is true on from information that you already have. *I inferred from the tone of her voice that she was angry.*
inference NOUN
✔ Do not use *infer* to mean the same as *imply*.

inferior
ADJECTIVE not as good as something else.
inferiority NOUN

Antonym: superior

inferno **infernos**
NOUN a very large, dangerous fire.

infertile
ADJECTIVE **1** Infertile land has poor soil, and little grows on it.
2 An infertile human or other animal or plant is unable to reproduce.
infertility NOUN

infested
ADJECTIVE something or somewhere that is infested has a large number of animals such as insects living in or on it and causing damage.
infestation NOUN

infinite
ADJECTIVE without any limit, never-ending.
infinitely ADVERB

infinitive **infinitives**
NOUN In grammar, the infinitive is the base form of the verb. It often has "to" in front of it: *to go*; *to see*.

infinity
NOUN **1** an infinite or indefinitely great number or amount.
2 an unreachable point, further away than any other point. *The skies seem to stretch on to infinity.*

infirm
ADJECTIVE An infirm person is weak in health or body, especially from old age.

infirmary **infirmaries**
NOUN a hospital.

inflamed
ADJECTIVE If part of your body is inflamed, it is red and swollen, usually because of infection.

inflammable
ADJECTIVE An inflammable material burns easily.
✔ *Inflammable* and *flammable* both mean likely to catch fire, although *flammable* is used more often.

inflammation
NOUN painful redness or swelling of part of the body.

inflate **inflates inflating inflated**
VERB to fill something with gas, such as helium or air, to make it swell.
inflatable ADJECTIVE

inflation
NOUN an overall increase in the price of goods and services in a country.

inflection **inflections**; also spelt **inflexion**
NOUN a change in the form of a word that shows its grammatical function. For example, a change that makes a noun plural: "song" becomes "songs".

inflexible
ADJECTIVE fixed and unable to be altered or to alter. *When it came to the rules, Mai was inflexible.*

inflict **inflicts inflicting inflicted**
VERB If you inflict something unpleasant on someone, you make them suffer it.

influence **influences influencing influenced**
NOUN **1** the power to make other people do what you want.
2 the effect that someone or something has: *the influence of alcohol.*
VERB **3** to have an effect on someone or something.
[from Latin *influentia* meaning power flowing from the stars]

Synonyms: (sense 1) hold, power, sway

influential
ADJECTIVE having a lot of influence over people.

influenza
NOUN; FORMAL flu.

 ► Joke. St Peter: "How did you get up to heaven?" New arrival: "Flu!"

inform informs informing informed
VERB **1** to tell someone about something; to notify.
2 If you inform on a person, you tell the police about a crime they have committed.
informant NOUN

informal
ADJECTIVE relaxed and casual; not formal.
informally ADVERB **informality** NOUN

information
NOUN knowledge and facts about something; data.

information technology
NOUN the production, storage and communication of information using computers and other electronic equipment; also the study and knowledge of how to achieve this.

informative
ADJECTIVE An informative book, television programme, etc. gives you a lot of useful information.

informer informers
NOUN someone who tells the police that another person has committed a crime.

infuriate infuriates infuriating infuriated
VERB to make someone very angry.
infuriating ADJECTIVE **infuriatingly** ADVERB

ingenious
Said "in-**jeen**-yuss" ADJECTIVE very clever at inventing new ideas and methods.
ingeniously ADVERB **ingeniousness** NOUN

ingot ingots
NOUN a brick-shaped lump of solid metal formed in a mould and cooled from its hot liquid state.

ingrained
ADJECTIVE If you have an ingrained characteristic, it is a strong and deep part of your personality.

ingratitude
NOUN not being grateful.

ingredient ingredients
NOUN Ingredients are the things that something is made from, especially in cookery.

inhabit inhabits inhabiting inhabited
VERB to live in a place.
inhabited ADJECTIVE

inhabitant inhabitants
NOUN someone who lives in a particular place.

Synonyms: citizen, dweller, resident

inhale inhales inhaling inhaled
VERB to breathe in.
inhalation NOUN

inherit inherits inheriting inherited
VERB **1** to receive money or property from someone who has died.
2 If you inherit a characteristic from a parent or ancestor, you are born with it.
inheritance NOUN **inheritor** NOUN

inhibited
ADJECTIVE People who are inhibited find it difficult to relax and to show their emotions.
inhibition NOUN

Synonyms: shy, repressed

inhospitable
ADJECTIVE **1** An inhospitable place is unpleasant or difficult to live in.
2 If someone is inhospitable, they do not make people who visit them feel welcome.

inhuman
ADJECTIVE not human or not behaving as a human being should.

initial initials
Said "in-**nish**-l" ADJECTIVE **1** first; early: *an initial reaction.*
NOUN **2** Your initials are the capital letters which begin each word of your name.
initially ADVERB

initiate initiates initiating initiated
Said "in-**ish**-ee-ate" VERB **1** to start or make happen.
2 If you initiate someone into a group or club, you make them a member – usually by means of a special ceremony.
initiation NOUN

initiative initiatives
Said "in-**nish**-at-ive" NOUN **1** an ability to decide what needs to be done, and to do it without needing the advice or assistance of other people.
PHRASE **2** If you **take the initiative**, you are the first person to do something.

inject injects injecting injected
VERB to use a needle and syringe to put a substance into a person's body.
injection NOUN

injure injures injuring injured
VERB If you are injured, part of your body is damaged.
injured ADJECTIVE

injury injuries
NOUN damage or hurt to the body.

injustice injustices
NOUN **1** unfairness and lack of justice.
2 If you do someone an injustice, you judge them too harshly.

ink
NOUN the coloured liquid used for writing or printing.
inky ADJECTIVE

A B C D E F G H I J K L M N O P Q R S T U V W X Y Z

inkling
NOUN a suspicion or slight suggestion. *I had an inkling I was right.*

inland
ADVERB OR ADJECTIVE **1** towards or near the middle of a country, away from the coast.
2 The Inland Revenue is the authority that collects income tax in the UK.

in-law **in-laws**
NOUN In-laws are members of a husband's or wife's family.

inlet **inlets**
NOUN a narrow opening of the coastline, for example, a creek.

inmate **inmates**
NOUN someone who lives in a prison or psychiatric hospital.

inn **inns**
NOUN a small hotel or pub.

inner
ADJECTIVE **1** contained inside or within a place or object. *Open the shell to reveal the inner lining.*
2 further inside. *North London has both a ring motorway and an inner ring road.*

Antonym: outer

innings
NOUN In cricket, an innings is a period when a particular team is batting.

innocent
ADJECTIVE **1** not guilty of a crime.
2 without experience of evil or unpleasant things: *young and innocent.*
3 not involved in a conflict, harmless. *They are killing innocent people.*
innocently ADVERB **innocence** NOUN

innovation **innovations**
NOUN a completely new idea, product or system of doing things.
✔ Do not use the word *new* before *innovation.*

innumerable
ADJECTIVE too many to be counted.

inoculate **inoculates inoculating inoculated**
VERB to inoculate someone means to inject them with a weak form of a disease in order to protect them from the disease.
inoculation NOUN

Synonym: vaccinate

input **inputs inputting input**
NOUN **1** all the money, information, and other resources that are put into a job, project or company to make it work.
2 In computing, input is information which is fed into a computer.
VERB **3** to feed information into a computer.

Antonym: output

inquest **inquests**
NOUN an official inquiry to find out what caused a person's death.

inquire **inquires inquiring inquired**; also spelt **enquire**
VERB to ask for information about something.

inquiry **inquiries**; also spelt **enquiry**
NOUN **1** a request for information; a question.
2 an investigation into an issue of public concern, such as finding the causes of a major accident.

inquisitive
ADJECTIVE keen to find out about things.
inquisitively ADVERB **inquisitiveness** NOUN

insane
ADJECTIVE mentally disturbed, mad.
insanely ADVERB **insanity** NOUN

insanitary
ADJECTIVE if conditions are insanitary, they are not clean or healthy.

inscribe **inscribes inscribing inscribed**
VERB **1** to write or carve words on an object.
2 If you inscribe a book, you write your name or a short message at the front.

inscription **inscriptions**
NOUN the words that are written or carved on something, often in a formal way.

insect **insects**
NOUN a small animal with three pairs of legs and usually two pairs of wings.
[from Latin *insectum* meaning animal that has been cut into (because of its shape)]

insecticide **insecticides**
NOUN a poisonous chemical used to kill insects.

insecure
ADJECTIVE **1** feeling unsure of yourself and doubting whether other people like you.
2 not safe or well protected.
insecurely ADVERB **insecurity** NOUN

insensitive
ADJECTIVE If you are insensitive, you do not notice when you are upsetting people.
insensitively ADVERB **insensitivity** NOUN

inseparable
ADJECTIVE Two people, or a group of people, who are inseparable always seem to be together.

insert **inserts inserting inserted**
VERB to put something inside something else.

inside **insides**
ADVERB, PREPOSITION OR ADJECTIVE **1** Inside refers to the inner part of something: *an inside pocket.*
NOUN **2** the part of something enclosed by the walls, sides, etc.: *the inside of the house.*
PHRASE **3** **Inside out** means with the inside part facing outwards.
✔ Do not use *of* after *inside.* You should write *she was waiting inside the school* and not *inside of the school.*

 ► Inscription is derived from the Latin *scriptio* meaning writing.

insight **insights**
NOUN the ability to see and understand what is happening in a situation.

insignificant
ADJECTIVE small and unimportant.
insignificantly ADVERB **insignificance** NOUN

insincere
ADJECTIVE Someone who is insincere pretends to have feelings which they do not really have.
insincerely ADVERB **insincerity** NOUN

insist **insists insisting insisted**
VERB to demand something strongly.

insistent
ADJECTIVE An insistent person is always making demands or wanting attention.

insolent
ADJECTIVE very rude and disrespectful.
insolence NOUN

insoluble
Said "in-**soll**-yoo-bl" ADJECTIVE **1** impossible to solve.
2 unable to dissolve.

insomnia
NOUN difficulty in sleeping.
insomniac NOUN

inspect **inspects inspecting inspected**
VERB to examine or check something carefully.
inspection NOUN

inspector **inspectors**
NOUN **1** someone whose job it is to inspect things or check on the work of others.
2 a police officer just above a sergeant in rank.

inspire **inspires inspiring inspired**
VERB **1** If someone or something inspires you, they give you new ideas, hope and enthusiasm.
2 to make somebody want to act or feel in a certain way.
inspiration NOUN

install **installs installing installed**
VERB to put a piece of equipment, software, etc. in its new, permanent place, and make it ready to use.
installation NOUN

instalment **instalments**
NOUN **1** If you pay for something in instalments, you pay small amounts of money regularly over a period of time.
2 one of the parts of a story or television series.
✔ There is only one *l*.

instance **instances**
NOUN **1** a particular example or occurrence of something.
PHRASE **2** You use **for instance** to give an example of something you are talking about. *Some counties, for instance Cornwall, are popular holiday places.*

instant **instants**
NOUN **1** a moment or short period of time.
ADJECTIVE **2** immediate and without delay, instantaneous.
instantly ADVERB

instantaneous
ADJECTIVE happening immediately and without delay.
instantaneously ADVERB

instead
ADVERB as an alternative to another. *He ate all the chocolate, instead of sharing it with his sister.* [from Middle English *in stead* meaning in place]

instep **insteps**
NOUN the arched middle part of your foot.

instinct **instincts**
NOUN a natural tendency to do something.
instinctive ADJECTIVE **instinctively** ADVERB

institute **institutes instituting instituted**
NOUN **1** an organization for teaching or research.
VERB **2** FORMAL If you institute a rule or system, you introduce it.

institution **institutions**
NOUN **1** a large, important organization, for example a university or bank.
2 a place such as a mental hospital, children's home or prison, where people are looked after as part of an organization.

instruct **instructs instructing instructed**
VERB **1** to tell someone to do something.
2 to teach someone a subject or a skill.

instruction **instructions**
NOUN **1** a piece of information on how to do something; a direction.
2 the act of instructing someone in a subject or skill.
3 Instructions are a set of directions telling you how to do something or get somewhere.
instructional ADJECTIVE

instrument **instruments**
NOUN **1** a tool or device.
2 an object, such as a piano or guitar, which you play in order to make music.

instrumental **instrumentals**
NOUN **1** a piece of music for instruments only, with no singing.
ADJECTIVE **2** If you are instrumental in doing something, you help to make it happen.

insufficient
ADJECTIVE not enough for a particular purpose.
insufficiently ADVERB

Synonyms: inadequate, meagre

A B C D E F G H I J K L M N O P Q R S T U V W X Y Z

insulate **insulates insulating insulated**
VERB **1** If materials such as feathers, fur or foam insulate something, they keep it warm or cold for longer, because they do not conduct heat well.
2 You insulate metal wires along which electricity will flow with materials such as rubber or plastic because they do not conduct electricity.
insulation NOUN **insulator** NOUN
[from Latin *insulatus* meaning made into an island

insulin
Said "**inss**-yoo-lin" NOUN a substance which controls the level of sugar in the blood. People with diabetes do not have enough insulin or are unable to use it efficiently.

insult **insults insulting insulted**
VERB **1** If you insult someone, you offend them by being rude to them.
NOUN **2** a rude remark which offends someone.

Synonyms: (sense 1) abuse, affront, offend (sense 2) abuse, affront, offence

insurance **insurances**
NOUN a system by which people make regular small payments to a company to cover their costs if things are stolen, damaged or stop working.

insure **insures insuring insured**
VERB If you insure something, or yourself, you pay money regularly to a company so that if there is damage or an accident, the company will pay for repairs or medical treatment.

intact
ADJECTIVE complete and undamaged.

intake **intakes**
NOUN **1** a person's intake of food, drink or air is the amount they take in.
2 In a school, college, etc., an intake is any group of students taken in at the beginning of their course.

integer **integers**
NOUN In mathematics, an integer is any whole number.

integral
ADJECTIVE If something is an integral part of a whole thing, it is an essential part.

integrate **integrates integrating integrated**
VERB to combine things so that they become closely linked or form one thing.
integration NOUN **integrated** ADJECTIVE

integrity
NOUN the quality of being honest and following your principles.

intellect **intellects**
NOUN Intellect is the ability to understand ideas and information.

intellectual **intellectuals**
NOUN **1** someone who enjoys and has a capacity for thinking about complicated ideas.
ADJECTIVE **2** involving thought, ideas and understanding: *the intellectual development of children.*

intelligence
NOUN A person's intelligence is their ability to understand and learn things quickly and well.

Synonyms: brains, intellect, understanding

intelligent
ADJECTIVE able to understand things quickly and well.
intelligently ADVERB

intelligible
ADJECTIVE able to be understood.

intend **intends intending intended**
VERB **1** If you intend to do something, you have decided or planned to do it; to mean to do something.
2 If something is intended for a particular purpose, it is planned to have that purpose.

intense
ADJECTIVE **1** very great in strength or amount.
2 Someone who is intense about something takes it very seriously.
intensely ADVERB **intensity** NOUN

intensive
ADJECTIVE involving a lot of effort over a short time: *an intensive training course.*

intent **intents**
NOUN; FORMAL **1** A person's intent is what they intend to do.
ADJECTIVE **2** If you are intent on doing something, you are determined to do it.

intention **intentions**
NOUN Your intention is your idea or plan of what you are going to do.

intentional
ADJECTIVE done on purpose; deliberate.
intentionally ADVERB

interact **interacts interacting interacted**
VERB The way that two people or things interact is the way they work together, communicate or react with each other.
interaction NOUN

interactive
ADJECTIVE allowing two-way communication: *interactive TV.*

intercept **intercepts intercepting intercepted**
Said "in-ter-**sept**" VERB to stop or deflect someone or something that is going from one place to another before they reach their destination.
interceptor NOUN **interception** NOUN

 ► Some poets use internal rhymes, making a word in the middle of a line rhyme with the end word. ►

interchange interchanges
NOUN the act or process of exchanging things or ideas.

interchangeable
ADJECTIVE able to be change places.

intercom intercoms
NOUN a device consisting of a microphone and a loudspeaker, which you use to speak to people in another room.

intercourse
NOUN Intercourse or sexual intercourse is the act of having sex.

interest interests interesting interested
NOUN 1 If you have an interest in something, you want to know more about it.
2 Your interests are the things you enjoy doing.
3 If something is in the interests of a person or group, it will benefit them.
4 an extra payment that you receive in return for lending or investing your money, or an extra payment that you make in return for having borrowed money.
VERB 5 If something interests you, you want to know more about it.
interested ADJECTIVE **interesting** ADJECTIVE

interface interfaces
NOUN The interface between two subjects or systems is the area in which they affect each other or are linked.

interfere interferes interfering interfered
VERB to try to influence a situation, although it does not concern you.
interfering ADJECTIVE

Synonyms: butt in, intrude, meddle

interference
NOUN 1 the act of interfering.
2 Interference on the television means that you receive a poor signal from the transmitter, resulting in poor sound and pictures.

interior interiors
NOUN The interior of something is its inside.

Antonym: exterior

interjection interjections
NOUN a word or phrase spoken suddenly, often to express surprise, pain or anger.

WHAT IS AN INTERJECTION?
Interjections often stand alone rather than as part of a sentence. They can express:
Greetings – *Hello. Hi. Congratulations!*
Agreement or disagreement – *Indeed. No. Yes.*
Pain, anger or annoyance – *Ouch! Blast! Ooh!*
Approval, pleasure or excitement – *Bravo! Hooray! Yippee!*
Surprise or relief – *Wow! Phew!*
Noises – *Sh! Psst! Ugh!*
When an interjection is used within a sentence, it is usually separated by commas or dashes:
I turned the key and, bingo, the engine started.

interlude interludes
*Rhymes with "**rude**"* NOUN a short break from an activity.

intermediate
ADJECTIVE An intermediate level occurs in the middle, between lower and higher stages.

intermission intermissions
NOUN an interval between two parts of a film or play.

intermittent
ADJECTIVE happening only occasionally.
intermittently ADVERB

internal
ADJECTIVE happening inside a person, place or object.
internally ADVERB

international
ADJECTIVE involving different countries.
internationally ADVERB

Internet
NOUN the single worldwide computer network that interconnects other computer networks, allowing data and other information to be exchanged through websites, e-mail, newsgroups, etc.

Synonym: the World Wide Web

interpret interprets interpreting interpreted
VERB 1 to immediately translate what someone is saying into another language so that someone else may understand what is being said.
2 If you interpret what someone says or does, you decide what it means. *I interpreted his silence as a "no".*
interpreter NOUN **interpretation** NOUN

interrogate interrogates interrogating interrogated
VERB to question someone thoroughly to get information from them, to cross-examine.
interrogation NOUN **interrogator** NOUN

interrupt interrupts interrupting interrupted
VERB 1 If you interrupt someone, you start talking while they are talking.
2 to stop a process or activity for a time. *Her holiday was interrupted.*
interruption NOUN

Synonym: (sense 1) to butt in

intersect intersects intersecting intersected
VERB When two roads or lines intersect, they cross each other.

intersection intersections
NOUN 1 the point at which two things, such as lines or roads, cross.
2 In mathematics, the area of overlap in a Venn diagram.

A B C D E F G H I J K L M N O P Q R S T U V W X Y Z

interval intervals
NOUN **1** a period of time between two events or dates.
2 a short break during a play or concert.

intervene intervenes intervening intervened
VERB If you intervene in a situation, you become involved in it and try to change it.
intervention NOUN

Synonyms: mediate, step in

interview interviews interviewing interviewed
NOUN **1** a meeting at which an employer asks you questions in order to find out if you are suitable for a job.
2 a conversation in which a journalist or broadcaster asks someone questions.
VERB **3** to conduct an interview.

intestine intestines
NOUN Your intestines are part of your digestive system, and consist of a very long tube folded up inside your abdomen that carries food from your stomach.
intestinal ADJECTIVE

intimate
ADJECTIVE **1** If two people are intimate, there is a close relationship between them.
2 An intimate matter is very private and personal.
intimately ADVERB **intimacy** NOUN

intimidate intimidates intimidating intimidated
VERB to make someone timid or frightened.
intimidation NOUN

into
PREPOSITION **1** to the interior, towards the middle; against. *We went into the hall. Police are looking into the theft. A car ran into the wall.*
2 INFORMAL If you are into something, you like it very much.

intolerable
ADJECTIVE so bad that it is difficult to put up with.
intolerably ADVERB

intolerant
ADJECTIVE not tolerant of people who are different from you in some way.
intolerance NOUN

intonation
NOUN the way that your voice rises and falls as you speak.

intoxicated
ADJECTIVE; FORMAL drunk.
intoxicating ADJECTIVE **intoxication** NOUN

intransitive
ADJECTIVE An intransitive verb is one that does not have a direct object. For example, "laughs" is an intransitive verb (because you can't laugh someone or something).

Antonym: transitive

intrepid
ADJECTIVE not worried by danger: *an intrepid explorer.*
intrepidly ADVERB

intricate
ADJECTIVE having many fine details.
intricately ADVERB **intricacy** NOUN

intrigue intrigues intriguing intrigued
VERB If something intrigues you, you are fascinated by it and curious about it.
intriguing ADJECTIVE

introduce introduces introducing introduced
VERB **1** If you introduce one person to another, you tell them each other's name so that they can get to know each other.
2 to bring something in for the first time; to establish. *Sir Walter Raleigh is supposed to have introduced the potato to England.*
3 If someone introduces a programme or a concert, they say a few words at the beginning, and perhaps during the course of it.
introductory ADJECTIVE

introduction introductions
NOUN **1** the act of presenting someone or something for the first time.
2 a piece of writing at the beginning of a book, which usually tells you what the book is about or why it was written.

Synonyms: (sense 2) foreword, opening, preface

intrude intrudes intruding intruded
VERB to disturb people by entering a situation or place without being asked.
intruder NOUN **intrusion** NOUN
intrusive ADJECTIVE

Synonyms: butt in, trespass

intuition intuitions
Said "int-yoo-**ish**-n" NOUN a feeling you have about somebody or something that you cannot explain; a hunch, a sixth sense.
intuitive ADJECTIVE **intuitively** ADVERB

Inuit Inuits
NOUN An Eskimo who comes from North America or Greenland.

inundated
ADJECTIVE **1** If you are inundated by letters or requests, you receive so many that you cannot deal with them all.
2 If land is inundated, it becomes flooded with water.
inundation NOUN

invade invades invading invaded
VERB **1** to enter another country by force.
2 If you invade someone's privacy, you intrude on them when you are not wanted.

 ► Anorak is an Inuit word meaning coat. But what sort of person is a "computer anorak"?

invalid invalids
Said "**in**-va-lid" NOUN **1** someone who is so ill that they need to be looked after.
Said "in-**val**-id" ADJECTIVE **2** If an action, process or document is invalid, it cannot be accepted because the correct procedure has not been followed.

invaluable
ADJECTIVE extremely useful.

invariably
ADVERB almost always.

invasion invasions
NOUN **1** the act of entering another country by military force.
2 the act of going into places that are not your own and where you are not wanted: *an invasion of ants*.
invasive ADJECTIVE **invasively** ADVERB

invent invents inventing invented
VERB **1** If you invent something, you are the first person to think of it or make it.
2 If you invent a story or excuse, you make it up.
invention NOUN **inventor** NOUN

Synonyms: (sense 1) conceive, create, devise

inventive
ADJECTIVE An inventive person is skilled and quick at thinking of ideas and solutions.
inventiveness NOUN

inverse
ADJECTIVE **1** FORMAL If there is an inverse relationship between two things or numbers, one decreases as the other increases, or vice versa.
2 In mathematics, the inverse of addition is subtraction, the inverse of multiplication is division, and vice versa.
inversely ADVERB

invert inverts inverting inverted
VERB to turn something upside down.

invertebrate invertebrates
NOUN a creature which does not have a backbone.

inverted comma inverted commas
NOUN Inverted commas are the punctuation marks " " or ' '. See **speech marks**, **quotation marks**.

INVERTED COMMAS
Inverted commas mark the beginning of a speaker's exact words or thoughts:
"It's hot in there," thought John.
Inverted commas are not used when a speaker's words are reported indirectly, rather than in their exact form:
John thought that it was hot in there.
Inverted commas can also be used to indicate the title of a story, piece of music or a painting:
The class has been reading "Clock" by Jim Hill.
Inverted commas are also used to draw attention to the fact that a word or phrase is being used in an unusual way, or that the word itself is the subject of discussion:
Braille allows blind people to "see" with their fingers.

invest invests investing invested
VERB **1** If you invest money, you try to increase its value, for example by buying property or shares.
2 If you invest in something useful, you buy it because it will help you do something better. *The company has invested in a huge new computer system.*

investigate investigates investigating investigated
VERB to try to find out all the facts about something that exists or has happened.
investigator NOUN **investigation** NOUN
investigative ADJECTIVE

Synonyms: examine, look into, study

invincible
ADJECTIVE too strong to be defeated.
invincibly ADVERB **invincibility** NOUN

invisible
ADJECTIVE If something is invisible, you cannot see it.
invisibly ADVERB **invisibility** NOUN

Antonym: visible

invitation invitations
NOUN a written or spoken request to someone to come to an event or to stay, etc.

invite invites inviting invited
VERB **1** to ask someone to come to an event or to stay.
2 to ask someone to do something. *He invited Jim to speak at the conference.*

invoice invoices
NOUN a bill for services or goods.
invoice VERB

involuntary
ADJECTIVE sudden and uncontrollable.
involuntarily ADVERB

involve involves involving involved
VERB **1** If a situation involves something, that thing is a necessary part of it.
2 If a situation involves someone, they are taking part in it.

involved
ADJECTIVE complicated and difficult to understand.

inward or **inwards**
ADJECTIVE OR ADVERB **1** moving towards the inside or centre of something.
ADJECTIVE **2** Your inward thoughts and feelings are private.
inwardly ADVERB

IQ IQs
NOUN your level of intelligence shown by the results of a special test. IQ is an abbreviation for intelligence quotient.

ir-
PREFIX used to give the opposite form of adjectives beginning with "r". For example, "relevant" becomes "irrelevant" and "reversible" becomes "irreversible".

irate
Said "eye-**rate**" **ADJECTIVE** very angry.

iris irises
NOUN 1 the round, coloured part of your eye.
2 a tall plant with long leaves and large blue, yellow or white flowers.

iron irons ironing ironed
NOUN 1 a hard magnetic metal which is used for making structures such as bridges and gates. Iron is used to make steel.
2 a device which you heat up and rub over clothes in order to remove creases.
VERB 3 If you iron clothes, you use a hot iron to remove creases from them.

irony
Said "**eye**-ron-ee" **NOUN 1** a form of humour in which you say the opposite of what you really mean. *Wake up, you bright and shining pupils!*
2 There is irony in a situation when there is an unexpected or unusual connection between things or events. *It's a sad irony of life: once you are lost, a map is useless.*
ironic ADJECTIVE **ironical** ADJECTIVE
ironically ADVERB

irrational
ADJECTIVE Irrational feelings are not based on logical reasons: *an irrational fear of spiders.*
irrationally ADVERB **irrationality** NOUN

irregular
ADJECTIVE 1 not smooth or straight, or not forming a regular pattern.
2 In mathematics, an irregular shape does not have sides the same size.
irregularly ADVERB **irregularity** NOUN

Synonyms: haphazard, random, variable

irrelevant
ADJECTIVE not directly connected with a subject, or important to that subject.
irrelevance NOUN

irresistible
ADJECTIVE 1 unable to be controlled: *an irresistible urge.*
2 extremely attractive.
irresistibly ADVERB

irresponsible
ADJECTIVE An irresponsible person does things without considering the consequences.
irresponsibly ADVERB **irresponsibility** NOUN

Synonyms: careless, reckless, thoughtless

irreversible
ADJECTIVE An irreversible decision or action cannot be changed.

irrigate irrigates irrigating irrigated
VERB To irrigate land is to supply it with water brought through pipes or ditches.
irrigated ADJECTIVE **irrigation** NOUN

irritable
ADJECTIVE An irritable person is easily annoyed.
irritably ADVERB **irritability** NOUN

irritate irritates irritating irritated
VERB to annoy, to get on your nerves.

is
the third person, present tense of **be**.

Islam
Said "**iz**-lahm" **NOUN** the Muslim religion, which teaches that there is only one God, Allah, and Mohammed is his prophet.
Islamic ADJECTIVE
[from Arabic *islam* meaning surrender to God]

island islands
Said "**eye**-land" **NOUN** a piece of land surrounded on all sides by water.

isle isles
Rhymes with "**mile**" **NOUN**; **FORMAL** an island.

isn't
contraction of **is not**.

isolate isolates isolating isolated
VERB 1 If you isolate something or someone, you separate them from everything else.
2 If you are isolated, you are set apart from other people.
isolated ADJECTIVE **isolation** NOUN

isosceles
Said "eye-**soss**-il-eez" **ADJECTIVE** An isosceles triangle has two of its three sides the same length and two of its three angles of equal size.
[from Greek *iso* meaning equal + *skelos* meaning leg]

issue issues issuing issued
Said "**ish**-yoo" **NOUN 1** an important subject that people are talking about.
2 a particular edition of a newspaper or magazine.
VERB 3 If someone issues a statement or warning, they say it formally and publicly.
4 If you are issued with something, it is officially given to you.

Synonyms: (sense 4) distribute, give out

it
PRONOUN 1 "It" is used to refer to something that has already been mentioned, or to a situation or fact. *It was a difficult decision.*
2 "It" is used to refer to people or animals whose sex is not known. *If a baby is thirsty, it feeds more often.*
3 You use "it" to make statements about the weather, time or date. *It was raining.*

 ► IQ, CD, DVD: think of some more initials that we use as words.

IT
abbreviation for **information technology**.

italics
PLURAL NOUN letters printed in a special sloping way, often used to emphasize something. *All the examples in this dictionary are in italics.*
italic ADJECTIVE

itch **itches**
NOUN an unpleasant feeling that makes you want to scratch.
itch VERB **itchy** ADJECTIVE

item **items**
NOUN one of a collection or list of objects. [from Latin *item* meaning in the same manner; once used to introduce each item on a list]

itinerary **itineraries**
NOUN a plan of a route to be travelled.

its
ADJECTIVE OR PRONOUN "Its" means belonging to it. *The dog fetched its ball.*
✔ *It's* with an apostrophe means *it is* or *it has*.

it's
contraction of **it is** or **it has**. *It's raining today. It's been very hot lately.*
✔ It is important not to confuse *it's* with the possessive *its* which means "belonging to it" and has no apostrophe.

itself
PRONOUN **1** "Itself" refers to the same thing, child, or animal that has already been mentioned. *The cat scratched itself.*
2 "Itself" is used to emphasize the thing you are referring to. *Life itself is a learning process.*

I've
contraction of **I have**.

ivory
NOUN **1** the creamy-white bone of elephant tusks.
NOUN OR ADJECTIVE **2** creamy-white.

ivy
NOUN an evergreen plant which creeps along the ground and up walls.

a b c d e f g h i j k l m n o p q r s t u v w x y z

Jj

jab jabs jabbing jabbed
VERB 1 to poke at something roughly.
NOUN 2 a sharp, sudden poke.
3 INFORMAL an injection.

jabber jabbers jabbering jabbered
VERB; INFORMAL to talk so fast that you cannot be understood.

jack jacks jacking jacked
NOUN 1 a piece of equipment for lifting heavy objects, especially for lifting a car when changing a wheel.
2 In a pack of cards, a jack is a picture card whose value is between a ten and a queen.
VERB 3 To jack up an object means to raise it, especially by using a jack.

jackal jackals
NOUN a wild animal related to the dog.

jacket jackets
NOUN 1 a short coat.
2 an outer covering for something: *a book jacket.*

jackpot jackpots
NOUN 1 the top prize in a gambling game.
PHRASE 2 INFORMAL If you **hit the jackpot**, you win the top prize or have a stroke of good luck.

Jacuzzi Jacuzzis
NOUN; TRADEMARK a type of bath which refreshes the skin with strong jets of water.

jade
NOUN Jade is a hard green stone used for making jewellery and ornaments.

jagged
ADJECTIVE sharp and spiky.

Synonyms: serrated, spiked, uneven

jaguar jaguars
NOUN a large spotted member of the cat family, similar to a leopard.

jail jails jailing jailed; also spelt **gaol**
NOUN 1 a building where people convicted of a crime are locked up.
VERB 2 to send someone to jail or to lock them up in a jail.

Synonyms: (sense 1) nick, prison, penitentiary

jailer jailers; also spelt **gaoler**
NOUN; OLD-FASHIONED a person in charge of prisoners in a jail.

jam jams jamming jammed
NOUN 1 a food made by boiling fruit and sugar together until it sets.
2 a situation where it is so crowded that you cannot move.
VERB 3 to push something roughly somewhere. *I jammed my hat on.*
4 to crowd somewhere, squashing people. *Crowds jammed the streets.*
5 to become stuck or unable to work properly: *the door jammed.*
PHRASE 6 INFORMAL If someone is **in a jam**, they are in a difficult situation.

Synonyms: (sense 6) fix, predicament, tight spot

jamboree jamborees
NOUN a gathering of large numbers of people enjoying themselves.

jammy
ADJECTIVE; INFORMAL If you say someone is jammy, you mean they are lucky, but perhaps do not deserve to be so.

jangle jangles jangling jangled
VERB to make a harsh metallic ringing noise.
jangle NOUN

janitor janitors
NOUN the caretaker of a building.

January
NOUN the first month of the year.

jar jars jarring jarred
NOUN 1 a glass container used for storing food.
VERB 2 If something jars on you, you find it unpleasant or annoying.

jargon
NOUN specialized or technical language which is often difficult to understand.

jaundice
NOUN an illness affecting the liver, in which the skin and the whites of the eyes become yellow.

jaunt jaunts
NOUN; INFORMAL a journey or trip you go on for pleasure.

jaunty jauntier jauntiest
ADJECTIVE cheerful and self-confident: *a jaunty tune.*
jauntily ADVERB

javelin javelins
NOUN a long spear that is thrown in sports competitions.

jaw jaws
NOUN 1 the bone in which your lower teeth are set.
2 A person's or other animal's jaws are their mouth and teeth. Some animals, such as crocodiles, have very powerful jaws.

jazz jazzes jazzing jazzed
NOUN 1 a style of popular music with a strong rhythm, often involving improvisation.
VERB 2 INFORMAL If you jazz up something, you make it livelier, brighter or more exciting.

 ► The letter J developed by adding a tail to the letter I.

jealous
ADJECTIVE If you are jealous of another person's possessions or qualities, you feel angry or bitter because you do not have them.
jealously ADVERB **jealousy** NOUN

Synonyms: covetous, envious

jeans
PLURAL NOUN casual denim trousers.

Jeep Jeeps
NOUN; TRADEMARK a small, sturdy, open-topped road vehicle with four-wheel drive, built for military use.

jeer jeers jeering jeered
VERB **1** to insult or mock someone in a loud, unpleasant way.
NOUN **2** Jeers are rude and insulting remarks.
jeering ADJECTIVE

jelly jellies
NOUN **1** a clear, sweet food usually eaten as a dessert.
2 Any clear rubbery substance can be described as a jelly.

jellyfish jellyfishes
NOUN a sea animal with a clear soft body and tentacles which may sting.

jeopardy
NOUN If someone or something is in jeopardy, they are in danger of failing or of being destroyed.
jeopardize VERB

jerk jerks jerking jerked
VERB **1** to give something a sudden, sharp pull.
2 to move suddenly and sharply.
NOUN **3** INFORMAL If you call someone a jerk, you mean that they are stupid.
jerky ADJECTIVE **jerkily** ADVERB

jersey jerseys
NOUN a knitted garment for the upper half of the body.
[knitting is an industry in Jersey, one of the Channel Islands]

jest jests jesting jested
NOUN **1** a joke.
VERB **2** to speak jokingly.

jester jesters
NOUN In the past, a jester was an entertaining man who was kept to amuse the king or queen.

jet jets jetting jetted
NOUN **1** a plane which is powered by jet engines.
2 a stream of liquid, gas or flame forced out under pressure.
ADJECTIVE **3** A jet engine works by heating air and thrusting it out behind in a powerful jet.
4 Jet is a hard black stone, usually highly polished and used in jewellery and ornaments.
VERB **5** INFORMAL to travel by jet plane. *They jetted off to the Alps.*

jet lag
NOUN a feeling of tiredness or confusion after a long flight.

jetty jetties
NOUN a wide stone wall or wooden platform at the edge of the sea or a river, where boats can be moored.

Jew Jews
Said "**joo**" NOUN a person who practises the religion of Judaism, or is of Hebrew descent.

jewel jewels
NOUN a precious stone used to decorate valuable things such as rings or necklaces.
jewelled ADJECTIVE

jeweller jewellers
NOUN a person who makes jewellery or who sells and repairs jewellery and watches.

jewellery
NOUN ornaments that people wear, such as rings and necklaces.

Jewish
ADJECTIVE to do with Jews.

jig jigs jigging jigged
NOUN **1** a type of lively folk dance.
VERB **2** to dance or jump around in a lively bouncy manner.

jiggle jiggles jiggling jiggled
VERB to move something around with quick jerky movements.

jigsaw jigsaws
NOUN a puzzle consisting of a picture on card that has been cut up into small pieces, which have to be put together again.

jingle jingles jingling jingled
NOUN **1** a short, catchy phrase or rhyme set to music and used to advertise something on radio or television.
2 the sound of something jingling.
VERB **3** to make a tinkling sound like small bells.

jinx jinxes jinxing jinxed
NOUN **1** someone or something that is thought to bring bad luck.
VERB **2** If you think someone has put a jinx on you or you are jinxed, you believe that someone has cursed you with bad luck.

job jobs
NOUN **1** the work that someone does to earn money.
2 a duty or responsibility.

Synonyms: (sense1) employment, occupation, work

jockey jockeys jockeying jockeyed
NOUN **1** someone who rides a horse in a race.
VERB **2** To jockey for position means to manoeuvre in order to gain an advantage over other people.

a b c d e f g h i j k l m n o p q r s t u v w x y z

What's the difference between a jeweller and a prison warder? One sells watches, the other watches cells.

jodhpurs
Said "**jod**-purz" PLURAL NOUN close-fitting trousers worn when riding a horse.
[from *Jodhpur*, the name of a town in northern India]

joey joeys
NOUN; INFORMAL In Australian English, a young kangaroo or wallaby.

jog jogs jogging jogged
VERB **1** to run at a slow easy pace.
PHRASE **2** If you **jog someone's memory**, you tell them about something they need to remember.
jogger NOUN **jogging** NOUN

join joins joining joined
VERB **1** When two things join, or when one thing joins another, they come together.
2 to fasten or connect things.
3 If you join someone, you go to where they are.
4 If you join a club or organization, you become a member or start taking part in it.
join in VERB If you join in an activity, you take part in it.
join up VERB to become a member of the armed forces.

Synonyms: (senses 1 and 2) connect, link, unite
(sense 4) enlist, enrol, sign up

joiner joiners
NOUN a person who makes wooden window frames, doors and furniture.
joinery NOUN

joint joints
NOUN **1** a part of your body such as your elbow or knee where two bones meet. Most of your joints enable you to bend different parts of your skeleton and move.
ADJECTIVE **2** shared by or belonging to two or more people: *a joint bank account*.
jointly ADVERB **jointed** ADJECTIVE

joist joists
NOUN a large beam used to support floors or ceilings.

joke jokes joking joked
NOUN **1** a funny story or witty question that you say to make people laugh.
2 anything you think is ridiculous and not worthy of respect. *The decision was a joke.*
VERB **3** to tell a funny story or ask a witty question to make people laugh.
4 If you are joking, you are teasing someone.
jokingly ADVERB

Synonyms: (sense 1) gag, jest
(sense 4) jest, kid, tease

joker jokers
NOUN **1** In a pack of cards, a joker is an extra card that does not belong to any of the four suits, but is used in some games.
2 a person who plays jokes on people.

jolly jollier jolliest
ADJECTIVE **1** happy, cheerful and pleasant.
ADVERB **2** INFORMAL very, extremely: *jolly lucky*.

jolt jolts jolting jolted
VERB **1** to move or shake roughly and violently.
2 If you are jolted by something, it gives you an unpleasant surprise.
jolt NOUN

jostle jostles jostling jostled
VERB to push roughly against people in a crowd.

jot jots jotting jotted
VERB **1** If you jot something down, you write it quickly in the form of a short informal note.
NOUN **2** a very small amount.
jotting NOUN

jotter jotters
NOUN a pad or notebook.

journal journals
NOUN **1** a magazine that deals with a particular subject, trade or profession.
2 a diary which someone keeps regularly.

journalist journalists
NOUN a person whose job is to collect news and to write or talk about it.
journalism NOUN

journey journeys journeying journeyed
NOUN **1** the act of travelling from one place to another.
VERB **2** FORMAL to travel somewhere, especially a long way away.

Synonyms: voyage, trek, trip

joust jousts jousting jousted
NOUN **1** In medieval times, a joust was a competition between knights fighting on horseback, using lances.
VERB **2** to fight in a joust.

jovial
ADJECTIVE cheerful and friendly.
jovially ADVERB **joviality** NOUN

joy joys
NOUN **1** a feeling of great happiness.
2 something that gives you pleasure. *Tasting food is one of the joys of being a chef.*

joyful
ADJECTIVE **1** causing pleasure and happiness.
2 Someone who is joyful is extremely happy.
joyfully ADVERB

joyride joyrides
NOUN a drive in a stolen car.
joyriding NOUN **joyrider** NOUN

joystick joysticks
NOUN **1** a lever in an aircraft which the pilot uses to control height and direction.
2 a lever that controls the cursor on a computer screen, especially in computer games.

 ► All these words contain the sound "er": journey, earn, person, firm, church, word, popular.

jubilation
NOUN a feeling of great happiness and triumph.

jubilee **jubilees**
NOUN a special anniversary of an event such as a coronation.
[from Hebrew *yobhel* meaning a ram; rams' horns were blown during festivals and celebrations]

judge **judges judging judged**
VERB 1 to form an opinion about someone or something, based on the information that you have.
2 to choose the winner of a competition.
NOUN 3 the person in a law court who decides how the law should be applied and how criminals should be punished.
4 the person who chooses the winner of a competition.

Synonyms: (sense 2) adjudicate, referee, umpire
(sense 4) adjudicator, referee, umpire

judgement **judgements**; also spelt **judgment**
NOUN 1 the act of judging something.
2 Someone who shows judgement, or good judgement, is able to make sensible and wise decisions.

judo
NOUN a sport in which two people try to force each other to the ground using special throwing techniques.
[from Japanese *ju* meaning gentleness + *do* meaning way]

jug **jugs**
NOUN a container used for holding or pouring liquids.

juggernaut **juggernauts**
NOUN a large heavy lorry.
[from Hindi *Jagannath*, the name of a huge idol of the god Krishna, which every year is wheeled through the streets of Puri in India]

juggle **juggles juggling juggled**
VERB to throw objects into the air, catching them in sequence, and tossing them up again so there are several in the air at one time.
juggler NOUN

juice **juices**
NOUN the liquid obtained from fruit or other food.

juicy
ADJECTIVE 1 Juicy food has a lot of juice in it.
2 interesting and exciting. *Mark passed on a juicy bit of gossip.*

jukebox **jukeboxes**
NOUN a music machine which automatically plays a selected piece of music when coins are inserted.

July
NOUN the seventh month of the year.
[named after the Roman emperor Julius Caesar, who in 46 BC added two months, July and August, to the calendar]

jumble **jumbles jumbling jumbled**
NOUN 1 an untidy muddle of things.
2 used household articles that are for sale. *They donated jumble to a local charity shop.*
VERB 3 to mix things up in an untidy way. *The speaker jumbled up his notes.*

jumble sale **jumble sales**
NOUN an event at which cheap second-hand clothes and other articles are sold to raise money, usually for a charity.

jumbo **jumbos**
NOUN 1 A jumbo or jumbo jet is a very large passenger jet aircraft.
ADJECTIVE 2 very large.
[from *Jumbo*, the name of a famous 19th-century elephant at London Zoo; it was sold to a circus]

jump **jumps jumping jumped**
VERB 1 to spring off the ground using your leg muscles.
2 To jump something means to spring off the ground and move over or across it.
3 If something makes you jump, you make a short, sudden movement of surprise.
4 If an amount or level jumps, it suddenly increases. *The population jumped to nearly 10 000.*
5 If you jump at an opportunity, you eagerly take up the opportunity.
jump NOUN

Synonyms: (sense 1) bound, leap, spring

jumper **jumpers**
NOUN a knitted piece of clothing for the top half of the body.

Synonyms: pullover, sweater

jumpy **jumpier jumpiest**
ADJECTIVE nervous and worried.

junction **junctions**
NOUN a place where roads or railway lines meet or cross.

June
NOUN the sixth month of the year.
[from Latin *Junius* meaning sacred to Juno, chief goddess and wife of Jupiter]

jungle **jungles**
NOUN a dense tropical forest.
[from Hindi *jangal* meaning wasteland]

junior
ADJECTIVE 1 younger.
2 A junior official or employee holds a lower position in an organization.
junior NOUN

a b c d e f g h i j k l m n o p q r s t u v w x y z

Some words from India: jungle, khaki, polo, bungalow, dinghy, shampoo, loot.

A B C D E F G H I J K L M N O P Q R S T U V W X Y Z

junk **junks**
NOUN **1** old or second-hand things which are sold cheaply or thrown away.
2 If you say something is junk, you mean that it is no good.
3 a Chinese sailing boat with a flat bottom and square sails.

junk food
NOUN food low in nutritional value which is eaten as well as or instead of proper meals.

jury **juries**
NOUN a group of people in a court of law who have been selected to listen to the facts about a crime and to decide whether the accused person is guilty or not.
juror NOUN

just
ADVERB **1** If something has just happened, it happened a very short time ago.
2 If you just do something, you do it by a very small amount.
3 simply or only. *It was just an excuse.*
4 exactly: *just what she wanted.*
ADJECTIVE **5** fair and reasonable: *a just decision.*
justly ADVERB

justice
NOUN fairness in the way that people are treated.

justify **justifies justifying justified**
VERB If you justify an action or idea, you prove or explain why it is reasonable or necessary.
justification NOUN **justifiable** ADJECTIVE

jut **juts jutting jutted**
VERB If something juts out, it sticks out beyond or above a surface or edge.

Synonyms: project, protrude, stick out

juvenile **juveniles**
NOUN **1** a young person not old enough to be considered an adult.
ADJECTIVE **2** suitable for young people.
3 childish and rather silly: *food fights are juvenile.*

juvenile delinquent **juvenile delinquents**
NOUN a young person guilty of a crime or of violent behaviour.
juvenile delinquency NOUN

 ► What is junk mail? What is a junk fax? What is a Chinese junk?

kaleidoscope kaleidoscopes
Said "kal-**eye**-dos-skope" NOUN a toy that is a tube you look into while twisting it around to see a changing pattern of colours.

kangaroo kangaroos
NOUN a large Australian marsupial with very strong back legs which it uses for jumping.

karaoke
NOUN A karaoke machine plays a prerecorded backing tape of songs while you sing the words.
[from Japanese meaning empty orchestra]

karate
Said "kar-**raht**-ee" NOUN a sport in which people fight each other using only their hands, elbows, feet and legs.
[from Japanese *kara* + *te* meaning empty hand]

kayak kayaks
Said "**ky**-ak" NOUN a covered canoe with a small opening for the person sitting in it, originally used by the Inuit.

kebab kebabs
NOUN meat or vegetable stuck on a stick and grilled.

keel keels keeling keeled
NOUN **1** the heavy, pointed part of the bottom of a boat that holds the boat stable in the water.
VERB **2** If someone or something keels over, they fall down sideways.

keen keener keenest
ADJECTIVE **1** enthusiastic.
2 fond.
3 sharp: *a keen sense of smell; a keen knife.*

Synonyms: (sense 1) avid, eager

keep keeps keeping kept
VERB **1** to continue to have something.
2 to maintain someone or something in a particular condition.
3 to store something in a particular place.
4 If you keep doing something or keep on doing it, you do it repeatedly or continuously.
5 If someone or something keeps you from doing something, they prevent you from doing it.
6 If you keep a promise or appointment, you do what you said you would do.
7 If you keep a record of events, you write down what happened.
NOUN **8** the main tower inside the walls of a castle.
keep up VERB If you keep up with other people, you move or work at the same speed they do.

keeper keepers
NOUN **1** a person whose job is to look after the animals in a zoo.
2 a goalkeeper in soccer or hockey.

keg kegs
NOUN a small barrel.

kennel kennels
NOUN **1** a small hut for a dog to sleep in.
2 A kennels is a place where dogs are bred and trained, or looked after when their owners are away.

kenning
NOUN a compound expression used in Old English and Norse poetry, which named something without using its name. For example, a possible kenning for cat is mouse catcher.

kept
past tense and past participle of **keep**.

kerb kerbs
NOUN the raised edge of a pavement, which separates it from the road.

kernel kernels
NOUN the part of a nut that is inside the shell.

kerosene
NOUN another name for paraffin.

kestrel kestrels
NOUN a type of small falcon that kills and eats small animals, including other birds.

ketchup
NOUN a cold sauce, usually made from tomatoes.

kettle kettles
NOUN a covered metal container with a spout, in which you boil water.

key keys keying keyed
NOUN **1** a shaped piece of metal used to turn a lock.
2 The keys on a computer, typewriter or piano are the buttons that you press in order to operate it.
3 In music, a key is a particular scale of notes: *in the key of A minor.*
ADJECTIVE **4** The key person or thing in a group is the most important one.
VERB **5** If you key in something to a computer or word processor, you enter it using a keyboard.

keyboard keyboards
NOUN **1** a set of keys on a computer, typewriter or piano.
2 an electronic musical instrument played in the same way as a piano.

keyhole keyholes
NOUN a hole in a door through which a key is put to turn a lock.

kg
abbreviation for **kilogram**.

khaki
Said "**kah**-kee" **NOUN 1** a strong yellowish-brown material, used especially for army uniforms.
NOUN OR ADJECTIVE 2 yellowish-brown.
[from Urdu *kaki* meaning dusty]

kick kicks kicking kicked
VERB 1 to hit someone or something with your foot.
NOUN 2 If you give something a kick, you hit it with your foot.
3 INFORMAL If you get a kick out of something, you enjoy it very much.

kick-off kick-offs
NOUN the time when a football match begins.

kid kids kidding kidded
NOUN 1 INFORMAL a child.
2 a young goat.
VERB 3 INFORMAL If you are kidding, you say something that is not true as a joke.

kidnap kidnaps kidnapping kidnapped
VERB To kidnap someone is to take them away by force and demand something in exchange for returning them.
kidnapper NOUN
[from *kid* + *nap* meaning child stealing; in the 17th century children were kidnapped to work on American plantations]

Synonyms: abduct, seize

kidney kidneys
NOUN Your kidneys are two organs in your body that remove waste products from your blood.

kill kills killing killed
VERB 1 To kill a person, another animal or a plant is to cause them to die.
2 INFORMAL If you say something is killing you, it is causing you a lot of pain.
killer NOUN

Synonyms: (sense 1) murder, slay

kiln kilns
NOUN an oven for baking china or pottery until it becomes hard and dry.

kilo kilos
NOUN a kilogram, abbreviated to "kg".

kilogram kilograms
NOUN a unit of weight equal to 1000 grams, abbreviated to "kg".

kilometre kilometres
NOUN a unit of distance equal to 1000 metres, abbreviated to "km".

kilowatt kilowatt
NOUN a unit of power equivalent to one thousand watts or 1·34 horsepower, abbreviated to "kW".

kilt kilts
NOUN a tartan skirt worn by men as part of Scottish Highland dress.

kimono kimonos
NOUN a long, loose garment with wide sleeves and a sash, worn in Japan.

kin
PLURAL NOUN Your kin are your relatives.

kind kinds; kinder kindest
NOUN 1 a type or sort. *All kinds of people were there.*
ADJECTIVE 2 caring and helpful towards other people.

Synonyms: (sense 2) considerate, generous

THAT KIND AND THOSE KINDS
When you use kind in its singular form, the adjective before it should also be singular:
that kind of dog
When you use the plural form kinds, the adjective before it should be plural:
those kinds of dog; those kinds of dogs

kindergarten kindergartens
NOUN a school for children who are too young to go to primary school; a nursery school.

kind-hearted
ADJECTIVE considerate and sympathetic.

kindle kindles kindling kindled
VERB 1 If you kindle a fire you light it and get it burning well.
2 to cause or arouse. *The conversation kindled hope.*

kindly kindlier kindliest
ADJECTIVE having a warm and sympathetic nature.
kindliness NOUN

kinetic
ADJECTIVE relating to movement. Kinetic energy is energy produced when something moves.

king kings
NOUN 1 a man who is the head of state in a country, having inherited his position from his parents.
2 the most important piece in a chess game.
3 in a pack of cards, a card with a picture of a king on it.

kingdom kingdoms
NOUN a country that is governed by a king or queen.

kingfisher kingfishers
NOUN a brightly coloured bird that lives near water and feeds on fish.

kiosk kiosks
Said "**kee**-osk" **NOUN** a very small shop or hut where you can buy newspapers, snacks and cigarettes.

kip kips kipping kipped
VERB; INFORMAL 1 to have a sleep.
NOUN 2 INFORMAL a period of sleep.

 ► Some words from Japan: kimono, judo, karate, haiku.

kipper **kippers**
NOUN a smoked herring.

kiss **kisses kissing kissed**
VERB 1 When you kiss someone, you touch them with your lips in order to show your affection.
NOUN 2 The **kiss of life** is a method of reviving someone by blowing air into their lungs.
kiss NOUN

kit **kits**
NOUN 1 a collection of clothes and other things that you use for a sport or other activity.
2 a set of parts that you put together in order to make something.

kitchen **kitchens**
NOUN a room used for cooking and preparing food.

kite **kites**
NOUN 1 a light frame covered with paper or cloth, which you fly in the air at the end of a long string.
2 the mathematical term for a diamond shape.
3 a large bird of prey with a long tail and long wings.

kitten **kittens**
NOUN a very young cat.

kitty **kitties**
NOUN 1 a fund of money that has been given by a group of people who will use it to pay for or do things together.
2 INFORMAL another word for a cat.

kiwi **kiwis**
Said "**kee**-wee" **NOUN 1** a type of flightless bird found in New Zealand.
2 INFORMAL a person who comes from New Zealand.

kiwi fruit **kiwi fruits**
NOUN a fruit with a brown hairy skin and green flesh.

km
abbreviation for **kilometres**.

knack
NOUN an ability to do something difficult whilst making it look easy: *the knack of blowing bubble gum bubbles.*

knead **kneads kneading kneaded**
VERB If you knead dough, you press it and squeeze it with your hands before baking it.

knee **knees**
NOUN Your knees are the joints in your legs between your ankles and your hips.

kneecap **kneecaps**
NOUN Your kneecaps are the bones at the front of your knee.

kneel **kneels kneeling knelt**
VERB When you kneel or kneel down, you bend your legs and lower your body until your knees are touching the ground.

knew
the past tense of **know**.

knickers
PLURAL NOUN Knickers are underwear for the lower part of the body, worn by women and girls.

knife **knives**
NOUN 1 a sharp metal tool used for cutting things.
VERB 2 To knife someone is to stab them with a knife.

knight **knights knighting knighted**
NOUN 1 In medieval times, a knight was a nobleman who served his king or lord in battle.
2 a chess piece shaped like a horse's head that moves either two squares horizontally and one square vertically or one square horizontally and two squares vertically.
VERB 3 If someone is knighted, they are given the title "Sir" before their name.
knighthood NOUN

knit **knits knitting knitted**
VERB to make a piece of clothing from wool or similar yarn, by twisting the yarn with knitting needles or using a knitting machine.

knives
plural of **knife**.

knob **knobs**
NOUN a round handle or switch.

knock **knocks knocking knocked**
VERB 1 If you knock on a door or window, you hit it with your hand.
2 If you knock something, you touch it or hit it roughly and it moves or falls over.
3 INFORMAL to knock someone is to criticize them.
NOUN 4 a firm blow on something solid. *There was a knock on the door.*
knock out **VERB** To knock someone out is to cause them to become unconscious.

knocker **knockers**
NOUN a metal device with a hinge, fixed to a door, which you use for knocking.

knockout **knockouts**
NOUN 1 a punch in boxing which knocks a boxer unconscious.
2 a competition in which competitors are eliminated in each round until only the winner is left.

knot **knots knotting knotted**
NOUN 1 a fastening made by tying the ends of string or rope together.
2 a circular pattern or small lump visible on the surface of a piece of wood.
3 a unit of speed for ships, aircraft and winds, equal to about 1·85 kilometres per hour.
VERB 4 If you knot a piece of string, you tie a knot in it.

a b c d e f g h i j k l m n o p q r s t u v w x y z

A B C D E F G H I J K L M N O P Q R S T U V W X Y Z

know **knows knowing knew known**
VERB **1** If you know something, you have it in your mind and you do not need to learn it.
2 If you know a person, place, or thing, you are familiar with them.
PHRASE **3** INFORMAL If you are **in the know**, you are one of a small number of people who share a secret.

knowing
ADJECTIVE A knowing look is one which shows that you know or understand something that others do not.

knowledge
NOUN all the information that someone knows about a subject.

knowledgeable
ADJECTIVE Someone who is knowledgeable knows a lot about a subject.
knowledgeably ADVERB

knuckle **knuckles**
NOUN Your knuckles are the joints where your fingers join your hand, and where they bend.

koala **koalas**
NOUN an Australian marsupial with grey fur and small tufted ears. Koalas live in trees and eat eucalyptus leaves.

Koran or **Qur'an**
Said "kaw-**rahn**" NOUN The Koran is the holy book of Islam.

kosher
Said "said **koh**-sher" ADJECTIVE Kosher food has been specially prepared to be eaten according to Jewish law.

kung fu
Said "kung-**foo**" NOUN a Chinese style of fighting which involves using your hands and feet.

 ► The Torah, the Upanishads and the Guru Granth Sahib are holy books. But of which religions?

Ll

lab labs
NOUN; INFORMAL a laboratory

label labels labelling labelled
NOUN 1 a piece of paper or plastic attached to something and giving information about it.
VERB 2 to put a label on something.
3 If you label someone, you judge them to be a certain type of person. *I could tell she labelled me a liar.*

laboratory laboratories
NOUN a place where scientific experiments are carried out; a lab.
[from Latin *laboratorium* meaning workshop]

laborious
ADJECTIVE needing a lot of effort or time.
laboriously ADVERB

labour labours labouring laboured
NOUN 1 hard work.
2 a general word for the people who work in a country or industry: *the labour force; skilled labour.*
3 the last stage of pregnancy when a woman gives birth to a baby.
4 In Britain, the Labour Party is one of the main forces in politics.
VERB 5 OLD-FASHIONED to work very hard, usually at a physical task.

Synonyms: (sense 1) toil, work
(sense 5) slave, toil, work

labourer labourers
NOUN a workman doing a job that requires no special skill.

labrador labradors
NOUN a large dog with short black or golden hair.

labyrinth labyrinths
Said "**lab**-er-inth" NOUN a complicated series of paths or passages, like a maze.

lace laces lacing laced
NOUN 1 a very fine decorated cloth, made with a lot of holes in it.
2 Laces are the thin pieces of material that are used to fasten shoes.
VERB 3 to tie up your shoes.
4 To lace someone's food or drink means to put a small amount of alcohol, a drug or poison in it. *The fruit cake was laced with whiskey.*
lacy ADJECTIVE

lack lacks lacking lacked
NOUN 1 If there is a lack of something, there is not enough of it or there is none of it.
VERB 2 to be short of or have none of something.

Synonyms: (sense 1) absence, scarcity, shortage

lacquer lacquers lacquering lacquered
Said "**lak**-er" NOUN 1 Hair lacquer is a liquid sprayed onto the hair to hold it in place.
2 a thin, clear varnish put on wood to protect it and make it shiny.
VERB 3 to apply lacquer.

lacrosse
NOUN an outdoor ball game in which two teams try to score goals using long sticks with nets on the end of them and a small, heavy ball.

lad lads
NOUN a boy or young man.

ladder ladders
NOUN 1 a tall wooden or metal frame used for climbing walls.
2 If your tights have a ladder in them, they have a rip in them.

laden
Said "**lay**-den" ADJECTIVE To be laden with something means to be carrying a lot of it.

ladle ladles ladling ladled
NOUN 1 a long-handled spoon with a deep, round bowl, used to serve soup.
VERB 2 to serve food with a ladle.

lady ladies
NOUN 1 a woman, especially one who is well-mannered.
2 a title used in front of the names of certain women of the peerage, for example the wife of a lord or knight. *Lady Lavinia Stewart.*
ladylike ADJECTIVE

ladybird ladybirds
NOUN a small flying beetle with a round red body patterned with black spots.

lag lags lagging lagged
VERB 1 To lag behind means to make slower progress than other people or processes.
2 To lag pipes or water tanks means to wrap cloth round them to prevent the water inside freezing.
NOUN 3 A time lag is a period of time that passes between one event and another.

lager lagers
NOUN a kind of light beer.

lagoon lagoons
NOUN an area of tropical water separated from the sea by reefs or sand.

laid
the past tense and past participle of **lay**.

lain
the past participle of some meanings of **lie**.

lair lairs
NOUN a place where a wild animal lives.

lake lakes
NOUN an area of fresh water surrounded by land.

lamb lambs
NOUN a young sheep, and the meat from it.

lame
ADJECTIVE **1** Someone who is lame has an injured leg and cannot walk easily.
2 A lame excuse is unconvincing.
lamely ADVERB **lameness** NOUN

Synonyms: (sense 2) feeble, flimsy, weak

lament laments lamenting lamented
VERB **1** to express sorrow or regret about something that has happened, especially a death.
NOUN **2** a song or poem expressing grief at someone's death.

lamp lamps
NOUN a device that produces light.

lamppost lampposts
NOUN a tall column in a street, with a lamp at the top.

lampshade lampshades
NOUN a decorative covering over an electric light bulb.

lance lances lancing lanced
NOUN **1** a long spear that used to be used by soldiers on horseback.
VERB **2** To lance a boil or abscess means to stick a sharp instrument into it in order to release the fluid within.

land lands landing landed
NOUN **1** the part of the earth that is not covered by water.
2 an area of ground.
3 a country: *land of hope and glory*.
VERB **4** to reach the ground after moving through the air. *The plane landed safely.*

landing landings
NOUN **1** a flat area at the top or middle of a staircase.
2 the act of bringing an aircraft down to the ground.

landlady landladies
NOUN **1** a woman who owns a house or small hotel and who lets rooms to people.
2 a woman who owns or manages a pub.

landlord landlords
NOUN **1** a man who owns a house or small hotel and who lets rooms to people.
2 a man who owns or manages a pub.

landmark landmarks
NOUN **1** a noticeable feature in a landscape, which you can use to check your position.
2 an important stage in the development of something. *The jet engine was a landmark in aircraft design.*

landscape landscapes
NOUN everything you can see when you look across an area of land.

landslide landslides
NOUN **1** a large amount of loose earth and rocks falling down a steep slope.
2 a victory in an election won by a large number of votes.

lane lanes
NOUN **1** a narrow road, especially in the country.
2 one of the parallel strips into which a road is divided: *the inside lane on the motorway*.

language languages
NOUN **1** a system of words used by a particular group of people to communicate with each other.
2 the particular style of words used in a book, show or film, or by a person. *The film contained bad language. Karl's use of language was good.*
[from Latin *lingua* meaning tongue]

languish languishes languishing languished
VERB to lose physical or mental strength through having to endure an unpleasant situation for a long time: *languishing in the Tower of London*.

lanky lankier lankiest
ADJECTIVE tall and thin, and moving rather awkwardly.

lantern lanterns
NOUN a lamp in a metal frame with glass sides.

lap laps lapping lapped
NOUN **1** Your lap is the flat area formed by your thighs when you are sitting down. *She sat with her hands in her lap.*
2 one circuit of a running track or racecourse.
VERB **3** When water laps against something, it gently moves against it in little waves.
4 When an animal laps a drink, it uses its tongue to flick the liquid into its mouth.
5 If you lap someone in a race, you pass them when they are still on the previous lap.

lapel lapels
Said "lap-**el**" NOUN a flap which is joined on to the collar of a jacket or coat.

lapse lapses lapsing lapsed
NOUN **1** a moment of bad behaviour by someone who usually behaves well.
2 a slight mistake.
3 a period of time between two events.
VERB **4** If you lapse into a different way of behaving, you start behaving that way.
5 If a legal document or contract lapses, it is not renewed on the date when it expires: *my magazine subscription lapsed*.

laptop laptops
NOUN a personal computer small and light enough to be used on someone's lap; short for laptop computer.

lard
NOUN fat from a pig, used in cooking.

larder larders
NOUN a room in which you store food, often next to a kitchen.

 ► Laptop is a fairly new word. Think of some other new words introduced in the last 50 years.

large larger largest
ADJECTIVE **1** bigger than usual or average.
PHRASE **2** If a prisoner is **at large**, he or she has escaped from prison.

Synonyms: (sense 1) big, huge, vast

largely
ADVERB to a great extent.

lark larks larking larked
NOUN **1** a small brown bird with a distinctive song.
2 If you do something for a lark, you do it in a high-spirited or mischievous way for fun.

larva larvae
NOUN an insect, which looks like a short fat worm, at the stage before it becomes an adult. See **pupa**.

lasagne
Said "laz-**zan**-ya" NOUN an Italian dish made with wide, flat sheets of pasta, meat, and cheese sauce.

laser lasers
NOUN a machine which produces a narrow beam of concentrated light used to cut very hard materials and for surgery, also in CD players and digital video disks, etc.
[from the first letters of Light Amplification by Stimulated Emission of Radiation]

lash lashes lashing lashed
NOUN **1** Your lashes are the hairs growing on the edge of your eyelids.
2 Lashes are blows struck with a whip.
VERB **3** to beat someone with a whip.
4 If you lash things together, you tie them together.
lash out VERB **1** to criticize someone severely.
2 to spend extravagantly.

lass lasses
NOUN; INFORMAL a girl or young woman.

lasso lassoes; lassos lassoing lassoed
Said "las-**soo**" NOUN **1** a length of rope with a noose at one end, used by cowboys to catch horses and cattle.
VERB **2** to catch an animal by throwing the noose of a lasso around its neck.

last lasts lasting lasted
ADJECTIVE **1** most recent of all: *last year.*
2 final, remaining: *the last three pages; the last piece of pizza.*
ADVERB **3** If you last did something on a particular occasion, you have not done it since then. *They last met in Rome.*
4 finally. *He added the milk last.*
VERB **5** to continue to exist or happen. *The hot weather lasted for three weeks.*
PHRASE **6 at last** means after a long time.
lastly ADVERB

latch latches latching latched
NOUN **1** a simple door fastening consisting of a metal bar which falls into a hook.
2 a type of door lock which locks automatically when you close the door and which has to be opened with a key.
latch on VERB; INFORMAL **1** to attach yourself to a new acquaintance. *Mervyn latched on to the people from Crewe.*
2 to understand. *She latched on pretty quickly to what I was saying.*

late later latest
ADVERB OR ADJECTIVE **1** near the end of a period of time: *late in the evening.*
2 after the time that was arranged or expected. *Steve arrived late.*
ADJECTIVE **3** FORMAL dead; deceased: *my late grandmother.*

Synonyms: (sense 2) belated, overdue, tardy

lately
ADVERB recently.

lateral
ADJECTIVE **1** relating to the side or sides of something.
2 A lateral thinker tackles problems in an imaginative and unusual way.

lathe lathes
NOUN a machine which holds and turns a piece of wood against a tool to cut and shape it.

lather
NOUN the foam that you get when you rub soap in water.

Latin
NOUN the language that was spoken in ancient Rome.
[from Latin *Latinus* meaning of Latium, a region of central Italy]

latitude latitudes
NOUN The latitude of a place is its distance north or south of the equator measured in degrees. See **longitude**.

latter
ADJECTIVE OR NOUN **1** You use "latter" to refer to the second of two things that you have just mentioned. *We ate sandwiches and sausage rolls (the latter bought from Mrs Miggins' pieshop).*
ADJECTIVE **2** the second or later part of something: *the latter part of his career.*
latterly ADVERB
✔ You use *latter* to talk about the second of two items. To talk about the last of three or more items you should use *last-named.*

laugh laughs laughing laughed
VERB to make a noise which shows that you are amused or happy.
laugh NOUN

laughable
ADJECTIVE quite absurd, ridiculous.
laughably ADVERB

A B C D E F G H I J K L M N O P Q R S T U V W X Y Z

laughter
NOUN the action or noise of laughing.

launch launches launching launched
VERB 1 to put a ship into water for the first time.
2 to send a rocket into space.
3 When a company launches a new product, it makes it available to the public.
launch NOUN

launch pad launch pads
NOUN the place from which space rockets take off.

launderette launderettes; also spelt laundrette
NOUN a place where you can take your washing to clean it in coin-operated washing machines.

laundry laundries
NOUN 1 dirty clothes and sheets that are being washed or are about to be washed.
2 a business that washes and irons clothes and sheets.

laurel laurels
NOUN an evergreen tree with shiny leaves.

lava
NOUN the very hot liquid rock that pours from an erupting volcano, and becomes solid as it cools.

lavatory lavatories
NOUN a toilet.

lavender
NOUN 1 a small bush with bluish-pink flowers that have a strong, pleasant scent.
ADJECTIVE 2 bluish-pink.

lavish lavishes lavishing lavished
ADJECTIVE 1 If you are lavish, you are very generous with your time, money or gifts.
VERB 2 If you lavish money or affection on someone, you give them a lot of it.
lavishly ADVERB

law laws
NOUN 1 one of the rules established by a government, which tells people what they are allowed to do.
2 the system of rules for the people of a country.
3 the profession of people such as lawyers and judges, or the study of this subject. *She wants a career in law.*
4 a scientific rule which explains how things work in the physical world: *the law of gravity.*
lawful ADJECTIVE lawfully ADVERB

lawn lawns
NOUN an area of cultivated grass.

lawnmower lawnmowers
NOUN a small machine for cutting grass.

lawsuit lawsuits
NOUN a civil court case privately brought between two people, as opposed to the police prosecuting someone for a criminal offence.

lawyer lawyers
NOUN a person who is qualified to advise people about the law and represent them in court.

lax
ADJECTIVE careless and not keeping up the usual standards: *a lax policeman.*

lay lays laying laid
VERB 1 the past tense of some senses of **lie**.
2 to place something down.
3 If you lay the table, you get it ready for a meal.
4 When a bird lays an egg, an egg comes out of its body.
✔ The verb *lay* takes an object: *lay the table please; the hen laid an egg*. The verb *lie* does not take an object: *the book was lying on the table; I'm going to lie down.*

layer layers
NOUN a single thickness of something.

layout layouts
NOUN the pattern in which something is arranged.

laze lazes lazing lazed
VERB to relax and do no work.

lazy lazier laziest
ADJECTIVE not wanting to work or make an effort.
lazily ADVERB laziness NOUN

Synonyms: idle, indolent, slothful

lead leads leading led
*Rhymes with "***feed***"* VERB 1 to go in front of someone in order to show them the way.
2 If a road leads somewhere, you can go to the place by that road.
3 to cause to happen. *Her good results led to an excellent career.*
4 To lead your life is to live it. *As an explorer, Beth leads such an interesting life.*
5 to be in charge. *The president led the country.*
NOUN 6 If you take the lead in a race or competition, or if you are in the lead, you are winning.
7 a length of leather or chain used for controlling a dog.
8 If the police have a lead, they have a clue which might help them to solve a crime.
*Rhymes with "***fed***"* NOUN 9 a soft, grey, heavy metal.
10 the part of a pencil that makes a mark.

Synonyms: (sense 1) conduct, escort, guide

leader leaders
NOUN 1 the person who is in charge of an organization or group of people.
2 the person who is winning in a race or competition.

leadership
NOUN 1 the ability to be a good leader.
2 the group of people in charge of an organization.

 ► What is a leading light, a leading lady, a leading question, a leading article?

leaf **leaves; leafs leafing leafed**
NOUN 1 a flat, usually green, part of a plant growing from its stem.
2 one of the sheets of paper in a book.
VERB 3 If you leaf through a book or magazine, you turn the pages over quickly.

leaflet **leaflets**
NOUN a piece of paper containing information about a particular subject.

league **leagues**
Said "**leeg**" **NOUN** a group of people, clubs or countries that have joined together for a particular purpose or because they share a common interest.

leak **leaks leaking leaked**
VERB 1 to escape from a container. *The water had leaked from the car's engine.*
2 to give official information to someone who is not supposed to have it. *The letter to the MP was leaked to the press.*
leak NOUN **leaky** ADJECTIVE
[from Old Norse *leka* meaning to drip]

lean **leans leaning leant** or **leaned; leaner leanest**
VERB 1 to bend your body in a particular direction.
2 When you lean on something, you rest your body against it for support.
3 to prop an object against something.
ADJECTIVE 4 If meat is lean, it does not have very much fat.
5 A lean period is a time when food or money is short.

leap **leaps leaping leapt** or **leaped**
VERB to jump a long distance or high in the air.
leap NOUN

Synonyms: bound, spring

leapfrog
NOUN a game in which you jump over people who are bending over.

leap year **leap years**
NOUN a year, usually occurring every four years, in which there are 366 days. (Century years not divisible by 400 are not leap years).

learn **learns learning learnt** or **learned**
VERB 1 to gain knowledge or a skill through study, training or experience.
2 If you learn of something, you get to know about it.

Synonyms: (sense 2) discover, find out, hear about

learner **learners**
NOUN a person who is learning to do something such as drive or swim.

lease **leases leasing leased**
VERB 1 to use property or equipment in return for a regular payment.
NOUN 2 a legal agreement which allows someone to use property or equipment in return for a regular payment.
leasing NOUN

leash **leashes**
NOUN another name for a dog's lead.

least
NOUN 1 the smallest possible amount of something.
ADJECTIVE OR ADVERB 2 a superlative form of **little**.
PHRASE 3 You use **at least** to indicate a minimum amount of something, and that the true amount may be greater.
4 You use **at least** when you are mentioning an advantage that still exists in a bad situation. *At least Ali didn't lose his money.*

leather
NOUN treated animal skin, used to make shoes, clothes and other things.

leave **leaves leaving left**
VERB 1 to go away from somewhere or somebody.
2 to put something down or away before you go elsewhere. *Did I leave my trainers in your car?*
3 to stop being a part of a job or organization.
4 to cause or allow to remain.
5 If you leave money or property to someone, they will receive it after you die.
NOUN 6 a period of holiday or absence from a job.

Synonyms: (sense 1) depart, exit, go

lecture **lectures**
NOUN 1 a formal talk to teach people about a particular subject, especially at a university.
2 a talk intended to tell someone off.
lecture VERB **lecturer** NOUN

led
the past tense and past participle of **lead**.

ledge **ledges**
NOUN a narrow shelf.

lee
NOUN the side of a place which is sheltered from the wind.
lee ADJECTIVE

leek **leeks**
NOUN a long vegetable of the onion family.

leer **leers leering leered**
VERB to smile at someone in an unpleasant and menacing way.
leer NOUN

left **1** the past tense and past participle of **leave**.
NOUN 2 The left is one of two opposite sides, positions or directions.
ADJECTIVE OR ADVERB 3 on or towards the left.
ADJECTIVE 4 remaining. *There was only one piece of cake left.*

a b c d e f g h i j k l m n o p q r s t u v w x y z

A B C D E F G H I J K L M N O P Q R S T U V W X Y Z

left-handed
ADJECTIVE OR ADVERB Someone who is left-handed does things such as writing with their left hand.

leftovers
PLURAL NOUN the food that is left after a meal.

leg legs
NOUN **1** the two long parts of your body that you stand on and walk with.
2 The legs of a pair of trousers are the parts that cover your legs.
3 The legs of an object such as a chair are the parts which rest on the floor and support the weight of the object.
4 A leg of a journey or a sports fixture is one part of it, where there is more than one.

legacy legacies
NOUN **1** property or money that someone gets in the will of a dead person.
2 something that exists as a result of a previous event or time: *the legacy of having a strict father.*

Synonyms: (sense 1) bequest, inheritance

legal
ADJECTIVE **1** allowed by the law.
2 relating to the law.

legalize legalizes legalizing legalized
VERB to make something legal which has previously been against the law.
legalization NOUN

legend legends
NOUN **1** a very old story which is not necessarily true, but has been handed down for many generations.
2 someone who is very famous. *Hollywood legend Gene Kelly.*
legendary ADJECTIVE

legible
ADJECTIVE clear enough to be read.
legibly ADVERB **legibility** NOUN

legion legions
NOUN **1** In ancient Rome, a legion was a military unit of between 3000 and 6000 soldiers.
2 a large military force: *the French Foreign Legion.*
3 Legions of people are large numbers of them.

legislation
NOUN the act of creating new laws, and the set of laws themselves.

legitimate
Said "lij-**it**-tim-it" ADJECTIVE reasonable or acceptable according to existing laws or standards. *It's legitimate to feel excited when you go on holiday.*
legitimately ADVERB **legitimacy** NOUN

leisure
Rhymes with "**measure**" NOUN spare time.

leisurely
ADJECTIVE OR ADVERB done in a relaxed, unhurried and calm way.

lemon lemons
NOUN a yellow citrus fruit with a sour taste.

lemonade
NOUN a clear, sweet, lemon-flavoured drink.

lend lends lending lent
VERB **1** to let someone borrow something for a period of time.
2 If a person or a bank lends you money, they let you have money now and you agree to pay it back later.
PHRASE **3** If you **lend someone a hand**, you help them.
lender NOUN

length lengths
NOUN **1** the distance from one end to the other of something.
2 the amount of time something continues.
3 the fact that something is long rather than short: *the length of her fingernails was amazing.*
PHRASE **4** If you **go to great lengths** to achieve something, you do extreme things in order to achieve it.

lengthen lengthens lengthening lengthened
VERB to make something longer or to become longer.

Synonyms: elongate, extend, prolong

lengthways or **lengthwise**
ADVERB If you measure something lengthways, you measure the distance from end to end.

lengthy lengthier lengthiest
ADJECTIVE lasting a long time.

lenient
ADJECTIVE If someone in authority is lenient, they are less severe than expected.
leniently ADVERB **leniency** NOUN
lenience NOUN

lens lenses
NOUN **1** a thin, curved piece of glass or plastic which makes things appear larger or clearer, found in glasses, cameras, binoculars and projectors.
2 a part of your eye which focuses light.
[from Latin *lens* meaning lentil, because of its convex shape]

lent
the past tense and past participle of **lend**.

Lent
NOUN a 40-day period before Easter when Christians remember the time Jesus spent fasting in the wilderness.

lentil lentils
NOUN Lentils are small, dried red, green or brown seeds used in cooking.

leopard leopards
NOUN a wild Asian or African big cat, with yellow fur and black or brown spots.

 ► Make sure you know the difference between lend and borrow. May I borrow your pencil?

leotard leotards
Said "**lee**-oh-tard" NOUN a tight-fitting costume worn for dancing or exercise.
[named after Jules Léotard, a French trapeze artist who was one of the first to wear one]

leper lepers
NOUN someone who has leprosy.

leprosy
NOUN an infectious disease which attacks the skin and nerves, and which can lead to fingers or toes dropping off.

lesbian lesbians
NOUN a homosexual woman.

less
ADJECTIVE OR ADVERB **1** a smaller amount of something. *Showers use less water than baths.*
2 to a smaller extent. *She was less frightened of the dark now.*
3 Less is a comparative form of **little**.
PREPOSITION **4** You use "less" to show that one number or amount is to be subtracted from another. *Jack was given his pocket money less the cost of replacing the window he'd broken.*
✔ Use *less* for things that can't be counted: *less time*. Use *fewer* for amounts that can be counted: *fewer apples*.

lessen lessens lessening lessened
VERB to reduce in amount, size or quality.

Synonyms: decrease, diminish, reduce

lesson lessons
NOUN **1** a fixed period of time during which people are taught.
2 an experience that makes you understand something important.

let lets letting let
VERB **1** to allow someone to do something. *Jim let me borrow his pen.*
2 to rent out a house, flat, etc.
3 You can say "let's" or "let us" when you are making a suggestion. *Let's go to the pictures.*
let off VERB **1** If someone lets you off, they do not punish you for something you have done wrong.
2 to detonate a firework.

lethal
Said "**lee**-thal" ADJECTIVE Something that is lethal can kill you.

Synonym: deadly

let's
contraction of **let us**.

letter letters
NOUN **1** a message written on paper and sent to someone, usually through the post.
2 Letters are written symbols which go together to make words.

letter box letter boxes
NOUN a flap or a box into which letters are delivered.

lettering
NOUN **1** the letters used in writing, and the way they are written: *bold lettering*.
2 the action of writing letter shapes.

lettuce lettuces
NOUN a vegetable with large green leaves, eaten in salads.

leukaemia
NOUN cancer of the blood.

level levels
NOUN **1** a point on a scale which measures the amount, importance or difficulty of something.
2 the height of something.
ADJECTIVE **3** flat and even: *level ground*.
ADVERB **4** If you draw level with someone, you get closer to them until you are beside them.

Synonyms: (sense 1) grade, position, stage

level crossing level crossings
NOUN a place where road traffic is allowed to drive across a railway track.

lever levers
NOUN **1** a long bar that you wedge underneath a heavy object and press down on to make the object move.
2 a handle on a machine that you pull in order to make the machine work.

liability liabilities
NOUN **1** Someone's liability is their responsibility for something they have done wrong.
2 If you say someone is a liability you mean that they are a hindering your progress in some way.

liable
ADJECTIVE **1** If something is liable to happen, it will probably happen.
2 legally responsible for something. *He was liable for the damage he had caused.*

liar liars
NOUN a person who tells lies.
lying ADJECTIVE

liberal
ADJECTIVE **1** Someone who is liberal is tolerant of a wide range of behaviour or opinions, and supports individual freedom.
2 To be liberal with something is to be generous with it.
liberal NOUN **liberally** ADVERB

liberate liberates liberating liberated
VERB to set free.
liberation NOUN **liberator** NOUN

liberty
NOUN the freedom to do what you want and go where you want.

librarian librarians
NOUN a person who works in, or is in charge of, a library.

a b c d e f g h i j k **l** m n o p q r s t u v w x y z

A B C D E F G H I J K L M N O P Q R S T U V W X Y Z

library libraries
NOUN a building in which books are kept, usually for people to borrow.

lice
plural of **louse**.

licence licences
NOUN an official document which gives you permission to do, use or own something.
✔ The noun *licence* ends in *ce*.

license licenses licensing licensed
VERB To license an activity means to give official permission for it to be carried out.
licensed ADJECTIVE
✔ The verb *license* ends in *se*.

lichen lichens
Said "**lie**-ken or **litch**-en" NOUN a green, moss-like growth on rocks or tree trunks.

lick licks licking licked
VERB to move your tongue over something.
lick NOUN

lid lids
NOUN the top of a container, which you open to reach what is inside.

lie lies lying lay lain; lies lying lied
VERB **1** to rest in a flat position; to be on the floor or ground.
2 to say something that you know is not true.
NOUN **3** something you say which you know is not true.
✔ (sense 1) The past tense of this verb *lie* is *lay*. Do not confuse it with the verb *lay* meaning put.

lieutenant lieutenants
Said "lef-**ten**-ent" NOUN a junior officer in the army or navy.

life lives
NOUN **1** the state of being alive.
2 Your life is your existence from the time you are born until the time you die.
3 the amount of activity in a place. *The town was full of life.*

lifeboat lifeboats
NOUN **1** a boat which is sent out to rescue people who are in danger at sea.
2 a small boat kept on a ship, which is used if the ship starts to sink.

life cycle life cycles
NOUN The life cycle of a plant or animal including a human being is the series of changes it goes through during its life.

lifeguard lifeguards
NOUN a person whose job is to rescue people who are in difficulty in the sea or in a swimming pool.

life jacket life jackets
NOUN a sleeveless inflatable jacket that helps to keep you afloat in water.

lifeless
ADJECTIVE **1** Someone who is lifeless is dead.
2 If you describe a place or person as lifeless, you mean that they are dull and unexciting.
lifelessly ADVERB **lifelessness** NOUN

lifelike
ADJECTIVE A picture or sculpture that is lifelike looks very real or alive.

lifelong
ADJECTIVE existing throughout someone's life.

life span life spans
NOUN the length of time that someone or something lives.

lifestyle lifestyles
NOUN the attitudes, habits and possessions which go with the way someone lives.

lifetime lifetimes
NOUN the period of time during which you are alive.

lift lifts lifting lifted
VERB **1** to move something to a higher position.
2 When fog or mist lifts, it clears away.
3 If people in authority lift a rule or law, they end it.
NOUN **4** a device that carries people or goods from one floor to another in a building.
5 If you give someone a lift, you drive them from one place to another.

Synonyms: (sense 1) elevate, raise
(sense 4) elevator

liftoff liftoffs
NOUN the action of a space rocket being launched.
lift off VERB

light lights lighting lighted or lit; lighter lightest
NOUN **1** a form of energy. You need light to see.
2 the brightness from the sun, moon, fire or lamps.
3 a lamp or other device that gives out brightness.
4 If someone asks for a light, they want a match or lighter.
VERB **5** to fill a place with light, to illuminate.
6 To light a fire means to make a fire start burning.
ADJECTIVE **7** If it is light, there is enough light from the sun to see things.
8 A light colour is pale.
9 A light object does not weigh much.
lightly ADVERB **lightness** NOUN

lighten lightens lightening lightened
VERB **1** to become less dark.
2 to make something less heavy.

lighter lighters
NOUN a device that sparks up a flame for setting things alight.

light-headed
ADJECTIVE slightly dizzy or drunk.
light-headedness NOUN

► Library words: fiction, non-fiction, reference, periodicals, catalogue, browse.

light-hearted
ADJECTIVE cheerful and without worries.
light-heartedly ADVERB **light-heartedness** NOUN

Synonyms: blithe, carefree, happy-go-lucky

lighthouse lighthouses
NOUN a tower by the sea, which sends out a powerful light to guide ships and warn them of danger.

lighting
NOUN the way that a room or building is lit.

lightning
NOUN bright flashes of light you see in the sky during a thunderstorm. Lightning is caused by electrical activity in the atmosphere.
✔ *Lightning* is often wrongly spelt with an *e* in the middle.

lightweight
ADJECTIVE 1 not weighing very much.
2 INFORMAL If you say something or someone is lightweight, you mean that they are not to be taken too seriously.

light year light years
NOUN a unit of distance equal to the distance that light travels in a year.

like likes liking liked
VERB 1 to think that someone or something is interesting, enjoyable or attractive.
2 If you would like something, you mean that you want it.
PREPOSITION 3 similar to.
4 If you talk about what someone or something is like, you are talking about their qualities.
5 You use "like" to give an example. *I have seen the big cities of the world – like New York, Rome and Paris.*
PHRASE 6 If you **feel like** doing something, you want to do it.

likable or **likeable**
ADJECTIVE very pleasant and friendly.

likely likelier likeliest
ADJECTIVE Something that is likely will probably happen or is probably true.
likelihood NOUN

liken likens likening likened
VERB If you liken one thing to another, you say that they are similar.

likeness likenesses
NOUN If two things have a likeness to each other, they are similar in appearance.

likewise
ADVERB similarly.

liking
NOUN If you have a liking for something, you like it.

lilac
NOUN 1 a shrub with large clusters of pink, white or mauve flowers.
ADJECTIVE 2 pale mauve.

lily lilies
NOUN a plant with trumpet-shaped flowers of various colours.

limb limbs
NOUN 1 Your limbs are your arms and legs.
2 a branch of a tree.

lime limes
NOUN 1 a small, green citrus fruit, rather like a lemon.
2 a large tree with pale green leaves.
3 a chemical substance made from limestone and chalk which is used in cement and as a fertilizer.
ADJECTIVE 4 bright acid green.

limelight
NOUN If someone is in the limelight, they are getting a lot of public attention.
[so called because stage lighting used to be produced by a lamp which heated lime to a white heat]

limerick limericks
NOUN an amusing nonsense poem of five lines.

limestone
NOUN a white rock which is used for building and making cement.

limit limits limiting limited
NOUN 1 a boundary or extreme beyond which something cannot go.
VERB 2 to prevent something from developing or becoming bigger.

limousine limousines
NOUN a very large luxury car, usually driven by a chauffeur.

limp limps limping limped; limper limpest
VERB 1 to walk in an uneven way because you have hurt your leg or foot.
2 to move far more slowly than usual: *the damaged racing car limped back to the pit.*
NOUN 3 an uneven way of walking.
ADJECTIVE 4 soft and floppy.

limpet limpets
NOUN a shellfish with a pointed shell that attaches itself very firmly to rocks.

line lines lining lined
NOUN 1 a long, thin mark.
2 a number of people or things that are arranged in a row.
3 a railway route: *the London-Brighton line.*
4 a number of words together in a piece of writing.
5 Someone's line of work is the type of work they do.
6 The line someone takes is the attitude they have towards something. *She took a hard line on discipline.*
7 In a shop or business, a line is a type of product. *We'll be getting more of that line later in the month.*
VERB 8 to fill the edges of something. *Crowds lined the streets.*
line up VERB to form a queue.

a b c d e f g h i j k l m n o p q r s t u v w x y z

The word "verse" originally meant line but it has come to mean several lines, a stanza.

A B C D E F G H I J K L M N O P Q R S T U V W X Y Z

linen
NOUN a type of white cloth used in high quality sheets, pillowcases and tablecloths.

liner liners
NOUN a large ocean-going passenger ship.

linesman linesmen
NOUN an official at a sports match.

linger lingers lingering lingered
VERB to remain for a long time around the same place.
lingering ADJECTIVE

lingerie
Said "**lan**-jer-ee" NOUN women's nightwear and underclothes.

linguist linguists
NOUN someone who studies foreign languages or the way in which language works.

lining linings
NOUN any material used to line the inside of something.

link links linking linked
NOUN **1** a relationship or connection between two things: *the link between industry and pollution.*
2 a physical connection between two things or places: *a high-speed rail link.*
VERB **3** to connect.

lino
a short form of **linoleum**.

linoleum
NOUN a light floor covering with a shiny, washable surface.

lint
NOUN soft cloth made from linen, used to dress wounds.

lion lions
NOUN a large member of the cat family found in Africa.

lioness lionesses
NOUN a female lion.

lip lips
NOUN **1** Your lips are the two outer edges of your mouth.
2 The lip of a jug is its pointed spout.

lip-read lip-reads lip-reading lip-read
VERB to interpret what someone is saying by watching their lips. Deaf people often lip-read.

lipstick lipsticks
NOUN a coloured cosmetic for the lips.

liquid liquids
NOUN a substance such as water, which is not gas or solid and can be poured. Liquids take the shape of the container they are in.
liquify VERB

liquidizer liquidizers; also spelt **liquidiser**
NOUN a kitchen machine with rotating blades which you use to change solid food into a liquid or a pulp.
liquidize VERB

liquor
NOUN any strong alcoholic drink.

liquorice
Said "**lik**-ker-iss" NOUN a root used to flavour sweets; also the sweets themselves.

lisp lisps lisping lisped
NOUN **1** Someone who has a lisp pronounces the sounds "s" and "z" like "th".
VERB **2** to speak with a lisp.

list lists listing listed
NOUN **1** a set of words or items written one below the other.
VERB **2** to write or say a number of things one after another.
3 If a ship lists, it leans to one side.

listen listens listening listened
VERB to pay attention to what someone is saying or the sounds you can hear.
listener NOUN

listless
ADJECTIVE lacking energy and enthusiasm.
listlessly ADVERB

lit
past tense of **light**.

literacy
NOUN the ability to read and write.
literate ADJECTIVE

literal
ADJECTIVE The literal meaning of a word is its most basic meaning. For example, in a literal sense, someone whom we call a star would live in outer space, not in Hollywood.

literally
ADVERB You use "literally" to emphasize what you are saying. *There were literally hundreds of people there.*

LITERALLY RUBBISH
Be careful when you use the word "literally" that what you say is actually true. It can make nonsense of some things. For example:
John was literally dying to meet me.
This sentence is ridiculous unless John actually died when he met the speaker.

literate
ADJECTIVE able to read and write.

literature
NOUN a general word for novels, plays and poetry.

litmus
NOUN In chemistry, litmus is an indicator used to tell how acid or alkaline a substance is. It turns red with acids and blue with alkalis.

litre litres
NOUN a unit of liquid volume equal to about 1·76 pints, abbreviated to "l".

litter litters littering littered
NOUN **1** rubbish in the street and other public places.
VERB **2** If things litter a place, they are scattered all over it.

little less lesser least
ADJECTIVE, ADVERB OR PRONOUN small in size or amount.

live lives living lived
Said "**liv**" VERB **1** to be alive.
2 If you live in a place, that is where your home is.
3 The way someone lives is the kind of life they have.
Said "**lyv**" ADJECTIVE OR ADVERB **4** Live television or radio is broadcast while the event is taking place.
ADJECTIVE **5** alive, rather than dead or artificial.

livelihood livelihoods
NOUN someone's job or the source of their income.

lively livelier liveliest
ADJECTIVE full of life and enthusiasm.

Synonyms: brisk, energetic, vigorous

liver livers
NOUN a large organ in your body which cleans your blood and helps digestion.

lives
plural of **life**.

livestock
NOUN a general name for farm animals.

livid
ADJECTIVE extremely angry.

living
ADJECTIVE **1** alive.
NOUN **2** The work that you do for a living is the work that you do in order to earn an income.

living room living rooms
NOUN the room where people relax in their homes.

lizard lizards
NOUN a reptile with short legs and a long tail.

llama llamas
NOUN a South American mammal related to the camel.

load loads loading loaded
VERB **1** to put things into a vehicle or container.
2 If you load a gun, you put a bullet or cartridge into it.
NOUN **3** something large or heavy which is being carried.
4 INFORMAL A load of something, or loads of something, means a lot of it.

loaf loaves; loafs loafing loafed
NOUN **1** a large piece of bread for cutting into slices.
VERB **2** to lounge about lazily.

loan loans loaning loaned
NOUN **1** a sum of money that you borrow.
VERB **2** to lend.

loathe loathes loathing loathed
VERB to feel a strong dislike for someone or something.
loathing NOUN

loathsome
ADJECTIVE very unpleasant.

loaves
plural of **loaf**.

lob lobs lobbing lobbed
VERB **1** to throw something high in the air.
NOUN **2** A tennis stroke in which the player hits the ball high in the air.

lobby lobbies
NOUN The lobby in a large building is the main entrance area with corridors and doors leading off it.

lobe lobes
NOUN The lobe of your ear is the rounded soft part at the bottom.

lobster lobsters
NOUN a crustacean with a hard shell, two large front claws, and eight legs, which lives in the sea.

local locals
ADJECTIVE **1** existing in or belonging to the area where you live.
2 A local anaesthetic deadens the pain in one particular area of the body only.
NOUN; INFORMAL **3** The locals are the people who live in a particular area.
4 The local is another name for the local pub.
locally ADVERB

Synonyms: (sense 1) community, provincial, regional

locality localities
NOUN The locality is the district around a particular place.

locate locates locating located
VERB **1** to find someone or something after looking for them.
2 If something is located in a place, it is in that place.

location locations
NOUN a place, especially the place or position where something is situated.

loch lochs
NOUN a Scottish word for lake.

a b c d e f g h i j k l m n o p q r s t u v w x y z

A B C D E F G H I J K L M N O P Q R S T U V W X Y Z

lock locks locking locked
VERB **1** to fasten something with a key.
2 to secure someone in a place. *They locked her in a cell.*
NOUN **3** a device which prevents something from being opened except with a key.

locker lockers
NOUN a small, lockable cupboard for someone's personal belongings.

locket lockets
NOUN a neck-chain with a small case in which you can keep a reminder of someone, such as a tiny photo or wisp of hair.

locomotive locomotives
NOUN a railway engine.

locust locusts
NOUN an insect like a large grasshopper, which travels in huge swarms and eats crops.

lodge lodges lodging lodged
VERB **1** If you lodge in someone else's house, you live there and pay them rent.
2 to get stuck somewhere. *The fish bone lodged in her throat.*
3 If you lodge a complaint, you formally make it.
NOUN **4** a small house in the grounds of a country estate.

lodger lodgers
NOUN a person who lives in someone's house and pays rent.

loft lofts
NOUN the space immediately under the roof of a house, often used for storing things.

lofty loftier loftiest
ADJECTIVE **1** very high: *lofty ceilings.*
2 noble and important: *lofty plans.*
3 proud and superior: *a lofty manner.*
loftily ADVERB

log logs logging logged
NOUN **1** a thick piece of wood which has been cut from a tree.
2 an official written account of what happens each day: *the starship's log.*
VERB **3** If you log something, you make an official written record of it.
4 If you log onto or into a computer system, you gain access to it.
PHRASE **5** If you **sleep like a log** you sleep very deeply.

Antonyms: (sense 4) exit, log off

logic
NOUN a way of reasoning step by step, using facts.

logical
ADJECTIVE **1** A logical conclusion or result is the only reasonable one.
2 A logical person works things out sensibly and reasonably.
logically ADVERB

logo logos
Said "**loh**-goh" NOUN The logo of an organization is a special design that is put on all its products.

loiter loiters loitering loitered
VERB to stand about idly with no real purpose.

lollipop lollipops
NOUN a hard sweet on the end of a stick.

lolly lollies
NOUN **1** a lollipop.
2 a piece of flavoured ice or ice cream on a stick.
3 INFORMAL money.

lone
ADJECTIVE unaccompanied.
loner NOUN

Synonyms: alone, single, solitary

lonely lonelier loneliest
ADJECTIVE **1** If you are lonely, you are unhappy because you are alone.
2 A lonely place is one which very few people visit.
loneliness NOUN

long longer longest; longs longing longed
ADJECTIVE OR ADVERB **1** continuing for a great amount of time.
2 You use "long" to talk about indefinite amounts of time. *How long can you stay?*
ADJECTIVE **3** great in length or distance.
4 You use "long" to talk about an indefinite distance. *How long is the tunnel?*
VERB **5** If you long for something, you want it very much.
PHRASE **6** If something **no longer** happens, it used to happen but does not happen now.
7 If one thing is true **as long as** another thing is true, it is true only if the other thing is true. *As long as there's no more rain, the match will go ahead.*

long division
NOUN in arithmetic, calculations that involve division, which are written down in a standard way: $13\overline{)396}$.

longitude longitudes
NOUN The longitude of a place is its distance east or west of a line passing through Greenwich, measured in degrees. See **latitude**.

long jump
NOUN an athletics event involving jumping as far as possible into a pit of sand.

long-range
ADJECTIVE **1** able to be used over a great distance.
2 extending a long way into the future: *a long-range weather forecast.*

long-sighted
ADJECTIVE A long-sighted person has difficulty in seeing things that are close.

 ► All these words contain the long "a"sound: bake, raid, say, gaol, gauge, break, rein, grey, reign, weight.

long-term
ADJECTIVE extending a long way into the future: *a long-term plan.*

long-winded
ADJECTIVE long and boring.

loo loos
NOUN; INFORMAL a toilet.

look looks looking looked
VERB **1** to turn your eyes towards something so that you can see it.
2 to search for someone or something.
3 to study or judge a situation. *Let's look at this closely.*
4 If you describe the way that something looks, you are describing its appearance.
5 If you look forward to something, you want it to happen because you think you will enjoy it.
NOUN **6** If you have a look at something, you look at it.
7 The look on your face is the expression on it.
look after VERB to take care of someone or something.
look out VERB You say look out to warn someone of danger.

Synonyms: (sense 1) gaze, watch, study
(sense 6) glance, glimpse, peek
(sense 7) expression

lookalike lookalikes
NOUN a person who looks very like someone else. *He's an Elvis lookalike.*

lookout lookouts
NOUN **1** someone who is keeping watch for danger.
2 a place where people keep watch for danger.
PHRASE **3** If you are **on the lookout** for something, you are watching for it or waiting expectantly for it.

loom looms looming loomed
NOUN **1** a machine for weaving cloth.
VERB **2** If something looms in front of you, it suddenly appears as a tall, unclear and sometimes frightening shape.
3 If a situation or event is looming, it is likely to happen soon and is rather worrying.

loony loonies
ADJECTIVE; INFORMAL mad or eccentric.
loony NOUN
[from *lunatic*]

loop loops looping looped
NOUN **1** a curved or circular shape in something long such as a piece of string.
VERB **2** If you loop rope or string around an object, you place it in a loop around the object.

loophole loopholes
NOUN **1** a small mistake or omission in a law that enables you to do something which the law really intends you should not do.
2 an arrow slit in a medieval castle.

loose looser loosest
ADJECTIVE **1** not firmly held or fixed in place.
ADVERB **2** If people or animals break loose or are set loose, they are freed after they have been restrained.
loosely ADVERB
✔ Do not confuse *loose* with the verb *lose.*

loosen loosens loosening loosened
VERB to make something looser.

loot loots looting looted
VERB **1** to steal goods from shops and houses during a battle or riot.
NOUN **2** stolen money or goods.

Synonyms: (sense 1) pillage, plunder, ransack
(sense 2) booty, plunder, spoils

lopsided
ADJECTIVE Something which is lopsided is uneven because its two sides are different sizes or shapes.
lopsidedly ADVERB

lord lords
NOUN a man who has inherited or has been granted a peerage, or an official of very high rank. *Lord Crumbleigh of Cheddar; the Lord Mayor of London.*

lorry lorries
NOUN a large vehicle for transporting goods by road.

lose loses losing lost
VERB **1** If you lose something, you cannot find it or you no longer have it because it has been taken from you.
2 If you lose an argument or a game, you are beaten.
3 If you lose something, you have less of it. *I need to lose weight. The company is losing money.*
loser NOUN **losing** ADJECTIVE
✔ Do not confuse *lose* with the adjective and adverb *loose.*

loss losses
NOUN **1** The loss of something is the losing of it.
PHRASE **2** If you are **at a loss**, you do not know what to do.

lost
ADJECTIVE **1** If you are lost, you do not know where you are.
2 If something is lost, you cannot find it.
VERB **3** the past tense and past participle of lose.

lot lots
NOUN **1** a large amount of something.
2 very often. *They go out quite a lot.*
3 a group of people or things. *There were three lots of tourists.*
4 The lot means the whole of an amount.

Synonyms: (sense 1) abundance, plenty, a great deal

A B C D E F G H I J K L M N O P Q R S T U V W X Y Z

lotion lotions
NOUN a liquid that you put on your skin to protect or soften it.

lottery lotteries
NOUN a method of raising money by selling tickets by which one or more winners are selected at random.

loud louder loudest
ADJECTIVE OR ADVERB producing a lot of sound.
loudly ADVERB **loudness** NOUN

loudspeaker loudspeakers
NOUN a piece of equipment that converts the electrical signals from a hi-fi system, microphone, etc. into sounds that you can hear. See **speaker**.

lounge lounges lounging lounged
NOUN **1** a room in a house, hotel or airport where people can sit and relax.
VERB **2** to spend time in a relaxed and lazy way.

louse lice
NOUN **1** Lice are small insects that live on people's bodies.
2 INFORMAL If you call someone a louse, you think they are unpleasant or mean.

lousy lousier lousiest
ADJECTIVE **1** INFORMAL of bad quality or very unpleasant.
2 ill or unhappy. *I woke up feeling lousy.*

lout louts
NOUN a young man who behaves in a rude or aggressive way.
loutish ADJECTIVE

lovable or **loveable**
ADJECTIVE having very attractive qualities and therefore easy to love.

love loves loving loved
VERB **1** to have strong feelings of affection for someone.
2 to like something very much.
3 If you would love to do something, you want very much to do it.
NOUN **4** a strong feeling of affection.
PHRASE **5** If a person is **in love** with someone else, they feel strongly attracted to them romantically.

Synonyms: (sense 1) adore, dote on

lovely lovelier loveliest
ADJECTIVE very beautiful or pleasant.
loveliness NOUN

low lower lowest; lows
ADJECTIVE OR ADVERB **1** close to the ground or measuring a short distance from the ground to the top: *a low coffee table.*
ADJECTIVE **2** small in value or amount.
3 poor in quality: *low standards.*
NOUN **4** A low is a level or amount that is less than before. *The euro fell to a new low today.*

lower lowers lowering lowered
VERB to move something downwards, or make it less in amount.

lower case
NOUN The lower case is the set of small letters used in printing or on a typewriter, as opposed to the capital letters.
lower-case ADJECTIVE

Antonyms: upper case, capital

lowlands
PLURAL NOUN an area of flat, low land.
lowland ADJECTIVE

lowly lowlier lowliest
ADJECTIVE low in importance, rank or status.

low tide low tides
NOUN On a coast, low tide is the time, usually twice a day, when the sea is at its lowest level.

loyal
ADJECTIVE firm in your friendship or support for someone or something.
loyally ADVERB **loyalty** NOUN

lozenge lozenges
NOUN a type of sweet which is sucked to relieve a sore throat or cough.

lubricate lubricates lubricating lubricated
VERB to put oil or grease onto a machine, wheel or other equipment so that it moves smoothly.
lubrication NOUN **lubricant** NOUN

lucid
ADJECTIVE **1** Lucid writing or speech is clear and easy to understand.
2 able to think clearly.
lucidly ADVERB **lucidity** NOUN

luck
NOUN **1** Luck or good luck is anything good that happens to you which is not a result of your own efforts.
2 Bad luck is anything bad that happens to you which is not a result of your own efforts.
PHRASE **3** You say **good luck** to someone when you are wishing them success.

Synonyms: (sense 1) chance, fortune

lucky luckier luckiest
ADJECTIVE **1** having a lot of good luck.
2 Something that is lucky has good effects or consequences. *It's lucky that no one was injured.*
3 If you say someone is lucky, you mean that they are in a desirable situation. *I'm lucky in having an excellent teacher.*
luckily ADVERB

ludicrous
ADJECTIVE completely foolish, unsuitable or ridiculous.
ludicrously ADVERB

lug lugs lugging lugged
VERB to carry something heavy with difficulty.

► Capital letters are said to be in upper case. Small letters are in lower case.

luggage
NOUN the bags and suitcases that you take with you when you travel.

lukewarm
ADJECTIVE 1 slightly warm, tepid.
2 not very enthusiastic or interested.

lull lulls lulling lulled
NOUN 1 a pause in something or a short time when it is quiet and nothing much happens.
VERB 2 If you are lulled into feeling safe, someone or something causes you to feel safe at a time when you are not safe: *lulled into a false sense of security.*

lullaby lullabies
NOUN a song used for sending a baby or child to sleep.

lumber lumbers lumbering lumbered
NOUN 1 wood that has been roughly cut up.
VERB 2 to move heavily and clumsily.
3 INFORMAL If you are lumbered with something, you are given it to deal with even though you do not want it.

lumberjack lumberjacks
NOUN a man whose job is to chop down trees in forests.

luminous
ADJECTIVE a substance that glows in the dark without being hot.
luminously ADVERB **luminosity** NOUN

lump lumps
NOUN 1 a solid piece of something, usually irregular in shape.
2 a small, hard piece of flesh on someone's body.
lumpy ADJECTIVE

lunar
ADJECTIVE relating to the moon.

lunatic lunatics
NOUN 1 If you call someone a lunatic, you mean that they are very foolish.
2 OLD-FASHIONED someone who is insane.
lunatic ADJECTIVE
[from Latin *luna* meaning moon. The moon has a strong influence on many people's behaviour, and the time of full moon can have a marked effect on the mentally ill]

lunch lunches lunching lunched
NOUN 1 a meal eaten in the middle of the day.
VERB 2 FORMAL to eat lunch.

lung lungs
NOUN Your lungs are the pair of spongy bag-like organs inside your chest with which you breathe.

lunge lunges lunging lunged
VERB 1 to make a sudden movement in a particular direction.
NOUN 2 a sudden forward movement.

lurch lurches lurching lurched
VERB 1 to make a sudden, jerky movement. *The train lurched, and my juice spilled everywhere.*
NOUN 2 a sudden, jerky movement.
PHRASE 3 If someone **leaves you in the lurch**, they leave you in a difficult situation instead of helping you.

lure lures luring lured
VERB 1 to attract someone or something into going somewhere or doing something.
NOUN 2 something that you find very attractive and tempting.

lurk lurks lurking lurked
VERB To lurk somewhere means to remain there hidden from the person you are waiting for.

luscious
ADJECTIVE very tasty and juicy.
lusciously ADVERB

lush lusher lushest
ADJECTIVE In a lush field or garden, the grass and plants are healthy and growing thickly.

lust lusts
NOUN 1 A lust for something is a strong desire to have it.
2 a very strong feeling of sexual desire for someone.

lustre
Said "**lus**-ter" NOUN a soft shining light reflected from the surface of something.

lute lutes
NOUN an old-fashioned stringed musical instrument which is plucked like a guitar.

luxury luxuries
NOUN 1 great comfort, especially among expensive and beautiful surroundings.
2 something that you enjoy very much but do not often have, usually because it is expensive. *Eating out is a luxury.*
luxurious ADJECTIVE **luxuriously** ADVERB

Synonyms: (sense 2) extravagance, indulgence, treat

Lycra
NOUN; TRADEMARK a synthetic shiny stretch fabric used for swimming costumes, leotards, etc.

lying
1 the present participle of **lie**.
NOUN 2 telling lies.
ADJECTIVE 3 A lying person often tells lies.

lynch lynches lynching lynched
VERB If a crowd lynches someone, they kill them in a violent way without any proper trial.

lyre lyres
NOUN a stringed instrument rather like a small harp, which was used in ancient Greece.

lyric lyrics
NOUN 1 The lyric or lyrics of a song are the words.
ADJECTIVE 2 Lyric poetry is written in a simple and direct style, usually about love.
lyrical ADJECTIVE

A B C D E F G H I J K L M N O P Q R S T U V W X Y Z

Mm

macaroni
NOUN short hollow tubes of pasta.

machine machines
NOUN a piece of equipment which uses electricity or power from an engine to make it work.
machine VERB

machine gun machine guns
NOUN a gun that works automatically while the trigger is pressed, firing bullets one after the other.
machine-gun VERB

machinery
NOUN Machinery is machines in general.

mackerel mackerels
NOUN a sea fish with blue and silver stripes.

mackintosh mackintoshes
NOUN a raincoat made from specially treated waterproof cloth.

mad madder maddest
ADJECTIVE **1** Someone who is mad has a severe mental illness which causes them to behave strangely. When used in this way, the word can sometimes cause offence.
2 very foolish, daft. *We were mad to go out in the storm.*
3 INFORMAL angry. *Dad was mad at me for waking him up.*
4 INFORMAL If you are mad about someone or something, you like them very much.
madly ADVERB **madness** NOUN

Synonyms: (sense 1) crazy, deranged, insane

madam
a formal way of addressing a woman. *Please come this way, madam.*
[from Old French *ma dame* meaning my lady]

maddening
ADJECTIVE irritating or frustrating.

made
past tense of **make**.

magazine magazines
NOUN a weekly or monthly publication with written articles and photographs.
[from Arabic *makhzan* meaning storehouse]

maggot maggots
NOUN an insect larva before it becomes an adult fly. Maggots look like short, fat worms and live on decaying things.

magic
NOUN **1** In fairy stories, magic is a special power that can make things happen that seem to be impossible.
2 the art of performing tricks to entertain people.
magic ADJECTIVE **magical** ADJECTIVE
magically ADVERB

magician magicians
NOUN **1** a person who performs tricks as entertainment.
2 In fairy stories, a magician is a man with magical powers.

Synonym: (sense 1) conjuror
(sense 2) enchanter, sorcerer

magistrate magistrates
NOUN an official in a law court who judges less serious offences.

magnet magnets
NOUN a piece of iron which attracts iron or steel towards it.
magnetism NOUN

magnetic
ADJECTIVE If something is magnetic, it attracts metal by magnetism.

magnificent
ADJECTIVE extremely beautiful or impressive.
magnificently ADVERB **magnificence** NOUN

Synonyms: grand, splendid

magnify magnifies magnifying magnified
VERB **1** When a microscope or lens magnifies something, it makes it appear bigger than it actually is.
2 to make something seem more important than it actually is. *You're magnifying the problem out of all proportion.*
magnification NOUN

magnifying glass magnifying glasses
NOUN a hand-held lens that makes things appear bigger.

magnitude
NOUN the great size or importance of something.

magpie magpies
NOUN a fairly large black-and-white bird with a long tail.

mahogany
NOUN **1** a hard reddish-brown wood used for making furniture.
ADJECTIVE **2** reddish-brown.

maid maids
NOUN a female servant.

maiden maidens
NOUN **1** LITERARY a young woman.
ADJECTIVE **2** first: *a maiden voyage.*
3 A maiden aunt is one who has never married.
4 A married woman's maiden name is her surname before she married.

mail mails mailing mailed
NOUN **1** the letters and parcels delivered to you by the post office.
VERB **2** to send something by post.

mail order
NOUN a system of buying goods from a catalogue, for home delivery.

 ► The letter M seems to have developed from a picture of the waves of the sea.

maim **maims maiming maimed**
VERB to injure someone very badly for life.

main
ADJECTIVE **1** most important.
PLURAL NOUN **2** The mains are the large pipes or cables that carry gas, water or electricity to a building.

Synonyms: (sense 1) chief, major, principal

mainland
NOUN the main part of a country, rather than the islands around its coast.

mainly
ADVERB for the most part, to the greatest extent.

maintain **maintains maintaining maintained**
VERB **1** to make something continue or keep at a particular rate or level. *We must maintain high standards.*
2 to keep something in good condition.
3 If you maintain that something is true, you believe it is true and say so.

maintenance
NOUN **1** the process of keeping something in good condition.
2 the money a person sends regularly to someone to provide for the things they need.

maize
NOUN a tall plant which produces sweet corn.

majestic
ADJECTIVE in a dignified and grand style.
majestically ADVERB

majesty **majesties**
NOUN **1** great dignity and impressiveness.
2 When people speak to a king or a queen, they use the title "Your Majesty".

major **majors**
ADJECTIVE **1** more important or more serious than other things.
NOUN **2** an army officer of the rank immediately above captain.

Antonym: (sense 1) minor

majority **majorities**
NOUN **1** The majority of a group of people or things is the greater part of them, that is more than half of them.
2 In an election or vote, a majority is the difference between the number of votes gained by the winner and the number gained by the person or party that comes second. *The decision was passed by a majority of eight to two.*
✔ Use *majority* for things that can be counted: *the majority of car owners*. For an amount that cannot be counted, use *most*: *most of the harvest was saved.*

Antonym: minority

make **makes making made**
VERB **1** to produce or prepare something. *I'll make some salad dressing.*
2 to cause or force someone to do something. *The smoke made him cough. She made him tidy his room.*
3 to do or to offer. *He was about to make a speech. Can I make a suggestion?*
NOUN **4** The make of a product is the name of the company that made it. *"What make of trainers are those?"*
PHRASE **5** INFORMAL If you **make it**, you succeed in achieving something difficult. *After 10 years, he finally made it as a singer.*
make of VERB If you ask someone what they make of something, you are asking them what they think of it. *What did you make of his speech?*
make up VERB **1** to form the members or parts of something. *One hundred years make up a century.*
2 to invent. *Will you make up a story for me?*
3 If two people make up or make it up, they become friends again after a quarrel.
4 To make up for something that is lost or damaged means to replace it or compensate for it.
5 If you make up your mind, you come to a decision.

Synonyms: (make, sense 1) create, produce

make-believe
NOUN **1** fantasy, unreality.
ADJECTIVE **2** imaginary.

makeshift
ADJECTIVE Something makeshift is arranged or built in a hurry to meet a temporary need: *a makeshift shelter.*

make-up
NOUN Make-up is the coloured creams and powders some women and performers use on their faces.

malaria
Said "mal-**air**-ree-a" NOUN a tropical disease carried by mosquitoes which causes fever and shivering.

male **males**
NOUN **1** an animal, including a human being, belonging to the sex that cannot have babies or lay eggs. The male part of a flowering plant contains pollen.
ADJECTIVE **2** concerning or affecting men rather than women.

Antonym: female

malevolent
Said "mal-**lev**-oh-lent" ADJECTIVE; FORMAL wanting or intending to cause harm.
malevolence NOUN **malevolently** ADVERB

Synonyms: malicious, spiteful, vindictive

a b c d e f g h i j k l m n o p q r s t u v w x y z

The prefix "mal-" means something which is wrong or bad.

A B C D E F G H I J K L M N O P Q R S T U V W X Y Z

malfunction **malfunctions malfunctioning malfunctioned**
VERB If a machine malfunctions, it fails to work properly.
malfunction NOUN

malice
NOUN a desire to cause harm to people.

Synonym: spite

malicious
ADJECTIVE deliberately harmful.
maliciously ADVERB

mall **malls**
NOUN Short for a shopping mall, a covered shopping area with pedestrian access only.

mallet **mallets**
NOUN a wooden hammer with a square head.

malnutrition
NOUN a condition of ill health that results from not eating enough healthy food.

malt
NOUN roasted grain, usually barley, which is used in making beer and whisky and sometimes bread.

mammal **mammals**
NOUN any animal that gives birth to live babies and feeds its young with milk from the mother's body. Human beings, dogs and whales are all mammals.

mammoth **mammoths**
ADJECTIVE **1** very large indeed.
NOUN **2** a huge animal that became extinct a long time ago. Mammoths looked like hairy elephants with long tusks.

man **men; mans manning manned**
NOUN **1** an adult male human being.
PLURAL NOUN **2** Human beings in general are sometimes referred to as man or men. *This is the most poisonous snake known to man.*
VERB **3** If you man something, you are in charge of it or you operate it. *The police station is not manned in the evening.*

Synonyms: (sense 1) bloke, chap, guy
(sense 2) humanity, humankind, mankind

manage **manages managing managed**
VERB **1** If you manage an organization or business, you are responsible for controlling it.
2 to succeed in doing something, after some effort; to cope. *We managed to find somewhere to sit.*

Synonyms: (sense 2) accomplish, succeed

manageable
ADJECTIVE If a task is manageable, you can deal with it.

management
NOUN **1** the controlling and organizing of a business or organization.
2 the people who control a business or organization.

manager **managers**
NOUN a person responsible for running a business or organization.
managerial ADJECTIVE
✔ In business, the word *manager* can apply to either a man or a woman.

mandarin **mandarins**
NOUN a type of small orange which is easy to peel.

mane **manes**
NOUN the long hair growing from the neck of a lion or horse.

manger **mangers**
NOUN a feeding box in a barn or stable.

mangle **mangles mangling mangled**
VERB **1** to crush and twist something: *a mangled tin can.*
NOUN **2** an old-fashioned piece of equipment consisting of two large rollers which squeezed water out of wet clothes.

mango **mangoes** or **mangos**
NOUN a sweet yellowish tropical fruit.

manhole **manholes**
NOUN a covered hole in the ground leading to a drain or sewer.

mania **manias**
NOUN **1** a very strong liking for something: *a mania for football stickers.*
2 a mental illness involving hyperactive behaviour.

maniac **maniacs**
NOUN **1** a person who is violent and dangerous through severe mental illness.
2 INFORMAL a person who is obsessively keen on something. *She's a ballet maniac.*
maniacal ADJECTIVE

manic
ADJECTIVE Manic behaviour is energetic and excited.

manifesto **manifestoes** or **manifestos**
NOUN a published statement of the aims and policies of a political party.

manipulate **manipulates manipulating manipulated**
VERB **1** to control or influence people for selfish reasons.
2 If you manipulate a piece of equipment, you control it in a skilful way.
manipulation NOUN **manipulative** ADJECTIVE
manipulator NOUN

mankind
NOUN a general word for all human beings.

manly **manlier manliest**
ADJECTIVE having qualities that are typically masculine. *He laughed a deep, manly laugh.*
manliness NOUN

manner **manners**
NOUN the way in which something is done. *Most of the time, we behave in a sensible manner.*

 ► Why does manageable have an "e" when managing doesn't?

mannerism mannerisms
NOUN a gesture or a way of speaking which is characteristic of a person.

manners
PLURAL NOUN If you have good manners, you behave very politely.

manoeuvre manoeuvres manoeuvring manoeuvred
Said "man-**noo**-ver" VERB **1** to move something skilfully in a difficult situation. *He manoeuvred the lifeboat close to the sinking ship.*
NOUN **2** a clever move you make in order to change a situation to your advantage.
PHRASE **3** If you have **room for manoeuvre**, you have the opportunity to change your plans if it becomes necessary or desirable.
manoeuvrable ADJECTIVE
manoeuvrability NOUN

manor manors
NOUN a large country house with land.

mansion mansions
NOUN a very large house.

manslaughter
NOUN the accidental killing of a person.

mantelpiece mantelpieces
NOUN the shelf directly above a fireplace.

manual manuals
ADJECTIVE **1** Manual work mainly involves physical effort rather than mental effort.
2 Manual equipment is operated by hand rather than by electricity, by a motor or by any automatic device. *My old car has manual gears.*
NOUN **3** a book which tells you how to use a machine or to do other practical tasks.
manually ADVERB
[from Latin *manus* meaning hand]

manufacture manufactures manufacturing manufactured
VERB to make goods in a factory.
manufacture NOUN **manufacturer** NOUN

manure
NOUN animal dung used to fertilize the soil.

manuscript manuscripts
NOUN a handwritten or typed document, especially a version of a book before it is printed.

many
ADJECTIVE OR PRONOUN **1** If there are many people or things, there are a large number of them. *Many people owed their lives to the few pilots who fought in the Battle of Britain.*
2 You use "many" to talk about how great a number or quantity is. *How many tickets do you require? No one knows how many were killed.*

Maori Maoris
NOUN someone descended from the people who lived in New Zealand before Europeans arrived; also the language that they speak.

map maps mapping mapped
NOUN **1** a detailed drawing of an area, representing in diagram form what you would see from directly above.
VERB **2** to draw a map of an area.
map out VERB to plan or design. *We mapped out our ideas for the new playground.*

maple maples
NOUN a tree that has large leaves with five points.

mar mars marring marred
VERB to spoil something. *The afternoon rain marred an otherwise good day out.*

marathon marathons
NOUN a race in which people run just over 26 miles (nearly 42 km) along roads.
[from *Marathon*, a place in Greece from which a messenger in 490 BC ran to Athens bringing news of a victory against Persian invaders]

marble
NOUN a very hard, patterned form of limestone used in buildings or sculptures.

march marches marching marched
VERB **1** to walk quickly in a determined way. *She marched out of the room.*
NOUN **2** an organized protest in which a large group of people walk somewhere together.
3 a piece of music written for people of the armed forces to march to when they are on parade.

March
NOUN the third month of the year.
[from Latin *Martius* the month of Mars, god of war]

mare mares
NOUN an adult female horse.

margarine
Said "**mar**-jar-reen" NOUN a substance similar to butter, made from vegetable oil and animal fats.

margin margins
NOUN **1** the blank space at each side on a written or printed page.
2 If you win a contest by a large or small margin, you win it by a large or small amount.

marginal
ADJECTIVE **1** small and not very important: *a marginal increase.*
2 A marginal result or decision is won by a very small majority.
marginally ADVERB

marigold marigolds
NOUN a type of yellow or orange garden flower.

marijuana
Said "mar-rih-**hwan**-a" NOUN Marijuana is an illegal drug which is smoked in cigarettes.

a b c d e f g h i j k l m n o p q r s t u v w x y z

marina marinas
NOUN a harbour for pleasure boats and yachts.

marine marines
ADJECTIVE 1 relating to or involving the sea.
NOUN 2 a soldier who is trained for duties on land or at sea.

mark marks marking marked
NOUN 1 a small stain or damaged area on a surface.
2 a written or printed symbol.
3 a score given to a student for homework or for an exam.
4 a sign of something. *When the funeral passed, they removed their hats as a mark of respect.*
VERB 5 to stain or damage.
6 to write a symbol on something or identify it in some other way.
7 to check a student's work, and perhaps give it a mark.
8 to be a sign of something. *The ceremony marked the end of the games.*
marking NOUN

market markets marketing marketed
NOUN 1 a place where goods are bought and sold, usually outdoors.
2 The market for a product is the number of people who want to buy it: *the housing market.*
VERB 3 To market a product is to sell it in an organized way.
marketing NOUN

Synonyms: (sense 1) bazaar, fair, mart

marksman marksmen
NOUN someone who can shoot very accurately.

marmalade
NOUN a type of jam made from oranges or lemons.

maroon
NOUN OR ADJECTIVE dark reddish-purple.

marquee marquees
Said "mar-**kee**" **NOUN** a very large tent used at a fair, a camp, a wedding or other outdoor event.

marriage marriages
NOUN 1 the relationship between a husband and wife. *Jim and Mo have a happy marriage.*
2 the act of marrying someone, a wedding.

Synonyms: (sense 1) matrimony, wedlock

married 1 the past tense of **marry**.
ADJECTIVE 2 having a husband or wife.

marrow marrows
NOUN a long, thick green vegetable with cream-coloured flesh.

marry marries marrying married
VERB 1 to become someone's husband or wife during a special ceremony.
2 to take charge of a marriage ceremony.

marsh marshes
NOUN an area of land which is permanently wet, a bog.
marshy ADJECTIVE

marshmallow marshmallows
NOUN a type of soft, spongy, pink or white sweet.

marsupial marsupials
Said "mar-**soo**-pee-al" **NOUN** an animal that carries its young in a pouch. Koalas and kangaroos are marsupials.
[from Greek *marsupion* meaning purse]

martial
Said "**mar**-shal" **ADJECTIVE** related to fighting or war.

martial arts
PLURAL NOUN the techniques of self-defence that come from the Far East, for example karate or judo.

Martian Martians
Said "**mar**-shun" **NOUN** an imaginary creature from the planet Mars.
Martian ADJECTIVE

martyr martyrs martyring martyred
NOUN 1 someone who suffers or is killed rather than change their religious beliefs.
VERB 2 If someone is martyred, they are killed because of their religious beliefs.
martyrdom NOUN

marvel marvels marvelling marvelled
VERB 1 If you marvel at something, it fills you with surprise or admiration.
NOUN 2 something that makes you feel great surprise or admiration. *The Pyramids are marvels of early building achievement.*

marvellous
ADJECTIVE wonderful or excellent.
marvellously ADVERB

marzipan
NOUN a paste made of almonds, sugar and egg. It is put on top of cakes before icing or used to make small sweets.

mascot mascots
NOUN a person, animal or toy which is thought to bring good luck.

masculine
ADJECTIVE 1 relating to men or considered to be typical of men.
2 in some languages, belonging to a particular class of nouns that are associated with being male.
masculinity NOUN

Antonym: feminine

WHAT IS THE MASCULINE?
Masculine nouns refer to male people and animals:
The boy put on his coat – boy is masculine.
Also look at the grammar boxes at gender, feminine, neuter and common nouns.

 ► Some words from Portuguese: marmalade, veranda, albatross.

mash **mashes mashing mashed**
VERB If you mash vegetables, you crush them after they have been cooked.
mashed ADJECTIVE

mask **masks masking masked**
NOUN 1 something you wear over your face for protection or as a disguise.
VERB 2 If you mask something, you cover it so that it is protected or cannot be seen.

mason **masons**
NOUN a person who is skilled at building and working with stone.

masonry
NOUN pieces of stone which form part of a wall or building.

mass **masses**
NOUN 1 a large amount of something. *She had a mass of red hair.*
2 the amount of matter in an object. Mass is measured in grams.
3 The masses are the ordinary people of the world.
4 Mass is a Roman Catholic religious service in which people eat bread and drink wine in remembrance of Jesus Christ.
ADJECTIVE 5 involving or affecting a large number of people. *Nuclear weapons could cause mass destruction.*

massacre **massacres massacring massacred**
Said "**mass**-ik-ker" **NOUN 1** the killing of a large number of people in a violent and cruel way.
VERB 2 to kill large numbers of people in a violent and cruel way.

massage **massages massaging massaged**
VERB to rub someone's body in order to help them relax or to relieve pain.
massage NOUN

massive
ADJECTIVE extremely large.
massively ADVERB

Synonyms: enormous, huge, vast

mast **masts**
NOUN 1 the tall upright pole that supports the sails of a boat.
2 a very tall pole that acts as an aerial to transmit sound, television pictures or telephone communications.

master **masters mastering mastered**
NOUN 1 a man who has authority over others, such as the employer of servants or the owner of slaves or animals.
VERB 2 If you master something, you succeed in learning how to do it or understand it.
mastery NOUN

masterful
ADJECTIVE showing control and authority.
masterfully ADVERB

masterly
ADJECTIVE extremely clever or well done: *a masterly exhibition of skill.*

mastermind **masterminding masterminded**
VERB to plan and organize a complicated activity.
mastermind NOUN

masterpiece **masterpieces**
NOUN an extremely good painting, novel, film or other work of art.

mat **mats**
NOUN 1 a small piece of cloth, card or plastic placed on a table to protect it.
2 a small piece of carpet or other thick material placed on the floor.

match **matches matching matched**
NOUN 1 an organized game of football, netball or some other sport.
2 a small, wooden stick that produces a flame when you strike it against a rough surface.
VERB 3 If one thing matches another or if they match, the two things look the same or similar or look good together.
matching ADJECTIVE

mate **mates mating mated**
NOUN 1 INFORMAL a friend.
2 an animal's partner.
VERB 3 When animals mate, they have sex in order to produce young.

material **materials**
NOUN 1 cloth, fabric.
2 any substance from which things are made, for instance, glass, metal, wood, plastic, etc.

materialistic
ADJECTIVE Someone who is materialistic has the attitude that money and possessions are the most important things in life.
materialism NOUN

maternal
ADJECTIVE relating to or involving a mother: *maternal instincts.*

maternity
ADJECTIVE relating to or involving pregnant women and birth: *a maternity hospital.*

mathematics or **maths**
NOUN the study of numbers, quantities and shapes. See **arithmetic**, **algebra**, **geometry**.
mathematical ADJECTIVE **mathematically** ADVERB
mathematician NOUN

maths
short for **mathematics**.

matinée **matinées**
NOUN an afternoon performance of a show.

matrimony
NOUN; FORMAL marriage.
matrimonial ADJECTIVE

matrix **matrices**
Said "**may**-trix" **NOUN** In mathematics, a matrix is a set of numbers or elements set out in rows and columns; a table.

A B C D E F G H I J K L M N O P Q R S T U V W X Y Z

matron **matrons**
NOUN **1** In some private hospitals, a senior nurse in charge of all the nursing staff is known as the matron; this was formerly the case in state hospitals also.
2 In a boarding school, the matron is the person who looks after the health of the pupils.

matt
ADJECTIVE dull rather than shiny.

matted
ADJECTIVE Hair that is matted is tangled with the strands sticking together.

matter **matters mattering mattered**
NOUN **1** a task or situation that you have to deal with.
2 In a scientific sense, matter is any substance.
VERB **3** If something matters, it is important.
PHRASE **4** If you ask **what's the matter?**, you are asking what is wrong.

Synonyms: (sense 1) affair, business, subject

mattress **mattresses**
NOUN a large flat pad, often with springs inside, which is put on a bed to make it comfortable to sleep on.

mature **matures maturing matured**
ADJECTIVE **1** fully grown or developed.
2 responsible and sensible: *mature behaviour.*
VERB **3** When a child or other young animal matures, they become adults.
maturity NOUN **maturely** ADVERB

Antonym: (senses 1 and 2) immature

maul **mauls mauling mauled**
VERB If someone is mauled by an animal, they are savagely attacked and badly injured by it.

mauve
Said "**moav**" NOUN OR ADJECTIVE pale purple.

maximum
ADJECTIVE **1** the most possible or allowed. *The old car's maximum speed was 80 kph.*
NOUN **2** the largest amount that is possible or allowed. *The lift takes a maximum of eight people.*

Antonym: minimum

may
VERB **1** If something may happen, it is possible. *It may rain later.*
2 If someone may do something, they are allowed to do it. *You may go out later, if you work now.*
3 used as "is". *He may only be 10 but he's a good batsman.*

MAY OR CAN?
It used to be that you always used *may* instead of *can* when asking for or giving someone permission to do something:
You may leave the table.
Nowadays *may* is usually only used as a polite form:
May I open the window?

May
NOUN the fifth month of the year.
[from the Roman goddess *Maia*]

maybe
ADVERB possibly, perhaps. *I met him once, maybe twice. Maybe you should wait for another month or two.*

mayonnaise
Said "may-on-**nayz**" NOUN a thick salad dressing made with egg yolks and oil.

mayor **mayors**
NOUN a person who has been elected to represent the people of a town or city.
mayoral ADJECTIVE

maze **mazes**
NOUN a system of complicated passages through which it is difficult to find your way, a labyrinth.

me
PRONOUN A speaker or writer uses "me" to refer to themselves. *He gave me the book. Are you talking to me?*

I OR ME?
When other people are mentioned in the sentence it is important to remember this rule: in written English "I" is always used when you are the subject of the sentence; "me" is used when you are the object:
Fiona and I went to the seaside.
Dad took Fiona and me to the seaside.

meadow **meadows**
NOUN a field of grass.

meagre
Said "**mee**-ger" ADJECTIVE very small and poor. *She only received a meagre pension.*

meal **meals**
NOUN **1** an occasion when people eat.
2 the food eaten at a meal time.

mean **means meaning meant; meaner meanest**
VERB **1** to signify or refer to. *What does that word actually mean?*
2 If you mean what you say, you believe it and you are serious about it. *I'm going to scream, I really mean it!*
3 If something means a lot to you, it is important to you.
4 to intend to do something. *I didn't mean to hurt you.*
ADJECTIVE **5** unwilling to spend much money.
6 unkind. *It was mean of Kevin to laugh at his friend's new hairstyle.*
NOUN **7** In mathematics, the mean is the average of a set of numbers. See **means**.

Synonyms: (sense 4) aim, intend, plan
(sense 5) miserly, stingy, tight-fisted

 ► Some surnames mean "son of". Examples include Richardson, O'Brien, MacDonald, Wilson, Fitzjohn.

meander **meanders meandering meandered**
Said "mee-**an**-der" VERB If a road or river meanders, it winds around, with a lot of bends in it.
[from *Maiandros*, the name of a Greek river]

meaning **meanings**
NOUN The meaning of a word or action is the thing that it refers to or expresses.
meaningful ADJECTIVE **meaningfully** ADVERB
meaningless ADJECTIVE

Synonyms: gist, sense, significance

means
NOUN 1 A means of doing something is a method or thing which makes it possible to do it. *I had no means of transport to get to the show.*
2 someone's means is their income.
PHRASE 3 If you do something **by means of** a particular method or machine, you use that method or machine to do it. *The tests were marked by means of a computer.*
4 **By all means** means without hesitation or doubt, certainly.

meantime
PHRASE **In the meantime** means in the period of time between two events. *I'll call an ambulance; in the meantime, just lie still.*

meanwhile
ADVERB while something else is happening. *Jane was still at school; meanwhile Sunil and Leroy were sitting on the doorstep waiting for her to return.*

measles
PLURAL NOUN an infectious illness in which you have red spots on your skin.
[from Germanic *masele* meaning spot on the skin]

measly
ADJECTIVE; INFORMAL very small or inadequate, stingy. *She gave him only a measly portion.*

measure **measures measuring measured**
VERB 1 to find out how big something is. *Use a ruler to measure the plant.*
2 to be a certain size. *The worm measured only a few millimetres in length.*

measurement **measurements**
NOUN the result obtained when you measure something.

meat **meats**
NOUN the flesh of animals that people cook and eat.

mechanic **mechanics**
NOUN 1 a person who repairs and maintains engines and machines.
PLURAL NOUN 2 The mechanics of something are the way in which it works.
3 the scientific study of movement and the forces that affect objects.

mechanical
ADJECTIVE 1 relating to machines and engines.
2 happening automatically and without thought or feeling.
mechanically ADVERB

mechanism **mechanisms**
NOUN a part of a machine that does a particular task.

medal **medals**
NOUN a metal disc given as an award for bravery or as a prize in a competition.

medallion **medallions**
NOUN a round piece of metal worn on a chain round the neck.

medallist **medallists**
NOUN a person who has won a medal in a competition.

meddle **meddles meddling meddled**
VERB to interfere and try to change things without being asked.
meddler NOUN **meddlesome** ADJECTIVE

media
PLURAL NOUN a general word for television, radio and newspapers.
✔ It is becoming more common for *media* to be used as a singular noun: *the media is obsessed with celebrities.*

median
Said "**mee**-dee-an" ADJECTIVE The median value of a set is the middle value when the set is arranged in order.

medical **medicals**
ADJECTIVE 1 relating to the treatment and prevention of illness and injuries.
NOUN 2 a thorough examination of your body by a doctor. *He failed his army medical.*

medication **medications**
NOUN a substance that is used to treat illness, for example, a medicine, drug or ointment.

medicine **medicines**
NOUN 1 a substance that you drink to help cure an illness.
2 a general word for the treatment of illness and injuries by doctors.

medieval or **mediaeval**
Said "med-dee-**ee**-vul" ADJECTIVE relating to the period between about 1100 AD and 1500 AD, especially in Europe. See **Middle Ages**.
[from Latin *medium aevum* meaning the middle age]

mediocre
Said "meed-dee-**oh**-ker" ADJECTIVE of rather poor quality. *Her project work was disappointingly mediocre.*
mediocrity NOUN

meditate **meditates meditating meditated**
VERB 1 to think very deeply about something.
2 to remain in a calm silent state for some time in order to let the mind relax.

People who acted in medieval plays acquired surnames such as King or Knight from their roles.

A B C D E F G H I J K L M N O P Q R S T U V W X Y Z

Mediterranean
NOUN 1 the large sea between southern Europe and northern Africa.
NOUN OR ADJECTIVE 2 a term for the countries and cultures that border this sea.

medium mediums or media
ADJECTIVE 1 If something is of medium size or degree, it is neither large nor small.
NOUN 2 a means that you use to communicate something. *They got their message across through the medium of television.*
3 A person who claims to be able to communicate with the spirits of the dead.

meek meeker meekest
ADJECTIVE A meek person is timid and does what other people say.
meekly ADVERB **meekness** NOUN

Synonyms: submissive, timid

meet meets meeting met
VERB 1 If you meet someone, you happen to be in the same place as them.
2 If you meet a visitor, you go to be with them when they arrive.
3 to come together for a purpose. *I'll meet you at the beach tomorrow.*
4 If something meets a need or requirement, it fulfils it.

meeting meetings
NOUN 1 an event at which people discuss things or make decisions.
2 an occasion when you meet someone. *He remembers his first meeting with Lisa.*

melancholy
ADJECTIVE sad.

mellow mellower mellowest; mellows mellowing mellowed
ADJECTIVE 1 Mellow light is soft and golden.
2 A mellow sound is smooth and pleasant to listen to.
VERB 3 If someone mellows, they become more pleasant or relaxed.

melodrama melodramas
NOUN a story or play in which people's emotions are deliberately exaggerated. *Many of the old silent films are melodramas.*

melodramatic
ADJECTIVE behaving in an exaggerated, emotional way.
melodramatically ADVERB

Synonyms: overdramatic, theatrical

melody melodies
NOUN a tune.
melodious ADJECTIVE

melon melons
NOUN a large, juicy fruit with a green or yellow skin and many seeds inside.

melt melts melting melted
VERB When something melts or when you melt it, it changes from a solid to a liquid because it has been heated.

member members
NOUN one of the people or things belonging to a group.

Member of Parliament Members of Parliament
NOUN a person who has been elected to represent people in a country's parliament.

membrane membranes
NOUN a very thin piece of skin or tissue which connects or covers plant or animal organs or cells.

memorable
ADJECTIVE likely to be remembered because it is special or unusual.
memorably ADVERB

memorial memorials
NOUN 1 a structure built to remind people of a famous event or person.
ADJECTIVE 2 A memorial event or prize is held or awarded in honour of someone who has died, so that they will be remembered.

memorize memorizes memorizing memorized; also spelt **memorise**
VERB to commit to memory, learn.

memory memories
NOUN 1 the ability to remember things. *The old lady had an excellent memory.*
2 something you remember about the past. *The old man had happy memories of his schooldays.*
3 A computer's memory is its capacity to store information.

Synonyms: (sense 1) recall, recollection, remembrance

men
the plural of **man**.

menace menaces menacing menaced
NOUN 1 someone or something who is threatening.
2 INFORMAL a nuisance.
VERB 3 to threaten to harm.
menacing ADJECTIVE **menacingly** ADVERB

mend mends mending mended
VERB to repair something that is broken.

menstruation
NOUN the monthly discharge of blood from a woman's womb.
menstruate VERB **menstrual** ADJECTIVE
[from Latin *mensis* meaning month]

mental
ADJECTIVE relating to the mind and the process of thinking: *mental arithmetic; mental illness.*
mentally ADVERB **mentality** NOUN

 ► Working from memory, how many road and traffic signs can you draw and explain?

mention mentions mentioning mentioned
VERB to say something about a subject, usually briefly.
mention NOUN

Synonyms: bring up, refer to, touch upon

menu menus
NOUN 1 a list of the food and drink you can buy in a restaurant.
2 In computer software, a list of choices.

mercenary mercenaries
NOUN a soldier who is paid to fight for a certain cause.

merchandise
NOUN; FORMAL goods which are for sale.

merchant merchants
NOUN someone who trades in a particular type of product: *a coal merchant.*

merchant navy
NOUN the boats and sailors involved in carrying goods for trade.

merciful
ADJECTIVE showing kindness and forgiveness.
mercifully ADVERB

Synonyms: compassionate, humane, kind

merciless
ADJECTIVE showing no kindness or forgiveness.
mercilessly ADVERB

Synonyms: cruel, heartless, ruthless

mercury
NOUN a silver-coloured metal that is liquid at room temperature, and is used in thermometers.

mercy mercies
NOUN 1 If you show mercy, you show kindness and forgiveness and do not punish someone as severely as you could.
2 a fortunate occurrence. *What a mercy we weren't spotted.*
PHRASE 3 If you are **at the mercy of** someone or something, they have complete power over you.

Synonyms: (sense 1) compassion, kindness, pity

mere merest
ADJECTIVE You use "mere" to emphasize how unimportant or small something is. *The racing car was doing a mere 20 kph as it limped back to the pits.*

merely
ADVERB only, simply. *She was merely joking.*

merge merges merging merged
VERB to combine together to make one thing. *The schools merged in 1999.*
merger NOUN

meridian meridians
NOUN one of the lines drawn on a map or globe running from the North Pole to the South Pole. *The Greenwich meridian is 0°.*

meringue meringues
Said "mer-**rang**" NOUN a type of crisp, sweet cake made with egg whites and sugar.

merit merits meriting merited
NOUN 1 If something has merit, it is good or worthwhile.
VERB 2 If something merits a particular treatment, it deserves that treatment. *Lucy merits a place on the hockey team.*

mermaid mermaids
NOUN In stories, a mermaid is a woman with a fish's tail instead of legs, who lives in the sea.

merry merrier merriest
ADJECTIVE happy and cheerful.
merrily ADVERB **merriment** NOUN

merry-go-round merry-go-rounds
NOUN a rotating platform with models of vehicles or animals on it, on which children ride at a fair.

mesh meshes meshing meshed
NOUN 1 threads of wire or plastic twisted together like a net.
VERB 2 to fit together closely.

mess messes messing messed
NOUN 1 a dirty or untidy place.
2 a situation full of problems. *I've made a real mess of things.*
3 In the armed forces, a mess is where servicemen live or spend recreation time.
mess about or **mess around** VERB to spend time doing silly or casual things.
mess up VERB to spoil something or do it wrong.

message messages
NOUN a piece of information or a request that you send someone or leave for them.

messenger messengers
NOUN someone who carries and delivers a message.

Synonyms: courier, emissary, envoy

Messiah
Said "miss-**eye**-ah" NOUN 1 For Jews, the Messiah is the king of the Jews who will be sent by God.
2 For Christians, the Messiah is Jesus Christ.

messy messier messiest
ADJECTIVE dirty, confused or untidy.

metal metals
NOUN a chemical element such as iron, steel, copper or lead. Metals are good conductors of heat and electricity.
[from Latin *metallum* meaning a mine]

A B C D E F G H I J K L M N O P Q R S T U V W X Y Z

metamorphosis metamorphoses
Said "met-am-**mor**-fuss-iss" NOUN; FORMAL a complete change or transformation in somebody or something: *the metamorphosis of a caterpillar into a butterfly.*
metamorphose VERB

metaphor metaphors
NOUN an imaginative way of describing something directly as something else: *clumsy as a disaster area; shy as a mouse.* See **simile**.
metaphorical ADJECTIVE **metaphorically** ADVERB

meteor meteors
NOUN a piece of rocky material that burns very brightly when it enters the earth's atmosphere from space. See **meteorite**.

meteorite meteorites
NOUN a piece of rocky material from space that has landed on earth.

meteorology
NOUN the study and forecasting of weather.
meteorological ADJECTIVE **meteorologist** NOUN

meter meters
NOUN a device that measures and records something, such as a gas meter.

method methods
NOUN a particular way of doing something.

methodical
ADJECTIVE Someone who is methodical does things carefully and in an organized way.
methodically ADVERB

meticulous
ADJECTIVE being very particular and precise about details: *the meticulous Miss Prinne even ironed the daily paper.*
meticulously ADVERB

metre metres
NOUN a unit of length equal to 100 centimetres, abbreviated to "m".

metric
ADJECTIVE relating to the system of measurement that uses metres, grams and litres. See **imperial**.

metronome metronomes
NOUN an adjustable device producing a regular ticking beat, used to help musicians keep in time as they practise playing.

metropolitan
ADJECTIVE relating or belonging to a large, busy city.

mew mews mewing mewed
VERB When a cat mews, it makes a short, high-pitched sound.
mew NOUN

miaow miaows miaowing miaowed
VERB When a cat miaows, it makes a short, high-pitched sound.
miaow NOUN

mice
the plural of **mouse**.

micro-
PREFIX very small.
[from Greek *micros* meaning small]

microbe microbes
NOUN a very small living thing which you can see only if you use a microscope.

microchip microchips
NOUN a small piece of silicon on which electronic circuits for a computer are printed.

microphone microphones
NOUN a device that you speak, sing or play music into when recording or amplifying sounds.

microscope microscopes
NOUN a piece of equipment which magnifies very small objects so that you can study them.

microscopic
ADJECTIVE very small indeed.
microscopically ADVERB

microwave microwaves
NOUN an oven which cooks food very quickly by means of radiation.
microwave VERB **microwaveable** ADJECTIVE

mid-
PREFIX "Mid-" is used to form words that refer to the middle part of a place or period of time. For example, "summer" becomes "midsummer".

midday
NOUN twelve o'clock in the middle of the day, or the time around then.

Synonym: noon

middle middles
NOUN **1** the part of something which is furthest from the edges, ends or surface.
2 The middle of an event is the part that comes after the beginning and before the end.
middle ADJECTIVE

middle-aged
ADJECTIVE aged between 40 and 60.

Middle Ages
NOUN in European history, the period between 1100 AD and 1500 AD. See **medieval**.

Middle East
NOUN the area around the eastern Mediterranean, including Israel, Egypt, Iran and the Arabian peninsula.
Middle Eastern ADJECTIVE

middle school middle schools
NOUN In England and Wales, a middle school is for children aged between about 8 and 12 in years 5, 6, 7 and 8.

midge midges
NOUN a small flying insect which can bite people.

 ▶ Miaow has three vowels together. A word beginning with "o" has four vowels in a row. What is it?

midget midgets
NOUN an extremely short person.

midnight
NOUN **1** twelve o'clock at night.
PHRASE **2** If you **burn the midnight oil** you work very late at night.

midst
NOUN If you are in the midst of a crowd or an event, you are in the middle of it.

midsummer
ADJECTIVE relating to the period in the middle of summer.

midway
ADVERB in the middle of a distance or period of time.

midwife midwives
NOUN a nurse who is trained to care for women through pregnancy and at the birth of a baby.
midwifery NOUN

might
VERB **1** You use "might" to say that something will possibly happen or is possibly true. *I might be back later than usual.*
2 Might is also the past tense of **may**.
NOUN **3** great strength.
✔ You can use *might* or *may* to make a polite request: *might I ask a favour; may I ask a favour?*

mighty mightier mightiest
ADJECTIVE; LITERARY very powerful or strong.
mightily ADVERB

migraine migraines
Said "**mee**-grane" NOUN a severe headache that makes you feel very ill.
[from Greek *hemikrania* meaning half-skull; migraine often occurs or starts on one side of the head]

migrant migrants
NOUN a person or animal that moves from one place to another permanently or seasonally.

migrate migrates migrating migrated
VERB **1** to move home from one place to another, especially to find work.
2 When animals migrate, they move at a particular season to a different place, usually to breed or to find new feeding grounds.
migration NOUN **migratory** ADJECTIVE

mike mikes
NOUN; INFORMAL a microphone.

mild milder mildest
ADJECTIVE gentle; not strong or powerful: *a mild shampoo; a mild voice; mild weather.*
mildly ADVERB **mildness** NOUN

mildew
NOUN a soft white fungus that grows on things when they are warm and damp.

mile miles
NOUN a unit of distance equal to about 1·6 kilometres.

mileage mileages
NOUN Your mileage is the distance that you have travelled, measured in miles.

militant militants
NOUN a person who is very active or aggressive in trying to bring about extreme political or social change.
militant ADJECTIVE **militantly** ADVERB
militancy NOUN

military
ADJECTIVE related to or involving the armed forces of a country.

milk milks milking milked
NOUN **1** the nourishing liquid produced by female mammals for their young. Babies drink the milk from their mother's breasts.
2 the white liquid produced by cows, goats and sheep which people drink and make into butter, cheese and yogurt.
VERB **3** to remove milk from an animal.

milkman milkmen
NOUN a man who delivers milk from door to door.

milk tooth milk teeth
NOUN Your milk teeth are your first teeth which fall out and are replaced by a permanent set.

milky milkier milkiest
ADJECTIVE **1** pale creamy white.
2 containing a lot of milk.

Milky Way
NOUN a cluster of stars that appear as a pale band in the night sky.

mill mills
NOUN **1** a building where grain is crushed to make flour.
2 a factory for processing materials such as steel, wool or cotton.
3 a small device for grinding coffee or spices: *a pepper mill.*

millennium millennia or millenniums
NOUN a period of 1000 years.

milligram milligrams
NOUN a unit of mass or weight equal to one thousandth of a gram, abbreviated to "mg".

millilitre millilitres
NOUN a unit of liquid volume equal to one thousandth of a litre, abbreviated to "ml".

millimetre millimetres
NOUN a unit of length equal to one tenth of a centimetre or one thousandth of a metre, abbreviated to "mm".

million millions
the number 1 000 000.
millionth ADJECTIVE

millionaire millionaires
NOUN someone who has money or property worth at least a million pounds or dollars.

mime mimes miming mimed
NOUN 1 the use of movements and gestures to express something or to tell a story without using speech.
VERB 2 to describe or express something using mime.

mimic mimics mimicking mimicked
VERB 1 to imitate someone's actions or voice in an amusing way.
NOUN 2 a person who can imitate other people.
mimicry NOUN

minaret minarets
NOUN a tall thin tower on a mosque.

mince minces mincing minced
NOUN 1 meat which has been chopped into very small pieces in a mincer.
VERB 2 to chop something such as meat into very small pieces.
PHRASE 3 If you **do not mince your words**, you tell someone something unpleasant in a very forceful and direct way.

mincemeat
NOUN a sticky mixture of pieces of dried fruit, apples, and suet, used to make mince pies.

mind minds minding minded
NOUN 1 Your mind is your ability to think, together with all the thoughts you have and your memory.
PHRASE 2 If you **change your mind**, you change a decision that you have made or an opinion that you have.
VERB 3 If you do not mind something, you are not annoyed or bothered by it.
4 If you say that you wouldn't mind something, you mean that you would quite like it. *I wouldn't mind another bun.*
5 to be careful of something. *Mind that plate, it's hot.*
6 to look after someone or something. *Please would you mind the shop while I nip out?*

mindless
ADJECTIVE 1 Mindless actions are regarded as stupid and thoughtless.
2 A mindless job or activity is simple and repetitive.
mindlessly ADVERB

mine mines
PRONOUN 1 belonging or relating to the person who is speaking or writing. *Carla is a good friend of mine.*
NOUN 2 a place where minerals are dug out and extracted from underground.
3 a bomb hidden in the ground or underwater, which explodes when something touches it.
mining NOUN

minefield minefields
NOUN an area of land or water where mines have been hidden.

miner miners
NOUN a person who works to extract coal or other substances from a mine.

mineral minerals
NOUN a solid substance formed naturally, which makes up different rocks. Some rocks contain different minerals. Rock salt, quartz and diamonds are minerals.

mineral salts
PLURAL NOUN chemicals found in the earth that are needed by plants and animals for healthy growth.

mineral water mineral waters
NOUN water from a natural spring in which some minerals have dissolved. It is often bottled for sale and is used in some soft drinks.

mingle mingles mingling mingled
VERB If things mingle, they become mixed together.

mini-
PREFIX smaller or less important.

miniature
Said "**min**-nit-cher" ADJECTIVE copying something much larger. A miniature version of something is a small copy of it.
miniature NOUN

minibus minibuses
NOUN a van with seats in the back which is used as a small bus.

minimum
NOUN the smallest amount that is possible or allowed. *This will take a minimum of one hour.*
minimum ADJECTIVE

Antonym: maximum

minister ministers
NOUN 1 a person who is in charge of a particular government department: *the Minister of Defence.*
2 a member of the clergy, especially in a Protestant church: *a Baptist minister.*
ministerial ADJECTIVE

ministry ministries
NOUN 1 a government department.
2 the work of a member of the clergy, such as a priest or vicar.

mink minks
NOUN 1 an animal similar to an otter, the fur of which is used to make expensive coats.

minnow minnows
NOUN a very small freshwater fish.

minor
ADJECTIVE less important or serious than other things.

Antonym: major

 ► New meanings. If a topic is said to be a minefield, what does this mean?

minority minorities
NOUN 1 A minority of a group of people or things is a smaller part of them, that is less than half of them. *Only a minority of people want this.*
2 a group of people of a particular race or religion living in a place where most people are of a different race or religion. *The council should have representatives from all ethnic minorities.*

Antonym: majority

minstrel minstrels
NOUN a singer and entertainer in medieval times.

mint mints minting minted
NOUN 1 a herb used for flavouring in cooking.
2 a peppermint-flavoured sweet.
3 the place where the official coins of a country are made.
VERB 4 When coins or medals are minted, they are made.
ADJECTIVE 5 If something is in mint condition, it is in very good condition, like new.

minus
PREPOSITION 1 You use "minus" to show that one number is being subtracted from another. The symbol (–) means "minus". *Ten minus six equals four.*
ADJECTIVE 2 "Minus" before a number means that the number is less than zero: *temperatures of –20 °C.*

Antonym: plus

minute minutes
Said "**min**-it" NOUN 1 a unit of time equal to sixty seconds.
2 a short period of time. *See you in a minute.*
3 The minutes of a meeting are notes of what has been discussed and decided.

minute
Said "my-**nyoot**" ADJECTIVE extremely small.
minutely ADVERB

miracle miracles
NOUN a surprising and fortunate event, especially one believed to have been caused by God.
miraculous ADJECTIVE **miraculously** ADVERB

mirage mirages
NOUN an image that you can see in the distance in very hot weather, but which does not actually exist.

mirror mirrors
NOUN a sheet of silvered glass in which you can see your reflection.

mis-
PREFIX wrong, bad or involving an error.

misbehave misbehaves misbehaving misbehaved
VERB to be naughty or behave badly.
misbehaviour NOUN

miscalculate miscalculates miscalculating miscalculated
VERB to make a wrong judgement or calculation.
miscalculation NOUN

miscarriage miscarriages
NOUN 1 If a woman has a miscarriage, she gives birth to a baby before it is properly formed, and it dies.
2 A miscarriage of justice is a wrong decision made by a court, which causes an innocent person to be punished.

miscellaneous
ADJECTIVE A miscellaneous group is made up of people or things that are different from each other.
miscellaneously ADVERB

Synonyms: assorted, various

mischief
NOUN eagerness to have fun by teasing people or playing tricks.

mischievous
Said "**miss**-chee-vus" ADJECTIVE eager to have fun by teasing people or playing tricks.
mischievously ADVERB
✔ Be careful that you do not pronounce *mischievous* as if it ends in *-ious*.

miser misers
NOUN a person who enjoys saving money but hates spending it.
miserly ADJECTIVE

miserable
ADJECTIVE 1 If you are miserable, you are very unhappy.
2 If a place or a situation is miserable, it makes you feel depressed: *miserable weather.*
miserably ADVERB

Synonyms: (sense 1) dejected, unhappy, wretched
(sense 2) gloomy, wretched

misery miseries
NOUN great unhappiness.

misfire misfires misfiring misfired
VERB 1 If a plan misfires, it goes wrong.
2 If a gun misfires, it goes off accidentally.

misfit misfits
NOUN a person who is not accepted by other people because of being different.

misfortune misfortunes
NOUN an unpleasant occurrence that is regarded as bad luck. *I had the misfortune to fall off my bike.*

mishap mishaps
Said "**miss**-hap" NOUN an unfortunate but not very serious accident.

misjudge misjudges misjudging misjudged
VERB to form a wrong idea or opinion about someone or something.
misjudgement NOUN

a b c d e f g h i j k l m n o p q r s t u v w x y z

The word "minute" is a homograph. The same spelling has different meanings and pronunciations.

A B C D E F G H I J K L M N O P Q R S T U V W X Y Z

mislay **mislays mislaying mislaid**
VERB to lose something for a while because you have forgotten where you put it.

mislead **misleads misleading misled**
VERB to make someone believe something which is not true.
misleading ADJECTIVE

misprint **misprints**
NOUN a mistake, such as a wrong spelling, in something that has been printed.

miss **misses missing missed**
VERB **1** to fail to hit something that you are aiming at. *I missed the penalty kick!*
2 to fail to notice something. *You can't miss the red door.*
3 to feel sad because someone or something is no longer with you. *The boys miss their father.*
4 to arrive too late to catch a bus, plane or train. *He missed the last bus home.*
5 to fail to attend an event or activity. *Because of a dentist's appointment, I had to miss games.*
NOUN **6** an occasion when you miss something that you were aiming at.

Miss **Misses**
NOUN the title used before the name of a girl or unmarried woman.

missile **missiles**
NOUN **1** a weapon that moves long distances through the air and explodes when it reaches its target.
2 any object thrown as a weapon.

mission **missions**
NOUN an important task that someone has to do.

missionary **missionaries**
NOUN a Christian who has been sent to a foreign country to work for the church.

misspell **misspells misspelling misspelt** or **misspelled**
VERB to spell a word wrongly.

mist **mists**
NOUN many tiny drops of water in the air, which make it hard to see clearly.

mistake **mistakes mistaking mistook mistaken**
NOUN **1** something you do wrong without intending to.
VERB **2** to get a person's identity wrong. *With the baby's long hair, I mistook him for a girl.*
[from Old Norse *mistaka* meaning to take something by mistake]

Synonyms: (sense 1) blunder, miscalculation, error

mistaken
ADJECTIVE to be wrong about something.
mistakenly ADVERB

mister
NOUN A man is sometimes addressed in a very informal way as "mister".

mistletoe
Said "**mis**-sel-toe" NOUN a plant which grows on trees and has white berries on it, used as a Christmas decoration.

mistook
past tense of **mistake**.

mistreat **mistreats mistreating mistreated**
VERB to treat someone or something badly and make them suffer.
mistreatment NOUN

mistress **mistresses**
NOUN **1** a female teacher, especially at a secondary girls' school.
2 A married man's mistress is a woman he is having a sexual relationship with, but who is not his wife.

mistrust **mistrusts mistrusting mistrusted**
VERB If you mistrust someone, you do not feel that you can trust them.
mistrust NOUN

misty **mistier mistiest**
ADJECTIVE full of or covered with mist.

misunderstand **misunderstands misunderstanding misunderstood**
VERB to fail to understand properly what someone says or does.
misunderstood ADJECTIVE

misunderstanding **misunderstandings**
NOUN a slight quarrel or disagreement.

misuse **misuses misusing misused**
Said "**miss**-yooz" VERB to use something incorrectly or dishonestly.
misuse NOUN

mite **mites**
NOUN **1** a very small animal that lives in the fur of animals and household dust.
2 OLD-FASHIONED a very small amount. *Anyone with a mite of common sense would have realized that!*
3 a small child, especially one you feel sorry for. *He was orphaned at six weeks, poor mite.*

mitten **mittens**
NOUN a glove with one section that covers your thumb and another for the rest of your fingers together.

mix **mixes mixing mixed**
VERB If you mix things, you combine them or shake them or stir them together.
mix up VERB If you mix up two things or people, you confuse them.

Synonyms: (mix) blend, combine

mixed
ADJECTIVE **1** combining two or more different types: *"mixed bathing" means swimming for males and females.*
2 A mixed number is a number which includes both a whole number and a fraction: $3\frac{1}{2}$.

 ▶ Which silent letters are missing from these words: _night, _nome, thum_, _neumatic, ha_f, _nit?

mixed up
ADJECTIVE **1** If you are mixed up, you are confused. *I'm mixed up about which country I want to play for.*
2 If you are mixed up in a crime or a scandal, you are involved in it.

mixer mixers
NOUN a machine for mixing things together.

mixture mixtures
NOUN two or more things mixed together.

Synonyms: blend, medley, mix

mix-up mix-ups
NOUN a mistake in something that was planned: *a mix-up in our bookings.*

moan moans moaning moaned
VERB **1** to make a low, miserable sound because you are in pain or unhappy.
2 to complain in an irritating and persistent way.
NOUN **3** a low cry of pain or unhappiness.

moat moats
NOUN a wide, water-filled ditch around a building such as a castle.

mob mobs mobbing mobbed
NOUN **1** a large, disorganized crowd of people.
VERB **2** If someone is mobbed, a disorderly crowd of people gathers closely around them. *The band was mobbed by fans.*

mobile mobiles
ADJECTIVE **1** able to move or be moved easily.
NOUN **2** a decoration consisting of several small objects which hang from threads and move around when the breeze blows.
mobility NOUN

mobile phone mobile phones
NOUN a small, hand-held, portable phone.

moccasin moccasins
NOUN flat, soft leather shoes with raised stitching over the toes.

mock mocks mocking mocked
VERB **1** to tease someone or try to make them look foolish.
ADJECTIVE **2** not genuine; used to describe a copy or imitation. *His voice was raised in mock horror.*
mockery NOUN **mocking** ADJECTIVE

Synonyms: (sense 1) laugh at, make fun of, ridicule

mode modes
NOUN **1** A mode of something is one of the different forms it can take: *road, rail and other modes of transport.*
2 In a set of data, the mode is the most frequently occurring number.

Synonyms: (sense 1) type, style

model models modelling modelled
NOUN OR ADJECTIVE **1** a smaller copy of something that shows what it looks like or how it works. *His hobby is building model aircraft.*
NOUN **2** a person who poses for a painter or photographer or who demonstrates clothes or other goods in a show: *a fashion model.*
3 a type or version of a machine. *Which model of washing machine did you choose?*
ADJECTIVE **4** A model student is an excellent student.
VERB **5** If one thing is modelled on another, the first thing is made so that it is like the second thing. *Most of the characters are modelled on the author's friends.*
6 to make models.

modem modems
Said "**mo**-dem" NOUN a piece of equipment that links a computer to the telephone system so that data can be transferred via the telephone line.

moderate moderates moderating moderated
Said "**mod**-er-ut" ADJECTIVE **1** not too little or too much.
Said "**mod**-er-ayt" VERB **2** When teachers or examiners moderate, they compare a number of completed exam papers in order to achieve a fair and consistent standard of marking.
moderately ADVERB **moderation** NOUN

modern
ADJECTIVE relating to the latest ideas or the present time.
modernity NOUN

Synonyms: contemporary, current, present-day

modernize modernizes modernizing modernized; also spelt **modernise**
VERB to replace old methods, designs or equipment with new ones.
modernization NOUN

modest
ADJECTIVE **1** Someone who is modest does not boast about their abilities or possessions.
2 quite small in size or amount. *She has made a modest improvement in her work.*
modestly ADVERB **modesty** NOUN

modify modifies modifying modified
VERB to change something slightly in order to improve it. *The computer was modified to take the latest software.*
modification NOUN

module modules
NOUN one of the parts which when put together form a whole unit or object. *You must pass module one of the exam before moving on to modules two and three.*
modular ADJECTIVE

Some words from North American Indians: moccasin, tomahawk, wigwam, papoose, tepee.

A B C D E F G H I J K L M N O P Q R S T U V W X Y Z

moist moister moistest
ADJECTIVE slightly wet.

moisten moistens moistening moistened
VERB to make something moist.

moisture
NOUN moisture is tiny drops of water or other liquid in the air or on a surface.

molar molars
NOUN one of the large teeth at the back of your mouth. See **canine**, **incisor**.

mole moles
NOUN **1** a dark, slightly raised spot on your skin.
2 a small mammal with black fur which lives in tunnels underground.

molecule molecules
NOUN the smallest amount of a substance that can exist, made up of two or more atoms held together by chemical bonds.
molecular ADJECTIVE

molehill molehills
NOUN **1** A molehill is a small pile of earth left by a mole that has been digging underground.
PHRASE **2** If someone is **making a mountain out of a molehill**, they are exaggerating a problem.

mollusc molluscs
NOUN an animal with a soft body and no backbone, such as a slug or snail.

molten
ADJECTIVE Molten rock or metal is a solid that has been heated to a very high temperature and has changed into a thick liquid that can flow.

moment moments
NOUN **1** a very short period of time.
2 The moment at which something happens is the point in time at which it happens.
PHRASE **3** If something is happening **at the moment**, it is happening now.

Synonyms: (sense 1) instant, second

momentary
ADJECTIVE Something that is momentary lasts for only a few seconds.
momentarily ADVERB

momentous
ADJECTIVE; FORMAL very important, often because of its future effect. *The coronation was a momentous occasion.*
momentously ADVERB

momentum
NOUN the ability that something has to keep on moving. This depends on its present speed and its mass. *The bike gathered momentum as it went downhill.*

monarch monarchs
Said "**mon**-nark" NOUN a king, queen or other royal person who reigns over a country.

monarchy
NOUN the system by which a royal person rules a country. See **republic**.

monastery monasteries
NOUN a building in which monks live, work, pray and worship God.
monastic ADJECTIVE

Monday Mondays
NOUN the day between Sunday and Tuesday.
[from Old English *monandaeg* meaning moon's day]

money
NOUN the coins or banknotes that you use to buy something.

mongrel mongrels
NOUN a dog with parents of different breeds.

monitor monitors monitoring monitored
VERB **1** to check regularly the condition and progress of something.
NOUN **2** a machine used to check or record things: *a heart monitor.*
3 a pupil given responsibility for a simple routine task in the classroom: *register monitor.*
4 a screen on which changing information is viewed: *a computer monitor.*

monk monks
NOUN a member of a male religious community, such as a monastery.

monkey monkeys
NOUN an animal that has a long tail and climbs trees.

monologue monologues
Said "**mon**-nol-og" NOUN a long speech by one person.

monopoly monopolies
NOUN the control of the supply of a product by one company.

monotonous
ADJECTIVE having a regular pattern which is very dull and boring.
monotonously ADVERB **monotony** NOUN

monsoon monsoons
NOUN the season of very heavy rain in South-east Asia.

monster monsters
NOUN a large, imaginary creature that looks very frightening.

monstrous
ADJECTIVE extremely shocking or unfair. *It was monstrous to expect people to pay for the mayor's limousine.*
monstrously ADVERB

month months
NOUN one of the twelve periods that a year is divided into.
[from an Old English word *monath* related to *moon*; the time between each full moon (a lunar month) is 28 days]

 ► Proverbs: a fool and his money are soon parted; out of the frying pan into the fire.

monthly
ADJECTIVE Monthly describes something that happens or appears once a month.

monument monuments
NOUN a large stone structure built to remind people of a famous person or event.

moo moos mooing mooed
VERB When a cow moos it makes a long deep sound.

mood moods
NOUN 1 Your mood is the way you are feeling at a particular time.
2 If someone is **in a mood** they are bad-tempered and sulky.

moody moodier moodiest
ADJECTIVE 1 unhappy and bad-tempered.
2 Moody people often change their moods for no apparent reason.
moodily ADVERB **moodiness** NOUN

Synonyms: (sense 1) morose, sulky, sullen
(sense 2) changeable, mercurial, temperamental

moon moons
NOUN the object moving round the earth that we see as a bright circle or crescent. Several other planets, such as Jupiter and Mars, have moons also.

moonlight moonlights moonlighting moonlighted
NOUN 1 Moonlight is the light that seems to come from the moon at night.
VERB 2 INFORMAL If someone is moonlighting, they have a second job as well as their main one.
moonlit ADJECTIVE

moor moors mooring moored
NOUN 1 a high area of open land.
VERB 2 If you moor a boat, you attach it to the land with a rope.
mooring NOUN

moose
NOUN a North American elk.

mop mops mopping mopped
NOUN 1 a tool for washing floors, consisting of a sponge, string or cloth head attached to a long handle.
VERB 2 to clean something with a mop.
3 to wipe a surface with a dry cloth to remove liquid.

mope mopes moping moped
VERB to feel miserable and not interested in anything.

moped mopeds
Said "**mo**-ped" NOUN a type of small motorcycle.
[from the first letters of *motor* + *pedal*]

moral morals
NOUN 1 a strong belief about the right way to behave.
2 the moral of a story is a lesson that can be learned from the story.
PLURAL NOUN 3 Morals are values based on beliefs about the correct and acceptable way to behave.
ADJECTIVE 4 concerned with people's values about what is right and wrong: *moral values.*
PHRASE 5 If you give someone **moral support**, you encourage them in what they are doing.

morale
Said "mor-**rahl**" NOUN the amount of confidence and hope that people have. *After several victories, the team's morale was high.*

morbid
ADJECTIVE having a great interest in unpleasant things, especially death.
morbidly ADVERB

more
ADJECTIVE OR PRONOUN 1 a greater number or extent than something else. *He's got more biscuits than I have!*
2 an additional amount. *Would you like some more?*
ADVERB 3 to a greater degree or extent. *I was more scared than I had been before.*
4 again. *Repeat the exercise once more.*
5 You use "more" in front of adjectives and adverbs to form comparatives. *You look more ridiculous than ever in that hat.*
PHRASE 6 **more or less** means almost but not completely. *The lesson was more or less over; we just had to hand in our work and we could go.*

moreover
ADVERB in addition.

morgue morgues
Said "**morg**" NOUN a building where dead bodies are kept before being buried or cremated. See **mortuary**.

morning mornings
NOUN 1 the early part of the day until lunchtime.
2 the part of the day between midnight and noon. *He was born at three in the morning.*

Synonym: a.m.

moron morons
NOUN; INFORMAL a very stupid person.
moronic ADJECTIVE

morose
ADJECTIVE miserable and bad-tempered.
morosely ADVERB

morphine
NOUN a strong drug used to relieve severe pain.

Morse code
NOUN an old system of sending coded messages along wires by electric telegraph, using long and short sounds known as dots and dashes.

Joke. How did Vikings send messages to each other? Norse code.

A B C D E F G H I J K L M N O P Q R S T U V W X Y Z

morsel **morsels**
NOUN a small piece of food.

mortal **mortals**
ADJECTIVE **1** unable to live forever.
2 A mortal wound kills the person it happens to.
NOUN **3** an ordinary person. *Kings and queens, like the rest of us, are mere mortals.*
mortally ADVERB

Antonym: immortal

mortar **mortars**
NOUN **1** a mixture of cement, sand and water used to hold bricks firmly together.
2 a short cannon which fires missiles high into the air for a short distance.

mortgage **mortgages**
Said "**mor**-gij" NOUN a loan which you get from a bank or building society in order to buy a house.

mortuary **mortuaries**
NOUN a special room in a hospital where dead bodies are kept before being buried or cremated. See **morgue**.

mosaic **mosaics**
Said "moe-**zay**-yik" NOUN a design made of small coloured stones or square pieces of coloured glass set into concrete or plaster.

Moslem
another spelling of **Muslim**.

mosque **mosques**
Said "**mosk**" NOUN a building where Muslims go to worship.

mosquito **mosquitoes** or **mosquitos**
Said "moss-**skee**-toe" NOUN Mosquitoes are small flying insects which bite people in order to suck their blood; some mosquitoes spread the disease malaria.

moss **mosses**
NOUN a soft, low-growing, green plant which grows on damp soil or stone.
mossy ADJECTIVE

most
ADJECTIVE OR PRONOUN **1** the larger part, the majority. *Most of the book is true.*
ADVERB **2** You use "most" in front of adjectives or adverbs to form superlatives: *the most spectacular view in the world.*
3 more often or more than anything else. *What she feared most was spiders.*
PHRASE **4** You say **at most** or **at the most** when stating the maximum number that is possible or likely. *It will take me three hours at the most.*
5 If you **make the most** of something, you get the maximum use or advantage from it. *Let's make the most of the sunshine and go to the beach.* See **majority**.

mostly
ADVERB mainly, chiefly. *My friends are mostly girls.*

motel **motels**
NOUN a hotel for people who are travelling by car.
[formed from *motor* + *hotel*]

moth **moths**
NOUN an insect with a stout body and antennae, which usually flies at night. Moths can be fairly large, like a butterfly, or quite small, like clothes moths.

mother **mothers**
NOUN a female parent.

mother-in-law **mothers-in-law**
NOUN the mother of a person's husband or wife.

motion **motions**
NOUN **1** movement.
2 an action or gesture. *Apply your paint with a brush, using circular motions.*

motionless
ADJECTIVE not moving at all.

motivate **motivates motivating motivated**
VERB **1** If you motivate someone, you make them feel determined to do something: *a manager who knows how to motivate her players.*
2 If you are motivated by something, it makes you behave in a particular way. *The player was motivated by greed rather than love of the game.*

Synonyms: (sense 1) drive, inspire, prompt

motive **motives**
NOUN a reason or purpose for doing something.

motor **motors**
NOUN **1** a part of a vehicle or a machine that uses electricity or fuel to produce movement so that the machine can work.
2 an informal name for a motor car.
ADJECTIVE **3** relating to vehicles with an engine.
motorized ADJECTIVE

motorbike **motorbikes**
NOUN another name for a **motorcycle**.

motorcycle **motorcycles**
NOUN a two-wheeled vehicle with an engine, which is ridden by someone sitting on it.

motorist **motorists**
NOUN a person who drives a car.

motorway **motorways**
NOUN a wide road built for fast travel over long distances.

mottled
ADJECTIVE covered with patches of different colours.

motto **mottoes** or **mottos**
NOUN a short sentence or phrase that is a rule for good or sensible behaviour. *The school's motto is "Do unto others as you would have them do unto you".*

mould moulds moulding moulded
VERB **1** to make a substance into a particular shape.
NOUN **2** Mould is a soft grey or green fungus that can form on old food or damp walls.
3 a container used to make something into a particular shape: *a jelly mould.*

mouldy mouldier mouldiest
ADJECTIVE covered with mould.

moult moults moulting moulted
VERB When an animal moults, it loses its hair or feathers so new ones can grow.

mound mounds
NOUN **1** a small man-made hill.
2 a large, untidy pile.

mount mounts mounting mounted
VERB **1** If you mount a horse or bicycle, you climb on to it.
2 to increase: *mounting excitement.*
3 FORMAL to go to the top of something. *She mounted the staircase.*
NOUN **4** "Mount" is used as part of the name of a mountain: *Mount Everest.*

mountain mountains
NOUN a very big, steep hill.
mountainous ADJECTIVE

mountaineer mountaineers
NOUN a person who climbs mountains.
mountaineering NOUN

mourn mourns mourning mourned
VERB If you mourn for someone who has died, you are very sad and think about them a lot.

Synonym: grieve

mourner mourners
NOUN a person who attends a funeral.

mournful
ADJECTIVE very sad.

mouse mice
NOUN **1** a small rodent with a long tail.
2 a computer device that you move by hand in order to perform operations without using the keyboard.

mousse mousses
Said "**moose**" NOUN **1** a light, fluffy food made from whipped eggs and cream.
2 a light, foamy product that squirts out of a can, such as hairstyling mousse or bathroom cleaning mousse.

moustache moustaches
Said "mus-**stahsh**" NOUN the hair that grows on a man's upper lip.
[from Greek *mustax* meaning upper lip]

mouth mouths mouthing mouthed
NOUN **1** Your mouth is your lips and the space behind them where your tongue and teeth are.
VERB **2** If you mouth something, you form words with your lips without making any sound.

mouthful mouthfuls
NOUN as much as you can hold in your mouth at one time: *a mouthful of jelly.*

mouth organ mouth organs
NOUN a small hand-held musical instrument played by blowing and sucking, similar to a harmonica.

mouthpiece mouthpieces
NOUN the part of a musical instrument or telephone that you put to your mouth.

movable
ADJECTIVE able to be moved from one place to another.

move moves moving moved
VERB **1** to change position.
2 to go to live in a different place. *We moved to Devon.*
3 If something moves you, it causes you to feel a deep emotion. *Her story moved us to tears.*
NOUN **4** movement.
5 a turn in a game.
movable ADJECTIVE

Synonyms: (sense 1) budge, go, shift, stir

movement movements
NOUN **1** changing position or going from one place to another.
2 a group of people who share the same beliefs or aims: *the peace movement.*

movie movies
NOUN another name for a film.

moving
ADJECTIVE inspiring deep sadness or emotion.

mow mows mowing mowed mown
VERB **1** To mow grass is to cut it with a lawnmower.
2 To mow down a large number of people is to kill them all quickly and violently.
mower NOUN

MP
abbreviation for **Member of Parliament**.

Mr
Said "**miss**-ter" "Mr" is used before a man's surname when you are speaking or referring to him.

Mrs
Said "**miss**-iz" "Mrs" is used before the surname of a married woman when you are speaking or referring to her.

Ms
Said "**mis**" "Ms" is used before a woman's surname when you are speaking or referring to her. It does not specify whether a woman is married or not.

A B C D E F G H I J K L M N O P Q R S T U V W X Y Z

much
ADVERB **1** A lot. *He's much taller than you.*
2 If something does not happen much, it does not happen often. *He doesn't go out much.*
ADJECTIVE OR PRONOUN **3** You use "much" to talk about the size or amount of something. *How much money do you need?*

muck **mucks mucking mucked**
NOUN **1** INFORMAL dirt or some other unpleasant substance.
2 manure.
VERB **3** INFORMAL If you muck about, you behave in a silly way and waste time.
4 To muck out farmyard buildings or stables means to clean them.
[from Old Norse *myki* meaning dung]

mucky **muckier muckiest**
ADJECTIVE; INFORMAL dirty.

mud
NOUN wet, sticky earth.
muddy ADJECTIVE

muddle **muddles muddling muddled**
NOUN **1** a state of disorder or untidiness.
VERB **2** to mix things up, jumble.
3 to confuse someone. *Don't muddle me, I'm trying to count.*
muddled ADJECTIVE

muesli
Said "**myooz**-lee" NOUN a mixture of chopped nuts, cereal flakes and dried fruit that you can eat with milk for breakfast.

muffin **muffins**
NOUN a type of bread roll or cake.

muffled
ADJECTIVE a muffled sound is quiet or difficult to hear.

mug **mugs mugging mugged**
NOUN **1** a large, deep cup.
2 INFORMAL a person who is easily fooled or taken advantage of.
VERB **3** INFORMAL If someone mugs a person, they attack them in order to steal their money.
mugger NOUN **mugging** NOUN

muggy **muggier muggiest**
ADJECTIVE Muggy weather is unpleasantly warm and damp.

mule **mules**
NOUN the offspring of a female horse and a male donkey.

multiple
ADJECTIVE **1** consisting of many parts or having many uses. *He died from multiple injuries.*
2 In mathematics, a multiple of a number is any number that it will divide into exactly: for example, six is a multiple of three.

multiplication **multiplications**
NOUN the process of multiplying a number.

multiply **multiplies multiplying multiplied**
VERB **1** to increase greatly in number or amount.
2 to add the same number several times, for example: 4 multiplied by 3 is 12 because 4 + 4 + 4 = 12. The symbol for "multiply" is ×. See **times**.

Antonym: divide

multitude **multitudes**
NOUN; FORMAL a very large number of people or things.

mum **mums**
NOUN; INFORMAL Your mum is your mother.

mumble **mumbles mumbling mumbled**
VERB to speak very quietly and indistinctly.

mummy **mummies**
NOUN **1** INFORMAL "Mummy" or "Mum" is used to mean "mother", especially by children.
2 a dead body which was preserved long ago by being rubbed with special oils and wrapped in cloth, particularly associated with Egypt.
mummify VERB
[sense 2 is from Persian *mum* meaning wax]

mumps
NOUN an infectious illness that causes painful swelling in the neck glands.

munch **munches munching munched**
VERB to chew food steadily and thoroughly.

mural **murals**
NOUN a picture painted on a wall.

murder **murders murdering murdered**
NOUN **1** the deliberate killing of a person.
VERB **2** to kill someone deliberately.
murderer NOUN **murderous** ADJECTIVE

Synonyms: (sense 1) homicide, killing

murky **murkier murkiest**
ADJECTIVE dark or dirty and unpleasant. *He rushed through the murky streets. The gangster had a very murky past.*

murmur **murmurs murmuring murmured**
VERB **1** to say something very quietly.
NOUN **2** something that someone says which can hardly be heard.

muscle **muscles**
NOUN an internal part of the body that contracts or relaxes to enable you to move other parts of your body. Pairs of muscle are attached to your bones by tendons. You also have muscles in other parts of your body, such as your heart and bladder.
[from Latin *musculus* meaning little mouse, because muscles were once thought to look like mice]

muscular
ADJECTIVE **1** involving or affecting your muscles.
2 having well-developed muscles.

 ► Classical music words: orchestra, instrument, melody, harmony, tempo, overture.

museum museums
NOUN a public building where interesting or valuable objects from the past are kept and displayed.

mushroom mushrooms mushrooming mushroomed
NOUN 1 a fungus with a short stem and a round top. Some types of mushroom are edible.
VERB 2 to grow very rapidly. *The population of Mexico City has mushroomed in the last ten years.*

mushy mushier mushiest
ADJECTIVE 1 very soft.
2 too sentimental.

music
NOUN 1 the pattern of sounds performed by people singing or playing instruments.
2 the written symbols that represent musical sounds.

musical musicals
ADJECTIVE 1 concerned with playing or studying music.
2 If you say that someone is musical, you mean that they have a natural ability for music.
NOUN 3 a play or film that uses singing and dancing in the story.
musically ADVERB

musician musicians
NOUN someone who plays music on an instrument.

musket muskets
NOUN an old-fashioned gun with a long barrel.

Muslim Muslims; also spelt **Moslem**
NOUN 1 a person who believes in Islam and lives according to its rules.
ADJECTIVE 2 relating to Islam.

muslin
NOUN a very thin cotton fabric.

mussel mussels
NOUN a kind of shellfish with a black shell.

must
VERB 1 If something must happen, it is very important or necessary that it happens. *You must switch the electricity off before changing a light bulb.*
2 You use "must" to show that you are fairly sure about something. *She must be her daughter.*
NOUN 3 something that is absolutely necessary. *The museum is a must for all visitors.*

mustard
NOUN a spicy-tasting yellow or brown paste made from seeds and used to add flavour to food.

muster musters mustering mustered
VERB to gather together.

musty mustier mustiest
ADJECTIVE smelling stale and damp.

mutate mutates mutating mutated
VERB If something mutates, its structure or appearance alters in some way.
mutation NOUN **mutant** NOUN OR ADJECTIVE

mute
ADJECTIVE; FORMAL not giving out sound or speech.

mutilate mutilates mutilating mutilated
VERB 1 If someone is mutilated, their body is badly injured.
2 to deliberately damage or spoil something.
mutilation NOUN

mutiny mutinies mutinying mutinied
VERB 1 If a group of sailors or soldiers mutiny, they rebel against their officers.
NOUN 2 a rebellion against someone in authority.
mutinous ADJECTIVE

mutter mutters muttering muttered
VERB to speak very quietly so that you cannot easily be heard.

mutton
NOUN the meat of an adult sheep.

mutual
ADJECTIVE used to describe something that two or more people do to each other or share. *They had a mutual interest in painting.*
✔ It used to be that mutual could only be used of something shared between two people or groups. You can now use *mutual* for something that's shared between two or more people or groups.

muzzle muzzles muzzling muzzled
NOUN 1 the nose and mouth of an animal.
2 a cover or a strap for a dog's nose and mouth to prevent it from biting.
3 the open end of a gun through which the bullets come out.
VERB 4 To muzzle a dog is to put a muzzle on it.

my
PRONOUN belonging or relating to the person speaking or writing. *I lent her my ruler.*

myself
PRONOUN 1 "Myself" is used to refer to the person speaking or writing. *When I'm working I often talk to myself.*
2 "Myself" is used to emphasize "I". *I don't understand it myself.*

mysterious
ADJECTIVE when something is strange.
mysteriously ADVERB

mystery mysteries
NOUN something that is not understood or known about.

a b c d e f g h i j k l m n o p q r s t u v w x y z

Rock music words: guitar, amplifier, keyboards, bass vocals, rhythm, gig, audience.

A B C D E F G H I J K L M N O P Q R S T U V W X Y Z

mystify **mystifies mystifying mystified**
VERB If something mystifies you, you find it impossible to understand.
mystifying ADJECTIVE

myth **myths**
NOUN 1 stories from long ago which explain natural events or religious beliefs.
2 an untrue belief or explanation. *It's a myth that men are better drivers than women.*
mythical ADJECTIVE

mythology **mythologies**
NOUN A group of stories from long ago that use the same characters and ideas to explain natural events and religious beliefs.
mythological ADJECTIVE

► Continue this word chain: myth, through, ghost, stood, odour... Can you do eight more?

Nn

nag **nags nagging nagged**
VERB 1 If you nag someone, you keep complaining to them about something.
2 If something nags at you, it keeps worrying you.

nail **nails nailing nailed**
NOUN 1 a small piece of metal with a sharp point, which you hammer into objects to hold them together.
2 the thin hard areas at the ends of your fingers and toes.
VERB 3 If you nail something somewhere, you fit it there using a nail.

naive or **naïve**
Said "said ny-**eev**" **ADJECTIVE** foolishly believing that things are easier or less complicated than they are.
naively ADVERB **naivety** NOUN

naked
ADJECTIVE not wearing any clothes, nude.
nakedness NOUN

name **names naming named**
NOUN 1 a word that you use to identify a person, place or thing.
2 Someone's name is also their reputation. *Don't spread rumours, or you'll damage my good name.*
VERB 3 If you name someone or something, you give them a name or you say their name.
4 If you name a price or a date, you say what you want it to be.

nameless
ADJECTIVE You describe someone as nameless if either they do not have a name, you do not know it, or you are not going to say what it is.

namely
ADVERB that is; used to introduce more detailed information. *We shall have games at the party, namely Pass the Parcel and Musical Chairs.*

nan **nans**
NOUN; INFORMAL another word for grandmother.

nanny **nannies**
NOUN 1 a woman whose job is looking after young children.
2 INFORMAL another word for grandmother.

nap **naps napping napped**
VERB When you nap you have a short sleep.
nap NOUN

napkin **napkins**
NOUN a small piece of cloth or paper used to wipe your hands and mouth after eating.

nappy **nappies**
NOUN a piece of thick cloth or paper worn round a baby's bottom.

narcotic **narcotics**
NOUN a drug which makes you sleepy and unable to feel pain.
[from Greek *narkoun* meaning to make numb]

narrate **narrates narrating narrated**
VERB to tell a story.
narration NOUN

narrative **narratives**
Said "**nar**-rat-tiv" **NOUN** a story or an account of events.

narrator **narrators**
NOUN in a book, play, film or television programme, someone who tells the story by talking directly to the reader or audience.

narrow **narrower narrowest; narrows narrowing narrowed**
ADJECTIVE 1 measuring a small distance from one side to the other.
2 concerned with only a few aspects of something: *a narrow point of view; a narrow knowledge of the subject.*
3 a narrow escape, victory or result is one you only just achieve.
VERB 4 If something narrows, it becomes less wide.
narrowly ADVERB

Antonym: (sense 1) wide

narrow-minded
ADJECTIVE unwilling to consider new ideas or opinions.

Synonyms: bigoted, intolerant

nasal
Said "**nay**-zal" **ADJECTIVE 1** relating to the nose: *a nasal spray.*
2 Nasal sounds are made by breathing out through your nose as you speak.

nasty **nastier nastiest**
ADJECTIVE very unpleasant.
nastily ADVERB **nastiness** NOUN

nation **nations**
NOUN a country and its people.

national **nationals**
ADJECTIVE 1 belonging or related to a whole country. *This oil painting is of national importance.*
NOUN 2 A national of a country is a citizen of that country: *British nationals.*

national anthem **national anthems**
NOUN a country's official song.

nationalism
NOUN love of your own country.
nationalist NOUN **nationalistic** ADVERB

nationality **nationalities**
NOUN the fact of being a citizen of a particular country. *Derek's nationality is Australian.*

The letter N was taken from the shape of a snake. *Nahas* was an early word for snake.

A B C D E F G H I J K L M N O P Q R S T U V W X Y Z

nationalize nationalizes nationalizing nationalized; also spelt **nationalise**
VERB To nationalize an industry means to bring it under the control and ownership of the state.
nationalized ADJECTIVE **nationalization** NOUN

nationwide
ADJECTIVE OR ADVERB happening all over a country: *a nationwide search.*

native natives
ADJECTIVE **1** Your native country is the country where you were born.
2 Your native language is the language that you first learned to speak.
NOUN **3** A native of a place is someone who was born there.

Nativity
NOUN In Christianity, the Nativity is the birth of Christ and the festival celebrating this.

natural naturals
ADJECTIVE **1** normal and to be expected. *It is only natural for dogs to chase cats.*
2 existing or happening in nature: *a natural disaster like an earthquake.*
3 A natural ability is one that you were born with: *her natural talent as a skater.*
NOUN **4** someone who is born with a particular ability. *Sunil is a natural at horseriding.*

Synonyms: (sense 3) inborn, inherent, innate

natural gas
NOUN a gas found underground or under the sea and used as a fuel.

natural history
NOUN the study of animals and plants.

nature natures
NOUN **1** Nature is animals, plants and all the other things in the world not made by people.
2 The nature of someone or something is their basic quality or character. *She liked his warm, generous nature.*

naughty naughtier naughtiest
ADJECTIVE behaving badly.
naughtiness NOUN

nausea
Said "**naw**-zee-ah" NOUN the feeling that you are going to be sick.
nauseous ADJECTIVE

nautical
Said "**naw**-tik-kl" ADJECTIVE relating to ships or navigation.

naval
ADJECTIVE relating to a navy.

nave naves
NOUN the main part of a church or cathedral where the congregation usually sits.

navel navels
NOUN your belly-button.

navigate navigates navigating navigated
VERB to work out the direction in which a ship, plane or car should go, using maps and sometimes instruments.
navigation NOUN **navigator** NOUN

navy navies
NOUN **1** the part of a country's armed forces that fights at sea.
ADJECTIVE **2** dark blue.

near nearer nearest; nears nearing neared
PREPOSITION, ADJECTIVE OR ADVERB **1** not far from. *Our school is quite near here. It was a night of near disaster. The wedding occurs near the end of the play.*
VERB **2** to approach. *The dog began to bark as he neared the door.*
nearness NOUN

nearby
ADJECTIVE OR ADVERB a short distance away.

nearly
ADVERB not completely but almost. *I've nearly finished.*

neat neater neatest
ADJECTIVE tidy and smart.
neatly ADVERB **neatness** NOUN

necessarily
ADVERB as a certain and natural consequence. *Artists are necessarily very observant.*

necessary
ADJECTIVE Something that is necessary is needed or must be done.

Synonyms: essential, needed, requisite

necessity necessities
NOUN **1** the need to do something. *Eating food is a necessity for human life.*
2 something which is needed. *I remembered to pack the necessities: underwear, towel and a toothbrush.*

neck necks
NOUN **1** Your neck is the part of your body which joins your head to the rest of your body.
2 The neck of a bottle is the long narrow part at the top of it.

necklace necklaces
NOUN a piece of jewellery to be worn around the neck.

nectar
NOUN a sweet liquid produced by flowers which is attractive to insects.

nectarine nectarines
NOUN a kind of peach with a smooth skin.

 ► Navy words: admiral, captain, lieutenant, destroyer, submarine, frigate, merchant... ►

need needs needing needed
VERB 1 If you need something, you believe that you must have it or do it. *I need to go out.*
2 to be necessary, to require. *The building needs some repairs.*
NOUN 3 a strong feeling that you must have or do something.
4 If a person is in need, they are poor.
5 Your needs are the things that you need to have. *The pay wasn't sufficient to meet his needs.*
needless ADJECTIVE **needlessly** ADVERB

Synonyms: (sense 5) essentials, necessities, requirements

needle needles needling needled
NOUN 1 a small thin piece of metal used to pull a thread in sewing.
2 Knitting needles are long thin pieces of steel or plastic used for knitting.
3 the part of a syringe which a doctor or nurse sticks into your body to give an injection.
4 the thin piece of metal or plastic on a dial which moves to show a measurement.
5 The needles of a pine tree are its leaves.
VERB 6 If someone or something needles you, it annoys or provokes you.

needlework
NOUN sewing or embroidery.

needy needier neediest
ADJECTIVE very poor.

negative negatives
ADJECTIVE 1 A negative answer means "no".
2 unpleasant or harmful. *The negative effects of car travel include exhaust fumes.*
3 Someone who is negative sees only the bad aspects of a situation. *Why are you so negative about everything?*
4 If a medical or scientific test is negative, it shows that something has not happened or is not present.
5 A negative number is less than zero and written with a minus sign in front of it: *–10.*
NOUN 6 the image that is first produced when you take a photograph.
negatively ADVERB

neglect neglects neglecting neglected
VERB 1 If you neglect someone or something, you do not look after them properly.
2 FORMAL If you neglect to do something, you fail to do it. *Phil neglected to post the letter.*
NOUN 3 failure to look after something or someone properly. *The plants died from neglect.*
neglectful ADJECTIVE

negligent
ADJECTIVE not taking enough care.
negligently ADVERB **negligence** NOUN

negotiate negotiates negotiating negotiated
VERB When people negotiate, they have formal discussion in order to reach an agreement about something.
negotiation NOUN **negotiator** NOUN

neigh neighs neighing neighed
*Rhymes with "***day***"* VERB When a horse neighs, it makes a loud high-pitched sound.
neigh NOUN

neighbour neighbours
NOUN someone who lives near to you.

neighbourhood neighbourhoods
NOUN Your neighbourhood is the area near your house; a district.

neighbourly
ADJECTIVE kind and friendly, as a neighbour should be.

neither
CONJUNCTION, ADJECTIVE OR PRONOUN You use "neither" to show that a negative statement refers to each of two things or people. *Jan spoke neither English nor German.*

HOW TO MAKE "NEITHER" AGREE
When **neither** is followed by a plural noun, the verb can be plural too:
neither of these books are useful.
When you have two singular subjects the verb should be singular too:
neither Jack nor John has done the work.

neon
*Said "***nee***-yon"* NOUN a gas used in glass tubes to make bright electric lights and signs.

nephew nephews
NOUN Someone's nephew is the son of their sister or brother.

nerve nerves
NOUN 1 Nerves are long thin fibres that send messages between your brain and other parts of your body.
2 If you talk about someone's nerves, you mean their ability to remain calm in a difficult situation. *Firefighting needs confidence and strong nerves.*
3 courage. *Patrick didn't have the nerve to ask Indira out.*
4 INFORMAL boldness or rudeness. *The pupil had the nerve to swear at the teacher.*
PHRASE 5 If someone or something **gets on your nerves**, they irritate you.

nerve-racking
ADJECTIVE making you feel very worried and tense.

nervous
ADJECTIVE worried and perhaps frightened.
nervously ADVERB **nervousness** NOUN

Synonyms: apprehensive, edgy, jumpy

nervous breakdown nervous breakdowns
NOUN an illness in which someone suffers from deep depression and needs psychiatric treatment.

nest nests
NOUN a place that birds, insects and other animals make to lay eggs in or rear their young in.
nest VERB

nestle nestles nestling nestled
Said "**ness**-sl" VERB to settle somewhere comfortably, often pressing up against someone else. *The new puppy nestled in her lap.*

nestling nestlings
NOUN a young bird that has not yet learned to fly and so has not left the nest.

net nets
NOUN 1 a piece of material consisting of threads woven together with small spaces in between.
2 the Net is the same as the **Internet**.
3 a net is the flat template that, when folded, forms a three-dimensional shape: *the net of a cube; the net of a pyramid.*
ADJECTIVE 4 A net result or amount is final, after everything has been considered or included. *The jumble sale made a net profit of £2100.*
5 The net weight of something is its weight without its wrapping.

netball
NOUN a game played by two teams in which each team tries to score goals by throwing a ball through a high net.

nettle nettles nettling nettled
NOUN 1 a wild plant covered with little hairs that sting.
VERB 2 to annoy someone.

network networks
NOUN 1 a large number of lines or roads which connect and cross at many points: *the telephone network.*
2 a large number of people or things that work together as a system: *our network of offices throughout the UK.*

neuter neuters neutering neutered
Said "**nyoo**-ter" VERB 1 When an animal is neutered, its reproductive organs are removed.
ADJECTIVE 2 In some languages, a neuter noun or pronoun has no gender, that is, it is one which is not masculine or feminine.

WHAT IS NEUTER?
Neuter nouns refer to inanimate objects and abstract ideas (things which are not alive), for example:
The kettle will switch itself off – kettle is neuter.
Also look at the grammar boxes at **gender, masculine** and **feminine.**

neutral
ADJECTIVE 1 People who are neutral do not support either side in a disagreement or war.
2 A neutral colour is not definite or striking, for example, pale grey.
3 In chemistry, a neutral substance is neither acid nor alkaline.
neutrality NOUN

never
ADVERB at no time in the past, present or future.

nevertheless
ADVERB in spite of what has just been said. *It did rain, but we enjoyed ourselves nevertheless.*

new newer newest
ADJECTIVE 1 recently made, created or discovered: *a new house; a new plan; a new virus.*
2 different or unfamiliar. *The dance was new to me.*
3 not used or owned before: *a new car.*
newly ADVERB

Synonyms: (sense 1) latest, modern, recent

newcomer newcomers
NOUN someone who has recently arrived in a place.

new moon new moons
NOUN the moon when it looks like a thin crescent shape at the start of its four-week journey around the earth.

news
NOUN information about things that have happened recently.

newsagent newsagents
NOUN a person or shop that sells newspapers and magazines.

newsletter newsletters
NOUN a printed sheet of paper containing information about an organization and sent regularly to its members.

newspaper newspapers
NOUN a publication, on large sheets of folded paper, that is produced regularly and contains news and articles.

newt newts
NOUN a small amphibious creature with a moist skin, short legs and a long tail.
[from a mistaken division of Middle English *an ewt*]

newton newtons
NOUN the standard unit of force, abbreviated to "N".

New Year
NOUN the time when people celebrate the start of a year.

next
ADJECTIVE OR ADVERB 1 coming immediately after something else. *We'll catch the next train. They lived in the next street.*
PHRASE 2 If one thing is **next to** another, it is at the side of it. *Put your boots next to the door.*

Synonyms: (sense 1) following, subsequent

 The word "nice" is overused. Try to avoid using it. Some alternatives are...

A B C D E F G H I J K L M N O P Q R S T U V W X Y Z

next door
ADJECTIVE OR ADVERB in the house next to yours.

nib nibs
NOUN the detachable metal end of a fountain pen, which delivers the ink to the paper.

nibble nibbles nibbling nibbled
VERB to take small bites of something.
nibble NOUN

nice nicer nicest
ADJECTIVE pleasant or attractive.
nicely ADVERB

nick nicks nicking nicked
VERB **1** to make a small cut in the surface of something. *He nicked his chin while shaving.*
2 INFORMAL to steal.
NOUN **3** a small cut.
PHRASE **4** If something happens **in the nick of time**, it happens only just in time.
5 INFORMAL If something is **in good nick**, it is in good condition.

nickel
NOUN a silver-coloured, magnetic metal which is often used in making coins and steel.

nickname nicknames nicknaming nicknamed
NOUN **1** an informal name for someone or something. *John's nickname was Grump because he was always moaning.*
VERB **2** If you nickname someone, you give them a nickname.
[from Middle English *an ekename* meaning an additional name]

nicotine
NOUN an addictive substance found in tobacco.

niece nieces
NOUN Someone's niece is the daughter of their sister or brother.

night nights
NOUN the time between sunset and sunrise when it is dark.

nightdress nightdresses
NOUN a loose dress that a woman or girl wears to sleep in, a nightie.

nightfall
NOUN the time of day when it starts to go dark, dusk.

nightingale nightingales
NOUN a small brown European bird, the male of which sings very beautifully at night.

nightly
ADJECTIVE OR ADVERB happening every night.

nightmare nightmares
NOUN **1** a very frightening dream.
2 INFORMAL a very unpleasant or frightening situation. *The whole journey was a nightmare.*
nightmarish ADJECTIVE

nil
NOUN zero or nothing. *We lost by two goals to nil.*

nimble nimbler nimblest
ADJECTIVE able to move or think quickly and brightly.
nimbly ADVERB **nimbleness** NOUN

nine
the number 9.
ninth

nineteen
the number 19.
nineteenth

ninety nineties
the number 90.
ninetieth

nip nips nipping nipped
VERB **1** INFORMAL to go somewhere quickly. *I'll just nip round the corner to the shop.*
2 To nip someone means to pinch them slightly.
NOUN **3** a light pinch.

nipple nipples
NOUN one of the two small tips on your breasts. Babies suck milk through their mother's nipples.

nit nits
NOUN **1** Nits are the eggs of a kind of louse that sometimes lives in people's hair.
2 INFORMAL a stupid person.

nitrogen
NOUN a colourless gas with no smell which forms about 78% of the earth's atmosphere.

no
INTERJECTION **1** You use "no" to say that something is not true or to refuse something.
ADJECTIVE **2** none at all or not at all. *She gave no reason. You're no friend of mine.*
ADVERB **3** used with a comparative to mean "not": *no later than 24th July.*

nobility
NOUN **1** The nobility are all the people in society who have titles and high social rank, including lords, ladies, dukes, duchesses, earls, etc.
2 If you show nobility, you behave in a noble way.

noble nobler noblest; nobles
ADJECTIVE **1** honest and brave, and deserving admiration.
NOUN **2** a member of the nobility.
nobly ADVERB

nobleman noblemen
NOUN a man or woman who is a member of the nobility.
noblewoman ADVERB

nobody
PRONOUN not a single person, no one.

nocturnal
ADJECTIVE happening or active at night: *a nocturnal journey. Badgers tend to be nocturnal animals.*

a b c d e f g h i j k l m n o p q r s t u v w x y z

pleasant, attractive, enjoyable, tasty, delicious, fascinating, interesting. ◀

A B C D E F G H I J K L M N O P Q R S T U V W X Y Z

nod nods nodding nodded
VERB **1** to move your head down and up to greet someone or agree with them.
NOUN **2** A nod is a movement of your head up and down.
nod off VERB to gradually and gently fall asleep. *With the movement of the train I was soon nodding off.*

noise noises
NOUN a sound, often one that is loud or unpleasant.

Synonyms: din, racket, row

noisy noisier noisiest
ADJECTIVE making a lot of noise or full of noise.
noisily ADVERB **noisiness** NOUN

nomad nomads
NOUN a person who belongs to a tribe which travels from place to place rather than living in just one place.
nomadic ADJECTIVE

nominate nominates nominating nominated
VERB If you nominate someone for a job or position, you formally suggest that they have it.
nomination NOUN

Synonyms: name, propose, suggest

non-
PREFIX a prefix which is added to form the negative of the attached word: *a nonsmoker.*

nonchalant
Said "**non**-shal-nt" ADJECTIVE seeming calm and not worried.
nonchalantly ADVERB **nonchalance** NOUN

none
PRONOUN not a single thing or person, or not even a small amount of something. *None of us know how to treat her. They asked me for fresh ideas, but I had none.*

nonexistent
ADJECTIVE not existing, not actual. *I spent hours diving in search of what turned out to be a nonexistent wreck.*

non-fiction
ADJECTIVE Non-fiction books are about real people and events.

nonflammable
ADJECTIVE not easily set on fire.

nonsense
NOUN foolish or meaningless words or behaviour.
nonsensical ADJECTIVE

nonsmoking
ADJECTIVE A nonsmoking area is one in which people are not allowed to smoke.

nonstop
ADJECTIVE never stopping. *The action in the film was nonstop.*

noodle noodles
NOUN Noodles are a kind of pasta shaped into long thin pieces.

noon
NOUN 12 o'clock midday.

no one
PRONOUN not a single person, nobody.

noose nooses
NOUN a loop at the end of a piece of rope, with a knot that tightens when the rope is pulled.

nor
CONJUNCTION You use "nor" after "neither" or after a negative statement, to add something else that the negative statement applies to. *We had neither the time nor the money to go on holiday.*

normal
ADJECTIVE usual and ordinary.
normally ADVERB **normality** NOUN

Synonyms: conventional, ordinary, usual

north
NOUN **1** If you are looking towards the rising sun, north is the direction on your left.
2 the part of a place which is towards the north: *the north of England.*
ADJECTIVE OR ADVERB **3** in, towards or from the north.
northern ADJECTIVE **northward** ADVERB

north-east
NOUN, ADVERB OR ADJECTIVE halfway between north and east.
north-eastern ADJECTIVE

northerly
ADJECTIVE OR ADVERB to, from or towards the north.

northern
ADJECTIVE in or from the north.

North Pole
NOUN the most northerly point of the earth's surface.

northward or **northwards**
ADVERB **1** towards the north.
ADJECTIVE **2** The northward part of something is the north part.

north-west
NOUN, ADVERB OR ADJECTIVE halfway between north and west.
north-western ADJECTIVE

nose noses
NOUN the part of the body which you use for smelling and breathing.

nosedive nosedives
NOUN a sudden downward plunge by an aircraft.

 ▶ Which author wrote *The Dong with the Luminous Nose* and *The Pobble Who Had No Toes?*

nostalgia
Said "nos-**tal**-ja" NOUN a feeling of affection for the past, and sadness that things have changed.
nostalgic ADJECTIVE **nostalgically** ADVERB

nostril **nostrils**
NOUN Your nostrils are the two openings in your nose which you breathe through.

nosy **nosier nosiest**; also spelt **nosey**
ADJECTIVE trying to find out about things that do not concern you.
nosiness NOUN

Synonyms: curious, inquisitive

not
ADVERB Not is used in several ways to form negatives. *I do not want any fuss. I'm afraid not. Not every pupil had remembered their books. Farah's not only pretty, she's smart too. School holidays are a necessity, not a perk.*

notable
ADJECTIVE important or interesting. *The town is notable for its hat industry.*
notably ADVERB

notch **notches**
NOUN a small V-shaped cut in a surface.

note **notes noting noted**
NOUN **1** a short letter.
2 Notes are bits of information you write down to help you remember something.
3 In music, a note is a musical sound of a particular pitch, or a written symbol that represents it.
4 a piece of paper money.
VERB **5** If you note a fact, you become aware of it.
6 If you note something down, you write it down.
PHRASE **7** If you **take note** of something, you pay attention to it because you think that it is important.

notebook **notebooks**
NOUN a small book for writing notes in.

nothing
PRONOUN not anything.

Synonyms: nil, nought, zero

notice **notices noticing noticed**
VERB **1** to become aware of something.
NOUN **2** a written or printed announcement.
3 attention or awareness. *I'm glad Jean brought it to my notice.*
4 advance warning about something. *The teacher gave three weeks' notice that she would be leaving.*

Synonyms: (sense 1) detect, observe, perceive

noticeable
ADJECTIVE obvious and easy to see.
noticeably ADVERB

noticeboard **noticeboards**
NOUN a board for notices.

notify **notifies notifying notified**
VERB to tell someone officially or formally about something. *They notified us by letter of what school we were going to.*
notification NOUN

notion **notions**
NOUN an idea or belief.

notorious
ADJECTIVE well known for something bad: *a notorious gangster.*
notoriously ADVERB **notoriety** NOUN

nougat
Said "**noo**-gah" NOUN a kind of chewy sweet containing nuts and sometimes fruit.

nought **noughts**
the number 0.

noun **nouns**
NOUN a word which refers to a person, thing or idea. Examples of nouns are president, table and beauty.

NOUNS
A **noun** is a word that labels a person, thing or idea. They are sometimes called "naming words".
Common nouns indicate general objects and types of people. They always begin with small letters:
girl, city, pictures
Concrete nouns are common nouns that indicate things that you can touch:
tree, bicycle, house
Abstract nouns are common nouns that indicate things that you cannot touch:
beauty, thoughtfulness, popularity
Proper nouns are different from common nouns in that they name particular people, places or objects. They begin with capital letters:
Alan Mills, Los Angeles, The Mona Lisa

nourish **nourishes nourishing nourished**
Said "**nur**-rish" VERB If food nourishes you, it makes you strong and healthy.
nourishing ADJECTIVE

nourishment
NOUN food that your body needs in order to remain healthy.

novel **novels**
NOUN **1** a book that tells a long story about imaginary people and events.
ADJECTIVE **2** new and interesting: *a very novel experience.*

novelist **novelists**
NOUN a person who writes novels.

novelty **novelties**
NOUN **1** something new and interesting or exciting.
2 a small, unusual object sold as a gift or souvenir.

a b c d e f g h i j k l m n o p q r s t u v w x y z

November
NOUN the eleventh month of the year.

novice novices
NOUN someone who is not yet experienced at something. *Many older people are novices on the computer.*

now
ADVERB 1 at the present time or moment: *in three days from now.*
CONJUNCTION 2 You use "now" or "now that" to show that two events are connected or may be connected. *Things have got better now there is a new teacher.*
PHRASE 3 If something happens **now and then**, it happens sometimes but not regularly.
4 **Just now** means a very short time ago. *He was here just now.*

nowadays
ADVERB at the present time. *Nowadays many children come to school by car.*

nowhere
ADVERB not anywhere.

nozzle nozzles
NOUN a spout fitted on to the end of a pipe or hose to control the flow of a liquid.

nuclear
ADJECTIVE relating to the energy produced when atoms are split: *a nuclear power station; nuclear weapons.*

nucleus nuclei
Said "**nyoo**-klee-uss" NOUN 1 The nucleus of a cell is the part that controls the growth and reproduction of the cell.
2 the central part of an atom.
3 The nucleus of something is the basic central part of it to which other things are added. *They have kept the nucleus of the team, only swapping two players.*

nude
ADJECTIVE not wearing any clothes, naked.

nudge nudges nudging nudged
VERB to push someone gently, usually with your elbow.
nudge NOUN

nugget nuggets
NOUN a small lump of something valuable, especially gold.

nuisance nuisances
NOUN someone or something that is annoying or causing problems.

Synonyms: bother, inconvenience, problem

numb
ADJECTIVE unable to feel anything. *My legs felt numb with cold. I was numb with grief.*
numb VERB

number numbers numbering numbered
NOUN 1 a word or symbol that is used for counting or calculating.
2 A number of things or people is several of them.
VERB 3 If you number something, you give it a number in a series or write the number on it.
4 If things number a particular amount, there are that many of them.
5 To be numbered among a particular group means to be included in that group.

Synonyms: (sense 1) digit, figure, numeral

numeracy
NOUN the ability to understand basic arithmetic.

numeral numerals
NOUN a symbol that represents a number.

numerate
ADJECTIVE able to use numbers and to calculate.

numerator numerators
NOUN In mathematics, the numerator is the top part of a fraction. See **denominator**, **common denominator**.

numerical
ADJECTIVE expressed in numbers or relating to numbers: *in numerical order.*

numerous
ADJECTIVE existing or happening in large numbers.

nun nuns
NOUN a member of a female religious community.

nurse nurses nursing nursed
NOUN 1 a person whose job is to look after people who are ill.
VERB 2 to look after people when they are ill.
nursing NOUN

nursery nurseries
NOUN 1 a place where young children are looked after while their parents are working.
2 OLD-FASHIONED a room in a big house where the children of a family spent most of their time.

nursery rhyme nursery rhymes
NOUN a short poem or song for young children.

nursery school nursery schools
NOUN a school for children from three to five years old.

nursing home nursing homes
NOUN a privately run hospital, especially for old people.

nut nuts
NOUN 1 a fruit with a hard shell and an edible centre that grows on certain trees and bushes.
2 a piece of metal with a hole in the middle which a bolt screws into.

nutrient nutrients
NOUN substances that help plants or animals to grow better.

 ► Nursing words: patient, ambulance, ward, syringe, transfusion, donor, casualty, theatre.

nutrition
NOUN the food that you eat, considered from the point of view of how it helps you to grow and remain healthy.

nutritious
ADJECTIVE containing substances that help you to grow and remain healthy.

nutty **nuttier nuttiest**
ADJECTIVE **1** INFORMAL mad or very foolish.
2 tasting of nuts.

nuzzle **nuzzles nuzzling nuzzled**
VERB to push or rub gently against someone.

nylon **nylons**
NOUN **1** a type of strong artificial material.
2 Nylons are stockings made of nylon.

nymph **nymphs**
NOUN **1** a spirit of nature imagined as a beautiful maiden.
2 the larva of insects such as the dragonfly or the mayfly.

A B C D E F G H I J K L M N O P Q R S T U V W X Y Z

Oo

oak oaks
NOUN a large tree which produces acorns. Its wood is often used to make furniture.

oar oars
NOUN a wooden pole with a wide, flat end, used for rowing a boat.

oasis oases
Said "oh-**ay**-siss" NOUN a small area in a desert where water and plants are found.

oath oaths
NOUN a formal promise, especially a promise to tell the truth in a court of law.

Synonyms: pledge, promise, vow

oatmeal
NOUN a rough flour made from oats.

oats
NOUN a type of grain often used to make breakfast cereals.

obedient
ADJECTIVE doing what you are told to do.
obediently ADVERB **obedience** NOUN

obey obeys obeying obeyed
VERB If you obey a person or an order, you do what you are told to do.

obituary obituaries
NOUN a passage written for a newspaper or magazine about someone who has recently died.

object objects objecting objected
Said "**ob**-jekt" NOUN 1 anything solid that you can touch or see, and that is not alive.
2 an aim or purpose. *The object of the exercise is to raise money.*
3 In grammar, the object of a verb or preposition is the word or phrase which follows it and describes the person or thing affected. In the sentence "He loved chips", the word "chips" is the object.
Said "ob-**jekt**" VERB 4 If you object to something, you dislike it or disapprove of it.

Synonyms: (sense 4) oppose, protest, take exception

objection objections
NOUN If you have an objection to something, you dislike it or disapprove of it.

objective objectives
NOUN 1 an aim. *Our objective was to get home before it got dark.*
ADJECTIVE 2 not influenced by personal feelings. *A journalist should be fair and completely objective.*
objectively ADVERB **objectivity** NOUN

obligation obligations
NOUN something that you must do because it is your duty.

oblige obliges obliging obliged
VERB 1 If you are obliged to do something, you have to do it.
2 If you oblige someone, you help them.

oblique
Said "o-**bleek**" ADJECTIVE An oblique line slopes at an angle.
obliquely ADVERB

oblong oblongs
NOUN a four-sided shape with two parallel short sides, two parallel long sides, and four right angles; a rectangle.
oblong ADJECTIVE

obnoxious
Said "ob-**nok**-shuss" ADJECTIVE extremely unpleasant.
obnoxiously ADVERB

oboe oboes
NOUN a woodwind musical instrument with a double reed.
oboist NOUN

obscene
ADJECTIVE indecent and likely to upset people.
obscenity NOUN **obscenely** ADVERB

Synonyms: filthy, indecent

obscure obscurer obscurest; obscures obscuring obscured
ADJECTIVE 1 Something obscure is difficult to see or to understand. *The contract was written in obscure language.*
2 Something that is obscure is known by only a few people. *The genius knew many obscure facts.*
VERB 3 To obscure something is to make it difficult to see or understand. *The sun was obscured by clouds.*

Synonyms: (sense 1) cryptic, unclear, vague

observant
ADJECTIVE Someone who is observant notices things that are not easy to see.

observation observations
NOUN 1 the act of watching something carefully.
2 something that you have seen or noticed. *This report is based on my own observations.*
3 a remark. *The chairperson kept making quiet observations about the people who got up to speak.*

observatory observatories
NOUN a room or building containing telescopes and other equipment for studying the sun, moon, planets and stars.

observe observes observing observed
VERB 1 to watch something carefully.
2 to notice something. *Holmes observed that Watson had mud on his shoes.*
3 To observe a law or custom is to obey or follow it.
observer NOUN

 ► The letter O seems to have begun as a picture of an eye.

obsessed
ADJECTIVE If someone is obsessed with something, they cannot stop thinking about it.

obsession **obsessions**
NOUN If someone has an obsession about something, they cannot stop thinking about that thing.
obsessional ADJECTIVE **obsessive** ADJECTIVE

obsolete
ADJECTIVE out of date and no longer used.

Synonyms: outmoded, passé

obstacle **obstacles**
NOUN something which is in your way and makes it difficult to do something.

Synonyms: difficulty, problem, stumbling block

obstinate
ADJECTIVE Obstinate people are stubborn and unwilling to change their minds.
obstinately ADVERB **obstinacy** NOUN

obstruct **obstructs obstructing obstructed**
VERB to block. *The builder's lorry has completely obstructed the entrance.*
obstruction NOUN **obstructive** ADJECTIVE

obtain **obtains obtaining obtained**
VERB to get something, to acquire.
obtainable ADJECTIVE

obtuse
ADJECTIVE **1** An obtuse person is stupid or slow to understand things.
2 An obtuse angle is one that is between 90° and 180°. See **acute, reflex**.

obvious
ADJECTIVE easy to see or understand.
obviously ADVERB

Synonyms: clear, evident, plain

occasion **occasions**
NOUN **1** a time when something happens. *I met her on only one occasion.*
2 an important event. *The first night of the show was quite an occasion.*

occasional
ADJECTIVE happening sometimes but not often.
occasionally ADVERB

occupant **occupants**
NOUN The occupants of a building are the people who live and work in it.

occupation **occupations**
NOUN **1** a job or profession.
2 The occupation of a country is the act of a foreign army invading it and taking control of it.
occupational ADJECTIVE

occupy **occupies occupying occupied**
VERB **1** to take up and fill a position. *The school occupies a key role in the community.*
2 If something occupies you, you spend your time doing it.
3 to live or work in a building.
4 to move into a country and take control of it. *Before the Second World War the German army occupied Poland.*
occupier NOUN

occur **occurs occurring occurred**
VERB **1** to happen. *The incident occurred at the swimming pool.*
2 If a thought or idea occurs to you, you suddenly think of it.
✔ For planned events, do not use *occur* or *happen*, instead use, for example, *took place*: *the wedding took place on Saturday.* Only something unexpected *occurs* or *happens*.

ocean **oceans**
NOUN The five oceans are the five very large areas of sea in the world.
oceanic ADJECTIVE

o'clock
ADVERB used when the time is an exact number of hours: *four o'clock*.
[an abbreviation of *of the clock*]

oct-
PREFIX related to the number eight.

octagon **octagons**
NOUN a shape with eight straight sides.
octagonal ADJECTIVE
[from Greek *okto* + *gonos* meaning eight-angled]

octahedron **octahedrons**
NOUN a three-dimensional shape with eight flat faces.

octave **octaves**
NOUN the difference in pitch between the first note and the eighth note of a musical scale.

October
NOUN the tenth month of the year.
[from Latin *october* meaning the eighth month, as it used to be before emperor Julius Caesar added two extra months (July and August) in 45 BC]

octopus **octopuses**
NOUN a sea animal with eight long tentacles which it uses to catch food.

odd **odder oddest**
ADJECTIVE **1** strange or unusual.
2 not matching: *odd socks*.
3 Odd numbers are numbers that cannot be divided exactly by two, such as three, five and seven.
PHRASE **4** The **odd one out** in a group is the one that is different from all the others.
oddly ADVERB **oddness** NOUN **oddity** NOUN

oddment **oddments**
NOUN an odd piece or thing, usually which is left over.

a b c d e f g h i j k l m n o p q r s t u v w x y z

A B C D E F G H I J K L M N O P Q R S T U V W X Y Z

odds
PLURAL NOUN In gambling, the probability of something happening is called the odds. *The odds on England winning were given at 10:1.*

ode odes
NOUN a poem written in praise of someone or something.

odour odours
NOUN; FORMAL a strong smell.
odorous ADJECTIVE odourless ADJECTIVE

of
PREPOSITION 1 consisting of or containing: *a cup of tea.*
2 used when talking about things that are characteristic of something: *a woman of great importance.*
3 belonging to or connected with: *a friend of Rachel.*
✔ Where *of* means "belonging to", it can be replaced by an apostrophe: *Rachel's friend.*

off
PREPOSITION OR ADVERB 1 indicating movement away from or out of a place. *Keep off the grass.*
2 indicating separation or distance from a place. *The grass has been fenced off.*
3 not working. *Turn the radio off.*
4 not liking or not using something. *He went right off eggs.*
ADJECTIVE 5 cancelled or postponed. *The concert is off.*
6 Food that is off has gone bad.

USING "OFF"
Don't use *of* after **off.** You should say:
he stepped off the bus,
not he stepped off of the bus.
Beware of using **off** when you really mean *from.* You should say:
they bought milk from a farmer,
not they bought milk off a farmer.

offence offences
NOUN 1 a crime. *Blackmail is a serious offence.*
2 If you take offence at what somebody says or does, you are upset and perhaps annoyed by it.

offend offends offending offended
VERB 1 If you offend someone, you upset and perhaps annoy them.
2 to commit an offence. *He had offended twice before the break-in which put him in jail.*

offender offenders
NOUN a person who has committed an offence against the law.

offensive
ADJECTIVE rude and upsetting.
offensively ADVERB

offer offers offering offered
VERB 1 to ask someone if they would like something.
NOUN 2 something that someone says they will give you or do for you. *He refused the offer of a drink.*
3 a specially low price for something in a shop.

office offices
NOUN 1 a place where people work at desks.
2 Someone who holds an office has an important job or position in government or in an organization.

officer officers
NOUN a person with a position of authority in the armed forces, the police or a government organization.

official officials
ADJECTIVE 1 to do with approval from someone in authority: *official notepaper; the official results.*
NOUN 2 a person who holds a position of authority in an organization.
officially ADVERB

officious
ADJECTIVE Officious people assert their authority in a dominating and aggressive way.

off-licence off-licences
NOUN a shop which sells alcoholic drinks.

offshore
ADJECTIVE OR ADVERB in or from the part of the sea near the shore.

offside
ADJECTIVE 1 If a soccer, rugby or hockey player is offside, they have broken the rules by moving too far forward.
NOUN 2 the side of a vehicle that is furthest from the pavement.

offspring
NOUN A person's or animal's offspring are their children.

often
ADVERB happening many times or a lot of the time.

ogre ogres
Said "**oh**-gur" NOUN a cruel, frightening giant in a fairy story.

oh
INTERJECTION a word used to express surprise.

oil oils oiling oiled
NOUN 1 a thick, sticky liquid found underground that is used as a fuel for lubricating machines and as a basis for many industrial and domestic products.
2 a thick, greasy liquid made from plants or animals and used for cooking.
VERB 3 If you oil something, you put oil in it or on it.

oil painting
NOUN painting done using a thick paint made from a coloured powder and linseed oil.

 ► You should say "the nut came off the bolt" **not** "the nut came off of the bolt".

oilskin oilskins
NOUN a piece of clothing made from a thick, waterproof material, worn especially by fishermen.

oily
ADJECTIVE covered with or containing oil: *an oily rag; oily skin.*

ointment ointments
NOUN a smooth, thick substance that you put on sore skin to heal it.

okay or **OK**
ADJECTIVE OR ADVERB; INFORMAL all right. *Tell me if this sounds OK.*

Synonyms: acceptable, satisfactory

old older oldest
ADJECTIVE **1** having lived or existed for a long time.
2 "Old" is used to give the age of someone or something. *This photo is five years old.*
3 former. *This was the old main road before the bypass was built.*

old-fashioned
ADJECTIVE no longer fashionable.

Synonyms: dated, outmoded, passé

olive olives
NOUN **1** a small green or black fruit containing a stone.
ADJECTIVE OR NOUN **2** dark yellowish-green.

Olympic Games
Said "ol-**lim**-pik" PLURAL NOUN a set of sporting contests held in a different city every four years.

omelette omelettes
Said "**om**-lit" NOUN a dish made by beating eggs together and cooking them in a flat pan.

omen omens
NOUN something that is thought to be a sign of what will happen in the future. *Red sky at night is an omen for good weather in the morning.*

Synonyms: portent, sign

ominous
ADJECTIVE An ominous event or sign suggests that something unpleasant is going to happen.
ominously ADVERB

Synonyms: sinister, threatening

omission omissions
NOUN **1** something that has not been included or done. *There are some striking omissions in this piece of homework.*
2 the act of not including or not doing something. *The apostrophe in "I'm" indicates the omission of the letter "a".*

omit omits omitting omitted
VERB **1** to leave out, to exclude.
2 FORMAL If you omit to do something, you do not do it.

omni-
PREFIX all.
[Latin *omnis* meaning all]

omnibus omnibuses
NOUN **1** a book containing a collection of stories or articles by the same author.
ADJECTIVE **2** The omnibus edition of a radio or television programme is a broadcast of several episodes together.
3 OLD-FASHIONED the original name for a bus.

omnivore omnivores
NOUN an animal that eats all types of food including meat and plants.
omnivorous ADJECTIVE

on
PREPOSITION **1** touching or attached to something. *The woman was sitting on the sofa.*
2 If you are on a bus, plane or train, you are inside it.
3 If something happens on a particular day, that is when it happens.
4 If something is done on a particular machine or instrument, it is done using that machine or instrument.
5 A book or talk on a particular subject is about that subject.
ADVERB **6** If you have a piece of clothing on, you are wearing it.
ADJECTIVE **7** If a machine or switch is on, it is working.
8 If an event is on, it is happening or taking place. *The race is definitely on.*

once
ADVERB **1** happening one time only.
2 If something was once true, it was true in the past, but is no longer true.
CONJUNCTION **3** If something happens once another thing has happened, it happens immediately afterwards. *The team must go back to the hotel once the game is over.*
PHRASE **4** If you do something **at once**, you do it immediately.
5 If several things happen **at once**, they all happen at the same time.

one ones
1 the number 1.
PRONOUN **2** one refers to a particular thing or person. *May I have a smaller one?*
3 people in general. *One never knows what the future may bring.*
ADJECTIVE **4** If you refer to the one person or thing, you mean only that person or thing. *The deputy president was the one man who could save the country.*

oneself
PRONOUN Oneself is used when you are talking about people in general, or as an alternative to myself. *One could hardly hear oneself talk.*

In English "off" and "of" hardly ever go together.

A B C D E F G H I J K L M N O P Q R S T U V W X Y Z

one-way
ADJECTIVE **1** One-way streets are streets along which vehicles can drive in only one direction.
2 A one-way ticket is a single ticket which allows you to travel to a place, but not back again.

onion onions
NOUN a small, round vegetable with a very strong taste.

online
ADJECTIVE OR ADVERB to do with being controlled by or connected to a central computer. *Is the computer online yet?*

Antonym: offline

onlooker onlookers
NOUN someone who is watching something happen.

only
ADVERB **1** You use "only" to indicate the one thing or person involved. *Of the group, only Tony was able to continue.*
2 You use "only" to introduce a condition which must happen before something else can happen. *The workers will be paid only if the produce is sold.*
3 You use "only" to emphasize that something is unimportant or small. *Dilip is only a little boy.*
4 You can use "only" to introduce something which happens immediately after something else. *She started to turn left, only to change her mind at the last minute.*
ADJECTIVE **5** single, solitary. *It was their only hit record.*
6 An only child has no brothers or sisters.
CONJUNCTION **7** but or except. *He was like you, only with blond hair.*
PHRASE **8** **Only too** means extremely. *I would be only too happy to swap places.*

onomatopoeia
Said "on-o-mat-o-**pee**-a" NOUN the use of words which sound like the thing that they represent, such as "hiss", "buzz", "smack".

onwards or **onward**
ADVERB **1** continuing to happen from a particular time. *From that moment onwards, he never spoke a word.*
2 travelling forwards. *The explorers trekked onwards to the Pole.*

ooze oozes oozing oozed
VERB to flow slowly. *The cold mud oozed over my bare feet.*

opaque
Said "oh-**pake**" ADJECTIVE If something is opaque, you cannot see through it.
opacity NOUN

open opens opening opened
VERB **1** to move a lid, door, etc. so that it is no longer closed.
2 to start business for the public. *The bank opens at nine o'clock.*
ADJECTIVE **3** not closed or fastened.
4 If you have an open mind, you are willing to consider new ideas or suggestions.
5 honest and frank. *The bankrupt shop-owner was quite open about his debts.*
6 available for the public to go in. *This restaurant is open on Sundays.*
7 an open area of sea or land is a large, empty area.
8 If a situation is still open, it is still being considered. *Even if the case remains open, we may never know the full facts.*
PHRASE **9** **In the open** means outside.
10 **In the open** also means not secret.

opener openers
NOUN a device for opening cans or bottles.

opening openings
ADJECTIVE **1** coming first. *It was the opening day of the cricket season.*
NOUN **2** the first part of a book, film, etc. *That would be a great opening for a novel.*
3 a hole or gap.
4 an opportunity.

Synonyms: (sense 3) aperture, gap, hole

openly
ADVERB If you do something openly, you do not hide what you are doing.

open-minded
ADJECTIVE willing to consider new ideas and suggestions.
open-mindedness NOUN

opera operas
NOUN a play in which the words are sung rather than spoken.

operate operates operating operated
VERB **1** to work, to function. *A healthy diet makes your body operate more effectively.*
2 to make a machine work.
3 When surgeons operate, they cut open a person's body to remove or repair a damaged part.

operation operations
NOUN **1** a complex, planned event: *a full-scale military operation.*
2 a form of medical treatment in which a surgeon cuts open a person's body to remove or repair a damaged part.
PHRASE **3** If something is **in operation**, it is working or being used.

operator operators
NOUN **1** someone who operates a machine.
2 someone who works at a telephone exchange or on a switchboard.

opinion opinions
NOUN a belief or view. *What's your opinion on nuclear power stations?*

Synonyms: belief, judgement, view

 ► Every time he opens his mouth he puts his foot in it. What does this mean? ►

opium
NOUN a drug made from the seeds of the poppy, used to relieve pain.

opponent opponents
NOUN someone who is against you in an argument or a contest.

opportunity opportunities
NOUN a chance to do something.

oppose opposes opposing opposed
VERB If you oppose something, you disagree with it and try to prevent it.
opposing ADJECTIVE **opposed** ADJECTIVE

opposite opposites
PREPOSITION OR ADVERB 1 If one thing is opposite another, it is facing it.
ADJECTIVE 2 If things are opposite, they are completely different. *Tall is opposite to short.*
NOUN 3 something which is as different as it is possible to get. *The two brothers are complete opposites.*

Synonyms: (sense 3) antithesis, contrary, reverse

opposition
NOUN 1 If there is opposition to an issue, people disagree with the issue.
2 In a game, the opposition is the person or team you are competing against.

oppress oppresses oppressing oppressed
VERB 1 To oppress people means to treat them cruelly or unfairly.
2 If something oppresses you, it makes you feel depressed and worried.
oppression NOUN **oppressor** NOUN

oppressive
ADJECTIVE 1 If the weather is oppressive, it is hot and humid.
2 An oppressive situation makes you feel depressed and worried.
3 An oppressive government treats people cruelly or unfairly.

opt opts opting opted
VERB 1 To opt for something is to choose it.
2 To opt out of something is to choose not to be involved in it.

optical
ADJECTIVE concerned with vision, light or images. *Mirages in the desert are an optical illusion.*
optic ADJECTIVE

optician opticians
NOUN someone who tests people's eyes and sells glasses and contact lenses.

optimist optimists
NOUN a person who tends to be positive and hopeful about life.
optimism NOUN

Antonym: pessimist

optimistic
ADJECTIVE Optimistic people tend to be positive and hopeful about life.
optimistically ADVERB

Antonym: pessimistic

option options
NOUN a choice between two or more things.

optional
ADJECTIVE If doing something is optional, you have a choice of whether to do it or not.

or
CONJUNCTION 1 used to link two different alternatives. *Moira didn't know whether to laugh or cry.*
2 used to introduce a warning. *Do what I say or I will shoot.*

oral orals
ADJECTIVE 1 spoken rather than written, verbal. *Oral history is recorded on tapes not written in books.*
2 related to the mouth: *oral hygiene.*
NOUN 3 an examination that is spoken rather than written.
orally ADVERB

orange oranges
NOUN 1 a round citrus fruit that is juicy and sweet.
ADJECTIVE 2 reddish-yellow.

orang-utan orang-utans; also spelt **orang-utang**
NOUN a large ape with reddish-brown hair from the forests of Borneo and Sumatra. [from Malay *orang* meaning man + *hutan* meaning forest]

orator orators
NOUN someone who is good at making speeches.

orbit orbits
NOUN the curved path followed by an object going round a planet, the sun or another star.
orbit VERB **orbiter** NOUN

orchard orchards
NOUN a piece of land where fruit trees are grown.

orchestra orchestras
Said "**or**-kess-tra" NOUN a large group of musicians who play together.
orchestral ADJECTIVE **orchestrate** VERB

orchid orchids
NOUN Orchids are a variety of plants with beautiful and unusual flowers.

ordeal ordeals
NOUN a difficult and extremely unpleasant experience.

Synonyms: hardship, torture, tribulation

A B C D E F G H I J K L M N O P Q R S T U V W X Y Z

order orders ordering ordered
NOUN **1** a command given by someone in authority.
2 a particular sequence or arrangement: *alphabetical order; numerical order; chronological order.*
3 a situation in which everything is in the correct place or done at the correct time. *Rosie checked that everything was in order.*
4 something that you ask to be brought or sent to you. *The waiter returned with their order.*
VERB **5** to tell someone firmly to do something.
6 to ask for something to be brought or sent to you.
PHRASE **7** If you do something **in order to** achieve a particular thing, you do it because you want to achieve that thing. *Naseem came to Britain in order to study.*
8 If something is **out of order**, it is not working.

orderly
ADJECTIVE well organized and arranged.

Synonyms: neat, methodical

ordinary
ADJECTIVE not special or different in any way.
ordinarily ADVERB

Synonyms: conventional, normal, usual

ore ores
NOUN rock or earth from which metal can be obtained.

organ organs
NOUN **1** Your organs are parts of your body that have a particular purpose. For example, your heart and lungs are organs.
2 a large musical keyboard instrument, often with large cylindrical pipes.

organic
ADJECTIVE **1** produced by or found in plants or animals: *decaying organic matter.*
2 Organic food is produced without the use of artificial fertilizers or pesticides.
organically ADVERB

organism organisms
NOUN any living animal, plant, or other living thing, such as bacteria or fungus.

organist organists
NOUN someone who plays the organ.

organization organizations; also spelt **organisation**
NOUN **1** any group or business with a shared purpose.
2 the act of planning and arranging an event, system, etc.
organizational ADJECTIVE

Synonyms: (sense 1) body, company, group

organize organizes organizing organized; also spelt **organise**
VERB **1** to plan and arrange an event, system, etc.
2 to arrange things in a sensible order.
organizer NOUN **organized** ADJECTIVE

oriental
ADJECTIVE relating to eastern or south-eastern Asia.

orienteering
NOUN a sport in which people run from one place to another in the countryside by the quickest route, using a map and compass to guide them.

origami
NOUN the Japanese art of paper folding.

origin origins
NOUN **1** the beginning or cause of something. *Rail travel had its origin in the tramways that brought coal out of the mines.*
2 You can refer to someone's family background as their origin or origins. *She was of Swedish origin.*
3 In mathematics, the origin of a graph is the point where the X axis and Y axis meet.

Synonyms: (sense 1) root, source

original originals
ADJECTIVE **1** existing at the beginning, rather than later: *the original owner of the cottage.*
2 imaginative and clever: *a stunningly original idea.*
NOUN **3** a work of art or a document that is the one that was first produced and not a copy. *The pictures on the walls were all originals.*
originally ADVERB **originality** NOUN

originate originates originating originated
VERB When something originates or you originate it, it begins to happen or exist.
originator NOUN

ornament ornaments
NOUN a small, attractive object which you display in your home.
ornament VERB **ornamental** ADJECTIVE
ornamentally ADVERB **ornamentation** NOUN

ornithology
NOUN the study of birds.
ornithologist NOUN

orphan orphans
NOUN a child whose parents are dead.
orphan VERB **orphaned** ADJECTIVE

orphanage orphanages
NOUN; OLD-FASHIONED a home for children who otherwise have no one to look after them, a children's home.

orthodox
ADJECTIVE **1** Orthodox beliefs or methods are the ones that most people have or use.
2 The Orthodox church is the main church in Greece and Russia.

 ► Think of an original way to say: the house was scary; she felt very cold.

ostrich ostriches
NOUN the largest bird in the world. Ostriches cannot fly.

other others
ADJECTIVE OR PRONOUN Other people or things are different people or things. *All the other children had gone home. One of the pictures is genuine, but the other is a copy.*

otherwise
ADVERB **1** You use "otherwise" to say a different situation would exist if a particular fact or occurrence was not the case. *You had to learn to swim pretty quickly, otherwise you would have sunk.*
2 "Otherwise" means apart from the thing mentioned. *Lee had written her name on the test paper, but otherwise had done nothing.*
3 in a different way. *The majority voted otherwise.*

otter otters
NOUN a small, furry mammal with a long tail. Otters swim well and eat fish.

ouch
INTERJECTION used to express sudden pain. *Ouch! You're standing on my toe.*

ought
Said "**awt**" VERB **1** If you say that someone ought to do something, you mean that they should do it. *You ought to see a dentist.*
2 If you say that something ought to be the case, you mean that you expect it to be the case. *It ought to be quite easy.*
✔ Do not use *did* and *had* with *ought*. *He ought not to come* is correct; *he didn't ought to come* is not correct.

ounce ounces
NOUN a unit of weight equal to one sixteenth of a pound or about 28·35 grams, abbreviated to "oz".

our
PRONOUN "Our" refers to something belonging and relating to the speaker or writer and one or more other people. *We recently sold our house.*

ours
PRONOUN "Ours" refers to something belonging or relating to the speaker or writer and one or more other people. *Frank is a friend of ours from Hampshire.*

ourselves
PRONOUN **1** us. *Let's cheer ourselves up.*
2 "Ourselves" can be used to emphasize "we". *They went to see the film last week, while we ourselves are going today.*

out
ADVERB **1** towards the outside of a place. *Two dogs rushed out of the house.*
ADVERB OR ADJECTIVE **2** not at home. *Ellie was out when I rang last night.*
3 no longer shining or burning. *All the lights went out.*
4 available to buy. *The video is out next week.*
ADJECTIVE **5** unacceptable or unfashionable. *My dear, pink is absolutely out this year.*
6 incorrect. *Ian's calculations were out by a few centimetres.*
PHRASE **7** If you do something **out of** a particular feeling, that feeling causes you to do it. *She went along out of curiosity.*
8 **Out of** means from: *old instruments made out of wood.*
9 If you are **out of** something, you no longer have any of it. *We're out of milk again.*
10 If you are **out of** the rain, sun or wind, you are sheltered from it.

Antonym: in

outback
NOUN the remote parts of Australia where very few people live.

Synonym: the bush

outboard motor outboard motors
NOUN a motor that can be fixed to the back of a small boat or cruiser.

outbreak outbreaks
NOUN If there is an outbreak of something unpleasant, such as a disease, it suddenly occurs.

outburst outbursts
NOUN a sudden, strong expression of an emotion, especially anger.

outcast outcasts
NOUN someone who is rejected by other people.

outcome outcomes
NOUN a result. *What was the outcome of the election?*

outcry outcries
NOUN If there is an outcry about something, a lot of people are angry about it.

outdated
ADJECTIVE no longer in fashion.

outdo outdoes outdoing outdid outdone
VERB To outdo someone else is to do better than them.

Synonyms: better, surpass, top

outdoor
ADJECTIVE happening or used outside. *Sailing and rock-climbing are outdoor activities.*

Antonym: indoor

outdoors
ADVERB outside. *In summer we often have a meal outdoors.*

Antonym: indoors

outer
ADJECTIVE The outer parts of something are the parts furthest from the centre.

Antonym: inner

A B C D E F G H I J K L M N O P Q R S T U V W X Y Z

outer space
NOUN everything beyond the earth's atmosphere.

outfit outfits
NOUN a set of clothes.

outgrow outgrows outgrowing outgrew outgrown
VERB **1** If you outgrow your clothes, you grow too big to wear them.
2 If you outgrow a way of behaving, you stop it because you have grown older and more mature.

outing outings
NOUN a trip made for pleasure.

outlandish
ADJECTIVE very unusual or odd. *Deirdre wore outlandish clothes.*

outlaw outlaws outlawing outlawed
NOUN **1** In the past, an outlaw was a criminal.
VERB **2** If something is outlawed, it is made illegal.

outlet outlets
NOUN **1** a hole or pipe through which water or air can flow away.
2 An outlet for your feelings or ideas is a way of expressing them.

outline outlines outlining outlined
NOUN **1** The outline of something is its overall shape.
2 a general explanation or description of something. *I don't want the details of your plan; just give me an outline.*
VERB **3** to explain something in a general way.

outlive outlives outliving outlived
VERB To outlive someone or something is to live longer than they do.

outlook
NOUN **1** your general attitude towards life. *Mick always had an optimistic outlook.*
2 the way something is likely to develop. *The weather outlook for Saturday is rather poor.*

outnumber outnumbers outnumbering outnumbered
VERB If there are more of one group than of another, the first group outnumbers the second.

outpatient outpatients
NOUN a patient who receives treatment at a hospital without staying overnight.

output outputs
NOUN **1** the amount of something produced by a person or organization: *the factory's daily output of products was enormous.*
2 the information that a computer produces.

Antonym: input

outrage outrages outraging outraged
VERB If something outrages you, it angers and shocks you.
outrage NOUN

outrageous
ADJECTIVE Outrageous behaviour is violent or uncontrolled, and likely to cause great offence to others.
outrageously ADVERB

outright
ADJECTIVE **1** complete and total: *an outright lie.*
ADVERB **2** in an open and direct way. *Have you asked Pete outright?*

outside
NOUN **1** the part of something which surrounds or encloses the rest of it: *the outside of the building.*
ADVERB, ADJECTIVE OR PREPOSITION **2** not inside. *Anwar stood outside and shouted. The house had an outside toilet. The houses were just outside the perimeter fence.*
3 not included in something. *The emergency phone number is only for use outside office hours.*
✔ Do not use *of* after *outside*. You should write *she was waiting outside the school* and not *outside of the school.*

Antonym: inside

outsider outsiders
NOUN **1** someone who does not belong to a particular group. *To outsiders, the little village was a sleepy, boring place.*
2 a competitor that people think will not win in a race.

outskirts
PLURAL NOUN the parts around the edge of a city or town.

outspoken
ADJECTIVE Outspoken people give their opinions openly, even if they shock other people.

outstanding
ADJECTIVE **1** extremely good.
2 Money that is outstanding is still owed. *I fully intend to repay the outstanding debt.*

outward
ADJECTIVE **1** moving towards the outside or away from something. *The outward journey was easier than the return.*
2 The outward features of someone are the ones they appear to have, rather than the ones they actually have. *The teacher had never showed any outward signs of stress, until one day she locked herself in the stock cupboard.*

outwardly
ADVERB by the outside appearance. *Outwardly they appeared confident, but inwardly they were terrified.*

outwards
ADVERB towards the outside.

outweigh outweighs outweighing outweighed
VERB If you say that the advantages of something outweigh its disadvantages, you mean that the advantages are more important than the disadvantages.

 ► What word would we normally use to describe a "retail outlet"?

outwit **outwits outwitting outwitted**
VERB to use your intelligence to beat someone in some way.

oval **ovals**
NOUN a rounded shape, similar to a circle but wider in one direction than the other.
oval ADJECTIVE

ovary **ovaries**
Said "**oh**-var-ree" **NOUN** A woman's ovaries are the two reproductive organs in her body that produce human eggs.
[from Latin *ovum* meaning egg]

ovation **ovations**
NOUN 1 a long burst of applause.
PHRASE 2 If someone gets a **standing ovation**, the audience stand up and applaud them.

oven **ovens**
NOUN the part of a cooker used for baking or roasting food.

over **overs**
PREPOSITION 1 directly above it or covering it: *the picture over the fireplace.*
2 more than. *It cost over a million dollars.*
3 "Over" indicates a topic which is causing concern. *A hotel guest was arguing over his bill.*
4 during. *I went to New Zealand over Christmas.*
ADVERB OR PREPOSITION 5 If you lean over, you bend your body in a particular direction.
ADVERB 6 "Over" is used to indicate a position. *Come over here.*
7 If something rolls or turns over, it is moved so the other side is facing upwards.
ADJECTIVE 8 completely finished. *Finally, in 1945, the war was over.*
NOUN 9 In cricket, an over is a unit of play, usually of six balls, bowled by a single bowler.

over-
PREFIX too much: *overprotective parents. I overate at the party.*

overall
ADJECTIVE OR ADVERB taking into account all the parts or aspects of something. *The overall quality of pupils' work was very good.*

overalls
PLURAL NOUN a single piece of clothing worn to protect your other clothes when you are working.

overboard
ADVERB 1 If you fall overboard, you fall over the side of a ship into the water.
PHRASE 2 INFORMAL If you **go overboard**, you are excessively enthusiastic.

overcast
ADJECTIVE If the weather is overcast, the sky is covered by cloud.

overcoat **overcoats**
NOUN a thick, warm coat.

overcome **overcomes overcoming overcame overcome**
VERB 1 to deal with or control a difficulty or problem successfully. *My mother managed to overcome her fear of flying.*
2 If you are overcome by something, it makes you powerless to act. *The fireman was overcome by the heat.*

overcrowded
ADJECTIVE If a place is overcrowded, there are too many things or people in it.
overcrowding NOUN

overdo **overdoes overdoing overdid overdone**
VERB If you overdo something, you do it too much or in an exaggerated way.

overdose **overdoses**
NOUN a larger dose of a drug than is safe.

overdue
ADJECTIVE If someone or something is overdue, they are late. *Our next payment on the widescreen television is overdue.*

overflow **overflows overflowing overflowed**
VERB 1 If a liquid overflows, it spills over the edges of its container. If a river overflows, it flows over its banks.
NOUN 2 a hole or pipe through which liquid can flow out of a container when it gets too full.

overgrown
ADJECTIVE A place that is overgrown is covered with weeds because it has not been looked after.

overhang **overhangs overhanging overhung**
VERB If one thing overhangs another, it sticks out sideways above it: *Low branches overhang the footpaths.*

overhaul **overhauls overhauling overhauled**
VERB to examine something thoroughly and repair any faults in it.
overhaul NOUN

overhead **overheads**
ADVERB OR ADJECTIVE 1 above: *seagulls flying overhead.*
PLURAL NOUN 2 The overheads of a business are the regular costs of running it.

overhear **overhears overhearing overheard**
VERB to hear someone else's conversation by chance.

overjoyed
ADJECTIVE extremely pleased.

Synonyms: delighted, over the moon

overlap **overlaps overlapping overlapped**
VERB If one thing overlaps another, one part of it covers part of the other thing.

overleaf
ADVERB on the next page. *Write to us at the address shown overleaf.*

overload **overloads overloading overloaded**
VERB If you overload someone or something, you give them too much to do or to carry.
overload NOUN

overlook **overlooks overlooking overlooked**
VERB 1 If a building or window overlooks a place, you can see that place from it. *Our hotel room overlooked the swimming pool.*
2 to ignore or not notice something. *The head teacher is willing to overlook this foolish behaviour.*

overnight
ADJECTIVE OR ADVERB 1 during the night.
2 sudden or suddenly. *The singer was an overnight success.*

overpower **overpowers overpowering overpowered**
VERB 1 to bring someone under control in a struggle, because you prove to be stronger than they are; to overcome. *It took six policemen to overpower the drunken man.*
2 If a feeling overpowers you, it affects you very strongly.
overpowering ADJECTIVE

overrun **overruns overrunning overran overrun**
VERB 1 to occupy very quickly. *Mice will soon overrun the house when we move out.*
2 If an event overruns, it continues for longer than it was meant to.

overseas
ADJECTIVE OR ADVERB 1 happening or existing abroad.
ADJECTIVE 2 from abroad: *overseas students.*

oversight **oversights**
NOUN something which you forget to do or fail to notice.

oversleep **oversleeps oversleeping overslept**
VERB to sleep for longer than you meant to.

overtake **overtakes overtaking overtook overtaken**
VERB to move past another moving vehicle or person.

overthrow **overthrows overthrowing overthrew overthrown**
VERB to remove a ruler or government from power by force.

overtime
NOUN time that someone works in addition to their normal working hours.
overtime ADVERB OR ADJECTIVE

overture **overtures**
NOUN a piece of music played as an introduction to an opera or play.

overturn **overturns overturning overturned**
VERB 1 to turn something upside down or onto its side.
2 If someone gets a legal decision overturned, they use higher authority to change it.

overweight
ADJECTIVE too fat and therefore unhealthy.

overwhelm **overwhelms overwhelming overwhelmed**
VERB If you are overwhelmed by something, it affects you very strongly; to be overcome or overpowered.
overwhelming ADJECTIVE
overwhelmingly ADVERB

ovum **ova**
Said "**oh**-vum" **NOUN** a reproductive cell of a woman or other female animal. The ovum is fertilized by a male sperm to produce young. [a Latin word meaning egg]

owe **owes owing owed**
VERB 1 If you owe someone money, they have lent it to you and you have not yet paid it back.
2 If you owe someone gratitude or loyalty, you mean that they deserve it from you.
PHRASE 3 **Owing to** something means because of that thing. *I was late owing to a traffic jam.*

owl **owls**
NOUN a bird of prey that hunts at night. Owls have large eyes and short, hooked beaks.

own **owns owning owned**
ADJECTIVE OR PRONOUN 1 If something is your own, it belongs to you or is associated with you.
VERB 2 If you own something, it belongs to you.
PHRASE 3 **On your own** means alone.

owner **owners**
NOUN The owner of something is the person it belongs to.
ownership NOUN

ox **oxen**
NOUN Oxen are cattle which are used for carrying or pulling things.

oxygen
NOUN a colourless gas which makes up about 21% of the earth's atmosphere. Animals and plants need oxygen for respiration. Fire cannot burn without oxygen.

oyster **oysters**
NOUN a large, flat shellfish. Some oysters can be eaten and others produce pearls.

ozone
NOUN a colourless gas. Ozone is a form of oxygen that is poisonous and has a strong smell.

ozone layer
NOUN a layer of ozone, forming the part of the earth's atmosphere, that protects living things from the harmful radiation of the sun.

 ► Plurals such as oxen, children and brethren come from Anglo-Saxon.

Pp

pace paces pacing paced
NOUN **1** the speed at which something moves or happens.
2 the distance you move when you take one step.
VERB **3** to keep walking around because you are anxious or impatient.

Pacific
ADJECTIVE relating to the Pacific Ocean.

pacifist pacifists
NOUN someone who is opposed to all violence and war.
pacifism NOUN

pacify pacifies pacifying pacified
VERB to calm someone who is angry.
pacification NOUN **pacifier** NOUN

Synonyms: appease, calm, placate

pack packs packing packed
VERB **1** to put your belongings into a bag before leaving a place.
2 to crowd into a place.
NOUN **3** a bag or rucksack carried on your back.
4 a packet or collection of something: *a pack of cards; a pack of wolves.*

package packages
NOUN a small parcel.

package holiday package holidays
NOUN a holiday bought from a travel company which includes travel and accommodation.

packet packets
NOUN a small box or bag in which something is sold.

pact pacts
NOUN a formal agreement, a treaty.

pad pads padding padded
NOUN **1** a thick, soft piece of material.
2 a number of pieces of paper fixed together at one end.
VERB **3** If you pad something, you put a pad inside it or over it to protect or change its shape.
4 If you pad around, you walk softly.
padding NOUN **padded** ADJECTIVE

paddle paddles paddling paddled
NOUN **1** a short pole with a broad blade at one or both ends, used to move a canoe or small boat.
VERB **2** to move a canoe or boat using a paddle.
3 to walk in shallow water.
paddling NOUN

paddock paddocks
NOUN a small field where horses are kept.

paddy paddies
NOUN A paddy or paddy field is an area in which rice is grown.

padlock padlocks
NOUN a lock made up of a metal case with a U-shaped bar attached to it, which can be put through a metal loop and then closed. It is unlocked by turning a key in the lock on the case.
padlock VERB

pagan pagans
NOUN a person who has spiritual beliefs outside the main religions of the world, which often involve the worship of aspects of nature.
pagan ADJECTIVE **paganism** NOUN

page pages paging paged
NOUN **1** one side of one of the pieces of paper in a book or magazine.
2 a single sheet of paper.
3 In medieval times, a page was a young boy servant who was learning to be a knight.
VERB **4** to call someone by a small electronic device called a pager to give them a message.

pageant pageants
Said "**paj**-jent" NOUN a grand, colourful show or parade.
pageantry NOUN

pagoda pagodas
NOUN a tall, richly decorated temple in the Far East or India.

paid
past tense and past participle of **pay**.

pail pails
NOUN a bucket.

pain pains
NOUN **1** a feeling of discomfort in your body caused by an illness or injury.
2 unhappiness: *the pain of losing a loved one.*
[from Latin *poena* meaning punishment]

painful
ADJECTIVE causing physical or emotional pain.
painfully ADVERB

painkiller painkillers
NOUN a drug that reduces or stops pain.

painless
ADJECTIVE not causing pain.
painlessly ADVERB

painstaking
ADJECTIVE very careful and thorough: *years of painstaking research.*
painstakingly ADVERB

paint paints
NOUN a coloured liquid used to decorate buildings and make pictures.
paint VERB

painter painters
NOUN **1** an artist who produces paintings.
2 a person whose job it is to put paint on buildings, structures, etc.

A B C D E F G H I J K L M N O P Q R S T U V W X Y Z

painting paintings
NOUN a piece of art that someone has painted.

pair pairs pairing paired
NOUN **1** two things of the same type that are meant to be used together: *a pair of socks.*
2 You use "pair" when referring to certain objects which have two main matching parts: *a pair of scissors; a pair of trousers.*
VERB **3** If you pair or pair up two people or things, you put them together to make a pair.

> **USING "PAIR" IN A SENTENCE**
> The verb following **pair** can be singular or plural. If **pair** refers to a unit, the verb is singular:
> *A pair of good shoes is essential.*
> If **pair** refers to two individual things, the verb is plural:
> *The pair are said to dislike each other.*

pal pals
NOUN; INFORMAL a friend.

palace palaces
NOUN a large, grand house, especially the home of a king or queen.

palate palates
Said "**pall**-lat" NOUN **1** the top of the inside of your mouth.
2 a person's ability to judge good food and wine. *There were dishes to tempt every palate.*

pale paler palest
ADJECTIVE not strong or bright in colour.

palette palettes
NOUN a flat piece of wood on which an artist mixes colours.

palm palms
NOUN **1** a tropical tree with no branches and a crown of long leaves.
2 the flat inner surface of your hand.

pamper pampers pampering pampered
VERB to give someone too much kindness and comfort.

pamphlet pamphlets
NOUN a very thin book in paper covers giving information about something.

pan pans
NOUN a round metal container with a long handle, used for cooking.

pancake pancakes
NOUN a thin, flat piece of fried batter which can be served with savoury or sweet fillings.

panda pandas
NOUN a large black and white bear-like mammal found in China.

pandemonium
Said "pan-dim-**moan**-ee-um" NOUN a state of noisy confusion.

pane panes
NOUN a sheet of glass in a window or door.

panel panels
NOUN **1** a flat piece of wood or other material that is part of a larger object.
2 a small group of people who are chosen to do something: *a panel of judges.*
panelled ADJECTIVE

pang pangs
NOUN a sudden strong feeling: *the pangs of hunger.*

panic panics panicking panicked
VERB to become suddenly so afraid or anxious that you cannot act sensibly.
panic NOUN **panicky** ADJECTIVE

panorama panoramas
NOUN an extensive view over a wide area of land.
panoramic ADJECTIVE

pansy pansies
NOUN a small garden flower with large round petals.

pant pants panting panted
VERB to breathe quickly and loudly through your mouth.

panther panthers
NOUN a large wild mammal belonging to the cat family, especially the black leopard.

pantomime pantomimes
NOUN a funny musical play, usually based on a fairy story and performed at Christmas.

pantry pantries
NOUN a small room where food is kept.

pants
PLURAL NOUN an item of underwear for the lower body.
✔ In American English, *pants* are trousers.

paper papers
NOUN **1** a material that you write on or wrap things with.
2 a newspaper.
3 part of a written examination.
PLURAL NOUN **4** Papers are official documents, such as a passport or identity card. *The officer asked him for his papers.*
[from *papyrus*, the plant from which paper was made in ancient Egypt, Greece and Rome]

paperback paperbacks
NOUN OR ADJECTIVE a book with a thin cover.

Antonym: hardback

papier-mâché
Said "pap-yay **mash**-shay" NOUN a wet mixture of mashed paper and glue that can be moulded into such things as bowls and ornaments and left to harden.
[from French *papier-mâché* meaning literally chewed paper]

parable parables
NOUN a short story which makes a moral or religious point.

parachute parachutes
Said "**par**-rash-oot" NOUN a piece of fabric attached by lines to a person or package so that they can fall safely to the ground from an aircraft.
parachuting NOUN **parachutist** NOUN

parade parades parading paraded
NOUN 1 a line of people or vehicles moving together through a public place in order to celebrate something.
VERB 2 When people such as soldiers parade, they walk together in a group, usually in front of spectators.

paradise
NOUN According to some religions, paradise is a wonderful place where good people go when they die.

paraffin
NOUN a strong-smelling liquid which is used as a fuel. See **kerosene**.

paragraph paragraphs
NOUN a section of a piece of writing. Paragraphs begin on a new line and usually comprise several sentences on the same subject.

parallel parallels
NOUN 1 If something has a parallel, or if there are parallels between two or more things, they are similar to each other.
ADJECTIVE 2 If two lines or objects are parallel, they are the same distance apart along the whole of their length.

parallelogram parallelograms
NOUN a four-sided shape in which each side is parallel to the opposite side.

paralyse paralyses paralysing paralysed
VERB If someone is paralysed by an accident or illness, they have no feeling in part or all of their body and are unable to move.
paralysed ADJECTIVE

Synonyms: freeze, immobilize, numb

paralysis paralyses
NOUN a state in which someone or something is unable to move.

paramedic paramedics
NOUN an ambulance person specially trained in life-saving skills.

parapet parapets
NOUN a low wall along the edge of a bridge or roof.

paraphernalia
Said "par-raf-fan-**ale**-yah" NOUN all someone's belongings or equipment.

paraphrase paraphrases paraphrasing paraphrased
VERB If you paraphrase what someone has said or written, you express it in your own words.

parasite parasites
NOUN a small animal or plant that lives on or inside a larger animal or plant.
parasitic ADJECTIVE
[from Greek *parasitos* meaning someone who eats at someone else's table]

parasol parasols
NOUN an umbrella that provides shelter from the sun.

paratroops or **paratroopers**
PLURAL NOUN soldiers trained to be dropped by parachute.

parcel parcels
NOUN something wrapped up in paper.
parcel VERB

parched
ADJECTIVE something that is parched is dry and in need of water. *I'm parched, I need a drink. The sun-baked ground was parched.*

parchment
NOUN thick yellowish paper of very good quality.

pardon pardons pardoning pardoned
PHRASE 1 You say **pardon** or **I beg your pardon** when you want someone to repeat something they have said.
2 You say **I beg your pardon** as a way of apologizing for accidentally doing something wrong.
VERB 3 If someone who has been found guilty of a crime is pardoned, they are allowed to go free.

parent parents
NOUN Your parents are your father and mother.
parental ADJECTIVE

parenthesis parentheses
Said "par-**renth**-iss-iss" NOUN 1 a phrase or remark inside brackets, dashes or commas which is inserted into a piece of writing or speech. *Wilberforce was trying – not very successfully as it happened – to remove his finger from the plughole.*
2 Parentheses are a pair of brackets put round a word or phrase.
parenthetical ADJECTIVE

parish parishes
NOUN an area with its own church and often its own elected council.
parochial ADJECTIVE

park parks parking parked
NOUN 1 a public area with grass and trees.
VERB 2 When you park a vehicle, you drive it into a position where it can be left.
parked ADJECTIVE **parking** NOUN

parliament parliaments
NOUN the group of people who are elected or appointed to make or change the laws of a country.

a b c d e f g h i j k l m n o p q r s t u v w x y z

A B C D E F G H I J K L M N O P Q R S T U V W X Y Z

parody parodies parodying parodied
VERB If you parody a book, film, play or familiar situation, you create an amusing imitation of it.
parody NOUN

Synonyms: send-up, take-off

parole
NOUN When prisoners are given parole, they are released early on condition that they behave well.

parrot parrots
NOUN **1** a brightly coloured tropical bird with a curved beak.
PHRASE **2** If you learn or repeat something **parrot fashion**, you do it accurately without understanding it.

parsley
NOUN a herb with very small curly or flat leaves, used for flavouring in cooking.

parsnip parsnips
NOUN a long, pointed, cream-coloured root vegetable.

parson parsons
NOUN; OLD-FASHIONED a vicar or other clergyman.

part parts parting parted
NOUN **1** one of the pieces or aspects of something. *Part of the door handle came off in my hand. It's all part of living in the 21st century.*
2 one of the roles in a play or film.
3 Someone's part in something is their involvement in it.
VERB **4** If things that are next to each other part or if they are parted, they move away from each other. *The tow rope parted and the stricken ship drifted helplessly away.*
5 If people part, they leave each other.
PHRASE **6** If you **take part** in an activity, you do it together with other people.

Synonyms: (sense 1) bit, component, piece

partial
ADJECTIVE **1** not complete or whole. *He gave me only a partial explanation for his behaviour.*
2 If you are partial to something, you like it. *Dad is partial to chocolate cake.*
3 supporting one side in a dispute, rather than being fair and unbiased.
partially ADVERB

participate participates participating participated
VERB If you participate in an activity, you do it together with other people.
participant NOUN **participation** NOUN

Synonyms: be involved in, join in, take part

participle participles
NOUN In grammar, a participle is a form of a verb used with an auxiliary verb in compound tenses and often as an adjective.

IDENTIFYING A PARTICIPLE
English has two participles: the past participle and the present participle.
The **past participle** describes a completed action:
He has gone – "gone" is a past participle.
The **present participle** describes a continuing action:
She is winning – "winning" is a present participle.

particle particles
NOUN a very small piece of something.

particular particulars
ADJECTIVE **1** You use particular to emphasize that you are talking about one thing rather than other similar ones. *Could I have that particular cake, please?*
2 greater or more intense than usual. *Pay particular attention to the following advice.*
3 If you are particular about something, you set high standards and are not easily satisfied.
PHRASE **4** You use **in particular** to show that what you are saying applies especially to one thing or person. *The man wearing the bobble hat interested him in particular.*
PLURAL NOUN **5** Particulars are facts or details.
particularly ADVERB

parting partings
NOUN **1** an occasion when one person leaves another.
2 When someone combs two parts of their hair in opposite directions, the line dividing the parts is called a parting.

partition partitions partitioning partitioned
NOUN **1** a screen separating one part of a room or vehicle from another.
VERB **2** to divide something into separate parts.

partly
ADVERB to some extent but not completely.

partner partners
NOUN **1** the person someone is married to or living with.
2 the person you are doing something with, such as in a dance or a game.
3 In business, a partner is someone who owns the business jointly with another person.
partner VERB **partnership** NOUN

part of speech parts of speech
NOUN one of the chief classes of words that make up a language, such as "noun" or "verb".

PARTS OF SPEECH
Every word in the dictionary is classified into a group known as a **part of speech**. (In this dictionary, the part of speech appears directly after the main entry word.) The most common parts of speech are noun, verb, adjective, adverb, pronoun, preposition, interjection and conjunction. If you know what part of speech a word is, it helps you use it correctly and understand its function in sentences.

 ► Test whether a partner can spell these useful words: colonel, corporal, interest, different.

partridge partridges
NOUN a brown game bird with a round body and a short tail.

part-time
ADJECTIVE OR ADVERB involving work for only a part of each normal working day or week.

party parties
NOUN **1** a social event, often in order to celebrate something.
2 an organization whose members share the same political beliefs and campaign for election to government: *the Labour Party.*
3 a group who are doing something together: *a coach party.*

pass passes passing passed
VERB **1** to move past something. *I passed the flower shop.*
2 to move in a particular direction. *They passed through the gate.*
3 If you pass something to someone, you hand it to them or transfer it to them.
4 to spend time in a particular way. *The children passed the time playing in the street.*
5 When a period of time passes, it happens and ends. *Minutes passed before anyone spoke.*
6 to succeed in a test.
7 When a new law or proposal is passed, it is formally approved.
8 When judges pass sentence, they state what the criminal's punishment will be.
NOUN **9** in a ball game, the transfer of the ball to another player in the same team. *Owen's pass was intercepted by Bridges.*
10 an official document that allows you to go somewhere.
11 a narrow route between mountains.
pass out VERB to faint or collapse.
pass away or **pass on** VERB to die.

Synonyms: (sense 1) go past, overtake (sense 5) elapse, go by, lapse

passable
ADJECTIVE of an acceptable standard, but not very good. *The soup was passable, but no better.*
passably ADVERB

passage passages
NOUN **1** a long, narrow corridor or space that connects two places.
2 a section of a book or piece of music. *The minister read a passage from the Bible.*

passenger passengers
NOUN a person travelling in a vehicle, aircraft or ship.

passer-by passers-by
NOUN someone who happens to be walking past.

passion passions
NOUN a very strong feeling for something or somebody, usually of love. *Mary had a passion for gardening.*

Synonyms: emotion, fervour, intensity

passionate
ADJECTIVE A passionate person has very strong feelings about something.
passionately ADVERB

Synonyms: emotional, fervent, intense

passive
ADJECTIVE **1** remaining calm and showing no feeling even when provoked.
2 Someone who is passive does not take action but instead lets things happen to them.
NOUN **3** In grammar, the passive or passive voice is a verb form.
passively ADVERB

Synonyms: (senses 1 and 2) inactive, submissive

THE PASSIVE VOICE
When a sentence is in the **passive voice**, the subject of the verb is affected by the action rather than doing it:
The cat is being fed by Carol – "is being fed" is in the passive voice.
The passive can sometimes sound clumsy, and it is often more natural to use the active voice instead. However, the passive is very useful if you want to avoid giving blame, and essential if you don't know the name of the person doing the action:
A book in our library has been damaged.
Also look at the grammar box for **active voice**.

Passover
NOUN an eight-day Jewish festival held in spring.

passport passports
NOUN an official document which you need to show when you enter or leave most countries.

password passwords
NOUN a secret word known only to a few people, which allows you access to something such as private computer files or the Internet.

past
NOUN **1** The past is the period of time before the present.
ADJECTIVE **2** happening or existing before the present.
PREPOSITION OR ADVERB **3** You use "past" when you are telling the time. If you say "It's ten past eleven", you mean it is 10 minutes past 11 o'clock.
4 If you go past something, you move towards it and continue until you are on the other side. *Winnie ran past the car without seeing us.*

pasta
NOUN a dried mixture of flour, eggs and water, formed into different shapes.

paste pastes pasting pasted
NOUN **1** a soft, sticky, spreadable mixture. *I used paste to stick the picture in the book. I had crab paste on my sandwiches.*
VERB **2** to stick something with glue

Dialect words for a narrow, outside passage include: alley, entry, ginnel, snicket, giddle-gaddle.

pastel pastels
ADJECTIVE **1** Pastel colours are pale and soft.
NOUN **2** Pastels are small sticks of coloured crayon, used for drawing pictures.

pasteurized or **pasteurised**
*Said "***past***-yoor-ized"* ADJECTIVE Pasteurized milk has been treated in a special heating process to kill bacteria.
pasteurization NOUN
[named after French scientist Louis Pasteur (1822–95) who invented the process]

pastille pastilles
*Said "***pass***-till"* NOUN a small, soft, round sweet with a fruit flavour.

pastime pastimes
NOUN an activity you do for pleasure in your spare time, a hobby.

past participle past participles
NOUN In grammar, the past participle of a verb is the form, usually ending in "ed" or "en", that is used to make some past tenses and the passive. For example, "killed" in *she has killed the goldfish* and "broken" in *my leg was broken* are past participles.

pastry pastries
NOUN **1** a mixture of flour, fat and water used for making pies.
2 a small cake.

past tense past tenses
NOUN In grammar, the past tense refers to one of the tenses of a verb that you use mainly to refer to things that happened or existed before the time of writing or speaking.

PAST TENSES
You can talk about the past by using simple past tenses or compound tenses. The **simple past tense** is usually formed by taking the dictionary form of the verb and adding **-ed** or **-d**:
cook: I ***cooked*** *the lunch.*
like: My sister ***liked*** *it.*
You can also use **compound tenses** to talk about actions that have happened.
To show a continuous action, you use **was** or **were** with the main verb plus **-ing**:
I ***was cooking*** *the lunch.*
My sister ***was tasting*** *it.*
To show that the action has been completed, you use a form of the verb **to have** in front of the main verb plus **-ed**:
I ***have cooked*** *the lunch.*
My sister ***has tasted*** *it.*
To show that the action has been completed before something else took place, you use **had** in front of the main verb plus **-ed**:
I ***had cooked*** *the lunch.*
My sister ***had tasted*** *it.*
To add emphasis, you can use **did** in front of the basic form of the verb:
We ***did enjoy*** *our lunch!*

pasture pastures
NOUN an area of grass on which farm animals graze.

pasty pasties
*Rhymes with "***hasty***"* ADJECTIVE **1** looking pale and unhealthy.
*Said "***pass***-tee"* NOUN **2** a small pie containing meat, potato and other vegetables.

pat pats patting patted
VERB to tap something lightly with your hand held flat.

patch patches patching patched
NOUN **1** a piece of material used to cover a hole in something.
2 an area of a surface that is different in appearance from the rest.
VERB **3** to mend a hole by fixing a patch of something over it.

patchwork
ADJECTIVE Something that is a patchwork is made up of many parts: *a patchwork quilt.*

patchy patchier patchiest
ADJECTIVE unevenly spread or incomplete in parts. *There will be patchy fog on the hills.*

pâté
*Said "***pa***-tay"* NOUN a mixture of meat, fish or vegetables blended into a paste and spread on bread or toast.

patent patents patenting patented
NOUN **1** an official right given to an inventor to be the only person or company allowed to make or sell a new product.
VERB **2** to protect an invention by obtaining a patent for it.
ADJECTIVE **3** obvious. *What the official said was patent nonsense.*
patently ADVERB

paternal
ADJECTIVE relating to or involving a father.

path paths
NOUN **1** a strip of ground for people to walk on.
2 the area ahead of you as you move along. *A large group of reporters blocked the president's path.*

pathetic
ADJECTIVE **1** If something is pathetic, it makes you feel pity.
2 very poor or unsuccessful: *a pathetic attempt to be funny.*
pathetically ADVERB

Synonyms: (sense 1) heart-rending, moving, sad

patience
NOUN **1** the ability to stay calm in a difficult or irritating situation.
2 a card game for one player.

Synonyms: (sense 1) forbearance, tolerance

 ► Verbs have three main tenses: past (I ran), present (I run) and future (I shall run).

patient **patients**
ADJECTIVE **1** able to stay calm in a difficult or irritating situation.
NOUN **2** a person receiving treatment from a doctor.
patiently ADVERB

patio **patios**
NOUN a paved area close to a house.

patriot **patriots**
NOUN a person who feels proud of and loyal towards their own country.
patriotic ADJECTIVE **patriotism** NOUN

patrol **patrols patrolling patrolled**
VERB **1** When soldiers, police or guards patrol an area, they walk or drive around it to make sure there is no trouble.
NOUN **2** a group of people patrolling an area.

patron **patrons**
NOUN **1** a person who supports or gives money to a particular good or deserving cause.
2 The patrons of a hotel, pub or shop are the people who use it.
patronage NOUN

patronize **patronizes patronizing patronized**; also spelt **patronise**
VERB **1** If someone patronizes you, they treat you kindly, but in a way that suggests that you are less intelligent than them or inferior to them.
2 If you patronize a hotel, pub or shop, you are a customer there.
patronizing ADJECTIVE

patron saint **patron saints**
NOUN The patron saint of a group of people or place is a saint who is believed to look after them and is particularly identified with them. *St Christopher is the patron saint of travellers.*

patter **patters pattering pattered**
VERB to make quick, light, tapping sounds on a surface: *the light rain pattered on the pebbles.*
patter NOUN

pattern **patterns**
NOUN **1** a design repeated at regular intervals.
2 a diagram or shape used as a guide for making something: *a knitting pattern.*
3 a particular way in which something is usually or repeatedly done. *All three contests followed the same pattern.*
patterned ADJECTIVE

pause **pauses pausing paused**
VERB to stop speaking or doing something for a short time.
pause NOUN

pave **paves paving paved**
VERB **1** When an area of ground is paved, it is covered with flat blocks of stone or concrete.
PHRASE **2** If something **paves the way** for a change, it creates conditions which will help it to happen.

pavement **pavements**
NOUN a path with a hard surface at the side of a road.

pavilion **pavilions**
NOUN a building at a sports ground where players can wash and change.

paw **paws**
NOUN the foot of an animal such as a cat, dog or bear.

pawn **pawns pawning pawned**
NOUN **1** the smallest and least important piece in a chess game.
VERB **2** If you pawn something, you leave it with a pawnbroker in exchange for money.

pawnbroker **pawnbrokers**
NOUN a dealer who lends money in return for personal property left with them, which may be sold if the loan is not returned on time.

pay **pays paying paid**
VERB **1** to hand over money to someone because you are buying something or because you owe it to them.
2 If it pays to do something, it is to your advantage to do it. *It pays to do your homework early rather than put it off.*
3 to suffer because of a wrong you have done. *Rani will have to pay for her mistake!*
4 If you pay attention to something, you look and listen carefully.
5 If you pay a visit to someone, you visit them.
NOUN **6** your wages or salary.

Synonyms: (sense 1) give, reimburse, settle

payment **payments**
NOUN **1** the act of paying money.
2 a sum of money paid.

PC **PCs**
NOUN **1** abbreviation for police constable.
2 abbreviation for personal computer.

pea **peas**
NOUN small round green seeds that are eaten as a vegetable.

peace
NOUN **1** a state of undisturbed calm and quiet.
2 When a country is at peace, it is not at war.

Synonyms: (sense 1) stillness, tranquillity

peaceful
ADJECTIVE quiet and calm.
peacefully ADVERB

Synonyms: serene, tranquil

peach **peaches**
NOUN **1** a soft, round fruit with yellow flesh and a yellow and red skin.
ADJECTIVE **2** pale pinky-orange.

peacock **peacocks**
NOUN a large male bird with very long green and blue tail feathers, which it can spread out in a fan.

Can you write the main tenses of: to have, to do, to be, to think, to fly?

A B C D E F G H I J K L M N O P Q R S T U V W X Y Z

peak peaks peaking peaked
NOUN **1** the pointed top of a mountain.
2 The peak of an activity or process is the point at which it is strongest or most successful.
3 The peak of a cap is the stiff part which projects at the front to shade the eyes.
VERB **4** When something peaks, it reaches its highest value or its greatest level of success.
peaked ADJECTIVE

Synonyms: (sense 2) climax, culmination, high point

peal peals
NOUN A peal of bells is the musical sound made by bells ringing one after another.
peal VERB

peanut peanuts
NOUN **1** Peanuts are small nuts that grow under the ground.
PLURAL NOUN **2** INFORMAL If someone is paid peanuts, they get very little money indeed.

peanut butter
NOUN a sandwich spread made from peanuts.

pear pears
NOUN a juicy fruit with a clear white flesh.

pearl pearls
NOUN a hard, round, creamy-white object that grows inside the shell of an oyster and is used in jewellery.

peasant peasants
NOUN a person in a poor country who works on the land.

peat
NOUN a dark-brown decaying plant material found in cool, wet regions. Dried peat can be used as fuel.

pebble pebbles
NOUN a smooth, round stone.

peck pecks pecking pecked
VERB **1** If a bird pecks something, it bites at it quickly with its beak.
2 If you peck someone on the cheek, you give them a quick kiss.
peck NOUN

peckish
ADJECTIVE; INFORMAL hungry.

peculiar
ADJECTIVE strange and often unpleasant.
peculiarly ADVERB

pedal pedals pedalling pedalled
NOUN **1** The pedals on a bicycle are the two parts that you push with your feet in order to make the bicycle move.
2 a foot control; for example, in a car or on a sewing machine.
VERB **3** to propel a bicycle.

peddle peddles peddling peddled
VERB to sell something, especially by going round from house to house or from person to person.
peddler NOUN

pedestal pedestals
NOUN a base on which something stands, such as a statue or wash basin.

pedestrian pedestrians
NOUN someone who is walking.
pedestrian ADJECTIVE

pedigree pedigrees
ADJECTIVE **1** A pedigree animal is descended from a single breed and its ancestors are known and recorded.
NOUN **2** Someone's pedigree is their background or ancestry.
[from Old French *pe de grue*, the foot of the crane bird, because it looked like the spreading lines of a family tree]

pedlar pedlars
NOUN; OLD-FASHIONED a person who sells small simple household goods from door to door.

peek peeks peeking peeked
VERB to have a quick look at something.
peek NOUN

peel peels peeling peeled
NOUN **1** The peel of a fruit is its skin.
VERB **2** to remove the skin from fruit or vegetables.
3 If a layer of something is peeling, it is coming off from a surface.
peelings PLURAL NOUN

peep peeps peeping peeped
VERB **1** to have a quick look at something.
2 If something peeps out from behind something else, a small part of it becomes visible: *a handkerchief peeping out of his breast pocket.*
NOUN **3** a quick look.
4 If you have not heard a peep out of someone, they have not said anything or made any noise.

peer peers peering peered
VERB **1** If you peer at something, you look at it very hard, often because you have difficulty in seeing it properly.
NOUN **2** a member of the nobility.
3 Your peers are the people who are of the same age and social status as yourself.

peg pegs pegging pegged
NOUN **1** a small device which you use to fasten clothes to a washing line.
2 a hook on a wall where you can hang things.
VERB **3** If you peg washing out, you fasten it to a line with pegs.

pelican pelicans
NOUN a large water bird with a pouch below its beak in which it stores fish.

 ► Etymology. What links these words: pedal, pedestrian, expedition, pedestal, pedometer?

pellet pellets
NOUN a small ball of paper, lead or other material.

pelt pelts pelting pelted
VERB 1 to throw things hard. *The crowd pelted tomatoes at the politician.*
2 to run very fast.
NOUN 3 the skin and fur of an animal.

pelvis pelvises
NOUN the wide, curved group of bones at hip-level at the base of your spine.
pelvic ADJECTIVE

pen pens
NOUN 1 a instrument for writing with ink.
2 a small fenced area in which farm animals are kept for a short time.
[from Latin *penna* meaning feather; writing pens used to be made from feathers]

penalize penalizes penalizing penalized; also spelt **penalise**
VERB If you are penalized, you are made to suffer some disadvantage as a punishment for something. *Beattie was penalized for cheating.*

penalty penalties
NOUN 1 a punishment for breaking a rule or law. *The fixed penalty for bad parking is £30.*
2 a free shot at goal in team games such as football and hockey, to be taken without interference from the opposing side, given by the referee to make up for the opposing side having played unfairly.

pence
a plural form of **penny**.

pencil pencils
NOUN a long, thin stick of wood with graphite, a soft dark form of carbon, in the centre, used for drawing or writing.

pendant pendants
NOUN a piece of jewellery attached to a chain and worn round the neck.

pendulum pendulums
NOUN a rod with a weight at one end which swings regularly from side to side to control certain types of large clock.

penetrate penetrates penetrating penetrated
VERB To penetrate an area that is difficult to get into is to succeed in getting into it.
penetration NOUN **penetrating** ADJECTIVE

pen friend pen friends
NOUN someone living in a different place or country whom you write to regularly, although you may never have met each other.

penguin penguins
NOUN A penguin is a black and white flightless bird with webbed feet and small wings like flippers, found mainly in the Antarctic.

penicillin
NOUN a powerful antibiotic obtained from fungus and used to treat infections.

peninsula peninsulas
NOUN an area of land almost surrounded by water.
[from Latin *paene* meaning almost + *insula* meaning island]

penis penises
NOUN A man's penis is the part of his body that he uses when urinating and having sexual intercourse.

penknife penknives
NOUN a small knife with a blade that folds back into the handle.

pennant pennants
NOUN a small triangular flag.

penniless
ADJECTIVE having no money.
pennilessness NOUN

penny pennies or pence
NOUN a unit of currency, in Britain worth one-hundredth of a pound.

pension pensions
NOUN a regular sum of money paid to a retired, disabled or widowed person.
pensionable ADJECTIVE

pensioner pensioners
NOUN a retired person who receives a pension from the state.

pensive
ADJECTIVE deep in thought.
pensively ADVERB

Synonyms: dreamy, meditative, thoughtful

pentagon pentagons
NOUN a shape with five straight sides.
pentagonal ADJECTIVE

pentathlon pentathlons
Said "pen-**tath**-lon" NOUN a contest in which athletes compete in five different events.

people peoples peopling peopled
PLURAL NOUN 1 a general word for men, women and children.
2 all the men, women and children of a particular country or race.
VERB 3 If an area is peopled by a particular group, that group of people lives there.

Synonyms: (sense 1) humanity, mankind, persons
(sense 2) nation, population, race

pepper peppers
NOUN 1 a hot-tasting powdered spice used for flavouring in cooking.
2 a hollow green, red or yellow vegetable, with sweet-flavoured flesh.
peppery ADJECTIVE

a b c d e f g h i j k l m n o p q r s t u v w x y z

Pen comes from Latin *penna* meaning a feather. Early quill pens were cut from feathers.

A B C D E F G H I J K L M N O P Q R S T U V W X Y Z

peppermint peppermints
NOUN a plant with a strong taste, used for making sweets and in medicine.

per
PREPOSITION each; "per" is used when expressing rates and ratios. *The class meets two evenings per week.*

perceive perceives perceiving perceived
VERB to notice or realize something, especially something that isn't obvious.

Synonyms: notice, see, spot

per cent
PHRASE You use "per cent" (%) to talk about amounts as a proportion of a hundred. For example, 10 per cent (10%) is equal to 10 hundredths.
[from Latin *per* meaning each + *centum* meaning hundred]

percentage percentages
NOUN a fraction of an amount expressed as a number of hundredths. *A high percentage of students passed the exam.*

perceptible
ADJECTIVE able to be seen, noticeable. *The actress's slight nod was perceptible even to those sitting right at the back.*

perception perceptions
NOUN Perception is the recognition, noticing or understanding of things using the senses, especially the sense of sight.

perceptive
ADJECTIVE Someone who is perceptive realizes or notices things that are not obvious.
perceptively ADVERB

Synonyms: astute, observant, sharp

perch perches perching perched
VERB 1 When a bird perches on something, it stands on it.
2 If you perch on something, you sit on the edge of it.
NOUN 3 a short rod for a bird to stand on.
4 an edible freshwater fish.

percolator percolators
NOUN a special pot for making and serving coffee.
✔ Percolator is often wrongly pronounced with a *u* sound in the middle.

percussion
NOUN OR ADJECTIVE Percussion instruments are musical instruments that you hit to produce sounds, such as the drums and the xylophone.
percussionist NOUN

perennial perennials
ADJECTIVE 1 continually occurring or never ending. *The damp cellar was a perennial problem.*
NOUN 2 a plant that lives for several years.

perfect perfects perfecting perfected
Said "**per**-fect" ADJECTIVE 1 as good as it can possibly be, faultless.
Said "per-**fect**" VERB 2 to make something as good as it can possibly be.
perfectly ADVERB **perfection** NOUN

perfectionist perfectionists
NOUN someone who always tries to do everything perfectly.

perforated
ADJECTIVE Something that is perforated has had small holes made in it, such as a sheet of stamps or a tea bag.
perforation NOUN

perform performs performing performed
VERB 1 to dance, act, sing or play a piece of music in front of an audience.
2 to carry out a task or action, to do.
performer NOUN

performance performances
NOUN 1 an entertainment provided for an audience.
2 the doing of a task or action.
3 Someone's or something's performance is how successful they are. *The car's performance on hills was disappointing.*

perfume perfumes
NOUN 1 a pleasant-smelling liquid which people put on their bodies.
2 The perfume of something is its pleasant smell.
perfume VERB **perfumed** ADJECTIVE

perhaps
ADVERB maybe, possibly.

peril perils
NOUN; FORMAL great danger.
perilous ADJECTIVE **perilously** ADVERB

perimeter perimeters
Said "per-**im**-itt-er" NOUN the whole of the outer edge of an area or shape.

period periods
NOUN 1 a particular length of time. *The Tudor period was a time of invention and discovery.*
2 When a woman has a period, she bleeds from her womb, usually once a month.
3 In American English, a period is a full stop.
period ADJECTIVE

periodical periodicals
NOUN a magazine.

periscope periscopes
NOUN a tube with mirrors which is used in a submarine to see above the surface of the water.

perish perishes perishing perished
VERB 1 FORMAL to be killed or destroyed.
2 If fruit or fabric perishes, it rots.
perishable ADJECTIVE

 ► A homonym has different meanings, but the same spelling and pronunciation. Find one on this page.

perk **perks perking perked**
NOUN 1 an extra, such as a company car or health insurance, offered by an employer in addition to a salary.
VERB 2 INFORMAL When someone perks up, they become more cheerful.
perky ADJECTIVE

perm **perms**
NOUN a hairstyle created by the use of chemicals with heat and rollers to keep the hair in the same shape for a long time. Perm is short for permanent wave.
perm VERB

permanent
ADJECTIVE lasting forever or present all the time.
permanently ADVERB **permanence** NOUN

permissible
ADJECTIVE allowed by the rules.

Synonyms: allowable, permitted

permission
NOUN If you have permission to do something, you are allowed to do it.

Synonyms: authorization, go-ahead

permissive
ADJECTIVE allowing things which some people disapprove of. *The permissive parents allowed their five-year-old to stay up until midnight if she wanted to.*
permissiveness NOUN

permit **permits permitting permitted**
Said "per-**mit**" **VERB 1** to allow or make possible.
Said "**per**-mit" **NOUN 2** an official document which says that you are allowed to do something.

Synonyms: (sense 1) allow, give permission, let

perpendicular
ADJECTIVE upright or at right angles to a horizontal line.

perpetual
ADJECTIVE never ending.
perpetually ADVERB

perplexed
ADJECTIVE If you are perplexed, you are puzzled and do not know what to do.
perplexity NOUN

persecute **persecutes persecuting persecuted**
VERB to treat someone with continual cruelty and unfairness.
persecution NOUN **persecutor** NOUN

Synonyms: pick on, victimize

persevere **perseveres persevering persevered**
VERB If you persevere with something difficult, you keep trying to do it and do not give up.
perseverance NOUN **persevering** ADJECTIVE

Synonyms: carry on, continue, keep going

persist **persists persisting persisted**
VERB 1 If you persist in doing something, you continue in spite of opposition or difficulty.
2 If something undesirable persists, it continues to exist. *Her cough persisted, so she went to the doctor's.*
persistence NOUN **persistent** ADJECTIVE
persistently ADVERB

person **persons** or **people**
NOUN 1 a man, woman or child.
2 In grammar, the first person is the speaker (I or we), the second person is the person being spoken to (you) and the third person is anyone else being referred to (he, she, it, they).
3 If you do something in person, you do it yourself, rather than by some other means.
✔ The usual plural of *person* is *people. Persons* is only used in formal or official English.

personal
ADJECTIVE 1 belonging or relating to a particular person.
2 Personal matters relate to your private life.

Synonyms: (sense 1) individual, own, private

personality **personalities**
NOUN 1 Your personality is your character and nature.
2 a famous person. *The chef is a television personality.*

personally
ADJECTIVE 1 relating to or involving an individual person. *I delivered the note personally.*
2 If you take what someone says personally, you are upset because you think they are criticizing you.

personification
NOUN In literature, personification occurs where writers give human characteristics and powers to non-human subjects. Examples include "the trees whispered in the wind" and "the sun crept shyly below the horizon".

personnel
Said "per-son-**nell**" **PLURAL NOUN** the people who work for an organization.

perspective **perspectives**
NOUN 1 A particular perspective is one way of thinking about something.
2 In drawings and paintings, perspective is the technique of depicting three-dimensional objects on a flat surface. Amongst other things, this involves making "distant" things smaller.

a b c d e f g h i j k l m n o p q r s t u v w x y z

perspire **perspires perspiring perspired**
VERB to sweat.
perspiration NOUN

persuade **persuades persuading persuaded**
VERB If someone persuades you to do something or persuades you that something is true, they cause you to do it or believe it by giving you good reasons for it.
persuasive ADJECTIVE

Synonyms: convince, talk into

persuasion
NOUN the act of persuading someone.

perverse
ADJECTIVE Someone who is perverse deliberately does things that are unreasonable or harmful.
perversely ADVERB **perversity** NOUN

pervert **perverts perverting perverted**
Said "**per**-vert" NOUN **1** a person whose sexual behaviour is disgusting or harmful.
Said "per-**vert**" VERB **2** FORMAL To pervert something is to interfere with it so that it is no longer what it should be: *a conspiracy to pervert the course of justice.*
perversion NOUN

pessimist **pessimists**
NOUN a pessimist is someone who always expects the worst.
pessimism NOUN

Antonym: optimist

pessimistic
ADJECTIVE expecting the worst.
pessimistically ADVERB

Antonym: optimistic

pest **pests**
NOUN **1** an insect or other small animal which damages plants or food supplies.
2 someone who keeps bothering or annoying you.
[from Latin *pestis* meaning plague]

pester **pesters pestering pestered**
VERB to keep bothering someone or asking them to do something.

Synonyms: annoy, badger, hassle

pesticide **pesticides**
NOUN Pesticides are chemicals sprayed onto plants to kill insects and grubs.

pet **pets**
NOUN **1** a tame animal that you keep at home.
2 someone who is treated as a favourite: *teacher's pet.*
ADJECTIVE **3** Someone's pet theory or pet project is something that they particularly support or feel strongly about.

petal **petals**
NOUN The petals of a flower are the coloured outer parts. The petals of some flowers are scented.

petition **petitions**
NOUN **1** a document demanding official action which is signed by a lot of people.
2 a formal request to a court for legal action to be taken.
petition VERB

petrified
ADJECTIVE very frightened.
petrify VERB
[from Greek *petra* meaning stone; "petrify" literally means to turn to stone]

petrol
NOUN a liquid which is used as a fuel for motor vehicles.

petroleum
NOUN another word for **petrol**.

petticoat **petticoats**
NOUN a piece of women's underwear like a very thin skirt.

petty **pettier pettiest**
ADJECTIVE **1** small and unimportant. *Deciding what to wear is a petty problem.*
2 Petty behaviour consists of doing small things which are selfish and unkind.

pew **pews**
NOUN a long wooden seat with a back, which people sit on in church.

pH
NOUN The pH value of a solution is a measurement of how acid or alkaline it is. pH is an abbreviation for potential for hydrogen.

phantom **phantoms**
NOUN **1** a ghost.
ADJECTIVE **2** imagined or unreal: *a phantom outline on the photograph.*

pharaoh **pharaohs**
Said "**fair**-oh" NOUN The pharaohs were the royal rulers of Ancient Egypt.

pharmacy **pharmacies**
NOUN a shop where medicines are sold, a chemist's.

phase **phases**
NOUN a particular stage in the development of something.

pheasant **pheasants**
NOUN a large, long-tailed game bird.

phenomenal
Said "fin-**nom**-in-nal" ADJECTIVE extraordinarily great or good.
phenomenally ADVERB

phenomenon **phenomena**
NOUN **1** something that happens or exists, especially something remarkable or something being considered in a scientific way. *Lightning is an extraordinary natural phenomenon.*
2 If you say that someone is a phenomenon, you mean that they are remarkable in some way. *The sports star is a goal-scoring phenomenon.*

A B C D E F G H I J K L M N O P Q R S T U V W X Y Z

► Words with "ph", making an "f" sound, come from the language of Ancient Greece.

philosophical
ADJECTIVE Someone who is philosophical does not get upset when disappointing things happen.
philosophically ADVERB

philosophy **philosophies**
NOUN **1** the study or creation of ideas about existence, knowledge or beliefs.
2 a set of beliefs that someone has.
philosopher NOUN

phobia **phobias**
NOUN a great fear or hatred of something.

phoenix **phoenixes**
Said "**fee**-nix" NOUN a mythical bird which is said to burn itself to ashes every five hundred years and rise from the fire again.

phone **phones**
NOUN a telephone.
phone VERB

phoneme **phonemes**
NOUN any of the units of sound in a language that enable us to distinguish one word from another. For example, the letters "p" and "b" are phonemes in the words "pet" and "bet".

phoney **phonier phoniest; phoneys**; also spelt **phony**
ADJECTIVE **1** INFORMAL false and intended to deceive.
NOUN **2** Someone who is a phoney pretends to have qualities they do not possess.

phonics
NOUN one element of teaching reading: the training of pupils to associate printed letters with the sounds they make.

photo **photos**
NOUN a photograph.

photo-
PREFIX related to light.

photocopier **photocopiers**
NOUN a machine which makes instant copies of documents by photographing them.

photocopy **photocopies photocopying photocopied**
VERB to make a copy of a document using an electronic and photographic copying machine.
photocopy NOUN

photograph **photographs photographing photographed**
NOUN **1** a still picture that is made using a camera.
VERB **2** to take a picture of someone or something using a camera.
photographer NOUN **photographic** ADJECTIVE

photography
NOUN the practice and art of taking photographs.

photosynthesis
NOUN the process by which green plants produce their own food using carbon dioxide from the air in the presence of sunlight and chlorophyll.

phrase **phrases phrasing phrased**
NOUN **1** a group of words shorter than a clause.
VERB **2** If you phrase something in a particular way, you say or write it in that way.
[from Greek *phrasis* meaning speech]

WHAT IS A PHRASE?
A **phrase** is a group of words which combine together but which cannot stand on their own to make complete sense.
Some phrases act as nouns:
We drank a cup of tea.
My sister's friend *is from Canada.*
Some phrases act as verbs:
She was always complaining *about the weather.*
I used to play *the piano.*
Some phrases act as adjectives:
The food here is of the highest quality.
He asked for an up-to-the-minute *report.*
Some phrases act as adverbs:
He disappeared in the blink of an eye.
They played with great gusto.
Some phrases are accepted as substitutes for sentences:
Happy birthday!
Good morning.
All right?

physical
ADJECTIVE **1** concerning the body rather than the mind.
2 Physical things are real things that can be touched or seen.
physically ADVERB

Antonym: (sense 1) mental

physical education
NOUN all the sport and physical activity that you do as part of the school curriculum.

physician **physicians**
NOUN a doctor.

physics
NOUN the scientific study of forces such as heat, light, sound and electricity.
physicist NOUN

pi
Rhymes with "**fly**" NOUN a number, approximately 3·142, and symbolized by the Greek letter π. The circumference of a circle is 3·142 times greater than its diameter. The area of a circle is 3·142 times greater than the radius squared.

pianist **pianists**
NOUN someone who plays the piano.

a b c d e f g h i j k l m n o p q r s t u v w x y z

Find out what these "phobias" are fears of: claustrophobia, cynophobia, xenophobia.

A B C D E F G H I J K L M N O P Q R S T U V W X Y Z

piano pianos
NOUN a large musical instrument with a row of black and white keys, which you strike with your fingers.
[originally called *pianoforte*, from Italian *piano* meaning soft + *forte* meaning loud]

piccolo piccolos
NOUN a high-pitched wind instrument like a small flute.

pick picks picking picked
VERB **1** to choose something.
2 to remove a flower, fruit, etc. with your fingers.
3 If someone picks a lock, they open it with wire instead of a key.
pick on VERB to criticize someone unfairly or treat them unkindly.
pick up VERB to collect someone or something from a place where they are waiting.

pickaxe pickaxes
NOUN a long-handled tool with a curved, pointed iron bar, used for breaking up hard ground.

picket pickets picketing picketed
VERB When a group of people picket a place of work, they stand outside to persuade other workers to join a strike.
picket NOUN

pickle pickles pickling pickled
NOUN **1** vegetables or fruit preserved in vinegar or salt water.
2 If you are **in a pickle**, you are in a difficult situation.
VERB **3** to preserve food in vinegar or salt water.

pickpocket pickpockets
NOUN a thief who steals from people's pockets or handbags.

picnic picnics
NOUN a meal eaten out of doors, usually elsewhere than at home.
picnic VERB **picnicker** NOUN

pictogram pictograms
NOUN a chart similar to a graph, but in which symbols of different sizes are used instead of lines, bars, etc. to illustrate different values.

pictorial
ADJECTIVE relating to or using pictures.
pictorially ADVERB

picture pictures picturing pictured
NOUN **1** any visual image, real or imagined. *She drew me a picture. I had a picture of his new bike in my mind.*
PLURAL NOUN **2** Going to the pictures means going to the cinema.
VERB **3** to show someone or something in a picture. *The team are pictured on the back page.*
4 to imagine something clearly. *I can picture now the town where I grew up.*

picturesque
Said "pik-chur-**esk**" ADJECTIVE A place that is picturesque is very attractive and unspoiled.

pie pies
NOUN a dish of meat, vegetables or fruit covered with pastry.

piece pieces piecing pieced
NOUN **1** a portion or part of something.
2 an individual thing of a particular kind: *a sturdy piece of furniture.*
3 something that has been written or created, such as a newspaper article, work of art or musical composition. *They played the piece very well.*
4 a coin: *a 50 pence piece.*
piece together VERB If you piece together a number of things, you gradually put them together to make something complete.

pie chart pie charts
NOUN a circular diagram to show how the whole of something is divided up. The size of the sectors of the circle matches the proportions of the quantities represented.

pier piers
NOUN a large platform which sticks out into the sea and which people can walk along.

pierce pierces piercing pierced
VERB If a sharp object pierces something, it goes through it, making a hole.

Synonyms: penetrate, puncture

piercing
ADJECTIVE **1** A piercing sound is high-pitched and unpleasant; shrill.
2 Someone with piercing eyes seems to look at you very intensely.

pig pigs
NOUN a mammal, with pink or black skin and a curly tail, that is kept as a farm animal for its meat: pork, ham or bacon.

pigeon pigeons
NOUN a largish bird with grey feathers, often seen in towns.

piggyback piggybacks
NOUN If you give someone a piggyback, you carry them on your back, supporting them under their knees.

pig-headed
ADJECTIVE Pig-headed people are stubborn and refuse to change their mind.
pig-headedness NOUN

piglet piglets
NOUN a young pig.

pigment pigments
NOUN a substance that gives something a particular colour.
pigmentation NOUN

 ► Joke. How do you spell "blind pig"? Answer: blnd pg (because it's got no eyes).

pigsty pigsties
NOUN 1 a hut with a small enclosed area where pigs are kept.
2 INFORMAL a very untidy and dirty room, house, etc.

pigtail pigtails
NOUN a length of plaited hair.

pike pikes
NOUN 1 a large, freshwater fish with strong teeth, found in northern countries.
2 a medieval weapon consisting of a pointed metal blade attached to a long pole.

pilchard pilchards
NOUN a small sea fish.

pile piles piling piled
NOUN 1 a quantity of things lying on top of one another.
VERB 2 to put things one on top of another in a heap.

pilfer pilfers pilfering pilfered
VERB to steal little things in small quantities over a period of time.

pilgrim pilgrims
NOUN a person who travels to a holy place for religious reasons.

pilgrimage pilgrimages
NOUN a journey to a shrine or other sacred place.

pill pills
NOUN 1 a small, round tablet of medicine that you swallow.
2 The pill is a type of contraceptive drug that women take regularly to prevent pregnancy. [from Latin *pilula* meaning little ball]

pillar pillars
NOUN a tall, narrow, solid structure, usually supporting part of a building.

pillar box pillar boxes
NOUN A pillar box is a free-standing box in which to post mail.

pillow pillows
NOUN a cushion which you rest your head on when you are in bed.

pillowcase pillowcases
NOUN a cover for a pillow which can be removed and washed.

pilot pilots
NOUN a person who is trained to fly an aircraft or to guide ships into harbour.
pilot VERB

pimple pimples
NOUN a small spot on the skin.
pimply ADJECTIVE

pin pins
NOUN a thin, pointed piece of metal that is used to fasten things together.
pin VERB

pinafore pinafores
NOUN 1 an apron.
2 a dress with no sleeves, worn over a blouse.

pincers
PLURAL NOUN 1 a tool used for gripping and pulling things.
2 The pincers of a crab or lobster are its front claws.

pinch pinches pinching pinched
VERB 1 to squeeze something between your thumb and first finger.
2 INFORMAL to steal something.
NOUN 3 A pinch of something is the amount that you can hold between your thumb and first finger.

pine pines pining pined
NOUN 1 The pine is an evergreen tree with very thin leaves.
VERB 2 If you pine for something, you are sad because you cannot have it.

pineapple pineapples
NOUN a large, oval fruit with sweet, yellow flesh and thick, brown skin.

ping-pong
NOUN; INFORMAL another name for the game of table tennis.

pink pinker pinkest
ADJECTIVE a pale reddish-white colour.

pinpoint pinpoints pinpointing pinpointed
VERB If you pinpoint something, you explain or discover exactly what or where it is.

pint pints
NOUN a unit of measurement for liquids equal to one eighth of a gallon or about 0·568 litres.

pioneer pioneers
Said "pie-on-**ear**" NOUN one of the first people to develop a particular activity or invention.
pioneer VERB **pioneering** ADJECTIVE

pious
Said "**pie**-uss" ADJECTIVE very religious and moral.
piously ADVERB

pip pips pipping pipped
NOUN 1 the hard seeds in a fruit.
VERB 2 If you pip someone, or pip them at the post, you narrowly beat them in a contest.

pipe pipes piping piped
NOUN 1 a long, hollow tube through which liquid or gas can flow.
2 an object that is used for smoking tobacco, consisting of a small, hollow bowl attached to a thin tube.
3 a long, hollow, woodwind musical instrument.
PLURAL NOUN 4 "Pipes" are another name for bagpipes.
VERB 5 to transfer liquid or gas through a pipe.
6 to play music on a pipe.

a b c d e f g h i j k l m n o p q r s t u v w x y z

"Ping-pong" is an example of onomatopoeia: words which are derived from a sound.

A B C D E F G H I J K L M N O P Q R S T U V W X Y Z

pipeline pipelines
NOUN **1** a large underground pipe that carries oil or gas over a long distance.
PHRASE **2** If something is **in the pipeline**, it is already planned or has begun.

piper pipers
NOUN someone who plays a pipe or the bagpipes.

piping
NOUN **1** a general word for pipes and tubes.
PHRASE **2** If food is **piping hot**, it has just been cooked and is very hot indeed.

pirate pirates
NOUN **1** Pirates are sailors who attack and rob other ships.
ADJECTIVE **2** Pirate videos, CDs, tapes, etc. have been copied and sold illegally.

pistol pistols
NOUN a small hand gun.

piston pistons
NOUN a cylinder or disc within an engine that slides up and down to make other parts of the engine move.

pit pits
NOUN **1** a large hole in the ground.
2 a coalmine.
3 INFORMAL If you say that somewhere, someone or something is the pits, you mean they are the worst possible place, person or thing.

pitch pitches pitching pitched
NOUN **1** an area of ground marked out for playing a game such as football or cricket.
2 The pitch of a sound is how high or low it is.
VERB **3** If you pitch something somewhere, you throw it there with a lot of force.
4 If you pitch something at a certain level of difficulty, you set it at that level.
5 If you pitch a tent, you fix it in an upright position so you can live in it.
ADJECTIVE **6** If something or somewhere is pitch black, it is very dark indeed.

pitcher pitchers
NOUN a large jug.

pitchfork pitchforks
NOUN a long-handled fork with long curved prongs for turning and tossing hay.

pitfall pitfalls
NOUN the pitfalls of a situation are its difficulties or dangers.

pitiful
ADJECTIVE **1** If someone or something is pitiful, they are in such a sad or weak situation that you feel pity for them.
2 very poor indeed. *That was a pitiful excuse.*
pitifully ADVERB

pitiless
ADJECTIVE A pitiless person shows no pity for anyone.

pitta
NOUN a flat bread with a pocket inside into which fillings can be put.

pity pities pitying pitied
VERB **1** to feel very sorry for someone.
NOUN **2** the feeling that you are very sorry for someone.
3 If you say that something is a pity, you are disappointed about it.

pivot pivots pivoting pivoted
VERB **1** to balance or turn on a central point. *Ali's future pivoted on passing the exam.*
NOUN **2** the central point on which something balances or turns.

pixie pixies; also spelt **pixy**
NOUN an imaginary little creature in fairy stories.

pizza pizzas
Said "**peet**-sah" NOUN a flat piece of dough covered with cheese, tomato and other savoury food and baked in an oven.

placard placards
NOUN a large notice carried at a demonstration or displayed in a public place.

place places placing placed
NOUN **1** any point, building or area.
2 the position where something belongs. *Put the book back in its place on the shelf.*
3 a seat or position that is available for someone to occupy. *Yusuf sat down in his place. Carol got a place at York University.*
4 a particular position in a race, competition or series: *first place.*
5 The place value of a numeral is how many units, tens, hundreds, etc. it represents. For example, in the number 423, the place value of 3 is three units or 3, the place value of 2 is two tens or 20, the place value of 4 is four hundreds or 400.
VERB **6** to put something somewhere carefully.
PHRASE **7** When something **takes place**, it happens.

Synonyms: (sense 1) location, site, spot

placid
ADJECTIVE calm and not easily excited or upset.
placidly ADVERB **placidity** NOUN

plague plagues plaguing plagued
Said "**playg**" NOUN **1** a very infectious disease that kills large numbers of people.
2 A plague of unpleasant things is a large number of them occurring at the same time.
VERB **3** If a problem plagues you, it keeps causing you trouble.

plaice
NOUN an edible European flat fish.

plaid plaids
Said "**plad**" NOUN woven material with a tartan design.

 ► Some surnames, such as Hill, Wood, Hall and Ford, come from the places where people lived.

plain **plainer plainest; plains**
ADJECTIVE 1 very simple in style with no pattern or decoration.
2 obvious or easy to understand.
3 a plain person is not attractive.
NOUN 4 a large, flat area of land with very few trees.
plainly ADVERB **plainness** NOUN

Synonyms: (sense 1) bare, simple, unadorned

plain clothes
PLURAL NOUN ordinary clothes, not in uniform.

plait **plaits plaiting plaited**
VERB 1 If you plait three lengths of hair or rope together, you twist them over each other in turn to make one thick length.
NOUN 2 a length of hair that has been plaited.

plan **plans planning planned**
VERB 1 If you plan something, you decide in detail what you are going to do.
2 to intend to do something. *They plan to marry.*
NOUN 3 a method you have worked out in order to achieve something.
planner NOUN

Synonyms: (sense 1) devise, scheme, think
(sense 2) intend, mean, propose
(sense 3) scheme, strategy

plane **planes**
NOUN 1 an aircraft with wings, an aeroplane.
2 In mathematics, a plane is a completely flat surface.
3 a tool for smoothing wood.

planet **planets**
NOUN a spherical body, such as the earth or Mars, in space which orbits a star, for example, the sun.
planetary ADJECTIVE

plank **planks**
NOUN a long rectangular piece of wood.

plankton
NOUN a layer of tiny plants and animals which live just below the surface of a sea or lake.

plant **plants planting planted**
NOUN 1 a living thing that grows in the earth and has a stem, leaves and roots.
2 a factory or power station: *a nuclear power plant.*
VERB 3 to put a seed, plant or tree into the ground so it can grow.
4 If you plant something somewhere, you put it there firmly or secretly.

plantation **plantations**
NOUN a large area of land where many trees are planted together, or where crops such as tea, cotton or sugar are grown.

plaque **plaques**
*Rhymes with "**black**"* **NOUN 1** a flat piece of metal which is fixed to a wall and has an inscription in memory of a famous person or event.
2 a substance which forms around your teeth and consists of bacteria, saliva and food.

plaster **plasters plastering plastered**
NOUN 1 a paste which hardens to form a smooth surface for inside walls and ceilings; also, in a different form, to keep fractured bones stable.
2 a strip of sticky material with a small pad, used for covering cuts on your body.
VERB 3 to cover a wall or a limb with a layer of plaster.

plasterer **plasterers**
NOUN someone whose job it is to put a smooth plaster finish on walls.

plaster of Paris
NOUN a quick-setting plaster used mainly for keeping broken bones in place while they heal.

plastic **plastics**
NOUN 1 a light but strong material made by a chemical process.
ADJECTIVE 2 made of plastic.

Plasticine
NOUN; TRADEMARK Plasticine is a soft coloured substance which can be used for modelling.

plastic surgery
NOUN surgery to replace or repair damaged skin or to improve a person's appearance.

plate **plates**
NOUN 1 a flat dish used to hold food.
2 a flat piece of any hard material: *a plate of glass.*

plateau **plateaus** or **plateaux**
*Rhymes with "**snow**"* **NOUN** an area of high and fairly flat land.

platform **platforms**
NOUN 1 a raised structure on which someone or something can stand.
2 the raised area in a railway station where passengers get on and off trains.
3 the declared policies of a political party or group.

platinum
NOUN a valuable silver-coloured metal.

platoon **platoons**
NOUN a small group of soldiers commanded by a lieutenant.

platypus **platypuses**
NOUN A platypus, or duck-billed platypus, is an Australian mammal which lives in rivers. It has brown fur, webbed feet and a snout like a duck.

plausible
ADJECTIVE likely to be true.
plausibility NOUN

A B C D E F G H I J K L M N O P Q R S T U V W X Y Z

play plays playing played
VERB **1** to take part in children's games or use toys.
2 to take part and compete in a sport or game.
3 to perform a role in a play or film. *His ambition is to play King Lear.*
4 If you play a part in something, you have an effect on it. *You really played a part in our success.*
5 to produce music from a musical instrument.
6 If you play a CD, tape, etc., you listen to it.
NOUN **7** a drama performed in the theatre or on television.
player NOUN

playful
ADJECTIVE **1** friendly and light-hearted. *She quickly gave him a playful kiss.*
2 lively: *a playful puppy.*
playfully ADVERB

playground playgrounds
NOUN a special area for children to play in.

playgroup playgroups
NOUN an informal kind of school for very young children where they learn by playing.

playing card playing cards
NOUN Playing cards are cards printed with numbers or pictures which are used to play various games.

playing field playing fields
NOUN an area of grass where people play sports.

playscript playscripts
NOUN the text of a play printed out.

playtime playtimes
NOUN a time for play or recreation, such as a school break.

playwright playwrights
NOUN a person who writes plays.

plea pleas
NOUN an emotional request. *The kidnapped girl's mother made a plea for her return.*

plead pleads pleading pleaded
VERB **1** If you plead with someone, you ask them in an intense emotional way to do something.
2 to state in court whether you are guilty or not guilty of a crime. *Morris had pleaded guilty to robbery.*

pleasant
ADJECTIVE nice, enjoyable or attractive.
pleasantly ADVERB **pleasantness** NOUN

Synonyms: agreeable, pleasing

please pleases pleasing pleased
1 You say "please" when you are asking someone politely to do something. *Can you help me, please?*
VERB **2** If something pleases you, it makes you feel happy and satisfied.

Synonyms: (sense 2) delight, gladden, satisfy

pleasure pleasures
NOUN **1** a feeling of happiness, satisfaction or enjoyment.
2 an activity that you enjoy.
pleasurable ADJECTIVE

pleat pleats pleating pleated
VERB to make permanent folds in fabric by folding one part over another.
pleat NOUN **pleated** ADJECTIVE

pledge pledges pledging pledged
VERB to make a solemn promise.
pledge NOUN

Synonyms: promise, swear, vow

plentiful
ADJECTIVE existing in large numbers or amounts and readily available.
plentifully ADVERB

plenty
NOUN OR PRONOUN If there is plenty of something, there is a lot of it.

pliable
ADJECTIVE You can bend something pliable without breaking it.

Synonyms: bendy, flexible, supple

pliers
PLURAL NOUN Pliers are a small tool with metal jaws for holding small objects and bending wire.

plight
NOUN Someone's plight is the very difficult or dangerous situation that they are in.

plod plods plodding plodded
VERB **1** to walk slowly and heavily.
2 to work slowly and patiently, but without enthusiasm or inspiration.
plodder NOUN

plonk plonks plonking plonked
VERB If you plonk something down, you put it down heavily and carelessly.

plop plops plopping plopped
NOUN to drop into a liquid with a gentle sound.
plop NOUN

plot plots plotting plotted
NOUN **1** a secret plan made by a group of people.
2 the story of a film, novel or play.
VERB **3** to plan secretly.
4 In mathematics, to place points accurately on a graph or grid.
PHRASE **5** INFORMAL If you say someone has **lost the plot**, they have gone completely wrong in what they are doing.

Synonyms: (sense 1) conspiracy, scheme
(sense 3) conspire, plan, scheme

 ► Shakespeare is England's most famous playwright. He is believed to have been born and to have died on 23 April.

plough ploughs
*Rhymes with "**cow**"* NOUN a large farming tool that is pulled across a field to turn the soil over before planting seeds.
plough VERB

pluck plucks plucking plucked
VERB **1** To pluck a fruit or flower is to remove it with a sharp pull.
2 To pluck a chicken or other dead bird means to pull its feathers out before cooking it.
3 When you pluck a stringed instrument, you pull the strings and let them go.
NOUN **4** courage. *The girl showed great pluck in rescuing the boy from the lake.*
PHRASE **5** If you **pluck up courage** to do something that you regard as frightening, you make an effort to do it.
plucky ADJECTIVE

plug plugs plugging plugged
NOUN **1** a plastic object with metal pins that connects a piece of electrical equipment to an electric socket.
2 a thick circular piece of rubber or plastic that you use to block the hole in a sink or bath.
VERB **3** If you plug a hole, you block it with something.
4 INFORMAL to mention something on television, radio or in the newspapers in order to attract public interest. *On the game show, the singer kept plugging his new album.*

plum plums
NOUN a small fruit with a smooth red or yellow skin and a stone in the middle.

plumage
*Said "**ploom**-mage"* NOUN A bird's plumage is its feathers.

plumber plumbers
NOUN a person who installs and repairs water and heating systems.

plumbing
NOUN **1** the system of water pipes within a building.
2 the activity of installing or repairing water and heating systems.

plume plumes
NOUN a large, brightly coloured feather.

plump plumper plumpest; plumps plumping plumped
ADJECTIVE **1** rather fat.
VERB **2** INFORMAL When you plump for a particular thing, you choose it.

Synonyms: (sense 1) chubby, podgy, tubby

plunder plunders plundering plundered
VERB to steal things from a place in a wild and forceful way.
plunder NOUN

plunge plunges plunging plunged
VERB **1** to fall quickly or rush into something, especially into water.
2 If you plunge an object into something, you push it in quickly.
NOUN **3** a sudden fall.

Synonyms: (sense 1) dive, drop, plummet

plural plurals
NOUN The plural of a word is the form that is used when referring to more than one person or thing.
[from Latin *pluralis* meaning concerning many]

FORMING THE PLURAL
Never use an apostrophe to form a plural. For example, the plural of *tomato* is not *tomato's* but *tomatoes*.
There are several ways to form the plural correctly.
Most plurals are formed simply by adding -*s* to the singular form of the noun:
book – books, sausage – sausages
To form the plural of singular words that end in -*s*, -*z*, -*x*, -*ch* or -*sh*, add the letters -*es*:
cross – crosses, box – boxes
To form the plural of singular words that end in a consonant + -*y*, remove the -*y* and add -*ies*:
pony – ponies, party – parties
To form the plural of singular words that end in -*ife*, remove the -*fe* and add -*ves*:
knife – knives, life – lives
Some singular words that end in -*f* are made plural by adding -*ves*. Others just add -*s*:
hoof – hooves, roof – roofs
Some words that have come from foreign languages have plurals that don't end in -*s*.
Latin: *cactus – cacti, medium – media, formula – formulae*
Greek: *phenomenon – phenomena*
French: *gateau – gateaux, bureau – bureaux*
Some plurals, but very few, do not follow any rule:
child – children, deer – deer, fish – fish or fishes, foot – feet, man – men, mouse – mice, ox – oxen, sheep – sheep, woman – women

plus
PREPOSITION **1** added to (often written as +). *Two plus two equals four* (2 + 2 = 4).
2 in addition to. *He wrote a travel book plus a history of British literature.*
ADJECTIVE **3** slightly more than the number mentioned: *a career of 25 years plus.*
[from Latin *plus* meaning more]
✔ Although you can use *plus* to mean additionally in spoken language, you should avoid it in written work: *plus, you could win a holiday in Florida.*

plywood
NOUN wooden board made from several thin sheets of wood glued together under pressure.

p.m.
used to specify times between 12 noon and 12 midnight, i.e. afternoon and evening.
[abbreviation for Latin *post meridiem* meaning after noon]

a b c d e f g h i j k l m n o p q r s t u v w x y z

A B C D E F G H I J K L M N O P Q R S T U V W X Y Z

pneumatic
Said "new-**mat**-ik" ADJECTIVE operated by or filled with compressed air.

pneumonia
Said "new-**moan**-ee-ah" NOUN a serious disease which affects a person's lungs and makes breathing difficult.

poach poaches poaching poached
VERB 1 to catch animals illegally from someone else's land.
2 When you poach food, you cook it gently in hot liquid.
poacher NOUN

pocket pockets
NOUN a small pouch that forms part of a piece of clothing.

pocket money
NOUN spending money that a child receives regularly from a parent or guardian.

pod pods
NOUN a long narrow seed container that grows on plants such as peas or beans.

podgy podgier podgiest
ADJECTIVE rather fat, plump.

poem poems
NOUN a concentrated piece of writing, usually in short lines, in which the words are chosen for their beauty, sound, and ability to communicate feelings and ideas; a verse.

poet poets
NOUN a person who writes poems.

poetry
NOUN poems, considered as a form of literature.

Antonym: prose

point points pointing pointed
NOUN 1 the thin, sharp end of something such as a needle or knife.
2 an opinion or fact expressed by someone. *You've made a very good point.*
3 the purpose of something. *The point of insulation is to stop heat from escaping.*
4 the essential meaning of something. *Good! You've grasped the point.*
5 a quality. *Julie is good at English, but French has never been her strong point.*
6 a position or time: *at various points along the road. At some point during the party, a fight started.*
7 a single mark in a competition. *It's three points all.*
8 In spoken English, you use "point" to refer to the decimal point, which separates whole numbers from decimals: *nine point four* (9·4).
9 The points of a compass are the directions indicated on it (north, north-east, east, etc.).
VERB 10 to hold out your index finger to show where something is.
11 If something points in a particular direction, it faces that way.
point out VERB to draw someone's attention to something by pointing to it or by explaining it.

point-blank
ADJECTIVE 1 Something that is shot at point-blank range is shot with a gun held very close to it.
ADVERB 2 If you say something point-blank, you say it directly without explanation or apology. *Gill refused point-blank to come.*

pointed
ADJECTIVE a pointed object has a thin sharp end.

pointer pointers
NOUN a clue or other piece of information which helps you to understand something. *I'll give you a few pointers to get you on the right track.*

pointless
ADJECTIVE having no purpose.
pointlessness NOUN **pointlessly** ADVERB

point of view points of view
NOUN your opinion about something or your attitude towards it.

poise
NOUN Someone who has poise is calm and dignified.

poised
ADJECTIVE 1 If you are poised to do something, you are ready to do it.
2 A poised person is calm, dignified and unhurried in what they do.

poison poisons poisoning poisoned
NOUN 1 a substance that harms or kills you if you swallow it or absorb it.
VERB 2 to harm someone by giving them poison.
poisonous ADJECTIVE

poke pokes poking poked
VERB 1 to push someone or something with your finger or a sharp object.
2 If something is poking out of another thing, a small part of it is visible.

Synonyms: (sense 1) prod, dig, jab

poker pokers
NOUN 1 a tool for poking the coals on an open fire.
2 a card game in which players bet money on how good their cards are and try to bluff their opponents into quitting.

polar
ADJECTIVE relating to the area around the North and South Poles.

polar bear polar bears
NOUN a large white bear which is found around the North Pole.

 ► Each line of a poem usually begins with a capital letter.

pole poles
NOUN **1** a long rounded piece of wood or metal.
2 The earth's poles are the two opposite ends of its axis.

pole vault
NOUN an athletics event in which contestants run up and propel themselves over a high bar using a long flexible pole.

police
PLURAL NOUN the official organization that is responsible for making sure that people obey the law, and the men and women who make up its members.
policeman NOUN **policewoman** NOUN

police officer police officers
NOUN a policeman or policewoman.

policy policies
NOUN **1** a set of plans and ideas, especially in politics or business.
2 An insurance policy is the document you receive when you take out insurance against something bad happening to you or your property.

polio
NOUN an infectious disease caused by a virus, which often results in paralysis. Polio is short for poliomyelitis.

polish polishes polishing polished
NOUN **1** a substance that you put on an object to clean it and make it shine.
VERB **2** to put polish on something or rub it with a cloth to make it shine.
3 If you polish something off, you finish it or consume it all. *The dog polished off the food that was left over.*
polished ADJECTIVE

polite
ADJECTIVE having good manners.
politely ADVERB **politeness** NOUN

Antonym: rude

political
ADJECTIVE relating to politics, the government or administration of a place.
politically ADVERB

politician politicians
NOUN a person whose job is in politics, especially a Member of Parliament.

politics
NOUN the activity and planning concerned with achieving power and control in a country or organization.

polka polkas
NOUN a fast dance in which couples dance together in circles around the room.

poll polls
NOUN a survey in which people are asked their opinions about something.
poll VERB

pollen
NOUN a fine yellow powder produced by flowers in order to fertilize other flowers of the same species.

pollinate pollinates pollinating pollinated
VERB to fertilize a plant with pollen.
pollination NOUN

pollute pollutes polluting polluted
VERB To pollute water, air or land means to make it dirty and dangerous to use or live in.
pollution NOUN **pollutant** NOUN
polluted ADJECTIVE

Synonyms: contaminate, foul, poison

polo
NOUN a game played between two teams of players on horseback. The players use wooden mallets with long handles to hit a ball through goals.

poltergeist poltergeists
Said "**pol**-ter-gye-st" NOUN a mischievous spirit which haunts a place by rattling doors, turning furniture over, etc.

poly-
PREFIX many or much.
[from Greek *polus* meaning many or much]

polyester
NOUN a man-made fibre, used especially to make clothes.

polygon polygons
NOUN any two-dimensional shape whose sides are all straight.

polyhedron polyhedrons or polyhedra
NOUN a solid shape with four or more flat faces.

polystyrene
NOUN a very light plastic, used especially as insulating material or to make containers and models.

polythene
NOUN a type of plastic that is used to make thin sheets or bags.

pomp
NOUN the use of ceremony, fine clothes and decorations on special occasions.

pompous
ADJECTIVE behaving in a way that is too serious and self-important.
pompously ADVERB **pomposity** NOUN

pond ponds
NOUN a small, usually man-made area of water.

ponder ponders pondering pondered
VERB to think about something deeply.

Synonyms: consider, mull over, think

pony ponies
NOUN a small horse.

a b c d e f g h i j k l m n o p q r s t u v w x y z

Police words: arrest, criminal, statement, trial, defendant, witness.

A B C D E F G H I J K L M N O P Q R S T U V W X Y Z

ponytail ponytails
NOUN a hairstyle in which long hair is tied at the back of the head and hangs down like a tail.

poodle poodles
NOUN a type of dog with curly hair.

pool pools pooling pooled
NOUN **1** a small area of still water or liquid.
2 a swimming pool.
3 a game in which players knock coloured balls into pockets around a table using long sticks called cues.
PLURAL NOUN **4** The pools are a competition in which people try to guess the results of football matches.
VERB **5** If people pool their resources, they share them or put them together for a particular purpose.

poor poorer poorest
ADJECTIVE **1** having very little money and few possessions.
2 You use poor to show sympathy. *Poor Wesley!*
3 of a low quality or standard. *This essay is a poor effort.*

Antonyms: (sense 1) affluent, rich, well-off

poorly
ADJECTIVE **1** feeling unwell or ill.
ADVERB **2** badly: *a poorly planned operation.*

pop pops popping popped
NOUN **1** a short, sharp sound.
2 modern music played and enjoyed especially by young people.
3 fizzy, non-alcoholic drinks.
VERB **4** to make a sudden sharp sound.
5 to put something quickly into a place. *I'd just popped the pie in the oven.*
6 to go somewhere quickly. *I'm just popping to the shops.*

popcorn
NOUN a snack consisting of grains of maize heated until they puff up and burst.

Pope Popes
NOUN the head of the Roman Catholic Church.
[from Latin *papa* meaning bishop or father]

poppadom poppadoms; also spelt **poppadum**
NOUN a large, circular crisp made of flour and spices and eaten with Indian food.

poppy poppies
NOUN a plant with a large red flower on a hairy stem.

popular
ADJECTIVE liked or approved of by a lot of people.
popularly ADVERB **popularity** ADJECTIVE

Synonyms: fashionable, well-liked

populated
ADJECTIVE A populated place has people living there.

population populations
NOUN the people who live in a place or the number of people living there.

porcelain
NOUN a delicate, hard material used to make crockery and ornaments.

porch porches
NOUN a covered area at the entrance to a building.

porcupine porcupines
NOUN a large rodent with long spines covering its body.

pore pores poring pored
NOUN **1** The pores in your skin or on the surface of a plant are very small holes which allow moisture to pass through.
VERB **2** If you pore over a piece of writing or a diagram, you study it carefully.

pork
NOUN meat from a pig, which has not been salted or smoked.

porous
ADJECTIVE containing many holes through which water and air can pass.

porpoise porpoises
Said "**por**-pus" NOUN a sea mammal related to the dolphin.
[from Latin *porcus* meaning pig and *piscis* meaning fish]

porridge
NOUN a thick, sticky food made from oats cooked in water or milk.

port ports
NOUN **1** a town or area which has a harbour or docks.
ADJECTIVE **2** The port side of a ship is the left side when you are facing the front.

portable
ADJECTIVE designed to be easily carried.

portcullis portcullises
NOUN a large metal gate above the entrance to a castle, which was lowered to keep out enemies.

porter porters
NOUN **1** a person whose job is to be in charge of the entrance of a building, such as in a university college.
2 a person whose job is to carry things, such as in a hotel or at a railway.

porthole portholes
NOUN a small window in the side of a ship or aircraft.

portion portions
NOUN a measured part of something: *a portion of stew big enough for one person.*

 ▸ Lewis Carroll invented portmanteaus, new words which are formed by combining other words. ▸

portrait portraits
NOUN a picture or photograph of someone.

portray portrays portraying portrayed
VERB When an actor, artist or writer portrays someone or something, they represent or describe them.
portrayal NOUN

pose poses posing posed
VERB **1** If something poses a problem or danger, it causes it.
2 If you pose a question, you ask it.
3 to pretend to be someone else.
4 If you pose for a photograph or painting, you stay still so that someone can photograph or paint you.
NOUN **5** a way of standing, sitting or lying for a picture to be taken.

posh posher poshest
ADJECTIVE **1** INFORMAL smart, fashionable and expensive.
2 upper class. *He spoke with a posh voice.*

position positions positioning positioned
NOUN **1** the place where someone or something is.
2 the way that someone or something is sitting or lying.
3 a job or post in an organization.
4 the situation that someone is in. *The fraud case puts the company in a difficult position.*
VERB **5** to place something carefully.

positive
ADJECTIVE **1** completely sure about something.
2 confident, encouraging and hopeful: *a positive attitude.*
3 a positive number is one that is greater than zero.
4 If a medical test is positive, it shows that a particular medical condition is present. *The pregnancy test was positive.*

posse posses
Said "**poss**-ee" NOUN **1** INFORMAL a group of friends or associates.
2 in the days of the Wild West in the USA, a group of people who helped a sheriff track down a criminal.

possess possesses possessing possessed
VERB to own or have.

possessed
ADJECTIVE under the influence of a powerful force such as a spirit or strong emotion.

possession possessions
NOUN **1** If something is in your possession, or if you are in possession of it, you have it.
2 Your possessions are the things that you own.

Synonyms: (sense 2) belongings, property

possessive
ADJECTIVE **1** A person who is possessive about someone or something wants to keep them to themselves.
NOUN **2** In grammar, the possessive is the form of a noun or pronoun used to show ownership: *my car; that's hers.*
possessiveness NOUN

FORMING THE POSSESSIVE CASE

The **possessive case** is used when a noun indicates a person or thing that owns another person or thing. It is formed by adding an apostrophe ' and the letter *s* to the dictionary form of the word:
The dog's coat was wet.
If the noun already ends in *-s*, the possessive is formed by simply adding an apostrophe:
The dogs' coats were wet.
When a possessive is not followed by another noun, it refers to a place where that person lives or works:
I am going to stay at my gran's.
I bought some carrots at the greengrocer's.
You can also show the possessive by putting the word **of** in front of the noun. This is usually used when you are talking about something that is not alive or that you cannot touch:
We climbed to the top of the hill.
He is a master of disguise.

possibility possibilities
NOUN something that might be true or might happen; chance, likelihood.

possible
ADJECTIVE **1** if it is possible to do something, it can be done. *It's possible to get there earlier by train.*
2 If something is possible, it might happen or be true. *It's quite possible that I'm wrong.*
3 If you do something as soon as possible or as quickly as possible, you do it as soon or as quickly as you can.

Synonyms: (sense 1) feasible, practicable

possibly
ADVERB maybe, perhaps.

possum possums
NOUN a possum is a marsupial with thick fur and a long tail.

post posts posting posted
NOUN **1** an upright pole fixed into the ground.
2 the system by which letters and parcels are collected and delivered, and the letters and parcels themselves.
3 a job or official position in an organization. *Our head teacher was well qualified for the post.*
VERB **4** to send a letter through the post.
5 If you are posted somewhere, you are sent by your employers to work there.

post-
PREFIX after.

postage
NOUN the money you pay to send a letter or parcel by post.
postage stamp NOUN

postal
ADJECTIVE relating to the post and its delivery.

A B C D E F G H I J K L M N O P Q R S T U V W X Y Z

postal order **postal orders**
NOUN a piece of paper representing a sum of money, which you can buy at a post office to send to someone by post. The person who receives it can cash the order for the amount of money concerned.

postbox **postboxes**
NOUN a box into which you post mail that is to be sent.

postcard **postcards**
NOUN a single piece of card, sometimes with a picture on one side, designed to be written on and sent by post without an envelope.

postcode **postcodes**
NOUN the numbers and letters you write at the end of an address which helps the post office sort out the post.

poster **posters**
NOUN a large notice or picture that you stick on a wall.

postman **postmen**
NOUN someone whose job it is to deliver mail.

postmark **postmarks**
NOUN a mark printed on envelopes showing when and where they were posted.

post office **post offices**
NOUN a building where you can buy stamps and letters, and also make payments of different kinds.

postpone **postpones postponing postponed**
VERB to put off a planned event until a later date.
postponement NOUN

Synonyms: delay, put off, shelve

posture **postures**
NOUN the position or manner in which you hold your body.

posy **posies**
NOUN a small bunch of flowers.

pot **pots**
NOUN a deep round container for cooking food.

potassium
NOUN a soft alkaline metal that reacts strongly with other chemicals. It is used in fertilizers, in batteries, and for cooling nuclear reactors.

potato **potatoes**
NOUN a white vegetable that has a brown or red skin and grows underground.
✔ Be careful not to spell *potato* with an *e* at the end.

potent
ADJECTIVE effective or powerful: *a potent medicine.*
potency NOUN

potential
ADJECTIVE **1** possible for the future. *The young lad driving the go-kart was a potential racing car world champion.*
NOUN **2** If someone or something has potential, they are capable of being successful or useful.
potentially ADVERB

pothole **potholes**
NOUN **1** a hole in the surface of a road caused by bad weather or traffic.
2 an underground cavern.

potion **potions**
NOUN a drink containing medicine, poison or supposed magical powers.

potter **potters pottering pottered**
NOUN **1** a person who makes pottery.
VERB **2** If you potter about, you pass the time doing pleasant but unimportant things.

pottery **potteries**
NOUN **1** pots, dishes and other items made from clay and fired in a kiln.
2 the craft of making pottery.
3 a workshop where pottery is made.

potty **potties; pottier pottiest**
NOUN **1** a bowl which a small child can sit on and use instead of a toilet.
ADJECTIVE **2** INFORMAL crazy or foolish.

pouch **pouches**
NOUN **1** a small, soft container with a fold-over top.
2 Marsupials such as kangaroos have a pouch, a pocket of skin in which they carry their young.

poultry
NOUN a general word for chickens, turkeys and other birds kept for their meat or eggs.

pounce **pounces pouncing pounced**
VERB If an animal or person pounces on something, they leap and grab it.

pound **pounds pounding pounded**
NOUN **1** the main unit of currency in Britain and in some other countries.
2 a unit of weight equal to 16 ounces or about 0·454 kilograms, often abbreviated to "lb".
VERB **3** to hit something repeatedly with your fist. *Someone was pounding on the door.*

pour **pours pouring poured**
VERB **1** to make liquid flow from a container by tipping it. *The waitress poured the tea into the cups.*
2 If something pours somewhere, it flows there quickly and in large quantities. *Sweat poured down his face.*
3 When it is raining heavily, you can say that it is pouring.

pout **pouts pouting pouted**
VERB to stick out your lips or bottom lip.

poverty
NOUN the state of being very poor.
poverty-stricken ADJECTIVE

powder **powders**
NOUN Powder consists of many tiny particles of a solid substance.
powdery ADJECTIVE **powdered** ADJECTIVE

power **powers powering powered**
NOUN **1** Someone who has power has rights or control over people and events. *Teachers have the power to give you detention.*
2 Your power to do something is your ability to do it. *I will do everything in my power to help.*
3 the physical strength of someone or something.
4 the rate of transfer of energy from one form to another: for example, electrical energy into light energy. Power is measured in watts.
VERB **5** to provide the energy for a machine to work. *The planes are powered by Rolls Royce engines.*

powerful
ADJECTIVE **1** having a lot of strength.
2 having control or influence over others.
powerfully ADVERB

powerless
ADJECTIVE unable to control or influence events.
powerlessness NOUN

Synonyms: helpless, impotent, incapable

power station **power stations**
NOUN a place where electricity is generated and distributed.

practical
ADJECTIVE **1** involving real situations rather than ideas or theories. *There are practical difficulties in teaching medical students how the brain works.*
2 sensible and likely to be effective, or the ability to be like this. *These are practical low-heeled shoes. We need a guide who's practical.*
practicality NOUN

practical joke **practical jokes**
NOUN a trick that is intended to make someone look ridiculous.

practically
ADVERB almost, very nearly. *With just the sweeping up to do, we had practically finished clearing up after the party.*

practice **practices**
NOUN **1** regular training in a skill or activity.
2 something that people do regularly. *I don't like the practice of footballers kissing each other when they score.*
✔ The noun *practice* ends in *ice*.

practise **practises practising practised**
VERB **1** to do something regularly in order to do it better.
2 When people practise a religion, custom or craft, they take part in the activities associated with it.
✔ The verb *practise* ends in *ise*.

prairie **prairies**
NOUN a large area of flat, grassy land in North America.

praise **praises praising praised**
VERB **1** to express your strong approval of someone or something.
NOUN **2** Praise is what you say or write when you praise someone.

Synonyms: (sense 1) acclaim, approve, compliment
(sense 2) acclaim, approval, commendation

pram **prams**
NOUN a cot-like four wheeled carriage for a baby.

prance **prances prancing pranced**
VERB to walk or jump around with exaggerated movements.

prank **pranks**
NOUN a childish trick.

prawn **prawns**
NOUN a small, pink, edible shellfish with a long tail.

pray **prays praying prayed**
VERB When someone prays, they speak to God to give thanks or praise, to confess sins or to ask God for help.

prayer **prayers**
NOUN **1** the activity of praying.
2 the words that someone says when they pray.

pre-
PREFIX before: *prefabricated; prewar.*

preach **preaches preaching preached**
VERB **1** to give a short talk on a religious or moral subject as part of a church service.
2 Someone who preaches a set of ideas tries to persuade people to accept them.
preacher NOUN

precarious
ADJECTIVE **1** If your situation is precarious, you are in danger of failing at any time.
2 Something precarious is likely to fall because it is not well balanced or secured.
precariously ADVERB

Synonyms: (sense 2) insecure, shaky, unsafe

precaution **precautions**
NOUN an action that is intended to prevent something from happening.
precautionary ADJECTIVE

precede **precedes preceding preceded**
VERB to happen or occur before something else. *The flash of lightning usually precedes the clap of thunder.*
preceding ADJECTIVE

precinct precincts
NOUN A shopping precinct is a pedestrian shopping area.

precious
ADJECTIVE Precious things are valuable and important, and should be looked after or used carefully.

precipice precipices
Said "**press**-sip-piss" NOUN a very steep rock face.

precise
ADJECTIVE exact rather than vague. *I want precise details of how to get there.*
precision NOUN **precisely** ADVERB

predator predators
Said "**pred**-dat-tor" NOUN an animal that kills and eats other animals.
predatory ADJECTIVE

predecessor predecessors
NOUN Someone's predecessor is the person who did the same job before them.

predicament predicaments
NOUN a difficult situation, a dilemma, a fix.

predicate
NOUN the part of a simple sentence that is not the subject and which contains the verb. In the sentence "She went to school", "went to school" is the predicate.

predict predicts predicting predicted
VERB to say what will happen in the future.
prediction NOUN

Synonyms: forecast, foretell, prophesy

predictable
ADJECTIVE If a situation is predictable, you can easily tell what is going to happen.
predictably ADVERB

predominant
ADJECTIVE more frequent, important or more noticeable than anything else in a set of people or things. *Yellow is the predominant colour in the house.*
predominantly ADVERB **predominance** NOUN

Synonyms: chief, main, prevailing

preen preens preening preened
VERB When a bird preens its feathers, it cleans and smooths them using its beak.

preface prefaces
Said "**pref**-fiss" NOUN an introduction at the beginning of a book explaining what the book is about or why it was written.

prefect prefects
NOUN a senior pupil who has special duties at a school.

prefer prefers preferring preferred
VERB If you prefer one thing to another, you like it better than the other thing.
preference NOUN

prefix prefixes
NOUN a letter or group of letters added to the beginning of a word to make a new word, for example, "semi-", "pre-" and "un-".

pregnant
ADJECTIVE A woman or other female animal who is pregnant has a baby developing in her body.
pregnancy NOUN

prehistoric
ADJECTIVE existing at a time in the past before anything was written down.

prejudice
NOUN an unreasonable dislike of someone or something, or an unreasonable preference for one group over another: *racial prejudice.*
prejudiced ADJECTIVE

preliminary
ADJECTIVE Preliminary activities take place before something starts and in preparation for it: *the preliminary rounds of the competition.*

Synonyms: first, initial, preparatory

premature
ADJECTIVE happening too early or earlier than expected.
prematurely ADVERB

premier premiers
NOUN **1** The leader of a government is sometimes referred to as the premier.
ADJECTIVE **2** considered to be the best or most important: *the city's premier hotel.*

premiere premieres
NOUN the first public performance of a play, film, etc.

premises
PLURAL NOUN the buildings and land on one enclosed site, especially those owned by a business. *The burglar was caught on the premises with the jewels in his bag.*

premium premiums
NOUN **1** an extra sum of money that has to be paid: *paying a premium for a top seat was worth it for the best view of the star.*
2 the amount you pay regularly to insure something.

premonition premonitions
Said "prem-on-**ish**-on" NOUN a feeling that something unpleasant is going to happen.

Synonyms: foreboding, presentiment

preoccupied
ADJECTIVE deep in thought and totally involved with something.

preparation preparations
NOUN the activity involved in getting something or someone ready.

preparatory
ADJECTIVE Preparatory activities are done before doing something else in order to prepare for it.

 ► "Pre-" is a prefix which means before. But why is a prefix called a prefix?

preparatory school preparatory schools; also spelt **prep school**
NOUN a private school for children up to the age of 11 or 13.

prepare prepares preparing prepared
VERB to get ready or get something ready.

prepared
ADJECTIVE **1** If you are prepared for something to happen, you expect it and are ready for it.
2 If you are prepared to do something, you are willing to do it.

preposition prepositions
NOUN a word such as "by", "for", "into" or "with", which usually has a noun as its object.

PREPOSITIONS
A **preposition** is a word that is used before a noun or pronoun to relate it to other words.
Prepositions may tell you the **place** of something in relation to another thing:
I saw my dog in the garden.
The dog was sheltering under the hedge.
Prepositions may indicate movement:
The train came into the station.
We pushed through the crowd.
Prepositions may indicate time:
They will arrive on Friday.
They will stay for two days.

preposterous
ADJECTIVE absurd, ridiculous.

prescribe prescribes prescribing prescribed
VERB If a doctor prescribes a medicine, they suggest you take it and write out a form for you to obtain it.

prescription prescriptions
NOUN a form on which a doctor writes the details of a medicine needed by a patient, so that a pharmacist can supply it.

presence
NOUN **1** Someone's presence in a place is the fact that they are there.
2 If you are in someone's presence, you are in the same place as they are.
3 Someone who has presence has an impressive appearance or manner that commands your attention.

present presents presenting presented
Said "**prez**-ent" ADJECTIVE **1** If someone is present somewhere, they are there.
2 A present situation is one that exists now rather than in the past or future; current or existing.
Said "**prez**-ent" NOUN **3** the period of time that is taking place now, as opposed to the past or the future.
4 something that you give to someone for them to keep.
Said "pri-**zent**" VERB **5** to give something to someone in a formal way. *She presented an award to the girl.*
6 Something that presents a difficulty or a challenge causes it or provides it.
7 If a person presents a show, they introduce it or host it.
presenter NOUN

presentation presentation
NOUN **1** the act of giving something. *We're having a presentation for Mrs Mogridge who is retiring.*
2 the act of demonstrating or explaining something. *Fiona has to do a presentation on a book she has read.*

presently
ADVERB **1** soon. *Andy will finish the job presently.*
2 now, at the moment. *Work is presently going on to repair the track.*

present participle present participles
NOUN In grammar, the present participle of an English verb is the form that ends in "-ing". It is used to form some tenses and can be used to form adjectives and nouns from a verb. *She loved running. The flowing river carried the boat along swiftly.*

present tense
NOUN In grammar, you use the present tense of a verb to talk about things that happen or exist at the time of writing or speaking.

THE PRESENT TENSE
You can talk about events that are happening now by using simple tenses or compound tenses.
The simple present tense is formed by using the verb on its own. It is the same as the main form given in the dictionary – *I cook the lunch* – except for the third person singular, when you need to add an *s* to the dictionary form:
She cooks the lunch.
Compound present tenses are formed by adding an auxiliary verb to a form of the main verb. The auxiliary verb is most often **to be**, and when using this, you need to add the ending *-ing* to the main verb. This shows that the action is going on at the present time and is continuous:
I am listening to the radio.
You can also talk about the present using a form of the verb **to do** in front of the basic form of the verb. This can add emphasis:
I do like classical music.

preservative preservatives
NOUN a substance or chemical that stops things decaying.

preserve preserves preserving preserved
VERB **1** to make sure that something stays as it is and doesn't change.
NOUN **2** Preserves are foods such as jam or chutney that have been made with a lot of sugar or vinegar.
preservation NOUN

president presidents
NOUN **1** The president of a country that has no king or queen (a republic) is the leader of the country.
2 the person who has the highest position in an organization.

a b c d e f g h i j k l m n o p q r s t u v w x y z

A B C D E F G H I J K L M N O P Q R S T U V W X Y Z

press presses pressing pressed
VERB **1** to push something or hold it firmly against something else.
2 If you press clothes, you iron them.
3 If you press for something, you try hard to persuade someone to agree to it.
NOUN **4** The press is a general term for newspapers and the journalists who work for them.

pressure pressures
NOUN **1** the force that is produced by pushing on something.
2 If there is pressure on you to do something, you have too much to do and not enough time, or someone is trying to make you do it.

prestige
Said "press-**teezh**" NOUN If you have prestige, people admire you because of your position.
prestigious ADJECTIVE

Synonyms: honour, standing, status

presumably
ADVERB If you say that something is presumably the case, you mean that you assume it is. *Presumably the front door was locked?*

presume presumes presuming presumed
Said "priz-**yoom**" VERB If you presume something, you think that it is the case although you have no proof.
presumption NOUN

Synonyms: assume, believe, suppose

presumptuous
ADJECTIVE Someone who behaves in a presumptuous way does things they have no right to do.

pretend pretends pretending pretended
VERB If you pretend that something is the case, you behave as if something is true or real when it isn't.
pretence NOUN

Synonyms: affect, feign, sham

pretty prettier prettiest
ADJECTIVE **1** attractive and pleasant.
ADVERB **2** INFORMAL quite or rather. *He spoke pretty good English.*
prettily ADVERB **prettiness** NOUN

prevent prevents preventing prevented
VERB to stop something from happening.
prevention NOUN

preview previews
NOUN an opportunity to see something, such as a film or exhibition, before it is shown to the public.

previous
ADJECTIVE A previous time or thing is one that occurred before the present one: *previous reports; the previous year.*
[from Latin *praevius* meaning going before]

prey preys preying preyed
Rhymes with "**say**" NOUN **1** The creatures that an animal hunts and eats are called its prey.
VERB **2** An animal that preys on a particular kind of animal lives by hunting and eating it.

price prices pricing priced
NOUN **1** the amount of money you have to pay in order to buy something.
VERB **2** If something is priced at a particular amount, that is what it costs.

Synonyms: (sense 1) charge, cost, expense

priceless
ADJECTIVE Something that is priceless is so valuable that it is impossible to work out how much it is worth.

prick pricks pricking pricked
VERB **1** to stick a sharp object into something.
NOUN **2** a small, sharp pain caused when something pricks you.

prickle prickles prickling prickled
NOUN **1** Prickles are small sharp points or thorns on plants.
VERB **2** If your skin prickles, it feels as if a lot of sharp points are being stuck into it.
prickly ADJECTIVE

pride prides priding prided
NOUN **1** a feeling of satisfaction that you have when you or people close to you have done something well.
2 a sense of dignity and self-respect.
3 a feeling of being better than other people.
VERB **4** if you pride yourself on something, you are pleased and satisfied with yourself for a particular reason.

priest priests
NOUN a member of the clergy in some Christian churches.

prim primmer primmest
ADJECTIVE Someone who is prim always behaves very correctly and is easily shocked by anything rude.

Synonyms: priggish, prudish, strait-laced

primary
ADJECTIVE extremely important or most important. *Saving lives was the primary aim of his research.*
primarily ADVERB

primary colour primary colours
NOUN In art, red, yellow and blue are called the primary colours because all other colours can be mixed from these. In science, red, green and blue are primary colours because a mixture of these produces white light.

primary school primary schools
NOUN a school for children between the ages of 5 and 11.

primate primates
NOUN a member of the group of animals which includes humans, monkeys and apes.

 ► The word endings "-cal" and "-cle" can be confused. Usually "-cal" ends adjectives, "-cle" ends nouns. ►

prime **primes priming primed**
ADJECTIVE **1** main or most important.
NOUN **2** Someone who is in their prime is at the best time of their lives for strength, knowledge, experience, etc.
VERB **3** If you prime someone, you give them information in advance to prepare them.

Synonyms: (sense 2) height, heyday, peak

prime minister **prime ministers**
NOUN the leader of a government.
prime ministerial ADJECTIVE

prime number **prime numbers**
NOUN a whole number greater than 1 which cannot be divided exactly by any whole number except itself and 1. For example, 2, 3, 7 and 11 are prime numbers.

primitive
ADJECTIVE **1** connected with a society in which people live very simply.
2 very simple, basic or old-fashioned: *a primitive cottage.*

primrose **primroses**
NOUN a small plant that has pale yellow flowers in spring.
[from Latin *prima rosa* meaning first rose]

prince **princes**
NOUN a male member of a royal family, especially the son of a king or queen.

princess **princesses**
NOUN a female member of a royal family, especially the daughter of a king or queen, or the wife of a prince.

principal **principals**
ADJECTIVE **1** main or most important.
NOUN **2** the person in charge of a school or college.
principally ADVERB
✔ Do not confuse *principal* with *principle.*

principle **principles**
NOUN **1** a belief you have about the way you should behave.
2 a general rule or scientific law.
✔ Do not confuse *principle* with *principal.*

print **prints printing printed**
VERB **1** to reproduce letters and numbers on paper in a mechanical way.
2 to reproduce books, newspapers, etc. in large quantities using a mechanical process.
3 to publish something. *The paper did not print my letter of complaint.*
4 If you are asked to print your name, you write each letter separately, not joined up.
NOUN **5** the letters and numbers on the pages of a book or newspaper.

printer **printers**
NOUN **1** a person or company whose job it is to print books, newspapers, documents, etc.
2 a machine for printing out data from computer files.

print-out **print-outs**
NOUN a printed copy of information from a computer.
print out VERB

prior
ADJECTIVE **1** arranged at an earlier time. *I won't be able to make it, I have a prior engagement.*
2 before, earlier than. *The presentation happened immediately prior to my arrival.*

priority **priorities**
NOUN something that needs to be dealt with before everything else. *An athlete's first priority is to stay fit and well.*

prise **prises prising prised**
VERB to force something open by forcing it, often with a levering tool.

prism **prisms**
NOUN an object made of clear glass with many flat sides. It separates light coming through it into the colours of the rainbow.

prison **prisons**
NOUN a building where criminals are kept.

prisoner **prisoners**
NOUN someone who is kept in prison or held in captivity against their will.

privacy
NOUN the state of being private, being left alone by other people.

private **privates**
ADJECTIVE **1** for the use of one person or group rather than for the general public.
2 taking place between a small number of people and kept secret from others: *a private conversation.*
3 owned or run by individuals or companies rather than by the state: *a private company.*
4 A private school does not receive any money from the government; parents pay fees for their children to attend it.
NOUN **5** a soldier of the lowest rank.
privately ADVERB

privatize **privatizes privatizing privatized**; also spelt **privatise**
VERB If the government privatizes an industry or organization previously owned by the state, it allows it to be bought and owned by private individuals or companies.
privatization NOUN

privet
NOUN a shrub with oval, dark green leaves, very commonly used in hedges.

privilege **privileges**
NOUN a special right or advantage that is given to a person or group.
privileged ADJECTIVE

prize **prizes prizing prized**
NOUN **1** a reward given to the winner of a competition or game; an award.
VERB **2** Something that is prized is wanted and admired because of its value or quality.

A B C D E F G H I J K L M N O P Q R S T U V W X Y Z

pro pros
NOUN 1 INFORMAL a professional, especially a professional sportsperson.
PHRASE 2 The **pros and cons** of a situation are its advantages and disadvantages.

pro-
PREFIX supporting or in favour of: *pro-hunting.*

probability probabilities
NOUN The probability of something happening is how likely it is to happen.

Synonyms: chance, likelihood, odds

probable
ADJECTIVE likely to be true or likely to happen.

probably
ADVERB Something that is probably going to happen is likely but not certain.

probation
NOUN 1 a period of time during which a person convicted of a crime is supervised by a probation officer instead of being sent to prison.
2 a period of time after someone starts a job during which their work is assessed and before they are given the job permanently.
probationary ADJECTIVE **probationer** NOUN

probe probes probing probed
VERB 1 to explore something by gently pushing a long thin object into it.
2 to ask a lot of questions to discover the facts about something.
NOUN 3 a long thin instrument used by doctors and dentists when examining a patient.

problem problems
NOUN 1 an unsatisfactory situation that causes difficulties.
2 a puzzle or question that you solve using logical thought or mathematics.
problematic ADJECTIVE

procedure procedures
NOUN a way of doing something, especially the correct or usual way.

proceed proceeds proceeding proceeded
VERB 1 If you proceed to do something, you start doing it or continue doing it. *She broke the news that she was married, then proceeded to tell them all about the wedding. Before we can proceed any further, I must say...*
2 FORMAL If you proceed in a particular direction, you move in that direction.

proceedings
PLURAL NOUN 1 an organized event that is in progress. *The proceedings were interrupted by a sudden shout.*
2 Legal proceedings are legal action taken against someone.

proceeds
PLURAL NOUN the proceeds of a sale, event, etc. are the profit it makes.

process processes processing processed
NOUN 1 a series of actions or events intended to achieve a particular result: *the cake-making process.*
PHRASE 2 If you are **in the process** of doing something, you have started doing it but have not yet finished.
VERB 3 When something such as food or information is processed, it is treated or dealt with in a particular way.

procession processions
NOUN a group of people or vehicles moving in a line, often as part of a ceremony or parade.

proclaim proclaims proclaiming proclaimed
VERB to announce or make something known publicly.
proclamation NOUN

prod prods prodding prodded
VERB to give something or someone a push with your finger or with something pointed; to poke.
prod NOUN

prodigy prodigies
Said "**prod**-dij-ee" NOUN someone who shows an extraordinary natural ability at an early age.

produce produces producing produced
Said "prod-**yooce**" VERB 1 to make something or cause it to happen.
2 to show something so that it can be seen. *Out of the hat, the magician produced a rabbit.*
Said "**prod**-yooce" NOUN 3 food that is grown to be sold.

producer producers
NOUN The producer of a record, film, play or programme is the person in charge of making it.

product products
NOUN 1 something that is made to be sold.
2 In mathematics, the product of two or more numbers or quantities is the result of multiplying them together.

production productions
NOUN 1 the process of manufacturing or growing something in large quantities.
2 a series of performances of a play, opera, programme or other show.

productive
ADJECTIVE 1 producing a large number of things.
2 If something such as a meeting is productive, good or useful things happen as a result of it.

productivity
NOUN the rate at which things are produced or dealt with.

profession professions
NOUN 1 a type of job that requires advanced education or training.
2 all the people who have the same profession: *the medical profession.*

 ► Write a list of the pros and cons of making school compulsory for everybody under 16.

professional **professionals**
ADJECTIVE 1 relating to the work of someone who is qualified in a particular profession. *I think you need professional advice.*
2 relating to activities which are done to earn money rather than as a hobby: *a professional footballer.*
3 A professional piece of work is of a high standard.
NOUN 4 a person who has been trained in a profession.
5 a person who plays sport to earn money rather than a hobby.
professionally ADVERB **professionalism** NOUN

professor **professors**
NOUN the most senior teacher in a department of a British university.

proficient
ADJECTIVE If you are proficient at something, you can do it well.
proficiently ADVERB **proficiency** NOUN

profile **profiles**
NOUN 1 the outline of your face seen from the side.
2 a short description of someone's life, character and abilities.

profit **profits profiting profited**
NOUN 1 the amount of money that you gain when you sell something for more than it cost you.
VERB 2 If you profit from something, you gain or benefit from it.
profitable ADJECTIVE

Synonyms: (sense 1) gain, proceeds, return

profound
ADJECTIVE 1 great in degree or intensity: *a profound mystery.*
2 showing deep thought or understanding.
profoundly ADVERB **profundity** NOUN

program **programs programming programmed**
NOUN 1 a set of instructions that a computer follows in order to perform a particular task.
VERB 2 If you program a computer, you write a program and install it in the computer.
programmer NOUN

programme **programmes**
NOUN 1 something that is broadcast on television or radio.
2 a planned series of events. *The duchess had a heavy programme of official engagements.*
3 a booklet giving information about a play, concert or show.

Synonyms: (sense 2) agenda, plan, schedule

progress **progresses progressing progressed**
Said "**pro**-gress" **NOUN 1** the process of gradually improving or getting near to achieving something. *You are making real progress in your schoolwork.*
2 the way that something develops. *I want a progress report on the building work.*
PHRASE 3 Something that is **in progress** has started and is still continuing.
Said "pro-**gress**" **VERB 4** to become more advanced or skilful at something.
5 to continue. *As the trip progressed, they relaxed more.*
progression NOUN **progressive** ADJECTIVE
progressively ADVERB

prohibit **prohibits prohibiting prohibited**
VERB to forbid something or make it illegal.
prohibition NOUN
✔ You *prohibit* a person *from* doing something.

project **projects projecting projected**
Said "**prod**-jekt" **NOUN 1** a carefully planned task that requires a lot of time or effort.
Said "prod-**jekt**" **VERB 2** Something that projects sticks out beyond a surface or an edge.
3 If you project an image onto a screen, you make it appear there.
4 Something that is projected is planned or expected: *projected exam results; projected financial returns.*
projection NOUN

projector **projectors**
NOUN a machine for showing films or transparencies on a screen.

prologue **prologues**
NOUN a speech or section that introduces a play or book.

prolong **prolongs prolonging prolonged**
VERB to make something last longer.
prolonged ADJECTIVE

promenade **promenades**
Said "prom-min-**ahd**" **NOUN** a road or path next to the sea at a seaside resort.

prominent
ADJECTIVE 1 important or well known. *We need a prominent person at the opening of the shop, such as the mayor.*
2 very noticeable. *Pinocchio had a prominent nose.*
prominently ADVERB **prominence** NOUN

promise **promises promising promised**
VERB 1 to say that you will definitely do something.
2 to show signs of having a particular quality. *From its reviews, the show promises to be very entertaining.*
NOUN 3 a statement made by someone that they will definitely do something.
4 Someone or something that shows promise seems likely to be successful. *The young actress gave a performance full of promise.*

Synonyms: (sense 1) guarantee, pledge, vow
(sense 3) guarantee, oath, vow

a b c d e f g h i j k l m n o p q r s t u v w x y z

A B C D E F G H I J K L M N O P Q R S T U V W X Y Z

promising
ADJECTIVE likely to be successful in the future.

promote **promotes promoting promoted**
VERB **1** If someone is promoted, they are given a more important job at work.
2 If someone promotes something, they try to make it happen or become more popular. *The pop group did a tour to promote their latest album.*
promotion NOUN

prompt **prompts prompting prompted**
ADJECTIVE **1** without any delay: *a prompt reply.*
VERB **2** If something prompts someone to do something, it makes them decide to do it. *Curiosity prompted him to push at the door.*
3 If you are prompted while acting in a play, someone tells you the lines you have forgotten.
ADVERB **4** exactly at the time mentioned. *I'll see you on Wednesday at 10 o'clock prompt.*
promptly ADVERB

prone
ADJECTIVE If you are prone to something, you have a tendency to be affected by it or to do it. *She was prone to have sneezing fits.*

Synonyms: inclined, liable, subject

prong **prongs**
NOUN the long, narrow, pointed parts of a fork or similar tool.

pronoun **pronouns**
NOUN a word that is usually used to replace a noun. Personal pronouns refer to people and things: examples include he, she, it, yourself, us. Possessive pronouns show ownership: examples include my, her, his, our, their, mine, ours, theirs.

pronounce **pronounces pronouncing pronounced**
VERB **1** When you pronounce a word, you say it.
2 to state or announce something formally. *I now pronounce you man and wife.*

pronounced
ADJECTIVE very noticeable. *He talks with a pronounced Scottish accent.*

pronunciation **pronunciations**
Said "pron-nun-see-**ay**-shn" NOUN the way a word is usually said.
✔ There is no *o* before the *u* in *pronunciation*. Compare this with *pronounce*. Strangely, the word *pronunciation* is often wrongly pronounced!

proof **proofs**
NOUN evidence which shows that something is true or exists.

Synonyms: confirmation, evidence, verification

proofread **proofreads proofreading proofread**
VERB to check a piece of writing through for mistakes.
proofreading NOUN **proofreader** NOUN

prop **props propping propped**
VERB **1** If you prop or prop up something, you stop it from falling down by pushing against it or by wedging something against it.
NOUN **2** A prop is a piece of wood or metal used to support something which might otherwise fall down.
3 The props in a play are all the objects and furniture used by the actors.

propaganda
NOUN exaggerated or false information that is published or broadcast in order to influence people.

propel **propels propelling propelled**
VERB to cause something to move in a particular direction.

propeller **propellers**
NOUN a device with large rotating blades connected to an engine, which move a boat or aircraft by a screwing action.

proper
ADJECTIVE **1** correct or suitable. *Put things in their proper place.*
2 real or satisfactory. *He was no nearer having a proper job.*

properly
ADVERB in the correct way.

proper noun **proper nouns**
NOUN the name of a particular person, place or institution, for example: Cedric, Berlin, Tuesday, Sydney Opera House. Proper nouns always start with a capital letter.

property **properties**
NOUN **1** A person's property is the things that belong to them.
2 a characteristic or quality. *Mint has powerful healing properties.*
3 a building and the land belonging to it.

prophecy **prophecies**
NOUN a statement about what someone believes will happen in the future.
✔ The noun *prophecy* ends in *cy*.

prophesy **prophesies prophesying prophesied**
VERB If someone prophesies something, they say it will happen.
✔ The verb *prophesy* ends in *sy*.

prophet **prophets**
NOUN **1** a religious person who is believed to speak the word of God.
2 someone who can predict the future.

 ► You should always proofread anything you write.

proportion **proportions**
NOUN 1 A proportion of an amount or group is a part of it. *A large proportion of the population drive cars.*
2 The proportion of one amount to another is its size in comparison with the other amount. *In the nursing profession, the proportion of women to men is around 4 to 1.*
PLURAL NOUN 3 You can refer to the size of something as its proportions. *She carried a red umbrella of vast proportions.*

proportional or **proportionate**
ADJECTIVE If one thing is proportional to another, it remains the same size in comparison with the other. *Sales increased, and there were proportional increases in profits.*
proportionally or **proportionately** ADVERB

propose **proposes proposing proposed**
VERB 1 to suggest a plan or idea.
2 If you propose to do something, you intend to do it. *The students propose to work their way round the world.*
3 If you propose to someone, you ask them to marry you.
proposal NOUN **proposition** NOUN

proprietor **proprietors**
NOUN the owner of a business.

propulsion
NOUN Propulsion is the power that moves something.

prose
NOUN ordinary written language, as distinct from poetry.

prosecute **prosecutes prosecuting prosecuted**
VERB If someone is prosecuted, they are charged with a crime and put on trial.
prosecution NOUN **prosecutor** NOUN

prospect **prospects**
NOUN 1 If there is a prospect of something, there is a possibility that it will happen.
2 Someone's prospects are their chances of being successful in future.

prosper **prospers prospering prospered**
VERB to be successful and make a lot of money.
prosperity NOUN

prosperous
ADJECTIVE A prosperous person is successful and wealthy.

prostitute **prostitutes**
NOUN a person, usually a woman, who has sex with men in exchange for money.
prostitution NOUN

protect **protects protecting protected**
VERB to prevent someone or something from being harmed.
protection NOUN **protective** ADJECTIVE

protein **proteins**
NOUN a substance from which living things are made, and which is needed for growth. Meat, fish, eggs, milk and pulses contain protein.

protest **protests protesting protested**
Said "pro-**test**" **VERB 1** to say or show that you disapprove of something.
Said "**pro**-test" **NOUN 2** a demonstration or statement showing that you disapprove of something.

Protestant **Protestants**
NOUN OR ADJECTIVE someone who belongs to the branch of the Christian church which separated from the Catholic church in the sixteenth century.
Protestantism NOUN

prototype **prototypes**
NOUN a first model of something that is made so that the design can be tested and improved.

protractor **protractors**
NOUN a flat, semicircular object used for measuring angles.

protrude **protrudes protruding protruded**
VERB; FORMAL to stick out.
protrusion NOUN

proud **prouder proudest**
ADJECTIVE 1 If you are proud of something, you feel satisfaction at something you own or have achieved.
2 Someone who is proud has a lot of dignity and self-respect.
proudly ADVERB

prove **proves proving proved** or **proven**
VERB to show by means of argument or evidence that something is definitely true.

Synonyms: confirm, show, verify

proverb **proverbs**
NOUN a short sentence which gives advice or makes a comment about life. *The early bird catches the worm.*
proverbial ADJECTIVE **proverbially** ADVERB

provide **provides providing provided**
VERB If you provide something for someone, you give it to them or make it available for them; to supply.
provision NOUN

province **provinces**
NOUN 1 one of the areas into which some large countries are divided.
2 You can refer to the parts of a country which are not near the capital as the provinces.

provision
NOUN If you make provision for something, you allow and prepare for it.

a b c d e f g h i j k l m n o p q r s t u v w x y z

provisional
ADJECTIVE A provisional arrangement has not yet been made definite and so might be changed; temporary.
provisionally ADVERB

provisions
PLURAL NOUN supplies of food and other basic requirements for a household, journey, etc.

provocation **provocations**
NOUN an act done deliberately to annoy someone.

provocative
ADJECTIVE intended to annoy other people or make them react in some way.
provocatively ADVERB

provoke **provokes provoking provoked**
VERB **1** If you provoke someone, you deliberately try to make them angry.
2 to cause an unpleasant reaction. *The programme provoked a storm of criticism.*

prow **prows**
NOUN the pointed front of a boat; the bow.

prowl **prowls prowling prowled**
VERB If a person or animal prowls around, they move around quietly and secretly.

proximity
NOUN; FORMAL nearness to someone or something.

prune **prunes pruning pruned**
NOUN **1** a dried plum.
VERB **2** When someone prunes a tree or shrub, they cut back some of the branches.

pry **pries prying pried**
VERB to try to find out about something secret or private.

psalm **psalms**
Said "**sahm**" NOUN one of the 150 songs, poems and prayers which together form the Book of Psalms in the Bible.
[from Greek *psalmos* meaning song accompanied on the harp]

pseudonym **pseudonyms**
Said "**syoo**-doe-nim" NOUN a name an author, actor, pop star, etc. uses rather than their real name.

psychiatrist **psychiatrists**
Said "sigh-**kye**-a-trist" NOUN a doctor whose job it is to treat mental illness.
psychiatry NOUN **psychiatric** ADJECTIVE

psychic
Said "**sigh**-kick" ADJECTIVE Psychic people have an unusual awareness of supernatural things. They often have mental powers such as the ability to read people's minds or predict the future.

psychologist **psychologists**
Said "sigh-**kol**-o-jist" NOUN a person qualified to understand the human mind and the reasons for people's behaviour.

psychology
Said "sigh-**kol**-oh-jee" NOUN the scientific study of the mind and of the reasons for people's behaviour.
psychological ADJECTIVE **psychologically** ADVERB

pub **pubs**
NOUN a building where people can buy and drink alcoholic drinks. Pub is short for public house.

puberty
Said "**pyoo**-ber-tee" NOUN the stage when a person's body changes from that of a child into that of an adult.

public
NOUN **1** people in general. *The gardens are open to the public.*
2 If you do or say something in public, you do or say it where everyone can see or hear you.
ADJECTIVE **3** relating to, or provided for, people in general: *public transport.*
publicly ADVERB

publication **publications**
NOUN **1** The publication of a book is the act of printing it and making it available.
2 a book or magazine.

publicity
NOUN information or advertisements about an item or event.

publicize **publicizes publicizing publicized**; also spelt **publicise**
VERB to advertise an event, information, etc. and make it widely known.

public school **public schools**
NOUN In Britain, a public school is a school that is privately run and that charges fees for the pupils to attend.

publish **publishes publishing published**
VERB When a company publishes a book, newspaper or magazine, they print copies of it and distribute it.
publisher NOUN **publishing** NOUN

pudding **puddings**
NOUN **1** a cooked sweet food, usually served hot.
2 another name for the dessert course of a meal.

puddle **puddles**
NOUN a small, shallow pool of rain or other liquid.

puff **puffs puffing puffed**
VERB **1** If you are puffing, you are breathing loudly and quickly with your mouth open.
2 If something puffs out or puffs up, it swells and becomes larger and rounder.
NOUN **3** a small amount of air or smoke that is released.

puffin **puffins**
NOUN a black and white sea bird with a large brightly coloured beak.

 ► Pseudonyms: who are or were Tom Mapother, Samuel Clemens, Charles Dodgson, Marion Morrison?

pull pulls pulling pulled
VERB 1 to hold and move something towards you.
2 If you pull a muscle, you injure it by stretching it too far or too quickly.
pull away VERB When a vehicle pulls away, it moves away from the kerb.
pull out VERB 1 When a vehicle pulls out, it moves away from the kerb.
2 If you pull out of a plan or arrangement, you decide to quit and not continue with it.
pull up, **pull over** or **pull in VERB** When a vehicle pulls up, pulls over or pulls in, it stops at the kerb.
pull through VERB to recover from a serious illness.

pulley pulleys
NOUN a device which uses ropes and wheels to lift heavy weights.

pullover pullovers
NOUN a piece of clothing that covers the top part of your body, made from wool or similar material.

Synonyms: jersey, jumper, sweater

pulp pulps pulping pulped
NOUN 1 a soft, moist mass, such as the inner part of a passion fruit.
VERB 2 to crush something into a pulp.

pulpit pulpits
NOUN the small raised platform in a church where a member of the clergy stands to preach.

pulse pulses pulsing pulsed
NOUN 1 the wave of pressure that passes through your arteries every time your heart pumps blood through your body. You can feel it at your wrists, your neck and elsewhere. Your pulse rate is a measure of how fast your heart is beating.
2 The seeds of beans, peas and lentils are called pulses when they are used for food.
VERB 3 If something is pulsing, it is moving or vibrating with rhythmic, regular movements. *The constant pulsing of the disco lights was giving her a headache.*

puma pumas
NOUN a wild animal belonging to the cat family.

pumice
Said "**pum**-iss" **NOUN** very lightweight grey stone, originally volcanic lava, that can be used to soften areas of hard skin.

pump pumps
NOUN a machine that is used to force a liquid or gas to move in a particular direction.
pump VERB

pumpkin pumpkins
NOUN a very large, round, orange vegetable.

pun puns
NOUN a clever and amusing use of words, so that what you say has two different meanings, such as: *did you hear the one about the cross-eyed teacher who couldn't control his pupils?*

punch punches punching punched
VERB 1 to hit someone or something hard with your fist.
2 If you punch holes in something, you make holes in it using a hole punch.
NOUN 3 a hard blow with the fist.
4 A hole punch is a device for pressing out holes in paper, leather, etc.
5 a drink usually made from wine or spirits mixed with fruit.

punch line punch lines
NOUN the last, and most important, line of a joke.

punctual
ADJECTIVE arriving at the correct time.
punctually ADVERB **punctuality** NOUN

Synonyms: on time, prompt

punctuate punctuates punctuating punctuated
VERB 1 to put the correct punctuation marks into a piece of writing.
2 Something that is punctuated by a particular thing is interrupted by it at intervals: *a grey day punctuated by bouts of rain.*

punctuation
NOUN The marks in writing such as full stops, question marks and commas are called punctuation or punctuation marks.

puncture punctures
NOUN a small hole in a car or bicycle tyre, made by a sharp object.
puncture VERB

punish punishes punishing punished
VERB to make someone suffer, usually because they have done something wrong.
punishing ADJECTIVE **punishment** NOUN

Synonyms: chastise, discipline, penalize

punt punts
NOUN a long, flat-bottomed river boat you move along by pushing a pole against the river bottom.

puny punier puniest
ADJECTIVE very small and weak.

pup pups
NOUN a young dog, or puppy. Some other young animals such as seals are also called pups.

pupa pupae
Said "**pyoo**-pa" **NOUN** an insect that is at the stage of development between a larva and a fully developed adult. See **larva**.

Punctuate: *what do you think I will feed you and clothe you for nothing.* Do you notice anything?

A B C D E F G H I J K L M N O P Q R S T U V W X Y Z

pupil pupils
NOUN 1 The pupils of a school are the children who attend it.
2 Your pupils are the small round black openings at the centre of your eyes.

puppet puppets
NOUN a doll that can be moved by pulling strings or by putting your hand inside its body.
[from Old French *poupette* meaning little doll]

puppy puppies
NOUN a young dog.

purchase purchases purchasing purchased
VERB 1 to buy.
NOUN 2 the act of buying something.
3 something which you have bought. *The shop assistant put my purchases in a bag.*
purchaser NOUN

pure purer purest
ADJECTIVE 1 Something that is pure is not mixed with anything else: *pure wool.*
2 clean and free from harmful substances: *pure water.*
3 complete and total: *pure luck.*
4 A pure person has not done anything sinful.
purity NOUN

Synonyms: (sense 4) chaste, innocent, virtuous

purely
ADJECTIVE involving only one feature and not including anything else. *I need this purely for my work - nothing else.*

purge purges purging purged
VERB To purge something is to remove undesirable things from it: *to purge the country of criminals.*

purify purifies purifying purified
VERB to remove all dirty or harmful substances from something.
purification NOUN

purple
ADJECTIVE OR NOUN a reddish-blue colour.

purpose purposes
NOUN 1 the reason for or function of something. *Just what is the purpose of your visit?*
2 the thing that you want to achieve. *Her only purpose in life was to get rich.*
PHRASE 3 If you do something **on purpose**, you do it deliberately.
purposeful ADJECTIVE **purposefully** ADVERB

purposely
ADVERB on purpose.

purr purrs purring purred
VERB When a cat purrs, it makes a low vibrating sound because it is contented.

purse purses pursing pursed
NOUN 1 a very small bag for carrying money.
2 In American English, a purse is a handbag.
VERB 3 If you purse your lips, you press them together in a tight, rounded shape.

pursue pursues pursuing pursued
VERB 1 If you pursue someone, you follow them in order to catch them.
2 If you pursue an activity, you do it or make efforts to achieve it. *Rashid decided to pursue a career in photography.*
pursuer NOUN

pursuit pursuits
NOUN 1 If you are in pursuit of someone, you are following them to try to catch them.
2 an occupation, hobby or pastime: *leisure pursuits.*

pus
NOUN a thick yellowish liquid that forms in an infected wound.

push pushes pushing pushed
VERB 1 to use force to make something or someone move away from you; to shove or thrust.
2 If you push someone into doing something, you encourage or force them to do it.
3 A person who pushes drugs tries to get people addicted to the drugs in order to sell them more in future.
NOUN 4 the act of pushing something.

pushchair pushchairs
NOUN a small folding chair on wheels in which a baby or toddler can be wheeled around.

pussy pussies
NOUN; INFORMAL another word for **cat**.

put puts putting put
VERB 1 When you put something or someone somewhere, you move it into that place, position or situation. *I put the books on the shelf. Susan has put me under a lot of stress.*
2 If you put an idea or remark in a particular way, you express it that way. *I think Anwar put that very well.*
put down VERB 1 If you have an animal put down, you have it painlessly killed.
2 to criticize someone in a way that makes them appear foolish.
put off VERB 1 to delay doing something, to postpone.
2 to cause someone to dislike something. *The bout of food poisoning put me off fish for life.*
put out VERB 1 to make a fire, light, etc. stop burning, to extinguish.
2 If you are put out, you are annoyed or upset.
put up VERB 1 to build or erect.
2 To put up the price of something means to increase it.
3 If you put up resistance to something, you fight it.
4 If you put up with something, you tolerate it even though you find it unpleasant.

 ► Modern proverb: never put off today what you can put off tomorrow.

putt **putts**
NOUN In golf, a putt is a gentle stroke made when the ball is fairly near the hole.
putt VERB

putty
NOUN a type of paste used to fix panes of glass into frames.

puzzle **puzzles puzzling puzzled**
VERB 1 If something puzzles you, it confuses you and you do not understand it. *There was something about the film that puzzled me.*
NOUN 2 a game or question that requires thought to complete or solve: *crossword puzzles.*
puzzled ADJECTIVE **puzzlement** NOUN

Synonyms: (sense 1) baffle, mystify, perplex

PVC
NOUN a tough form of plastic. PVC is an abbreviation of polyvinyl chloride.

pygmy **pygmies**; also spelt **pigmy**
Said "**pig**-mee" **NOUN** a very small person, especially one who belongs to a racial group in which all the people are small.

pyjamas
PLURAL NOUN loose trousers and a loose jacket that are worn in bed.

pylon **pylons**
NOUN a very tall metal structure which carries overhead electricity cables.

pyramid **pyramids**
NOUN 1 a three-dimensional shape with a flat base and flat triangular sides sloping upwards to a point.
2 The Pyramids are ancient stone structures built over the tombs of Egyptian kings and queens.

python **pythons**
NOUN a large snake that kills animals by squeezing them with its body.

A B C D E F G H I J K L M N O P Q R S T U V W X Y Z

Qq

quack **quacks quacking quacked**
VERB When a duck quacks, it makes a loud harsh sound.
quack NOUN

quad **quads**
Said "**kwod**" NOUN **1** an abbreviation for **quadruplet**.
2 an abbreviation for **quadrangle**.

quadrangle **quadrangles**
Said "**kwod**-rang-gl" NOUN a courtyard with buildings all round it.

quadrant **quadrants**
Said "**kwod**-rant" NOUN a quarter section of a circle or a quarter of the circumference of a circle.
[from Latin *quadrans* meaning quarter]

quadrilateral **quadrilaterals**
Said "kwod-ril-**lat**-ral" NOUN a two-dimensional shape with four straight sides.

quadruple **quadruples quadrupling quadrupled**
Said "kwod-**roo**-pl" VERB When an amount or number quadruples, it becomes four times as large.
quadruple ADJECTIVE

quadruplet **quadruplets**
Said "kwod-**roo**-plet" NOUN Quadruplets are four children born at the same time to the same mother.

quail **quails quailing quailed**
NOUN **1** a type of small game bird with a round body and short tail.
VERB **2** If you quail, you feel or look afraid.

quaint **quainter quaintest**
ADJECTIVE attractively old-fashioned or unusual.
quaintly ADVERB **quaintness** NOUN

quake **quakes quaking quaked**
VERB **1** to shake and tremble because you are very frightened.
NOUN **2** INFORMAL an earthquake.

Quaker **Quakers**
NOUN a member of a Christian group, the Society of Friends.

qualification **qualifications**
NOUN Your qualifications are your skills and achievements, particularly those officially recognized at the end of a course of training or study.

qualify **qualifies qualifying qualified**
VERB **1** to pass the examinations needed to do a particular job.
2 If you qualify for something, you have the right to do it or have it. *As a regular customer, Mrs Bloggs, you qualify for a discount.*

quality **qualities**
NOUN **1** The quality of something is how good it is.
2 a characteristic. *Even when young, Mark had leadership qualities.*

quantity **quantities**
NOUN an amount.
[from Latin *quantus* meaning how much]

quarantine **quarantines**
Said "**kwor**-an-teen" NOUN If an animal is in quarantine, it is kept away from other animals for a time because it might have an infectious disease.
quarantine VERB
[from Italian *quarantina* meaning forty days]

quarrel **quarrels quarrelling quarrelled**
VERB to have an angry argument, to fall out.
quarrel NOUN

quarrelsome
ADJECTIVE A quarrelsome person often quarrels or disagrees with others.

quarry **quarries quarrying quarried**
Said "**kwor**-ree" NOUN **1** a place where stone is removed from the ground by digging or blasting.
2 A person's or animal's quarry is the animal that they are hunting.
VERB **3** to remove stone from a quarry by digging or blasting.

quarter **quarters**
NOUN **1** one of four equal parts in a whole one.
2 When you are telling the time, "quarter" refers to the fifteen minutes before or after the hour.
3 an American or Canadian coin worth 25 cents.
4 A soldier's or servant's quarters are the rooms that they live in.
[from Latin *quartarius* meaning a fourth part]

quartet **quartets**
Said "kwor-**tet**" NOUN a group of four musicians who sing or play together; also a piece of music written for four instruments or singers.

quartz
NOUN a kind of hard, shiny crystal found in many rocks, used in industry and in making very accurate watches and clocks.

quaver **quavers quavering quavered**
Said "**kway**-ver" VERB If your voice quavers, it sounds unsteady, usually because you are nervous.
quavery ADJECTIVE

quay **quays**
Said "**kee**" NOUN a place where boats are tied up and loaded or unloaded.

queasy **queasier queasiest**
Said "**kwee**-zee" ADJECTIVE feeling slightly sick.
queasiness NOUN

 ► The letter Q is a puzzle. It seems to have had connections with K or might have been a monkey.

queen **queens**
NOUN **1** a female monarch or a woman married to a king.
2 a female bee or ant which can lay eggs.
3 the most powerful chess piece, which can move any number of squares in any direction.

queer **queerer queerest**
ADJECTIVE very strange, odd, peculiar.
queerly ADVERB

quench **quenches quenching quenched**
VERB If you quench your thirst, you have a drink so that you are no longer thirsty.

query **queries querying queried**
Said "**qweer**-ree" NOUN **1** a question.
VERB **2** If you query something, you ask about it because you think it might not be correct.

quest **quests**
NOUN a long, hard search for something important.

question **questions questioning questioned**
NOUN **1** a sentence which asks for information; an enquiry.
2 a problem that needs to be discussed; an issue. *We must solve the difficult question of unemployment.*
3 If there is no question about something, there is no doubt about it.
VERB **4** to ask someone questions.
5 to express doubts about something; to dispute or challenge. *The manager questioned whether his player was offside.*
PHRASE **6** If something is **out of the question**, it is impossible.

Synonyms: (sense 1) enquiry, query

QUESTIONS
Questions are used to ask for information. They are often introduced by adverbs such as **what, who, where, when, why,** and **how**.
What is your name?
If a sentence does not already contain an auxiliary verb, a form of the auxiliary verb **do** may be placed at the start to turn it into a question:
Does your mum know about this?
If there is already an auxiliary verb in the sentence, you can turn it into a question by reversing the word order so the auxiliary verb comes before the subject instead of after it.
You are going to the pictures.
Are you going to the pictures?
They must keep doing that.
Must they keep doing that?
A question can also be made by adding a phrase such as **isn't it** or **don't you** on to the end of a statement:
It's hot today, isn't it?
You like chocolate, don't you?
All questions have a question mark **?** at the end of the sentence.

questionable
ADJECTIVE doubtful.
questionably ADVERB

question mark **question marks**
NOUN the punctuation mark (?) used at the end of a question.

questionnaire **questionnaires**
NOUN a list of questions which asks for information.

queue **queues queuing** or **queueing queued**
Said "**kyoo**" VERB When people or vehicles queue or queue up, they wait in a line.
queue NOUN

quibble **quibbles quibbling quibbled**
VERB **1** to argue about something unimportant.
NOUN **2** a minor objection.

quiche **quiches**
Said "**keesh**" NOUN a tart with a savoury filling.

quick **quicker quickest**
ADJECTIVE **1** moving or doing things with great speed.
2 lasting only a short time: *a quick chat.*
3 intelligent and able to understand things easily.
quickness NOUN **quickly** ADVERB

quicken **quickens quickening quickened**
VERB to go faster or to make something faster.

quicksand **quicksands**
NOUN an area of deep wet sand that you sink into if you walk on it.

quid
NOUN; INFORMAL in British English, one pound in money.

quiet **quieter quietest**
ADJECTIVE **1** making very little noise.
2 calm and peaceful. *We had a quiet evening at home.*
3 A quiet event happens with very little fuss or publicity: *a quiet wedding.*
NOUN **4** silence. *The librarian asked for quiet.*
quietly ADVERB **quietness** NOUN

Antonyms: (sense 1) noisy, loud, rowdy

quieten **quietens quietening quietened**
VERB to go quieter or to make something quieter.

quill **quills**
NOUN **1** an old-fashioned pen made from a feather.
2 A porcupine's quills are the spines on its back.

quilt **quilts**
NOUN A quilt for a bed is a cover, especially a cover that is padded.

a b c d e f g h i j k l m n o p q r s t u v w x y z

quintet **quintets**
Said "kwin-**tet**" NOUN a group of five musicians who sing or play together; also a piece of music written for five instruments or singers.

quit **quits quitting quit**
VERB to leave or stop doing something. *Leigh quit his job as a lifeguard.*

quite
ADVERB **1** fairly but not very. *It's quite a long way away.*
2 completely. *Our position is quite clear.*

quiver **quivers quivering quivered**
VERB **1** to tremble.
NOUN **2** a trembling movement.
3 a container for arrows.

quiz **quizzes quizzing quizzed**
NOUN **1** a game in which someone tests your knowledge by asking you questions.
VERB **2** to question someone intensively.

quota **quotas**
NOUN a number or quantity of something which is officially allowed.

quotation **quotations**
NOUN **1** an extract from a book or speech which is quoted.
2 an estimate of how much a piece of work will cost.

quotation mark **quotation marks**
NOUN Quotation marks are the punctuation marks "..." that show where a speech or quotation begins and ends. See **inverted comma**, **speech marks**.

quote **quotes quoting quoted**
VERB **1** If you quote something that someone has written or said, you repeat their words.
NOUN **2** an extract from something that has been written or said. *The article began with a quote from Churchill.*
3 an estimate of how much a piece of work will cost.

quotient
NOUN in mathematics, the result you get from a division.

Qur'an
another spelling of **Koran**.

The letter "q" must be followed by "u" in English words. "U must join the queue."

Rr

rabbi rabbis
Said "**rab**-by" NOUN a Jewish religious leader.

rabbit rabbits
NOUN a small, furry, mammal with long ears.

rabble
NOUN a noisy, disorderly crowd.

rabies
Said "**ray**-beez" NOUN an infectious disease which causes people and animals, especially dogs, to go mad and die.

raccoon raccoons; also spelt **racoon**
NOUN a small North American mammal with a long striped tail.

race races racing raced
NOUN **1** a competition to see who is fastest, for example in running or driving.
2 one of the major groups that human beings can be divided into according to their physical features.
VERB **3** to take part in a race.
4 If something or someone races, they go at their quickest rate possible. *Britney's heart raced. Malik raced after the others.*

racecourse racecourses
NOUN a track, sometimes with jumps, along which horses race.

racehorse racehorses
NOUN a horse trained to run in races.

racial
ADJECTIVE relating to the different races that people belong to.
racially ADVERB

racist
ADJECTIVE If someone is racist, they believe that people of certain other races are inferior, and they often behave aggressively towards them.
racist NOUN **racism** NOUN

rack racks racking racked
NOUN **1** a piece of equipment for holding things or hanging things on.
VERB **2** If you are racked by something such as pain or guilt, you suffer because of it.
PHRASE **3** INFORMAL If you **rack your brains**, you try hard to think of or remember something.

racket rackets
NOUN **1** a lot of noise.
2 an illegal way of making money.
3 another spelling of **racquet**.

racquet racquets
NOUN a type of long bat used in tennis, badminton and squash that has a network of tight strings with which the ball is hit.

radar
NOUN a way of discovering the position or speed of objects such as ships or aircraft by using radio signals.
[an acronym from RA(dio) D(etecting) A(nd) R(anging)]

radiant
ADJECTIVE **1** Someone who is radiant is so happy that it shows in their face.
2 glowing brightly.
radiantly ADVERB **radiance** NOUN

radiate radiates radiating radiated
VERB **1** to form a pattern like lines spreading out from the centre of a circle.
2 If you radiate a quality or emotion, it shows clearly in your face and behaviour.

radiation
NOUN **1** the stream of particles given out by a radioactive substance.
2 the energy given out by something. The sun gives out heat and light radiation.

radiator radiators
NOUN **1** a metal panel for heating a room, often as part of a central heating system.
2 part of a car which prevents the engine from overheating.

radical radicals
ADJECTIVE **1** Radical changes are far-reaching, significant and dramatic.
NOUN **2** a person who thinks there should be great changes in society.
radically ADVERB

radii
the plural of **radius**.

radio radios radioing radioed
NOUN **1** a system of sending sound over a distance by transmitting electrical signals.
2 the broadcasting of programmes for the public to listen to.
3 a piece of equipment for listening to radio programmes.
VERB **4** to send a message by two-way radio.

radioactive
ADJECTIVE Radioactive substances produce energy in the form of powerful and harmful rays.
radioactivity NOUN

radish radishes
NOUN a small salad vegetable with a red skin and white flesh and a hot taste.

radius radii
NOUN a straight line drawn from the centre of a circle to its circumference.
[from Latin *radius* meaning ray or spoke]

raffia
NOUN a thin, stringy material made from palm leaves and used for making mats and baskets.

The letter R began as a picture of a human head, perhaps a man with a beard.

A B C D E F G H I J K L M N O P Q R S T U V W X Y Z

raffle raffles
NOUN a competition in which people buy numbered tickets and win a prize if they have the ticket that is chosen.
raffle VERB

raft rafts
NOUN a floating platform made from long pieces of wood tied together.

rafter rafters
NOUN Rafters are the sloping pieces of wood that support a roof.

rag rags
NOUN **1** a piece of old cloth used to clean or wipe things.
2 If someone is dressed in rags, they are wearing old torn clothes.

rage rages raging raged
NOUN **1** complete, uncontrollable anger, fury.
VERB **2** To rage about something means to speak angrily about it.
3 If something such as a storm or battle rages, it continues with great force or violence.

ragged
ADJECTIVE Ragged clothes are old and torn.

raid raids raiding raided
VERB When people raid a place, they enter it by force in order to attack it or look for something.
raid NOUN
[from Old English *rad* meaning military expedition]

rail rails railing railed
NOUN **1** a fixed horizontal bar used as a support or for hanging things on.
2 Rails are the steel bars which trains run along.
3 railway transport: *travelling by rail.*
PHRASE **4** If someone goes **off the rails** they lose control of their actions, perhaps by having a nervous breakdown.
VERB **5** to complain or protest strongly about something.

railings
PLURAL NOUN Railings are a fence made from metal bars.

railway railways
NOUN a route along which trains travel on steel rails.

rain rains
NOUN water falling from the clouds in small drops.
rain VERB

rainbow rainbows
NOUN an arch of different colours that sometimes appears in the sky after it has been raining.

raincoat raincoats
NOUN a long waterproof coat.

raindrop raindrops
NOUN a drop of rain.

rainfall
NOUN the amount of rain that falls in a place during a particular period.

rainforest rainforests
NOUN a dense forest of tall trees in a tropical area where there is warmth and a lot of rain.

raise raises raising raised
VERB **1** to make something higher.
2 If you raise the level or standard of something, you increase it or improve it.
3 If you raise your voice, you speak more loudly.
4 To raise money for a cause means to get people to donate money towards it.
5 If you raise a child, you look after it until it is grown up.
6 If you raise a subject, you mention it.

raisin raisins
NOUN Raisins are dried grapes.

rake rakes raking raked
NOUN **1** a garden tool with a row of metal teeth and a long handle.
VERB **2** To rake leaves or soil means to use a rake to gather the leaves or make the soil level.
rake up VERB If you rake up something embarrassing from the past, you remind someone about it.

rally rallies rallying rallied
NOUN **1** a large public meeting held to show support for something.
2 a competition in which vehicles are raced over public roads.
3 In tennis or squash, a rally is a continuous series of shots exchanged by the players.
VERB **4** When people rally to something, they gather together to continue a struggle or to support something or someone.

ram rams ramming rammed
VERB **1** to deliberately crash heavily into something. *The robbers' car rammed the security van.*
2 to push something firmly into place. *He rammed filler into the hole in the plaster.*
NOUN **3** an adult male sheep.

Ramadan
NOUN the ninth month of the Muslim year, during which Muslims eat and drink nothing during the hours of daylight.

ramble rambles rambling rambled
NOUN **1** a long walk in the countryside.
VERB **2** to go for a ramble.
3 to talk in a confused and long-winded way.
rambler NOUN

ramp ramps
NOUN a sloping surface connecting two different levels.

 ► Muslims observe Ramadan. Who would celebrate Diwali, Hanukkah, Advent?

rampage rampages rampaging rampaged
VERB **1** to rush about wildly causing damage.
PHRASE **2** To **go on the rampage** means to rush about in a wild or violent way.

Synonyms: (sense 1) go berserk, run amok

rampart ramparts
NOUN Ramparts are earth banks, often with a wall on top, built to protect a castle or city.

ramshackle
ADJECTIVE in very poor condition: *a ramshackle house.*

ran
past tense of **run**.

ranch ranches
NOUN a large farm where cattle or horses are reared, especially in the USA.
[from Mexican Spanish *rancho* meaning small farm]

rancid
Said "**ran**-sid" ADJECTIVE Rancid food, such as butter or bacon, has gone bad.
[from Latin *rancere* meaning to stink]

random
ADJECTIVE Something that is done in a random way, or at random, is done without a definite plan.
randomly ADVERB

Synonyms: chance, haphazard, incidental

rang
past tense of **ring**.

range ranges ranging ranged
NOUN **1** a number of different things of the same kind. *A wide range of colours is available.*
2 The range of a set of numbers or values is expressed by stating the lowest and highest numbers in that range. *The age range is between 35 and 55.*
3 The range of something is the maximum distance over which it can reach things or detect things: *a missile with a range of 2000 kilometres.*
4 a range of mountains is a line of them.
VERB **5** When a set of things ranges between two points, they vary within these points on a scale.

Synonyms: (sense 1) series, variety

ranger rangers
NOUN someone whose job is to look after a forest or park.

rank ranks ranking ranked
NOUN **1** Someone's rank is their position or grade in an organization, such as one of the armed forces.
2 a row of people or things: *a taxi rank.*
VERB **3** If someone or something is ranked at a particular position on a scale, they are at that position. *The tennis player was ranked number one in the world.*
ADJECTIVE **4** having a strong, unpleasant smell: *the unwashed clothes smelt really rank.*
ranking NOUN

ransack ransacks ransacking ransacked
VERB To ransack a place means to disturb everything and leave it in a mess, in order to search for or steal something.
[from Old Norse *rann* meaning house + *saka* meaning to search]

ransom ransoms
NOUN money that is demanded to free someone who has been kidnapped.

rant rants ranting ranted
VERB to talk loudly in an excited or angry way.

rap raps rapping rapped
NOUN **1** a quick knock or blow on something. *A rap on the door signalled his arrival.*
2 a type of music in which the words are spoken in a rapid, rhythmic way.
VERB **3** to hit with a series of quick blows.
4 to perform rap music.

rape rapes raping raped
VERB **1** If someone is raped, they are forced to have sex.
NOUN **2** the crime of forcing someone to have sex.
rapist NOUN

rapid
ADJECTIVE happening or moving very quickly: *rapid industrial expansion; rapid dance steps.*
rapidly ADVERB **rapidity** NOUN

rapids
PLURAL NOUN an area of a river where water moves extremely fast over rocks.

rapier rapiers
NOUN a long thin sword with a sharp point.

rare rarer rarest
ADJECTIVE **1** not common or not happening often.
2 Meat that is rare is cooked very lightly.
rarely ADVERB **rarity** NOUN

rascal rascals
NOUN someone who does bad or mischievous things.
rascally ADJECTIVE

rash rashes; rasher rashest
NOUN **1** an area of red spots that appear on your skin when you are ill or have an allergy.
ADJECTIVE **2** If you are rash, you do something without thinking carefully about it.

Synonyms: (sense 2) foolhardy, reckless

rasher rashers
NOUN a thin slice of bacon.

raspberry raspberries
NOUN a small soft red fruit that grows on a bush.

A B C D E F G H I J K L M N O P Q R S T U V W X Y Z

rat rats ratting ratted
NOUN **1** a long-tailed animal which looks like a large mouse.
2 INFORMAL an unpleasant and untrustworthy person.
VERB **3** INFORMAL If you rat on somebody, you desert or betray your associates.
PHRASE **4** If you **smell a rat**, you suspect there is something not right about the situation.

rate rates rating rated
NOUN **1** The rate at which something happens is the speed or frequency with which it happens.
2 A rate is the amount of money that is charged for goods or services. *We offer a special rate for students.*
PHRASE **3** If you say **at this rate** something will happen, you mean it will happen if things continue in the same way.
4 You say **at any rate** when you want to add something to qualify what you have just said. *He's the best character in the book, to me at any rate.*
VERB **5** The way you rate someone or something is your opinion of their worth. *I rate her as one of the UK's finest actresses.*

rather
ADVERB **1** to a fair degree. *We got along rather well.*
PHRASE **2** If you **would rather** do something, you would prefer to do it.
3 If you do one thing **rather than** another, you do the first thing in preference to the second. *I like to play tennis rather than watch it.*

Synonyms: (sense 1) quite, relatively, somewhat
(sense 2) preferably

ratio ratios
NOUN a relationship which shows how many times one thing is bigger than another, expressed in its lowest terms. *There were 30 children and 5 adults on the trip, so the adult to child ratio was 1 to 6.*

ration rations
NOUN Your ration of something is the amount you are allowed to have, particularly of food or other such necessities when they are in short supply.
rationing NOUN

rational
ADJECTIVE based on reason rather than emotion. *It was a rational and kind decision to have the injured dog put down, but it broke her heart.*
rationality NOUN

rattle rattles rattling rattled
VERB to make short, regular knocking sounds, for example if something is shaking.

rattlesnake rattlesnakes
NOUN a poisonous American snake.

rave raves raving raved
VERB **1** to talk in an excited and uncontrolled way, perhaps because you are angry.
2 INFORMAL If you rave about something, you talk about it very enthusiastically.
ADJECTIVE **3** INFORMAL A rave review for a play or film is a very enthusiastic one.
NOUN **4** INFORMAL a large dance event with electronic music.

raven ravens
NOUN **1** a large black bird with a deep, harsh call.
ADJECTIVE **2** Raven hair is black and shiny.

ravenous
ADJECTIVE very hungry.
ravenously ADVERB

ravine ravines
Said "rav-**een**" NOUN a deep, narrow valley with steep sides.

ravioli
Said "rav-ee-**oh**-lee" NOUN small squares of pasta filled with meat and served with a sauce.

raw rawer rawest
ADJECTIVE **1** Raw food is uncooked.
2 A raw substance is in its natural state before being processed.

raw material raw materials
NOUN Raw materials are the original substances used to make something.

ray rays
NOUN **1** a beam of light.
2 a large, flat sea fish with eyes on the top of its body and a long tail.

razor razors
NOUN a tool that people use for shaving.

re-
PREFIX again: *repeat; reread.*

reach reaches reaching reached
VERB **1** to arrive at a place.
2 to stretch your arm out and touch or hold something.
3 to extend as far as a place or point. *Her cloak reached the ground.*
4 When people reach an agreement or decision, they succeed in achieving it.
5 to contact someone, usually by telephone. *You can reach me on the usual number.*
PHRASE **6** If a place or thing is **within reach**, it is possible to get to it.
7 If something is **out of reach**, you cannot get to it.

react reacts reacting reacted
VERB **1** When you react to something, you behave in a particular way because of it.
2 If one substance reacts with another, a chemical change takes place when they are put together.

 ► What do these animal phrases mean: underdog, dark horse, to cry wolf, lame duck?

reaction **reactions**
NOUN 1 Your reaction to something is what you feel, say or do because of it.
2 Your reactions are your ability to move quickly in response to something that happens. *The game of squash requires fast reactions.*
3 In a chemical reaction, a chemical change takes place when two substances are put together.

reactor **reactors**
NOUN a device which is used to produce nuclear energy.

read **reads reading read**
VERB 1 When you read, you look at something written and follow it or say it aloud.
2 If you can read someone's mind or moods, you can judge what they are feeling or thinking.
3 When you read a meter or gauge, you look at it and record the figure on it.

reader **readers**
NOUN 1 The readers of a newspaper or magazine are the people who read it regularly.
2 a person who reads something aloud.

readily
ADVERB 1 willingly and eagerly. *Katriona would readily have jumped into the river to save the child.*
2 easily done or quickly obtainable. *Help is readily available.*

reading **readings**
NOUN 1 the activity of reading a book.
2 the figure or measurement shown by a dial or gauge is its reading.

ready
ADJECTIVE 1 properly prepared for something. *Your glasses will be ready in a fortnight. I'll be ready in a minute.*
2 willing to do something. *I'm ready to do any job you give me.*
readiness NOUN

ready-made
ADJECTIVE already made and therefore able to be used immediately.

real
ADJECTIVE 1 Something that is real actually exists and is not imagined or invented.
2 genuine and not artificial or imitation.
3 true or actual. *This was the real reason for her call.*
realist NOUN **reality** NOUN

Synonyms: authentic, genuine, true

realistic
ADJECTIVE 1 like real life. *Her sculptures of people are very realistic.*
2 If you are realistic about a situation, you recognize and accept its true nature. *Being realistic, we haven't got time to go shopping now.*
realistically ADVERB

realize **realizes realizing realized**; also spelt **realise**
VERB 1 to become aware of something. *Suddenly, she realized she loved him!*
2 FORMAL If your hopes or fears are realized, what you hoped for or feared actually happens.
realization NOUN

really
ADVERB 1 You use "really" to emphasize a statement or to reduce the force of a negative statement. *That was a really good film. I'm not really surprised.*
2 actually or truly. *What is really going on?*
3 You can say "Really?" to express surprise.

reap **reaps reaping reaped**
VERB 1 to cut and gather a grain crop.
2 When people reap benefits or rewards, they get them as a result of hard work or careful planning.
reaper NOUN

reappear **reappears reappearing reappeared**
VERB to come back into view after having disappeared or gone away.
reappearance NOUN

rear **rears rearing reared**
NOUN 1 the part of something at its back. *You'll find it at the rear of the garage.*
ADJECTIVE 2 back. *My rear bumper fell off.*
VERB 3 to bring up children or young animals.
4 When a horse rears, it raises its front legs in the air.

rearrange **rearranges rearranging rearranged**
VERB to organize or arrange something in a different way.
rearrangement NOUN

reason **reasons reasoning reasoned**
NOUN 1 the fact or situation which explains why something happens; cause or motive.
2 the ability to think and make judgements; logical thought. *It stands to reason.*
VERB 3 to decide something is true after considering all the facts. *I reasoned that if he could do it, so could I.*
4 If you reason with someone, you persuade them to accept sensible arguments.

reasonable
ADJECTIVE 1 fair and sensible. *Palvinder is a reasonable person, he won't mind.*
2 A reasonable amount is a fairly large amount.
3 fairly good, but not very good. *The food is reasonable here.*
4 A reasonable price is fair and not too high.
reasonably ADVERB

reassure **reassures reassuring reassured**
VERB If you reassure someone, you say or do things to make them stop worrying.
reassurance NOUN **reassuring** ADJECTIVE

a b c d e f g h i j k l m n o p q r s t u v w x y z

Wacky anagram: "the countryside" can be rearranged to "no city dust here".

rebel **rebels rebelling rebelled**
Said "**reb**-ul" **NOUN 1** Rebels are people who are fighting against their own country's army in order to change the political system.
2 someone who rejects the values of the society around and behaves differently from other people.
Said "rib-**bell**" **VERB 3** to reject society's values and behave differently from other people.

rebellion **rebellions**
NOUN organized and often violent opposition to authority.

Synonyms: mutiny, revolution, uprising

rebellious
ADJECTIVE unwilling to obey, and likely to rebel against authority.

rebound **rebounds rebounding rebounded**
VERB to spring or bounce back after hitting something.
rebound NOUN

rebuild **rebuilds rebuilding rebuilt**
VERB to build something again after it has been taken down or damaged in some way.

rebuke **rebukes rebuking rebuked**
Said "rib-**yook**" **VERB** to tell someone off in a severe way.
rebuke NOUN

recall **recalls recalling recalled**
VERB 1 to remember.
2 If you are recalled to a place, you are ordered to return there.
3 If a company recalls products, it asks people to return them because they are faulty.

recap **recaps recapping recapped**
VERB to repeat and summarize the main points of an explanation or discussion.
recap NOUN

recapture **recaptures recapturing recaptured**
VERB to catch or possess something again when it had gone away or been lost. *Don't try to recapture the past. The soldiers recaptured their garrison from the enemy. The groom recaptured the escaped racehorse.*

recede **recedes receding receded**
VERB 1 When something recedes, it moves away into the distance.
2 If a man's hair is receding, he is starting to go bald at the front.

receipt **receipts**
Said "ris-**seet**" **NOUN** a piece of paper confirming that money or goods have been received.

receive **receives receiving received**
VERB 1 When you receive something, you get it after someone has given or sent it to you.
2 To receive something also means to have it happen to you. *He received severe injuries in the car crash.*
3 If something is received in a particular way, people react to it in that way. *The decision was received with jubilation.*
receptive ADJECTIVE

receiver **receivers**
NOUN the part of a telephone you hold near to your ear and mouth.

recent
ADJECTIVE Something recent happened a short time ago.
recently ADVERB

reception **receptions**
NOUN 1 In a hotel or office, reception is the place near the entrance where appointments and enquiries are dealt with.
2 a formal party: *a wedding reception.*
3 The reception that someone or something gets is the way that people react to them. *The film got an enthusiastic reception from the public.*
4 If your radio or television gets good reception, the sound or picture is clear.

receptionist **receptionists**
NOUN someone in an office, hotel, etc. who deals with people as they arrive, answers the phone and arranges appointments.

recess **recesses**
NOUN 1 a period when no work is done by a committee, parliament, etc.: *the Christmas recess.*
2 a place where part of a wall has been built further back than the rest.

recession **recessions**
NOUN a period when a country's economy is less successful and more people become unemployed.

recipe **recipes**
Said "**res**-sip-ee" **NOUN 1** a list of ingredients and instructions for cooking something.
2 If something is a recipe for disaster or for success, it is likely to result in disaster or success.

recital **recitals**
NOUN a performance of music or poetry, usually by one person.

recite **recites reciting recited**
VERB to say aloud a poem or something you have learnt.
recitation NOUN

reckless
ADJECTIVE showing a lack of care about danger or damage.
recklessly ADVERB **recklessness** NOUN

reckon **reckons reckoning reckoned**
VERB 1 to estimate or calculate. *About 20% of the population is reckoned to be illiterate.*
2 INFORMAL to think. *I reckon Sally likes me.*
reckon with **VERB** If you had not reckoned with something, you had not expected it and therefore were unprepared when it happened.

 ► Verso means the left-hand page of an open book, having an even number. ◄

reclaim **reclaims reclaiming reclaimed**
VERB 1 When you reclaim something, you collect it after leaving it somewhere or losing it.
2 To reclaim land means to make it suitable for use, for example, by draining it.

recline **reclines reclining reclined**
VERB to lie or lean back at an angle.

recognize **recognizes recognizing recognized**; also spelt **recognise**
VERB 1 to realize who somebody is or what something is, to identify, to know.
2 to accept. *The council have been slow to recognize the traffic problem.*
recognition NOUN **recognizable** ADJECTIVE
recognizably ADVERB

recoil **recoils recoiling recoiled**
VERB to jerk back from something.

recollect **recollects recollecting recollected**
VERB If you recollect something, you remember it.
recollection NOUN

recommend **recommends recommending recommended**
VERB If you recommend something to someone, you think it is good and suggest that they try it.
recommendation NOUN

reconcile **reconciles reconciling reconciled**
VERB If two people are reconciled after a quarrel, they make friends again.

reconstruct **reconstructs reconstructing reconstructed**
VERB 1 To reconstruct something that has been damaged means to build it again.
2 To reconstruct a past event means to get a complete description of it from small pieces of information.
reconstruction NOUN

record **records recording recorded**
Said "**rec**-cord" **NOUN 1** If you keep a record of something, you keep a written account of the details concerning it.
2 a round, flat piece of plastic on which music has been recorded.
3 an achievement which is the best of its type. *The high-jumper set a new world record.*
4 Your record is what is known about your achievements or past activities. *You have an excellent school record.*
Said "rec-**cord**" **VERB 5** to write information down so that it can be referred to later.
6 to put music or speech on tape, record or CD.
ADJECTIVE 7 higher, lower, better or worse than ever before. *Profits were at a record high.*

Synonyms: (sense 1) document, file, register
(sense 5) note, register, write down

recorder **recorders**
NOUN a small woodwind instrument.

recount **recounts recounting recounted**
Said "re-**count**" **VERB 1** If you recount a story, you tell it.
Said "**re**-count" **NOUN 2** a second counting of votes at an election in order to check the result.

recover **recovers recovering recovered**
VERB 1 to get well again after illness.
2 to stop being upset after an unhappy experience.
3 to get something back that you once had. *Most of the stolen goods were recovered.*
recovery NOUN

Synonyms: (sense 1) convalesce, recuperate
(sense 3) regain, retrieve

recreation **recreations**
Said "rek-kree-**ay**-shn" **NOUN** the things that you do for enjoyment in your spare time.
recreational ADJECTIVE

recruit **recruits recruiting recruited**
VERB 1 to get people to join a group or help with something.
NOUN 2 someone who has joined the army or some other organization.
recruitment NOUN

rectangle **rectangles**
NOUN a four-sided, two-dimensional shape with four right angles.
rectangular ADJECTIVE

rectify **rectifies rectifying rectified**
VERB; FORMAL If you rectify something that is wrong, you put it right.

recuperate **recuperates recuperating recuperated**
VERB to recover gradually after being ill or injured.
recuperation NOUN **recuperative** ADJECTIVE

recur **recurs recurring recurred**
VERB If something recurs, it happens again.
recurrence NOUN **recurrent** ADJECTIVE

recurring
ADJECTIVE 1 happening or occurring many times.
2 In arithmetic, if the decimal answer to a division sum contains a number or numbers that repeat over and over again indefinitely, these numbers are said to be recurring. For example, 1 divided by 3 gives the answer 0·33333... and so on. This is described as "point three recurring".

recycle **recycles recycling recycled**
VERB to process used products so that the materials they contain can be used again.

red **redder reddest**
NOUN OR ADJECTIVE the colour of blood or ripe tomatoes.

redeem redeems redeeming redeemed
VERB **1** If a feature redeems an unpleasant thing or situation, it makes it seem less bad.
2 If you redeem yourself after having done something wrong, you do something that gives people a good opinion of you again.
3 If you redeem a voucher for money, goods or services, you hand over the voucher and receive the money, goods or services in exchange.
4 In Christianity, to redeem someone means to free them from sin by giving them faith in Jesus Christ.
redemption NOUN

red-handed
PHRASE To **catch someone red-handed** means to catch them in the act of doing something wrong.

red herring red herrings
NOUN something that is irrelevant and distracts people's attention from what is important.

redraft redrafts redrafting redrafted
VERB to make a second version of a piece of writing.
redraft NOUN

red tape
NOUN official rules and procedures that seem unnecessary and cause delay.
[in the 18th century, red tape was used to bind official government documents]

reduce reduces reducing reduced
VERB **1** to make something smaller in size or amount.
2 You can use "reduce" to say that someone or something is changed to a weaker or inferior state. *She reduced them to tears. The village was reduced to rubble.*

Synonyms: (sense 1) cut, decrease, lessen

reduction reductions
NOUN When there is a reduction in something, it is made smaller.

redundant
ADJECTIVE **1** When people are made redundant, they lose their jobs because there is no more work for them or no money to pay them.
2 When something becomes redundant, it is no longer needed.
redundancy NOUN

reed reeds
NOUN **1** Reeds are hollow stemmed plants that grow in shallow water or wet ground.
2 a thin piece of cane or metal inside some wind instruments which vibrates when air is blown over it.

reef reefs
NOUN a long line of rocks or coral close to the surface of the sea.

reek reeks reeking reeked
VERB To reek of something means to smell strongly and unpleasantly of it.
reek NOUN

reel reels reeling reeled
NOUN **1** a cylindrical object around which you wrap something; often part of a device which you turn as a control: *the reel of a fishing rod.*
2 a fast Scottish dance.
VERB **3** When someone reels, they move unsteadily as if they are going to fall.
4 If your mind is reeling, you are confused because you have too much to think about.
reel off VERB If you reel off information, you repeat it from memory quickly and easily.

refer refers referring referred
VERB **1** to mention. *Here's the picture I referred to earlier.*
2 If you refer to a book, document, etc., you look at it to find something out.
3 When a problem is referred to someone, they are formally asked to deal with it. *My doctor referred me to the hospital.*
referral NOUN
✔ Do not use *back* after *refer: This refers to what has already been said* not *refers back.*

referee referees
NOUN the official who controls a football or boxing match.
referee VERB

reference references
NOUN **1** A reference to someone or something is a mention of them.
2 a number or name that tells you where to find information, or identifies a document.
3 the act of referring to someone or something for information or advice.
4 If someone gives you a reference when you apply for a job, they write a letter about your abilities.

reference book reference books
NOUN a book of facts in which you look things up.

referendum referendums or referenda
NOUN a vote in which all the people in a country are officially asked whether they agree with an important policy or proposal.

refill refills refilling refilled
VERB to fill up something which was full but is now empty.
refill NOUN

refine refines refining refined
VERB To refine a raw material such as oil or sugar means to process it to remove impurities.

refined
ADJECTIVE very polite, well-mannered and with good taste.
refinement NOUN

 ► It is very important in any writing you do, to make time to check through and redraft.

refinery **refineries**
NOUN a factory or plant where substances such as oil or sugar are refined.

reflect **reflects reflecting reflected**
VERB 1 When something is reflected in a mirror or in water, you can see its image there.
2 If a surface reflects light or heat, the light or heat bounces back from the surface instead of passing through.
3 If something reflects an attitude or situation, it shows what it is like. *My choice of light blue wallpaper reflected my love for Manchester City.*
4 When you reflect, you think about something.
reflective ADJECTIVE

reflection **reflections**
NOUN 1 an image in a mirror or on water.
2 the process by which light and heat are bounced off a surface.
3 Reflection is careful thought. *After a period of reflection, I've decided to retire.*

reflector **reflectors**
NOUN a piece of glass or plastic which glows when light shines on it.

reflex **reflexes**
NOUN 1 A reflex or reflex action is a sudden uncontrollable movement that you make as a result of pressure or a blow.
2 If you have good reflexes, you respond very quickly when something unexpected happens.
ADJECTIVE 3 A reflex angle is between 180° and 360°. See **acute, obtuse**.

reform **reforms reforming reformed**
NOUN 1 Reforms are major changes to laws or institutions.
VERB 2 When laws or institutions are reformed, major changes are made to them.
3 When people reform, they stop committing crimes or doing other unacceptable things.
reformer NOUN

refraction
NOUN the bending of a ray of light, for example, when it enters water or glass.
refract VERB

refrain **refrains refraining refrained**
VERB 1 FORMAL If you refrain from doing something, you do not do it. *Please refrain from running in the corridor.*
NOUN 2 The refrain of a song is a short, simple part, repeated many times.

refresh **refreshes refreshing refreshed**
VERB 1 If something refreshes you when you are hot or tired, it makes you feel cooler or more energetic.
PHRASE 2 To **refresh someone's memory** means to remind them of something they had forgotten.

refreshing
ADJECTIVE 1 Something refreshing, such as a cold drink or a shower, makes you feel fresher when you are tired or hot.
2 You say that something is refreshing when it is pleasantly different from usual.

refreshments
PLURAL NOUN drinks and small amounts of food provided at an event.

refrigerator **refrigerators**
NOUN an electrically cooled container in which you store food to keep it fresh; a fridge.
refrigerate VERB **refrigeration** NOUN

refuel **refuels refuelling refuelled**
VERB to fill a vehicle, aircraft, etc. with more fuel.
refuelling NOUN

refuge **refuges**
NOUN 1 a place where you go for safety.
PHRASE 2 If you **take refuge**, you go somewhere for safety or behave in a way that will protect you. *The hikers took refuge in a barn during the storm.*

Synonyms: (sense 1) haven, sanctuary, shelter

refugee **refugees**
NOUN Refugees are people who have been forced to leave their country and live elsewhere.

refund **refunds refunding refunded**
VERB If someone refunds money that you have spent, they return it to you.
refund NOUN **refundable** ADJECTIVE

refuse **refuses refusing refused**
Said "ref-**yooze**" **VERB 1** to say or decide firmly that you will not do something.
2 If you refuse something, you do not allow it or do not accept it. *They offered me a tip but, thanking them politely, I refused it.*
Said "**ref**-yoos" **NOUN** rubbish or waste.
refusal NOUN

regain **regains regaining regained**
VERB to get something back that you had before.

regal
ADJECTIVE very grand and suitable for a king or queen.

regard **regards regarding regarded**
VERB 1 to think of someone or something in a particular way, or to have an opinion about someone or something. *We regard our teacher as a friend.*
2 LITERARY to look at someone in a particular way. *Miss Bennett regarded the stranger with curiosity.*
NOUN 3 If you have a high regard for someone, you respect them greatly.
PHRASES 4 **As regards, with regard to** and **in regard to** are all used to indicate what you are writing and talking about.

a b c d e f g h i j k l m n o p q r s t u v w x y z

George Bernard Shaw believed that the apostrophe was unnecessary and he refused to use it.

A B C D E F G H I J K L M N O P Q R S T U V W X Y Z

regarding
PREPOSITION about, to do with, concerning. *I received the note regarding your absence.*

regardless
PREPOSITION OR ADVERB happening in spite of something else. *They ate the cake, regardless of the fact that it was stale.*

regards
PLURAL NOUN If you give or send your regards to someone, you express friendly greetings and good wishes.

regatta **regattas**
NOUN a race meeting for sailing or rowing boats.

reggae
NOUN a type of music originally from the West Indies, with a strong beat.

regiment **regiments**
NOUN a large group of soldiers commanded by a lieutenant colonel.
regimental ADJECTIVE

region **regions**
NOUN **1** a large area of land with its own identity, a territory.
PHRASE **2** **In the region of** means approximately.
regional ADJECTIVE

register **registers registering registered**
NOUN **1** an official list or record.
VERB **2** When something is registered, it is recorded on an official list.
3 When something registers on a scale, it shows a particular value.
registration NOUN

regret **regrets regretting regretted**
VERB **1** If you regret something, you wish that it had not happened.
2 You can say that you regret something as a way of apologizing. *We regret any inconvenience to passengers.*
regret NOUN

Synonyms: (sense 1) repent, rue

regretful
ADJECTIVE If you are regretful about something, you are sorry that it happened.
regretfully ADVERB

regrettable
ADJECTIVE unfortunate and undesirable: *a regrettable accident.*
regrettably ADVERB

regular **regulars**
ADJECTIVE **1** equal and evenly spaced. *The music had a strong, regular beat.*
2 Regular events happen at equal or frequent intervals.
3 If you are a regular visitor somewhere, you go there often.
4 usual or normal. *Regular services will be resumed as soon as possible.*
5 In geometry, a regular shape has sides which are the same size.
NOUN **6** People who go to a place often are known as its regulars.
regularly ADVERB **regularity** NOUN

Synonyms: (sense 1) even, steady, uniform

regulate **regulates regulating regulated**
VERB to control the way something operates.
regulator NOUN

regulation **regulations**
NOUN **1** Regulations are official rules.
2 control. *Public houses are subject to strict regulation.*

rehearse **rehearses rehearsing rehearsed**
VERB to practise a performance in preparation for the actual event.
rehearsal NOUN

reign **reigns reigning reigned**
Said "**rain**" VERB When a king or queen reigns, he or she rules the country.
reign NOUN

rein **reins**
NOUN **1** Reins are the thin leather straps which you hold when you are riding a horse.
PHRASE **2** To **keep a tight rein** on someone or something means to control them firmly.

reincarnation
NOUN People who believe in reincarnation believe that when you die, you are born again as another person or creature.

reindeer
NOUN deer with large antlers, which live in northern regions.

reinforce **reinforces reinforcing reinforced**
VERB **1** to strengthen something physically. *They poured in concrete to reinforce the sea wall.*
2 to give added evidence to an idea, claim, etc. that has been put forward. *This reinforces what I was saying.*

reinforcement **reinforcements**
NOUN **1** Reinforcements are additional soldiers sent to join an army in battle.
2 Reinforcement is the reinforcing of something.

reject **rejects rejecting rejected**
Said "ree-**ject**" VERB **1** If you reject a proposal or request, you do not accept it or agree to it.
Said "**ree**-ject" NOUN **2** a product that cannot be used because there is something wrong with it.
rejection NOUN

Synonyms: (sense 1) decline, refuse, turn down

rejoice **rejoices rejoicing rejoiced**
VERB to be very pleased about something, to celebrate.
rejoicing NOUN

► "Reign" and "rain" are homophones: they sound the same but are different in spelling and meaning.

relate relates relating related
VERB **1** If something relates to something else, it is connected or concerned with it.
2 If you relate to someone, you understand their thoughts and feelings.
3 to tell a story.

related
ADJECTIVE **1** If you are related to someone, they are in some way part of your family.
2 connected, associated. *Are there any related matters to discuss?*

relation relations
NOUN **1** Your relations are the members of your family.
2 If there is a relation between two things, they are connected in some way.
3 Relations between people are their feelings and behaviour towards each other. *It is important to maintain good relations with other countries.*

relationship relationships
NOUN **1** The relationship between two things is the way in which they are connected.
2 The relationship between two people or groups is the way they feel and behave towards each other.
3 a close friendship, especially one involving romantic feelings.

relative relatives
ADJECTIVE **1** You use "relative" when comparing the size or quality of two or more things. *The short wrestler and the tall wrestler had equal relative strengths. Sally is a relative beginner.*
NOUN **2** Your relatives are the members of your family.

relax relaxes relaxing relaxed
VERB **1** If you relax or if something relaxes you, you become calm and less worried or tense.
2 If you relax your grip, you loosen your hold on something.
3 If you relax a rule, you make it less strict.
relaxation NOUN **relaxed** ADJECTIVE

Synonyms: (sense 1) rest, take it easy, unwind

relay relays relaying relayed
Said "**ree**-lay" NOUN **1** A relay or relay race is a race between teams, with each team member running one part of the race.
Said "ree-**lay**" VERB **2** If you relay information, you tell it to someone else.

release releases releasing released
VERB **1** to set free.
2 to let go.
3 to make something publicly available. *She is releasing a new album this month.*
NOUN **4** the act of setting someone free or being set free.
5 the act of making a recording or film, etc. available.
6 A press release is an official written statement given to reporters.

relegate relegates relegating relegated
VERB If a sports team is relegated, it is moved to a lower division because of its poor performance.
relegation NOUN

relent relents relenting relented
VERB If someone relents, they agree to something they had previously not allowed.

relentless
ADJECTIVE never stopping and never becoming less intense: *the relentless buzz of the big city.*
relentlessly ADVERB **relentlessness** NOUN

relevant
ADJECTIVE If something is relevant to a situation or person, it is important in that situation or to that person.
relevance NOUN

Synonyms: appropriate, pertinent, significant

reliable
ADJECTIVE **1** able to be trusted to do what you want or to work well.
2 Reliable information is likely to be correct, because it comes from a source that you can trust.
reliably ADVERB **reliability** NOUN

reliant
ADJECTIVE dependent on someone or something.
reliance NOUN

relic relics
NOUN **1** an objects or custom that has survived from an earlier time.
2 an object regarded as holy because it is thought to be connected with a saint.

relief
NOUN **1** If you feel relief, you feel glad and thankful because a bad situation is over or has been avoided.
2 money, food and clothing provided for poor or hungry people.
3 a way of making part of a design, map or sculpture stand out from the surface.

relief map relief maps
NOUN a map showing the shape of mountains and hills by shading.

relieve relieves relieving relieved
VERB **1** If something relieves an unpleasant feeling, it makes it less unpleasant.
2 FORMAL If you relieve someone, you do their job or duty for a period.
3 If someone is relieved of their duties, they are dismissed from their job.
4 If you relieve yourself, you urinate.

relieved
ADJECTIVE If you are feeling relieved, you are glad that a situation you were worried about is over or has turned out well.

religion religions
NOUN belief in a god or gods, and all the activities connected with such a belief.

A B C D E F G H I J K L M N O P Q R S T U V W X Y Z

religious
ADJECTIVE **1** connected with religion.
2 having a strong belief in a god or gods.

Synonyms: (sense 2) devout, pious

relish **relishes relishing relished**
VERB **1** to enjoy an experience or thought.
NOUN **2** enjoyment. *She threw herself into the dancing with relish.*
3 a savoury sauce or pickle.

reluctant
ADJECTIVE If you are reluctant to do something, you are unwilling to do it.
reluctantly ADVERB **reluctance** NOUN

rely **relies relying relied**
VERB **1** If you rely on someone or something, you need them in order to do something.
2 If you can rely on someone, you can trust them.
reliance NOUN

remain **remains remaining remained**
VERB **1** to stay as or where you are. *They remained silent. She remained behind.*
2 to continue to exist. *Some of the work is finished, but other tasks still remain.*
PLURAL NOUN **3** The remains of something are the parts that are left after most of it has been destroyed.

Synonyms: (sense 3) debris, remnants

remainder
NOUN **1** The remainder of something is the part that is left after the rest has gone.
2 In a division sum, if a number cannot be divided exactly, the remainder is the amount left over.

remark **remarks remarking remarked**
VERB If you remark on something, you make a comment about it, often in a casual way.
remark NOUN

remarkable
ADJECTIVE impressive and unexpected, extraordinary.
remarkably ADVERB

Synonyms: extraordinary, outstanding, wonderful

remedial
ADJECTIVE Something that is remedial helps you to get better, either in health or in ability.

remedy **remedies**
NOUN something that cures an illness or corrects a problem.
remedy VERB

remember **remembers remembering remembered**
VERB **1** If you remember someone or something from the past, you still have an idea of them and you are able to think about them.
2 If you remember to do something, you do it when you intended to.

Synonyms: (sense 1) recall, recollect

remembrance
NOUN If you do something in remembrance of a dead person, you are showing that they are remembered with respect and affection.

remind **reminds reminding reminded**
VERB **1** to jog someone's memory about something they need to remember.
2 If someone reminds you of another person, they look similar and make you think of them.
reminder NOUN

remnant **remnants**
NOUN a small part of something left after the rest has been used or destroyed.

remorse
NOUN a strong feeling of guilt and regret.
remorseful ADJECTIVE **remorsefully** ADVERB

Synonyms: contrition, regret, repentance

remote **remoter remotest**
ADJECTIVE **1** far away in distance or time.
2 If there is only a remote possibility that something will happen, it is unlikely to happen.
remoteness NOUN

remote control
NOUN a system of controlling a machine or vehicle from a distance using radio or electronic signals.

removal **removals**
NOUN **1** the act of removing something.
2 A removal company transports someone's belongings and furniture from one home to a new one.

remove **removes removing removed**
VERB If you remove something, you take it off or away.
removable ADJECTIVE

rendezvous
Said "**ron**-day-voo" NOUN **1** a meeting.
2 a place where you have arranged to meet someone. *The shopping centre became a popular rendezvous for truants.*
rendezvous VERB

renew **renews renewing renewed**
VERB **1** If you renew a library book or a licence, you extend the period of time for which it is valid to have it.
2 To renew an activity or a friendship means to begin it again.
renewal NOUN

renewable
ADJECTIVE Renewable resources are those which never run out, such as wind and water.

renovate **renovates renovating renovated**
VERB to repair and restore something to good condition.
renovation NOUN

 ► Repeat quickly: does this shop still sell shiny silk shirts?

renowned
ADJECTIVE well known for something good, famous.
renown NOUN

rent **rents renting rented**
VERB **1** If you rent something, such as a house or a car, you pay the owner a regular sum of money in exchange for being able to use it.
NOUN **2** the amount of money that you pay regularly for the use of something.

rental **rentals**
ADJECTIVE **1** concerned with the renting out of something: *a TV rental company.*
NOUN **2** the amount paid to rent or hire something.

repair **repairs repairing repaired**
VERB **1** to mend something.
NOUN **2** something that you do to mend something that is broken, damaged or worn.
repairer NOUN

repay **repays repaying repaid**
VERB **1** To repay money means to give it back to the person who lent it.
2 If you repay a favour, you do something to help the person who helped you.
repayment NOUN

repeat **repeats repeating repeated**
VERB to do or say something again.
repeat NOUN **repeated** ADJECTIVE
repetition NOUN

repeatedly
ADVERB over and over again.

repel **repels repelling repelled**
VERB **1** If something repels you, you find it horrible and disgusting.
2 When soldiers repel an attack, they successfully defend against it.
3 When a magnetic pole repels an opposite pole, it forces the opposite pole away.
repulsion NOUN

repellent **repellents**
ADJECTIVE **1** FORMAL horrible and disgusting.
NOUN **2** Repellents are chemicals used to keep insects or other creatures away.

repent **repents repenting repented**
VERB; FORMAL to be extremely sorry for something bad you have done.
repentance NOUN **repentant** ADJECTIVE

repetition **repetitions**
NOUN If there is a repetition of something, it happens again.
repetitious ADJECTIVE

repetitive
ADJECTIVE A repetitive activity involves a lot of repetition and is boring.

replace **replaces replacing replaced**
VERB **1** to put something back where it was before.
2 to take the place of something or someone else.
3 If you replace something that is damaged or lost, you get a new one.
replacement NOUN

Synonyms: (sense 2) supersede, supplant

replay **replays replaying replayed**
VERB **1** to play something again, such as a sports match or a video tape.
NOUN **2** a match that is played for a second time.

replica **replicas**
NOUN an accurate copy of something.
replicate VERB

reply **replies replying replied**
VERB to say or write an answer.
reply NOUN

report **reports reporting reported**
VERB **1** If you report what has happened, you tell someone about it.
2 If you report someone to an authority, you make an official complaint about them.
3 If you report to a person or place, you go there and say you are ready for work.
NOUN **4** an account of an event or situation.

reporter **reporters**
NOUN someone who writes news articles or broadcasts news reports.

repossess **repossesses repossessing repossessed**
VERB If a shop or company repossesses goods that have not been paid for, they take them back.
repossession NOUN

represent **represents representing represented**
VERB **1** If a sign or symbol represents something, it is accepted as meaning that thing.
2 If someone represents you, they act on your behalf.
3 If something or someone is represented in a certain way, they are suggested to be that way. *He is represented in the press as a hero.*
representation NOUN

representative **representatives**
NOUN **1** a person who acts on behalf of another person or group of people.
2 a salesman, often abbreviated to "rep".
ADJECTIVE **3** If something is representative of a group, it is typical of that group.

reprieve **reprieves reprieving reprieved**
Said "rip-**preev**" VERB **1** If someone who has been sentenced to death is reprieved, their sentence is changed and they are not killed.
NOUN **2** a delay before something unpleasant happens. *The zoo won a reprieve from closure.*

reprimand **reprimands reprimanding reprimanded**
VERB to tell someone officially that they should not have done something.
reprimand NOUN

A B C D E F G H I J K L M N O P Q R S T U V W X Y Z

reprisal reprisals
NOUN Reprisals are violent actions taken by one group of people against another group that has harmed them.

reproach reproaches
NOUN; FORMAL If you express reproach to someone, you show that you feel sad and angry about something they have done wrong.
reproach VERB **reproachful** ADJECTIVE
reproachfully ADVERB

reproduce reproduces reproducing reproduced
VERB 1 to copy something.
2 When living things reproduce, they produce more of their own kind.

reproduction reproductions
NOUN 1 the process by which living things produce more of their kind.
2 a copy of something such as an antique or a painting.
reproductive ADJECTIVE

reptile reptiles
NOUN a cold-blooded animal such as a snake or lizard, which has scales on its skin and lays eggs.
[from Latin *reptilis* meaning creeping]

republic republics
NOUN a country which has a president rather than a king or queen.
republican ADJECTIVE OR NOUN
republicanism NOUN

repulsive
ADJECTIVE horrible and disgusting.
repulsively ADVERB

reputation reputations
NOUN the opinion that people have of someone or something. *The school had a good reputation.*

Synonyms: name, renown, standing

request requests requesting requested
VERB to ask for something politely or formally.
request NOUN

require requires requiring required
VERB 1 If you require something, you need it.
2 If a law or rule requires you to do something, you have to do it.

requirement requirements
NOUN something that you must have or must do.

reread rereads rereading reread
VERB to read something again.

rescue rescues rescuing rescued
VERB to save someone or something from a dangerous or unpleasant situation.
rescue NOUN **rescuer** NOUN

research researches
NOUN work that tries to discover facts about something.
research VERB **researcher** NOUN

resemblance resemblances
NOUN If there is a resemblance between two things, they are similar to each other.

Synonyms: likeness, similarity

resemble resembles resembling resembled
VERB If one thing or person resembles another, they are similar to each other.

resent resents resenting resented
VERB If you resent something, you feel bitter and angry about it.
resentment NOUN

reservation reservations
NOUN 1 If you make a reservation, you book a travel ticket, hotel room, restaurant table, etc.
2 If you have reservations about something, you are not sure that it is good or right.

reserve reserves reserving reserved
VERB 1 If something is reserved for a particular person or purpose, it is kept specially for them.
NOUN 2 a supply of something for future use.
3 In sport, a reserve is someone who is available to play in case one of the first team is unable to play.
4 an area of land where animals and plants are officially protected.

Synonyms: (sense 1) put by, save, set aside

reserved
ADJECTIVE Reserved people are shy and keep their feelings hidden.

reservoir reservoirs
Said "**rez**-ev-wahr" NOUN a lake used for storing water before it is supplied to people.

reside resides residing resided
VERB; FORMAL to live in a particular place.

residence residences
NOUN; FORMAL a house, especially a large and important one.

resident residents
NOUN 1 the people who live in a house or area.
ADJECTIVE 2 If someone is resident in a town or country, they live there.

resign resigns resigning resigned
VERB 1 If you resign from a job, you formally announce that you are leaving it.
2 If you resign yourself to an unpleasant situation, you accept it.
resignation NOUN

resin resins
NOUN 1 a sticky substance produced by some trees.
2 a chemically-produced substance used to make plastic and adhesives.

 ▶ Reservoir is a French *and* an English word. Others include avalanche, beret, bouquet and camouflage.

resist resists resisting resisted
VERB 1 to refuse to accept a situation and try to prevent it.
2 to stop yourself from doing something that you want to do. *She resisted the temptation to have another chocolate.*

resistance
NOUN 1 If you put up resistance to something, you oppose it strongly and actively.
2 If you have resistance to a disease, your body has a natural ability to fight it.
3 the property of substances that oppose the flow of electricity in a circuit.
resistant ADJECTIVE

resolute
ADJECTIVE; FORMAL determined not to change your mind.
resolutely ADVERB

resolution resolutions
NOUN 1 a formal decision taken at a meeting.
2 determination. *The brave nurse acted with great resolution.*
3 If you make a resolution, you decide to try very hard to do something.
4 FORMAL The resolution of a problem is the solving of it.

resolve resolves resolving resolved
VERB 1 If you resolve a problem, you find a solution to it.
2 to make a firm decision to do something.
NOUN 3 absolute determination.

resort resorts resorting resorted
VERB 1 If you resort to doing something, you do it because you have no other choice.
NOUN 2 a place where people spend their holidays: *a seaside resort.*
PHRASE 3 If you do something **as a last resort**, you do it because you can find no other way of solving a problem.

resource resources
NOUN The resources of a country, organization or person are the materials, money or skills they have.

resourceful
ADJECTIVE A resourceful person is good at finding ways to deal with problems.
resourcefulness NOUN **resourcefully** ADVERB

respect respects respecting respected
VERB 1 If you respect someone, you have a good opinion of their character or ideas.
2 If you respect someone's rights or wishes, you avoid doing things that they would dislike or regard as wrong.
NOUN 3 a good opinion of someone's character or ideas.
PHRASE 4 You can say **in this respect, in many respects**, etc. to show that what you are saying applies to a particular thing or number of things. *In some respects, nothing has changed.*

respectable
ADJECTIVE 1 approved of by society and regarded as honest and decent.
2 adequate or reasonable. *We were going at a respectable speed.*
respectably ADVERB **respectability** NOUN

respectful
ADJECTIVE showing respect for someone.
respectfully ADVERB

respective
ADJECTIVE belonging or relating individually to the people or things just mentioned. *Bill and Ben went into their respective rooms to pack.*

respectively
ADVERB in the same order as the items just mentioned. *Their sons, Bill and Ben, were three and six respectively.*

respiration
NOUN 1 Your respiration is your breathing.
2 the process by which living organisms obtain energy from their food. Respiration takes place in cells.
respiratory ADJECTIVE

respond responds responding responded
VERB When you respond to something, you react to it by doing or saying something.

response responses
NOUN the reaction or reply to an event. *The charity's plea for help got a good response.*

responsibility responsibilities
NOUN 1 If you have responsibility for something, it is your duty to deal with it.
2 If you have a responsibility to someone, it is your duty to help them.
3 If you accept responsibility for something that has happened, you agree that you were to blame for it.

responsible
ADJECTIVE 1 A responsible person behaves properly, without needing to be supervised.
2 If you are responsible for something that has happened, it is your fault.
3 If you are responsible for something, it is your duty to deal with it.
4 If you are responsible to someone, that person is your superior and tells you what to do.
responsibly ADVERB

Synonyms: (senses 2 and 3) accountable, answerable, liable

rest rests resting rested
NOUN 1 the remaining parts of something.
2 a time when you do not do anything active for a while.
VERB 3 to relax and not do anything active for a while.
4 If you rest something somewhere or if it rests there, its weight is supported there.

a b c d e f g h i j k l m n o p q r s t u v w x y z

Oscar Wilde claimed to be able to resist everything except temptation.

restaurant **restaurants**
Said "**rest**-ront" NOUN a place where you can buy and eat a meal.

restful
ADJECTIVE something that is restful helps you feel calm and relaxed.
restfully ADVERB

restless
ADJECTIVE finding it hard to remain still or relaxed because of boredom or impatience.
restlessly ADVERB **restlessness** NOUN

restore **restores restoring restored**
VERB to cause something to exist again or to return to its previous state. *In 1660 Charles II was restored to the throne of England. We asked her to restore an antique chair.*
restoration NOUN

restrain **restrains restraining restrained**
VERB to hold someone or something back or prevent them from doing what they want to.
restraint NOUN

restrict **restricts restricting restricted**
VERB **1** If you restrict something, you put a limit on it to prevent it becoming too large or varied. *We restricted the numbers inside the club, to prevent overcrowding.*
2 To restrict someone's movements or actions means to prevent them from moving or acting freely.
restriction NOUN **restricted** ADJECTIVE
restrictive ADJECTIVE

result **results resulting resulted**
NOUN **1** The result of an action or situation is the outcome or consequence of it.
2 The result of a contest, calculation or exam is the final score, figures or marks at the end of it.
VERB **3** to cause. *Half of all road accidents result in head injuries.*

resume **resumes resuming resumed**
Said "riz-**yoom**" VERB If you resume an activity or if it resumes, it begins again after a break.
resumption NOUN

Resurrection
NOUN The Resurrection is the Christian belief that Jesus Christ returned to life three days after he had died.

resuscitate **resuscitates resuscitating resuscitated**
Said "ris-**suss**-it-tate" VERB to assist an unconscious person physically, so they become conscious again.
resuscitation NOUN

retail **retails retailing retailed**
VERB To retail goods means to sell them to the public. See **wholesale**.
retailer NOUN

retain **retains retaining retained**
VERB to keep or hold. *The plant retains moisture well.*
retention NOUN **retentive** ADJECTIVE

retaliate **retaliates retaliating retaliated**
VERB to fight back against someone who has harmed you or tried to harm you.
retaliation NOUN **retaliatory** ADJECTIVE

retire **retires retiring retired**
VERB **1** to leave a job and stop working because of old age.
2 FORMAL If you retire to another room or place, such as bed, you go there.
retirement NOUN

retort **retorts retorting retorted**
VERB to reply angrily to someone.
retort NOUN

retrace **retraces retracing retraced**
VERB If you retrace your steps, you carefully go back the way that you came.

retreat **retreats retreating retreated**
VERB **1** to move away from something or somebody.
NOUN **2** If an army moves away from the enemy, this is referred to as a retreat.
3 a quiet place you can go to rest or do things in private.

retrieve **retrieves retrieving retrieved**
VERB to get something back. *My dog retrieved the ball from the stream.*
retrieval NOUN

retriever **retrievers**
NOUN a large dog often used by hunters to bring back animals which they have shot.

retrospect
NOUN When you think about something in retrospect, you consider it afterwards and often have a different opinion from the one you had at the time.

return **returns returning returned**
VERB **1** to go back to a place or condition. *We returned to Britain by ferry. At last, life returned to normal.*
2 to give something back. *He returned her passport.*
NOUN **3** arrival back at a place or at a former condition.
4 the act of giving or putting something back.
5 A return or a return ticket is a ticket for a journey to a place and back again.
PHRASE **6** If you do something **in return** for what someone has done for you, you do it because of what they did.

reunion **reunions**
NOUN a party or meeting for people who have not seen each other for a long time.
reunite VERB

 ► Food words: diet, menu, vegetarian, organic, restaurant, protein, carbohydrate.

rev revs revving revved
VERB 1 INFORMAL When you rev the engine of a vehicle, you press the accelerator to increase the engine speed.
NOUN 2 The speed of an engine is measured in revolutions per minute, referred to as revs.

reveal reveals revealing revealed
VERB 1 to uncover something that has been hidden.
2 to tell people about something that has been a secret.
revelation NOUN **revealing** ADJECTIVE

revel revels revelling revelled
VERB If you revel in a situation, you enjoy it very much.
reveller NOUN **revelry** NOUN

revenge
NOUN the act of getting your own back on someone who has hurt you; retaliation, vengeance.

revenue revenues
NOUN money that a government, company or organization receives.

revere reveres revering revered
VERB If you revere somebody, you respect and admire them very greatly.
revered ADJECTIVE

Reverend
a title used before the name of a member of the clergy, often abbreviated to "Rev".

reverent
ADJECTIVE showing great respect.
reverence NOUN **reverently** ADVERB

reverse reverses reversing reversed
VERB 1 When you reverse a car, you drive it backwards.
2 When someone reverses a process, decision or order, they change it to its opposite.
NOUN 3 the opposite of what has just been said or done.
ADJECTIVE 4 opposite to what has just been described.
reversal NOUN

reversible
ADJECTIVE able to be reversed. Reversible clothing can be worn with either side on the outside.

review reviews
NOUN 1 an article or a talk on television or radio, giving an opinion of a new book, play or film.
2 When there is a review of a situation or system, it is examined again to decide whether changes are needed.
review VERB **reviewer** NOUN

revise revises revising revised
VERB to look at what you have done either to learn it or to correct it.
revision NOUN

revive revives reviving revived
VERB 1 to help someone become conscious again, after they have been unconscious.
2 When something is revived, it becomes active or successful again. *We revived the tradition of maypole dances on the green.*
revival NOUN

revolt revolts revolting revolted
NOUN 1 a violent attempt by a group of people to change their country's political system.
VERB 2 If something revolts you, it is so horrible that you feel disgust.
3 When people revolt, they fight against the authority that governs them.

revolting
ADJECTIVE horrible and disgusting.

revolution revolutions
NOUN 1 an attempt by a large group of people to change their country's political system, using force.
2 an important change in an area of human activity: *the computer revolution.*
3 a complete turn of 360°.

revolutionary revolutionaries
ADJECTIVE 1 new and very different. *A century ago electric power was revolutionary.*
NOUN 2 a person who takes part in a revolution.

revolutionize revolutionizes revolutionizing revolutionized; also spelt **revolutionise**
VERB to change things in an important and permanent way. *Computers have revolutionized the way people work.*

revolve revolves revolving revolved
VERB 1 to turn in a circle around a central point. *The earth revolves on its own axis.*
2 If something revolves round something else, it centres on that as the most important thing. *Their lives revolve around their children.*
revolving ADJECTIVE

revolver revolvers
NOUN a small gun held in the hand.

reward rewards
NOUN something you are given because you have done something good.
reward VERB

rewarding
ADJECTIVE Something that is rewarding gives you a lot of satisfaction.

rewind rewinds rewinding rewound
VERB If you rewind a tape on a tape recorder or video, you make the tape go backwards.

rewrite rewrites rewriting rewrote
VERB to write something again in a different way.
rewritten ADJECTIVE

a b c d e f g h i j k l m n o p q r s t u v w x y z

These words make new words when read backwards: lever, knits, evil, time, meet, parts.

rhetorical
ADJECTIVE 1 A rhetorical question is one which is asked in order to make a statement rather than to get an answer, such as "What's that got to do with you?"
2 Rhetorical language is intended to be grand and impressive.
rhetorically ADVERB

rheumatism
Said "**room**-at-izm" NOUN an illness that makes your joints and muscles stiff and painful.
rheumatic ADJECTIVE

rhinoceros **rhinoceroses**
NOUN a large African or Asian mammal with one or two horns on its nose.

rhombus **rhombuses** or **rhombi**
NOUN a shape with four equal sides and no right angles.

rhubarb
NOUN a plant with long red stems which can be cooked with sugar and eaten.

rhyme **rhymes rhyming rhymed**
VERB 1 If one word rhymes with another or if two words rhyme, they have a very similar sound; for example, "Molly" rhymes with "trolley".
NOUN 2 a word that rhymes with another. *He couldn't find a rhyme for "orange".*

rhyming couplet **rhyming couplets**
NOUN two lines of poetry together that rhyme.

rhythm **rhythms**
NOUN a regular series of sounds, movements or actions.
rhythmic ADJECTIVE **rhythmically** ADVERB

rib **ribs**
NOUN Your ribs are the curved bones that go from your spine to your chest, protecting your lungs.
ribbed ADJECTIVE

ribbon **ribbons**
NOUN a long, narrow piece of cloth used as a fastening or decoration.

rice
NOUN white or brown grains taken from a cereal plant.

rich **richer richest**
ADJECTIVE 1 having a lot of money or possessions.
2 containing a large amount of something. *Oranges are rich in vitamin C.*
3 Rich food is highly flavoured and contains a large amount of fat, oil or sugar.
4 Rich colours, smells and sounds are strong and pleasant.
richly ADVERB **richness** NOUN

riches
PLURAL NOUN valuable possessions or large amounts of money.

richly
ADVERB 1 If someone is richly rewarded, they are rewarded with something very valuable.
2 greatly. *The snooty lady richly deserved to be splashed with mud by the tractor.*

rickety
ADJECTIVE likely to collapse or break.

rickshaw **rickshaws**
NOUN a hand-pulled cart used in Asia for carrying passengers.

ricochet **ricochets ricocheting** or **ricochetting ricocheted** or **ricochetted**
Said "**rik**-osh-ay" VERB When a bullet ricochets, it hits a surface and bounces away from it.
ricochet NOUN

rid **rids ridding rid**
PHRASE 1 When you **get rid** of something you do not want, you remove it or destroy it. *He had to get rid of the smell in the kitchen.*
VERB 2 FORMAL To rid a place of something unpleasant means to succeed in removing it.

riddance
PHRASE; INFORMAL If you say **good riddance** when someone leaves, you mean you are glad they have gone.

riddle **riddles**
NOUN 1 a puzzle which seems to be nonsense, but which has an entertaining solution.
2 something which puzzles and confuses you, a mystery.

Synonyms: (sense 2) enigma, mystery

ride **rides riding rode ridden**
VERB 1 When you ride a horse or bicycle, you sit on it and control it as it moves along.
2 When you ride in a car or bus, you travel in it.
NOUN 3 a journey on a horse or bicycle or in a vehicle.
rider NOUN

ridge **ridges**
NOUN 1 a long, narrow piece of high land.
2 a raised line on a flat surface.

ridicule **ridicules ridiculing ridiculed**
VERB 1 to make fun of someone in an unkind way.
NOUN 2 unkind laughter and mockery.

ridiculous
ADJECTIVE very foolish.
ridiculously ADVERB

rife
ADJECTIVE; FORMAL very common. *Unemployment was rife in the 1930s.*

rifle **rifles**
NOUN a hand-held gun with a long barrel.

 ► Try a *bout-rimé*: choose any three or four pairs of rhyming words and write a verse to fit.

rig **rigs rigging rigged**
VERB **1** If you rig up a device or structure, you erect it quickly and fix it in place.
2 If someone rigs a contest, they dishonestly arrange for a particular person to succeed.
NOUN **3** a large structure used for extracting oil or gas from the ground or the sea bed.
4 any arrangement of equipment or apparatus.

rigging
NOUN the ropes supporting the mast and sails of a sailing boat.

right **rights righting righted**
ADJECTIVE OR ADVERB **1** correct and in accordance with the facts.
2 Right refers to actions that are considered to be morally or legally correct.
ADJECTIVE **3** The right decision, action or person is the best or most suitable one.
NOUN **4** If you have a right to do something, you are morally or legally entitled to do it.
5 the direction right. In the number 56, the 6 is on the right and the 5 is on the left.
ADVERB **6** You can use "right" to emphasize the exact position or time of something. *I had to decide right there and then.*
VERB **7** If you right something, you correct it or put it back in an upright position.
rightly ADVERB

Antonym: (sense 1) wrong
(sense 5) left

right angle **right angles**
NOUN an angle of 90°.

righteous
ADJECTIVE; OLD-FASHIONED Righteous people behave in a way that is morally good and religious.

rightful
ADJECTIVE Someone's rightful possession is one which they have a moral or legal right to own.
rightfully ADVERB

right-handed
ADJECTIVE Someone who is right-handed does things such as writing with their right hand.

rigid
ADJECTIVE **1** A rigid object is stiff and does not bend easily.
2 Rigid laws or systems cannot be changed and are considered severe.
rigidly ADVERB **rigidity** NOUN

Synonyms: (sense 2) inflexible, strict

rim **rims**
NOUN the outside or top edge of an object such as a wheel or a cup.

rind **rinds**
NOUN the thick outer skin of fruit, cheese or bacon.

ring **rings ringing rang rung**
VERB **1** When a telephone or bell rings, it makes a clear, loud sound.
2 If you ring someone, you phone them.
3 If something is ringed with something else, it has that thing all around it. *The court was ringed with police.*
NOUN **4** the sound made by a telephone or bell.
5 a small circle of metal that you wear on your finger, sometimes as a decoration but often as a token of marriage.
6 an object or group of things in the shape of a circle.
7 At a boxing match or circus, the ring is the place where the fight or performance takes place.
8 an organized group of people who are involved in an illegal activity. *The agent was part of an international spy ring.*
✔ The past tense of *ring* is *rang* and the past participle is *rung*: *she rang the bell; I had rung the police.*

ringleader **ringleaders**
NOUN the leader of a group of troublemakers or criminals.

ringlet **ringlets**
NOUN Ringlets are long, hanging curls of hair.

rink **rinks**
NOUN a large indoor area for ice-skating or roller-skating.

rinse **rinses rinsing rinsed**
VERB to wash something in clean water.

riot **riots**
NOUN When there is a riot, a crowd of people behave violently in a public place.
riot VERB

rip **rips ripping ripped**
VERB **1** to tear something with force.
2 If you rip something away or off, you remove it quickly and with force.
NOUN **3** a long split in a piece of cloth or paper.

ripe **riper ripest**
ADJECTIVE Ripe fruit or grain is fully developed and ready to be harvested.
ripeness NOUN

ripen **ripens ripening ripened**
VERB When fruit or crops ripen, they become ripe.

rip-off **rip-offs**
NOUN; INFORMAL If you say that something you bought was a rip-off, you mean it was not worth what you paid.

ripple **ripples**
NOUN **1** Ripples are little waves on the surface of calm water.
2 If there is a ripple of laughter or applause, people laugh or applaud gently for a short time.
ripple VERB

Rip-off is a modern expression. Find other phrases coined in the last 50 years. ◀

rise **rises rising rose risen**
VERB 1 to move upwards, to ascend.
2 FORMAL to stand up.
3 to get out of bed.
4 When the sun or moon rises, it appears from below the horizon.
5 If a sound or wind rises, it becomes higher or stronger.
6 If an amount rises, it increases.
7 If you rise to a challenge or a remark, you respond to it instead of ignoring it. *She accepted the challenge with enthusiasm.*
8 When people rise up, they start fighting against people in authority.
NOUN 9 an increase: *a pay rise.*
10 the process by which someone becomes more powerful or successful: *the writer's rise to fame.*
PHRASE 11 If something **gives rise to** an event or situation, it causes it to happen.

Synonyms: (sense 1) ascend, climb, go up

risk **risks risking risked**
NOUN 1 If there is a risk of something unpleasant, there is a possibility that it will happen.
2 someone or something likely to cause harm or have undesirable results. *Policemen face many risks these days.*
VERB 3 If you risk something, you do it knowing that something unpleasant may happen as a result.
[from Italian *rischiare* meaning to be in danger]

rite **rites**
NOUN a religious ceremony.

ritual **rituals**
NOUN 1 a series of actions which must be carried out in a certain way, according to the custom of a particular society or group.
ADJECTIVE 2 Ritual activities happen as part of a tradition or ceremony.
ritualistic ADJECTIVE

rival **rivals rivalling rivalled**
NOUN 1 the person you are competing with.
VERB 2 If something rivals something else, it is of a similar high standard or quality.
rivalry NOUN

Synonyms: (sense 1) adversary, opponent

river **rivers**
NOUN a natural feature consisting of water draining off the land down to the sea, flowing between two banks for a long distance.

road **roads**
NOUN a long piece of hard ground built for vehicles to travel along.

roam **roams roaming roamed**
VERB to travel or walk around without any particular purpose.

roar **roars roaring roared**
VERB If something roars, it makes a very loud noise.
roar NOUN

roast **roasts roasting roasted**
VERB When you roast meat or other food, you cook it using dry heat in an oven or over a fire.
roast ADJECTIVE OR NOUN

rob **robs robbing robbed**
VERB to steal someone's possessions.
robber NOUN **robbery** NOUN

robe **robes**
NOUN a long, loose piece of clothing which covers the body.

robin **robins**
NOUN a small bird with a red breast.

robot **robots**
NOUN a machine which moves and performs tasks automatically.
robotic ADJECTIVE
[from Czech *robota* meaning forced labour]

robust
ADJECTIVE very strong and healthy.
robustly ADVERB **robustness** NOUN

rock **rocks rocking rocked**
NOUN 1 Rock is made up of small pieces of one or more minerals. Granite, sandstone and shale are common rocks. The earth's surface is made up of rock.
2 a piece of rock.
3 Rock or rock music is music with a strong beat, usually involving electric guitars and drums.
4 Rock is also a sweet shaped into long, hard sticks, sold at the seaside.
VERB 5 to move regularly backwards and forwards or from side to side.
6 If something rocks people, it shocks or upsets them.

rocket **rockets rocketing rocketed**
NOUN 1 a vehicle for launching spacecraft, usually shaped like a long pointed tube.
2 an explosive missile: *an anti-tank rocket.*
3 a firework that explodes when it is high in the air.
VERB 4 If prices rocket, they increase very quickly.

rod **rods**
NOUN a long, thin bar made of wood or metal.

rode
past tense of **ride**.

rodent **rodents**
NOUN any of several small mammals with sharp front teeth which they use for gnawing, for example, the mouse, rat or squirrel.

rodeo **rodeos**
NOUN a public entertainment in which cowboys show different skills, especially horseriding and using a lasso.

 ► There are several rivers named Avon in England. Avon is an old Celtic word meaning water.

roe
NOUN the eggs of a fish.

rogue rogues
NOUN an affectionate term for a man who behaves dishonestly.

role roles
NOUN 1 the character that an actor plays; a part in a play, film, etc. *He was excited to get his first leading role.*
2 the position or function of someone or something in a situation. *She played a major role in the peace talks.*

roll rolls rolling rolled
VERB 1 to move along a surface, turning over many times.
2 If you roll something or roll it up, you wrap it around itself so that it has a rounded shape.
NOUN 3 a long piece of something that has been rolled into a tube.
4 a very small, circular loaf of bread.
5 a roll on a drum is a long, rumbling sound made on it.
PHRASE 6 If you are **on a roll** you are having a time of consistent successes at the moment.

roller rollers
NOUN 1 a cylinder that turns round in a machine or piece of equipment.
2 Rollers are tubes which you can wind your hair around to make it curly.

Rollerblade Rollerblades
NOUN; TRADEMARK Rollerblades are roller skates which have the wheels set in one straight line on the bottom of the boot.

roller coaster roller coasters
NOUN a pleasure ride at a fair, consisting of a small railway that goes up and down very steep slopes.

roller skate roller skates
NOUN Roller skates are shoes with four small wheels underneath.
roller-skate VERB

rolling pin rolling pins
NOUN a long tube of wood or other heavy material used for flattening out pastry.

Roman Romans
NOUN The Romans were Latin-speaking people of Rome who controlled an empire around the Mediterranean, north to France and Britain, and east to the Caspian and Red Seas, which lasted from 510 BC to 476 AD.
Roman ADJECTIVE

Roman Catholic Roman Catholics
NOUN someone who belongs to a branch of the Christian church which accepts the Pope in Rome as its leader.
Roman Catholic ADJECTIVE
Roman Catholicism NOUN

romance romances
NOUN 1 a relationship between two people who are in love with each other.
2 a novel about a love affair.

Roman numeral Roman numerals
NOUN Roman numerals are the letters used by the Romans in ancient times to write numbers. For example, V means five, VI means six, X means ten and IX means nine.

romantic
ADJECTIVE 1 connected with love. *She had romantic thoughts about the boy next door.*
2 Something romantic is beautiful in a way that strongly affects your feelings. *It was a romantic scene with the moon shining across the still ocean.*
romantically ADVERB

romp romps romping romped
VERB to play and jump around in a happy, noisy way.

roof roofs
NOUN 1 the covering on top of a building, car, etc.
2 The roof of your mouth or of a cave is the highest part.

rook rooks
NOUN 1 a large black bird of the crow family.
2 a chess piece which looks like the tower of a castle and can move any number of squares in a straight but not diagonal line.

room rooms
NOUN 1 a separate section in a building, divided from other rooms by walls.
2 If there is room for something, there is enough space for it.

roomy roomier roomiest
ADJECTIVE having ample room, spacious.

roost roosts roosting roosted
VERB 1 When birds roost, they settle somewhere for the night.
NOUN 2 a place where birds rest or build their nests.
PHRASE 3 Someone who **rules the roost** has authority over the people in a particular place.

root roots rooting rooted
NOUN 1 The parts of a plant that grow underground and anchor it in the soil. Roots carry water and minerals from the soil to the rest of the plant.
2 The root of a hair or tooth is the part beneath the skin.
3 You can refer to the place or culture that you come from as your roots.
4 The root of a problem is the thing that caused it.
VERB 5 To root through things means to search through them, pushing them aside.
root out VERB If you root out something or someone, you find them and force them out from where they are.

A B C D E F G H I J K L M N O P Q R S T U V W X Y Z

root word root words
NOUN the basic word or part of a word that remains when all prefixes and suffixes are removed.

rope ropes roping roped
NOUN 1 a thick cord, made by twisting together several thinner cords.
VERB 2 to tie things together with rope.
PHRASE 3 If you **know the ropes** in a particular situation, you are experienced at dealing with it.

rosary rosaries
NOUN a string of beads that Roman Catholics use for counting prayers.

rose roses
NOUN a flower which has a pleasant smell and grows on a bush with thorns.

rosette rosettes
NOUN a large badge of coloured ribbons gathered into a circle, which is worn as a prize in a competition or to support a political party.

Rosh Hashanah or **Rosh Hashana**
NOUN the festival celebrating the Jewish New Year.

rosy rosier rosiest
ADJECTIVE 1 reddish-pink.
2 If a situation seems rosy, it is likely to be good or successful.

rot rots rotting rotted
VERB 1 to decay and fall apart, to decompose.
NOUN 2 the condition that affects wood and other former living things when they decay.

rota rotas
NOUN a list of people who take turns to do a particular job.

rotary
ADJECTIVE moving in a circular direction.

rotate rotates rotating rotated
VERB to turn with a circular movement.
rotation NOUN

rotor rotors
NOUN The rotors or rotor blades of a helicopter are the four long flat pieces of metal on top of it which rotate and lift it off the ground.
[short for rotator]

rotten
ADJECTIVE 1 Something that is rotten has decayed: *rotten eggs*.
2 INFORMAL bad, unpleasant or unfair. *I think it's a rotten idea.*

rough rougher roughest
Said "**ruff**" ADJECTIVE 1 uneven and not smooth.
2 using too much force. *Don't be so rough or you'll break it.*
3 dangerous or violent: *a rough part of town.*
4 difficult or unpleasant. *You've had a rough time.*
5 approximate. *At a rough guess, they are five kilometres away.*
NOUN OR ADJECTIVE 6 A rough or a rough sketch is a drawing or description that shows the main features but does not show the details.
roughness NOUN

roughage
NOUN Roughage is the fibre in food that makes digestion easier and helps your bowels work properly.

roughly
ADVERB 1 in a rough way.
2 approximately. *There were roughly 3000 people at the concert.*

round rounder roundest; rounds rounding rounded
ADJECTIVE 1 shaped like a ball or a circle; circular or spherical.
PREPOSITION OR ADVERB 2 If something is round something else, it surrounds it.
3 The distance round something is the length of its circumference or boundary.
4 You can use "round" to refer to an area near a place. *There's nothing to do round here.*
PREPOSITION 5 If something moves to the other side of something else, you say it has gone round it: *a car came round the corner.*
6 If you go round a place, you go to different parts of it to look at it. *We went round the museum.*
ADVERB 7 If you turn or look round, you turn so you are facing in a different direction.
8 When someone comes round, they visit you.
NOUN 9 one of a series of events, especially in a sporting competition.
VERB 10 to move in the direction of the corner or bend.
round down VERB If you round down a number, you decrease it to the nearest lower number. For example, 1·3 may be rounded down to 1.
round up VERB 1 to gather people or animals together.
2 If you round up a number, you increase it to the nearest higher number. For example, 1·8 may be rounded up to 2.

roundabout roundabouts
NOUN 1 a meeting point of several roads with a circle in the centre which vehicles have to travel around.
2 a rotating ride in a playground or fairground.
ADJECTIVE 3 If someone speaks of something in a roundabout way, they do not mention it directly.

rounders
NOUN a game played by two teams, in which a player scores points by hitting a ball and running around four sides of a square pitch.

rouse rouses rousing roused
Said "**rowze**" VERB 1 to wake someone up.
2 If you rouse yourself to do something, you make yourself get up and do it.
3 If something, such as music, rouses you, it makes you feel very emotional and excited.
rousing ADJECTIVE

 ► When syllables rhyme with "bee", spell i before e except straight after c: believe receive achieve. ►

rout routs routing routed
*Rhymes with "**out**"* VERB to defeat your opponents completely and easily.
rout NOUN

route routes
*Said "**root**"* NOUN a way from one place to another.

routine routines
NOUN 1 the usual way or order in which you do things.
2 a boring repetition of tasks.
ADJECTIVE 3 Routine activities are done regularly.
routinely ADVERB

rove roves roving roved
VERB; LITERARY to roam about.
roving ADJECTIVE

row rows rowing rowed
*Rhymes with "**snow**"* NOUN 1 several people or things arranged in a line.
VERB 2 to use oars to make a small boat move through the water.
*Rhymes with "**now**"* NOUN 3 a serious argument.
4 If someone makes a row, they make too much noise.
VERB 5 If people row, they have a noisy argument.

rowdy rowdier rowdiest
ADJECTIVE rough and noisy.
rowdily ADVERB

rowing boat rowing boats
NOUN a small, open boat propelled by pulling on oars.

royal
ADJECTIVE belonging to or involving a queen, a king or a member of their family.

royalty
NOUN The members of a royal family are sometimes referred to as royalty.

rub rubs rubbing rubbed
VERB to move your hand or a cloth backwards and forwards over something.
rub out VERB If you rub something out you erase or delete it.

rubber rubbers
NOUN 1 a strong, elastic substance used for making tyres, boots and other products.
2 a small piece of rubber used to rub out pencil mistakes; an eraser.
rubbery ADJECTIVE

rubbish
NOUN 1 unwanted things or waste material.
2 You can refer to something of very poor quality as rubbish.

Synonyms: (sense 1) garbage, refuse, trash

rubble
NOUN bits of old brick, stone and concrete.

ruby rubies
NOUN a type of red jewel.

rucksack rucksacks
NOUN a bag with shoulder straps for carrying things on your back.

rudder rudders
NOUN a piece of wood or metal at the back of a boat or plane which is moved to make the boat or plane turn.

rude ruder rudest
ADJECTIVE 1 not polite, ill-mannered.
2 embarrassing or offensive because of reference to sex or other bodily functions: *a rude joke.*
3 unexpected and unpleasant: *a rude awakening.*
rudely ADVERB **rudeness** ADJECTIVE

Antonyms: (sense 1) courteous, polite, well-mannered

ruffle ruffles ruffling ruffled
VERB 1 If you ruffle someone's hair, you move your hand quickly backwards and forwards over their head.
2 If something ruffles you, it makes you annoyed or upset.
NOUN 3 Ruffles are small folds made in a piece of material for decoration.

rug rugs
NOUN 1 a small carpet.
2 a blanket which you can use to cover your knees or to sit on outdoors.

rugby
NOUN a game played by two teams, who try to carry an oval ball past a line at their opponents' end of the pitch, or kick the ball through high posts there.

rugged
ADJECTIVE 1 A rugged coast is rocky, wild and unsheltered.
2 Rugged good looks are strong, masculine features.

ruin ruins ruining ruined
VERB 1 to destroy or spoil something completely.
NOUN 2 A ruin or the ruins of something refers to the parts that are left after it has been severely damaged.

rule rules ruling ruled
NOUN 1 Rules are instructions which tell you what you are allowed to do; regulations or laws.
VERB 2 to control the affairs of a country.
PHRASE 3 **As a rule** means usually or generally.
rule out VERB to reject an idea or course of action.

ruler rulers
NOUN 1 a person who rules a country.
2 an instrument used for measuring things or drawing straight lines.

ruling rulings
ADJECTIVE **1** controlling or exercising authority.
NOUN **2** a decision made by a court or other official body.

rum
NOUN a strong alcoholic drink made from sugar cane juice.

rumble rumbles rumbling rumbled
VERB **1** to make a continuous low noise.
2 INFORMAL If you rumble someone, you find out about something that they have been concealing.
NOUN **3** a continuous low noise.

rummage rummages rummaging rummaged
VERB to search for something, moving things about carelessly.

rumour rumours
NOUN a piece of information that people are talking about, which may or may not be true.
rumour VERB

rump rumps
NOUN the rear end of an animal, or meat cut from there.

run runs running ran
VERB **1** to move quickly, leaving the ground during each stride.
2 When a machine is running or when you are running it, it is operating.
3 If a liquid, river or road runs somewhere, it flows there or takes that particular course.
4 to be in charge of a business, organization or activity.
5 If a bus or train runs somewhere, it travels there at set times.
6 If you run your hand or finger over an object, you move it over it.
7 If someone runs in an election, they stand as a candidate for it.
8 If you run an experiment, computer program or tape, you start it and let it continue.
9 If you run water, you turn on a tap to make it flow.
10 If you run someone somewhere, you give them a lift in your car.
11 If an event or contract runs for a particular time, it lasts for that time.
12 If your nose is running, it is producing a lot of mucus.
13 If clothes run, dye comes out of them when they are washed.
NOUN **14** If you go for a run, you run for pleasure or exercise.
run away VERB to leave a place suddenly or secretly, to bolt or flee.
run out VERB to have no more left of something.
run over VERB If a vehicle runs over someone, it knocks them down.

Synonyms: (sense 1) dash, race, sprint

runaway runaways
NOUN a person or animal who has escaped from a place or left it secretly and hurriedly.

rung rungs
NOUN **1** one of the bars that form the steps of a ladder.
VERB **2** past participle of **ring**.

runner runners
NOUN **1** a person who is running, especially one in a race or one who takes messages.
2 A runner on a plant is a long shoot from which a new plant develops.
3 A thin strip on which something else slides and moves.

runner bean runner beans
NOUN Runner beans are long green pods eaten as a vegetable, which grow on a climbing plant.

runner-up runners-up
NOUN a person or team that comes second in a race or competition.

runny runnier runniest
ADJECTIVE **1** more liquid than usual.
2 If someone's nose or eyes are runny, liquid is coming from them.

runway runways
NOUN a long strip of ground used by aeroplanes for taking off or landing.

rural
ADJECTIVE relating to or involving the countryside.

rush rushes rushing rushed
VERB **1** to go somewhere quickly.
2 If you rush something or if you are rushed into something, you do it too quickly.
NOUN **3** a situation in which you need to go somewhere or do something very quickly.
4 If there is a rush for something, there is a sudden increase in demand for it.
5 Rushes are plants with long, thin stems that grow near water.

rush hour rush hours
NOUN The rush hour is one of the busy parts of the day when most people are travelling to or from work.

rusk rusks
NOUN a hard, dry biscuit given to babies.

rust
NOUN a reddish-brown substance that forms on iron or steel when it is exposed to water and oxygen.
rust VERB

rustic
ADJECTIVE simple in a way considered to be typical of the countryside.

rustle rustles rustling rustled
VERB When something rustles, it makes soft sounds as it moves.
rustling ADJECTIVE OR NOUN

A B C D E F G H I J K L M N O P Q R S T U V W X Y Z

 In the past, British sailors felt "groggy" after drinking their grog, a mixture of rum and water.

rusty **rustier rustiest**
ADJECTIVE **1** affected by rust.
2 If someone's knowledge or skills are rusty, they are not as good as they used to be because they have not been used for a long time.

rut **ruts**
NOUN **1** a deep, narrow groove in the ground made by the wheels of a vehicle.
PHRASE **2** If someone is **stuck in a rut**, they have become stuck in their way of doing things.

ruthless
ADJECTIVE very harsh or cruel.
ruthlessly ADVERB **ruthlessness** NOUN

rye
NOUN a type of grass that produces light brown grain.

A B C D E F G H I J K L M N O P Q R S T U V W X Y Z

Ss

Sabbath
NOUN the day of the week when members of some religious groups, especially Jews and Christians, do not work.
[from Hebrew *shabbath* meaning to rest]

sabotage **sabotages sabotaging sabotaged**
Said "**sab**-ot-ahj" VERB the damaging of things such as machinery and railway lines as an act of war, protest, etc.
sabotage NOUN **saboteur** NOUN

sabre **sabres**
NOUN 1 a heavy curved sword.
2 a light sword used in fencing.

sachet **sachets**
Said "**sash**-ay" NOUN a small closed packet, containing a small amount of something such as sugar or shampoo.

sack **sacks sacking sacked**
NOUN 1 a large bag made of rough material.
VERB 2 INFORMAL If you are sacked, you are told by your employer that you no longer work for them.
PHRASE 3 If someone **gets the sack**, they are dismissed from their job.

Synonyms: (sense 2) dismiss, fire

sacred
Said "**say**-krid" ADJECTIVE holy or connected with religion or religious ceremonies.
sacredness NOUN

sacrifice **sacrifices sacrificing sacrificed**
Said "**sak**-riff-ice" VERB to give up something which is valuable or important to you.
sacrifice NOUN **sacrificial** ADJECTIVE

Synonyms: forfeit, give up

sad **sadder saddest**
ADJECTIVE unhappy.
sadly ADVERB **sadness** NOUN

sadden **saddens saddening saddened**
VERB If something saddens you, it makes you feel sad.

saddle **saddles saddling saddled**
NOUN 1 a leather seat that you sit on when you are riding a horse.
2 the seat of a bicycle.
VERB 3 to put a saddle on a horse.

sadist **sadists**
NOUN someone who takes pleasure from hurting people in some way.
sadistic ADJECTIVE **sadism** NOUN

safari **safaris**
NOUN an expedition for hunting or observing wild animals.
[from Swahili *safari* meaning journey]

safari park **safari parks**
NOUN a large park where wild animals such as lions and elephants roam freely.

safe **safer safest; safes**
ADJECTIVE 1 not in any danger or at risk.
2 not causing harm or danger.
NOUN 3 a strong metal box with special locks, in which you can keep valuable things.
safely ADVERB

safeguard **safeguards**
NOUN a rule, law or action designed to protect something or someone.
safeguard VERB

safety
NOUN the state of being safe or protected.

safety belt **safety belts**
NOUN a belt fastened round a person in a vehicle to help prevent them from hurting themselves if an accident happens.

safety pin **safety pins**
NOUN a pin with a point protected by a cover.

sag **sags sagging sagged**
VERB to hang down loosely or sink downwards in the middle.
sagging ADJECTIVE

saga **sagas**
Said "**sah**-ga" NOUN a very long story, usually with many different adventures.
[from Old Norse *saga* meaning story]

sage **sages**
NOUN 1 a herb used for flavouring in cooking.
2 LITERARY a very wise person.

said
past participle of **say**.

sail **sails sailing sailed**
VERB 1 When a ship sails, it moves across water.
2 to go somewhere by ship.
NOUN 3 large pieces of material attached to a boat's mast. The wind blows against the sails and moves the boat.

sailboard **sailboards**
NOUN a board like a surfboard with a mast and sail attached, used for windsurfing.

sailor **sailors**
NOUN a member of a ship's crew.

saint **saints**
NOUN a person who after death is formally recognized by a Christian church as deserving special honour because of having lived a very holy life.
saintly ADJECTIVE

sake **sakes**
PHRASE 1 If you do something for someone's sake, you do it to help or please them.
2 You use **for the sake of** to say why you are doing something. *I took the kids to the cinema for the sake of a bit of peace and quiet.*

 ► The letter S might have been a picture of an extracted tooth. "Shin" was a word for tooth.

salad salads
NOUN a mixture of foods, often raw, eaten cold or warm.

salamander salamanders
NOUN an amphibious animal resembling a lizard.

salami
Said "sal-**lah**-mee" NOUN a type of spicy sausage.

salary salaries
NOUN the regular payment made to someone each month for the work they do. See **wage**.
salaried ADJECTIVE
[from Latin *salarium* meaning money given to soldiers to buy salt]

sale sales
NOUN 1 the selling of goods.
2 an occasion when a shop sells things at reduced prices.
3 The sales of a product are the numbers of it that are sold.

salesperson salespeople
NOUN someone who sells products for a company.
salesman NOUN **saleswoman** NOUN

saliva
Said "sal-**live**-a" NOUN the watery liquid in your mouth that helps you chew and swallow food.
salivate VERB

salmon salmons or salmon
Said "**sam**-on" NOUN a large, edible, silver-coloured fish with pink flesh.

salon salons
NOUN a place where hairdressers or beauty therapists work.

saloon saloons
NOUN 1 a car with a fixed roof and a separate boot.
2 In America, a place where alcoholic drinks are sold and drunk.

salt
NOUN a white substance used to flavour and preserve food.
salty ADJECTIVE **salted** ADJECTIVE

salute salutes
NOUN a formal sign of respect. Soldiers give a salute by raising their right hand to their forehead.
salute VERB

salvage salvages salvaging salvaged
VERB to save things; for example, from a wrecked ship or a destroyed building.
salvage NOUN

salvation
NOUN 1 the act of being saved from harm or evil.
2 To be someone's salvation means to save them from harm or evil.

same
ADJECTIVE 1 not different. *They were born in the same town.*
PRONOUN 2 If two things are the same, they are like one another.

samosa samosas
NOUN a small crisp pastry case filled with a spicy meat or vegetable mixture, eaten as a snack.

sample samples
NOUN a small amount of something that you can try or test.
sample VERB

sanctuary sanctuaries
NOUN 1 a place where you are safe from harm or danger.
2 a place where wildlife is protected.

sand sands sanding sanded
NOUN 1 Sand consists of minute pieces of stone and shells. Beaches are made of sand.
VERB 2 If you sand something, you rub sandpaper over it to make it smooth.

sandal sandals
NOUN light shoes with straps, worn in warm weather.

sandbag sandbags
NOUN Sandbags are sacks filled with sand which are piled up to protect against floodwater and explosives.

sandpaper
NOUN strong paper with a coating of sand on it, used for rubbing surfaces to make them smooth.

sands
PLURAL NOUN The sands is a word used for the beach.

sandstone
NOUN a type of rock formed from sand, often used for building.

sandwich sandwiches sandwiching sandwiched
NOUN 1 two slices of bread with a filling between them.
VERB 2 If one thing is sandwiched between two others, it is squashed into a narrow space between them.
[sandwiches are named after the scandalous gambler, the 4th Earl of Sandwich (1718–92), who invented them so that he could eat without having to leave the gambling table]

sandy sandier sandiest
ADJECTIVE 1 covered with sand.
2 Sandy hair is light orange-brown.

sane saner sanest
ADJECTIVE 1 If someone is sane, they have a normal and healthy mind.
2 A sane action is sensible and reasonable.

Antonym: insane

sang
past tense of **sing**.

sanitary
ADJECTIVE concerned with keeping things clean and hygienic.

sanitary towel sanitary towels
NOUN a pad of thick, soft material which women wear during their periods.

sanitation
NOUN the process of keeping places clean and hygienic, especially by providing a sewage system and clean water supply.

sanity
NOUN the condition of having a normal healthy mind.

sank
past tense of **sink**.

sap saps sapping sapped
NOUN **1** the watery liquid in plants.
VERB **2** If something saps your strength or confidence, it gradually weakens and destroys it.

sapling saplings
NOUN a young tree.

sapphire sapphires
NOUN a blue precious stone.

sarcastic
ADJECTIVE saying the opposite of what you really mean in order to mock or insult someone. *I wish I had a big nose like you!*
sarcastically ADVERB **sarcasm** NOUN
[from Greek *sarkazein* meaning to tear the flesh]

sardine sardines
NOUN a small edible sea fish.

sari saris
Said "**sah**-ree" NOUN a piece of clothing worn especially by Indian women, consisting of a long piece of material folded around the body.
[a Hindi word]

sash sashes
NOUN a long piece of cloth worn round the waist or over one shoulder.

sat
past tense of **sit**.

satchel satchels
NOUN a rectangular leather or cloth bag with shoulder straps, usually used for carrying school books.

satellite satellites
NOUN **1** a spacecraft sent into orbit round the earth to collect information or as part of a communications system.
2 a natural object in space that moves round a planet or star.

satellite dish satellite dishes
NOUN an aerial, shaped like a large bowl, fixed out of doors to receive satellite television signals.

satellite television
NOUN television services that are broadcast by satellite rather than by land-based television masts.

satin satins
NOUN a kind of smooth, shiny silk.

satire satires
NOUN **1** the use of mocking humour in literature, theatre, television, etc., to show how foolish, bad or incompetent some people are.
2 a play, novel, or poem containing satire.
satirical ADJECTIVE **satirically** ADVERB

satisfaction
NOUN the feeling of pleasure you get when you do or receive something you wanted or needed.

satisfactory
ADJECTIVE acceptable or adequate.
satisfactorily ADVERB

satisfy satisfies satisfying satisfied
VERB **1** to give someone enough of something to make them pleased or contented.
2 To satisfy the requirements for something means to fulfil or meet them.
3 to convince. *I satisfied the policeman that I wasn't a burglar but had locked myself out of our house.*
satisfied ADJECTIVE

Synonyms: (sense 1) content, indulge, please

satsuma satsumas
Said "sat-**soo**-ma" NOUN a fruit like a small orange.

saturated
ADJECTIVE **1** soaked, full of moisture.
2 In chemistry, if a liquid is saturated with a substance, the maximum amount possible of the substance has been dissolved in the liquid.
saturation NOUN

Saturday Saturdays
NOUN the day between Friday and Sunday.
[from Latin *Saturni dies* meaning day of Saturn]

sauce sauces
NOUN a liquid eaten with other food to give it more flavour and moisture.

saucepan saucepans
NOUN a deep metal cooking pot with a handle and a lid.

saucer saucers
NOUN a small curved plate for a cup.

saucy saucier sauciest
ADJECTIVE cheeky in an amusing way.

 ► What would you find in a: satchel, carafe, cruet, compact, caddy, scuttle?

sauna saunas
Said "**saw**-na" **NOUN** If you have a sauna, you go into a very hot room in order to sweat, then have a cold bath or shower.
[a Finnish word]

saunter saunters sauntering sauntered
VERB to walk slowly, casually and confidently.
saunter NOUN

sausage sausages
NOUN a mixture of minced meat and herbs formed into a tubular shape and served cooked.

savage savages savaging savaged
ADJECTIVE 1 cruel and violent.
NOUN 2 If you call someone a savage, you mean that they are violent and uncivilized.
VERB 3 If an animal savages you, it attacks you and bites you.
savagely ADVERB

savanna or **savannah**
NOUN open grassland with scattered bushes and trees, found in many parts of tropical Africa.

save saves saving saved
VERB 1 to rescue someone or help to keep them safe in some way.
2 If you save something, you keep it so that you can use it later. *They had saved up enough money for the deposit.*
3 To save time, money or effort means to prevent it from being wasted.
PREPOSITION 4 LITERARY except. *Robinson Crusoe was alone on the island save for his companion, Man Friday.*
saving NOUN

savings
PLURAL NOUN Your savings are the money you have saved.

saviour saviours
NOUN 1 If someone saves you from danger, you can refer to them as your saviour.
2 In Christianity, the Saviour is Jesus Christ.

savoury
ADJECTIVE Savoury food is salty or spicy.

Antonym: sweet

saw saws sawing sawed sawn
1 the past tense of **see**.
NOUN 2 a tool for cutting wood, with a blade with sharp teeth along one edge.
VERB 3 to cut using a saw.

sawdust
NOUN the dust created when you saw wood.

saxophone saxophones
NOUN a curved metal wind instrument often played in dance or jazz bands.
[named after Adolphe Sax (1814–94), who invented the instrument]

say says saying said
VERB 1 to speak words.
NOUN 2 If you have a say in something, you can give your opinion and influence decisions.

saying sayings
NOUN a well-known sentence or phrase that tells you something about human life.

Synonyms: adage, proverb

scab scabs
NOUN a hard, dry covering that forms over a wound.
scabby ADJECTIVE

scabbard scabbards
NOUN a cover for a sword.

scaffold scaffolds
NOUN a platform on which criminals used to be hanged or beheaded.

scaffolding
NOUN a framework of poles and boards used by workmen to stand on while they are working on the outside structure of a building.

scald scalds scalding scalded
Said "**skawld**" **VERB** If you scald yourself, you burn yourself with very hot liquid or steam.
scald NOUN **scalding** ADJECTIVE

scale scales scaling scaled
NOUN 1 The scale of something is its size or extent.
2 a set of levels or numbers used for measuring things.
3 The scale of a map is the relationship between the size of something in the map and its size in the real world. *The model railway had a scale of 1:25.*
4 Scales are the small pieces of hard skin on a fish's or reptile's body.
5 an upward or downward sequence of musical notes.
VERB 6 If you scale something high, you climb it.
scaly ADJECTIVE

scalene
ADJECTIVE A scalene triangle has sides which are all of different lengths.

scales
PLURAL NOUN Scales are a piece of equipment used for weighing things.

scalp scalps
NOUN the skin under the hair on your head.

scalpel scalpels
NOUN a knife with a short, thin blade used by surgeons during operations.

scamper scampers scampering scampered
VERB to move quickly and lightly.

scampi
PLURAL NOUN large prawns, usually eaten fried in breadcrumbs.

a b c d e f g h i j k l m n o p q r s t u v w x y z

scan scans scanning scanned
VERB **1** If you scan something, you look over all of it quickly. *I scanned the sky for signs of rain.*
2 If a machine scans something, it examines it with a beam of light or X-rays.
NOUN **3** an examination of part of the body with X-ray or laser equipment.

scandal scandals
NOUN a situation or event that people think is shocking and immoral.
scandalous ADJECTIVE **scandalously** ADVERB

scanner scanners
NOUN **1** a piece of electronic medical equipment which gives a very accurate image of the inside of the body.
2 a piece of equipment which scans images or print and converts them to be used as computer data.

scanty scantier scantiest
ADJECTIVE limited, barely enough.
scantily ADVERB

scapegoat scapegoats
NOUN If someone is made a scapegoat, they are blamed for something, although it may not be their fault.

scar scars scarring scarred
NOUN **1** a mark left on your skin after a wound has healed.
VERB **2** If an injury scars you, it leaves a permanent mark on your skin.
3 If an unpleasant experience scars you, it has a permanent effect on you.

scarce scarcer scarcest
ADJECTIVE If something is scarce, there is not very much of it.
scarcity NOUN

scarcely
ADVERB hardly, only just. *We scarcely got there in time.*
✔ As *scarcely* already has a negative sense, it is followed by *ever* or *any* and not by *never* or *no*.

scare scares scaring scared
VERB **1** to frighten.
NOUN **2** If there is a scare about something, a lot of people are worried about it.

scarecrow scarecrows
NOUN an object shaped like a person put in a field to scare birds away from crops.

scarf scarfs or scarves
NOUN a piece of cloth worn round your neck or head to keep you warm.

scarlet
NOUN OR ADJECTIVE bright red.

scary scarier scariest
ADJECTIVE; INFORMAL frightening.

scatter scatters scattering scattered
VERB **1** to throw or drop things all over an area.
2 If people scatter, they suddenly move away in different directions.

Synonyms: (sense 1) sprinkle, strew, throw about

scavenge scavenges scavenging scavenged
VERB If you scavenge for things, you search for them among waste and rubbish.
scavenger NOUN

scene scenes
NOUN **1** part of a play or film in which a series of events happen in one place.
2 the place where an action or event takes place; a situation. *The whole house was a scene of destruction.*
3 Pictures and views are sometimes called scenes: *a village scene.*

scenery
NOUN **1** In the countryside, you can refer to everything you see as the scenery.
2 In a theatre, the scenery is the painted cloth, wood, etc. which represents the place where the action is happening.
scenic ADJECTIVE

scent scents
NOUN a smell, especially a pleasant one.

sceptic sceptics
NOUN a person who always mistrusts other people or who doubts the things that most other people believe.
sceptical ADJECTIVE **scepticism** NOUN

schedule schedules
Said "**shed**-yool" NOUN a plan that gives a list of events or tasks, together with the times at which each thing should be done.
schedule VERB **scheduled** ADJECTIVE

scheme schemes scheming schemed
NOUN **1** a plan or arrangement.
VERB **2** to make secret plans.

scholar scholars
NOUN **1** a person who studies an academic subject and knows a lot about it.
2 a pupil or student who has a scholarship.
scholarly ADJECTIVE

scholarship scholarships
NOUN If you get a scholarship to a school or university, your studies are paid for by the school or university or by some other organization.

school schools
NOUN **1** a place where children are educated.
2 You can refer to a large group of fish or dolphins as a school.
schoolboy NOUN **schoolgirl** NOUN
schoolchildren PLURAL NOUN **schooling** NOUN

schooner schooners
NOUN a type of sailing ship with two masts.

 ► Homophones: scent, cent, sent; ail, ale; aisle, isle; brake, break; berry, bury.

science sciences
NOUN the systematic study of, and knowledge about, the characteristics and behaviour of living things, the properties of materials, and physical processes such as energy and forces. [from Latin *scientia* meaning knowledge]

science fiction or **sci-fi**
NOUN OR ADJECTIVE stories or films about events happening in the future or in other parts of the universe.

scientific
ADJECTIVE 1 relating to science.
2 done in a systematic way, using experiments and tests.
scientifically ADVERB

scientist scientists
NOUN an expert in one of the sciences who does work connected with it.

scissors
PLURAL NOUN a cutting tool with two sharp blades.

scoff scoffs scoffing scoffed
VERB 1 to speak in a scornful, mocking way about something.
2 INFORMAL to eat food quickly and greedily.

scold scolds scolding scolded
VERB to tell someone off.

Synonyms: rebuke, reprimand

scone scones
Said "**skon** or **skone**" **NOUN** Scones are small cakes made from flour and fat and usually eaten with butter, jam, cream, etc.

scoop scoops scooping scooped
VERB 1 If you scoop something up, you pick it up using a spoon or the palm of your hand.
NOUN 2 any object that works to scoop things up, such as the bucket on an excavator.
3 an important news story reported in one newspaper before it appears elsewhere.

scooter scooters
NOUN 1 a small, light motorcycle with some protective bodywork.
2 a simple cycle which a child rides by standing on it and pushing the ground with one foot.

scope
NOUN 1 If you have scope to do something, you have the chance to do it.
2 The scope of something is the whole subject area which it deals with or includes.

scorch scorches scorching scorched
VERB to burn something slightly.

score scores scoring scored
VERB 1 to get a goal, run or point in a game.
NOUN 2 the number of goals, runs or points in a game.
3 The score of a piece of music is the written version of it.
4 OLD-FASHIONED a score is twenty.
scorer NOUN

scorn scorns scorning scorned
NOUN 1 great contempt.
VERB 2 FORMAL If you scorn something, you refuse to accept it.

scornful
ADJECTIVE showing contempt: *a scornful look.*
scornfully ADVERB

scorpion scorpions
NOUN an animal which looks like a small lobster, with a long tail which has a poisonous sting on the end.

scoundrel scoundrels
NOUN; OLD-FASHIONED someone who cheats and deceives people.

scour scours scouring scoured
VERB 1 to clean a pan, plate, etc. by rubbing it with something rough.
2 If you scour a place, you look all over it in order to find something.

scout scouts scouting scouted
NOUN 1 a boy who is a member of the Scout Association.
2 someone who is sent to an area to find out the position of an enemy army.
VERB 3 If you scout around for something, you look around for it.

scowl scowls scowling scowled
VERB to frown because you are angry.
scowl NOUN

scrabble scrabbles scrabbling scrabbled
VERB 1 to scrape quickly at something with your hands or feet.
NOUN 2 TRADEMARK Scrabble is a word game played with letters on a board.

scramble scrambles scrambling scrambled
VERB 1 to climb over something using your hands to help you.
2 To scramble a radio or telephone transmission means to interfere with it so that it can only be understood using special equipment.
3 To scramble eggs means to beat them and cook them slowly in a pan with added milk and seasoning.
NOUN 4 a motorcycle race over rough ground; also called motocross.

scrap scraps scrapping scrapped
NOUN 1 a very small piece of something.
2 used material, such as metal or paper.
3 INFORMAL a fight.
VERB 4 If you scrap something, you throw it away, often for recycling.
5 INFORMAL to fight.

scrapbook scrapbooks
NOUN a book in which you stick things such as pictures or newspaper articles.

Scout can be a noun or a verb. List 10 more words that can be both.

A B C D E F G H I J K L M N O P Q R S T U V W X Y Z

scrape scrapes scraping scraped
VERB **1** If something scrapes something else, it rubs against it harshly.
2 If you scrape something off a surface, you remove it by pulling a rough or sharp object over the surface.
scraper NOUN

scrappy scrappier scrappiest
ADJECTIVE A scrappy piece of work consists of bits and pieces which are not properly organized.
scrappily ADVERB **scrappiness** NOUN

scratch scratches scratching scratched
VERB **1** to make a small cut on something.
2 to rub your skin with your nails because it is itching.
NOUN **3** a small cut.

scrawl scrawls scrawling scrawled
VERB If you scrawl something, you write it in a careless and untidy way.
scrawl NOUN

scrawny scrawnier scrawniest
ADJECTIVE thin and bony.

scream screams screaming screamed
VERB to shout or cry in a loud, high-pitched voice.
scream NOUN

Synonyms: cry, shriek, yell

screech screeches screeching screeched
VERB to make an unpleasant, high-pitched noise. *The car screeched to a halt.*
screech NOUN

screen screens screening screened
NOUN **1** a flat vertical surface on which a picture is shown.
2 a panel used to separate different parts of a room or to protect something.
VERB **3** To screen a film or television programme means to show it.

screenplay screenplays
NOUN the script of a film.

screw screws screwing screwed
NOUN **1** a small, sharp piece of metal used for fixing things together.
VERB **2** If you screw something onto something else, you fix it there by twisting it round and round.
screw up VERB to twist or squeeze something so that it no longer has its proper shape.

screwdriver screwdrivers
NOUN a tool for turning screws.

scribble scribbles scribbling scribbled
VERB **1** to write quickly and untidily.
2 to make meaningless marks with a crayon, pencil, etc. *Toddlers often like to scribble on bits of paper.*
scribble NOUN

script scripts
NOUN **1** the written version of a play or film. *The actor studied the script to learn his lines.*
2 a system of writing. *Arabic script is written from right to left.*
scripted ADJECTIVE

scripture scriptures
NOUN sacred writings, especially the Bible.
scriptural ADJECTIVE

scroll scrolls
NOUN a long roll of paper or parchment with writing on it.

scrounge scrounges scrounging scrounged
VERB; INFORMAL to get something by asking for it rather than by earning or buying it.
scrounger NOUN

Synonyms: cadge, sponge

scrub scrubs scrubbing scrubbed
VERB **1** to clean something vigorously with a stiff brush and water.
2 INFORMAL to delete or cancel. *When the team dropped out of the league, their matches were automatically scrubbed.*
NOUN **3** an area of low trees and bushes.

scruffy scruffier scruffiest
ADJECTIVE dirty and untidy.
scruffily ADVERB

Synonyms: tatty, unkempt

scrum scrums
NOUN When rugby players form a scrum, they form a group and push against each other with their heads down in an attempt to get the ball.

scuba diving
NOUN the sport of swimming underwater with tanks of compressed air on your back. [acronym of Self Contained Underwater Breathing Apparatus]

scuff scuffs scuffing scuffed
VERB If you scuff your shoes, you mark them by dragging them along the ground while walking.
scuffed ADJECTIVE

scuffle scuffles scuffling scuffled
VERB to have a short, rough fight.
scuffle NOUN

sculptor sculptors
NOUN someone who creates sculptures.

sculpture sculptures
NOUN **1** a work of art produced by carving or shaping stone or clay.
2 the art of making sculptures.

scum
NOUN a layer of a dirty substance on the surface of a liquid.

 ► Etymology. Find out how these words are connected: scribble, inscribe, inscription, describe?

scurry scurries scurrying scurried
VERB to move about in a hurry.

scuttle scuttles scuttling scuttled
VERB 1 to run or move about taking short, hasty steps.
NOUN 2 a container for coal used next to a fire.

scythe scythes
NOUN a tool with a long handle and a curved blade used for cutting grass or grain.

sea seas
NOUN 1 the salty water that covers much of the earth's surface.
2 A sea of people or things is a very large number of them: *a sea of waving flags.*

seafaring
ADJECTIVE working or travelling on the sea.
seafarer NOUN

seafood
NOUN edible sea fish or shellfish.

seagull seagulls
NOUN common white, grey and black birds that live near the sea.

seahorse seahorses
NOUN a small fish that swims upright, with a horse-like head.

seal seals sealing sealed
NOUN 1 a piece of wax or other material fixed over the opening of a container, scroll, etc.
2 a fish-eating mammal with four flippers. Seals live in the sea but come ashore to breed.
VERB 3 If you seal an opening, you cover it or stick it securely closed.

sea level
NOUN the average level of the surface of the sea in relation to the land.

sea lion sea lions
NOUN a type of large seal.

seam seams
NOUN 1 a line of stitches joining two pieces of cloth.
2 A seam of coal is a long, narrow layer of it beneath the ground.

seaman seamen
NOUN a sailor.

search searches searching searched
VERB to look hard for something.
search NOUN

Synonyms: look, hunt, scour

searchlight searchlights
NOUN a very powerful light whose beam can be turned in different directions.

seashore
NOUN the land along the edge of the sea.

seasick
ADJECTIVE feeling sick because of the movement of a boat.
seasickness NOUN

seaside
NOUN an area next to the sea.

season seasons seasoning seasoned
NOUN 1 one of the four periods into which a year is divided: spring, summer, autumn and winter.
2 a period of the year when something usually happens: *the cricket season.*
VERB 3 to add salt, pepper or spices to food.

seasonal
ADJECTIVE happening only during one season or one time of the year.
seasonally ADVERB

seasoning seasonings
NOUN flavouring such as salt and pepper.

season ticket season tickets
NOUN a ticket for a series of events, number of journeys, etc. within a specific period of time.

seat seats seating seated
NOUN 1 something you can sit on.
VERB 2 If you seat yourself, or are told to be seated, you sit down.
3 If a place seats a certain number of people, it has enough seats for that number.
seating NOUN

seat belt seat belts
NOUN a strap that you fasten across your body for safety when travelling in a car or aircraft.

seaweed
NOUN a general name for plants that grow in the sea.

secluded
ADJECTIVE quiet and hidden from view.
seclusion NOUN

second seconds
ADJECTIVE 1 The second item in a series is the one counted as number two.
NOUN 2 one of the sixty parts that a minute is divided into.
3 Seconds are goods sold cheaply because they are slightly faulty.
secondly ADVERB

secondary
ADJECTIVE 1 If something is secondary, it is less important than something else.
2 Secondary education is for pupils between the ages of eleven and eighteen. See **primary**.

secondary school secondary schools
NOUN a school for pupils between the ages of eleven and eighteen.

second-hand
ADJECTIVE OR ADVERB 1 Something that is second-hand has already been owned by someone else; used: *a second-had car; second-hand clothes.*
2 If you hear some news second-hand, you hear it from someone else, rather than directly from the people involved.

a b c d e f g h i j k l m n o p q r s t u v w x y z

A B C D E F G H I J K L M N O P Q R S T U V W X Y Z

second person
NOUN In English grammar, the second person is the form of the pronoun or the verb that goes with "you".

secrecy
NOUN the state of keeping something secret. If you are sworn to secrecy, you promise not to tell anyone else about something.

secret secrets
NOUN a fact known by only a small number of people and hidden from everyone else.
secret ADJECTIVE **secretly** ADVERB

secretary secretaries
NOUN a person employed by an organization to keep records, write letters and do office work.

secrete secretes secreting secreted
Said "sik-**kreet**" VERB 1 When part of a plant or animal secretes a liquid, it produces it.
2 FORMAL to hide. *The smuggled goods were secreted in a shed at the docks.*
secretion NOUN

secretive
ADJECTIVE Secretive people tend to hide their feelings and keep their thoughts secret.

Synonyms: reticent, tight-lipped

sect sects
NOUN a religious or political group which has broken away from a larger group.

section sections
NOUN one of the parts that something is divided into.

Synonyms: part, portion, segment

sector sectors
NOUN 1 A sector of something, especially a country's trade and industry, is one part of it: *the engineering sector; the health sector.*
2 A sector of a circle is one of the two parts formed when you draw two straight lines from the centre to the circumference.

secure secures securing secured
ADJECTIVE 1 firmly fixed in place.
2 If you feel secure, you feel safe and confident.
3 If a place is secure, it is tightly locked or well protected.
VERB 4 If you secure an object, you fasten it firmly.
5 If you secure a place, you make it safe from harm or attack.
6 If you secure something, you manage to get it. *He managed to secure the last crate in the shop.*
securely ADVERB

security
NOUN all the precautions taken to protect a place.

sedate sedates sedating sedated
Said "sid-**date**" ADJECTIVE 1 quiet and dignified.
VERB 2 To sedate someone means to give them a drug to calm them down or make them sleep.
sedately ADVERB

sediment sediments
NOUN 1 small particles of material that settle at the bottom of a liquid.
2 small particles of worn rock deposited by wind, ice and water.

sedimentary
ADJECTIVE Sedimentary rocks, such as sandstone and limestone, are formed from fragments of shells or rocks that have become compressed.

see sees seeing saw seen
VERB 1 If you see something, you are looking at it or you notice it.
2 to visit or meet someone.
3 to realize or understand. *I see what you mean.*
4 to find out. *We'll see what the weather's like before we buy tickets.*
5 to deal with. *I'll just see to this customer.*
PHRASE 6 INFORMAL **Seeing as** or **seeing that** means because. *I took my mum breakfast in bed, seeing as it was her birthday.*
see off VERB 1 If you see someone off, you are present as they depart on a train, aircraft, ship, etc.
2 to chase someone away. *Our dog soon saw off the burglar.*

Synonyms: (see, sense 1) glimpse, observe, perceive

seed seeds
NOUN 1 the fertilized part of a plant from which new plants can grow.
2 The seeds of a feeling or process are its beginning or origin: *the seeds of peace.*

seedling seedlings
NOUN a young plant grown from a seed.

seek seeks seeking sought
VERB 1 FORMAL To seek something means to try to find it, obtain it or achieve it.
2 If you seek to do something, you try to do it.

seem seems seeming seemed
VERB If something seems to be the case, it appears to be the case or you think it is the case.
seemingly ADVERB

seen
past participle of **see**.

seep seeps seeping seeped
VERB If a liquid or gas seeps through something, it flows through very slowly.

seesaw seesaws
NOUN a piece of playground equipment on which two children move up and down in turn.

 ► Idioms. What are: second sight, second thoughts, second nature, second-best?

seethe **seethes seething seethed**
VERB 1 If you seethe, you feel very angry but do not show it.
2 If a place is seething with people, there are a lot of them moving about.

segment **segments**
NOUN 1 one part of something. *This orange has eight segments.*
2 A segment of a circle is one of the two parts formed when you draw a straight line across it.

segregate **segregates segregating segregated**
VERB To segregate two groups of people means to keep them apart from each other.
segregated ADJECTIVE **segregation** NOUN

seize **seizes seizing seized**
VERB 1 to grab something firmly.
2 To seize a place means to take control of it quickly and suddenly.
3 If you seize an opportunity, you take advantage of it.
4 If you seize on something, you immediately show great interest in it.
seize up **VERB** If something seizes up, it stops working.

seizure **seizures**
Said "**seez**-yer" **NOUN 1** a sudden violent attack of an illness, such as a heart attack or fit.
2 the capture of something using force.

seldom
ADVERB not very often.

select **selects selecting selected**
VERB 1 to choose.
ADJECTIVE 2 of good quality: *a select hotel.*
selector NOUN

selection **selections**
NOUN 1 the choosing of people or things. *Team selection was done by Mr Gabriel.*
2 a set of people or things chosen from a larger group.
3 The selection of goods in a shop is the range of goods available.

self **selves**
NOUN Your self is your basic personality or nature.

self-centred
ADJECTIVE thinking only about yourself and not about other people.
self-centredly ADJECTIVE **self-centredness** NOUN

self-confident
ADJECTIVE confident of your own abilities or worth.
self-confidence NOUN

self-conscious
ADJECTIVE nervous and easily embarrassed and worried about what other people think of you.
self-consciously ADVERB
self-consciousness NOUN

self-control
NOUN the ability to restrain yourself and not show your feelings.
self-controlled ADJECTIVE

self-defence
NOUN 1 the use of special physical techniques to protect yourself when someone attacks you.
PHRASE 2 If you say something **in self-defence**, you say it to explain why you have done something.

self-employed
ADJECTIVE working for yourself and organizing your own finances, rather than working for an employer.
self-employment NOUN

selfish
ADJECTIVE caring only about yourself, and not about other people.
selfishly ADVERB **selfishness** NOUN

Antonym: selfless

selfless
ADJECTIVE putting other people's interests before your own.
selflessly ADVERB **selflessness** NOUN

Antonym: selfish

self-respect
NOUN a feeling of confidence and pride in your own abilities and worth.

self-righteous
ADJECTIVE convinced that you are better or more virtuous than other people.
self-righteousness NOUN

Synonyms: holier-than-thou, sanctimonious

self-service
ADJECTIVE A self-service shop or restaurant is one where you help yourself to what you want.

self-sufficient
ADJECTIVE 1 producing or making everything you need and so not needing to buy things.
2 able to live in a way in which you do not need other people.
self-sufficiency NOUN

sell **sells selling sold**
VERB to let someone have something in return for money.
sell out **VERB** If a shop has sold out of something, it has sold it all.
seller NOUN

Sellotape
NOUN; TRADEMARK a transparent sticky tape.

semaphore
Said "**sem**-ma-for" **NOUN** a system of sending messages using two flags held in different positions to represent the letters of the alphabet.

a b c d e f g h i j k l m n o p q r s t u v w x y z

Idioms. What kinds of persons are: self-conscious, self-made, self-possessed, self-controlled?

A B C D E F G H I J K L M N O P Q R S T U V W X Y Z

semen
Said "**see**-men" NOUN the liquid containing sperm produced by a man's or other male animal's sex organs.

semi-
PREFIX half or partly.
[from Latin *semi* meaning half]

semicircle semicircles
NOUN a half of a circle or something this shape.
semicircular ADJECTIVE

semicolon semicolons
NOUN the punctuation mark (;).

THE SEMICOLON
The **semicolon** is stronger than a comma but weaker than a full stop. It can be used to mark the break between two main clauses, especially where there is a balance or contrast between them:
I hate jazz; rock music is more my scene.
The semicolon can also be used instead of a comma to separate clauses or items in a long list:
They had a bad time on holiday: the weather was wet; the caravan leaked; the beach was mud not sand; and their money ran out after three days.
Also look at the grammar box at **colon**.

semidetached
ADJECTIVE A semidetached house is joined to another house on one side by a shared wall.

semifinal semifinals
NOUN Semifinals are the two matches of a knockout competition which decide who plays in the final.
semifinalist NOUN

Senate Senates
Said "**sen**-et" NOUN the smaller, more important of the two councils in the government of many countries including the USA, Australia and Canada.
senator NOUN

send sends sending sent
VERB **1** If you send something to someone, you have it delivered.
2 If you send someone somewhere, you tell them to go there or arrange for them to go.
3 If you send off for something, you write and ask for it to be sent to you.
4 If you send someone up, you imitate them in a funny way.

Synonyms: (sense 1) direct, dispatch, forward

senile
ADJECTIVE If old people become senile, they become confused and cannot look after themselves.
senility NOUN

senior seniors
NOUN someone who is higher in rank or older than someone else. *He is three years my senior.*
seniority NOUN

senior citizen senior citizens
NOUN an elderly person, especially one receiving an old age pension.

sensation sensations
NOUN **1** If something is a sensation, it causes great excitement and interest.
2 a feeling, especially a physical feeling.

sensational
ADJECTIVE **1** causing great excitement and interest.
2 INFORMAL extremely good. *That was a sensational party, Felicity.*
sensationally ADVERB

sense senses sensing sensed
NOUN **1** Your senses are the physical abilities of sight, hearing, smell, touch and taste.
2 a feeling: *a sense of excitement.*
3 the ability to think and behave sensibly. *Show a bit of sense!*
4 A sense of a word is one of its meanings.
VERB **5** If you sense something, you become aware of it.
PHRASE **6** If something **makes sense**, you can understand it or it seems sensible.

senseless
ADJECTIVE **1** having no meaning or purpose: *senseless destruction.*
2 unconscious.
senselessly ADVERB **senselessness** NOUN

sensible
ADJECTIVE showing good sense and judgment.
sensibly ADVERB

Synonyms: prudent, rational, wise

sensitive
ADJECTIVE **1** If you are sensitive about something, you are worried or easily upset about it.
2 If you are sensitive to other people's feelings, you understand them.
3 Something that is sensitive to a particular thing is easily affected or harmed by it. *The medicine was light-sensitive.*
sensitively ADVERB **sensitivity** NOUN

sensor sensors
NOUN an instrument which reacts to physical conditions such as light and heat.

sent
past tense and past participle of **send**.

sentence sentences sentencing sentenced
NOUN **1** a group of words which make a statement, question or command. When written down, a sentence begins with a capital letter and ends with a full stop.
2 In a law court, a sentence is a punishment given to someone who has been found guilty.
VERB **3** When a guilty person is sentenced, they are told officially what their punishment will be.

► We have five senses through which we experience our environment: sight, hearing, smell, touch, taste. ◄

WHAT IS A SENTENCE?
A sentence is a group of words which expresses an idea or describes a situation.
Sentences begin with a capital letter, like this one.
Sentences usually end with a full stop, like this one.
If a sentence is a question, it ends in a question mark:
Where's the dog gone to?
If a sentence is an exclamation of surprise, anger or excitement it ends with an exclamation mark:
You must be joking!
Sentences have a subject which indicates a person or thing:
James *laughed.*
The boys *love kicking a ball around.*
Most sentences have a verb. This shows what the subject of the sentence is doing or what is happening to them:
Jim **chased** *the ball.*
Most sentences have an object. This indicates who or what the action is happening to:
Robbie likes **bananas.**
Marina jumped up from **the chair.**

sentiment sentiments
NOUN **1** a feeling, attitude or opinion. *I share your sentiments exactly.*
2 Sentiment consists of feelings such as tenderness or sadness. *Some say that there's no room for sentiment in business.*

sentimental
ADJECTIVE **1** relating to a person's emotions. *These wedding photos are of great sentimental value.*
2 feeling or expressing tenderness or sadness in an exaggerated way. *The sentimental film made me weep.*
sentimentality NOUN

Synonyms: (sense 2) emotional, romantic, slushy

sentry sentries
NOUN a soldier who keeps watch and guards a camp or building.

separate separates separating separated
Said "**sep**-ar-ut" ADJECTIVE **1** not connected. *My brother and I have separate rooms.*
Said "**sep**-ar-ate" VERB **2** to cause people or things to be apart from each other. *The machine separated the cream from the milk.*

Synonyms: (sense 2) divide, split, part

sepal sepals
NOUN the part of a flower, usually green and leaf-like, which encloses the petals and protects the flower before it opens.

September
NOUN the ninth month of the year.

septic
ADJECTIVE If a wound becomes septic, it becomes infected with poison.

sequel sequels
NOUN **1** A sequel to a book or film is another book or film which continues the story.
2 The sequel to an event is a result or consequence of it.

sequence sequences
NOUN **1** The sequence in which things are arranged is the order in which they are arranged.
2 A sequence of events is a number of them coming one after the other.
3 In mathematics, a sequence is a set of numbers in a particular order.

sequin sequins
NOUN Sequins are small, shiny, coloured discs sewn on clothes to decorate them.

serene
ADJECTIVE peaceful and calm.
serenely ADVERB **serenity** NOUN

sergeant sergeants
NOUN **1** a noncommissioned officer of middle rank in the army or air force.
2 a police officer just above a constable in rank.

serial serials
NOUN a story which is broadcast or published in a number of parts over a period of time.

series
NOUN **1** A series of things is a number of them coming one after the other.
2 A radio or television series is a set of programmes with the same title.
PHRASE **3** In an electrical circuit, if two or more components are connected **in series**, the current flows first through one then the other.

Synonyms: (sense 1) sequence, set, succession

serious
ADJECTIVE **1** Serious matters are important and should be thought about carefully.
2 A serious problem or situation is very bad and worrying.
3 If you are serious about something, you are sincere about it.
4 Serious people are thoughtful, quiet, and do not laugh much.
seriously ADVERB **seriousness** NOUN

Synonyms: (sense 2) grave, severe

sermon sermons
NOUN a talk on a religious or moral subject given as part of a church service.

serpent serpents
NOUN; LITERARY a snake.

servant servants
NOUN someone who is employed to work in another person's house.

a b c d e f g h i j k l m n o p q r s t u v w x y z

A B C D E F G H I J K L M N O P Q R S T U V W X Y Z

serve serves serving served
VERB **1** If you serve food or drink to people, you give it to them.
2 To serve customers in a shop, restaurant, etc. means to help them and provide them with what they want.
3 If you serve a country, an organization or a person, you do useful work for them.
4 To serve as something means to act or be used as that thing. *The room serves as their office.*
5 to provide a facility for someone or something: *the hospital serves the whole of the county.*
6 If you serve at tennis, badminton, squash, etc., you are the first person to play the ball for a particular point.
NOUN **7** the act of serving at tennis, badminton, squash, etc.

service services
NOUN **1** a system organized to provide something for the public: *the bus service.*
2 If you give your services to a person or organization, you work for them or help them in some way.
3 a religious ceremony.
4 The services are the army, navy and air force.
5 Motorway services consist of a garage, restaurant, shop and toilets.
VERB **6** If a machine or vehicle is serviced, it is examined and adjusted so it will continue working efficiently.

service station service stations
NOUN a garage that sells petrol, oil, spare parts and snacks.

serviette serviettes
NOUN a square of cloth or paper used when you are eating to protect your clothes or to wipe your mouth.

session sessions
NOUN the period during which an activity takes place: *a photo session.*

set sets setting set
NOUN **1** a group of similar or matching things, or of people in the same situation: *a chess set. She was in the top maths set.*
2 In mathematics, a set is a collection of numbers or other things which are treated as a group.
3 The set for a play or film is the scenery and furniture on the stage or in the studio.
VERB **4** to decide or fix. *They set a date for their wedding.*
5 to adjust. *Set the volume as high as possible.*
6 If something is set somewhere, that is where it is. *The house was set back from the beach.*
7 When the sun sets, it goes below the horizon.
8 to become firm or hard. *The cat ran over the cement before it had set.*
ADJECTIVE **9** fixed and not varying: *a set menu.*
10 If you are set to do something, you are ready or likely to do it.
11 If a play or story is set at a particular time or in a particular place, the events in it take place at that time or in that place. *The play is set in a small American town.*
set off VERB **1** to start a journey.
2 to cause something to start. *My dad set off some rockets on New Year's Eve.*
set up VERB to make all the necessary preparations for something.

setback setbacks
NOUN something that delays or hinders you.

settee settees
NOUN a long comfortable seat for two or three people to sit on.

setting settings
NOUN **1** The setting of something is its surroundings or circumstances. *The South American setting made the story very interesting.*
2 The settings on a machine are the different positions to which the controls can be adjusted.

settle settles settling settled
VERB **1** If you settle yourself somewhere, you sit down and make yourself comfortable.
2 If something is settled, it has all been decided and arranged.
3 If you settle in a place, you make it your permanent home.
4 To settle an argument means to put an end to it.
5 When you settle a bill, you pay it.
6 If something settles, it sinks slowly down and comes to rest.
settle down VERB **1** to become quiet or calm.
2 When someone settles down, they start living a quiet life in one place, especially when they get married.

settlement settlements
NOUN **1** a place where people have settled and built homes.
2 an official agreement between people who have been involved in a conflict.

settler settlers
NOUN someone who settles in a new country or area, particularly one that has not been occupied before.

set-up set-ups
NOUN **1** the way in which something is organized or arranged. *I joined the youth club because I liked the set-up there.*
2 If you say that the outcome of a situation is a set-up, you mean that it was fixed unfairly in advance.

seven
the number 7.
seventh

 ► Seven words have mutated plurals. They become plural by changing the main vowel. ►

seventeen
the number 17.
seventeenth

seventy seventies
the number 70.
seventieth

sever severs severing severed
VERB to cut something off or cut right through it. *Mia severed the friendship. Eric severed the electricity cable.*

several
ADJECTIVE OR PRONOUN Several people or things means a small number of them.

severe
ADJECTIVE 1 extremely bad or unpleasant: *severe stomach pains.*
2 stern and harsh: *The judge handed out a severe punishment.*
severely ADVERB **severity** NOUN

sew sews sewing sewed sewn
Said "**so**" VERB to use a needle and thread to make or mend things.
sewing NOUN

sewage
NOUN dirty water and waste which is carried away in sewers.

sewer sewers
NOUN an underground channel that carries away sewage.

sex sexes
NOUN 1 The sexes are the two groups, male and female, into which humans and other animals are divided.
2 the physical activity by which people and animals produce young.
3 The sex of a person or animal is their characteristic of being either female or male.

sexism
NOUN discrimination against the members of one sex, usually women.
sexist ADJECTIVE OR NOUN

sextet sextets
NOUN a group of six musicians who sing or play together.

sexual
ADJECTIVE 1 connected with the act of sex or with the physical attraction between people.
2 relating to the difference between males and females.
sexually ADVERB

sexual intercourse
NOUN the physical act of sex between two people.

sexy sexier sexiest
ADJECTIVE sexually attractive or exciting.

shabby shabbier shabbiest
ADJECTIVE 1 old and worn in appearance: *a shabby overcoat.*
2 behaving in a mean or unfair way. *She received shabby treatment from her bosses.*
shabbily ADVERB

Synonyms: (sense 1) tatty, threadbare, worn

shack shacks
NOUN a small hut.

shade shades shading shaded
NOUN 1 an area that is relatively dark and cool which the sun does not reach. *They wanted a table in the shade.*
2 The shades of a colour are its different forms.
3 a lampshade.
VERB 4 If you shade in a drawing, you add pencil lines or colour to it.
5 If you shade your eyes, you put your hand in front of them to protect them from bright light.

shadow shadows shadowing shadowed
NOUN 1 the dark shape made when an object prevents light from reaching a surface.
2 Darkness caused by light not reaching a place.
VERB 3 to follow someone and watch them closely.

shady
ADJECTIVE 1 A shady place on a sunny day is one where the sun is not shining directly.
2 INFORMAL suspicious and probably dishonest. *The trader was well-known for his shady dealings.*

shaft shafts
NOUN 1 a vertical passage, such as one for a lift or one in a mine.
2 A shaft of light is a beam of light.
3 a rod in a machine: *the propeller shaft of a boat.*

shaggy shaggier shaggiest
ADJECTIVE Shaggy hair or fur is long and untidy.

shake shakes shaking shook shaken
VERB 1 to move vigorously from side to side or up and down.
2 to shock and upset. *She was severely shaken by the accident.*
NOUN 3 A shake of the head is an action that means "no".
4 A milk shake is a drink of milk, ice cream and flavouring whisked up together.
PHRASE 5 When you **shake hands** with someone, you grasp their hand as a way of greeting them.

Synonyms: (sense 1) quiver, tremble, vibrate

shaky shakier shakiest
ADJECTIVE rather weak and unsteady.
shakily ADVERB

a b c d e f g h i j k l m n o p q r s t u v w x y z

A B C D E F G H I J K L M N O P Q R S T U V W X Y Z

shall
VERB 1 If you say "I shall do something", you mean that you intend to do it or you are sure you will do it.
2 If I say something shall happen, I mean that it will definitely happen or I am ordering it to happen. *You shall go the ball, Cinderella!*
3 "Shall" is used in questions when you are asking what to do or making a suggestion. *Shall we sit down?*

SHALL AND WILL
The verbs **shall** and **will** have only one form. They are used as auxiliary verbs to form the future tense:
We shall arrive on Thursday.
She will give us a talk on wildlife.
Shall is always used in questions involving **I** and **we.** Will is avoided in these cases:
Shall I put the kettle on?
Shall we go to the pictures?
Will is always used when making polite requests, giving orders and indicating persistence. Shall is avoided in these cases:
Will you please help me?
She will keep going on about Tom Cruise.

shallow shallower shallowest
ADJECTIVE 1 Shallow means not deep. *The water is quite shallow.*
2 Feelings can also be described as shallow if they are not deeply felt or not sincere.

sham shams
NOUN something that is not real or genuine.
sham ADJECTIVE

shambles
NOUN If an event is a shambles, it is confused and badly organized.

shame shames shaming shamed
NOUN 1 the feeling of guilt or embarrassment you get when you know you have done something wrong or foolish.
2 If you say something is a shame, you mean you are sorry about it.
VERB 3 If you shame someone into doing something, you force them to do it by making them feel ashamed not to do it.

shameful
ADJECTIVE If someone's behaviour is shameful, they ought to be ashamed of it.
shamefully ADVERB

shampoo shampoos
NOUN a soapy liquid used for washing your hair.
shampoo VERB

shamrock shamrocks
NOUN a plant with three round leaves on each stem, which is the national emblem of Ireland.

shanty shanties
NOUN 1 A sea shanty is a song sailors used to sing.
2 a small, rough hut: *a shanty town.*

shape shapes shaping shaped
NOUN 1 the form or pattern of something's outline. *I could feel a hard shape inside the bag, but I didn't know what it was.*
2 something with a definite form, such as a circle.
VERB 3 to form into a particular shape. *Shape the clay into a ball.*
shape up VERB If you tell someone to shape up, you want them to try harder.
shaped ADJECTIVE

share shares sharing shared
VERB 1 If two people share something, they both use it, do it or have it.
NOUN 2 a portion of something.
3 If you buy shares in a company, you invest your money in the company in return for a share of the profit that it makes.

shark sharks
NOUN 1 a very large, powerful fish with sharp teeth.
2 INFORMAL a person who cheats people out of money.

sharp sharper sharpest; sharps
ADJECTIVE 1 A sharp object has a fine edge or point that is good for cutting or piercing things.
2 A sharp person is quick to notice and understand things.
3 sudden and significant: *a sharp rise in prices.*
4 A sharp taste is slightly sour.
5 If someone speaks to you in a sharp way, they speak briefly, firmly and rather angrily.
ADVERB 6 exactly. *Be outside the cinema at eight o'clock sharp.*
NOUN 7 In music, a sharp is a note or key slightly higher in pitch than others which have the same letter name. It is represented by the symbol #. *You're playing F sharp, when it should be F.*
sharply ADVERB **sharpness** NOUN

Synonyms: (sense 2) astute, perceptive, quick-witted

sharpen sharpens sharpening sharpened
VERB to make something sharp.
sharpener NOUN

shatter shatters shattering shattered
VERB 1 to break into a lot of small pieces.
2 If you are shattered by a piece of news, it causes you great surprise and distress.
3 If something shatters you, it tires you out.
shattered ADJECTIVE **shattering** ADJECTIVE

shave shaves shaving shaved
VERB 1 to remove hair with a razor.
2 to cut thin pieces off something, especially wood.
shave NOUN **shaven** ADJECTIVE

shavings
PLURAL NOUN small, very thin pieces of wood which have been cut from a larger piece.

 ► Hairdressing words: shampoo, salon, perm, style, scissors, mousse.

shawl **shawls**
NOUN a large piece of woollen cloth worn round a woman's head or shoulders or used to wrap a baby in.

she
PRONOUN "She" is used to refer to a woman, girl or any other female animal.

sheaf **sheaves**
NOUN a bundle: *a sheaf of papers; a sheaf of corn.*

shear **shears shearing sheared shorn**
VERB To shear a sheep means to cut the wool off it.

shears
PLURAL NOUN Shears are a tool like a large pair of scissors, used especially for cutting hedges.

sheath **sheaths**
NOUN **1** a covering for the blade of a knife.
2 a condom.

shed **sheds shedding shed**
NOUN **1** a small building used for storing things.
VERB **2** When an animal sheds hair or skin, some of its hair or skin drops off. When a tree sheds its leaves, its leaves fall off. If a lorry sheds its load, its load falls off and spills onto the road.

she'd
1 contraction of **she would**.
2 contraction of **she had**.

sheen
NOUN a gentle brightness on the surface of something.

sheep
NOUN an animal kept on farms for its wool and meat.
✔ The plural of *sheep* is *sheep*.

sheepdog **sheepdogs**
NOUN a breed of dog often used for controlling sheep.

sheepish
ADJECTIVE If you look sheepish, you look embarrassed because you feel shy or foolish.
sheepishly ADVERB

sheer **sheerer sheerest**
ADJECTIVE **1** complete and total: *sheer happiness.*
2 A sheer cliff or drop is vertical.
3 A sheer fabric is very thin, light and delicate.

sheet **sheets**
NOUN **1** a large rectangular piece of cloth used to cover a bed.
2 A sheet of paper is a rectangular piece of it.
3 A sheet of glass or metal is a large, flat piece of it.

sheik **sheiks**; also spelt **sheikh**
Said "**shake**" NOUN an Arab chief or ruler.

shelf **shelves**
NOUN a horizontal piece of wood, metal or glass fixed to a wall and used for putting things on.

shell **shells shelling shelled**
NOUN **1** The shell of an egg or nut is its hard covering.
2 The shell of a tortoise, snail or crab is the hard protective covering on its back.
VERB **3** If you shell peas or nuts, you remove their natural coverings.
4 If a building or place is shelled, it is bombed with explosives.

she'll
contraction of **she will**.

shellfish **shellfish** or **shellfishes**
NOUN a small sea animal with a shell.

shelter **shelters sheltering sheltered**
NOUN **1** a small building made to protect people from bad weather or danger.
2 protection from bad weather or danger. *The refugees were given food and shelter.*
VERB **3** If you shelter in a place, you stay there and are safe.
4 If you shelter someone, you provide them with a place to stay when they are in danger.

shelves
plural of **shelf**.

shepherd **shepherds**
NOUN a person who looks after sheep.

sherbet
NOUN a sweet fizzy powder used in sweets and drinks.

sheriff **sheriffs**
NOUN **1** In the United States, a sheriff is a person elected to enforce the law in a county.
2 In Scotland, a sheriff is a judge.

sherry **sherries**
NOUN a kind of strong wine.

she's
1 contraction of **she is**.
2 contraction of **she has**.

shield **shields shielding shielded**
NOUN **1** a large, flat piece of metal or plastic, which soldiers or policeman carry to protect themselves.
VERB **2** to protect. *He shielded his eyes from the sun.*

shift **shifts shifting shifted**
VERB **1** to move. *I want you to shift this rubble.*
NOUN **2** a set period during which people work.
3 A shift in opinion or situation is a slight change.

shimmer **shimmers**
NOUN a faint, flickering light.
shimmer VERB

a b c d e f g h i j k l m n o p q r s t u v w x y z

shin shins
NOUN Your shin is the front part of your leg between your knee and your ankle.

shine shines shining shone
VERB **1** to give out or reflect a bright light.
2 If you shine a torch somewhere, you point it there.

shingle
NOUN small pebbles on the seashore.

shiny shinier shiniest
ADJECTIVE Shiny things are bright and look as though they have been polished.

ship ships shipping shipped
NOUN **1** a large boat which carries passengers or cargo.
VERB **2** to transport. *Food is being shipped to poor areas.*

shipping
NOUN **1** the transport of cargo on ships.
2 a word for all ships generally.

shipwreck shipwrecks shipwrecking shipwrecked
NOUN **1** When there is a shipwreck, a ship is destroyed in an accident at sea.
VERB **2** If someone is shipwrecked, they survive a shipwreck and manage to reach land.

shipyard shipyards
NOUN a place where ships are built and repaired.

shirk shirks shirking shirked
VERB to avoid doing a task.
shirker NOUN

shirt shirts
NOUN a piece of clothing worn on the upper part of the body, having a collar, sleeves and buttons down the front.

shiver shivers shivering shivered
VERB to tremble slightly because you are cold or scared.
shiver NOUN **shivery** ADJECTIVE

shoal shoals
NOUN a large group of fish swimming together.

shock shocks shocking shocked
NOUN **1** a sudden upsetting experience.
2 a person's emotional and physical condition when something very unpleasant or upsetting has happened to them. *The accident victim is still in a state of shock.*
3 A shock of hair is a thick mass of it.
VERB **4** If something shocks you, it upsets you because it is unpleasant and unexpected, or rude and offensive.
shocked ADJECTIVE

shocking
ADJECTIVE **1** INFORMAL very bad. *It was a shocking display by the tiddlywinks team.*
2 rude or immoral.

shoddy shoddier shoddiest
ADJECTIVE badly made or done.
shoddily ADVERB

shoe shoes shoeing shod
NOUN **1** strong coverings for your feet.
VERB **2** to put horseshoes onto a horse's hooves.

shoelace shoelaces
NOUN Shoelaces are thin pieces of cord used to tie your shoes.

shone
past tense of **shine**.

shook
past tense of **shake**.

shoot shoots shooting shot
VERB **1** to kill or injure someone or something by firing a gun at them.
2 To shoot an arrow is to fire it from a bow.
3 If someone shoots somewhere, they move there very quickly.
4 In sports such as football and hockey, to shoot means to kick or hit the ball towards the goal.
5 to make a film.
NOUN **6** A shoot is a part of a plant that is beginning to grow from a seed, stem or branch.

shooting star shooting stars
NOUN a meteor.

shop shops shopping shopped
NOUN **1** a place where things are sold.
2 a place where a particular type of work is done: *the factory's machine shop.*
VERB **3** to go to the shops to buy things.
shopper NOUN

shopkeeper shopkeepers
NOUN someone who owns or manages a small shop.

shoplifting
NOUN stealing goods from shops.
shoplifter NOUN

shopping
NOUN the goods you have bought from the shops.

shore shores shoring shored
NOUN **1** the land along the edge of a sea, lake or wide river.
VERB **2** If you shore something up, you reinforce it or strengthen it.

shorn
past tense of **shear**.

short shorter shortest
ADJECTIVE **1** small in length, distance or height.
2 not lasting very long.
3 If you are short of something, you do not have enough of it.
4 If a name is short for another name, it is a short version of it.
PHRASE **5** **Short of** is used to say that a level or amount has not quite been reached: *a hundred votes short of a majority.*

 ► Shop words: stock, customer, service, courtesy, checkout, cash and carry, wholesale.

shortage shortages
NOUN If there is a shortage of something, there is not enough of it.

shortbread or **shortcake**
NOUN a crumbly biscuit made from flour and butter.

short circuit short circuits
NOUN a fault in an electrical circuit, which prevents the electricity flowing around the complete circuit. Instead, the electricity takes a shorter path between two points.
short-circuit VERB

shortcoming shortcomings
NOUN a fault or weakness.

shortcut shortcuts
NOUN a quicker way of doing something or getting somewhere.

shorten shortens shortening shortened
VERB to make something shorter or to become shorter.

shorthand
NOUN a way of writing down very quickly what someone is saying, using signs instead of letters.

shortly
ADVERB soon. *I'll be back shortly.*

shorts
PLURAL NOUN short trousers.

short-sighted
ADJECTIVE **1** unable to see distant things clearly.
2 A short-sighted decision does not take account of the way things may develop in the future.

short-tempered
ADJECTIVE Someone who is short-tempered loses their temper easily.

shot shots
1 the past tense and past participle of **shoot**.
NOUN **2** the act of firing a gun.
3 In football, golf and tennis, a shot is the act of kicking or hitting the ball.
4 a photograph or short film sequence. *We got a good shot of the volcanic eruption.*
5 INFORMAL If you have a shot at something, you try to do it.

shotgun shotguns
NOUN a gun that fires a lot of small pellets all at once.

should
VERB **1** You use "should" to say that something ought to happen. *People should respect the feelings of others.*
2 You use "should" to say that you expect something to happen. *We should get the results any day now.*
3 "Should" is used in questions where you are asking someone for advice about what to do. *Should we tell her about it?*
4 "Should" is used in conditional sentences, i.e. where the outcome is not certain. *If I should go to the shops, what do you want me to get you?*
✔ Note that in letters asking for something, the correct style is *I should be grateful if you would...*

shoulder shoulders
NOUN the parts of your body between your neck and the tops of your arms.

shouldn't
contraction of **should not**.

shout shouts shouting shouted
VERB to call something very loudly.
shout NOUN

Synonyms: bawl, bellow, yell

shove shoves shoving shoved
VERB **1** to push roughly.
NOUN **2** a rough push.
shove off VERB; INFORMAL If you tell someone to shove off, you are telling them angrily and rudely to go away.

shovel shovels
NOUN a tool similar to a spade, but larger and with curved side edges, used for moving earth or snow.
shovel VERB

show shows showing showed shown
VERB **1** to let someone see something.
2 to demonstrate something. *Gerald showed me how to hold a saw.*
3 to prove. *The survey shows that not enough people eat a proper breakfast.*
4 to represent, to depict. *The painting shows Granny Reilly in her rocking chair.*
5 to lead someone somewhere. *The usherette showed me to my seat.*
6 If something shows, it is visible. *Margaret was unhappy and it showed.*
NOUN **7** a form of entertainment at the theatre or on television.
8 an exhibition.
PHRASE **9** If something is **on show**, it is being exhibited for the public to see.
show off VERB; INFORMAL to try to impress people.
show up VERB **1** INFORMAL to arrive.
2 If something shows up, it can be seen clearly. *The broken leg showed up clearly in the X-ray.*
3 to embarrass. *Please don't show me up in public.*

shower showers showering showered
NOUN **1** a device which sprays you with water so that you can wash yourself.
2 the acting of washing in a shower.
3 a short period of rain.
VERB **4** to have a shower.
5 If you are showered with a lot of things, they fall on you.

I should have known that! "Should", "could" and "would" are followed by "have", not "of".

showjumping
NOUN a horse-riding competition in which riders and horses jump high fences as fast as they can.
showjumper NOUN

showroom showrooms
NOUN a shop where goods such as cars or electrical appliances are displayed.

showy showier showiest
ADJECTIVE large or bright, and intended to impress people.

Synonyms: flamboyant, flashy, ostentatious

shrank
past tense of **shrink**.

shrapnel
NOUN small pieces of metal scattered from an exploding shell.
[from General Henry Shrapnel (1761–1842) who invented it]

shred shreds shredding shredded
VERB **1** to cut or tear something into very small pieces.
NOUN **2** a small, narrow piece of material or paper.
3 If there is not a shred of something, there is absolutely none of it.

shrew shrews
Said "**shroo**" NOUN a small mouse-like animal with a long pointed nose.

shrewd shrewder shrewdest
ADJECTIVE Someone who is shrewd is intelligent and makes good judgements.
shrewdly ADVERB **shrewdness** NOUN

Synonyms: astute, clever, sharp

shriek shrieks shrieking shrieked
VERB to make a high-pitched scream.
shriek NOUN

shrill shriller shrillest
ADJECTIVE A shrill sound is unpleasantly high-pitched and piercing.
shrilly ADVERB

shrimp shrimps
NOUN a small, edible shellfish with a long tail and many legs.

shrine shrines
NOUN a place of worship associated with a sacred person or object.
[from Latin *scrinium* meaning bookcase; originally it referred to a container of sacred relics]

shrink shrinks shrinking shrank shrunk
VERB **1** to become smaller.
2 If you shrink away from something, you move away from it because you are afraid of it.

shrinkage
NOUN the amount by which something shrinks.

shrivel shrivels shrivelling shrivelled
VERB to become dry and withered.

shroud shrouds shrouding shrouded
NOUN **1** a cloth in which a dead body is wrapped before burial.
VERB **2** If something is shrouded in darkness or mist, it is hidden by it.

shrub shrubs
NOUN a low, bushy plant.

shrug shrugs shrugging shrugged
VERB If you shrug your shoulders, you raise them slightly as a sign that you do not know or do not care about something.
shrug NOUN

shrunk
past participle of **shrink**.

shrunken
ADJECTIVE Something that has shrunken is smaller than it used to be.

shudder shudders shuddering shuddered
VERB **1** to tremble with fear or horror.
2 to shake violently.
NOUN **3** a shiver of fear or horror.

shuffle shuffles shuffling shuffled
VERB **1** to walk without lifting your feet properly off the ground.
2 If you shuffle about, you move about and fidget because you feel uncomfortable or embarrassed.
3 If you shuffle a pack of cards, you mix them up before you begin a game.
shuffle NOUN

shun shuns shunning shunned
VERB to avoid someone or something deliberately.

shunt shunts shunting shunted
VERB; INFORMAL to move something or someone about from one place to another in a rather rough way. *We were shunted from room to room.*

shut shuts shutting shut
VERB **1** to close.
ADJECTIVE **2** closed.
shut up VERB; INFORMAL to stop talking.

shutter shutters
NOUN Shutters are hinged wooden or metal covers fitted on the outside or inside of a window.

shuttle shuttles
ADJECTIVE **1** A shuttle service is an air, bus or train service which makes frequent journeys between two places.
NOUN **2** A train, bus or plane that makes regular short journeys between two places.
3 a space shuttle.

shuttlecock shuttlecocks
NOUN the feathered object used as a ball in the game of badminton.

 ► Don't mix up past tense and past participle. Use "shrank" and "shrunk" correctly in sentences.

shy shyer shyest; shies shying shied
ADJECTIVE **1** nervous and uncomfortable in the company of other people.
VERB **2** If a horse shies, it moves away from something quickly because it is suddenly frightened.
3 If you shy away from doing something, you avoid doing it because you are afraid or nervous.
shyly ADVERB

Synonyms: (sense 1) bashful, self-conscious, timid

sibling siblings
NOUN; FORMAL Your siblings are your brothers and sisters.

sick sicker sickest
ADJECTIVE **1** ill, poorly.
2 If you feel sick, you feel as if you are going to vomit.
3 If you are sick, you vomit.
4 INFORMAL If you are sick of doing something, you feel you have been doing it too long.
5 INFORMAL A sick joke or story deals with death or suffering in an unpleasantly frivolous way.
PHRASE **6** If something **makes you sick**, it makes you angry.

Synonyms: (sense 2) nauseous, queasy

sicken sickens sickening sickened
VERB **1** If something sickens you, it makes you feel disgusted.
2 OLD-FASHIONED If you sicken, you become ill.
sickening ADJECTIVE

sickly sicklier sickliest
ADJECTIVE **1** weak and unhealthy.
2 very unpleasant to smell, taste or see: *sickly food; a sickly grin.*

sickness sicknesses
NOUN **1** the condition of being ill.
2 an illness or disease.

side sides siding sided
NOUN **1** a position to the left or right of something. *Sit by my side.*
2 the outside surfaces of something which are not top, bottom, front or back.
3 The two sides in a war, argument or relationship are the two people or groups involved.
VERB **4** If you side with someone in an argument, you support them.
side ADJECTIVE

sideboard sideboards
NOUN a long, low cupboard for plates and glasses.

sideshow sideshows
NOUN Sideshows are stalls at a fairground.

sideways
ADVERB from or towards the side of something or someone.

siding sidings
NOUN a section of railway off the main track where trains are stored or wait for other trains to pass.

siege sieges
Said "**seej**" NOUN a military operation in which an army surrounds a place and prevents food or help from reaching the people inside in order to make them surrender.

sieve sieves sieving sieved
Said "**siv**" NOUN **1** a kitchen tool made of mesh, used for sifting or straining things.
VERB **2** If you sieve a powder or liquid, you pass it through a sieve.

sift sifts sifting sifted
VERB **1** If you sift a powdery substance, you pass it through a sieve to remove lumps.
2 to examine thoroughly. *The professor sifted through the data.*

sigh sighs sighing sighed
VERB to let out a deep breath.
sigh NOUN

sight sights
NOUN **1** the ability to see, which is one of the five senses.
2 something you see: *a beautiful sight.*
3 Sights are interesting places which tourists visit.
PHRASE **4** If something is **in sight**, you can see it.
5 If something is **out of sight**, you cannot see it.

sightseeing
NOUN visiting the interesting places that tourists usually visit.
sightseer NOUN

sign signs signing signed
NOUN **1** a mark or symbol that always has a particular meaning, for example, in mathematics or music: *the multiplication sign; the minus sign.*
2 a movement or gesture with a particular meaning.
3 A sign can also consist of words, a picture or a symbol giving information or a warning. *The traffic sign instructed drivers to slow down.*
4 If there are signs of something, there is something that shows it exists or is happening. *Snowdrops are one of the first signs of spring.*
VERB **5** to write your name on a document, etc. *He signed autographs for the waiting fans.*
6 to communicate by using sign language.
sign on VERB If a person signs on, they officially state that they are unemployed and wish to claim benefit from the state.
sign up VERB If you sign up for a job or course, you officially agree to do it by signing a contract.

A B C D E F G H I J K L M N O P Q R S T U V W X Y Z

signal signals
NOUN 1 a gesture, sound or action intended to give a message to someone.
2 A railway signal is a piece of equipment beside the track which tells train drivers whether to stop or not.
signal VERB

signature signatures
NOUN If you write your signature, you write your name the way you usually write it.

significant
ADJECTIVE 1 important or full of meaning: *a significant victory.*
2 A significant amount is a large amount.
significantly ADVERB **significance** NOUN

signify signifies signifying signified
VERB A sign or gesture that signifies something has a particular meaning. *The raised flag signified that the starter was ready.*

sign language
NOUN a way of communicating using your hands, used especially by deaf people.

signpost signposts
NOUN a road sign showing the direction of a place and how far away it is.

Sikh Sikhs
Said "**seek**" NOUN a person who believes in Sikhism, an Indian religion which teaches that there is only one God.
Sikh ADJECTIVE
[from Hindi *sikh* meaning disciple]

silence silences silencing silenced
NOUN 1 complete quietness.
VERB 2 to stop someone talking or to stop something from making a noise.

silencer silencers
NOUN a device on a car exhaust or a gun which makes it quieter.

silent
ADJECTIVE 1 making no noise.
2 not saying anything.
silently ADVERB

Synonyms: (sense 2) dumb, mute, speechless

silhouette silhouettes
Said "sil-loo-**ett**" NOUN the outline of a dark shape against a light background.
silhouetted ADJECTIVE

silicon
NOUN Silicon is an element found in sand, clay and stone. It is used to make glass and also to make parts of computers.

silk silks
NOUN a fine, soft cloth made from a substance produced by silkworms.
silky ADJECTIVE **silkiness** NOUN

sill sills
NOUN a ledge at the bottom of a window.

silly sillier silliest
ADJECTIVE foolish or childish.
silliness NOUN

Synonyms: daft, stupid

silver
NOUN 1 a valuable, greyish-white metal used for making jewellery and ornaments.
2 coins made from silver, or from silver-coloured metal.
ADJECTIVE 3 greyish-white.
silvery ADJECTIVE

similar
ADJECTIVE 1 If one thing is similar to another or if two things are similar, they are like each other.
2 In mathematics, two triangles are similar if the angles in one correspond exactly to the angles in the other.
similarity NOUN
✔ *Similar* means alike but not identical, whereas *same* means identical. Do not put *as* after *similar*.

simile similes
Said "**sim**-ill-ee" NOUN a figure of speech where one thing is compared with another thing: *as pleased as Punch; as cold as a fridge in February.* See **metaphor**.

simmer simmers simmering simmered
VERB 1 to cook gently at or just below boiling point.
PHRASE 2 If you **simmer down**, you calm down.

simple simpler simplest
ADJECTIVE 1 not complicated, easy to understand or do.
2 plain in style.
simplicity NOUN

simplify simplifies simplifying simplified
VERB to make something easier to do or understand.
simplification NOUN

simply
ADVERB 1 merely. *The table is simply a piece of wood on a base. We watch television simply because we are bored.*
2 You use "simply" to emphasize what you are saying. *What he said is simply not true!*
3 If you say or do something simply, you do it in a way that makes it easy to understand.

simulate simulates simulating simulated
VERB to imitate. *The lino pattern simulated a real stone floor.*
simulation NOUN

simultaneous
ADJECTIVE happening at the same time.
simultaneously ADVERB

 ► Similes: flat as a pancake or as a fluke. Black as ...? Cool as ...? Clear as ...? Mad as ...?

sin sins sinning sinned
VERB to do something wicked and immoral.
sin NOUN **sinful** ADJECTIVE **sinner** NOUN

since
PREPOSITION, CONJUNCTION OR ADVERB **1** from a particular time until now. *I've been waiting since half past three.*
ADVERB **2** at some time after a particular time in the past. *The budgie escaped but has since been seen twice.*
CONJUNCTION **3** "Since" also means because. *I'm always on a diet, since I put on weight very easily.*
✔ Do not put *ago* before *since*, as it is not needed. *It is ten years since she wrote her book.*

sincere
ADJECTIVE If you are sincere, you say things that you really mean.
sincerely ADVERB **sincerity** NOUN
[from Latin *sincerus* meaning pure, genuine]

sing sings singing sang sung
VERB **1** to make musical sounds with your voice, usually producing words that fit a tune.
2 When birds or insects sing, they make pleasant sounds.
singer NOUN
✔ The past tense of *sing* is *sang* and the past participle is *sung. The team sang the national anthem. We have sung together many times.*

singe singes singeing singed
VERB **1** to burn something slightly so that it goes brown but does not catch fire.
NOUN **2** a slight burn. See **scorch**.
✔ Note that *singe* is one of the few verbs which keeps an *e* when forming the present participle "singeing". This is to differentiate it from "singing".

single singles
ADJECTIVE **1** only one and not more.
2 not married.
3 A single bed or bedroom is for one person.
4 A single or a single ticket is a ticket for a journey to a place but not back again.
NOUN **5** a recording of one or two short pieces of music on a small CD, cassette, etc.
PLURAL NOUN **6** A game of singles in tennis, badminton, etc. is between just two players.
single out VERB If you single someone out from a group, you give them special treatment.

single file
NOUN If a group walks in single file, they walk one behind the other.

single-handed
ADVERB on your own, without any help.
single-handedly ADVERB

singly
ADVERB If people do something singly they do it on their own, or one by one.

singular
NOUN In grammar, the singular is the form of a word that refers to just one person or thing.

Antonym: plural

sinister
ADJECTIVE looking harmful or evil.
[from Latin *sinister* meaning left-hand side, because the left side was considered unlucky]

sink sinks sinking sank sunk
VERB **1** to move downwards, especially through water.
NOUN **2** a basin with taps supplying water, usually in a kitchen or bathroom.
sink in VERB When a fact sinks in, you fully understand it or realize it.
✔ The past tense of *sink* is *sank* and the past participle is *sunk. The old ship turned over and sank. Enemy submarines have sunk a destroyer.*

sip sips sipping sipped
VERB to drink a small amount at a time.
sip NOUN

siphon siphons siphoning siphoned; also spelt **syphon**
Said "**sigh**-fn" VERB **1** If you siphon off a liquid, you draw it out of a container through a tube and transfer it to another place.
NOUN **2** a tube used for siphoning.

sir
NOUN a polite, formal way of addressing a man.

siren sirens
NOUN a warning device which makes a loud wailing or other distinctive noise.

sister sisters
NOUN a girl or woman who has the same parents as you.
sisterly ADJECTIVE

sister-in-law sisters-in-law
NOUN Someone's sister-in-law is the sister of their husband or wife, or their brother's wife.

sit sits sitting sat
VERB **1** If you are sitting, your weight is supported by your bottom, rather than your feet.
2 to take an examination.

site sites siting sited
NOUN a piece of ground where a particular thing happens or is: *a building site.*
VERB If something is sited in a place, it is built or positioned there.

sitting room sitting rooms
NOUN a room in a house used for relaxation and the entertainment of guests.

situated
ADJECTIVE If something is situated somewhere, that is where it is.

Joke. Why is a house full of married couples empty? There's not a single person there.

A B C D E F G H I J K L M N O P Q R S T U V W X Y Z

situation situations
NOUN 1 what is happening in a particular place at a particular time: *the political situation just now.*
2 The situation of a building or town is its surroundings: *a beautiful situation.*

Synonyms: (sense 1) circumstances, condition, state of affairs

six sixes
the number 6.
sixth

sixteen
the number 16.
sixteenth

sixty sixties
the number 60.
sixtieth

size sizes sizing sized
NOUN 1 The size of something is how big or small it is. *The organisers were surprised by the size of the audience.*
2 The size of something is also the fact that it is very large: *the sheer size of Australia.*
3 one of the standard graded measurements of clothes and shoes. *Patrick takes a size 6 in shoes.*

Synonyms: (sense 1) dimensions, proportions

sizeable
ADJECTIVE fairly large.

sizzle sizzles sizzling sizzled
VERB If something sizzles, it makes a hissing sound like the sound of frying food.

skate skates skating skated
NOUN 1 Skates are ice skates or roller skates.
2 a flat, edible sea fish.
VERB 3 to move about wearing skates.
4 If you skate round a difficult subject, you avoid discussing it.
skater NOUN **skating** NOUN

skateboard skateboards
NOUN a narrow board on wheels which you stand on and ride for fun.
skateboarder NOUN **skateboarding** NOUN

skeleton skeletons
NOUN the framework of bones in your body.

sketch sketches sketching sketched
NOUN 1 a quick, rough drawing.
2 a short piece of comic acting.
VERB 3 to draw something quickly and roughly.

sketchy sketchier sketchiest
ADJECTIVE giving only a rough description or account: *a sketchy idea.*

skewer skewers
NOUN a long metal pin which holds pieces of meat together while they are cooking.
skewer VERB

ski skis
Said "**skee**" **NOUN** Skis are long pieces of wood, metal or plastic that you fasten to special boots so you can move easily on snow.
ski VERB

skid skids skidding skidded
VERB to slide in an uncontrolled way, for example, because a playground or road is wet or icy.
skid NOUN **skiddy** ADJECTIVE

skilful
ADJECTIVE If you are skilful at something, you can do it very well.
skilfully ADVERB

Synonyms: able, expert, proficient

skill skills
NOUN 1 the knowledge and ability that enable you to do something well.
2 a type of work or technique which requires special training and knowledge. *I would like to learn some new skills.*
skilled ADJECTIVE

Synonyms: (sense 1) ability, expertise, proficiency

skim skims skimming skimmed
VERB 1 If something skims a surface, it moves along just above it.
2 If you skim something from the surface of a liquid, you remove it. *The cheesemaker skimmed the cream from the milk.*
3 If you skim a piece of writing, you look through it very quickly.

skimmed milk
NOUN Skimmed milk has had the cream removed.

skin skins skinning skinned
NOUN 1 the natural covering of your body.
2 An animal skin is the skin of a dead animal.
3 The skin of a fruit or vegetable is its outer covering.
VERB 4 to remove the skin from a dead animal.

skinny skinnier skinniest
ADJECTIVE extremely thin.

skint
ADJECTIVE; INFORMAL If you are skint, you have no money.

skip skips skipping skipped
VERB 1 If you skip along, you move along jumping from one foot to the other.
2 If you skip, you jump over a circling rope.
3 If you skip something, you miss it out or avoid doing it.
NOUN 4 a large metal container for holding rubbish and rubble.

skipper skippers
NOUN; INFORMAL the captain of a ship, boat or sports team.
skipper VERB

 ► Rhyming slang. What is the meaning of: apples and pears, mince pies, dog and bone, trouble and strife? ►

skirt skirts skirting skirted
NOUN **1** A woman's skirt is a piece of clothing which fastens at her waist and hangs down over her legs.
VERB **2** Something that skirts an area is situated around the edge of it.
3 If you skirt a problem, you avoid dealing with it.

skirting skirtings
NOUN Skirting or skirting board is the narrow strip of wood running along the bottom of walls in a room.

skittles
NOUN Skittles is a game in which players roll a heavy ball and try to knock down wooden objects called skittles.

skull skulls
NOUN the bony part of your head which surrounds your brain.

skunk skunks
NOUN a small black and white mammal from North America which gives off an unpleasant smell when it is frightened.

sky skies
NOUN the space around the earth which you can see when you look upwards.
[from Old Norse *sky* meaning cloud]

skylark skylarks
NOUN a bird often heard in summer, singing while it hovers above the fields.

skylight skylights
NOUN a window set in a roof or ceiling.

skyscraper skyscrapers
NOUN an extremely tall building.

slab slabs
NOUN a thick, flat piece of something.

slack slacker slackest; slacks
ADJECTIVE **1** loose and not firmly stretched or tightly in position.
2 A slack period is one when there is not much work to do.
PLURAL NOUN **3** Slacks are casual trousers.
slacken VERB

slain
past participle of **slay**.

slam slams slamming slammed
VERB **1** to shut a door, lid, etc. noisily and with great force.
2 to throw something down violently. *She slammed the phone down.*

slang
NOUN Slang consists of very informal words and expressions.

slant slants slanting slanted
VERB **1** to slope.
NOUN **2** a slope.
3 A slant on a subject is one way of looking at it, especially a biased one.

slap slaps slapping slapped
VERB to hit someone or something with the palm of your hand.
slap NOUN
[from German *Schlappe*, an imitation of the sound made by a slap]

slash slashes slashing slashed
VERB **1** to make a long deep cut in something.
NOUN **2** a long deep cut.
3 a diagonal line sloping forwards to the top that separates letters, words or numbers, for example in this code number E/436/VHS.

slate slates slating slated
NOUN **1** a dark grey rock that splits easily into thin layers.
2 Slates are small, flat pieces of slate used for covering roofs.
VERB **3** INFORMAL to criticize a play, film or book severely.

slaughter slaughters slaughtering slaughtered
VERB **1** To slaughter farm animals means to kill them for meat.
2 To slaughter a large number of people means to kill them unjustly or cruelly.
NOUN **3** the killing of many people.

Synonyms: (sense 3) carnage, massacre, murder

slave slaves slaving slaved
NOUN **1** someone who is owned by another person and must work for them.
VERB **2** to work very hard for someone.
slavery NOUN
[from Latin *sclavus* meaning a Slav; Slavonic races were frequently conquered and made into slaves]

slay slays slaying slew slain
VERB; LITERARY to kill.

sled sleds
another word for **sledge**.

sledge sledges
NOUN a vehicle on runners used for travelling over snow.
sledge VERB

sledgehammer sledgehammers
NOUN a large, heavy hammer with a long straight handle.

sleek sleeker sleekest
ADJECTIVE Sleek hair is smooth and shiny.

sleep sleeps sleeping slept
NOUN **1** the natural state of rest in which your eyes are closed and you are inactive and not conscious.
VERB **2** When you sleep, you rest in a state of sleep.
PHRASE **3** If a sick or injured animal is **put to sleep**, it is painlessly killed.

Synonyms: (senses 1 and 2) doze, nap, slumber

A B C D E F G H I J K L M N O P Q R S T U V W X Y Z

sleeping bag **sleeping bags**
NOUN a large, warm bag for sleeping in, especially when you are camping.

sleepless
ADJECTIVE unable to get to sleep.
sleeplessness NOUN

sleepwalk **sleepwalks sleepwalking sleepwalked**
VERB to walk around while you are asleep.
sleepwalker NOUN

sleepy **sleepier sleepiest**
ADJECTIVE feeling so tired that you could go to sleep.
sleepily ADVERB

sleet
NOUN a mixture of rain and snow.

sleeve **sleeves**
NOUN the parts of a piece of clothing that cover your arms.
sleeveless ADJECTIVE

sleigh **sleighs**
Said "**slay**" **NOUN** a large sledge.

slender
ADJECTIVE 1 attractively thin and graceful.
2 small in amount or degree: *slender hopes.*

Synonyms: (sense 1) slim, willowy

slept
past participle of **sleep**.

slew
past tense of **slay**.

slice **slices slicing sliced**
NOUN 1 A slice of cake, bread or other food is a piece of it cut from a larger piece.
2 In sport, a slice is a stroke in which the player makes the ball go to one side rather than straight ahead.
VERB 3 to cut into thin pieces.
4 to cut or move quickly through something, like a knife.
slicer NOUN

slick **slicker slickest; slicks**
ADJECTIVE 1 A slick action is done quickly and smoothly.
NOUN 2 An oil slick is a layer of oil floating on the surface of the sea or a lake.
slickly ADVERB **slickness** NOUN

slide **slides sliding slid**
VERB 1 When something slides, it moves smoothly over or against something else.
NOUN 2 a piece of playground equipment for children to slide down.
3 a small piece of photographic film which can be projected onto a screen so that you can see the picture.
4 a small piece of glass on which you put something that you want to examine through a microscope.

slight **slighter slightest; slights slighting slighted**
ADJECTIVE 1 small in amount or degree.
2 A slight person has a slim body.
PHRASE 3 Not in the slightest means not at all.
VERB 4 If you slight someone, you insult them.
slightly ADVERB

slim **slimmer slimmest; slims slimming slimmed**
ADJECTIVE 1 thin.
2 If there is only a slim chance that something will happen, it is unlikely to happen.
VERB 3 to try to lose weight.
slimmer NOUN

slime
NOUN any unpleasant, thick, gooey substance.
slimy ADJECTIVE

sling **slings slinging slung**
VERB 1 INFORMAL to throw something somewhere, often in a careless way.
NOUN 2 a piece of cloth tied round a person's neck to support a broken or injured arm.
3 a device made of ropes or cloth used for carrying things: *carrying the baby in a sling.*
4 a simple weapon made of string and leather, for hurling stones.

slink **slinks slinking slunk**
VERB to move a slow, quiet, secretive way.

slip **slips slipping slipped**
VERB 1 If you slip, you accidentally lose your balance and slide.
2 If something slips, it slides out of place accidentally.
3 to go somewhere or put something somewhere quickly and quietly. *She slipped out of the house. He slipped a £5 note into my hand.*
4 If something slips to a lower level or standard, it falls to that level or standard.
NOUN 5 a small mistake.
6 a piece of underclothing worn under a woman's dress or skirt.
7 A slip of paper is a small piece of paper.

slipper **slippers**
NOUN loose soft shoes that you wear indoors.

slippery
ADJECTIVE 1 smooth, wet or greasy and difficult to hold or walk on.
2 You describe a person as slippery when they cannot be trusted.

slit **slits slitting slit**
VERB to make a long, narrow cut in something.
slit NOUN

slither **slithers slithering slithered**
VERB to move by sliding along the ground in an uneven way.
slithery ADJECTIVE

sliver **slivers**
NOUN a small thin piece of something.

 ► Besides rain and snow, think of other "weather" words for what falls from the sky.

slob slobs
NOUN; INFORMAL a lazy, untidy person.

slog slogs slogging slogged
VERB; INFORMAL 1 to work hard and steadily at something, to toil.
2 to hit hard and wildly. *He slogged the ball for six.*

slogan slogans
NOUN a short, easily-remembered phrase used in advertising or by a political party.

Synonyms: catch-phrase, motto

slop slops slopping slopped
VERB If a liquid slops, it spills over the edge of a container in a messy way.

slope slopes
NOUN a surface that is at an angle, so that one end is higher than the other.
slope VERB

sloppy sloppier sloppiest
ADJECTIVE 1 INFORMAL very messy or careless.
2 foolishly sentimental. *I can't stand sloppy love films.*
sloppily ADVERB **sloppiness** NOUN

slot slots slotting slotted
NOUN 1 a narrow opening in a machine or container.
VERB 2 When you slot something into something else, you put it into a space where it fits. *She slotted a CD into the player.*

sloth sloths
*Rhymes with "**growth**"* NOUN 1 FORMAL laziness.
2 a South and Central American mammal that moves very slowly and hangs upside down from the branches of trees.

slouch slouches slouching slouched
VERB to stand or sit with your shoulders and head drooping forwards.

slow slower slowest; slows slowing slowed
ADJECTIVE 1 moving, happening or doing something with very little speed.
2 If a clock is slow, it shows a time that is earlier than the real time.
3 If you say someone is slow, you mean that they are not very intelligent or quick-witted.
VERB 4 to move or happen more slowly. *Traffic slowed to a halt.*
slowly ADVERB

Antonyms: (sense 1) quick, fast

sludge
NOUN thick mud or sewage.

slug slugs
NOUN a small, slow-moving animal with a slimy body, like a snail without a shell.

sluggish
ADJECTIVE moving slowly and without energy.
sluggishly ADVERB **sluggishness** NOUN

slum slums
NOUN a run-down, dirty overcrowded house or area of a city.

slumber slumbers slumbering slumbered
NOUN 1 LITERARY sleep.
VERB 2 to sleep.

slump slumps slumping slumped
VERB 1 If you slump somewhere, you fall or sit down heavily.
NOUN 2 a sudden drop in an amount or value: *a severe slump in house prices.*
3 a time when there is economic decline and high unemployment.

slung
past tense and past participle of **sling**.

slunk
past tense and past participle of **slink**.

slur slurs slurring slurred
NOUN 1 an insulting remark.
VERB 2 If someone slurs their speech they do not say words clearly, often because they are drunk or ill.

slush
NOUN wet, melting snow.
slushy ADJECTIVE

sly slyer or slier slyest or sliest
ADJECTIVE 1 A sly person is cunning and good at deceiving people.
2 A sly expression or remark shows that you know something other people do not know.
slyly ADVERB

Synonyms: (sense 1) crafty, cunning, devious

smack smacks smacking smacked
VERB to hit someone with your open hand as a punishment.
smack NOUN
[from German or Old Dutch *smacken*, probably an imitation of the sound made by a smack]

small smaller smallest
ADJECTIVE not large in size, number or amount.

Synonyms: little, slight

smart smarter smartest; smarts smarting smarted
ADJECTIVE 1 clean and neatly dressed.
2 clever.
3 a smart movement is quick and sharp.
VERB 4 If a wound smarts, it stings.
smartly ADVERB **smartness** NOUN **smarten** VERB

smash smashes smashing smashed
VERB 1 to break something into a lot of pieces by hitting it or dropping it.
2 to smash against something means to hit it with great force.
NOUN 3 INFORMAL If a play or film is a smash or smash hit, it is very successful.
4 a car crash.
5 a stroke in tennis in which the player hits the ball downwards very hard.

What kind of person would you be if you are: sluggish, waspish, shrewish, catty?

smashing
ADJECTIVE; INFORMAL excellent, first-rate, wonderful.

smear **smears smearing smeared**
NOUN 1 a dirty, greasy mark on a surface.
VERB 2 to make dirty, greasy marks on a surface.
3 If you smear something onto a surface, you cover the surface with a thin layer of the substance.

smell **smells smelling smelled** or **smelt**
NOUN 1 The smell of something is what you sense of it through your nose.
2 Your sense of smell is your ability to smell things.
VERB 3 If something smells, or if you can smell it, it has a quality you can perceive through your nose.
4 If you can smell danger or trouble, you feel it is present or likely to happen.

Synonyms: (sense 1) fragrance, odour, scent

smelly **smellier smelliest**
ADJECTIVE having a strong unpleasant smell.

smelt
past tense of **smell**.

smile **smiles smiling smiled**
VERB When you smile, the corners of your mouth move outwards and slightly upwards because you are pleased or amused.
smile NOUN **smiling** ADJECTIVE

smirk **smirks smirking smirked**
VERB to smile in a smug, sneering or sarcastic way.
smirk NOUN

smith **smiths**
NOUN someone who makes things out of iron, gold or another metal.

smock **smocks**
NOUN a loose garment like a long blouse.

smog
NOUN a mixture of smoke and fog which occurs in some industrial cities.
[a combination of smoke and fog]

smoke **smokes smoking smoked**
NOUN 1 a mixture of gas and small bits of solid material sent into the air when something burns.
VERB 2 If something is smoking, smoke is coming from it.
3 to light and use a cigarette, cigar or pipe.
4 To smoke fish or meat means to hang it over burning wood so that the smoke preserves it and gives it a pleasant flavour.
smoky ADJECTIVE **smoker** NOUN **smoking** NOUN

smooth **smoother smoothest; smooths smoothing smoothed**
ADJECTIVE 1 A smooth surface has no roughness and no holes in it.
2 A smooth liquid or mixture has no lumps in it.
3 A smooth movement or process happens evenly and steadily.
4 successful and without problems. *Can you look after the smooth running of the party?*
VERB 5 to make something smooth and flat.
smoothly ADVERB **smoothness** NOUN

smother **smothers smothering smothered**
VERB 1 If you smother a fire, you cover it with something to put it out.
2 To smother a person means to cover their face with something so that they cannot breathe.
3 To smother children means to give them too much love and protection.
4 If you smother an emotion, you control it so that people do not notice it.

smoulder **smoulders smouldering smouldered**
VERB 1 to burn very slowly, producing smoke but no flames.
2 If a feeling is smouldering inside you, you feel it very strongly but do not show it.

smudge **smudges smudging smudged**
VERB If you smudge something, you make it dirty or messy by touching it or marking it.
smudge NOUN

smug **smugger smuggest**
ADJECTIVE Someone who is smug is very pleased with how good or clever they think they are.
smugly ADVERB **smugness** NOUN

smuggle **smuggles smuggling smuggled**
VERB to take things into or out of a place illegally or secretly.
smuggler NOUN

snack **snacks**
NOUN 1 a small, quick meal.
2 something eaten between meals.
snack VERB

snag **snags snagging snagged**
NOUN 1 a small problem or disadvantage.
VERB 2 If you snag your clothing, you damage it by catching it on something sharp.

snail **snails**
NOUN a small, slow-moving animal with a long, shiny body and a shell on its back.

snake **snakes**
NOUN a long, thin reptile with scales and no legs.

snap **snaps snapping snapped**
VERB 1 to break with a sharp cracking noise.
2 to speak in a sharp, unfriendly way.
3 If an animal snaps, it shuts its jaws as if to bite you.
4 If you snap someone, you take a quick photograph of them.
NOUN 5 the sound of something snapping.
6 INFORMAL a photograph, particularly one that is taken quickly and casually.
ADJECTIVE 7 A snap decision is taken suddenly, with very little thought.

 ► Some words from Dutch: smuggle, yacht, boom, blunderbuss, skipper.

snappy **snappier snappiest**
ADJECTIVE Someone who is snappy speaks to people in a sharp, unfriendly way.

snare **snares**
NOUN a trap for catching animals.
snare VERB

snarl **snarls snarling snarled**
VERB 1 When an animal snarls, it bares its teeth and makes a fierce growling noise.
2 to say something in a fierce, angry way.
snarl NOUN

snatch **snatches snatching snatched**
VERB 1 to reach out for something quickly and take it, to grab.
NOUN 2 a quick grab.
3 A snatch of conversation or song is a very small piece of it.

sneak **sneaks sneaking sneaked**
VERB 1 to go somewhere quickly trying not to be seen or heard.
NOUN 2 INFORMAL someone who tells people in authority that someone else has done something wrong.

sneaky **sneakier sneakiest**
ADJECTIVE Someone who is sneaky does things secretly rather than openly.
sneakily ADVERB

sneer **sneers sneering sneered**
VERB 1 to show by your expression and your comments that you think someone or something is stupid or inferior.
NOUN 2 the expression on someone's face when they sneer.

sneeze **sneezes sneezing sneezed**
VERB to get rid of air from your nose involuntarily and suddenly, and usually noisily.
sneeze NOUN

sniff **sniffs sniffing sniffed**
VERB 1 to breathe in air through your nose hard enough to make a sound.
2 If you sniff something, you smell it by sniffing.
sniff NOUN

snigger **sniggers sniggering sniggered**
VERB to laugh quietly and disrespectfully.
snigger NOUN

snip **snips snipping snipped**
VERB 1 to cut something with scissors or shears in a single quick action.
NOUN 2 a small cut made by scissors or shears.
3 INFORMAL a bargain. *The antique chair was a snip at only £10.*

sniper **snipers**
NOUN someone who shoots a gun or rifle from a hidden place.

snippet **snippets**
NOUN a snippet of news or information is a small piece of it.

snivel **snivels snivelling snivelled**
VERB 1 to have a runny nose.
2 If you say that someone is snivelling, you are scornful that they are sniffing because they are upset.

snob **snobs**
NOUN someone who admires people of a higher social class and looks down on people of a lower social class. Snobs often believe that they are better than other people.
snobbery NOUN **snobbish** ADJECTIVE

snooker
NOUN a game played on a large table covered with smooth green cloth. Players score points by hitting different coloured balls into pockets using a long stick called a cue.

snoop **snoops snooping snooped**
VERB; INFORMAL to look secretly round a place to find out things.
snooper NOUN

snooze **snoozes snoozing snoozed**
VERB; INFORMAL to sleep lightly for a short time, especially during the day.
snooze NOUN

snore **snores snoring snored**
VERB When a sleeping person snores, they make a loud noise each time they breathe.
snore NOUN

snorkel **snorkels**
NOUN a tube you can breathe through when you are swimming just under the surface of the sea.
snorkel VERB **snorkelling** NOUN
[from German *Schnorchel*, originally an air pipe for a submarine]

snort **snorts snorting snorted**
VERB When people or animals snort, they force breath out through their nose in a noisy way.
snort NOUN

snout **snouts**
NOUN an animal's nose.

snow **snows**
NOUN soft white crystals of ice which fall from the sky in cold weather.
snow VERB

WORD FAMILY:snow
snowball **NOUN** snowball fight **NOUN**
snowboarding **VERB** snowdrift **NOUN**
snowfall **NOUN** snowflake **NOUN**
snowman **NOUN** snowplough **NOUN**
snowstorm **NOUN**

snowball **snowballs snowballing snowballed**
NOUN 1 a ball of snow for throwing.
VERB 2 When something such as a project snowballs, it grows rapidly.

snowdrop **snowdrops**
NOUN a small white flower which appears in early spring.

a b c d e f g h i j k l m n o p q r s t u v w x y z

A B C D E F G H I J K L M N O P Q R S T U V W X Y Z

snowflake snowflakes
NOUN a single crystal of snow.

snowman snowmen
NOUN a figure built out of packed snow.

snowshoe snowshoes
NOUN a frame like a tennis racket strapped to the shoe to enable someone to walk on snow.

snub snubs snubbing snubbed
VERB **1** To snub someone means to behave rudely towards them, especially by making an insulting remark or ignoring them.
NOUN **2** an insulting remark or a piece of rude behaviour.
ADJECTIVE **3** A snub nose is short and turned-up.

Synonyms: (sense 2) affront, insult, slap in the face

snug
ADJECTIVE **1** warm and comfortable.
2 If something is a snug fit, it fits very closely.
snugly ADVERB

snuggle snuggles snuggling snuggled
VERB to cuddle up more closely to something or someone.

so
ADVERB **1** "So" is used to refer back to what has just been said. *Had he locked the car? If so, where were the keys?*
2 also. *He laughed and so did Jarvis.*
3 therefore. *It's a bit expensive, so we won't get one.*
4 "So" is used when you are talking about the extent or degree of something. *Why are you so cruel?*
5 "So" is used before words like "much" and "many" to say that there is a definite limit to something. *I can only answer so many questions.*
CONJUNCTION **6** "So that" and "so as" are used to introduce the reason for doing something. *We go to school so that we can learn.*

soak soaks soaking soaked
VERB **1** to put something in a liquid and leave it there.
2 to make something or someone very wet.
3 When something soaks up a liquid, the liquid is drawn up into it.
soaked ADJECTIVE

soap soaps
NOUN a substance used with water for washing yourself.
soapy ADJECTIVE

soap opera soap operas
NOUN a popular television drama serial about people's daily lives.
[originally from daytime programmes in the USA which were sponsored by soap or detergent companies]

soar soars soaring soared
VERB **1** to go very quickly up into the air.
2 to increase suddenly and by a great deal: *prices soared.*
soaring ADJECTIVE

sob sobs sobbing sobbed
VERB **1** to cry in a noisy way, breathing in short breaths.
NOUN **2** the noise made when you cry.

sober soberer soberest
ADJECTIVE **1** not drunk.
2 serious and thoughtful.
soberly ADVERB

so-called
ADJECTIVE You use "so-called" to say that the name by which something is called is incorrect or misleading. *She was the so-called "queen of country music".*

soccer
NOUN a game played by two teams of eleven players kicking a ball in an attempt to score goals.

sociable
ADJECTIVE Sociable people are friendly and enjoy talking to other people.
sociability NOUN

Synonyms: friendly, gregarious, outgoing

social
ADJECTIVE **1** to do with society or life within a society.
2 to do with leisure activities that involve meeting other people rather than work: *social events.*
socially ADVERB

socialism
NOUN the political belief that the state should own industries on behalf of the people and that everyone should be equal.
socialist NOUN

social worker social workers
NOUN someone whose job it is to give help and advice to people with serious financial or family problems.
social work NOUN

society societies
NOUN **1** the people in a particular country or region.
2 an organization for people who have the same interest or aim. *We are starting a railway society at school.*
3 Society is also rich, upper-class, fashionable people.

Synonyms: (sense 1) civilization, culture

sock socks
NOUN pieces of clothing covering your foot and ankle.
[from Old English *socc* meaning light shoe]

 ► What is the full name of the game soccer?

socket sockets
NOUN **1** a place on a wall or on a piece of electrical equipment into which you can put a plug or bulb.
2 any hollow part or opening into which another part fits: *eye sockets*.

soda sodas
NOUN **1** soda water.
2 Soda is also sodium in the form of crystals or a powder, and is used for baking or cleaning.

soda water soda waters
NOUN a type of fizzy water used for mixing with alcoholic drinks or fruit juice.

sodium
NOUN a silvery-white chemical element which is found in common salt.

sofa sofas
NOUN a long comfortable seat with a back and arms, for two or three people.

soft softer softest
ADJECTIVE **1** Something soft is not hard, stiff or firm.
2 very gentle: *a soft breeze*.
3 A soft sound or voice is quiet and not harsh.
4 A soft colour or light is not bright.
softly ADVERB **softness** NOUN

soft drink soft drinks
NOUN any cold, non-alcoholic drink.

soften softens softening softened
VERB to make something softer or to become softer.

software
NOUN a general word for computer programs. See **hardware**.

soggy soggier soggiest
ADJECTIVE unpleasantly wet or full of water. [from American dialect *sog* meaning marsh]

soil soils soiling soiled
NOUN **1** the top layer of the land surface of the earth. Soil is a mixture of very small pieces of rock, bits of rotting plants and animals, air and water.
VERB **2** to make something dirty. *You have soiled your shirt.*
soiled ADJECTIVE

Synonyms: (sense 1) earth, ground

solar
ADJECTIVE relating or belonging to the sun.

solar system
NOUN the sun and all the planets, comets and asteroids that orbit round it.

sold
past tense of **sell**.

solder solders soldering soldered
VERB to join small pieces of metal together using molten metal.

soldier soldiers
NOUN a person in an army.

sole soles
ADJECTIVE **1** The sole thing or person of a particular type is the only one of that type.
NOUN **2** the underneath part of your foot or shoe.
3 a flat sea-water fish which you can eat.
solely ADVERB

solemn
ADJECTIVE serious rather than cheerful or humorous.
solemnly ADVERB **solemnity** NOUN

solicitor solicitors
NOUN a lawyer who gives legal advice and prepares legal documents and cases.

solid
ADJECTIVE **1** hard or firm.
2 You say that something is solid when it does not have any space in it: *a solid steel bar. The car park was packed solid.*
3 happening for a period of time without interruption, continuous. *She cried for two weeks solid.*
NOUN **4** a solid substance or object, and not a liquid or gas.
solidly ADVERB **solidity** NOUN

solidarity
NOUN If a group of people show solidarity, they show unity and support for each other.

solidify solidifies solidifying solidified
VERB to turn from liquid to solid.

solitary
ADJECTIVE **1** on your own, alone. *She spent a solitary day in the sun.*
2 single. *Susan was the solitary guest in the hotel.*

solitude
NOUN the state of being alone.

Synonyms: isolation, seclusion

solo
ADJECTIVE OR ADVERB A solo performance or activity is done by one person alone: *a solo flight; to sail solo around the world.*
solo NOUN

soloist soloists
NOUN a person who performs a solo.

solstice solstices
NOUN one of the two times in the year when the sun is at its furthest point south or north of the equator.

soluble
ADJECTIVE **1** able to dissolve in liquid.
2 A soluble problem can be solved.
solubility NOUN

solute solutes
NOUN a substance which is dissolved in a liquid, such as sugar in a cup of tea.

a b c d e f g h i j k l m n o p q r s t u v w x y z

solution solutions
NOUN 1 the answer to a problem or difficult situation.
2 a mixture of substances in which one or more are completely dissolved. *Salt dissolved in water forms a solution.*

solve solves solving solved
VERB to find a solution or answer to a problem.

Synonyms: answer, resolve, work out

solvent solvents
NOUN 1 a liquid in which other substances can be dissolved.
ADJECTIVE 2 If a person or company is solvent, they have enough money to pay all their debts.

sombre
ADJECTIVE 1 A sombre person is very serious, sad or gloomy.
2 Sombre colours are dark and dull.
sombrely ADVERB

some
ADJECTIVE OR PRONOUN 1 You use "some" to refer to a quantity or number when you are not stating the quantity or number exactly. *There's some money on the table.*
ADJECTIVE 2 You use "some" to emphasize that a quantity or number is fairly large. *She had been there for some days.*

WORD FAMILY: some
somebody **PRONOUN** somehow **ADVERB**
someone **PRONOUN** something **PRONOUN**
sometimes **ADVERB** somewhere **ADVERB**

somersault somersaults
NOUN a forwards or backwards roll in which the body is brought over the head.
somersault VERB

sometime
ADVERB at a time in the future or the past that is unknown or that has not yet been fixed. *He has to find out sometime.*

sometimes
ADVERB occasionally.

somewhat
ADVERB to some extent or degree. *Her future seemed somewhat doubtful.*

son sons
NOUN Someone's son is their male child.

sonar
NOUN equipment on a ship which calculates the depth of the sea or the position of an underwater object using sound waves. [from So(und) Na(vigation) R(anging)]

song songs
NOUN a piece of music with words that are sung to the music.

sonic
ADJECTIVE related to sound.

sonnet sonnets
NOUN a poem with 14 lines, in which lines rhyme according to fixed patterns.

soon sooner soonest
ADVERB in a short time, presently.

soot
NOUN black carbon powder which rises in the smoke from a fire.
sooty ADJECTIVE

soothe soothes soothing soothed
VERB 1 If you soothe someone who is angry or upset, you make them calmer.
2 to make pain or discomfort less severe.
soothing ADJECTIVE

sophisticated
ADJECTIVE 1 Sophisticated people have refined or cultured tastes or habits.
2 A sophisticated machine or device is made using advanced and complicated methods.
sophistication NOUN

sopping
ADJECTIVE soaking wet.

soppy soppier soppiest
ADJECTIVE; INFORMAL silly or foolishly sentimental.

soprano sopranos
NOUN a singer who can sing the highest range of notes.

sorbet sorbets
Said "**sor**-bay" **NOUN** a type of ice cream which has more water than milk in it, with fruit, egg white, etc. added.

sorcerer sorcerers
Said "**sor**-ser-er" **NOUN** a person who performs magic by using the power of evil spirits.
sorcery NOUN

sordid
ADJECTIVE 1 dishonest or immoral: *a sordid business.*
2 dirty, unpleasant or depressing: *a sordid guest house.*

Synonyms: (sense 2) seedy, sleazy, squalid

sore sorer sorest; sores
ADJECTIVE 1 painful.
2 annoyed or offended. *He was sore at me because I came late.*
NOUN 3 a painful place where your skin has become infected.
soreness NOUN

Synonyms: (sense 1) painful, sensitive, tender

sorely
ADVERB greatly, seriously. *I was sorely tempted to argue with the ref.*

 ► Poetry words: sonnet, ballad, epic, ode, metre, rhyme, scansion, stanza, laureate.

sorrow **sorrows**
NOUN 1 deep sadness or regret.
2 things that cause sorrow. *All the sorrows of the world seemed heaped upon him.*
sorrowful ADJECTIVE **sorrowfully** ADVERB

sorry **sorrier sorriest**
ADJECTIVE 1 to feel sadness, regret or sympathy because of something.
2 "Sorry" is used to describe people and things that are in a bad physical or mental state. *Alan's wilted bunch of flowers was a sorry sight.*

sort **sorts sorting sorted**
NOUN 1 type, kind, variety. *What sort of book have you chosen?*
VERB 2 to arrange things into different groups, sets or sorts.
sort out VERB to find a solution to a problem or misunderstanding.
✔ When you use *sort* in its singular form, the adjective before it should also be singular: *that sort of car.* When you use the plural form *sorts,* the adjective before it should be plural: *those sorts.*

sought
past participle of **seek**.

soul **souls**
NOUN 1 A person's soul is the spiritual part of them which some people think continues after their body is dead.
2 a person's mind, character, thoughts and feelings. *I put my heart and soul into the job.*
3 person. *There was not a soul there.*

sound **sounds sounding sounded; sounder soundest**
NOUN 1 anything that can be heard. Sound is a form of energy that travels as vibrations through solids, liquids and gases.
VERB 2 to make a noise. *The captain sounded the foghorn.*
3 The way someone sounds is the impression you have of them when they speak. *Indira sounded angry.*
ADJECTIVE 4 in good condition, reliable. *The car's engine was rough but the bodywork was sound. His work throughout the year has been sound.*

sound effect **sound effects**
NOUN Sound effects are sounds created artificially to make a play more realistic.

soundly
ADVERB 1 If you sleep soundly, you sleep deeply and well.
2 If you are soundly beaten at a game, you lose by a large margin.

soundproof **soundproofs soundproofing soundproofed**
ADJECTIVE 1 If a room is soundproof, sound cannot get into it or out of it.
VERB 2 to make something soundproof.

soundtrack **soundtracks**
NOUN the sound accompaniment to a film.

soup **soups**
NOUN liquid food made by boiling meat, fish or vegetables in water.

sour **sours souring soured**
ADJECTIVE 1 If something is sour, it has a sharp, acid taste.
2 If a person is sour, they are bad-tempered and unfriendly.
VERB 3 If a friendship, situation or attitude sours, it becomes less friendly, enjoyable or hopeful.

source **sources**
NOUN The source of something is the person, place or thing that it comes from. *The source of the river was a spring in the hills.*

south
NOUN 1 the direction on your right when you are looking towards the direction where the sun rises.
ADJECTIVE OR ADVERB 2 in or towards the south.

south-east
NOUN, ADVERB OR ADJECTIVE halfway between south and east.
south-eastern ADJECTIVE

southerly
ADJECTIVE OR ADVERB 1 to or towards the south.
2 A southerly wind blows from the south.

southern
ADJECTIVE in or from the south.

South Pole
NOUN the most southerly point of the earth's surface.

southward or **southwards**
ADVERB 1 towards the south.
ADJECTIVE 2 The southward part of something is the south part.

south-west
NOUN, ADVERB OR ADJECTIVE halfway between south and west.
south-western ADJECTIVE

souvenir **souvenirs**
NOUN something you keep to remind you of a holiday, place or event.
[from French *se souvenir* meaning to remember]

sovereign **sovereigns**
Said "**sov**-rin" **NOUN 1** a king, queen or royal ruler of a country.
2 a former British gold coin, then worth one pound.

sow **sows sowing sowed sown**
Said "**soh**" **VERB 1** to plant seeds in the ground.
Rhymes with "**now**" **NOUN 2** an adult female pig.

soya
NOUN Soya flour, margarine, oil and milk are made from the beans of the soya plant.

a b c d e f g h i j k l m n o p q r s t u v w x y z

Can you make anagrams of: south, north, east, west, skin, life, parts, verse, smile, mean?

space **spaces**
NOUN 1 the area or volume that is empty or available in a place, building or container, or between two things.
2 the area beyond the earth's atmosphere surrounding the stars and planets.
3 a period of time: *the space of a week.*

spacecraft **spacecraft**
NOUN a vehicle designed to orbit the earth or travel into outer space.

spaceship **spaceships**
NOUN a manned spacecraft.

space shuttle **space shuttles**
NOUN a spacecraft designed to be used many times for travelling out into space and back again.

space station **space stations**
NOUN a large satellite that orbits the earth and is used as a base by astronauts or scientists.

spacesuit **spacesuits**
NOUN a protective suit covering the whole of an astronaut's body.

spacious
ADJECTIVE having or providing a lot of space.
spaciousness NOUN

Synonyms: capacious, commodious, roomy

spade **spades**
NOUN 1 a tool with a flat metal blade and a long handle used for digging.
2 Spades is one of the four suits in a pack of playing cards.

spaghetti
Said "spag-**get**-ee" **NOUN** long, thin pieces of pasta.
[from Italian *spago* meaning string]

span **spans spanning spanned**
NOUN 1 The span of something is the total length of it from one end to the other.
2 the period of time during which something exists or functions.
3 Your span is the distance between the tips of your thumb and little finger when your fingers are stretched wide.
VERB 4 to last throughout a particular time. *The comedian's career spanned 50 years.*
5 A bridge that spans something stretches right across it.

spaniel **spaniels**
NOUN a dog with long drooping ears and a silky coat.

spank **spanks spanking spanked**
VERB If a child is spanked, it is punished by being slapped, usually on its leg or bottom.

spanner **spanners**
NOUN a tool with a specially shaped end that fits round a nut to turn it.

spare **spares sparing spared**
ADJECTIVE 1 extra to what is needed.
VERB 2 to make something available for a particular purpose. *Few teachers could be spared to go on the trip.*
3 If someone is spared an unpleasant experience, they are prevented from suffering it.
NOUN 4 something that is extra to what is needed.

spark **sparks sparking sparked**
NOUN 1 a tiny, bright piece of burning material thrown up by a fire.
VERB 2 If one thing sparks another off, it causes the second thing to start happening. *The win sparked off a wave of excitement.*

sparkle **sparkles sparkling sparkled**
VERB to shine with a lot of small, bright points of light.
sparkling ADJECTIVE

Synonyms: gleam, glitter, twinkle

sparkler **sparklers**
NOUN a hand-held firework which gives off bright sparks as it burns.

sparrow **sparrows**
NOUN a common, small bird with brown and grey feathers.

sparse **sparser sparsest**
ADJECTIVE small in number or amount and spread out over an area.
sparsely ADVERB

spasm **spasms**
NOUN 1 a sudden cramping of the muscles.
2 a sudden burst of activity, emotion, etc: *a spasm of fear.*

spat
past tense of **spit**.

spatter **spatters spattering spattered**
VERB to cover a surface with drops of liquid.
spatter NOUN **spattered** ADJECTIVE

spawn **spawns spawning spawned**
NOUN 1 a jelly-like substance containing the eggs of fish or amphibians such as frogs and newts.
VERB 2 When fish or amphibians spawn, they lay their eggs.
3 If something spawns something else, it causes it. *The depressed economy spawned the riots.*

speak **speaks speaking spoke spoken**
VERB 1 to use your voice to say words.
2 If you can speak a foreign language, you know it and can use it.
speak out VERB to state publicly your opinion about something.

Synonyms: (sense 1) communicate, talk, utter

speaker **speakers**
NOUN 1 a person who is speaking, especially someone making a speech.
2 a part of a sound system through which sound comes out; a loudspeaker.

 ► Some words from Italian: spaghetti, pasta, bandit, opera, piano.

spear spears
NOUN a weapon consisting of a long pole with a sharp point, for jabbing into things.
spear VERB

special
ADJECTIVE If someone or something is special, they are different from normal, often in a way that makes them more important or better than other things.

specialist specialists
NOUN someone who has a particular skill or who knows a lot about a particular subject, often a branch of medicine: *a specialist in tropical diseases.*

speciality specialities
NOUN A person's speciality is something they are especially good at or know a lot about.

specialize specializes specializing specialized; also spelt **specialise**
VERB If you specialize in something, you know a lot about it and spend a lot of time on it.
specialization NOUN

specially
ADVERB If something has been done specially for a particular person or purpose, it has been done only for that person or purpose.

species
Said "**spee**-sheez" NOUN a group of plants or animals whose members have the same characteristics and are able to breed with each other.

specific
ADJECTIVE 1 particular: *specific areas of difficulty.*
2 precise and exact, definite. *She will ask for specific answers.*
specifically ADVERB

specify specifies specifying specified
VERB to state or describe something precisely.

specimen specimens
NOUN an example or small amount of something, which gives an idea of what the whole is like.

speck specks
NOUN a very small stain or amount of something.

speckled
ADJECTIVE covered in very small marks or spots.

spectacle spectacles
PLURAL NOUN 1 Someone's spectacles are their glasses.
NOUN 2 a strange or interesting sight or scene. *The eclipse was an astonishing spectacle.*
3 a grand and impressive event or performance.

spectacular spectaculars
ADJECTIVE 1 very impressive or dramatic.
NOUN 2 a very impressive show.

Synonyms: (sense 1) impressive, sensational, stunning

spectator spectators
NOUN a person who is watching something, an onlooker.
spectate VERB

Synonyms: observer, onlooker, watcher

spectre spectres
NOUN a ghost.

spectrum spectra or spectrums
NOUN 1 the range of different colours when light passes through a prism or a drop of water. A rainbow shows the colours of the spectrum.
2 a complete range of opinions or emotions.

speech speeches
NOUN 1 the ability to speak or the act of speaking.
2 a formal talk given to an audience.

speech bubble speech bubbles
NOUN In a cartoon, speech bubbles are drawn to tell you what each character is saying.

speechless
ADJECTIVE unable to speak for a short time because of a shock.

speech marks
PLURAL NOUN Another term for **inverted commas**. See **quotation mark**.

speed speeds speeding sped or speeded
NOUN 1 the rate at which something moves or happens.
2 very fast movement or travel.
VERB 3 to move or travel somewhere quickly.
4 to drive a vehicle faster than the legal speed limit.

Synonyms: (sense 2) rapidity, swiftness, velocity

speedboat speedboats
NOUN a small, fast motorboat.

speedometer speedometers
NOUN an instrument which shows how fast a vehicle is moving.

speedway
NOUN the sport of racing lightweight motorcycles on special tracks.

speedy speedier speediest
ADJECTIVE very quick.
speedily ADVERB

spell spells spelling spelled or spelt
VERB 1 to name or write the letters of words in order.
NOUN 2 a short period: *a spell of good weather.*
3 a word or sequence of words used to perform magic.
spell out VERB to explain something in detail.

spellbound
ADJECTIVE so fascinated by something that you cannot think about anything else.

What is the difference between a spectacle and a pair of spectacles?

A B C D E F G H I J K L M N O P Q R S T U V W X Y Z

spelling spellings
NOUN the spelling of a word is the correct order of letters in it.

spend spends spending spent
VERB **1** When you spend money, you buy things with it.
2 To spend time or energy means to use it.
spent ADJECTIVE

sperm sperms
NOUN a cell produced in the sex organ of a male animal which can enter a female animal's egg and fertilize it.

sphere spheres
NOUN **1** a perfectly round object, such as a ball.
2 an area of activity or interest. *The designer was well known in the sphere of the theatre.*
spherical ADJECTIVE

sphinx sphinxes
Said "**sfingks**" NOUN In mythology, the sphinx was a monster with a person's head and a lion's body.

spice spices spicing spiced
NOUN **1** powder or seeds from a plant added to food to give it flavour.
VERB **2** to add spice to food.
3 If you spice something up, you make it more exciting or lively.
spiced ADJECTIVE

spicy spicier spicier
ADJECTIVE Spicy food is strongly flavoured with spices.

spider spiders
NOUN a small insect-like creature with eight legs that spins webs to catch insects for food.

spied
past tense of **spy**.

spike spikes spiking spiked
NOUN a long pointed piece of metal or other sharp material.
spiked ADJECTIVE **spiky** ADJECTIVE

spill spills spilling spilled or spilt
VERB to let something accidentally fall or run out of a container.

spin spins spinning spun
VERB **1** to turn quickly around a central point.
2 to make thread by twisting together pieces of fibre using a machine.
3 When a spider spins a web, it gives out a sticky substance and makes it into a web.
4 If your head is spinning, you feel dizzy or confused.
NOUN **5** a rapid turn around a central point.

spinach
Said "**spin**-ij" NOUN a vegetable with large green leaves.

spine spines
NOUN **1** the row of bones down your back, also called the spinal column.
2 The spine of a book is the binding that runs from top to bottom, holding all the pages together.
3 Spines are long, sharp points on an animal's body or on a plant.
spinal ADJECTIVE

Synonym: (sense 1) backbone

spinning wheel spinning wheels
NOUN a wooden machine for spinning flax or wool.

spin-off spin-offs
NOUN something useful that unexpectedly results from an activity.

spinster spinsters
NOUN a woman who has never married.

spiral spirals spiralling spiralled
NOUN **1** a continuous curve which winds round and round, with each curve above or outside the previous one.
ADJECTIVE **2** in the shape of a spiral.
VERB **3** to move up or down in a spiral curve.
4 to rise or fall quickly at an increasing rate. *Prices have spiralled recently.*

spire spires
NOUN the tall cone-shaped structure on top of a church tower.

spirit spirits
NOUN **1** the part of you that is not physical and that is connected with your deepest thoughts and feelings.
2 a ghost or supernatural being.
3 liveliness, energy and self-confidence.
4 Spirits are strong alcoholic drinks made by distilling.
spirited ADJECTIVE

spiritual
ADJECTIVE **1** to do with people's thoughts and beliefs, rather than their bodies and physical surroundings.
2 to do with people's religious beliefs.
spiritually ADVERB **spirituality** NOUN

spit spits spitting spat
NOUN **1** saliva.
2 a long stick made of metal or wood which is pushed through a piece of meat so that it can be hung over a fire and cooked.
3 a long, flat, narrow piece of land sticking into the sea.
VERB **4** to force saliva or some other substance out of your mouth.

spite spites spiting spited
NOUN **1** a feeling that you wish to hurt or annoy someone.
PHRASE **2** **In spite of** is used to introduce a fact which makes the other part of the sentence surprising; despite. *In spite of having a cold, she still won the race.*
VERB **3** If you do something nasty to spite someone, you do it deliberately to hurt or annoy them.

 ► Collective nouns. Can you make up your own nouns for a collection of: spiders, teachers, vampires?

spiteful
ADJECTIVE A spiteful person does or says nasty things to others in order to hurt them.
spitefully ADVERB

Synonyms: malicious, nasty, vindictive

splash **splashes splashing splashed**
VERB **1** to disturb liquid in a noisy way.
NOUN **2** the sound made when something hits or falls into water.
splash out VERB If you splash out on something, you spend more money on it than you can really afford.

splatter **splatters splattering splattered**
VERB When something is splattered with a substance, the substance is splashed all over it.

splendid
ADJECTIVE very good or impressive.
splendidly ADVERB

Synonyms: grand, magnificent

splendour **splendours**
NOUN the beauty and impressiveness of something.

splint **splints**
NOUN a long piece of wood or metal fastened to a broken limb to hold it in place.

splinter **splinters**
NOUN a thin, sharp piece of wood or glass which has broken off a larger piece.
splinter VERB

split **splits splitting split**
VERB **1** to divide or share something into two or more parts.
2 If something splits, a long crack or tear appears in it.
NOUN **3** a split in a piece of wood or fabric is a crack or tear.
4 a split between two things is a division or difference between them: *the split between rugby league and rugby union.*

splutter **splutters spluttering spluttered**
VERB **1** If something splutters, it makes a series of short, sharp sounds.
2 If someone splutters, they speak in a confused way because they are embarrassed.

spoil **spoils spoiling spoiled** or **spoilt**
VERB **1** If you spoil something, you prevent it from being successful or satisfactory; to ruin.
2 To spoil children means to give them everything they want, with harmful effects on their character.
3 To spoil someone means to give them something nice as a treat.
PLURAL NOUN **4** Spoils are valuable things obtained during war or as a result of violence.

Synonyms: (sense 1) mess up, ruin, wreck
(sense 2) overindulge, pamper

spoilsport **spoilsports**
NOUN someone who spoils people's fun.

spoke **spokes**
1 past tense of **speak**.
NOUN **2** The spokes of a wheel are the bars which connect the hub to the rim.

spoken
past participle of **speak**.

sponge **sponges sponging sponged**
NOUN **1** a sea animal made up of many cells.
2 a piece of a light absorbent substance used for washing or cleaning.
VERB **3** to clean a surface with a sponge.
4 If you sponge money, favours, etc. off somebody, you get it from them without doing anything in return.

spongy **spongier spongiest**
ADJECTIVE soft and porous like a sponge.

sponsor **sponsors sponsoring sponsored**
VERB **1** If an organization sponsors an event, etc., it gives money to pay for it.
2 If you sponsor someone who is doing something for charity, you agree to give them a sum of money for the charity if they manage to do it.
NOUN **3** a person or organization that sponsors something or someone
sponsored ADJECTIVE **sponsorship** NOUN

spontaneous
ADJECTIVE Spontaneous acts are not planned or arranged, but are done because you feel like it: *a spontaneous eruption.*
spontaneously ADVERB **spontaneity** NOUN

spooky **spookier spookiest**
ADJECTIVE eerie and frightening.

spool **spools**
NOUN a reel on which film, tape, cotton, etc. is wound.

spoon **spoons**
NOUN an object used for eating, stirring and serving food.

spoonful **spoonfuls** or **spoonsful**
NOUN the amount held by a spoon.

sport **sports**
NOUN **1** Sports are games and other enjoyable activities which need physical effort and skill.
2 You say that someone is a sport when they cheerfully accept defeat or teasing. *Go on, be a sport!*

sports car **sports cars**
NOUN a fast, two-seater car, usually built low to the ground and with an open top.

sportsman **sportsmen**
NOUN a person who plays sport regularly and well.
sportswoman NOUN

a b c d e f g h i j k l m n o p q r s t u v w x y z

Splatter, wheeze and hum are examples of onomatopoeia. What does onomatopoeia mean?

sportsmanship
NOUN good behaviour and attitudes when playing sport, such as fairness, generosity, and cheerfulness when losing.

spot **spots spotting spotted**
NOUN **1** Spots are small, round, coloured areas on a surface.
2 Spots on a person's skin are small lumps, usually caused by infection or allergy.
3 A spot of something is a small amount of it.
4 a place. *This is the most beautiful spot for a picnic.*
VERB **5** to notice something. *He spotted his friend in the distance.*
PHRASE **6** If you do something **on the spot**, you do it immediately.

spotless
ADJECTIVE perfectly clean, immaculate.
spotlessly ADVERB

spotlight **spotlights spotlighting spotlit** or **spotlighted**
NOUN **1** a powerful light which can be directed to light up a small area.
VERB **2** If something spotlights a situation or problem, it draws the public's attention to it.

spotted
ADJECTIVE Something spotted has a pattern of spots on it.

spotter **spotters**
NOUN a person whose hobby is looking out for things of a particular kind: *a train spotter.*

spotty **spottier spottiest**
ADJECTIVE Someone who is spotty has spots or pimples on their skin, especially on their face.

spouse **spouses**
NOUN Someone's spouse is the person they are married to.

spout **spouts spouting spouted**
NOUN **1** a tube with a lip-like end for pouring liquid: *a teapot with a long spout.*
VERB **2** When liquid or flame spouts out of something, it shoots out in a long stream.
3 INFORMAL When someone spouts what they have learned, they say it in a boring way.

sprain **sprains spraining sprained**
VERB to damage one of your joints accidentally by twisting it violently.
sprain NOUN

sprang
past tense of **spring**.

sprawl **sprawls sprawling sprawled**
VERB **1** to sit or lie somewhere with your legs and arms spread out.
2 A place that sprawls is spread out over a large area. *London sprawls over an area of 1600 square kilometres.*
NOUN **3** anything that spreads in an untidy and uncontrolled way.
sprawling ADJECTIVE

spray **sprays spraying sprayed**
NOUN **1** many small drops of liquid splashed or forced into the air.
2 a liquid kept under pressure in a container: *hair spray.*
3 A spray of flowers or leaves consists of several of them on one stem.
VERB **4** to cover something with drops of liquid.

spread **spreads spreading spread**
VERB **1** If you spread something out, you open it out or arrange it so that it can be seen or used easily.
2 to go in all directions at once. *The news spread quickly.*
3 to distribute evenly. *She spread butter and marmalade on her toast.*
NOUN **4** The spread of something is its increasing presence or occurrence: *the spread of Buddhism.*
5 A spread of ideas, interests, or other things is a wide variety of them.
6 soft food put on bread: *cheese spread.*

spreadsheet **spreadsheets**
NOUN a piece of computer software for entering and arranging figures, usually for financial planning.

sprightly **sprightlier sprightliest**
ADJECTIVE lively and active.

spring **springs springing sprang sprung**
NOUN **1** the season between winter and summer.
2 a coil of wire which returns to its original shape after being pressed or pulled.
3 a place where water comes up through the ground.
VERB **4** to jump upwards or forwards.
5 If one thing springs from another, it is a result of it.

springboard **springboards**
NOUN a flexible board on which a diver or gymnast jumps to gain height.

springbok **springboks**
NOUN a small South African antelope which moves in leaps.

springy **springier springiest**
ADJECTIVE Springy surfaces and materials spring back to their original shape when squashed or stretched.

sprinkle **sprinkles sprinkling sprinkled**
VERB to scatter liquid or powder in small, fine quantities.
sprinkle NOUN

sprint **sprints sprinting sprinted**
VERB to run fast over a short distance.
sprint NOUN **sprinter** NOUN

sprout **sprouts sprouting sprouted**
VERB **1** to grow.
2 to appear rapidly. *Houses sprouted up in all the suburbs.*
NOUN **3** vegetables that look like tiny cabbages, sometimes called Brussels sprouts.

 ► Find three words on this page that are nouns and also verbs. Write sentences using them as both.

spruce **spruces sprucing spruced; sprucer sprucest**
NOUN 1 an evergreen tree with needle-like leaves.
VERB 2 To spruce something up means to make it neat and smart.
ADJECTIVE 3 Someone who is spruce is very neatly and smartly dressed.

sprung
past participle of **spring**.

spun
past tense and past participle of **spin**.

spur **spurs spurring spurred**
NOUN 1 Spurs are sharp metal points attached to the heels of a rider's boots and used to urge a horse on.
VERB 2 If something spurs you to do something or spurs you on, it encourages you to do it.
PHRASE 3 If you do something **on the spur of the moment**, you do it suddenly, without planning it.

spurt **spurts spurting spurted**
VERB 1 When a liquid or flame spurts out of something, it comes out quickly in a thick, powerful stream.
NOUN 2 a thick powerful stream of liquid or flame.
3 A spurt of activity or effort is a sudden, brief period of it.

spy **spies spying spied**
NOUN 1 a person sent to find out secret information about a country or organization.
VERB 2 If you spy on someone, you watch them secretly.

squabble **squabbles squabbling squabbled**
VERB to quarrel about something trivial.
squabble NOUN

squad **squads**
NOUN a small group chosen to do a particular activity: *the fraud squad.*

squadron **squadrons**
NOUN a section of one of the armed forces, especially the air force.
[from Italian *squadrone* meaning soldiers drawn up in a square formation]

squalid
ADJECTIVE A squalid home is dirty, untidy and in bad condition.

squall **squalls**
NOUN a brief, violent storm.
squally ADJECTIVE

squander **squanders squandering squandered**
VERB to waste money or resources.

square **squares squaring squared**
NOUN 1 a shape with four equal sides and four right angles.
2 In a town or city, a square is a flat, open place, bordered by buildings or streets.
3 The square of a number is the product of the number multiplied by itself. For example, the square of 6 is 36 (6 × 6).
ADJECTIVE 4 shaped like a square.
5 "Squared", or the symbol (^{2}) is used when talking about the area of something: *24 m*^{2}.
VERB 6 If you square a number, or a number is squared, it is multiplied by itself. For example, 4 squared is 16 (4 × 4).

squarely
ADVERB If you look at someone squarely, you face them directly.

square root
NOUN a number that when multiplied by itself makes a given number. For example, the square root of 25 is 5, that of 49 is 7. Square root can be written as the symbol $\sqrt{}$.

squash **squashes squashing squashed**
VERB 1 to press something so that it becomes flat or loses its shape.
NOUN 2 a game on an enclosed indoor court in which two players hit a small rubber ball against a wall using rackets.
3 a drink made with fruit juice, sugar and water.

squat **squats squatting squatted**
VERB 1 If you squat or squat down you crouch, balancing on your feet with your legs bent.
2 to live in an unused building without owning it and without permission.
ADJECTIVE 3 short and thick.
squatter NOUN

squawk **squawks squawking squawked**
VERB When a bird squawks, it makes a loud, harsh noise.
squawk NOUN

squeak **squeaks squeaking squeaked**
VERB to make a short high-pitched sound.
squeak NOUN **squeaky** ADJECTIVE

squeal **squeals squealing squealed**
VERB to make a long high-pitched sound.
squeal NOUN

squeamish
ADJECTIVE easily upset by unpleasant sights or situations.

squeeze **squeezes squeezing squeezed**
VERB 1 to press something firmly from two sides.
2 If you squeeze something into a small amount of time or space, you just manage to fit it in.
squeeze NOUN

squelch **squelches squelching squelched**
VERB to make a wet, sucking sound.
squelch NOUN

squid **squids**
NOUN a sea creature with a long soft body and many tentacles.

squiggle **squiggles**
NOUN a wiggly line.

a b c d e f g h i j k l m n o p q r s t u v w x y z

Squelch is an example of onomatopoeia. Others are murmur, thud, crunch and click.

A B C D E F G H I J K L M N O P Q R S T U V W X Y Z

squint squints squinting squinted
VERB If you squint at something, you look at it with your eyes screwed up.

squirm squirms squirming squirmed
VERB to wriggle and twist your body about, usually because you are nervous or embarrassed.

squirrel squirrels
NOUN a small furry mammal with a long bushy tail.

squirt squirts squirting squirted
VERB If a liquid squirts, it comes out of a narrow opening in a thin, fast stream.
squirt NOUN

stab stabs stabbing stabbed
VERB **1** to wound someone by pushing a knife into their body.
PHRASE **2** If you **have a stab** at something, you try to do it.
NOUN **3** You can refer to a sudden unpleasant feeling as a stab of something: *a stab of guilt.*

stabilizer stabilizers
NOUN Stabilizers are devices added to something, such as a ship or a bicycle, to keep them steady as they move.

stable stables
NOUN **1** a building in which horses are kept.
ADJECTIVE **2** not likely to change or move. *Make sure your ladder is stable before you climb it.*
stability NOUN **stabilize** VERB

stack stacks stacking stacked
NOUN **1** a pile of things, one on top of the other.
VERB **2** to pile things up.
PLURAL NOUN; INFORMAL **3** If someone has stacks of something, they have a lot of it.

stadium stadiums
NOUN a sports ground with rows of seats around it; an arena.

staff staffs staffing staffed
NOUN **1** The staff of an organization are the people who work for it.
2 A staff is a long, sturdy, wooden stick, used in the past for fighting.
VERB **3** To staff an organization means to find and employ people to work in it.

stag stags
NOUN an adult male deer.

stage stages staging staged
NOUN **1** a part of a process that lasts for a period of time: *the final stage of the cycle race.*
2 a raised platform where the actors or entertainers perform.
VERB **3** If someone stages a play or event, they organize it and present it.

Synonyms: (sense 1) period, phase, point

stagecoach stagecoaches
NOUN a large carriage pulled by horses which used to carry passengers and mail.

stagger staggers staggering staggered
VERB **1** to walk unsteadily because you are ill or drunk.
2 If something staggers you, it amazes you.
3 If events are staggered, they are arranged so that they do not all happen at the same time.
staggering ADJECTIVE

Synonyms: (sense 1) lurch, reel, totter

stagnant
ADJECTIVE Stagnant water is not flowing and is unhealthy and dirty.

stain stains
NOUN a mark on something that is difficult to remove.
stain VERB

stair stairs
NOUN a set of steps, usually inside a building, going from one level to another.

staircase staircases
NOUN a set of stairs.

stairway stairways
NOUN a set of stairs.

stake stakes staking staked
VERB **1** to risk. *I'd stake my life that my team will win this match.*
PHRASE **2** If something is **at stake**, it might be lost or damaged if something else is not successful. *The whole future of the company was at stake.*
PLURAL NOUN **3** The stakes involved in something are the things that can be lost or gained. *The poker players were playing for very high stakes.*
NOUN **4** If you have a stake in something such as a business, you own part of it.
5 a pointed wooden post that can be hammered into the ground and used as a support.

stalactite stalactites
NOUN a piece of rock like a huge icicle hanging from the roof of a cave, caused by the dripping of water laden with minerals.

stalagmite stalagmites
NOUN a pointed piece of rock sticking up from the floor of a cave, caused by the dripping of water laden with minerals.

stale staler stalest
ADJECTIVE **1** Stale food or air is no longer fresh.
2 If you feel stale, you have no new ideas and are bored.

stalk stalks stalking stalked
Said "**stawk**" NOUN **1** The stalk of a flower or leaf is its stem.
VERB **2** If you stalk along, you walk in a proud, stiff or angry way.
3 to follow someone or something quietly in order to catch, observe or kill them.

 ► What is the feminine of: stag, dog, fox, boar (pig), gander, lion?

stall stalls stalling stalled
NOUN 1 a large table containing goods for sale or information.
VERB 2 When a vehicle stalls, the engine suddenly stops.
3 If you stall when someone asks you to do something, you try to avoid doing it until later.

stallion stallions
NOUN an adult male horse that can be used for breeding.

stalls
PLURAL NOUN In a theatre or cinema, the stalls are the seats at the lowest level, in front of the stage.

stamen stamens
NOUN the male part of a flower consisting of a stalk (the filament) and an anther in which pollen is produced.

stamina
NOUN the physical or mental energy needed to do something for a very long time.

stammer stammers stammering stammered
VERB When someone stammers, they speak with difficulty, repeating words and sounds and hesitating awkwardly.
stammer NOUN

stamp stamps stamping stamped
NOUN 1 a small piece of paper which you stick on a letter or parcel before posting it.
2 a small block with a pattern cut into it which you press onto an inky pad, then make a mark with it on paper.
VERB 3 to make a mark with a stamp.
4 to bang your foot hard on the ground.
stamp out VERB to put an end to something. *We must stamp out bullying in schools.*

stampede stampedes stampeding stampeded
VERB When a group of animals stampede, they run in a wild, uncontrolled way.
stampede NOUN

stand stands standing stood
VERB 1 to be upright with your weight on your feet.
2 to be in a certain position somewhere. *The house stands on top of a small hill.*
3 to place something in an upright position.
4 If a decision or offer still stands, it is still valid.
5 to represent. *Dr stands for Doctor.*
6 to be strong enough to survive a situation or test. *This bridge can stand heavy tanks going over it.*
7 If you cannot stand someone or something, you hate them.
NOUN 8 a stall or small shop as part of an exhibition, fair, etc.
9 a sloping structure containing seating at a sports ground.
10 a piece of furniture designed to hold or support something else: *an umbrella stand; a television stand.*
stand by VERB 1 to get ready for something to happen or to do something.
2 to support someone. *My friends stood by me when I was having problems.*
stand in VERB to take someone's place, to deputize.
stand out VERB to be clearly visible.
stand up VERB 1 If something stands up to rough treatment, it remains undamaged.
2 If you stand up to someone who is attacking you, you defend yourself.
stand up for VERB to defend or support someone or something. *Stand up for what you believe is right.*

standard standards
ADJECTIVE 1 usual, normal and correct: *standard procedure.*
NOUN 2 a level of quality or achievement that is considered acceptable. *The work is not up to your usual standard.*
PLURAL NOUN 3 Standards are moral principles of behaviour.

standstill
NOUN If something comes to a standstill, it stops completely.

stank
past tense of **stink**.

stanza stanzas
NOUN a verse of a poem.
[from Italian *stanza* meaning stopping place]

staple staples stapling stapled
NOUN 1 Staples are small pieces of wire that hold sheets of paper firmly together.
VERB 2 to fasten things together with staples.
ADJECTIVE 3 A staple food forms a regular and basic part of someone's everyday diet.

stapler staplers
NOUN a machine for inserting staples.

star stars starring starred
NOUN 1 a large ball of burning gas in space that appears as a point of light in the sky at night. Our sun is a star.
2 a shape with four, five or more points sticking out in a regular pattern.
3 Famous actors, sports players and musicians are referred to as stars.
VERB 4 If a film stars a person, that person is the leading actor in the film.
PLURAL NOUN 5 The horoscope in a newspaper or magazine can be referred to as your stars.
starry ADJECTIVE

starboard
ADJECTIVE OR NOUN The starboard side of a ship is the right side when you are facing the front.
[from Old English *steorbord* meaning steering side, because boats were formerly steered with a paddle over the right-hand side]

a b c d e f g h i j k l m n o p q r s t u v w x y z

A B C D E F G H I J K L M N O P Q R S T U V W X Y Z

starch **starches starching starched**
NOUN **1** a substance used for stiffening fabric such as cotton and linen.
2 a carbohydrate found in foods such as bread, rice, pasta and potatoes.
VERB **3** to stiffen fabric with starch.

stare **stares staring stared**
VERB to look hard at something for a long time.
stare NOUN

Synonyms: gawp, gaze, goggle

starfish **starfishes** or **starfish**
NOUN a flat, star-shaped sea animal with five limbs.

starling **starlings**
NOUN a common European bird with shiny dark feathers.

start **starts starting started**
VERB **1** to begin or commence.
2 to cause something to work. *I started the engine.*
3 If you start, your body suddenly jerks because of surprise or fear.
NOUN **4** the point or time at which something begins.
5 If you do something with a start, you do it with a sudden jerky movement because of surprise or fear.

startle **startles startling startled**
VERB to surprise and frighten.
startled ADJECTIVE **startling** ADJECTIVE

starve **starves starving starved**
VERB to suffer from a serious lack of food.
starving ADJECTIVE **starvation** NOUN

state **states stating stated**
NOUN **1** the condition of something: what it is like or its circumstances. *Your bedroom is in a terrible state!*
2 a country, a nation. *Luxembourg is a small European state.*
3 Some countries are divided into regions called states which make some of their own laws.
ADJECTIVE **4** A state ceremony involves the ruler or leader of a country.
VERB **5** to say or write something, especially in formal way.
PHRASE **6** If you are **in a state**, you are nervous or upset, and unable to control your emotions.

stately **statelier stateliest**
ADJECTIVE impressive, graceful and dignified.

statement **statements**
NOUN something said or written which gives information in formal way.

static
ADJECTIVE never moving or changing. *The temperature remains fairly static.*

static electricity
NOUN an effect caused when certain materials are rubbed together, resulting in the build-up of electrically-charged particles.

station **stations stationing stationed**
NOUN **1** a building by a railway line where trains stop for passengers.
2 A bus or coach station is a place where some buses start their journeys.
3 a particular radio or television company or channel: *Radio 1, your favourite station.*
VERB **4** Someone who is stationed somewhere is sent there to work or do a particular job: *her son was stationed in Vienna.*

stationary
ADJECTIVE not moving.

stationery
NOUN a general word for paper, pens and other writing equipment.
✔ Do not confuse *stationary* with *stationery*. One way to remember is that "e" is for envelopes.

statistic **statistics**
NOUN Statistics are facts obtained by analysing information which is expressed in numbers.
statistical ADJECTIVE

statue **statues**
NOUN a sculpture of a person or animal.

status
Said "**stay**-tuss" NOUN A person's status is their position and importance in society.

staunch **stauncher staunchest**
ADJECTIVE A staunch supporter is a strong and loyal supporter.

stay **stays staying stayed**
VERB **1** to remain in a place, not move away from it.
2 to continue to be in a particular condition. *I stayed awake all night.*
3 to spend time in a place as a guest or visitor. *I went to stay with my friend Susan for the weekend.*
NOUN **4** a short time spent somewhere. *We had a pleasant stay at the seaside.*

steady **steadier steadiest**
ADJECTIVE **1** continuing or developing gradually without interruptions or changes: *steady progress.*
2 firm and not moving about. *Keep the boat steady while I climb in.*
3 A steady look or voice is calm and controlled.
steady VERB **steadily** ADVERB

Synonyms: (sense 2) firm, secure, stable

steak **steaks**
NOUN **1** good quality beef without much fat.
2 a thick slice of meat or fish: *pork steaks; cod steaks.*

 ► Americans say "status" differently to the British. How do they say "tomato" and "missile"?

steal **steals stealing stole stolen**
VERB **1** to take something without permission and without intending to return it.
2 To steal somewhere means to move there quietly and secretly.

Synonyms: nick, take

stealth
*Rhymes with "**health**"* NOUN **1** If you do something with stealth, you do it quietly and secretly.
2 A stealth aircraft is one that is virtually undetectable by radar or sight.
stealthy ADJECTIVE **stealthily** ADVERB

steam
NOUN the gas or vapour which condenses into a mist in the air when liquid water boils.
steamy ADJECTIVE

steam-engine **steam-engines**
NOUN any engine that uses the energy of steam to produce mechanical work.

steamer **steamers**
NOUN **1** a boat or ship driven by steam.
2 a pan with layers inside it used to cook food in steam.

steamroller **steamrollers**
NOUN; OLD-FASHIONED a steam-powered vehicle with heavy rollers for preparing road surfaces.

steel **steels steeling steeled**
NOUN **1** a very strong metal made mainly from iron.
VERB **2** If you steel yourself, you prepare to deal with something unpleasant. *Johnny steeled himself for bad news.*

steel band **steel bands**
NOUN a group of people who play music on special metal drums.

steep **steeper steepest**
ADJECTIVE **1** A steep slope rises sharply and is difficult to go up.
2 A steep increase is large and sudden.
steeply ADVERB

Synonyms: (sense 1) precipitous, sheer

steeple **steeples**
NOUN a tall pointed structure on top of a church tower.

steeplechase **steeplechases**
NOUN a long horse race or running race, in which the contestants jump over obstacles such as water jumps.
[originally a race with a church steeple in sight as the goal]

steer **steers steering steered**
VERB to control the direction of a vehicle or boat.

Synonyms: direct, guide, pilot

stem **stems stemming stemmed**
NOUN **1** the thin upright part of a plant that grows above ground, from which leaves and flowers grow, and through which water travels.
VERB **2** If a problem stems from a particular situation, that situation is the cause of the problem.
3 If you stem the flow of something, you restrict it or stop it from spreading. *The nurse applied the bandage to stem the bleeding.*

stench **stenches**
NOUN a very strong, unpleasant smell.

stencil **stencils**
NOUN a thin sheet with a cut-out pattern through which ink or paint passes to form the pattern on the surface below.
stencil VERB

step **steps stepping stepped**
NOUN **1** If you take a step, you lift your foot and put it down somewhere else.
2 a raised flat surface, usually one of a series, that you can walk up or down.
3 one of a series of actions that you take in order to achieve something.
VERB **4** to pick up your foot and put it down in a different spot.
5 If someone steps down or steps aside from an important position, they resign.

stepladder **stepladders**
NOUN a folding portable set of steps that can stand on their own.

stepping stone **stepping stones**
NOUN **1** one of a series of stones used to walk on when crossing a shallow stream, river, etc.
2 a job or event that is regarded as a stage in your progress. *Passing the exam was a great stepping stone in her career.*

stereo **stereos**
NOUN a piece of equipment that reproduces sound from CDs, tapes or records. Stereo sound is reproduced on two channels and sends separate sound information from two speakers.
[short for stereophonic]

sterile
ADJECTIVE **1** completely clean and free from germs.
2 A sterile person or animal is unable to have young.
sterility NOUN

sterilize **sterilizes sterilizing sterilized**; also spelt **sterilise**
VERB **1** To sterilize something means to make it completely clean and free from germs, usually by boiling it or treating it with an antiseptic.
2 If a person or animal is sterilized, they have an operation that makes it impossible for them to produce offspring.

a b c d e f g h i j k l m n o p q r s t u v w x y z

How many anagrams can you make from the letters STEP?

A B C D E F G H I J K L M N O P Q R S T U V W X Y Z

sterling
NOUN 1 the money system of Great Britain.
ADJECTIVE 2 excellent in quality: *sterling work.*

stern sterner sternest; sterns
ADJECTIVE 1 very serious and strict.
NOUN 2 The stern of a boat or ship is its back end.

Antonym: (sense 2) bow

stethoscope stethoscopes
NOUN a device used by doctors to listen to a patient's heart and breathing.

stew stews stewing stewed
NOUN 1 a dish of small pieces of savoury food cooked together slowly in a liquid.
VERB 2 To stew meat, vegetables or fruit means to cook them slowly in a liquid.

stick sticks sticking stuck
NOUN 1 a long, thin piece of wood, but also of other things such as celery or dynamite.
VERB 2 If you stick a long or pointed object into something, you push it in.
3 If you stick one thing to another, you attach it with glue or tape.
4 If one thing sticks to another, it becomes attached or fixed and will no longer move or work properly. *My gears are sticking.*
5 If you stick to a task, you keep at it until it is done.
6 When people stick together, they stay together and support each other.
7 INFORMAL to put. *Stick that tennis racquet in the cupboard.*
stick out VERB to be further forward than the main part of something, to protrude, to project.
stick up VERB 1 to be further upward than the main part of something.
2 INFORMAL If you stick up for someone, you support or defend them.
NOUN 3 INFORMAL an armed robbery in a bank. *Hand over your money, it's a stick-up!*

sticker stickers
NOUN a small piece of paper or plastic with writing or a picture on it that you stick onto a surface.

sticky stickier stickiest
ADJECTIVE 1 covered with a substance that can stick to other things.
2 INFORMAL A sticky situation is difficult or embarrassing to deal with.

stiff stiffer stiffest
ADJECTIVE 1 firm and not easily bent.
2 If you are stiff, your muscles or joints ache when you move.
3 Stiff behaviour is formal and not friendly or relaxed.
4 difficult or severe: *stiff competition.*
ADVERB 5 INFORMAL If you are bored stiff or scared stiff, you are very bored or very scared.
stiffly ADVERB **stiffness** NOUN

stiffen stiffens stiffening stiffened
VERB to make something stiffer or to become stiffer.

stifle stifles stifling stifled
Said "**sty**-fl" VERB 1 If the atmosphere stifles you, you feel you cannot breathe properly.
2 to prevent something from happening or continuing naturally. *I stifled a yawn.*
stifling ADJECTIVE

stile stiles
NOUN a step on either side of a wall or fence to enable you to climb over.

still stiller stillest; stills
ADJECTIVE 1 A still place is peaceful and quiet with no signs of activity.
ADVERB OR ADJECTIVE 2 staying in the same position without moving.
ADVERB 3 If a situation still exists, it has continued to exist and it exists now.
4 If something could still happen, it might happen although it has not happened yet.
5 "Still" emphasizes that something is the case in spite of other things. *Despite the bad weather, we still played netball.*
NOUN 6 A still is a photograph taken from a cinema film or video.
stillness NOUN

stilt stilts
NOUN Stilts are long pieces of wood or metal on which people balance and walk.

stimulate stimulates stimulating stimulated
VERB to encourage something to begin or develop. *The book stimulated many exciting ideas.*
stimulating ADJECTIVE **stimulation** NOUN

Synonyms: arouse, encourage, inspire

sting stings stinging stung
VERB 1 If a creature or plant stings you, it pricks your skin and injects a substance which causes pain.
2 If someone's remarks sting you, they make you feel upset or hurt.
sting NOUN

stingy stingier stingiest
Said "**stin**-jee" ADJECTIVE; INFORMAL very mean.

stink stinks stinking stank stunk
VERB 1 to smell very unpleasant.
2 INFORMAL If you say that a situation stinks, you mean there is something very unpleasant or suspicious about it.
stink NOUN

stir stirs stirring stirred
VERB 1 to move liquid around using a spoon or a stick.
2 to move slightly. *She shook him, but he did not stir.*
3 If something stirs you, it makes you feel strong emotions.
PHRASE 4 If something **causes a stir**, it causes general excitement or shock.

 ► Find out where these bones are in the human body: sternum, mandible, scapula, femur, pelvis?

stir-fry stir-fries stir-frying stir-fried
VERB to fry small pieces of food quickly in oil over a high heat.

stirrup stirrups
NOUN Stirrups are two metal loops hanging by leather straps from a horse's saddle, which you put your feet in when riding.

stitch stitches stitching stitched
VERB **1** to use a needle and thread to sew pieces of material or flaps of skin together.
NOUN **2** a visible length of thread where something has been sewn.
3 If you have a stitch when you are running or laughing, you feel a sharp pain in your abdomen.

stoat stoats
NOUN a small wild mammal with a long body and brown fur.

stock stocks stocking stocked
NOUN **1** a supply of something ready for use or for sale.
2 Stock is farm animals.
3 Stock is a liquid made from boiling meat, bones or vegetables together in water, used as a base for soups, stews and sauces.
4 A stock is a share bought as an investment in a company.
VERB **5** A shop that stocks particular goods keeps a supply of them to sell.
6 If you stock a shelf or cupboard, or stock up, you fill it with food or other things.

stocking stockings
NOUN Stockings are long pieces of thin clothing that cover a woman's legs.

stock market stock markets
NOUN the organization and activity involved in buying and selling stocks and shares.

stocks
PLURAL NOUN a heavy wooden frame with holes in, usually to hold the feet, in which offenders used to be locked as a public punishment.

stocky stockier stockiest
ADJECTIVE A stocky person is rather short, but broad and solid-looking.

stodgy stodgier stodgiest
ADJECTIVE Stodgy food is very solid and makes you feel very full.

stoke stokes stoking stoked
VERB to keep a fire burning by moving or adding fuel.

stole
past tense of **steal**.

stolen
past participle of **steal**.

stomach stomachs stomaching stomached
NOUN **1** the organ inside your body that helps in the digestion of food.
2 the front part of your body below your waist.
VERB **3** If you cannot stomach something, you strongly dislike it and cannot accept it.

stone stones stoning stoned
NOUN **1** the hard solid substance found in the ground and used for building.
2 a small piece of rock.
3 The stone in a fruit such as a plum or cherry is the large seed in the centre.
4 a unit of weight equal to 14 pounds or about 6·35 kilograms.
5 You can refer to a jewel as a stone: *a diamond ring with three stones.*
VERB **6** To stone someone means to throw stones at them.

stony stonier stoniest
ADJECTIVE **1** Stony ground is rough and hard, and contains a lot of stones or rocks.
2 If someone's expression is stony, it shows no friendliness or sympathy.

stood
past tense and past participle of **stand**.

stool stools
NOUN a seat with legs but no back or arms.

stoop stoops stooping stooped
VERB **1** to stand or walk with your shoulders bent forwards.
2 If you will not stoop to something, you won't lower yourself or disgrace yourself by doing it.

stop stops stopping stopped
VERB **1** to come to an end, to halt. *The rain had stopped.*
2 to prevent something from happening or continuing. *Stewards tried to stop the crowd from running onto the pitch.*
3 If you stop somewhere, you stay there for a short while.
NOUN **4** a place where a bus, train or other vehicle stops during a journey.
5 If something that is moving comes to a stop, it no longer moves.

Synonyms: (sense 1) cease, desist

stoppage stoppages
NOUN an unscheduled stop during an activity, such as in a sports match because of an injury.

stopper stoppers
NOUN a piece of glass or cork that fits into the neck of a jar or bottle.

stopwatch stopwatches
NOUN a watch that can be started and stopped by pressing buttons, used to time events.

storage
NOUN The storage of something is the keeping of it somewhere until it is needed.

A B C D E F G H I J K L M N O P Q R S T U V W X Y Z

store stores storing stored
NOUN **1** a shop.
2 a supply of something kept until it is needed.
3 a place where things are kept while they are not used.
VERB **4** When you store something somewhere, you keep it there until it is needed.
PHRASE **5** Something that is **in store** for you is going to happen to you in the future.

Synonyms: (sense 2) hoard, stockpile, supply

storey storeys
NOUN one of the floors or levels of a building.

stork storks
NOUN a very large white and black bird with long red legs and a long bill.

storm storms storming stormed
NOUN **1** When there is a storm, there is heavy rain, a strong wind and often thunder and lightning.
2 A storm of protest is a wild, angry reaction to something.
VERB **3** If someone storms out, they leave quickly and angrily.
4 If people storm a place, they attack it.
stormy ADJECTIVE

story stories
NOUN **1** a description of imaginary people and events written or told to entertain people.
2 an account of the important events that have happened to someone or something. *I read her life story.*
[from Latin *historia* meaning narrative or history]

Synonyms: (sense 1) anecdote, tale, yarn

stout stouter stoutest
ADJECTIVE **1** rather fat.
2 thick, strong and sturdy. *Wear stout walking shoes.*
3 determined, firm and strong: *stout opposition.*
stoutly ADVERB

stove stoves
NOUN a piece of equipment for heating a room or for cooking.

stow stows stowing stowed
VERB If you stow something somewhere or stow it away, you store it until it is needed.

stowaway stowaways
NOUN someone who hides in a ship or plane in order to go somewhere secretly without paying.

straddle straddles straddling straddled
VERB If you straddle something, you stand or sit with one leg on either side of it.

straggle straggles straggling straggled
VERB **1** If people straggle somewhere, they move slowly in irregular and disorganized groups.
2 If something straggles over an area, it spreads over it in an untidy way.
straggly ADJECTIVE **straggler** NOUN

straight straighter straightest
ADJECTIVE OR ADVERB **1** continuing in the same direction without curving or bending.
ADJECTIVE **2** INFORMAL A straight person is honest and direct to deal with.
ADVERB **3** immediately and directly. *Go straight home.*

straighten straightens straightening straightened
VERB to make something straighter or to become straighter.

straightforward
ADJECTIVE easy and involving no problems.
straightforwardly ADVERB

strain strains straining strained
NOUN **1** If a strain is put on something, it is affected by a strong force which may damage it.
2 If strain is put on a person or organization, they have to do more than is reasonable or normal.
3 worry or nervous tension.
4 A particular strain of plant is a variety of it.
VERB **5** To strain something means to force it or use it more than is reasonable or normal. *Bob strained at the door.*
6 To strain food means to pour away the liquid from it.
7 If you strain a muscle, you injure it by moving it awkwardly.
strained ADJECTIVE

strainer strainers
NOUN a sieve used for straining sauces, vegetables, tea leaves, etc.

strait straits
NOUN **1** a narrow strip of sea.
PLURAL NOUN **2** If someone is in a bad situation, you can say they are in difficult straits.

strand strands
NOUN a single long piece of thread or hair.

stranded
ADJECTIVE If someone or something is stranded somewhere, they are stuck and cannot leave.

strange stranger strangest
ADJECTIVE **1** unusual or unexpected, curious, odd, peculiar.
2 not known, seen or experienced before.
strangely ADVERB **strangeness** NOUN

stranger strangers
NOUN someone you have never met before.

 ▶ Expressions. Do you know what is meant by: a storm in a teacup, a windfall, seeing red, feeling blue?

strangle **strangles strangling strangled**
VERB to kill someone by squeezing their throat.
strangulation NOUN

strap **straps strapping strapped**
NOUN **1** a narrow piece of leather or cloth, used to fasten or hold things together.
VERB **2** If you strap something together, you fasten it with a strap.

strategy **strategies**
NOUN **1** a plan for achieving something.
2 the skill of planning the best way to achieve something, especially in war.
strategic ADJECTIVE **strategically** ADVERB

straw **straws**
NOUN **1** the dry, yellowish stalks from some crops.
2 a hollow tube of paper or plastic which you use to suck a drink into your mouth.
PHRASE **3** If something is **the last straw** it is the latest in a series of bad events, and makes you feel you cannot stand any more.

strawberry **strawberries**
NOUN a small red fruit with small seeds in its skin.

stray **strays straying strayed**
VERB **1** When people or animals stray, they wander away from where they should be.
2 If your thoughts stray, you stop concentrating.
NOUN **3** a stray dog or cat.
stray ADJECTIVE

streak **streaks streaking streaked**
NOUN **1** a long, narrow mark or stain.
2 If you have a lucky streak, you have a series of experiences which are lucky.
3 If someone has a particular streak, they have that quality in their character: *a nasty streak.*
VERB **4** If something is streaked, it has lines of colour or stains on it.
5 to move very fast.
streaky ADJECTIVE

stream **streams streaming streamed**
NOUN **1** a small river.
2 a steady flow of something: *a stream of people.*
VERB **3** to move in a continuous flow in large quantities. *Rain streamed down the windscreen.*

streamer **streamers**
NOUN a long, narrow strip of coloured paper used for decoration.

street **streets**
NOUN a road in a town or village, usually with buildings along it.

strength **strengths**
NOUN **1** Your strength is your physical energy and the power of your muscles.
2 The strength of an object is the degree to which it can stand rough treatment.
3 Someone's strengths are their good qualities and abilities.
4 The strength of something is its intensity. *This coffee is the correct strength. The strength of feeling was very high.*
5 The strength of a group is the total number of people in it.

strengthen **strengthens strengthening strengthened**
VERB to improve something or add to its structure so that it can withstand rough treatment, to fortify, to reinforce.

strenuous
Said "**stren**-yoo-uss" ADJECTIVE involving a lot of effort or energy.
strenuously ADVERB

stress **stresses stressing stressed**
NOUN **1** worry and nervous tension.
2 emphasis placed on a syllable when pronouncing a word. For example, in the word "teacher", the stress is on "tea".
VERB **3** If you stress a point, you emphasize it and draw attention to its importance.

Synonyms: (sense 1) anxiety, pressure, strain

stretch **stretches stretching stretched**
VERB **1** To stretch something means to pull it or draw it out to make it longer or bigger.
2 When you stretch, you hold out part of your body as far as you can.
3 to cover an area. *Forests stretched the length of the valley.*
NOUN **4** A stretch of land or water is an area of it.
5 A stretch of time is a period of time.

stretcher **stretchers**
NOUN a long piece of material with a pole along each side, used to carry an injured person.

strict **stricter strictest**
ADJECTIVE **1** Someone who is strict controls other people very firmly.
2 A strict rule must always be obeyed.
3 You can use "strict" to describe someone who never breaks the principles of a particular religion: *a strict Muslim.*
strictly ADVERB **strictness** NOUN

Synonyms: (sense 1) severe, stern

stride **strides striding strode stridden**
VERB **1** to walk quickly with long steps.
NOUN **2** a long step; also the length of a step.
PHRASE **3** To take a problem **in your stride** means to deal with it calmly.

strife
NOUN; FORMAL trouble, conflict and disagreement.

a b c d e f g h i j k l m n o p q r s t u v w x y z

A B C D E F G H I J K L M N O P Q R S T U V W X Y Z

strike strikes striking struck
VERB **1** to hit.
2 to affect or attack suddenly. *The tourists was very struck by the beautiful autumn colours. A powerful earthquake struck Sicily.*
3 When a clock strikes, it makes a sound to indicate the time.
4 If you strike a match, you rub it against something to make it burst into flame.
NOUN **5** If there is a strike, people stop working as a protest.
strike off VERB If a professional person is struck off, they are punished for bad behaviour by having their name removed from an official register and not being allowed to work any more.
strike up VERB To strike up a conversation or a friendship means to begin it.

striker strikers
NOUN **1** Strikers are people who are refusing to work as a protest.
2 In soccer, a player whose function is to attack and score goals.

striking
ADJECTIVE very noticeable because of being unusual or very attractive.
strikingly ADVERB

string strings
NOUN **1** a thin cord made of twisted threads.
2 a row or series of similar things: *a string of islands.*
3 In an orchestra, the strings are the name given to the group of musicians playing instruments with strings.

stringy
ADJECTIVE Stringy meat has too many fibres and is difficult to chew.

strip strips stripping stripped
NOUN **1** a long, narrow piece of something.
2 A sports team's strip is the clothes that they wear when playing.
VERB **3** to remove whatever is covering a surface. *I stripped the paint off the door.*
4 to take off your clothes.

stripe stripes
NOUN Stripes are long, thin lines, usually of different colours.
striped ADJECTIVE

strive strives striving strove striven
VERB to make a great effort to achieve something.

strode
past tense of **stride**.

stroke strokes stroking stroked
VERB **1** If you stroke something, you move your hand smoothly and gently over it.
NOUN **2** The strokes of a brush or pen are the movements that you make with it and the marks that are left on the paper.
3 a particular style of swimming, such as backstroke.
4 If someone has a stroke, a blood vessel in the brain bursts or gets blocked, possibly causing death or paralysis.
PHRASE **5** If you have **a stroke of luck**, something fortunate happens to you.

stroll strolls strolling strolled
VERB to walk slowly in a relaxed way, to amble.
stroll NOUN

strong stronger strongest
ADJECTIVE **1** having powerful muscles.
2 able to withstand rough treatment.
3 having confidence, determination and courage.
4 great in degree or intensity: *a strong smell of soap.*
5 You can use "strong" to say how many people there are in a group. *The team was eleven strong.*
ADVERB **6** If someone or something is still going strong, they are still healthy or working well after a long time.
strongly ADVERB

Synonyms: (sense 1) beefy, brawny, powerful
(sense 2) durable, heavy-duty, tough
(sense 3) firm, forceful, resourceful

stronghold strongholds
NOUN a place that is held and defended by an army.

strove
past tense of **strive**.

struck
past tense and past participle of **strike**.

structure structures structuring structured
NOUN **1** the way something is made, built or organized.
VERB **2** To structure something means to arrange it into an organized pattern or system.
structural ADJECTIVE **structurally** ADVERB

struggle struggles struggling struggled
VERB **1** to try hard to do something, with difficulty.
2 When people struggle, they twist and move violently when they are being held.
NOUN **3** Something that is a struggle is difficult to achieve and takes a lot of effort.
4 a fight.

strum strums strumming strummed
VERB To strum a guitar means to play it by moving your fingers backwards and forwards across all the strings.

strut struts strutting strutted
VERB **1** to walk in a stiff, proud way with your chest out and your head high.
NOUN **2** A strut is a piece of wood or metal which strengthens or supports part of a building.

 ► Which animals could you use to help you to describe a very strong person?

stub **stubs stubbing stubbed**
NOUN **1** The stub of a pencil is the short piece that remains when the rest has been used.
VERB **2** If you stub your toe, you hurt it by accidentally kicking something.

stubble
NOUN **1** The short stalks remaining in the ground after a crop is harvested are called stubble.
2 If a man has stubble on his face, he has very short hair growing there because he has not shaved recently.

stubborn
ADJECTIVE **1** Someone who is stubborn is determined not to change their opinion or course of action; obstinate, pig-headed.
2 A stubborn stain is difficult to remove.
stubbornly ADVERB **stubbornness** NOUN

stuck
1 past tense and past participle of **stick**.
ADJECTIVE **2** fixed and unable to be moved.

stuck-up
ADJECTIVE; INFORMAL proud and conceited.

stud **studs**
NOUN a small piece of metal fixed into something.
studded ADJECTIVE

student **students**
NOUN a person studying at a university, college or school.

studio **studios**
NOUN **1** a room where an artist or craftsman works.
2 a room containing special equipment where records, films or radio or television programmes are made.

studious
Said "**styoo**-dee-uss" ADJECTIVE spending a lot of time studying.
studiously ADVERB

study **studies studying studied**
VERB **1** to spend time learning about a particular subject.
2 to look at something carefully.
NOUN **3** the activity of studying a subject.
4 Studies are subjects which are studied.
5 a room used for writing and studying.

stuff **stuffs stuffing stuffed**
NOUN **1** any material or substance.
2 You can refer to a group of things as stuff. *Put all that stuff in your bag.*
VERB **3** If you stuff something somewhere, you push it there quickly and roughly.

stuffing
NOUN **1** a mixture of small pieces of food put inside poultry or a vegetable before it is cooked.
2 material used to fill a cushion or soft toy.

stuffy **stuffier stuffiest**
ADJECTIVE **1** If it is stuffy in a room, there is not enough fresh air.
2 Someone who is stuffy is very formal and old-fashioned.

Synonyms: (sense 1) airless, close, fusty

stumble **stumbles stumbling stumbled**
VERB **1** to trip and nearly fall.
2 If you stumble across something or stumble on it, you find it unexpectedly.

stump **stumps stumping stumped**
NOUN **1** a small part of something that is left when the rest has been removed: *the stump of a dead tree.*
2 In cricket, the stumps are the three upright wooden sticks that support the bails, forming the wicket.
VERB **3** If a question or problem stumps you, you cannot think of an answer or solution.

stun **stuns stunning stunned**
VERB **1** to knock a person or animal unconscious.
2 If you are stunned by something, you are very shocked by it.

stung
past tense and past participle of **sting**.

stunk
past participle of **stink**.

stunning
ADJECTIVE very beautiful or impressive.

stunt **stunts stunting stunted**
NOUN **1** an unusual or dangerous and exciting action that someone does to get publicity or as part of a film.
VERB **2** To stunt the growth or development of something means to prevent it from developing as it should.
stunted ADJECTIVE

stupendous
ADJECTIVE very large or impressive.

stupid **stupider stupidest**
ADJECTIVE showing lack of good judgement or intelligence and not at all sensible; foolish, unintelligent.
stupidly ADVERB **stupidity** NOUN

sturdy **sturdier sturdiest**
ADJECTIVE strong and firm and unlikely to be damaged or injured.
sturdily ADVERB

stutter **stutters stuttering stuttered**
VERB When someone stutters, they hesitate or repeat sounds when speaking.
stutter NOUN

sty **sties**
NOUN a pigsty.

A B C D E F G H I J K L M N O P Q R S T U V W X Y Z

style styles styling styled
NOUN **1** The style of something is the general way in which it is done or presented. *The food was cooked in genuine Chinese style. I like her writing style.*
2 The style of something is its design: *Tudor style.*
3 A person or place that has style is smart, elegant and fashionable.
VERB **4** To style a piece of clothing or a person's hair means to design and create its shape.

Synonyms: (sense 3) elegance, flair, panache

stylish
ADJECTIVE smart, elegant and fashionable.
stylishly ADVERB

Synonyms: chic, smart

sub-
PREFIX under, below.

subdue subdues subduing subdued
VERB If soldiers subdue a group of people, they bring them under control by using force.

Synonyms: control, overcome, quell

subdued
ADJECTIVE **1** A subdued person is rather quiet and sad.
2 Subdued colours or lighting are not very noticeable or bright.

subheading subheadings
NOUN the heading to a portion of writing that is part of a larger section.

subject subjects subjecting subjected
Said "**sub**-jekt" NOUN **1** The subject of writing or a conversation is the thing or person being discussed.
2 an area of study.
3 In grammar, the subject is the word or words representing the person or thing doing the action expressed by the verb. In the sentence "My cat keeps catching birds", "my cat" is the subject.
4 A king or queen's subjects are the people who live in the country which they rule.
ADJECTIVE **5** Someone or something that is subject to something is affected by it. *We are all subject to the laws of the land.*
Said "sub-**jekt**" VERB **6** To subject someone to something unpleasant means to make them experience it.

submarine submarines
NOUN a ship that can travel beneath the surface of the sea.

submerge submerges submerging submerged
VERB **1** to go beneath or to place something beneath the surface of a liquid.
2 If you submerge yourself in an activity, you become totally involved in it.
submerged ADJECTIVE

submissive
ADJECTIVE behaving in a quiet, obedient way.

submit submits submitting submitted
VERB **1** If you submit to something, you accept it because you are not powerful enough to resist it.
2 If you submit an entry to a competition, you send it in.

subordinate
ADJECTIVE If one thing is subordinate to another, it is less important.
subordinate NOUN

subscribe subscribes subscribing subscribed
VERB **1** If you subscribe to something such as a magazine or club, you pay money to it regularly.
2 If you subscribe to a particular belief or opinion, you support it or agree with it.
subscriber NOUN

subscription subscriptions
NOUN a sum of money that you pay regularly to belong to an organization or to receive regular copies of a magazine.

subsequent
ADJECTIVE happening or coming afterwards. *All the snow in early February and the subsequent thaw made it a very bad month.*
subsequently ADVERB

subside subsides subsiding subsided
VERB **1** to become less intense or quieter. *The noise subsided.*
2 If water or the ground subsides, it sinks to a lower level.

subsidize subsidizes subsidizing subsidized; also spelt **subsidise**
VERB If a government subsidizes something, it provides part of the cost of it.
subsidized ADJECTIVE **subsidy** NOUN

substance substances
NOUN **1** any kind of material, solid, liquid or gas.
2 If a speech or piece of writing has substance, it is meaningful or important.

Synonym: (sense 1) stuff

substantial
ADJECTIVE **1** very large in degree or amount. *He received a substantial pay rise.*
2 large and strongly built: *a substantial stone building.*

substitute substitutes
NOUN If a thing or person is a substitute for another, they are used instead, or take their place; an alternative, a replacement.
substitute VERB **substitution** NOUN

subtitle subtitles
NOUN A television programme with subtitles has a printed version of the dialogue at the bottom of the screen for the use of people who are hard of hearing.

 ► Submit comes from the Latin *mitto* meaning I send; subscribe comes from *scribo* meaning I write.

subtle **subtler subtlest**
Said "**sut**-tl" **ADJECTIVE 1** not immediately obvious or understandable. *The changes have been so subtle, few have noticed them.*
2 using indirect methods to achieve something: *a subtle approach.*
subtly ADVERB **subtlety** NOUN

subtract **subtracts subtracting subtracted**
VERB If you subtract one number from another, you take away the first number from the second. The symbol for subtract is (–). *Five subtracted from eight leaves three* (8 – 5 = 3).
subtraction NOUN

suburb **suburbs**
NOUN an area of a town or city that is away from its centre.
suburban ADJECTIVE

subway **subways**
NOUN a footpath that goes underneath a road.

succeed **succeeds succeeding succeeded**
VERB 1 to achieve the result you want.
2 To succeed someone means to be the next person to have their job.
3 If one thing succeeds another, it comes after it in time. *The race was succeeded by the awards ceremony.*
succeeding ADJECTIVE

Synonyms: (sense 1) be successful, do well, make it

success **successes**
NOUN 1 the achievement of something you have been trying to do.
2 Someone who is a success has achieved an important position or has made a lot of money.

successful
ADJECTIVE 1 If you are successful in something, you achieve what you wanted to do.
2 If someone has become famous and wealthy, they are thought of as being successful.
successfully ADVERB

succession **successions**
NOUN 1 A succession of things is a number of them occurring one after the other.
2 When someone becomes the next person to have an important position, you can refer to this event as their succession to this position. *The prince was the next in succession to the throne.*
PHRASE 3 If something happens a number of weeks, months or years **in succession**, it happens that number of times without a break.

successive
ADJECTIVE occurring one after the other without a break.

successor **successors**
NOUN Someone's successor is the person who takes their job when they leave.

such
ADJECTIVE OR PRONOUN 1 You use "such" to refer to the person or thing you have just mentioned or to someone or something similar. *Such were the fashions in those days.*
PHRASE 2 You can use **such as** to introduce an example of something: *foods such as potatoes, vegetables and pasta.*
3 You can use **such as it is** to indicate that something is not great in quality or quantity. *The party, such as it is, is going well.*
4 You can use **such and such** when you want to refer to something that is not specific. *This is the point when you ask them such and such and they reply.*
ADJECTIVE 5 "Such" can be used for emphasizing the degree or extent of something. *Don't cross her, she has such a terrible temper.*

suck **sucks sucking sucked**
VERB 1 to pull at something with your mouth, usually to get liquid out of it.
2 If something is sucked up, it is forcibly drawn up by a disappearing rush of air.
3 INFORMAL To suck up to someone means to do things to please them in order to obtain praise or approval.

suction
NOUN 1 the effect you create when you draw up or pull air or liquid out of a space.
2 the process by which two surfaces stick together when the air between them is removed.

sudden
ADJECTIVE happening quickly and unexpectedly.
suddenly ADVERB **suddenness** NOUN

suds
PLURAL NOUN the bubbles made when soap, detergent, etc. and water are mixed together.

sue **sues suing sued**
VERB to start a legal case against someone, usually to claim money from them because, in your opinion, they have done something wrong against you.

suede
Said "**swayd**" **NOUN** a thin, soft leather with a rough surface.

suet
NOUN fat from certain parts of sheep, cattle, etc. used for cooking.

suffer **suffers suffering suffered**
VERB to be badly affected by physical or emotional pain or as a result of an unpleasant situation.
suffering NOUN **sufferer** NOUN

sufficient
ADJECTIVE enough, adequate.
sufficiently ADVERB

A B C D E F G H I J K L M N O P Q R S T U V W X Y Z

suffix suffixes
NOUN a group of letters which is added to the end of a word to form a new word, for example "-ology" or "-itis".

suffocate suffocates suffocating suffocated
VERB to die as a result of having too little air or oxygen to breathe.
suffocation NOUN

sugar
NOUN a sweet substance used to sweeten food and drinks.

suggest suggests suggesting suggested
VERB **1** If you suggest a plan or idea to someone, you ask them to consider doing it.
2 If something suggests a thought or impression to you, it gives you that idea. *His healthy appearance suggested that he had made a full recovery.*

Synonyms: (sense 1) advocate, propose, recommend
(sense 2) hint, imply

suggestion suggestions
NOUN **1** a plan or idea that is mentioned as a possibility for someone to consider, a proposal.
2 a slight indication or faint sign: *a suggestion of colour.*

Synonyms: (sense 1) proposal, recommendation

suicidal
ADJECTIVE A suicidal person is so worried or depressed that they are thinking of killing themselves.

suicide
NOUN People who commit suicide deliberately kill themselves.

suit suits suiting suited
NOUN **1** a matching jacket and trousers or skirt.
2 one of four different types of card in a pack of playing cards, such as spades.
VERB **3** to be appropriate or acceptable for someone's purpose. *They devised a scheme which would suit them both.*
4 If a piece of clothing or a colour suits you, you look good when you are wearing it.

suitable
ADJECTIVE right or acceptable for a particular purpose or occasion.
suitably ADVERB **suitability** NOUN

Synonyms: appropriate, apt, fitting

suitcase suitcases
NOUN a case in which you carry your clothes when you are travelling.

suite suites
Said "**sweet**" NOUN **1** a set of matching furniture or bathroom fittings.
2 In a hotel, a suite is a set of rooms together.

sulk sulks sulking sulked
VERB to show annoyance by being silent and moody.
sulky ADJECTIVE

sullen
ADJECTIVE behaving in a bad-tempered and disagreeably silent way.
sullenly ADVERB

sulphur
NOUN a pale yellow non-metallic element which burns with a very unpleasant smell.

sultan sultans
NOUN In some Muslim countries, the ruler of the country is called the sultan.

sultana sultanas
NOUN **1** a dried grape.
2 the wife of a sultan.

sum sums
NOUN **1** In arithmetic, a sum is a calculation.
2 The sum of two numbers is their total when you add them together. *The sum of four and five is nine.*
3 an amount of money. *The company spent a vast sum on advertising.*
sum up VERB to describe the main points of something, to summarize.

summarize summarizes summarizing summarized; also spelt **summarise**
VERB to give a short account of the main points, to sum up.

summary summaries
NOUN a short account covering the main points of something.

Synonyms: précis, résumé, synopsis

summer summers
NOUN the season between spring and autumn.

summit summits
NOUN **1** the top of a mountain.
2 a meeting between leaders of different countries to discuss important matters.

summon summons summoning summoned
VERB **1** If someone summons you, they order you to go to them.
2 If you summon up strength or energy, you make a great effort to be strong or energetic.
summons NOUN

sun suns
NOUN The sun is the star providing heat and light for the planets in our solar system.

WORD FAMILY: sun
sunbathe **VERB**
sunburn **NOUN** sunburnt **ADJECTIVE**
sunflower **NOUN** sunglasses **NOUN**
sunlight **NOUN** sunshine **NOUN**
suntan **NOUN** suntanned **ADJECTIVE**

 ► These words from Greek have a common ending: magician, politician, musician, electrician.

sundae sundaes
Said "**sun**-day" NOUN a dish of ice cream with cream and fruit or nuts.

Sunday Sundays
NOUN the day between Saturday and Monday. [from Old English *sunnandoeg* meaning day of the sun]

sundial sundials
NOUN an object used for telling the time by the sun, consisting of a pointer which casts a shadow on to a base marked with the hours.

sunflower sunflowers
NOUN a tall plant with very large yellow flowers.

sung
past participle of **sing**.

sunk
past participle of **sink**.

sunken
ADJECTIVE **1** having sunk to the bottom of the sea, a river or lake.
2 curving inwards: *sunken cheeks*.

sunlight
NOUN light from the sun.

sunny sunnier sunniest
ADJECTIVE When it is sunny, the sun is shining.

sunrise sunrises
NOUN the time in the morning when the sun first appears, and the colours produced in the sky at that time.

sunset sunsets
NOUN the time in the evening when the sun disappears from the sky, and the colours produced in the sky at that time.

sunshine
NOUN bright light from the sun when it is shining.

sunstroke
NOUN an illness caused by spending too much time in hot sunshine.

super
ADJECTIVE very nice or very good.

superb
ADJECTIVE very good indeed.
superbly ADVERB

superficial
ADJECTIVE **1** involving only the most obvious or most general aspects of something: *a superficial knowledge*.
2 not having a deep, serious or genuine interest in anything: *a superficial person*.
3 Superficial wounds are not very deep or severe.
superficially ADVERB **superficiality** NOUN

superfluous
Said "soo-**per**-floo-uss" ADJECTIVE unnecessary or no longer needed.

superintendent superintendents
NOUN **1** a police officer above the rank of inspector.
2 a person whose job is to be responsible for a particular thing: *the superintendent of a leisure centre*.

superior
ADJECTIVE **1** better or of higher quality than other similar things.
2 in a more important position than another person. *The clerk had to refer complicated cases to his superiors.*
superior NOUN **superiority** NOUN

Antonym: inferior

superlative superlatives
Said "soo-**per**-lat-tiv" NOUN **1** In grammar, the superlative is the form of an adjective which indicates that the person or thing described has the most of a particular quality. For example, "quickest", "best" and "easiest" are all superlatives. See **comparative**.
ADJECTIVE **2** FORMAL very good indeed. *The orchestra gave a superlative performance.*

supermarket supermarkets
NOUN a large self-service shop selling food and household goods.

supernatural
ADJECTIVE **1** Something that is supernatural, such as ghosts or witchcraft, cannot be explained by normal scientific laws.
NOUN **2** You can refer to supernatural things as the supernatural.

supersonic
ADJECTIVE able to travel faster than the speed of sound.
supersonically ADVERB

superstar superstars
NOUN You can refer to a very famous entertainer or sports player as a superstar.

superstition superstitions
NOUN a belief in things like magic and powers that bring good or bad luck.
[from Latin *superstitio* meaning dread of the supernatural]

superstitious
ADJECTIVE believing in things like magic and powers that bring good and bad luck.

supervise supervises supervising supervised
VERB to direct and check what someone is doing to make sure that they do it correctly.
supervision NOUN **supervisor** NOUN
supervisory ADJECTIVE

Synonyms: oversee, superintend

supper suppers
NOUN a meal eaten in the evening or a snack eaten before you go to bed.

supple
ADJECTIVE able to bend and move easily.

supplement supplements supplementing supplemented
NOUN **1** something that is added to something else to improve it. *A supplement on fashion came free with the magazine.*
VERB **2** to add to. *Vitamin tablets can supplement a healthy diet.*
supplementary ADJECTIVE

supply supplies supplying supplied
VERB **1** to provide someone with what they want or need.
NOUN **2** A supply of something is an amount available for use.
PLURAL NOUN **3** Supplies are food and equipment for a particular purpose.
supplier NOUN

support supports supporting supported
VERB **1** If something supports an object, it is underneath it and holding it up.
2 If you support someone, you agree with their aims and want them to succeed.
3 to provide the food, shelter, etc. necessary for someone else to live. *Sharon supported her children on her own.*
NOUN **4** If you give support to someone, you are kind, encouraging and helpful to them.
supportive ADJECTIVE

supporter supporters
NOUN someone who supports a particular cause, team, etc.

suppose supposes supposing supposed
VERB **1** If you suppose that something is the case, you think that it is likely.
PHRASE **2** You can say **I suppose** when you are not entirely certain or enthusiastic about something. *Yes, I suppose he could come.*
3 If something **is supposed** to be done, it should be done. *You are supposed to report it to the police.*
4 If something **is supposed** to happen, it is planned or expected to happen. *It was supposed to rain this afternoon.*
CONJUNCTION **5** You can use "suppose" or "supposing" when you are considering or suggesting a possible situation or action. *Supposing we were to break down on the way to the match?*
supposedly ADVERB **supposition** NOUN

suppress suppresses suppressing suppressed
VERB **1** If an army or government suppresses an activity, it prevents people from doing it.
2 If someone suppresses a piece of information, they prevent it from becoming generally known.
3 If you suppress your feelings, you stop yourself expressing them.
suppression NOUN

Synonyms: (sense 1) crush, quell, stop

supreme
ADJECTIVE a word used to emphasize the greatness of someone or something. *Red Rum was the supreme Grand National horse of the 20th century.*
supremely ADVERB **supremacy** NOUN

sure surer surest
ADJECTIVE without any doubts; certain, definite.
surely ADVERB

surf surfs surfing surfed
NOUN **1** the white foam that forms on the top of waves when they break near the shore.
VERB **2** to ride a big wave into the shore, balancing on a surfboard.
3 When you surf the net, you go from website to website on the Internet reading the information.
surfer NOUN

surface surfaces surfacing surfaced
NOUN **1** The surface of something is the top or outside area of it.
VERB **2** When a submarine or diver surfaces, they come up from under water to the surface.

surfing
NOUN a sport which involves riding towards the shore on the top of a large wave while standing on a surfboard.

surge surges surging surged
NOUN **1** a sudden great increase in the amount of something.
VERB **2** to move suddenly and powerfully. *The crowd surged forwards.*

surgeon surgeons
NOUN a doctor who performs operations.

surgery surgeries
NOUN **1** the room or building where doctors, dentists and nurses work.
2 medical treatment involving cutting open part of a person's body to treat the damaged part.

surgical
ADJECTIVE used in or involving a medical operation: *surgical gloves.*
surgically ADVERB

surly surlier surliest
ADJECTIVE rude and bad-tempered.
surliness NOUN

surname surnames
NOUN Your surname is your last name which you share with other members of your family.

surpass surpasses surpassing surpassed
VERB; FORMAL To surpass someone or something means to be much better than them.

surplus surpluses
NOUN If there is a surplus of something, there is more of it than is needed.

Synonyms: excess, surfeit

 ► People's forenames and surnames always begin with capital letters, such as John Brown, Michelle Stand.

surprise **surprises**
NOUN 1 an unexpected event.
2 the feeling caused when something unexpected happens. *They all looked at her in surprise.*
surprise VERB **surprising** ADJECTIVE
surprisingly ADVERB

surrender **surrenders surrendering surrendered**
VERB 1 to stop fighting and agree that the other side has won.
2 If you surrender something, you have to give it up. *Please surrender your ticket to the bus conductor.*
3 If you surrender to a temptation or feeling, you let it take control of you.
surrender NOUN

Synonyms: (sense 1) give in, submit, yield

surround **surrounds surrounding surrounded**
VERB 1 To surround someone or something means to be situated all around them.
NOUN 2 The surround of something is its outside edge or border.

Synonyms: (sense 1) encircle, enclose

surroundings
PLURAL NOUN The surroundings are the area and environment around a person or place.

survey **surveys surveying surveyed**
Said "**sur**-vay" **NOUN 1** A survey of something is a detailed examination of it, often in the form of a report.
Said "sur-**vay**" **VERB 2** If you survey something, you look carefully at the whole of it.

Synonyms: (sense 2) look over, scan, view

surveyor **surveyors**
NOUN a person whose job is to survey buildings and land.

survive **survives surviving survived**
VERB To survive means to continue to live or exist in spite of a great danger or difficulties.
survivor NOUN

sus-
PREFIX under.

suspect **suspects suspecting suspected**
Said "sus-**pekt**" **VERB 1** If you suspect something, you think that it is likely or is probably true.
2 If you suspect someone of doing something wrong, you think that they have done it.
Said "**sus**-pekt" **NOUN 3** someone who is thought to be guilty of a crime.
ADJECTIVE 4 If something is suspect, it cannot be trusted or relied upon.
suspicion NOUN

suspend **suspends suspending suspended**
VERB 1 If someone is suspended from going to school or from playing a game, they are not allowed to do it for a certain period of time.
2 To suspend an activity or event means to stop it for a while.
3 If something is suspended, it hangs downwards.
suspension NOUN

suspense
NOUN a state of excitement or anxiety caused by having to wait for something.

suspension bridge **suspension bridges**
NOUN a bridge that is supported by hanging under cables attached to towers.

suspicion **suspicions**
NOUN 1 the feeling of not trusting someone, or the feeling that something is wrong.
2 the feeling that something is likely to happen or is probably true: *a suspicion that more could have been done.*

Synonyms: (sense 1) distrust, misgiving, scepticism

suspicious
ADJECTIVE If you are suspicious of someone or something, you do not trust them: *a suspicious acquaintance; suspicious circumstances.*
suspiciously ADVERB

sustain **sustains sustaining sustained**
VERB 1 To sustain something means to continue it for a period of time. *The team sustained the pace for half an hour.*
2 If something sustains you, it gives you energy and strength.
3 FORMAL To sustain an injury or loss means to suffer it.

swagger **swaggers swaggering swaggered**
VERB to walk in a proud, boastful exaggerated way, to show off.
swagger NOUN **swaggeringly** ADVERB

swallow **swallows swallowing swallowed**
VERB 1 to make something go down your throat and into your stomach.
NOUN 2 a migrating bird with a long forked tail and pointed wings.

swam
past tense of **swim**.
✔ The past tense of the verb *to swim* is *swam*. It is correct to say "I swam" but not "I swum".

swamp **swamps swamping swamped**
NOUN 1 an area of permanently wet land.
VERB 2 If something is swamped, it is covered or filled with water.
3 If you are swamped by things, you have more than you are able to deal with.
swampy ADJECTIVE

swan **swans**
NOUN a large, usually white, bird with a long neck that lives on rivers or lakes.

a b c d e f g h i j k l m n o p q r s t u v w x y z

The word beginning "sus-" is a version of the Latin *sub* meaning under.

A B C D E F G H I J K L M N O P Q R S T U V W X Y Z

swap **swaps swapping swapped**; also spelt **swop**
*Rhymes with "**stop**"* VERB to exchange, to switch.
swap NOUN

swarm **swarms swarming swarmed**
NOUN **1** A swarm of insects is a large group of them flying together.
VERB **2** When bees or other insects swarm, they fly together in a large group.
3 If a place is swarming with people, there are a lot of people there.

swat **swats swatting swatted**
VERB To swat an insect means to hit it sharply in order to kill it.

sway **sways swaying swayed**
VERB **1** To sway means to lean or swing slowly from side to side.
2 If something sways you, it influences your judgment.

swear **swears swearing swore sworn**
VERB **1** to use words that are considered to be very rude or offensive.
2 If you swear to do something, you solemnly promise that you will do it.

swearword **swearwords**
NOUN a word which is considered to be rude or blasphemous, and which may cause offence to others.

sweat
NOUN the salty liquid which comes out of the pores of your skin when you are hot or afraid.
sweat VERB **sweaty** ADJECTIVE

sweater **sweaters**
NOUN a knitted piece of clothing covering your upper body and arms.

sweatshirt **sweatshirts**
NOUN a piece of clothing made of thick cotton, covering your upper body and arms.

swede **swedes**
NOUN a large round root vegetable with yellow flesh and a brownish-purple skin.
[from *Swedish turnip* because it was introduced to Scotland from Sweden in the 18th century]

sweep **sweeps sweeping swept**
VERB **1** to use a brush to gather up dust or rubbish.
2 To sweep things off a surface means to push them all off with a quick, smooth movement.
3 If something sweeps from one place to another, it moves there very quickly. *A gust of wind swept over the garden. The new fashion swept through America.*
PHRASE **4** If you do something with **a sweep of your arm**, you do it with a wide, curving movement of your arm.

sweet **sweeter sweetest; sweets**
ADJECTIVE **1** containing a lot of sugar.
2 A sweet sound is gentle and tuneful.
3 attractive and delightful, charming, cute.
4 pleasant and satisfying: *sweet success.*
NOUN **5** Things such as toffees, chocolates and mints are sweets.
6 something sweet that you eat at the end of a meal. *We had ice cream and meringue for sweet.*
sweetly ADVERB **sweetness** NOUN

Antonyms: (sense 1) bitter, savoury

sweet corn
NOUN a long stalk covered with juicy yellow seeds that can be eaten as a vegetable.

sweeten **sweetens sweetening sweetened**
VERB to make something sweeter.

sweetheart **sweethearts**
NOUN **1** You can call someone whom you are very fond of "sweetheart".
2 OLD-FASHIONED A young person's sweetheart is their boyfriend or girlfriend.

swell **swells swelling swelled swollen**
VERB **1** to become larger and rounder.
2 If an amount swells, it increases in number.
NOUN **3** the regular up and down movement of the sea.

swelling **swellings**
NOUN an enlarged area on your body as a result of injury or illness.

sweltering
ADJECTIVE If the weather is sweltering, it is very hot.

swept past tense and past participle of **sweep**.

swerve **swerves swerving swerved**
VERB to change direction suddenly to avoid colliding with something.
swerve NOUN

swift **swifter swiftest; swifts**
ADJECTIVE **1** happening or moving very quickly.
NOUN **2** a bird with narrow crescent-shaped wings and a short forked tail.
swiftly ADVERB **swiftness** NOUN

swill **swills swilling swilled**
VERB **1** to pour plenty of water over something to clean it.
NOUN **2** a liquid mixture containing waste food that is fed to pigs.

swim **swims swimming swam swum**
VERB to move through water by making movements with your arms and legs.

swimmer **swimmers**
NOUN a person who can swim.

swimming
NOUN **1** the activity of moving through water using your arms and legs.
ADJECTIVE **2** If everything is swimming, it seems as if everything you see is moving and you feel dizzy.

 ► In swap, the "a" makes an "o" sound. Find five other words where the same thing happens, such as halt.

swimming bath swimming baths
NOUN a public swimming pool, usually indoors.

swimming costume swimming costumes
NOUN the clothes that someone wears for swimming.

swimming pool swimming pools
NOUN a large, square pit, tiled and filled with water for swimming.

swimsuit swimsuits
NOUN a swimming costume.

swindle swindles swindling swindled
VERB 1 to cheat a person out of money or property.
NOUN 2 a trick in which someone is cheated out of money or property.
swindler NOUN

swine swines
NOUN 1 OLD-FASHIONED Swine are pigs.
2 INFORMAL If you call someone a swine, you mean they are nasty and spiteful.

swing swings swinging swung
VERB 1 to move evenly and repeatedly from side to side from a fixed point.
NOUN 2 a seat hanging from a frame or a branch, which moves backwards and forwards when you sit on it.
3 A swing in opinion is a significant change in it.

swipe swipes swiping swiped
VERB 1 to try to hit something by making a curving movement with the arm.
2 INFORMAL to steal.
3 To swipe a credit card means to pass it through a machine that electronically reads the information stored in the card.
swipe NOUN

swirl swirls swirling swirled
VERB When water swirls it moves quickly in circles.

swish swishes swishing swished
VERB 1 to move with a whistling or hissing sound.
ADJECTIVE 2 posh, smart.
swish NOUN

switch switches switching switched
NOUN 1 a small control for an electrical device or machine.
2 a change. *She made a switch between the nice present and the nasty present.*
VERB 3 to change from one thing to another. *Jack switched from English to geography.*
switch off VERB If you switch a light or machine off, you stop it working by pressing a switch.
switch on VERB If you switch a light or machine on, you start it working by pressing a switch.

switchboard switchboards
NOUN The part of an organization where all telephone calls are received.

swivel swivels swivelling swivelled
VERB to turn round on a central point.
swivel ADJECTIVE

swollen
ADJECTIVE Something that is swollen has swelled up; enlarged.

Synonyms: distended, enlarged, puffed up

swoon swoons swooning swooned
VERB to faint briefly.
swoon NOUN

swoop swoops swooping swooped
VERB 1 to move downwards through the air in a fast curving movement.
PHRASE 2 If you do something **in one fell swoop**, you achieve it in a single action.
✔ To say *foul* instead of *fell* in this phrase is a common mistake.

swop
another spelling of **swap**.

sword swords
NOUN a weapon consisting of a very long blade with a short handle.

swore
past tense of **swear**.

swot swots swotting swotted
VERB 1 INFORMAL to study or revise very hard.
2 If you swot up on a subject, you find out as much about it as possible in a short time.
NOUN 3 someone who spends a lot of time studying.

swum
past participle of **swim**.
✔ The past tense of the verb *to swim* is *swam*. It is correct to say "I swam" but not "I swum".

swung
past tense and past participle of **swing**.

sycamore sycamores
Said "**sik**-am-mor" NOUN a tree that has large leaves with five points.

syllable syllables
NOUN a part of a word that contains a single vowel sound and is pronounced as a unit. For example, "book" has one syllable, "reading" has two and "enjoyment" has three.
syllabic ADJECTIVE

syllabus syllabuses or syllabi
NOUN a general word for the subjects that are studied for a particular course or examination.
✔ The plural *syllabuses* is much more common than *syllabi*.

symbol symbols
NOUN a shape, design or idea that is used to represent something. *Apple blossom is a Chinese symbol of peace and beauty.*
symbolic ADJECTIVE

Synonyms: emblem, representation, sign

symbolize **symbolizes symbolizing symbolized**; also spelt **symbolise**
VERB to stand as a symbol for something. *A white dove often symbolizes peace.*
symbolism NOUN

symmetrical
ADJECTIVE If something is symmetrical, it has two halves which are exactly the same, except that one half is like a reflection of the other half.
symmetrically ADVERB

symmetry
NOUN Something has symmetry if it is symmetrical.

sympathetic
ADJECTIVE A sympathetic person shows kindness and understanding to other people.
sympathetically ADVERB

sympathize **sympathizes sympathizing sympathized**; also spelt **sympathise**
VERB to show understanding and care to someone who is in difficulties.

sympathy
NOUN kindness and understanding towards someone who is in difficulties.

Synonyms: compassion, pity

symphony **symphonies**
NOUN a piece of music for an orchestra, usually in four sections called movements.

symptom **symptoms**
NOUN **1** something wrong with your body that is a sign of an illness. *The child had all the symptoms of measles.*
2 a sign of a bad situation. *Unemployment is a symptom of a bad economy.*

synagogue **synagogues**
Said "**sin**-a-gog" NOUN a building where Jewish people meet for worship and religious instruction.

synchronize **synchronizes synchronizing synchronized**; also spelt **synchronise**
Said "**sing**-kron-nize" VERB **1** To synchronize watches means to set them to show exactly the same time as each other.
2 To synchronize two actions means to do them at the same time and speed: *synchronized swimming.*
synchronization NOUN

synonym **synonyms**
NOUN If two words have the same or a very similar meaning, they are synonyms. See **antonym**.
synonymous ADJECTIVE

synthetic
ADJECTIVE made from artificial substances rather than natural ones.
synthetically ADVERB

syringe **syringes**
Said "sir-**rinj**" NOUN a hollow tube with a plunger and a fine hollow needle, used for injecting or extracting liquids.

syrup **syrups**
NOUN a thick sweet liquid made by boiling sugar with water.

system **systems**
NOUN **1** an organized way of doing or arranging something according to a fixed plan or set of rules; a method or procedure.
2 People sometimes refer to the government and administration of a country as "the system".
3 In biology, a system of a particular kind is the set of organs that perform that function: *the immune system.*

Synonyms: (sense 1) method, procedure, routine

systematic
ADJECTIVE following a fixed plan and done in an efficient way; methodical.
systematically ADVERB

 ► George Mackay Brown claimed that the decay of language is always a symptom of a more serious sickness.

Tt

tab **tabs**
NOUN 1 a small extra strip or flap that is added to something, for example, on a curtain so it can be hung on a pole.
PHRASE 2 If you **keep tabs** on someone, you make sure you know what they are doing.

tabby **tabbies**
NOUN a cat whose fur has grey, brown or black stripes.
[from Old French *tabis* meaning striped silk cloth]

table
NOUN 1 a piece of furniture with a flat top supported by one or more legs.
2 a set of facts or figures arranged in rows or columns.
3 Tables or times tables are multiplication sums involving numbers twelve or less.

tablecloth **tablecloths**
NOUN a cloth used to cover a table and keep it clean.

tablespoon **tablespoons**
NOUN a large spoon used for serving food; also the amount that a tablespoon contains.
tablespoonful NOUN

tablet **tablets**
NOUN any small, round pill made of powdered medicine.

table tennis
NOUN a game for two or four people in which you use bats to hit a small hollow ball over a low net across a table; also called ping-pong.

tabloid **tabloids**
NOUN a newspaper with small pages, short news stories and lots of photographs.

Antonym: broadsheet

tack **tacks tacking tacked**
NOUN 1 a short nail with a broad, flat head.
2 If you change tack, you start to use a different method for dealing with something.
3 Tack is the equipment used for horseriding.
VERB 4 to fasten something with tacks.
5 to sew something with long loose stitches.
6 In sailing, to steer the boat into the wind in a series of zigzags.

tackle **tackles tackling tackled**
VERB 1 to start dealing with a difficult task in a determined way.
2 If you tackle someone in a game such as soccer, you try to get the ball away from them.
3 If you tackle someone about something, you talk to them about it in order to get something changed or dealt with.
NOUN 4 an attempt to get the ball away from your opponent.
5 Tackle is the equipment used in fishing.

Synonyms: (sense 1) confront, deal with, undertake

tacky **tackier tackiest**
ADJECTIVE 1 slightly sticky to touch. *This paint still feels tacky.*
2 INFORMAL badly made and in poor taste.

tact
NOUN the ability to handle delicate or difficult situations without upsetting people.
tactless ADJECTIVE **tactlessly** ADVERB

Synonyms: delicacy, diplomacy, discretion

tactful
ADJECTIVE Tactful people can handle difficult or delicate situations without upsetting others.
tactfully ADVERB

tactic **tactics**
NOUN Tactics are the methods you use to achieve the results you want, particularly in a competition or battle.
tactical ADJECTIVE **tactically** ADVERB

tadpole **tadpoles**
NOUN Tadpoles are the larvae of frogs and toads. They are black with round heads and long tails and live in water.
[from Middle English *tadde* meaning toad + *pol* meaning head]

tag **tags tagging tagged**
NOUN 1 a small label made of cloth, paper or plastic.
2 a children's game in which one child chases the others and tries to touch them.
VERB 3 to attach a tag to something.
4 If you tag along with someone, you go with them or behind them.

tail **tails tailing tailed**
NOUN 1 the rear part extending beyond the body of an animal.
2 the end part of something: *the tail of the plane.*
PLURAL NOUN 3 If a man is wearing tails, he is wearing a formal jacket which has two long pieces hanging down at the back.
ADJECTIVE OR ADVERB 4 The tails side of a coin is the side which does not have a person's head on it.
VERB 5 to follow someone.
tail off **VERB** If something tails off, it becomes gradually less.

tailback **tailbacks**
NOUN a long traffic queue.

tailor **tailors tailoring tailored**
NOUN 1 a person who makes, alters and repairs clothes, especially for men.
VERB 2 to design something specially for a particular purpose. *This kit is tailored to suit the DIY enthusiast.*
tailor-made ADJECTIVE

a b c d e f g h i j k l m n o p q r s t u v w x y z

T began as an X. This became an upright cross and later the top of the cross was removed.

take takes taking took taken
VERB **1** to put your hand round something and hold it or carry it.
2 to accept. *Dave took the job.*
3 to require or need. *It takes only one person to change a light bulb, except in jokes.*
4 to steal something. *Someone's taken our belongings!*
5 to drive someone by car or lead them to a place.
6 to bear or endure. *Boxers can take a lot of punches.*
7 to measure. *I took my own temperature.*
8 If you take a car or train, or a road or route, you use it to go from one place to another.
9 "Take" is also used to show what action or activity is being done. *Hannah took a bath. Alan was taking an interest in life again.*
10 If you take pills or medicine, you swallow them.
11 In mathematics, take away or take means subtract.
take after VERB If you take after someone in your family, you look or behave like them.
take down VERB to write down what someone is saying.
take in VERB **1** to deceive. *I was taken in by the bogus salesman.*
2 to understand, to comprehend.
take off VERB **1** When an aircraft takes off, it leaves the ground and begins to fly.
2 to make fun of someone by imitating them in a comical way, to parody.
takeoff NOUN
take over VERB to control something which other people have previously controlled. *The giant corporation took over the small company.*
takeover NOUN
take to VERB to like someone or something immediately. *She has really taken to our dogs.*

takeaway takeaways
NOUN **1** a shop or restaurant that sells hot cooked food to be eaten elsewhere
2 the hot cooked food you can buy from a takeaway.

talcum powder or **talc**
NOUN a soft perfumed powder used for absorbing moisture on the body.

tale tales
NOUN a story.

talent talents
NOUN the natural ability to do something well.
talented ADJECTIVE

Synonyms: ability, flair, gift

talk talks talking talked
VERB **1** When you talk, you say things to someone.
NOUN **2** a conversation, discussion or speech.

talkative
ADJECTIVE Talkative people talk a lot.
talkatively ADVERB

tall taller tallest
ADJECTIVE **1** of more than average or normal height.
2 having a particular height: *a wall four metres tall.*
PHRASE **3** If you describe what someone says as **a tall story**, you find it difficult to believe.

tally tallies tallying tallied
NOUN **1** an informal record of amounts which you keep adding to as you go along. *He kept a tally of the number of buses he passed on the journey.*
VERB **2** to count something up using simple strokes of the pen for each one and separating each bundle of five strokes.
3 If numbers or statements tally, they are exactly the same or they give the same results or conclusions.

Talmud
Said "**tal**-mood" NOUN The Talmud consists of the books containing the ancient Jewish ceremonies and civil laws.

talon talons
NOUN Talons are sharp, hooked claws, especially of a bird of prey.

tambourine tambourines
NOUN a percussion instrument made of a skin stretched tightly over a circular frame, with small cymbals attached, which is beaten or shaken.

tame tamer tamest; tames taming tamed
ADJECTIVE **1** A tame animal is not afraid of people.
2 weak or uninteresting. *The end of the film was pretty tame.*
VERB **3** to train a wild animal not to be afraid of humans.
tamely ADVERB **tamer** NOUN

tamper tampers tampering tampered
VERB to interfere or meddle with something in a physical way. *I caught him tampering with the car engine.*

tampon tampons
NOUN a firm, specially shaped piece of cotton wool that a female places inside her vagina to absorb the blood during her period.

tan tans tanning tanned
NOUN **1** If you have a tan, your skin is darker than usual because you have been in the sun.
VERB **2** to acquire a suntan.
3 to turn an animal's hide into leather by using chemicals.

tandem tandems
NOUN a bicycle designed for two riders sitting one behind the other.

tang tangs
NOUN a strong, sharp smell or flavour.
tangy ADJECTIVE

 ▶ Saying: talk is cheap because supply exceeds demand.

tangent tangents
NOUN 1 A tangent of a curve is any straight line that touches the curve at one point only.
PHRASE 2 If you **go off at a tangent**, you start talking away from the subject.
[from Latin *tangere* meaning to touch]

tangerine tangerines
NOUN 1 a type of small sweet orange with a loose rind.
NOUN OR ADJECTIVE 2 reddish-orange.

tangle tangles tangling tangled
NOUN 1 a mass of things such as hairs or fibres that are twisted together and difficult to separate.
VERB 2 If you are tangled up, you are trapped in a mass of something so that it is difficult to get free.

tank tanks
NOUN 1 a large container for storing liquid or gas.
2 an armoured military vehicle which moves on tracks and has guns or rockets.

tanker tankers
NOUN a ship or lorry designed to carry large quantities of gas or liquid.

tantalize tantalizes tantalizing tantalized; also spelt **tantalise**
VERB If something or someone tantalizes you, they tease you by making you feel hopeful and excited and then do not allow you to have what you want.
tantalizing ADJECTIVE **tantalizingly** ADVERB

tantrum tantrums
NOUN a noisy and sometimes violent outburst of temper, especially by a child.

tap taps tapping tapped
NOUN 1 a device that you turn to control the flow of liquid or gas from a pipe or container.
2 a gentle hit.
VERB 3 If you tap something or tap on it, you hit it lightly.
4 If a telephone is tapped, a device is fitted to it so that someone can listen secretly to the calls.

tap-dancing
NOUN a type of dancing in which the dancers wear special shoes with pieces of metal on the toes and heels which click against the floor.
tap-dance VERB **tap-dancer** NOUN

tape tapes taping taped
NOUN 1 a long, thin strip of fabric used for binding or fastening.
2 a strip of sticky plastic which you use for sticking things together.
3 a cassette with magnetic tape wound round it, used for recording sound.
VERB 4 If you tape one thing to another, you fasten them together using tape.
5 to record sounds or television programmes using a tape recorder or a video recorder.

tape measure tape measures
NOUN a strip of plastic or metal marked off in inches and centimetres and used for measuring.

taper tapers tapering tapered
NOUN 1 a thin candle.
VERB 2 Something that tapers becomes thinner towards one end.

tape recorder tape recorders
NOUN a machine used for recording sounds onto magnetic tape and for playing these sounds back.
tape recording NOUN

tapestry tapestries
NOUN a piece of heavy cloth with designs embroidered on it.

tar
NOUN a thick, black, sticky substance which is used in making roads.

tarantula tarantulas
Said "tar-**rant**-yoo-la" NOUN a large, hairy poisonous spider.

target targets
NOUN 1 something which you aim at when firing a weapon.
2 a result that you are trying to achieve. *The school set a target of £8000 for their annual appeal.*
3 The target of an action or remark is the person or thing at which it is directed. *Don't make me the target of your jokes!*
target VERB

Tarmac
NOUN; TRADEMARK a material used for making road surfaces. It consists of crushed stones mixed with tar.
tarmac VERB
[short for tarmacadam, from the name of John McAdam, the Scottish engineer who invented it]

tarnish tarnishes tarnishing tarnished
VERB 1 If metal tarnishes, it becomes stained and loses its shine.
2 If something tarnishes your reputation, it spoils it and causes people to lose their respect for you.

tarpaulin tarpaulins
NOUN a sheet of heavy waterproof material used as a protective covering.

tart tarts
NOUN 1 a pastry case with a sweet filling.
ADJECTIVE 2 Something that is tart is sour or sharp to taste.

tartan tartans
NOUN a woollen fabric from Scotland with checks of various colours and sizes, depending on which clan it belongs to.
tartan ADJECTIVE

A B C D E F G H I J K L M N O P Q R S T U V W X Y Z

task tasks
NOUN any piece of work which has to be done.

Synonyms: chore, duty, job

tassel tassels
NOUN a tuft of loose threads tied by a knot and used for decoration.

taste tastes tasting tasted
NOUN 1 Your sense of taste is the ability to recognize the flavour of things in your mouth.
2 the flavour of something.
3 If you have a taste for something, you enjoy it.
4 If you have a taste of something, you experience it: *my first taste of defeat.*
5 Your taste is your choice of the things you like to buy or have around you: *good taste.*
VERB 6 to be aware of the flavour of something in your mouth.
7 If you taste food or drink, you have a small amount of it to see what it is like.

tasteful
ADJECTIVE 1 showing good taste.
2 attractive and elegant.
tastefully ADVERB

tasteless
ADJECTIVE 1 Tasteless food has very little flavour.
2 vulgar and unattractive: *tasteless decoration.*
3 A tasteless remark or joke is offensive.
tastelessly ADVERB

tasty tastier tastiest
ADJECTIVE having a pleasant flavour.

tattered
ADJECTIVE Tattered clothes are ragged and worn.

tatters
PLURAL NOUN Clothes that are in tatters are badly torn.

tattoo tattoos tattooing tattooed
VERB 1 to draw a design on someone's skin by pricking little holes and filling them with coloured dye.
NOUN 2 a picture or design tattooed on someone's body.
3 a public military display of exercises and music.

tatty tattier tattiest
ADJECTIVE worn out or untidy and rather dirty.

taught
the past tense and past participle of **teach**.

taunt taunts taunting taunted
VERB 1 to speak to someone about their weaknesses or failures in order to make them angry or upset; to provoke or tease.
NOUN 2 an offensive remark intended to make a person angry or upset.

taut
ADJECTIVE stretched very tight.
tautly ADVERB

tavern taverns
NOUN; OLD-FASHIONED an inn.

tawny
ADJECTIVE brownish-yellow.

tax taxes taxing taxed
NOUN 1 money that people have to pay to a government so that it can provide public services such as health care and education.
VERB 2 If someone or something is taxed, a certain amount of money has to be paid to the government.
3 If a job taxes you, you find it difficult or strenuous.
taxation NOUN **taxing** ADJECTIVE

taxi taxis taxiing taxied
NOUN 1 a car with a driver which you hire, usually for a short journey.
VERB 2 When a plane taxis, it moves slowly around the airfield.

tea teas
NOUN 1 the dried leaves of a shrub found in Asia.
2 a drink made by brewing the leaves of the tea plant in hot water; also a cup of this.
3 a meal taken in the late afternoon or early evening.
teatime NOUN

teach teaches teaching taught
VERB to pass on information or skills to a pupil.
teaching NOUN

Synonyms: educate, instruct, train

teacher teachers
NOUN a person whose job it is to teach pupils.

teak
NOUN a hard wood that comes from a large Asian tree.

team teams teaming teamed
NOUN 1 a group of people who play together against another group in a sport or game.
VERB 2 If you team up with someone, you join them and work or play together.
teamwork NOUN

teapot teapots
NOUN a round pot with a lid, handle and spout, used for brewing tea.

tear tears tearing tore torn
Said "**teer**" NOUN 1 Tears are the drops of liquid that come out of your eyes when you cry.
Said "**tare**" 2 a hole that has been made in something.
VERB 3 If you tear something, it is damaged by being pulled so that a hole appears in it.
4 to remove something roughly and violently. *He tore the tie from his neck.*
5 If you tear somewhere, you dash there.

tearful
ADJECTIVE about to cry or crying gently.
tearfully ADVERB **tearfulness** NOUN

 ▶ Some words from Malaysia: teak, amok, bamboo, bantam, raffia.

tease teases teasing teased
VERB to make fun of someone deliberately, and try to embarrass them.
tease NOUN

teaspoon teaspoons
NOUN a small spoon used for stirring drinks; also the amount that a teaspoon holds.
teaspoonful NOUN

teat teats
NOUN **1** a nipple on a female animal.
2 a piece of rubber or plastic that is shaped like a nipple and fitted to a baby's feeding bottle.

technical
ADJECTIVE **1** involving machines, processes and materials used in industry, transport and communications.
2 involving a specialized field of activity: *technical language.*

technically
ADVERB If something is technically true or correct, it is true according to the facts, rules or laws although this may not be important in certain situations. *Technically, ambulances often break the law when they speed to emergencies.*

technique techniques
NOUN **1** a particular method of doing something.
2 skill and ability in an activity which are developed through training and practice.

technology technologies
NOUN Technology refers to practical things which are the result of knowledge of science: *computer technology.*
technological ADJECTIVE **technologically** ADVERB

teddy teddies
NOUN A teddy or teddy bear is a stuffed toy that looks like a friendly bear.
[named after the American President Theodore (Teddy) Roosevelt, who hunted bears]

tedious
Said "**tee**-dee-uss" **ADJECTIVE** boring and lasting for a long time.
tediously ADVERB

teem teems teeming teemed
VERB **1** If a place is teeming with people or things, there is a mass of them moving about.
2 to rain very heavily.
teeming ADJECTIVE

teenage
ADJECTIVE aged between thirteen and nineteen, or typical of this age group.

teenager teenagers
NOUN a person aged between thirteen and nineteen.

teens
PLURAL NOUN the period of your life when you are between thirteen and nineteen years old.

teeth
the plural of **tooth**.

teetotal
Said "tee-**toe**-tl" **ADJECTIVE** Someone who is teetotal never drinks alcohol.
teetotaller NOUN

tele-
PREFIX at or over a distance.
[from Greek *tele* meaning far]

telecommunications
NOUN the science and activity of sending signals and messages over long distances using electronic equipment.

telegram telegrams
NOUN a message sent by telegraph.

telegraph
NOUN; OLD-FASHIONED a system of sending messages over long distances using electrical or radio signals.
telegraph VERB

telepathy
Said "til-**lep**-ath-ee" **NOUN** the ability to know what someone is thinking without any words being spoken.
telepathic ADJECTIVE

telephone telephones telephoning telephoned
NOUN **1** a piece of electrical equipment for talking directly to someone who is in a different place.
VERB **2** to speak to someone using a telephone.

telescope telescopes
NOUN a long, optical instrument which makes distant objects appear larger and nearer.

teletext
NOUN an electronic system that broadcasts pages of information onto a television set.

televise televises televising televised
VERB If an event is televised, it is filmed and shown on television.

television televisions
NOUN a piece of electronic equipment which receives and reproduces pictures and sounds by electrical signals over a distance.

tell tells telling told
VERB **1** If you tell someone something, you let them know about it; to inform or notify. *The policeman told him to move his car.*
2 to judge correctly. *I could tell he was scared.*
3 If an unpleasant or tiring experience begins to tell, it begins to have a serious effect. *The pressure began to tell.*
tell off **VERB** to speak to someone strongly because they have done something wrong, to scold or chastise.
telling-off NOUN

telly tellies
NOUN; INFORMAL a television.

A B C D E F G H I J K L M N O P Q R S T U V W X Y Z

temper
NOUN 1 If someone has a temper, they become angry very easily.
PHRASE 2 If you **lose your temper**, you become very angry.

temperamental
ADJECTIVE Someone who is temperamental has moods that change often and suddenly.
temperamentally ADVERB

temperate
ADJECTIVE A temperate place has weather that is neither extremely hot nor extremely cold.

temperature **temperatures**
NOUN 1 a measure of how hot or cold something is.
2 Your temperature is the temperature of your body.
3 If you have a temperature, the temperature of your body is higher than it should be.

template **templates**
NOUN 1 a shape or pattern cut out in wood, metal, plastic or card which you draw or cut around to reproduce that shape or pattern.
2 In computing, a template is a basic layout for a certain type of document which you create in advance, then adapt it each time you use it for your requirements at that time.

temple **temples**
NOUN a building used for the worship of a god in various religions.

tempo **tempos** or **tempi**
NOUN The tempo of something is the speed at which it happens, particularly the speed of music.

temporary
ADJECTIVE lasting for only a short time.
temporarily ADVERB

Antonym: permanent

tempt **tempts tempting tempted**
VERB 1 to try to persuade someone to do something by offering them something they want.
2 If you are tempted to do something, you want to do it but you think it might be wrong or harmful.
temptation NOUN **tempting** ADJECTIVE

Synonyms: (sense 1) entice, lure

ten
the number 10.
tenth

tenant **tenants**
NOUN someone who pays rent for the place they live in or for land or buildings that they use.
tenancy NOUN

tend **tends tending tended**
VERB 1 If something tends to happen, it happens usually or often.
2 to look after something.

tendency **tendencies**
NOUN a trend or type of behaviour that happens very often. *The weather here has a tendency to be unpredictable.*

tender **tenderest; tenders tendering tendered**
ADJECTIVE 1 gentle and caring.
2 Tender meat is easy to cut or chew.
3 painful and sore: *a tender bruise.*
VERB 4 To tender an apology or a resignation is to offer it.
tenderly ADVERB **tenderness** NOUN

Synonyms: (sense 1) affectionate, gentle, loving

tendon **tendons**
NOUN a strong cord of tissue which joins a muscle to a bone.

tennis
NOUN a game played by two or four players on a rectangular court in which a ball is hit by players over a central net.

tenor **tenors**
NOUN 1 a man who sings in the middle to high range of voices.
ADJECTIVE 2 A tenor recorder, saxophone, or other musical instrument has a range of notes of a fairly low pitch.

tense **tenser tensest; tenses tensing tensed**
ADJECTIVE 1 nervous and unable to relax, or being made to feel like this: *a tense situation. I was very tense before the exam.*
2 tight: *tense muscles.*
VERB 3 to become tight and stiff. *Your muscles tense when you get cramp.*
NOUN 4 The tense of a verb is the form which shows whether you are talking about the past, present or future.

TENSES
Some forms of a verb indicate that the action has already happened. These forms are called **past tenses**:
She asked her doctor for advice.
She has asked her doctor for advice.
She was asking her doctor for advice this morning.
She had asked her doctor for advice that morning.
Some forms of the verb indicate that the action is happening at the present time. These forms are called **present tenses**:
I agree with you.
I do agree with you.
I am agreeing with you, whatever you think.
Some forms of the verb indicate that the action will happen in future. These forms are called **future tenses**:
They will play the Veterans in July.
They will have played the Veterans by mid-July.
Also look at the grammar boxes at **past tense** *and* **present tense**.

 ► Joke. When is it a good thing to lose your temper? When it is a bad one.

tension **tensions**
NOUN 1 the feeling of nervousness or worry that you have when something dangerous or important is happening.
2 The tension of a rope or wire is how tightly it is stretched.

tent **tents**
NOUN a shelter made of fabric held up by poles and pinned down at the bottom with pegs and ropes.

tentacle **tentacles**
NOUN the long, thin parts that octopuses, squid, etc. use to feel and hold things.

tepid
ADJECTIVE Tepid liquid is only slightly warm; lukewarm.

term **terms terming termed**
NOUN 1 a name or word used for a particular thing. *Rubella is the medical term for German measles.*
2 a fixed period of time: *a school term.*
3 The terms of an agreement are the conditions that have been accepted by the people involved in it.
4 If you express something in particular terms, you express it using a particular type of language or in a way that shows what you think of it. *In terms of the history of the earth, our life span is hardly anything.*
VERB 5 To term something is to give it a name or describe it. *They termed my performance memorable.*
PHRASE 6 If you **come to terms with** something difficult or unpleasant, you learn to accept it.

terminal **terminals**
ADJECTIVE 1 A terminal illness or disease cannot be cured and causes death gradually.
NOUN 2 a place where vehicles, passengers or goods begin or end a journey.
3 A terminal is one of the parts of an electrical device, through which electricity enters or leaves.
terminally ADVERB

terminate **terminates terminating terminated**
VERB When you terminate something or when it terminates, it stops or ends.
termination NOUN

terminology **terminologies**
NOUN Terminology is a set of special words and expressions used for a subject.

terminus **terminuses**
Said "**ter**-min-uss" **NOUN** a place where a bus or train route ends.

terrace **terraces**
NOUN 1 a row of houses joined together.
2 a flat area of stone next to a building where people can sit; a patio.
3 a sloping area of wide steps where spectators at a sports match stand.
4 one of a series of flat areas of ground built like steps so that crops can be grown there: *rice terraces.*
terraced ADJECTIVE

terrapin **terrapins**
NOUN a small North American freshwater turtle.

terrible
ADJECTIVE 1 serious and unpleasant: *a terrible accident.*
2 very bad or of poor quality: *Wayne sported a terrible haircut.*

terribly
ADVERB 1 done very badly.
2 INFORMAL extremely, very. *The children were terribly excited.*

terrier **terriers**
NOUN a small, active, short-bodied dog.

terrific
ADJECTIVE 1 very pleasing or impressive: *a terrific film.*
2 very great or strong: *a terrific crash.*
terrifically ADVERB

terrify **terrifies terrifying terrified**
VERB to make someone feel extremely frightened.
terrifying ADJECTIVE

territory **territories**
NOUN 1 The territory of a country is the land that it controls.
2 a specific large district, often belonging to someone or something. *The dog defended his territory against the local mongrels.*
territorial ADJECTIVE

terror **terrors**
NOUN great fear or panic.
terror-stricken ADJECTIVE

terrorism
NOUN the use of extreme violence to try to bring about change.
terrorist NOUN OR ADJECTIVE

terrorize **terrorizes terrorizing terrorized**; also spelt **terrorise**
VERB If someone terrorizes you, they frighten you by threatening you or being violent to you.

test **tests testing tested**
VERB 1 to try something to find out what it is, what condition it is in or how well it works.
2 to ask someone questions to find out how much they know.
NOUN 3 a deliberate action or experiment to find out whether something works or how well it works.
4 a set of questions or tasks given to someone to find out what they know or can do.

testicle **testicles**
NOUN A man's testicles are the two sex glands that produce sperm.

a b c d e f g h i j k l m n o p q r s t u v w x y z

A B C D E F G H I J K L M N O P Q R S T U V W X Y Z

testify testifies testifying testified
VERB 1 to make a formal statement, especially in a court of law.
2 To testify to something is to show that it is likely to be true. *The doctor's certificate testified to her good health.*

test match test matches
NOUN one of a series of international cricket or rugby matches.

test tube test tubes
NOUN a small cylindrical glass container that is used in chemical experiments.

tetanus
Said "**tet**-nuss" NOUN a painful, infectious disease caused by germs getting into wounds.

tether tethers tethering tethered
VERB 1 to tie up an animal to a post, etc. so that it cannot stray.
NOUN 2 a rope or chain used to tie an animal to a post, etc.
PHRASE 3 If you are **at the end of your tether**, you are extremely tired and have no more patience or energy left to deal with problems.

tetrahedron tetrahedrons or tetrahedra
NOUN a solid shape having four flat faces.

text texts
NOUN 1 The text of a book is the main written part of it, rather than the pictures or index.
2 any written material.
textual ADJECTIVE

textbook textbooks
NOUN a book about a particular subject for students to use.

textile textiles
NOUN a woven cloth or fabric.

texture textures
NOUN The texture of something is the way it feels when you touch it.

Synonyms: consistency, feel

than
PREPOSITION OR CONJUNCTION 1 You use "than" to link two parts of a comparison. *She was older than I was.*
2 You use "than" to link two parts of a contrast. *This tastes more like coffee than tea.*

thank thanks thanking thanked
VERB 1 to show that you are grateful for something.
PHRASE 2 If an occurrence happened **thanks to** someone or something, it happened because of them.
INTERJECTION 3 You say "thanks" or "thank you" to show that you are grateful for something.

thankful
ADJECTIVE grateful, happy and relieved that something has happened.
thankfully ADVERB

that those
ADJECTIVE OR PRONOUN 1 "That" or "those" is used to refer to things or people already mentioned or known about. *She returned to work later that week. Those shoes of yours are great.*
CONJUNCTION 2 "That" is used to introduce a clause. *I said that I was coming home.*
PRONOUN 3 You use "that" after a noun to introduce a clause which gives more information about the noun: *a car that won't start; a woman that I have known for ten years.*

thatch thatches
NOUN Thatch is straw and reeds used to make roofs.
thatch VERB **thatched** ADJECTIVE

thaw thaws thawing thawed
VERB 1 When snow or ice thaws, it melts.
2 When you thaw frozen food or when it thaws, it becomes unfrozen.
NOUN 3 a period of warmer weather in winter when snow or ice melts.

the
DEFINITE ARTICLE "The" is used when you are talking about something that is known about or when it is clear which thing you are talking about. *We sat in the sun. Where have you put the TV remote control?*

theatre theatres
Said "**theer**-ter" NOUN 1 a building where plays and other entertainments are performed on a stage.
2 a general word for plays and drama.

theatrical
ADJECTIVE 1 relating to the theatre.
2 Someone behaving in a theatrical way exaggerates their feelings and actions as if they were in a play.
theatrically ADVERB

thee
PRONOUN; OLD-FASHIONED you.

theft thefts
NOUN the crime of stealing, robbery.

their
ADJECTIVE belonging or relating to them. *It was their fault. Trees lose their leaves in autumn.*
✔ Be careful not to confuse *their* with *there*.

theirs
PRONOUN You use "theirs" to indicate that something belongs or relates to the group of people, animals or things which you are talking about. *I sat at the table next to theirs.*

them
PRONOUN "Them" refers to a group of people, animals or things which have already been mentioned. *His socks had stripes on them.*

theme themes
NOUN a main idea in a piece of writing, painting, film or music. *The main theme of the book is love.*

 ► Remember "theirs" does not have an apostrophe. It doesn't mean "belonging to their".

theme park theme parks
NOUN an area which people pay to visit, which has rides, displays and activities.

themselves
PRONOUN 1 "Themselves" refers to the same people, animals or things that have already been mentioned. *They were talking amongst themselves.*
2 "Themselves" is used to emphasize the plural subject or object of a clause. *Although the forest is big, the islands themselves are very small.*

then
ADVERB 1 at a particular time in the past or future. *I'll be there on Saturday, so I'll speak to you then.*
2 You use "then" to indicate that one thing happens after another thing. *Pour in the milk, then add the sugar.*

theology
NOUN the study of religion and God.

theoretical
ADJECTIVE based on the ideas behind a subject rather than on the practical aspects of it.
theoretically ADVERB

theory theories
NOUN 1 an idea or set of ideas that is meant to explain something: *the theory behind rocket science.*
PHRASE 2 You use **in theory** to say that although something is supposed to happen, it may not in fact happen. *In theory, if bacon goes up, pigs can fly.*

Synonyms: (sense 1) conjecture, hypothesis

therapy therapies
NOUN the treatment of mental or physical illness, often without the use of drugs or operations.
therapist NOUN

there
ADVERB 1 in, at or to a place that has already been mentioned or that you are looking at. *He's sitting over there.*
PRONOUN 2 "There" is used to say that something exists or does not exist, or to draw attention to something. *There is nothing to do here. There's a letter for you in my office.*
✔ Be careful not to confuse *there* with *their*. A good way to remember that *there* is connected to the idea of place is by remembering the spelling of two other place words, *here* and *where*.

therefore
ADVERB as a result. *This bottle is bigger and therefore more expensive.*

thermal
ADJECTIVE 1 to do with or caused by heat.
2 Thermal clothes are specially designed to keep you warm in cold weather.

thermometer thermometers
NOUN an instrument for measuring temperature.

Thermos or **Thermos flask**
NOUN; TRADEMARK an insulated container, usually used to keep drinks hot.

thermostat thermostats
NOUN a device used to control temperature, for example, on a central heating system.

thesaurus thesauruses
Said "this-**saw**-russ" NOUN a reference book in which words with similar meanings are grouped together.

these
the plural of **this**.

they
PRONOUN 1 You use "they" to refer to a group of people, animals or things that you have already mentioned. *They married two years ago.*
2 "They" is sometimes used instead of "he" or "she" when it is not known or is not important if the person is male or female. Some people consider this to be incorrect. *Someone could be hurt if they trip over that.*

they'd
1 contraction of **they would**.
2 contraction of **they had**.

they'll
contraction of **they will**.

they're
contraction of **they are**.

they've
contraction of **they have**.

thick thicker thickest
ADJECTIVE 1 Something thick has a large distance between its two sides.
2 measuring a certain amount between its two sides: *a folder two centimetres thick.*
3 close together and in a large number: *thick, dark hair.*
4 Thick liquids are quite solid and do not flow easily.
5 INFORMAL not very intelligent.
thickly ADVERB **thickness** NOUN

Antonym: (sense 1) thin

thicken thickens thickening thickened
VERB to become thicker or make something thicker.

thief thieves
NOUN a person who steals.
thieving ADJECTIVE

thigh thighs
NOUN the top parts of your legs, between your knees and your hips.

∴ is a short way to write "therefore" when you are taking notes. ◀

A B C D E F G H I J K L M N O P Q R S T U V W X Y Z

thimble **thimbles**
NOUN a small metal or plastic cap that you put on the end of your finger to protect it when you are sewing.

thin **thinner thinnest**
ADJECTIVE 1 Something that is thin is much narrower than it is long; not thick.
2 A thin person or animal has very little fat on their body.
3 Thin liquids contain a lot of water and flow easily.
thinly ADVERB

Antonyms: (sense 1) thick, wide, broad

thing **things**
NOUN 1 an object, rather than a plant, an animal or a person; an article.
2 You use "thing" instead of another word when you are not able or do not need to be more exact: *trees and flowers and things like that. A strange thing happened today.*
3 Your things are your clothes and possessions.

Synonyms: (sense 2) business, situation, subject

think **thinks thinking thought**
VERB 1 to use your mind to consider ideas or problems.
2 If you think something, you have the opinion that it is true or the case.
3 If you think of something, you remember it or it comes into your mind.
4 to consider doing something. *I'm thinking of going on holiday.*

third **thirds**
ADJECTIVE 1 The third item in a series is the one counted as number three.
NOUN 2 one of three equal parts.
thirdly ADVERB

third person
NOUN In English grammar, the third person is the form of the pronoun or the verb that goes with "he", "she", "it" or "they". *He drank some tea. She played with the puppy. They swam in the sea.*

Third World
NOUN a name for the poorer countries of Africa, Asia and South America.

thirst **thirsts**
NOUN 1 the condition of being thirsty.
2 a thirst for something is a great desire for it: *a thirst for knowledge.*

thirsty **thirstier thirstiest**
ADJECTIVE wanting or needing a drink.
thirstily ADVERB

thirteen
the number 13.
thirteenth

thirty **thirties**
the number 30.
thirtieth

this **these**
ADJECTIVE OR PRONOUN 1 You use "this" to talk about things or people that you have already referred to or that you can see. *I'd been on many holidays but never one like this. This is the ball we will use.*
2 You use "this" to refer to the present time. *I've been on holiday this week.*

thistle **thistles**
NOUN a wild plant with prickly-edged leaves and purple flowers.

thorn **thorns**
NOUN one of many sharp points growing on some plants.
thorny ADJECTIVE

thorough
Said "**thur**-ruh" **ADJECTIVE** done very carefully and completely.
thoroughly ADVERB

those
the plural of **that**.

thou
PRONOUN; OLD-FASHIONED "Thou" means you, when you are talking to only one person.

though
Rhymes with "**show**" **CONJUNCTION 1** in spite of the fact that. *Though we were poor, we were happy.*
2 "Though" is used when you are saying something which contrasts with something else that has been said; but. *I climbed the hill, though not very far.*
PHRASE 3 As though is used to say what seems to be happening or to compare two situations. *It looks as though you were right.*

thought **thoughts**
1 the past tense and past participle of **think**.
NOUN 2 an idea or opinion that you have.
3 the activity of thinking.

Synonyms: (sense 3) consideration, reflection, thinking

thoughtful
ADJECTIVE 1 quiet and serious, because you are thinking about something.
2 A thoughtful person remembers what other people want or need and tries to be kind to them.
thoughtfully ADVERB **thoughtfulness** NOUN

Synonyms: (sense 1) meditative, pensive, reflective
(sense 2) caring, considerate, kind

thoughtless
ADJECTIVE A thoughtless person forgets or ignores what other people want, need or feel.
thoughtlessly ADVERB **thoughtlessness** NOUN

 ► Think of a more vivid way to say: he ate hungrily; she had a lovely smile.

thousand **thousands**
the number 1000.
thousandth

thrash **thrashes thrashing thrashed**
VERB 1 to beat someone violently by hitting them with something.
2 To thrash someone in a contest or fight is to defeat them completely.
3 To thrash out a problem or an idea is to discuss it in detail until a solution is reached.
4 If you thrash around, you twist and turn your body violently because you are afraid or in pain.
thrashing NOUN

thread **threads threading threaded**
NOUN 1 a long, fine piece of cotton, silk, nylon or wool.
VERB 2 To thread a needle is to put thread through the eye of it.
3 If you thread your way through people or things, you carefully make your way through them.

threadbare
ADJECTIVE Threadbare cloth or clothing is old and thin.

threat **threats**
NOUN 1 a statement that someone will harm you, especially if you do not do what they want.
2 anything or anyone that seems likely to harm you. *Rain was a real threat to the progress of the building work.*
3 If there is a threat of something unpleasant happening, it seems likely that it will happen.

threaten **threatens threatening threatened**
VERB 1 If you threaten to harm someone or threaten to do something that will upset them, you say that you will do it.
2 If someone or something threatens a person or thing, they are likely to harm them.
threatening ADJECTIVE

Synonyms: (sense 2) endanger, jeopardize

three
the number 3.

three-dimensional
ADJECTIVE A three-dimensional object or shape is not flat, but has height or depth as well as length and width. Three-dimensional is often abbreviated to "3D".

thresh **threshes threshing threshed**
VERB When corn, wheat or rice is threshed, it is beaten in order to separate the grains from the rest of the plant.
thresher NOUN

threshold **thresholds**
NOUN a doorway or entrance.

threw
past tense of **throw**.

thrifty **thriftier thriftiest**
ADJECTIVE A thrifty person saves money and does not waste things.
thrift NOUN **thriftily** ADVERB

thrill **thrills**
NOUN a sudden feeling of great excitement, pleasure or fear; also any event or experience that gives you such a feeling.
thrill VERB **thrilled** ADJECTIVE **thrilling** ADJECTIVE

Synonyms: buzz, kick

thriller **thrillers**
NOUN Thrillers are a genre, or type, of fiction book or film depicting crime, mystery or espionage.

thrive **thrives thriving thrived** or **throve**
VERB to be healthy, happy or successful.
thriving ADJECTIVE

throat **throats**
NOUN 1 the back of your mouth and the top part of the tubes inside your neck.
2 the front part of your neck.

throb **throbs throbbing throbbed**
VERB 1 to vibrate and make a strong, rhythmic noise. *The engines throbbed.*
2 If a part of your body throbs, you feel a series of strong beats or dull pains.

throne **thrones**
NOUN 1 a ceremonial chair used by a king or queen on important official occasions.
2 The throne is a way of referring to the position of being king or queen. *Victoria was on the throne for 64 years.*

throng **throngs thronging thronged**
NOUN 1 a large crowd of people.
VERB 2 If people throng a place, they are there in a great numbers. *Hundreds of city workers thronged the square at lunchtime.*

throttle **throttles throttling throttled**
VERB to kill or injure someone by squeezing their throat.

through
*Said "**threw**"* **PREPOSITION 1** moving all the way from one side of something to the other: *a path through the woods.*
2 because of. *He was exhausted through lack of sleep.*
3 during. *During busy periods he has to work through the night.*
4 If you go through an experience, it happens to you.
ADJECTIVE 5 If you are through with something, you have finished doing it or using it.

throughout
PREPOSITION 1 during the whole of a period of time: *throughout the night.*
ADVERB 2 through the whole of a place: *throughout the house.*

a b c d e f g h i j k l m n o p q r s t u v w x y z

Tongue twister: there are thirty thousand feathers on every thrush's throat.

throw **throws throwing threw thrown**
VERB **1** to propel something through the air with your hand and arm.
2 to move somewhere suddenly and with force. *We threw ourselves on the ground.*
3 If you throw a tantrum or mood, you go into one.
4 To throw someone into an unpleasant situation is to put them there.
5 If you throw yourself into an activity, you become actively and enthusiastically involved in it.
throw away VERB to get rid of something.
throw up VERB to vomit.

Synonyms: (sense 1) chuck, fling, hurl

thrush **thrushes**
NOUN a small, brown songbird.

thrust **thrusts thrusting thrusted**
VERB to move or push something quickly with a lot of force. *Macbeth thrust the dagger into Duncan's heart. We thrust our way through the crowds.*
thrust NOUN

thud **thuds**
NOUN a dull sound, usually made by a solid, heavy object hitting something soft.
thud VERB

thug **thugs**
NOUN a very rough and violent person. [from Hindi *thag* meaning thief]

thumb **thumbs**
NOUN the short, thick finger on the side of your hand.

thump **thumps thumping thumped**
VERB **1** to hit someone or something hard with your fist.
2 If something thumps somewhere, it makes a fairly loud, dull sound, usually when it hits something else.
3 When your heart thumps, it beats strongly and quickly.
NOUN **4** a hard hit.
5 a fairly loud, dull sound.

thunder
NOUN the loud noise that you hear from the sky after a flash of lightning.
thunderous ADJECTIVE

thunderstorm **thunderstorms**
NOUN a storm with thunder and lightning.

Thursday **Thursdays**
NOUN the day between Wednesday and Friday. [from Old English *Thursdoeg* meaning Thor's day; Thor was the Norse god of thunder]

thus
ADVERB **1** therefore. *Some people will be more capable and thus better paid than others.*
2 FORMAL in this way. *He threw the ball thus.*

thy
ADJECTIVE; OLD-FASHIONED your. *Thy kingdom come, thy will be done.*

tick **ticks ticking ticked**
NOUN **1** a written mark to show that something is correct or has been dealt with.
2 a tiny, blood-sucking, insect-like animal that usually lives on the bodies of other animals, including occasionally humans.
VERB **3** to write a tick next to something.
4 When a clock ticks, it makes a regular series of short sounds as it works.
tick off VERB; INFORMAL If you tick someone off, you speak angrily to them because they have done something wrong.
ticking NOUN

ticket **tickets**
NOUN a piece of paper or card which shows that you have paid for a journey or have paid to enter a place of entertainment.

tickle
VERB When you tickle someone, you move your fingers lightly over their body in order to make them laugh.

ticklish
ADJECTIVE Someone who is ticklish laughs or wriggles easily when you tickle them.

tidal
ADJECTIVE to do with or produced by tides.

tidal wave **tidal waves**
NOUN a very large wave, often caused by an earthquake, which comes over land and destroys things.

tide **tides**
NOUN **1** the regular change in the level of the sea on the shore, caused by the pull of the moon's gravity.
2 A tide of something is a large amount of it: *a tide of public opinion; a tide of excitement; a tide of anger.*

tidings
PLURAL NOUN; FORMAL news. *We bring you glad tidings!*

tidy **tidier tidiest; tidies tidying tidied**
ADJECTIVE **1** Something that is tidy is neat and arranged in an orderly way. Someone that is tidy always keeps their things like this.
2 A tidy amount of money is a fairly large amount.
VERB **3** to make a place neat by putting things in their proper place.
tidily ADVERB **tidiness** NOUN

tie **ties tying tied**
VERB **1** to fasten using string, rope, etc., to bind.
2 If you tie with someone in a competition or game, you have the same number of points.
NOUN **3** a long, narrow piece of cloth worn around the neck under a shirt collar and tied in a knot at the front.
4 a connection or feeling that links you with a person, place or organization. *I had close ties with the family.*

 ► Joke. What did the sardine say when her baby saw a submarine? ◄

tier tiers
NOUN a layer or level, such as the parts on a wedding cake or the layers of seats in a theatre.

tiger tigers
NOUN a large animal of the cat family, with an orange-coloured coat with black stripes.

tight tighter tightest
ADJECTIVE **1** fitting closely: *tight shoes.*
2 firmly fastened and difficult to move: *a tight knot.*
3 INFORMAL mean with money.
ADVERB **4** held firmly and securely. *He held her tight and whirled her round.*
tightly ADVERB **tightness** NOUN

tighten tightens tightening tightened
VERB **1** If you tighten your hold on something, you hold it more firmly.
2 If you tighten a rope or chain, or if it tightens, it is stretched or pulled until it is straight, or made smaller and closer-fitting around something it is circling.
3 If someone tightens a rule or system, they make it stricter or more efficient.

tightrope tightropes
NOUN a tightly-stretched rope on which an acrobat balances and performs tricks.

tights
PLURAL NOUN a piece of clothing made of thin stretchy material that fits closely round a person's hips, legs and feet.

tile tiles
NOUN a small flat square piece of something, for example, slate or carpet, that is fixed onto surfaces to cover them.
tile VERB **tiled** ADJECTIVE

till tills
PREPOSITION OR CONJUNCTION **1** until. *We had to wait till Monday.*
NOUN **2** a drawer or box in a shop where money is kept, usually in a cash register.

tiller tillers
NOUN the handle fixed to the top of the rudder for steering a boat.

tilt tilts tilting tilted
VERB If you tilt an object or it tilts, it changes position so that one end or side is higher than the other.

Synonyms: incline, lean, tip

timber timbers
NOUN wood that has been cut and prepared ready for building and making furniture.

time times timing timed
NOUN **1** Time is what is measured in hours, days and years.
2 a particular point in the day. *The time is eight o'clock.*
3 a particular period when something was happening. *I enjoyed my time on holiday.*
4 the right moment. *It's time for a change.*
VERB **5** to arrange for or do something at a particular time. *The jockey timed his finish perfectly.*
6 to measure how long something lasts. *She timed me as I ran.*

Synonyms: (sense 3) interval, period, spell

timer timers
NOUN a device that measures time, especially one that is part of a machine.

times
PLURAL NOUN **1** multiplied by, often written ×. *Two times three is six* ($2 \times 3 = 6$).
2 "Times" is used after numbers to indicate how often something happens. *I bath the dog three times a year.*
3 "Times" is used after numbers when you are saying how much bigger, smaller, better or worse one thing is compared to another. *The Belgians drink three times as much beer as the French.*

timetable timetables
NOUN **1** a list of the times when particular trains, boats, buses or aircraft arrive and depart.
2 a plan of the times when particular activities or jobs should be done.
timetable VERB

timid
ADJECTIVE shy and having no courage or self-confidence.
timidly ADVERB **timidity** NOUN

Synonyms: fearful, shy, timorous

timing
NOUN skill in judging the right moment at which to do something.

tin tins
NOUN **1** a metal container which is filled with food and then sealed in order to preserve the food; a can.
2 a soft silvery-white metal often used in the making of cans.
3 a small metal container which may have a lid: *a cake tin.*
tinned ADJECTIVE

tingle tingles tingling tingled
VERB When a part of your body tingles, you feel a slight prickling feeling in it.
tingle NOUN **tingling** NOUN OR ADJECTIVE

tinker tinkers tinkering tinkered
VERB **1** to make a lot of small changes to something in order to repair or improve it. *All he wanted was to tinker with engines.*
NOUN **2** A person who travels from place to place, mending metal pots and pans or doing other small repair jobs.

tinkle tinkles tinkling tinkled
VERB to make a sound like a small bell ringing.

tinsel
NOUN long threads with strips of shiny paper attached, used as a decoration at Christmas.

tint tints tinting tinted
NOUN **1** a small amount of a particular colour.
VERB **2** If a person tints their hair, they change its colour.
tinted ADJECTIVE

tiny tinier tiniest
ADJECTIVE extremely small, minute.

tip tips tipping tipped
NOUN **1** the end of something long and thin.
2 a place where rubbish is dumped.
3 a piece of useful advice.
4 a gift of a small amount of money to thank someone such as a waiter or a taxi driver for their services.
VERB **5** to tilt an object so that it is no longer horizontal or upright.
6 to pour or dump something carelessly.
tipped ADJECTIVE

tiptoe tiptoes tiptoeing tiptoed
VERB to walk very quietly on your toes.

tire tires tiring tired
VERB **1** to make someone feel as if they have little energy left or are ready for sleep.
2 to become bored with something.
tiring ADJECTIVE

Synonyms: (sense 1) exhaust, fatigue, weary

tired
ADJECTIVE having less energy or enthusiasm than normal.

Synonyms: exhausted, weary, worn out

tireless
ADJECTIVE Someone who is tireless has a lot of energy and never seems to need a rest.

tiresome
ADJECTIVE Someone or something that is tiresome is irritating and boring.

tissue tissues
Said "**tiss**-yoo" NOUN **1** a small piece of soft paper that you use as a handkerchief.
2 The tissue in plants and animals consists of cells that are similar in appearance and function: *scar tissue; muscle tissue.*

title titles
NOUN **1** the name of a book, play or piece of music.
2 a word describing someone's rank or job, such as Mrs, captain and head teacher.
3 the position of champion in a sports competition: *the European featherweight title.*
titled ADJECTIVE

titter titters tittering tittered
VERB to laugh in a nervous or embarrassed way.
titter NOUN

to
PREPOSITION **1** "To" is used to indicate the place that someone or something is moving towards or pointing at. *The prime minister went to China.*
2 "To" is used to indicate the limit of something: *goods to the value of £500.*
3 "To" is used in ratios and rates when saying how many units of one type there are for each unit of another. *My car does 30 kilometres to the gallon.*
ADVERB **4** If you push or shut a door to, you close it but do not shut it completely.

toad toads
NOUN an amphibian that looks like a frog but has a drier skin and spends less time in the water.

toadstool toadstools
NOUN a type of poisonous fungus.

toast toasts toasting toasted
NOUN **1** slices of bread made brown and crisp by being grilled.
VERB **2** to grill bread at a high temperature.
3 To drink an alcoholic drink in honour of someone.
[from Latin *tostus* meaning parched]

toaster toasters
NOUN a piece of electrical equipment for toasting bread.

tobacco
NOUN the dried leaves of the tobacco plant which people smoke in pipes, cigarettes and cigars.

toboggan toboggans
NOUN a flat seat with two wooden or metal runners, used for sliding over the snow.
toboggan VERB

today
ADVERB OR NOUN **1** the day on which you are speaking or writing.
2 the present time. *The children of today are lucky in many respects.*

toddler toddlers
NOUN a small child who has just learned to walk.
toddle VERB

toe toes
NOUN Your toes are the five movable parts at the end of your foot.

toffee toffees
NOUN a sticky, chewy sweet made by boiling sugar and butter together with water.

toga togas
NOUN a long loose robe worn in ancient Rome.

 ► The main words in titles of books, plays, films, CDs, television programmes, etc. are capitalised.

together
ADVERB 1 If people do something together, they do it with each other.
2 If two things happen together, they happen at the same time.
3 If things are joined or fixed together, they are joined or fixed to each other.
4 If things or people are together, they are very near to each other.

Synonyms: (sense 1) collectively, jointly (sense 2) concurrently, simultaneously

✔ Two nouns joined by *together with* do not make a plural subject, so the following verb is not plural: *Jones, together with his partner, has had great success.*

toil toils toiling toiled
VERB 1 When people toil, they work hard doing unpleasant, difficult or tiring tasks or jobs.
NOUN 2 unpleasant, difficult or tiring work.

toilet toilets
NOUN 1 a large bowl, connected to the drains, which you use to get rid of waste from your body.
2 a small room containing a toilet, a lavatory.

token tokens
NOUN 1 a piece of paper, card, plastic or metal that is worth a particular amount of money and can be exchanged for goods: *a gift token; a car wash token.*
ADJECTIVE 2 If something is described as "token", it shows that it is not being treated as important: *a token contribution to your fees.*

told
the past tense and past participle of **tell**.

tolerable
ADJECTIVE 1 able to be put up with. *The noise was just about tolerable.*
2 fairly satisfactory. *We had a tolerable meal.*

Antonym: intolerable

tolerant
ADJECTIVE Tolerant people allow other people to have different attitudes and beliefs, or to behave in a different way, even if they do not agree or approve.
tolerance NOUN

Antonym: intolerant

tolerate tolerates tolerating tolerated
VERB 1 If you can tolerate something, you accept it, even though it is unsatisfactory or unpleasant.
2 If you tolerate things that you do not approve of or agree with, you allow them.
toleration NOUN

Synonyms: (sense 1) bear, endure, stand

toll tolls tolling tolled
NOUN 1 a sum of money that you have to pay in order to use a particular bridge or road.
2 The death toll in an accident is the number of people who have died in it.
VERB 3 When someone tolls a bell, it is rung slowly, often as a sign that somebody has died.

tomato tomatoes
NOUN a small round red fruit, used as a vegetable and eaten cooked or raw.

tomb tombs
NOUN a large grave to hold one or more bodies.

tombola
NOUN a type of lottery, in which tickets are pulled out of a revolving drum, some of which win prizes.

tomboy tomboys
NOUN a girl who likes playing rough or noisy games.

tombstone tombstones
NOUN a gravestone.

tomorrow
ADVERB OR NOUN 1 the day after today.
2 the future, especially the near future. *This is the computer of tomorrow.*

ton tons
NOUN a unit of weight equal to 2240 pounds or about 1016 kilograms.

tone tones toning toned
NOUN 1 a quality in someone's voice which shows what they are thinking or feeling. *She spoke in an anxious tone.*
2 The tone of a piece of writing is its style and the ideas or opinions in it.
3 a lighter or darker shade of the same colour.
4 The tone of a musical instrument or a singer's voice is the kind of sound it has.
VERB 5 If you tone down something, you make it less forceful or severe.

tongs
PLURAL NOUN two long narrow pieces of metal joined together at one end which you press together to pick an object up.

tongue tongues
NOUN 1 the soft part movable part of your mouth which you use for tasting, licking and speaking.
2 a language. *Spanish is his native tongue.*
3 The tongue of a shoe or boot is the piece of leather underneath the laces.

tongue twister tongue twisters
NOUN a sentence that is very difficult to say properly, especially when you are saying it quickly.

tonic tonics
NOUN 1 Tonic or tonic water is a colourless, fizzy, slightly bitter drink, often mixed with alcohol.
2 a medicine that makes you feel stronger, healthier, and less tired.

Tongue twister: Freddy the thrush flew through the thick fog thinking of his family.

A B C D E F G H I J K L M N O P Q R S T U V W X Y Z

tonight
ADVERB OR NOUN the evening or night that will come at the end of today.

tonne tonnes
Said "**tun**" NOUN a unit of weight equal to 1000 kilograms, a metric ton.

tonsillitis
Said "ton-sil-**lie**-tis" NOUN a painful swelling of the tonsils, caused by an infection.

tonsil tonsils
NOUN Your tonsils are the two small, soft lumps in your throat at the back of your mouth.

too
ADVERB 1 also or as well. *Fiona went and Angus too.*
2 You use "too" to indicate that there is more of something than is desirable or acceptable. *The tea was too hot to drink.*

took
past tense of **take**.

tool tools
NOUN any hand-held piece of equipment that you use to help you do a particular kind of work.

Synonyms: implement, instrument, utensil

tooth teeth
NOUN the small hard, white structures in the mouth of vertebrates used for biting and chewing food. See **canine**, **incisor**, **molar**.

toothache
NOUN a pain in your tooth.

toothbrush toothbrushes
NOUN a small brush for cleaning your teeth.

toothpaste
NOUN a substance which you use to clean your teeth.

top tops topping topped
NOUN 1 the highest point, part or surface of something.
2 a cap or lid.
3 a piece of clothing worn on the upper half of your body.
ADJECTIVE 4 highest in a series of things.
PHRASE 5 If one thing is **on top of** another thing, it is on its highest part.
VERB 6 If someone tops a poll, record chart, etc., they do better than anyone else. *The record topped the charts across Europe.*
7 If something tops a particular amount, it is greater than that amount. *The temperature topped 35 °C.*

Synonyms: (sense 1) apex, height, peak

topic topics
NOUN a particular subject that you write about or discuss.

topical
ADJECTIVE involving or related to events that are happening at the time you are speaking or writing.
topically ADVERB

topping toppings
NOUN food that is put on top of other food in order to decorate it or add to its flavour.

topple topples toppling toppled
VERB 1 to become unsteady and fall over.
2 to make something fall over.

top-secret
ADJECTIVE meant to be kept completely secret.

topsy-turvy
ADJECTIVE 1 upside down.
2 in a confused state.

Torah
NOUN Jewish law and teaching.

torch torches
NOUN 1 a small battery-powered light carried in the hand, a flashlight.
2 In the past, a torch was a long stick with burning material wrapped around one end. [from Old French *torche* meaning handful of twisted straw, which was set alight to see in the dark]

tore
past tense of **tear**.

torment torments tormenting tormented
VERB If something torments you, it causes you extreme pain or unhappiness.
torment NOUN

torn
1 the past participle of **tear**.
ADJECTIVE 2 If you are torn between two or more things, you cannot decide which one to choose.

tornado tornadoes or tornados
Said "tor-**nay**-doh" NOUN a violent storm with strong circular winds around a funnel-shaped cloud.

torpedo torpedoes torpedoing torpedoed
Said "tor-**pee**-doh" NOUN 1 a tube-shaped bomb that travels underwater and explodes when it hits a target.
VERB 2 If a ship is torpedoed, it is hit and usually sunk by a torpedo.

torrent torrents
NOUN When a lot of water is falling very rapidly, it can be said to be falling in torrents.

torrential
ADJECTIVE Torrential rain pours down very rapidly and in great quantities.

torso torsos
NOUN the main part of your body, excluding your head, arms and legs.

tortoise tortoises
NOUN a slow-moving reptile with a large, hard shell over its body.

► The main words ending "oo" are: igloo, shampoo, taboo, tattoo, too. Do you know any more?

torture **tortures**
NOUN **1** great physical pain that is deliberately caused to someone to punish them or get information from them.
2 Mental torture is extreme emotional upset and anguish.
torture VERB **torturer** NOUN

toss **tosses tossing tossed**
VERB **1** to throw something lightly and carelessly.
2 If you toss a coin, you decide something by spinning a coin into the air and guessing which side will face upwards when it lands.
3 To toss and turn is to sleep badly, moving continually from side to side.

Synonyms: (sense 1) fling, sling, throw

total **totals totalling totalled**
NOUN **1** the number you get when you add several numbers together.
VERB **2** When you total a set of numbers or objects, you add them all together.
ADJECTIVE **3** complete: *a total surprise.*
totally ADVERB

Synonyms: (sense 1) aggregate, sum, whole

totem pole **totem poles**
NOUN a long wooden pole with symbols and pictures carved and painted on it, traditional to Native Americans.

totter **totters tottering tottered**
VERB to walk in an unsteady way.

toucan **toucans**
Said "**too**-kan" NOUN a large tropical bird with a very large beak.

touch **touches touching touched**
VERB **1** If you touch something, you put your fingers or hand on it.
2 to come into contact. *The wires touched accidentally and the electrician flew across the room.*
3 If you are touched by something, you are emotionally affected by it. *I was touched by his thoughtfulness.*
NOUN **4** Your sense of touch is your ability to tell what something is like by touching it.
5 a detail which is added to improve something: *the finishing touch.*
6 a small amount of something: *a touch of salt.*
PHRASE **7** If you are **in touch with** someone, you are in contact with them.
8 If a situation is **touch and go**, it is very risky and critical.

touchdown **touchdowns**
NOUN the landing of an aircraft or spacecraft.

touching
ADJECTIVE causing feelings of sadness and sympathy; moving, poignant.

touchy **touchier touchiest**
ADJECTIVE **1** If someone is touchy, they are easily upset or irritated.
2 A touchy subject is one that needs to be dealt with carefully, because it might upset or offend people.

tough **tougher toughest**
Said "**tuff**" ADJECTIVE **1** A tough person is strong and able to put up with hardship.
2 Something that is tough is strong and difficult to break: *tough plastic.*
3 A tough task or way of life is difficult or full of hardship.
4 Tough actions are strict and firm.
toughly ADVERB **toughness** NOUN

Synonyms: (sense 2) durable, resilient, strong

toughen **toughens toughening toughened**
VERB to become tougher or to make something tougher.

tour **tours**
NOUN **1** a short trip round a place such as a city or famous building.
2 a long journey during which you visit several places.
tour VERB

tourist **tourists**
NOUN a person who visits places for pleasure or interest.
tourism NOUN

tournament **tournaments**
NOUN a sports competition in which players who win a match play further matches, until just one person or team is left as the winner.

tow **tows towing towed**
VERB If a vehicle tows another vehicle, it pulls it along behind it.
tow NOUN

towards
PREPOSITION **1** in the direction of. *She turned towards the door.*
2 about or involving. *My feelings towards poetry have changed.*
3 a contribution for: *a donation towards the opera house.*
4 near to. *We sat towards the back.*

towel **towels**
NOUN a piece of thick, soft cloth that you use to dry yourself with.

tower **towers towering towered**
NOUN **1** a tall, narrow building, sometimes attached to a larger building such as a castle or church.
VERB **2** If somebody towers over you, they are much taller than you are.
towering ADJECTIVE

town **towns**
NOUN a place with many streets and buildings where people live and work, and the central shopping and business part of that place.

town hall **town halls**
NOUN the chief building from which a town council organizes the town's public services.

a b c d e f g h i j k l m n o p q r s t u v w x y z

Pair these up with words on this page: centre, and go, Blackpool, the caber, luck.

A B C D E F G H I J K L M N O P Q R S T U V W X Y Z

towpath towpaths
NOUN a path along the side of a canal or river.

toxic
ADJECTIVE poisonous: *toxic waste.*
[from Greek *toxikon* meaning poison for putting on arrows]

toy toys toying toyed
NOUN 1 any object made to play with.
VERB 2 If you toy with an object, you fiddle with it. *Samantha was constantly toying with her glasses.*
3 If you toy with a plan, you consider it without being very serious about it. *Mike toyed with the idea of going for a run.*

trace traces tracing traced
VERB 1 to find something after looking for it. *We traced the owner of the lost puppy.*
2 If you trace a picture, diagram, etc., you copy its outline by drawing over it on transparent paper.
NOUN 3 a sign that shows you that someone or something has been there.
4 a very small amount of something.

track tracks tracking tracked
NOUN 1 a narrow road or path.
2 a strip of ground with rails on it that a train travels along.
3 a piece of ground, shaped like a ring, which horses, cars or athletes race around.
VERB 4 If you track animals or people, you go after them by following their footprints or other signs they have left behind.
5 If you track down someone or something, you find them after a search.

tracksuit tracksuits
NOUN a loose, warm suit of trousers and a top, for outdoor sports or casual wear.

tractor tractors
NOUN a vehicle with large wheels that is used on a farm for pulling machinery and other heavy loads.

trade trades trading traded
NOUN 1 the activity of buying, selling or exchanging goods or services.
2 If someone has a trade, they are skilled in a type of practical work. *He was a builder by trade.*
VERB 3 to buy, sell or exchange goods or services.
trader NOUN

trademark trademarks
NOUN a name or symbol that a manufacturer always uses on its products. Trademarks are usually protected by law so that no one else can use them.

trade union trade unions
NOUN an organization of workers who meet with their employers to represent the workers' interests.

tradition traditions
NOUN a custom or belief that has existed for a long time without changing.

traditional
ADJECTIVE 1 Traditional customs, beliefs or stories have existed for a long time without changing.
2 A traditional organization or institution is one in which older methods are are used rather than modern ones.
traditionally ADVERB

traffic traffics trafficking trafficked
NOUN 1 the movement of vehicles or people along a route at a particular time.
VERB 2 Someone who traffics in drugs or other goods buys and sells them illegally.

traffic lights
PLURAL NOUN the red, amber and green lights used to control traffic at junctions.

traffic warden traffic wardens
NOUN a person whose job is to make sure that cars are not parked in the wrong place or for longer than is allowed.

tragedy tragedies
Said "**traj**-id-ee" NOUN 1 an event or situation that is disastrous or very sad.
2 a serious story or play, that usually ends with the death of the main character.

tragic
ADJECTIVE Something tragic is very sad because it involves death, suffering or disaster.
tragically ADVERB

trail trails trailing trailed
NOUN 1 a rough path across open country or through forests.
2 a series of marks or other signs left by someone or something as they move along.
VERB 3 If you trail something or it trails, it drags along behind you as you move or it hangs down loosely.

trailer trailers
NOUN 1 a small vehicle which can be loaded with things and pulled behind a car.
2 A trailer for a film or a television or radio programme is a set of short extracts from it, which are shown in order to advertise it.

train trains training trained
NOUN 1 a number of carriages or trucks which move along a railway track.
VERB 2 to learn how to do a particular job.
3 If you train for a sports match or a race, you prepare for it by doing exercises.
training NOUN

trainer trainers
NOUN 1 Trainers are special shoes for running, jogging or casual wear.
2 a person who trains someone in sport or physical fitness.

 ► The adverb of tragic is tragically. Find five other "-ic" words that add "-ally" to make their adverb.

traitor traitors
NOUN someone who betrays their country or the group which they belong to.
traitorous ADJECTIVE **traitorously** ADVERB

tram trams
NOUN a vehicle which runs on rails along the street and is powered by electricity from an overhead wire.

tramp tramps tramping tramped
NOUN 1 a person who has no home, no job and very little money.
VERB 2 If you tramp from one place to another, you walk with slow, heavy footsteps.

trample tramples trampling trampled
VERB If you trample on something, you tread heavily on it so that it is damaged.

trampoline trampolines
NOUN a large piece of strong cloth held taut by springs in a frame, on which gymnasts jump and somersault.

trance trances
NOUN a mental state in which someone seems to be asleep but is conscious enough to be aware of their surroundings and to respond to questions and commands. See **hypnotize**.

tranquil
Said "**trang**-kwil" ADJECTIVE calm and peaceful.
tranquillity NOUN

tranquillizer tranquillizers; also spelt **tranquilliser**
NOUN a drug that makes people feel less anxious or nervous.

trans-
PREFIX across, through or beyond.

transaction transactions
NOUN a business deal which involves buying, selling or the transfer of money.

transatlantic
ADJECTIVE on, crossing, or on the other side of the Atlantic, especially to do with America.

transfer transfers transferring transferred
VERB 1 to move something or someone from one place to another.
NOUN 2 the act of moving someone or something from one place to another. *The player asked for a transfer.*
3 a piece of paper with a design on one side which can be ironed or pressed onto cloth, paper or china.
transferable ADJECTIVE

transform transforms transforming transformed
VERB If something is transformed, it is changed completely.
transformation NOUN

transformer transformers
NOUN a device for increasing or decreasing an electrical current.

transfusion transfusions
NOUN A transfusion or blood transfusion is a process in which blood from a healthy person is injected into the body of another person who is badly injured or ill.

transistor transistors
NOUN 1 a small electrical device in something such as a television or radio which is used to control electric currents.
2 A transistor or a transistor radio is a small portable radio.

transition transitions
NOUN a change from one form or state to another: *the transition from failure to success.*
transitional ADJECTIVE

translate translates translating translated
VERB To translate something that someone has said or written is to say it or write it in a different language.
translation NOUN **translator** NOUN

translucent
ADJECTIVE If an object or substance is translucent, it will allow light through, but you cannot see through it. See **opaque**, **transparent**.

transmit transmits transmitting transmitted
VERB to send an electronic signal by radio waves.
transmission NOUN

transmitter transmitters
NOUN a device for sending radio or television signals over a distance.

transparency transparencies
NOUN a small piece of photographic film which can be projected onto a screen.

transparent
ADJECTIVE 1 If an object or substance is transparent, you can see through it.
2 If something such as a statement, situation or feeling is transparent, it is easily understood or recognized. See **opaque**, **translucent**.
transparently ADVERB

transpire transpires transpiring transpired
VERB; FORMAL 1 When it transpires that something is the case, people discover that it is true.
2 When plants transpire they lose water, in vapour form, through their leaves.

transplant transplants transplanting transplanted
VERB 1 to remove a plant from one location and replant it in another.
2 the removal by a surgeon of a part from one person's body to put it in another.
transplant NOUN

transport
NOUN 1 the moving of goods or people from one place to another.
2 a general name for vehicles that you travel in: *public transport.*
transport VERB

Words beginning with "trans-" always have the idea of "across" in their meaning.

A B C D E F G H I J K L M N O P Q R S T U V W X Y Z

trap **traps trapping trapped**
NOUN 1 a piece of equipment or a hole used to catch animals.
2 a trick that is intended to catch or deceive someone.
VERB 3 to catch someone or something using a trap.
4 If you are trapped somewhere, you cannot move or escape for some reason.

trap door **trap doors**
NOUN a small horizontal door in a floor, ceiling or stage.

trapeze **trapezes**
NOUN a bar of wood or metal hanging from two ropes on which acrobats and gymnasts swing and perform skilful movements.

trapezium **trapeziums** or **trapezia**
Said "trap-**pee**-zee-um" **NOUN** a four-sided shape with two sides parallel to each other.

trash
NOUN rubbish.

traumatic
Said "traw-**mat**-ik" **ADJECTIVE** A traumatic experience is very powerful, distressing and long-lasting in its effect.
traumatize VERB

travel **travels travelling travelled**
VERB 1 to go from one place to another, to journey.
PLURAL NOUN 2 Someone's travels are the journeys that they make to places a long way from their home.
travel NOUN **traveller** NOUN

trawler **trawlers**
NOUN a deep-sea fishing boat that catches fish by trailing a type of large net bag behind it.
trawlerman NOUN

tray **trays**
NOUN a flat object with raised edges which is used for carrying food or drinks.

treacherous
ADJECTIVE 1 A treacherous person is likely to betray you and cannot be trusted.
2 The ground, the sea or conditions of different sorts can be described as treacherous when they are dangerous or unreliable.
treacherously ADVERB **treachery** NOUN

Synonyms: (sense 1) disloyal, untrustworthy

treacle
NOUN a thick, sweet syrup used to make cakes and toffee.
treacly ADJECTIVE

tread **treads treading trod trodden**
VERB 1 to walk or step on something.
NOUN 2 A person's tread is the sound they make with their feet as they walk.
3 The tread of a tyre or shoe is the pattern of ridges on it that stops it slipping.

treason
NOUN the crime of betraying your country, for example, by helping its enemies.

treasure **treasures treasuring treasured**
NOUN 1 a collection of gold, silver, jewels or other precious objects, especially one that has been hidden.
2 Treasures are valuable works of art or other artefacts.
VERB 3 If you treasure something, you think it is very special. *She treasures the signed photograph of her favourite pop star.*
treasured ADJECTIVE

treasurer **treasurers**
NOUN a person who is in charge of the finance and accounts of an organization.

treasury **treasuries**
NOUN 1 a secure place where valuable things are kept, often for display.
2 The Treasury is the government department that deals with the country's finances.

treat **treats treating treated**
VERB 1 If you treat someone or something in a particular way, you behave that way towards them.
2 When a doctor treats a patient or an illness, he or she gives them medical care and attention.
3 If you treat someone to something, you buy or arrange something special for them.
4 If something such as wood or cloth is treated, a special substance is put on it in order to protect it or give it special properties. *The carpet was treated with stain protector.*
treat NOUN

treatment **treatments**
NOUN 1 the application of medical or other therapies to someone who is sick or injured.
2 the way in which something is dealt with or handled: *fair treatment.*

treaty **treaties**
NOUN a written agreement between countries in which they agree to do something or to help each other.

treble **trebles trebling trebled**
VERB to become three times greater in number or amount.
treble ADJECTIVE

tree **trees**
NOUN a large plant with a hard trunk, branches and leaves.

trek **treks trekking trekked**
VERB to go on a long and difficult journey.
trek NOUN
[an Afrikaans word]

trellis **trellises**
NOUN a frame made of horizontal and vertical strips of wood or metal and used to support plants.

 ► Drivers travelling overseas must put their country's International Vehicle Registration sticker on their car. ►

tremble **trembles trembling trembled**
VERB to shake slightly, usually because you are frightened or cold.
trembling ADJECTIVE

tremendous
ADJECTIVE **1** large or impressive.
2 INFORMAL very good or pleasing: *tremendous fun.*
tremendously ADVERB

tremor **tremors**
NOUN **1** a small earthquake.
2 a shaking of your body or in your voice which you cannot control.

trench **trenches**
NOUN a long narrow channel dug into the ground.

trend **trends**
NOUN a change in an attempt to do or be something different, a fashion. *Ripped jeans are the latest trend.*

trendy **trendier trendiest**
ADJECTIVE; INFORMAL fashionable.
trendily ADVERB **trendiness** NOUN

trespass **trespasses trespassing trespassed**
VERB to go onto someone's private land or property without permission.
trespasser NOUN

tri-
PREFIX three.

trial **trials**
NOUN **1** an experiment in which something is tested.
2 a court case where an accused person is tried by a judge and jury.

triangle **triangles**
NOUN **1** a shape with three straight sides.
2 a percussion instrument consisting of a thin steel bar bent in the shape of a triangle. See **equilateral**, **isosceles**, **scalene**.
triangular ADJECTIVE

tribe **tribes**
NOUN a group of people of the same race, who have the same customs, religion, language or land.
tribal ADJECTIVE

tributary **tributaries**
NOUN a stream or river that flows into a larger river.

tribute **tributes**
NOUN **1** something said or done to show admiration and respect for someone. *The police paid tribute to her courage.*
2 If one thing is a tribute to another, it is the result of the other thing and shows how good it is. *The group's success was a tribute to the hard work of their producer.*

trick **tricks tricking tricked**
VERB **1** If someone tricks you, they deceive you.
NOUN **2** an action done to deceive someone.
3 Tricks are clever or skilful actions by magicians that are done in order to entertain people.
4 In card games such as whist or bridge, a trick is the cards won in one round of play.
trickery NOUN

trickle **trickles trickling trickled**
VERB When a liquid trickles somewhere, it flows slowly in a thin stream.
trickle NOUN

tricky **trickier trickiest**
ADJECTIVE difficult to do or deal with.
trickily ADVERB

tricycle **tricycles**
NOUN a vehicle similar to a bicycle but with two wheels at the back and one at the front.

tried
past tense and past participle of **try**.

trifle **trifles trifling trifled**
NOUN **1** A trifle means a little. *He seemed a trifle annoyed.*
2 something that is not very important or valuable. *Don't worry – it's a trifle.*
3 a cold pudding made of layers of sponge cake, fruit, jelly and custard.
VERB **4** If you trifle with someone or something, you treat them in a disrespectful way. *She trifled with his emotions.*

trigger **triggers triggering triggered**
NOUN **1** the small lever on a gun which is pulled in order to fire it.
VERB **2** If something triggers an event, or triggers it off, it causes it to happen.

trillion **trillions**
NOUN **1** a million million.
2 INFORMAL Trillions of things means an extremely large number of them.
✔ In Britain a trillion used to mean a million million million.

trilogy **trilogies**
NOUN a series of three books or plays that have the same characters or are on the same subject.

trim **trims trimming trimmed; trimmer trimmest**
VERB **1** to cut small amounts off something.
NOUN **2** a decoration along the edges of something: *a coat with a fur trim.*
ADJECTIVE **3** neat and attractive. *The gardens are tidy and trim.*
PHRASE **4** If you are **in trim**, you are in good health and shape.
trimly ADVERB **trimming** NOUN

Trinity
NOUN In the Christian religion, the Trinity is the three-in-one concept of God the Father, God the Son and God the Holy Spirit.

trinket **trinkets**
NOUN a cheap ornament or piece of jewellery.

trio trios
NOUN **1** a group of three musicians who sing or play together, also a piece of music written for three instruments or singers.
2 any group of three things or people together.

trip trips tripping tripped
NOUN **1** a journey made to a place.
VERB **2** If you trip or trip over, you catch your foot on something and fall over.
3 If you trip someone or trip them up, you make them fall over by making them catch their foot on something.

Synonyms: (sense 1) excursion, journey, outing

tripe
NOUN **1** the stomach lining of a pig, cow or ox, which is cooked and eaten.
2 INFORMAL anything that you consider to be silly or worthless.

triple triples tripling tripled
ADJECTIVE **1** consisting of three things or three parts.
VERB **2** If you triple something or if it triples, it becomes three times greater in number or size.

triple jump
NOUN an athletics event in which you do a hop, step and jump after taking a long run.

triplet triplets
NOUN Triplets are three children born at the same time to the same mother.

tripod tripods
Said "**try**-pod" NOUN a stand with three legs used to support something like a camera or telescope.

triumph triumphs
NOUN a great success or achievement, and the resulting feeling of great satisfaction.
triumph VERB

triumphant
ADJECTIVE Someone who is triumphant is very happy because they have won a victory or have achieved something.
triumphantly ADVERB

trivial
ADJECTIVE unimportant.
triviality NOUN

trod
past tense of **tread**.

trodden
past participle of **tread**.

troll trolls
NOUN an imaginary creature in fairy stories that lives in caves or mountains and is believed to turn to stone at daylight.

trolley trolleys
NOUN a small cart on wheels used for carrying heavy objects.

trombone trombones
NOUN a brass wind instrument with a U-shaped slide which you move to produce different notes.
trombonist NOUN

troop troops trooping trooped
PLURAL NOUN **1** Troops are soldiers.
NOUN **2** A troop of people or animals is a group of them.
VERB **3** If people troop somewhere, they go there on foot in a group.

trophy trophies
NOUN a cup or shield given as a prize to the winner of a competition.

tropical
ADJECTIVE belonging to or typical of the tropics.

tropics
PLURAL NOUN The tropics are the hottest parts of the world, situated between two lines of latitude, the Tropic of Cancer, $23\frac{1}{2}^{\circ}$ north of the equator, and the Tropic of Capricorn, $23\frac{1}{2}^{\circ}$ south of the equator.

trot trots trotting trotted
VERB **1** When a horse trots, it moves at a speed between a walk and a canter, lifting its feet quite high off the ground.
NOUN **2** a run or jog using small quick steps.
PHRASE **3** INFORMAL If things happen **on the trot**, they happen one after the other: *his fourth victory on the trot.*
trot out VERB If you trot out information or ideas, you repeat them in a boring way.

trouble troubles troubling troubled
NOUN **1** Troubles are difficulties or problems.
2 If there is trouble, people are arguing or fighting.
PHRASE **3** If you are **in trouble**, you are in a situation where you may be punished because you have done something wrong.
VERB **4** If something troubles you, it makes you feel worried or anxious.
5 If you trouble someone for something, you disturb them in order to ask them for it.
troubling ADJECTIVE **troubled** ADJECTIVE

Synonyms: (sense 5) bother, inconvenience

troublesome
ADJECTIVE causing problems or difficulties.

trough troughs
Said "**troff**" NOUN a long, narrow container from which animals drink or feed.

trousers
PLURAL NOUN a piece of clothing covering the body from the waist down, enclosing each leg separately.

trout
NOUN a type of freshwater fish.

trowel trowels
NOUN a small tool with a pointed blade used for gardening or spreading cement or plaster.

 ► Joke. How do you make trousers last? Make the jacket first.

truant **truants**
NOUN **1** a child who stays away from school without permission.
PHRASE **2** If children **play truant**, they stay away from school without permission.
truancy NOUN

truce **truces**
NOUN an agreement between two people or groups to stop fighting for a short time.

truck **trucks**
NOUN a large motor vehicle used for carrying heavy loads, a lorry.

trudge **trudges trudging trudged**
VERB **1** to walk with slow, heavy steps.
NOUN **2** a slow tiring walk: *the long trudge home.*

true **truer truest**
ADJECTIVE **1** factually correct and not invented, accurate.
2 real and genuine. *She was a true friend.*
PHRASE **3** If something **comes true**, something you have dreamed of or thought about actually happens.
truly ADVERB

trump **trumps**
NOUN **1** In a game of cards, trumps is one of the four suits chosen to have a higher value than the others, and a card belonging to that suit.
PHRASE **2** Your **trump card** is the most powerful thing that you can use or do to gain an advantage.
trump VERB

trumpet **trumpets trumpeting trumpeted**
NOUN **1** a brass wind instrument with a narrow tube ending in a bell-like shape.
VERB **2** to make a loud noise like an elephant.
trumpeter NOUN

truncheon **truncheons**
Said "**trunt**-shn" NOUN a short, thick stick that policemen carry as a weapon.

trundle **trundles trundling trundled**
VERB If you trundle something or it trundles somewhere, it moves or rolls along slowly.

trunk **trunks**
NOUN **1** the main stem of a tree from which the branches and roots grow.
2 the long, flexible nose of an elephant.
3 a large, strong case or box with a hinged lid, used for storing things.
PLURAL NOUN **4** A man's trunks are his bathing pants or shorts.

trust **trusts trusting trusted**
VERB **1** If you trust someone, you believe that they are honest and will not harm you.
2 If you trust someone to do something, you believe they will do it.
NOUN **3** the responsibility you are given to deal with or look after important or secret things.
trusting ADJECTIVE

trustworthy
ADJECTIVE reliable, responsible and able to be trusted.
trustworthiness NOUN

truth **truths**
NOUN the facts about something, rather than things that are imagined or invented; reality. *I know she was telling the truth.*

truthful
ADJECTIVE A truthful person is honest and tells the truth.
truthfully ADVERB **truthfulness** NOUN

try **tries trying tried**
VERB **1** to make an effort to do something.
2 to test how useful or enjoyable something is. *The waiter asked Howard to try the wine.*
3 When a person is tried, they appear in court and a judge and jury decide if they are guilty.
NOUN **4** an attempt to do something, a go or shot at doing something.
try on VERB If you try on a piece of clothing, you wear it to see if it fits you or if it looks nice.
✔ You can use *try to* in speech and writing: *try to get here on time for once. Try and* is very common is speech, but you should avoid it in written work.

Synonyms: (sense 1) attempt, endeavour, strive

T-shirt **T-shirts**; also spelt **tee shirt**
NOUN a simple, light, short-sleeved cotton shirt with no collar or fastenings.

tub **tubs**
NOUN a wide, circular container.

tuba **tubas**
NOUN a large brass musical instrument that can produce very low notes.

tubby **tubbier tubbiest**
ADJECTIVE rather fat.

tube **tubes**
NOUN **1** a long, hollow cylindrical object like a pipe.
2 a long, thin container: *a tube of toothpaste.*
tubing NOUN

tuck **tucks tucking tucked**
VERB **1** If you tuck something somewhere, you put it there so that it is safe or comfortable. *She tucked the letter into her handbag.*
2 to push the loose ends of fabric inside or under something to make it tidy. *He tucked his shirt into his trousers.*
3 If something is tucked away, it is in a quiet place where few people go. *We found a little house tucked away in a valley.*

tuck shop **tuck shops**
NOUN a small shop in a school that sells snacks and sweets to the pupils.

a b c d e f g h i j k l m n o p q r s t u v w x y z

"She is always blowing her own trumpet." You might know someone like this. What does it mean?

Tuesday **Tuesdays**
NOUN the day between Monday and Wednesday.
[from Old English *tiwesdoeg* meaning Tiw's day; Tiw was the Scandinavian god of war and the sky]

tuft **tufts**
NOUN A tuft of something such as hair is a bunch of it growing closely together.
tufted ADJECTIVE **tufty** ADJECTIVE

tug **tugs tugging tugged**
VERB **1** to give something a quick, hard pull.
NOUN **2** a quick, hard pull.
3 a small, very powerful boat that is used to tow larger ships.

tug-of-war
NOUN a contest in which two teams test their strength by pulling against each other on opposite ends of a rope.

tulip **tulips**
NOUN a brightly coloured spring flower.
[from Turkish *tulbend* meaning turban, because of its shape]

tumble **tumbles tumbling tumbled**
VERB to fall with a rolling or bouncing movement.
tumble NOUN

tumbler **tumblers**
NOUN **1** a drinking glass with straight sides.
2 an acrobat who performs on the ground, often with other members of a group.

tummy **tummies**
NOUN; INFORMAL stomach.

tumour **tumours**
Said "**tyoo**-mur" NOUN a mass of diseased or abnormal cells that has grown in a person's or animal's body.

tuna
Said "**tyoo**-na" NOUN Tuna are large fish that live in warm seas and are caught for food.

tundra
NOUN a vast, treeless, frozen Arctic region.

tune **tunes tuning tuned**
NOUN **1** a series of musical notes arranged in a particular way, usually to make a pleasant sound.
VERB **2** To tune a musical instrument is to adjust it so that it produces the right notes.
3 If you tune into a particular radio or television station, you turn or press the controls to select the station you want to listen to or watch.
PHRASE **4** If you sing **in tune**, your voice produces the right notes.

tuneful
ADJECTIVE having a pleasant and easily remembered tune.

tunic **tunics**
NOUN a sleeveless garment covering the top part of the body and reaching to the hips, thighs, or knees.

tunnel **tunnels tunnelling tunnelled**
VERB to dig or bore a long underground passage.
tunnel NOUN **tunneller** NOUN

turban **turbans**
NOUN a head-covering worn by a Hindu, Muslim or Sikh man, consisting of a long piece of cloth wound round his head.

turbine **turbines**
NOUN a machine or engine in which power is produced when a stream of air, water or steam pushes the blades of a wheel and makes it turn round.

turbulence
NOUN **1** a state of very unsettled air currents with unpredictable gusts of wind.
2 a state of confusion, movement and agitation.
turbulent ADJECTIVE

turf **turfs** or **turves; turfs turfing turfed**
NOUN **1** short thick even grass and the layer of soil beneath it.
VERB **2** To turf an area of ground means to lay turf on it.
turf out VERB; INFORMAL to force someone to leave a place.

turkey **turkeys**
NOUN a large bird kept for food; also the meat of this bird.

turn **turns turning turned**
VERB **1** to move yourself or something else so that you or it are facing or going in a different direction.
2 When something turns or is turned into something else, it becomes something different.
3 If you turn your attention or thoughts to someone or something, you start thinking about them or discussing them.
NOUN **4** an act of turning. *Take a right turn here.*
5 a change in the way something is happening or being done. *Her career took a turn for the better.*
6 If it is your turn to do something, you have the right, chance or duty to do it.
PHRASE **7 In turn** means in sequence, one after the other. *She spoke to each student in turn.*
turn down VERB to refuse or reject a request or an offer.
turn on VERB to cause heat, sound or water to be produced by using the controls.
turn over VERB **1** to move something so that the top part faces downwards.
2 If you turn over a new leaf, you decide to change your behaviour for the better.
turn up VERB to arrive or appear somewhere.

Synonyms: (sense 6) chance, go, opportunity

 ► Some words from Turkish: turban, tulip, kiosk, coffee, horse.

turnip turnips
NOUN a round root vegetable with a white or yellow skin.

turnstile turnstiles
NOUN a revolving mechanical barrier you pass through to enter somewhere.

turquoise
Said "**tur**-kwoyz" ADJECTIVE OR NOUN a light bluish green colour.

turret turrets
NOUN 1 a small narrow tower on top of a larger tower or other buildings.
2 a revolving structure on tanks and warships, on which guns are mounted.

turtle turtles
NOUN a large reptile with a thick shell covering its body and flippers for swimming. It lays its eggs on land but lives the rest of its life in the sea.

tusk tusks
NOUN The tusks of an elephant, wild boar or walrus are the pair of long curving pointed teeth it has.

tussle tussles
NOUN an energetic fight or argument between two people, especially about something they both want.
tussle VERB

tutor tutors
NOUN a private teacher.
tutor VERB

TV TVs
NOUN a television or television set.

tweak tweaks tweaking tweaked
VERB 1 to twist or pull something.
2 INFORMAL to make adjustments to something in order to improve it. *I think the engine needs tweaking.*
tweak NOUN

tweed tweeds
NOUN a thick woollen cloth.

tweet tweets tweeting tweeted
VERB to make a short, high-pitched sound like a bird.
tweet NOUN

tweezers
PLURAL NOUN Tweezers are a small tool with two arms which can be closed together by finger and thumb, and are used for pulling out hairs or picking up small objects.

twelve
the number 12.
twelfth

twenty twenties
the number 20.
twentieth

twice
ADVERB two times.

twiddle twiddles twiddling twiddled
VERB to twist or turn something quickly.

twig twigs twigging twigged
NOUN 1 a very small thin branch growing from a main branch of a tree or bush.
VERB 2 INFORMAL If you twig something, you realize or understand something.

twilight
Said "**twy**-lite" NOUN 1 the time after sunset when it is just getting dark.
2 the final stages of something: *the twilight of your career.*

twin twins twinned twinning
NOUN 1 If two people are twins, they have the same mother and were born on the same day.
2 "Twin" is used to describe two similar things that are close together or happen together: *a building with twin towers.*
VERB 3 to link one town with one in another country. If towns are twinned, they exchange cultural visits.

twine twines twining twined
NOUN 1 a type of string.
VERB 2 If you twine one thing round another, you twist or wind it round.

twinge twinges
NOUN a sudden, unpleasant feeling.

twinkle twinkles twinkling twinkled
VERB 1 to sparkle or seem to sparkle with an unsteady light.
NOUN 2 a sparkle or brightness that something has. *The kind old lady always had a twinkle in her eyes.*
twinkly ADJECTIVE

twirl twirls twirling twirled
VERB to spin or twist round and round.

twist twists twisting twisted
VERB 1 When you twist something, you turn the two ends in opposite directions. *Matilda twisted the lid off the jar.*
2 to move or bend into a strange shape. *Leon twisted the carrier bag into a knot.*
3 If you twist, you turn a part of your body while keeping the rest still.
4 You can say that you twist a part of your body if you injure it by turning it too sharply or in an unusual direction. *I've twisted my ankle.*
5 If you twist what somebody has said, you change the meaning slightly in telling someone else.
NOUN 6 a twisting action or motion.
7 an unexpected development or event in a story or film, especially at the end.

Synonyms: (sense 1) screw, coil, wind
(sense 2) contort, distort

twit twits
NOUN; INFORMAL a silly person.

a b c d e f g h i j k l m n o p q r s t u v w x y z

A B C D E F G H I J K L M N O P Q R S T U V W X Y Z

twitch **twitches twitching twitched**
VERB to make little jerky movements which you cannot control.
twitch NOUN **twitchy** ADJECTIVE

twitter **twitters twittering twittered**
VERB **1** When birds twitter, they make short high-pitched sounds.
2 If someone twitters, they speak very fast in a high-pitched voice.

two
the number 2.

two-dimensional
ADJECTIVE having only two dimensions, length and width; abbreviated to "2D".

two-faced
ADJECTIVE A two-faced person is not honest in the way they behave towards other people.

tying
present participle of **tie**.

type **types typing typed**
NOUN **1** A type of something is a group of those things that have the same qualities. *What type of dog should we get?*
VERB **2** to write using a typewriter or word processor, to key in.

Synonyms: (sense 1) kind, sort, variety

typewriter **typewriters**
NOUN a machine with keys which are pressed in order to produce letters and numbers on a page.
typewritten ADJECTIVE

typhoon **typhoons**
NOUN a very violent tropical storm.
[from Chinese *tai fung* meaning great wind]

typical
ADJECTIVE showing the most usual characteristics or behaviour of a particular person or type, characteristic.
typically ADVERB

Synonyms: characteristic, standard, usual

typist **typists**
NOUN a person whose job is typing.

tyrannosaurus **tyrannosauruses**
Said "tir-ran-oh-**saw**-russ" NOUN a very large meat-eating dinosaur which walked upright on its hind legs.

tyrant **tyrants**
NOUN a person in power who treats the people they have under them cruelly and unjustly.
tyranny NOUN

tyre **tyres**
NOUN a thick ring of rubber fitted round each wheel of a vehicle and filled with air.

► These phrases are always written as two separate words: in case, a lot, as well, no one.

Uu

udder **udders**
NOUN the baglike organ that hangs below a cow's body and produces milk.

UFO **UFOs**
NOUN a strange object seen in the sky which some people believe to be an alien spaceship. UFO is an abbreviation of unidentified flying object.

ugly **uglier ugliest**
ADJECTIVE very unattractive and unpleasant.

ulcer **ulcers**
NOUN a sore area on the skin or inside the body, which takes a long time to heal.

ultimate
ADJECTIVE **1** final or eventual: *the ultimate battle in the war.*
2 most important or powerful: *my ultimate ambition.*
NOUN **3** You can refer to the best or most advanced example of something as the ultimate: *the ultimate in bikes.*
ultimately ADVERB

ultraviolet
ADJECTIVE Ultraviolet light is not visible to the human eye. It is a form of radiation that causes your skin to darken on exposure to the sun.

umbrella **umbrellas**
NOUN a folding device that you use to protect yourself from the rain.

umpire **umpires**
NOUN The umpire in cricket or tennis is the person who makes sure that the game is played fairly and the rules of the game are not broken.
umpire VERB

un-
PREFIX "Un-" is added to the beginning of many words to form a word with the opposite meaning.

unable
ADJECTIVE If you are unable to do something you cannot do it.

unacceptable
ADJECTIVE too bad, or of too low a standard, to be acceptable.
unacceptably ADVERB

unaccustomed
ADJECTIVE not used to doing or experiencing something.

unaided
ADVERB OR ADJECTIVE without help.

unanimous
Said "yoon-**nan**-nim-mus" ADJECTIVE When people are unanimous, they all agree about something.
unanimously ADVERB **unanimity** NOUN

unattended
ADJECTIVE not being watched or looked after. *Do not leave your bags unattended in the airport.*

unauthorized or **unauthorised**
ADJECTIVE done without official permission.

unavoidable
ADJECTIVE An unavoidable occurrence is one that you cannot prevent.
unavoidably ADVERB

unaware
ADJECTIVE If you are unaware of something, you do not know about it.

unbearable
ADJECTIVE Something unbearable is so unpleasant or upsetting that you feel unable to put up with it.
unbearably ADVERB

Synonyms: insufferable, intolerable

unbeatable
ADJECTIVE Something that is unbeatable is the best thing of its kind.

unbelievable
ADJECTIVE **1** extremely great. *He won an unbelievable amount of money.*
2 so surprising and unlikely that you cannot believe it.
unbelievably ADVERB

Synonyms: (sense 1) astonishing, incredible (sense 2) far-fetched, implausible

unblock **unblocks unblocking unblocked**
VERB to clear something which is blocked.

unbroken
ADJECTIVE continuous or complete: *an hour of unbroken silence.*

uncalled-for
ADJECTIVE A remark that is uncalled-for is unkind and unfair.

uncanny
ADJECTIVE strange and difficult to explain: *an uncanny resemblance.*
uncannily ADVERB

uncertain
ADJECTIVE **1** not knowing what to do.
2 doubtful or not known: *an uncertain future.*
uncertainly ADVERB **uncertainty** NOUN

uncle **uncles**
NOUN the brother of your mother or father, or the husband of your aunt.

a b c d e f g h i j k l m n o p q r s t u v w x y z

The letters U and W were developed from V, which seems to have been another form of hook.

A B C D E F G H I J K L M N O P Q R S T U V W X Y Z

unclear
ADJECTIVE confusing and not obvious.

uncomfortable
ADJECTIVE **1** not physically relaxed and feeling slight pain or discomfort.
2 slightly worried or embarrassed.
uncomfortably ADVERB

uncommon
ADJECTIVE **1** not happening often or not seen often.
2 unusually great: *uncommon interest.*
uncommonly ADVERB

unconscious
ADJECTIVE **1** asleep or in a state similar to sleep as a result of a shock, accident or injury.
2 not aware of something. *The train driver ate his sandwich, unconscious that he had passed a signal at red.*
unconsciously ADVERB

uncouth
Said "un-**kooth**" ADJECTIVE An uncouth person has bad manners and is unpleasant.

Synonyms: boorish, coarse, vulgar

uncover uncovers uncovering uncovered
VERB **1** to remove the cover or lid from something.
2 If you uncover a secret, you find it out.

undecided
ADJECTIVE If you are undecided, you have not yet made a decision about something.

undeniable
ADJECTIVE certainly true.
undeniably ADVERB

under
PREPOSITION **1** below or beneath.
2 You can use "under" to say that a person or thing is affected by a particular situation or condition: *under the influence of alcohol.*
3 less than: *children under the age of 14.*
PHRASE **4** **Under way** means already started.

under-
PREFIX used in words that describe something as not being sufficient.

underarm
ADVERB If you throw underarm, you throw a ball without raising your arm over your shoulder.

undercarriage undercarriages
NOUN the part of an aircraft, including the wheels, that supports the aircraft when it is on the ground.

underclothes
PLURAL NOUN the clothes that you wear under your other clothes and next to your skin; underwear.

undercover
ADJECTIVE involving secret work and disguise to obtain information.

underdog underdogs
NOUN The underdog in a competition is the person who seems likely to lose.

underdone
ADJECTIVE Underdone food has not been cooked for long enough.

underestimate underestimates underestimating underestimated
VERB If you underestimate something or someone, you do not realize how large or great or capable they are.

underfoot
ADJECTIVE OR ADVERB under your feet.

undergo undergoes undergoing underwent undergone
VERB to experience something necessary, unpleasant or both. *He recently had to undergo surgery.*

undergraduate undergraduates
NOUN a person at university studying for their first degree.

underground
ADJECTIVE **1** below the surface of the ground.
2 secret, unofficial and usually illegal: *an underground political movement.*
NOUN **3** a railway system in which trains travel mostly in tunnels below ground.

undergrowth
NOUN Small bushes and other plants growing under trees.

underhand
ADJECTIVE secret and dishonest.

underline underlines underlining underlined
VERB **1** to put a line under a word, sentence, etc.
2 to emphasize. *The report underlines the dangers of smoking.*

undermine undermines undermining undermined
VERB If you undermine what someone is trying to do, you make their position weaker and more difficult.

Synonyms: subvert, weaken

underneath
ADVERB OR PREPOSITION **1** below or beneath.
2 "Underneath" describes feelings and qualities that do not show in your behaviour. *Alex knew that underneath she was unhappy.*
ADJECTIVE **3** The underneath part of something is the part that touches or faces the ground.

underpants
PLURAL NOUN a piece of clothing worn by men and boys next to their skin, under their trousers.

underpass underpasses
NOUN a road or footpath that goes under a road or railway.

► In "uncouth" the "ou" makes an "oo" sound. Find more words where the same thing happens.

underprivileged
ADJECTIVE having less money and fewer opportunities than other people.

understand **understands understanding understood**
VERB **1** If you understand what someone says, you know what they mean.
2 If you understand a situation, you know what is happening and why.
3 If you say that you understand that something is the case, you mean that you have heard that it is the case. *I understand that she's a lot better now.*

Synonyms: comprehend, follow, grasp, see

understandable
ADJECTIVE If something is understandable, people can easily understand or sympathize with it.
understandably ADVERB

understanding **understandings**
NOUN **1** knowledge about something. *I have a basic understanding of computers.*
2 an informal agreement between people. *Joe and Kim reached an understanding about cleaning the flat.*
ADJECTIVE **3** kind and sympathetic: *an understanding doctor.*

Synonyms: (sense 1) comprehension, grasp, perception

understudy **understudies**
NOUN a junior actor who stands in for someone playing a leading role in a play if they are ill or unavailable.

undertake **undertakes undertaking undertook undertaken**
VERB to agree to do a task or job.
undertaking NOUN

undertaker **undertakers**
NOUN someone whose job is to prepare bodies for burial and arrange funerals.

underwater
ADVERB OR ADJECTIVE **1** beneath the surface of the sea, a river or a lake.
ADJECTIVE **2** designed to work under water: *an underwater watch.*

underwear
NOUN the clothing that you wear under your other clothes, next to your skin; underclothes.

underworld
NOUN **1** In the mythology of some cultures, the Underworld is a place where people's souls go to after death.
2 INFORMAL organized crime and the people who are involved in it.

undesirable
ADJECTIVE unwelcome and likely to cause harm: *undesirable behaviour.*

undeveloped
ADJECTIVE **1** An undeveloped country has little industry and does not use modern farming methods.
2 Undeveloped land has not yet been built on.

undo **undoes undoing undid undone**
VERB **1** to unfasten, loosen or untie something.
2 to reverse the effect of something that has been done.

undoubted
ADJECTIVE definite, sure.
undoubtedly ADVERB

undress **undresses undressing undressed**
VERB to take off your clothes.

unearth **unearths unearthing unearthed**
VERB to discover something that is hidden.

unearthly
ADJECTIVE strange and unnatural: *unearthly noises.*

uneasy
ADJECTIVE feeling worried that something may be wrong.
unease NOUN **uneasily** ADVERB
uneasiness NOUN

unemployed
ADJECTIVE without a job.
unemployment NOUN

unequal
ADJECTIVE **1** Unequal things are different in size, strength or ability.
2 An unequal society does not offer the same opportunities and privileges to all people.
unequally ADVERB

uneven
ADJECTIVE **1** not level or smooth.
2 not the same or consistent. *They received very uneven shares.*
unevenly ADVERB

unexpected
ADJECTIVE Something unexpected is surprising because it was not thought likely to happen.
unexpectedly ADVERB

unfair
ADJECTIVE not right or just.
unfairly ADVERB **unfairness** NOUN

unfaithful
ADJECTIVE An unfaithful person is not loyal and does not keep the promises or vows they have made (particularly to remain true to a lover).
unfaithfulness NOUN

unfamiliar
ADJECTIVE If something is unfamiliar, you have not seen, heard or done it before.
unfamiliarity NOUN

unfasten **unfastens unfastening unfastened**
VERB If you unfasten something, you undo its buttons, straps or clips.

A B C D E F G H I J K L M N O P Q R S T U V W X Y Z

unfit
ADJECTIVE **1** If you are unfit, your body is not in good condition because you have not been taking enough exercise.
2 not suitable for a particular purpose.

unfold **unfolds unfolding unfolded**
VERB **1** If you unfold something that has been folded, you open it out so that it is flat.
2 When a situation unfolds, it develops and becomes known.
unfolding ADJECTIVE

unforeseen
ADJECTIVE happening unexpectedly.

unforgettable
ADJECTIVE so good or so bad that you are unlikely to forget it.
unforgettably ADVERB

unforgivable
ADJECTIVE Something unforgivable is so bad or cruel that it can never be forgiven or justified.
unforgivably ADVERB

unfortunate
ADJECTIVE **1** unlucky.
2 If you describe an event as unfortunate, you mean that it is a pity that it happened: *an unfortunate accident.*
unfortunately ADVERB

unfriendly
ADJECTIVE not friendly, hostile.

ungrateful
ADJECTIVE not thankful for something that has been done for you or given to you.
ungratefulness NOUN

unhappy **unhappier unhappiest**
ADJECTIVE **1** sad and miserable.
2 not pleased or satisfied. *Carl was unhappy at being left out of the team.*
3 If you describe a situation as an unhappy one, you are sorry that it exists. *It was an unhappy state of affairs.*
unhappily ADVERB **unhappiness** NOUN

unhealthy
ADJECTIVE **1** likely to cause illness: *an unhealthy diet.*
2 An unhealthy person is often ill.

unheard-of
ADJECTIVE never having happened before and therefore surprising or shocking.

unicorn **unicorns**
NOUN an imaginary animal that looks like a white horse with a straight horn growing from its forehead.

uniform **uniforms**
NOUN **1** a special set of clothes worn by people at work or school.
ADJECTIVE **2** Something that is uniform does not vary but is even and regular throughout: *a uniform performance.*
uniformity NOUN

unify **unifies unifying unified**
VERB to bring a number of things together.
unification NOUN

unimportant
ADJECTIVE having very little significance or importance, minor or trivial.

uninhabited
ADJECTIVE An uninhabited place is a place where nobody lives; unoccupied.

unintentional
ADJECTIVE not done on purpose.

uninterested
ADJECTIVE If you are uninterested in something, you are not interested in it.
✔ *Uninterested* should not be confused with *disinterested* which means impartial or neutral.

uninterrupted
ADJECTIVE continuing without breaks or interruptions.

union **unions**
NOUN **1** an organization of workers that aims to improve the working conditions, pay and benefits of its members; a trade union.
2 When the union of two things takes place, they are joined together to become one thing.
[from Latin *unus* meaning one]

unique
Said "yoo-**neek**" ADJECTIVE **1** Something that is unique is the only one of its kind.
2 If something is unique to one person or thing, it concerns or belongs to that person or thing only.
uniquely ADVERB **uniqueness** NOUN
✔ Something is either *unique* or *not unique*, so you should avoid saying things like *rather unique* or *very unique.*

unisex
ADJECTIVE designed to be used by both men and women.

unison
NOUN If people sing in unison, they all sing the same notes, with no harmonies.

unit **units**
NOUN **1** a single complete thing; in arithmetic this is normally called a whole one.
2 a group of people who work together at a particular job.
3 a machine or piece of equipment which has a particular function: *a remote control unit.*
4 a fixed standard that is used for measuring things. *The metre is the standard unit of measurement.*
[from Latin *unus* meaning one]

unite **unites uniting united**
VERB If a number of people unite, they join together and act as a group.

 ► Many words of French origin make a "k" sound by ending with "-que". ◄

unity
NOUN Where there is unity, people are in agreement and act together for a particular purpose.

universal
ADJECTIVE concerning or relating to everyone in the world or every part of the universe.
universally ADVERB

universe **universes**
NOUN the whole of space, including all the stars and planets.

university **universities**
NOUN a place where students study for degrees.

unjust
ADJECTIVE not fair or reasonable.
unjustly ADVERB

unkempt
ADJECTIVE untidy and not looked after properly.

unkind
ADJECTIVE unpleasant and rather cruel.
unkindly ADVERB **unkindness** NOUN

Synonyms: cruel, nasty, uncharitable

unknown
ADJECTIVE 1 If someone or something is unknown, people do not know about them or have not heard of them.
NOUN 2 You can refer to things that people in general do not know about as the unknown.

unleaded
ADJECTIVE Unleaded petrol contains a greatly reduced amount of lead in order to reduce environmental pollution.

unless
CONJUNCTION You use "unless" to introduce the only circumstances in which something will not take place or is not true. *I will not give you a lift unless you help me wash up first.*

unlike
PREPOSITION If one thing is unlike another, the two things are different.

unlikely
ADJECTIVE 1 If something is unlikely, it is probably not true or probably will not happen.
2 strange and unexpected. *There are wonderful antiques in unlikely places.*

unlimited
ADJECTIVE If a supply of something is unlimited, you can have as much as you want or need.

unload **unloads unloading unloaded**
VERB 1 to remove things from a container or vehicle.
2 If you unload a problem or worry onto someone, you tell them about it.

unlock **unlocks unlocking unlocked**
VERB to open something by turning a key in a lock.

unlucky
ADJECTIVE Someone who is unlucky has bad luck.
unluckily ADVERB

Synonyms: hapless, unfortunate

unmistakable or **unmistakeable**
ADJECTIVE Something unmistakable is so obvious that it cannot be mistaken for something else.
unmistakably ADVERB

unnatural
ADJECTIVE 1 strange and rather frightening because it is not usual.
2 artificial and not typical. *My voice sounded high-pitched and unnatural.*
unnaturally ADVERB

unnecessary
ADJECTIVE not needed.
unnecessarily ADVERB

unoccupied
ADJECTIVE If a house is unoccupied, there is nobody living in it; uninhabited.

unofficial
ADJECTIVE without the approval or permission of a person in authority.
unofficially ADVERB

unpack **unpacks unpacking unpacked**
VERB to take everything out of a suitcase or bag.

unpleasant
ADJECTIVE 1 Something unpleasant causes you to have bad feelings, for example, by making you uncomfortable or upset.
2 unfriendly or rude.
unpleasantly ADVERB

unplug **unplugs unplugging unplugged**
VERB If you unplug an electrical appliance, you take the plug out of the socket.

unpopular
ADJECTIVE disliked by most people.

unpredictable
ADJECTIVE If someone or something is unpredictable, you never know how they will behave or what they are going to do.
unpredictably ADVERB **unpredictability** NOUN

unravel **unravels unravelling unravelled**
VERB 1 to unwind something that is twisted and knotted, to untangle.
2 If you unravel a mystery, you work out the answer to it.

unreal
ADJECTIVE so strange that you find it difficult to believe.

unreasonable
ADJECTIVE unfair and difficult to deal with.
unreasonably ADVERB

a b c d e f g h i j k l m n o p q r s t u v w x y z

unreliable
ADJECTIVE If people, machines or methods are unreliable, you cannot trust them to do what you want.

unrest
NOUN If there is unrest, people are angry and dissatisfied.

unroll unrolls unrolling unrolled
VERB If you unroll a roll of cloth or paper, you open it up and make it flat.

unruly
ADJECTIVE difficult to control or organize: *unruly children.*

unsafe
ADJECTIVE potentially dangerous or harmful.

unscathed
ADJECTIVE not injured or harmed as a result of a dangerous experience.

unscrew unscrews unscrewing unscrewed
VERB to remove something by turning it or by removing the screws that are holding it.

unseen
ADJECTIVE You use "unseen" to describe things that you cannot see or have not seen.

unselfish
ADJECTIVE concerned about other people's wishes and needs rather than your own.
unselfishly ADVERB

unsettled
ADJECTIVE If you feel unsettled, you feel restless and worried.
unsettling ADJECTIVE

unskilled
ADJECTIVE Unskilled work does not require any special training.

unsteady
ADJECTIVE **1** If you are unsteady, you have difficulty in controlling the movement of your legs or hands.
2 not held or fixed securely and likely to fall over.
unsteadily ADVERB

unsuccessful
ADJECTIVE If you are unsuccessful, you do not succeed in what you are trying to do.
unsuccessfully ADVERB

unsuitable
ADJECTIVE not right for a particular purpose.
unsuitably ADVERB **unsuitability** NOUN

unthinkable
ADJECTIVE so shocking or awful that you cannot imagine it to be true.

untidy untidier untidiest
ADJECTIVE not neat or well arranged.
untidily ADVERB

untie unties untying untied
VERB If you untie something, you undo the knots in the string or rope around it.

until
PREPOSITION OR CONJUNCTION **1** If something happens until a particular time, it happens up to that time but not after it.
2 If something does not happen until a particular time, it does not begin before that time.

untold
ADJECTIVE so great that it cannot be described: *untold riches.*

untrue
ADJECTIVE not true.

untruthful
ADJECTIVE Someone who is untruthful tells lies.

unused
ADJECTIVE
Said "un-**yoozd**" **1** not yet used.
Said "un-**yoost**" **2** If you are unused to something, you have not often done or experienced it.

unusual
ADJECTIVE Something that is unusual does not happen very often.
unusually ADVERB

Synonyms: exceptional, extraordinary, rare

unveil unveils unveiling unveiled
VERB When someone unveils a new statue or plaque, they draw back a curtain that is covering it.

unwell
ADJECTIVE ill or sick.

unwieldy
ADJECTIVE difficult to move or carry, because of being large or an awkward shape.

unwilling
ADJECTIVE If you are unwilling to do something, you do not want to do it.
unwillingly ADVERB **unwillingness** NOUN

Synonyms: averse, loath, reluctant

unwind unwinds unwinding unwound
VERB **1** If you unwind something that is wrapped round something else, you undo it.
2 to relax after working hard.

unworthy
ADJECTIVE; FORMAL Someone who is unworthy of something does not deserve it; undeserving.

unwrap unwraps unwrapping unwrapped
VERB to take off the paper or covering around something.

unzip unzips unzipping unzipped
VERB to unfasten the zip of something.

 ► Remember that "until" has one "l", but "till" has two.

up
ADVERB OR PREPOSITION **1** towards or in a higher place.
2 towards or in the north. *I'm flying up to Darwin.*
PREPOSITION **3** along. *She ran up the road.*
4 You use "up to" to say how large something can be or what level it has reached. *You can spend up to £15 worth of vouchers.*
5 INFORMAL If someone is up to something, they are secretly doing something they should not be doing. *I didn't realize what they were up to.*
6 If it is up to someone to do something, it is their responsibility.
ADJECTIVE **7** not in bed. *Are you up yet, Heather?*
8 If a period of time is up, it has come to an end.
ADVERB **9** If an amount of something goes up, it increases.

upbringing
NOUN the way that your parents have taught you to behave.

update **updates updating updated**
VERB If you update something, you make it more modern or add new information to it, to bring it up to date.

upgrade **upgrades upgrading upgraded**
VERB If you upgrade something, you replace it with a newer, better version, or make it newer and better by adding something to it. *We upgraded our train ticket to first class.*
upgrade NOUN

upheaval **upheavals**
NOUN a big change which causes a lot of trouble.

uphill
ADVERB **1** If you go uphill, you go up a slope.
ADJECTIVE **2** Something that is an uphill struggle requires a lot of effort and determination.

uphold **upholds upholding upheld**
VERB to support and maintain a law, belief, etc.

upholstery
NOUN the soft covering on chairs and sofas that makes them comfortable.
upholstered ADJECTIVE

upkeep
NOUN the continual process and cost of keeping something in good condition.

upland **uplands**
ADJECTIVE **1** an upland area is an area of high land.
NOUN **2** Uplands are areas of high land.

upon
PREPOSITION on.

upper **uppers**
ADJECTIVE **1** above or higher: *the upper floor.*
NOUN **2** the top part of a shoe, above the sole.

upper case
ADJECTIVE Upper case letters are the capital letters used in printing or on a typewriter.

Antonym: lower case

upright
ADJECTIVE OR ADVERB **1** standing or sitting up straight, rather than bending or lying down.
2 behaving in a very respectable and moral way.

uprising **uprisings**
NOUN If there is an uprising, a large group of people begin fighting against the existing government to bring about political changes; a revolt.

uproar
NOUN If there is uproar, or an uproar, there is a lot of shouting and noise, often because people are angry.

Synonyms: commotion, pandemonium

upset **upsets upsetting upset**
ADJECTIVE **1** unhappy and disappointed.
VERB **2** If something upsets you, it makes you feel worried or unhappy.
3 If someone or something upsets a procedure or state of affairs, they cause things to go wrong. *The weather upset our plans.*
4 If you upset an object, you turn it over or spill it accidentally.
NOUN **5** A stomach upset is a slight stomach illness.

upside down
ADJECTIVE OR ADVERB the wrong way up.

upstairs
ADVERB **1** up to a higher floor.
NOUN **2** a higher floor.

Antonym: downstairs

upstream
ADVERB On a river, upstream means nearer or moving nearer to the source of the river.

Antonym: downstream

uptight
ADJECTIVE; INFORMAL tense or annoyed.

up-to-date
ADJECTIVE **1** being the newest of its kind.
2 having the newest information.

upturned
ADJECTIVE **1** pointing upwards.
2 upside down.

upwards
ADVERB towards a higher place or level.
upward ADJECTIVE

Antonym: downwards

uranium
Said "yoo-**ray**-nee-um" NOUN a radioactive, metallic element used as a source of nuclear energy.

The uplands of Southern England are called downs, from the Anglo-Saxon *dun* meaning hill.

urban
ADJECTIVE relating to a town or city.

urge **urges urging urged**
NOUN **1** a strong wish to do something.
VERB **2** If you urge someone to do something, you try hard to persuade them to do it.

Synonyms: (sense 1) compulsion, desire, impulse
(sense 2) beg, implore

urgent
ADJECTIVE needing to be dealt with as soon as possible.
urgently ADVERB **urgency** NOUN

Synonyms: crucial, pressing

urinate **urinates urinating urinated**
Said "**yoor**-rin-ate" VERB When you urinate, you go to the toilet and get rid of urine from your body.

urine
Said "**yoor**-rin" NOUN waste liquid that you get rid of from your body when you go to the toilet.

urn **urns**
NOUN a decorated container, especially one used to hold the ashes of a person who has been cremated.

us
PRONOUN A speaker uses "us" to refer to himself or herself and one or more other people.

usable
ADJECTIVE able to be used.

usage **usages**
NOUN **1** the degree to which something is used or the way in which it is used.
2 the way in which words are actually used. *The phrase soon entered common usage.*

use **uses using used**
Said "**yooze**" VERB **1** If you use something, you do something with it.
2 If you use someone, you take advantage of them by making them do things for you.
Said "**yoos**" NOUN **3** The use of something is the act of using it.
4 purpose. *I loved the fabric but I couldn't find a use for it.*
5 If you have the use of something, you have the ability or permission to use it.
PHRASE **6** If you say it's **no use** doing something, you are saying that it is pointless and will not succeed.
use up VERB If you use up a supply of something, you use it until it is finished.

Synonyms: (sense 1) apply, employ, utilize
(sense 3) application, employment, usage

used
Said "**yoost**" VERB **1** Something that used to be done or used to be true was done or was true in the past.
PHRASE **2** If you are **used to** something, you are familiar with it and have often experienced it.
Said "**yoozd**" ADJECTIVE **3** A used object has had at least one previous owner.

useful
ADJECTIVE If something is useful, you can use it in order to do something or to help you in some way.
usefully ADVERB **usefulness** NOUN

useless
ADJECTIVE **1** not suitable or helpful.
2 If a course of action is useless, it will not achieve what is wanted.
uselessly ADVERB

user-friendly
ADJECTIVE designed in a way that is easy to use and sympathetic to those who will use it.

usher **ushers ushering ushered**
NOUN **1** a person who shows people where to sit at a wedding or a concert.
VERB **2** If you usher someone somewhere, you show them where to go by going with them.

usual
ADJECTIVE **1** happening, done or used most often.
PHRASE **2** If something happens **as usual**, it normally happens or happens in the way that it normally does.
usually ADVERB

Synonyms: (sense 1) customary, normal, regular

utensil **utensils**
Said "yoo-**ten**-sil" NOUN a tool for practical use: *cooking utensils.*

uterus **uteruses**
Said "**yoo**-ter-us" NOUN a woman's uterus is her womb.

utility **utilities**
NOUN **1** The utility of something is its usefulness.
2 a service, such as water or gas, that is provided for everyone.

utilize **utilizes utilizing utilized**; also spelt **utilise**
VERB; FORMAL to use something.
utilization NOUN

utmost
ADJECTIVE used to emphasize a particular quality. *I have the utmost respect for Wendy.*

utter **utters uttering uttered**
VERB **1** When you utter sounds, you make or say them.
ADJECTIVE **2** complete or total: *utter nonsense.*
utterly ADVERB

 "Urk" used to be a word for a small, underdeveloped child. An urchin was even smaller.

Vv

vacant
ADJECTIVE **1** If something is vacant, it is not being used or no one is in it.
2 A vacant look suggests that someone does not understand something.
vacancy NOUN

vacate **vacates vacating vacated**
VERB; FORMAL If you vacate a room or job, you leave it and it becomes available for someone else.

vacation **vacations**
NOUN a holiday.

vaccinate **vaccinates vaccinating vaccinated**
Said "**vak**-sin-ate" VERB If someone vaccinates you, they give you a substance, usually by injection, to protect you against a disease.
vaccination NOUN

vaccine **vaccines**
Said "**vak**-seen" NOUN a substance made from the germs that cause a disease and given to people to protect them from that disease.

vacuum **vacuums vacuuming vacuumed**
Said "**vak**-yoom" NOUN **1** a space containing no air, gases or other matter.
VERB **2** If you vacuum something, you clean it using a vacuum cleaner.
[from Latin *vacuum* meaning empty space]

vacuum cleaner **vacuum cleaners**
NOUN an electric machine which cleans by sucking up dirt.

vagina **vaginas**
Said "vaj-**jy**-na" NOUN A woman's vagina is the passage that connects her outer sex organs to her womb.

vague **vaguer vaguest**
Said "**vayg**" ADJECTIVE **1** If something is vague, it is not expressed or explained clearly or you cannot see or remember it clearly.
2 Someone looks or sounds vague if they are not concentrating or thinking clearly.
vaguely ADVERB **vagueness** NOUN

Synonyms: (sense 1) imprecise, indefinite, unclear

vain **vainer vainest**
ADJECTIVE **1** unsuccessful: *a vain effort.*
2 A vain person is very proud of their looks, intelligence or other qualities.
PHRASE **3** If you do something **in vain**, you are unsuccessful.
vainly ADVERB

vale **vales**
NOUN; LITERARY a valley.

valentine **valentines**
NOUN **1** Your valentine is someone you love and send a card to on St Valentine's Day, 14 February
2 the card you send to someone you love on St Valentine's Day.

valiant
ADJECTIVE very brave.
valiantly ADVERB

valid
ADJECTIVE **1** Something that is valid is based on sound reasoning: *a valid excuse.*
2 A valid ticket or document is one which is current and can be used.
validity NOUN

valour
NOUN great bravery.

valley **valleys**
NOUN a long stretch of land between hills, often with a river flowing through it.

valuable **valuables**
ADJECTIVE **1** having great value.
PLURAL NOUN **2** Valuables are things that you own that cost a lot of money.

Synonyms: (sense 1) costly, expensive, precious

value **values valuing valued**
NOUN **1** the importance, worth or usefulness of something.
2 the amount of money that something is worth.
3 Someone's values are the moral principles and beliefs that they think are important.
VERB **4** If you value something, you think it is important and you appreciate it.
5 If an expert values something, they tell you what they think it is worth.
valued ADJECTIVE **valuation** NOUN
valuer NOUN

valve **valves**
NOUN a part attached to a pipe or tube which controls the flow of gas or liquid.
[from Latin *valva* meaning folding door]

vampire **vampires**
NOUN In horror stories, vampires are corpses that come out of their graves at night and suck the blood of living people.

van **vans**
NOUN a motor vehicle with closed sides and covered interior used for carrying goods.

vandal **vandals**
NOUN someone who deliberately damages or destroys things, particularly public property.
vandalize or **vandalise** VERB **vandalism** NOUN
[from the Germanic tribe the Vandals who plundered and partially destroyed Rome in 455 AD]

vanilla
NOUN a flavouring for food such as ice cream, which comes from the pods of a tropical plant.

vanish **vanishes vanishing vanished**
VERB to disappear or cease to exist.

Dracula, written in 1897 by Bram Stoker, is the world's best known vampire story.

A B C D E F G H I J K L M N O P Q R S T U V W X Y Z

vanity
NOUN a feeling of excessive pride about your looks or abilities.

vanquish vanquishes vanquishing vanquished
Said "**vang**-kwish" VERB; LITERARY to defeat someone completely.

vaporize vaporizes vaporizing vaporized; also spelt **vaporise**
VERB to turn something to vapour or to become vapour.

vapour
NOUN a mass of tiny drops of water or other liquids in the air, which looks like mist.

variable variables
ADJECTIVE **1** likely to change at any time. *The weather is very variable at present.*
NOUN **2** In any situation, a variable is something in it that can change or be controlled.
3 In mathematics, a variable is a symbol such as x which can represent any value or any one of a set of values.
variability NOUN

variation variations
NOUN a change from the usual.

varied
ADJECTIVE of different types, quantities or sizes.

variety varieties
NOUN **1** A variety of things is a number of different kinds of them.
2 If something has variety, it consists of things which are not all the same.
3 A variety of something is a type of it: *a variety of potato.*
4 Variety is a form of entertainment consisting of short, unrelated acts, such as singing, dancing and comedy.

Synonyms: (sense 1) assortment, mixture, range

various
ADJECTIVE of several different types, miscellaneous.
variously ADVERB
✔ You should avoid putting *different* after *various*: *the disease exists in various forms* not *various different forms.*

varnish varnishes
NOUN a liquid which when painted onto a surface gives it a hard clear protective finish.
varnish VERB

vary varies varying varied
VERB **1** If things vary, they change. *Weather patterns vary greatly.*
2 If you vary something, you introduce changes in it. *The security van varies its routes as much as possible.*
varying ADJECTIVE

vase vases
Said "**vahz**" NOUN a jar for flowers.

vast
ADJECTIVE extremely large.
vastly ADVERB **vastness** NOUN

vat vats
NOUN a large container for liquids.

vault vaults vaulting vaulted
Rhymes with "**salt**" NOUN **1** a strong secure room, often underneath a building, where valuables are stored, or underneath a church where people are buried.
VERB **2** If you vault over something, you jump over it using your hands or a pole to help.

veal
NOUN the meat from a calf.

Veda Vedas
Said "**vay**-da" NOUN an ancient sacred text of the Hindu religion; also these texts as a collection.
Vedic ADJECTIVE

veer veers veering veered
VERB to move suddenly in a different direction.

vegan vegans
Said "**vee**-gn" NOUN someone who does not eat any food made from animal products, such as meat, eggs, cheese or milk.
veganism NOUN

vegetable vegetables
NOUN Vegetables are plants, or parts of plants which can be eaten, such as carrots, cabbage or beans.

vegetarian vegetarians
NOUN a person who does not eat meat, poultry or fish.
vegetarianism NOUN

vegetation
NOUN the plants in a particular area.

vehicle vehicles
Said "**vee**-ik-kl" NOUN **1** a machine, often with an engine, used for moving people or goods.
2 something used to achieve a particular purpose or as a means of expression. *The play seemed an ideal vehicle for his music.*
vehicular ADJECTIVE

veil veils
Rhymes with "**male**" NOUN a piece of thin, soft cloth that women sometimes wear over their heads.
veiled ADJECTIVE

vein veins
Rhymes with "**rain**" NOUN **1** Veins are the tubes in your body through which blood flows back to the heart. See **artery**.
2 A vein of a metal or mineral is a layer of it in a rock.
3 Something that is in a particular vein is in that style or mood.

 ► VAT is an acronym used for value-added tax? Have you got a PIN?

Velcro
NOUN; TRADEMARK a fastening consisting of two strips of nylon fabric that form a strong bond when pressed together.

velocity velocities
NOUN the speed at which something is moving in a particular direction.

velvet
NOUN a very soft material which has a thick layer of short threads on one side.

vendetta vendettas
NOUN a long-lasting bitter quarrel which results in people trying to harm each other.

vending machine vending machines
NOUN a machine which provides things such as drinks or sweets when you put money in it.

venerable
ADJECTIVE 1 Someone who is venerable is respected because they are old and wise.
2 Something that is venerable is impressive because it is old and important historically.

venereal disease venereal diseases
NOUN Venereal diseases such as syphilis and gonorrhoea are caught through having unprotected sexual intercourse with an infected person. Often abbreviated to VD.

vengeance
NOUN 1 the act of harming someone because they have harmed you, the desire for revenge.
PHRASE 2 If something happens **with a vengeance**, it happens to a much greater degree than was expected. *It began to rain again with a vengeance.*

venison
NOUN the meat from a deer.

Venn diagram Venn diagrams
NOUN In mathematics, a Venn diagram is a drawing which uses circles to show the relationships between different sets of things.

venom
NOUN 1 the poison of a snake, scorpion or spider.
2 a feeling of great bitterness or spitefulness towards someone.
venomous ADJECTIVE **venomously** ADVERB

vent vents venting vented
NOUN 1 a hole in something through which gases and smoke can escape and fresh air can enter.
VERB 2 to express strong feelings. *She wanted to vent her anger upon me.*

ventilate ventilates ventilating ventilated
VERB To ventilate a room means to allow fresh air into it.

ventriloquist ventriloquists
Said "ven-**trill**-o-kwist" NOUN an entertainer who can speak without moving their lips so that the words seem to come from a dummy.
ventriloquism NOUN

venture ventures venturing ventured
NOUN 1 something new which involves the risk of failure or of losing money. *The business was a brave new venture.*
VERB 2 If you venture an opinion, you say it cautiously or hesitantly because you are afraid it might be foolish or wrong.
3 If you venture somewhere that might be dangerous, you go there.

Synonyms: (sense 1) enterprise, undertaking

veranda verandas; also spelt **verandah**
Said "ver-**ran**-da" NOUN a platform with a roof that is attached to an outside wall of a house at ground level.

verb verbs
NOUN In grammar, a verb is a word that expresses actions and states, such as "be", "become", "take" and "run".

VERBS
A **verb** is a word that describes an action or a state of being. They are sometimes called "doing words". **Verbs of state** indicate the way things are:
The weather is bad.
Anna has one sister.
Verbs of action indicate specific events that happen, have happened or will happen:
Mark visits the dentist.
Heather faxed her order.
Auxiliary verbs are used in combination with other verbs to allow the user to distinguish between different times, different degrees of completion and different amounts of certainty:
Mark will visit the dentist.
They may talk for up to three hours.
A **phrasal verb** consists of a verb followed by either an adverb or a preposition, which together have a special meaning:
My old car broke down again.
When did you take up cricket?
An **impersonal verb** is a verb that does not have a subject and is only used after **it** or **there**:
It rains here every day.
Can, could, may, might, must, should, would and ought are called **modal verbs**. They are usually used as auxiliary verbs to change the tone of the meaning of another verb:
I wonder if you can come?
We may have taken a wrong turning.
She must have thought I was stupid.

verbal
ADJECTIVE spoken rather than written: *a verbal agreement.*
verbally ADVERB

verdict verdicts
NOUN 1 In a law court, a verdict is the decision which states whether a prisoner is guilty or not guilty.
2 your opinion. *Give me your verdict on the film.*

A B C D E F G H I J K L M N O P Q R S T U V W X Y Z

verge **verges verging verged**
NOUN **1** The verge of a road is the narrow strip of grassy ground at the side.
PHRASE **2** If you are **on the verge of something**, you are going to do it soon or it is likely to happen soon.
VERB **3** Something that verges on something else is almost the same as it. *Her intelligence verged on genius.*

verify **verifies verifying verified**
VERB to check that something is true.
verifiable ADJECTIVE **verification** NOUN

vermin
PLURAL NOUN small animals, such as insects, rats and cockroaches, which carry disease and damage crops.

verruca **verrucas**
Said "ver-**roo**-ka" NOUN a small hard infectious growth rather like a wart, occurring on the sole of the foot.

versatile
ADJECTIVE If someone or something is versatile, they have many different skills.
versatility NOUN

verse **verses**
NOUN **1** poetry.
2 one part of a poem, song or chapter of the Bible.

version **versions**
NOUN **1** A version of something is a form of it in which some details are different from other forms: *a cheaper version of the dress.*
2 Someone's version of an event is their personal description of what happened.

versus
PREPOSITION competing against. *Arsenal versus Manchester City.*

vertebra **vertebrae**
Said "**ver**-tib-bra" NOUN Vertebrae are the small bones which form the backbone of a vertebrate.

vertebrate **vertebrates**
NOUN Vertebrates are animals which have a backbone. Mammals, birds, fish, amphibians and reptiles are vertebrates.

Antonym: invertebrate

vertex **vertexes** or **vertices**
NOUN The vertex of something such as a triangle or pyramid is the point opposite the base.

vertical
ADJECTIVE Something that is vertical points straight up.
vertically ADVERB

very
ADJECTIVE OR ADVERB **1** "Very" is used before words to emphasize them: *very good work; the very end of the book.*
PHRASE **2** You use **not very** to mean that something is not true or true only to a small degree. *I'm not very good at tennis. You're not very like your sister.*

Synonyms: (sense 1) extremely, greatly, really

vessel **vessels**
NOUN **1** a ship or large boat.
2 LITERARY any bowl or container in which a liquid can be kept.

vest **vests**
NOUN a piece of underwear worn for warmth on the top half of the body.

vestry **vestries**
NOUN the part of a church building where priests, ministers, choirs, etc. change into their official clothes.

vet **vets vetting vetted**
NOUN **1** an abbreviation for veterinary surgeon.
VERB **2** If you vet someone or something, you check them carefully to see if they are acceptable.

veteran **veterans**
NOUN someone who has been involved in a particular activity for a long time. *Tony was a veteran of British politics.*

veterinary
ADJECTIVE **1** a veterinary surgeon, often called a vet, is an animal doctor.
2 relating to the treatment of animals by vets.

veto **vetoes vetoing vetoed**
NOUN **1** the right that someone in authority has to say no to something.
VERB **2** If someone in authority vetoes something, they say no to it.
[from Latin *veto* meaning I forbid]

vex **vexes vexing vexed**
VERB If you vex someone, you annoy or worry them.
vexation NOUN **vexed** ADJECTIVE

via
PREPOSITION going by way of, going through. *He drove from Bonn to London via Paris.*

viaduct **viaducts**
NOUN a long high bridge that carries a road or railway across a valley.

vibrate **vibrates vibrating vibrated**
VERB to move very quickly up and down or backwards and forwards.
vibration NOUN

vicar **vicars**
NOUN a priest in the Church of England.
[from Latin *vicarius* meaning deputy]

vicarage **vicarages**
NOUN a house where a vicar lives.

vice **vices**
NOUN **1** a fault in someone's character, such as greed, or a weakness, such as smoking.
2 crimes connected with sexual activities.

 ► Proverbs which agree: empty vessels make most sound; every ass loves to hear himself bray.

vice president **vice presidents**
NOUN an official who is below the rank of president, who acts in place of them when necessary.

vice versa
"Vice versa" is used to indicate that the reverse of what you have said is also true. *Most dogs hate cats, and vice versa.*

vicinity
Said "vis-**sin**-it-ee" NOUN the surrounding or nearby area. *Is there a library in this vicinity?*

vicious
ADJECTIVE cruel and violent.
viciously ADVERB **viciousness** NOUN

victim **victims**
NOUN someone who has been harmed or injured by someone or something, usually through no fault of their own.

victimize **victimizes victimizing victimized**; also spelt **victimise**
VERB deliberately to treat someone unfairly over a period of time.
victimization NOUN

victor **victors**
NOUN the person who wins a fight or contest.

Victorian
ADJECTIVE happening or made during the reign of Queen Victoria.

victory **victories**
NOUN a success in a battle or competition.
victorious ADJECTIVE

Synonyms: conquest, triumph, win

video **videos videoing videoed**
NOUN **1** a sound and picture recording which can be played back on a television set.
2 a video recorder.
VERB **3** to record a television programme on tape to watch later.
[from Latin *video* meaning I see]

video recorder **video recorders**
NOUN A video recorder or video cassette recorder is a machine for recording and playing back programmes on television.

view **views viewing viewed**
NOUN **1** a belief or opinion. *What are your views on fighting crime?*
2 everything you can see from a particular place.
VERB **3** If you view something in a particular way, you think of it in that way. *They viewed the newcomer with suspicion.*
PHRASE **4** **With a view to** doing something means with the possible intention of doing that thing. *I looked at the adverts with a view to buying a bicycle.*
5 You use **in view of** to specify the main fact or event influencing your actions or opinions. *She wore a sundress in view of the heat.*
6 If something is **on view**, it is being shown or exhibited to the public.

Synonyms: (sense 2) prospect, scene, vista

viewer **viewers**
NOUN Viewers are the people who watch television.

viewpoint **viewpoints**
NOUN **1** your attitude towards something.
2 a place from which you get a good view of an area or event.

vigilant
ADJECTIVE watchful and alert to danger or trouble.
vigilance NOUN **vigilantly** ADVERB

vigorous
ADJECTIVE energetic, enthusiastic.
vigorously ADVERB

vigour
NOUN If you are full of vigour, you are strong, lively and energetic.

Viking **Vikings**
NOUN The Vikings were raiders who came by sea from Scandinavia to attack villages in north-western Europe from the 8th to the 11th centuries AD.
Viking ADJECTIVE

vile **viler vilest**
ADJECTIVE unpleasant or disgusting.

villa **villas**
NOUN a house, especially a pleasant holiday home in a country with a warm climate.

village **villages**
NOUN a small community of houses and other buildings in the countryside.

villain **villains**
NOUN someone who harms others or breaks the law.
villainous ADJECTIVE **villainy** NOUN

Synonyms: criminal, evildoer, rogue

vindictive
ADJECTIVE Someone who is vindictive is deliberately hurtful towards someone, often as an act of revenge.
vindictively ADVERB **vindictiveness** NOUN

vine **vines**
NOUN a climbing plant, especially one which produces grapes.

vinegar
NOUN a sharp-tasting liquid made from sour wine.
vinegary ADJECTIVE
[from French *vin* meaning wine + *aigre* meaning sour]

vineyard **vineyards**
Said "**vin**-yard" NOUN an area of land where grapes are grown.

a b c d e f g h i j k l m n o p q r s t u v w x y z

A B C D E F G H I J K L M N O P Q R S T U V W X Y Z

vintage vintages
ADJECTIVE **1** Vintage describes something which is the best or most typical of its kind.
2 A vintage car is one made between 1918 and 1930.
3 A vintage wine is a good quality wine which has been stored for a number of years to improve its quality.
NOUN **4** a grape harvest of one particular year and the wine produced from it. *The year 1987 was a great vintage.*

vinyl
NOUN a strong plastic used to make things such as floor coverings.

viola violas
Said "vee-**oh**-la" NOUN a musical instrument like a violin, but larger and with a lower pitch.

violate violates violating violated
VERB **1** to break an agreement, law or promise.
2 to disturb someone's peace or privacy.
3 to treat somewhere, especially a holy place, with disrespect or violence.
violation NOUN **violator** NOUN

violence
NOUN behaviour which is meant to hurt or kill people.
violent ADJECTIVE

violet violets
NOUN **1** a plant with dark purple flowers.
NOUN OR ADJECTIVE **2** bluish purple.

violin violins
NOUN a musical instrument with four strings that is held under the chin and played with a bow.
violinist NOUN

viper vipers
NOUN a type of poisonous snake.

virgin virgins
NOUN **1** someone who has never had sexual intercourse.
2 The Virgin, or the Blessed Virgin, is a name given to Mary, the mother of Jesus Christ.

virtual
Said "**vur**-tyool" ADJECTIVE **1** "Virtual" means that something has all the characteristics of a particular thing but it is not formally recognized as being that thing: *a virtual state of war.*
2 "Virtual" relates to the simulation by computers of real situations in a way that mimics the effect and essence of these situations. See **virtual reality**.

virtually
ADVERB almost, as good as. *This is virtually the same as being on the moon.*

virtual reality
NOUN a computer-generated environment which in many ways seems real and which allows a person wearing a headset or mask to "move" within it and interact with it.

virtue virtues
NOUN **1** a good quality in someone's character.
2 a general word for thinking and doing what is morally right and avoiding what is wrong, goodness or morality.
3 an advantage. *The virtue of her scheme is that we can start almost straight away.*
PHRASE **4 By virtue of** means because of. *He won the prize by virtue of his outstanding perseverance.*
virtuous ADJECTIVE

Synonyms: (sense 2) goodness, integrity, morality

virus viruses
Said "**vie**-russ" NOUN **1** a tiny organism that can cause disease, or the disease itself.
2 a program that damages the information stored in a computer system and can transfer from machine to machine in the same way that a real virus does among people.
viral ADJECTIVE
[from Latin *virus* meaning slime or poisonous liquid]

visa visas
NOUN an official stamp, usually put in your passport, that allows you to visit a particular country.

visibility
NOUN You use "visibility" to say how far or how clearly you can see in particular weather conditions. *Visibility in North Devon is good today.*

visible
ADJECTIVE **1** able to be seen.
2 noticeable or evident: *visible excitement.*
visibly ADVERB

vision visions
NOUN **1** the ability to see clearly.
2 Your vision of something is what you imagine it might be like.
3 an unusual experience that you have, in which you see things that other people cannot see.
visionary NOUN OR ADJECTIVE

visit visits visiting visited
VERB to go to see someone or a place.
visit NOUN

visitor visitors
NOUN someone who goes to see a person or a place.

visor visors
Said "**vyzor**" NOUN a transparent movable shield attached to a helmet, which can be pulled down to protect the eyes or face.

 ► Active voice: our team won the game. Passive voice: the game was won by our team. ►

visual
ADJECTIVE relating to sight: *visual problems*.
visually ADVERB

visualize **visualizes visualizing visualized;** also spelt **visualise**
Said "**viz**-yool-eyes" VERB to form a mental picture of something; to imagine.
visualization NOUN

vital
ADJECTIVE necessary or very important, essential.
vitally ADVERB

vitality
NOUN People who have vitality are energetic and lively.

vitamin **vitamins**
NOUN Vitamins are substances in food which you need in order to remain healthy.

vivid
ADJECTIVE very bright in colour or clear in detail.
vividly ADVERB **vividness** NOUN

Synonyms: intense, powerful

vivisection
NOUN the act of performing experiments on animals for medical research, involving cutting into or dissecting the body.

vixen **vixens**
NOUN a female fox.

vocabulary **vocabularies**
NOUN **1** the total number of words someone knows in a particular language.
2 The vocabulary of a language is all the words in it.

vocal
ADJECTIVE **1** involving or relating to the use of the human voice, especially in singing.
2 You say that someone is vocal if they express their opinions strongly and openly.
vocally ADVERB

vocalist **vocalists**
NOUN a singer, especially one who appears with a band, pop group, etc.

vocation **vocations**
NOUN **1** a strong wish to do a particular job, especially one which involves serving other people.
2 a profession or career.

vocational
ADJECTIVE "Vocational" is used to describe the skills needed for a particular job or profession.

vodka **vodkas**
NOUN a strong, clear alcoholic drink.
[from Russian *vodka* meaning little water]

voice **voices voicing voiced**
NOUN **1** Your voice is what you hear when you speak or sing.
VERB **2** If you voice an opinion or an emotion, you say what you think or feel.

VOICES
In grammar, there are two voices, the **active voice** and the **passive voice.**
The **active voice** involves the subject of the sentence performing the action of the verb, for example:
The boy pushed the girl into the pond.
With the **passive voice**, the action of the verb is done to the subject, for example:
The girl was pushed into the pond.
Also look at the grammar boxes at **active voice** and **passive voice.**

void **voids**
ADJECTIVE **1** If a match or competition is officially declared void, the result does not count.
NOUN **2** a situation which seems empty because it has no interest or excitement. *My dog filled a void in my life.*
3 a large empty hole or space. *Her feet dangled in the void.*

volcano **volcanoes**
NOUN an opening in the earth's crust, often in the shape of a conical mountain, through which lava, gas and ash sometimes burst out.
volcanic ADJECTIVE
[named after *Vulcan*, the Roman god of fire]

vole **voles**
NOUN a small mammal like a mouse with a short tail, which lives in fields and near rivers.

volley **volleys**
NOUN **1** In sport, a volley occurs when the player hits or kicks the ball before it bounces.
2 A volley of shots or gunfire is a lot of shots fired at the same time.

volleyball
NOUN a game in which two teams hit a large ball back and forth over a high net with their hands.

volt **volts**
NOUN a unit to measure the voltage of a battery.

voltage **voltages**
NOUN the measure of how much electrical current a battery can push through an electric circuit.

volume **volumes**
NOUN **1** The volume of something is the amount of space it contains or occupies, expressed in cubic measurements, for example, cubic metres or cubic centimetres.
2 The volume of something is also the amount of it that there is. *We received a large volume of letters.*
3 The volume of a radio, television or hi-fi is how loud it is.
4 a book or one of a series of books.

a b c d e f g h i j k l m n o p q r s t u v w x y z

Write short descriptions of the start of the school day. Use the active voice then the passive.

A B C D E F G H I J K L M N O P Q R S T U V W X Y Z

voluntary
ADJECTIVE **1** Voluntary actions are ones that you do because you choose to do them and not because you have been forced to do them.
2 Voluntary work is done by people who are not paid for what they do.
voluntarily ADVERB

volunteer volunteers volunteering volunteered
VERB **1** to offer to do something rather than being forced into it.
2 If you volunteer information, you give it without being asked.
NOUN **3** someone who does work for which they are not paid.

vomit vomits vomiting vomited
VERB If you vomit, you are sick and food and drink comes back up from your stomach and out through your mouth.
vomit NOUN

vote votes voting voted
VERB **1** When people vote, they indicate their choice or opinion, usually by writing on a piece of paper or by raising their hand.
NOUN **2** Someone's vote is their choice in an election or at a meeting where decisions are taken.
voter NOUN

voucher vouchers
NOUN a piece of paper that can be used instead of money to pay for something, a token.

vow vows vowing vowed
VERB to make a solemn promise to do something, or not to do something.
vow NOUN

vowel vowels
NOUN one of the letters a, e, i, o, u; also, and more correctly, the sound that these letters represent. See **consonant**.

voyage voyages
NOUN a long journey on a ship or in a spacecraft.
voyager NOUN

vulgar
ADJECTIVE rude or offensive, especially when referring to sex or the body.
vulgarly ADVERB **vulgarity** NOUN

vulnerable
ADJECTIVE weak and without protection.
vulnerability NOUN

Synonyms: defenceless, susceptible, weak

vulture vultures
NOUN a large bird which lives in hot countries and eats the flesh of dead animals.

Joke. When were there only two vowels? In the days of No-a before U and I were born!

Ww

wacky **wackier wackiest**
ADJECTIVE; INFORMAL odd or crazy.

wad **wads**
NOUN 1 a thick bundle of papers, banknotes, etc.
2 a lump of something: *a wad of cotton wool.*

waddle **waddles waddling waddled**
VERB When someone waddles, they walk with short, quick steps, swaying slightly from side to side, like a duck.

wade **wades wading waded**
VERB 1 to walk slowly through water or mud.
2 If you wade through a book or document, you spend a lot of time and effort reading it because you find it dull or difficult.

wafer **wafers**
NOUN a thin, crisp, sweet biscuit often eaten with ice cream.

waffle **waffles waffling waffled**
Said "**wof**-fl" **VERB 1** to talk or write a lot without being clear or without saying anything of importance.
NOUN 2 vague and lengthy speech or writing.
3 a thick, crisp pancake with squares marked on it, often eaten with syrup.

wag **wags wagging wagged**
VERB 1 When a dog wags its tail, it shakes it repeatedly from side to side.
2 If you wag your finger, you move it repeatedly up and down.
PHRASE 3 When **tongues wag**, people are gossiping.

wage **wages waging waged**
NOUN 1 the regular payment made to someone each week for the work they do.
VERB 2 If a person or country wages a campaign or war, they start it and carry it on over a period of time. See **salary**.

wager **wagers**
NOUN a bet.
wager VERB

waggle **waggles waggling waggled**
VERB If you waggle something or if it waggles, it moves up and down or from side to side with short, quick movements.

wagon **wagons**; also spelt **waggon**
NOUN a strong four-wheeled vehicle for carrying heavy loads, usually pulled by a horse or tractor.

wail **wails wailing wailed**
VERB to cry loudly with sorrow or pain.
wail NOUN

waist **waists**
NOUN the middle part of your body where it narrows slightly above your hips.

waistcoat **waistcoats**
NOUN a sleeveless piece of clothing, often worn under a suit or jacket, which buttons up the front.

wait **waits waiting waited**
VERB 1 If you wait, you spend time, usually doing little or nothing, before something happens.
2 If something can wait, it can be dealt with later.
3 To wait, wait on or wait tables is to act as a waiter or waitress.
NOUN 4 a period of time before something happens.
PHRASE 5 If you **can't wait** to do something, you are very excited and eager to do it.

waiter **waiters**
NOUN a man who works in a restaurant, serving people with food and drink.

waitress **waitresses**
NOUN a woman who works in a restaurant, serving people with food and drink.

wake **wakes waking woke woken**
VERB 1 To wake or wake up is to become conscious again after being asleep.
NOUN 2 The wake of a boat or other object moving in water is the track of waves it leaves behind it.
3 a gathering of people who have got together to mourn somebody's death.

Synonyms: (sense 1) awaken, rouse

walk **walks walking walked**
VERB 1 to move along on foot.
NOUN 2 a journey made by walking. *After Sunday lunch, they always went for a walk.*
PHRASE 3 If you **walk out on** someone, you leave them suddenly.
4 If workers **walk out** they go on strike.
5 If you **walk away with** something such as a prize, you win or achieve it easily.
walker NOUN

walkie-talkie **walkie-talkies**
NOUN a small portable radio used for sending and receiving messages.

walking stick **walking sticks**
NOUN a wooden stick which people can lean on while walking.

Walkman
NOUN; TRADEMARK a very small, portable cassette player with lightweight headphones.

walkover **walkovers**
NOUN; INFORMAL a very easy victory in a competition or contest.

A B C D E F G H I J K L M N O P Q R S T U V W X Y Z

wall walls
NOUN a structure made of stone or brick that surrounds or divides an area of land, or separates an indoor space into rooms.

wallaby wallabies
NOUN a marsupial like a small kangaroo.

wallet wallets
NOUN a small, flat case made of leather or plastic, used for keeping paper money and sometimes credit cards.

wallop wallops walloping walloped
VERB; INFORMAL to hit someone very hard.

wallow wallows wallowing wallowed
VERB 1 When an animal wallows in mud or water, it lies or rolls about in it slowly for pleasure.
2 If you wallow in an unpleasant feeling or situation, you allow it to continue longer than is reasonable or necessary.

wallpaper wallpapers
NOUN thick coloured or patterned paper for pasting on to the walls of rooms.
wallpaper VERB

walnut walnuts
NOUN 1 an edible nut with a wrinkled shape and a hard, round, light-brown shell.
2 wood from the walnut tree which is often used for making expensive furniture.

walrus walruses
NOUN a sea mammal which looks like a large seal with a tough skin, coarse whiskers and two tusks.

waltz waltzes waltzing waltzed
NOUN 1 an old-fashioned dance which has a rhythm of three beats to the bar.
VERB 2 to dance a waltz with someone.

wand wands
NOUN a long, thin rod that magicians wave when they are performing tricks and magic.

wander wanders wandering wandered
VERB 1 to walk around in a casual way without any particular aim or direction.
2 If your mind wanders or your thoughts wander, you lose concentration and start thinking about other things.
wanderer NOUN

Synonyms: (sense 1) ramble, roam, stroll

wane wanes waning waned
VERB 1 If a condition, attitude or emotion wanes, it becomes gradually weaker.
2 When the moon wanes, it gradually appears less bright.

wangle wangles wangling wangled
VERB; INFORMAL If you wangle something that you want, you manage to get it by being crafty or persuasive.

want wants wanting wanted
VERB 1 to feel a desire to have something or a need for it to happen.
2 If something wants doing, there is a need for it to be done. *He needed some new clothes and his hair wants cutting.*
NOUN 3 A want of something is a lack of it.

Synonyms: (sense 1) desire, long for, hanker after

wanted
ADJECTIVE If someone is wanted, they are being hunted by the police in connection with a crime that has been committed.

war wars
NOUN 1 a period of fighting between countries or states when weapons are used and many people may be killed.
2 a competition between groups of people or a campaign against something: *the war against crime.*
war VERB **warring** ADJECTIVE

warble warbles warbling warbled
VERB When a bird warbles, it sings pleasantly with high notes.
warbler NOUN

ward wards warding warded
NOUN 1 a room or set of rooms in a hospital with beds for several people who need similar treatment.
2 A ward or a ward of court is a child who is officially put in the care of an adult or of a court of law because their parents are dead or because they need protection.
VERB 3 If you ward off a danger or an illness, you do something to prevent it from affecting or harming you.

warden wardens
NOUN 1 a person in charge of a building or institution such as a youth hostel or prison.
2 an official who makes sure that certain laws or rules are obeyed in a particular place or activity: *a traffic warden.*

warder warders
NOUN a person who is in charge of prisoners in a jail.

wardrobe wardrobes
NOUN 1 a tall cupboard in which you can hang your clothes.
2 Someone's wardrobe is their collection of clothes.

warehouse warehouses
NOUN a large building where raw materials or manufactured goods are stored.

warfare
NOUN the activity of fighting a war.

warhead warheads
NOUN the front end of a missile, in which the explosive material is carried.

 ► Some words from German: waltz, blitz, lager, zinc, poodle, nickel, quartz.

warm **warmer warmest; warms warming warmed**
ADJECTIVE **1** having heat, but not enough to be hot.
2 Warm clothes, blankets, etc. provide warmth.
3 Warm people are friendly and affectionate.
VERB **4** to heat something up gently.
warm up VERB If you warm up for an event or activity, you practise or exercise gently to prepare for it.
warmth NOUN **warmly** ADVERB
warming ADJECTIVE

warn **warns warning warned**
VERB **1** to tell someone about a possible problem or danger.
2 to advise someone not to do something, in order that they should avoid possible danger or punishment.

Synonyms: (sense 1) alert, caution, notify

warning **warnings**
NOUN something said or written to tell people of a possible problem or danger.

warp **warps warping warped**
VERB **1** to become bent, often because of the effect of heat or water.
2 If something warps someone's mind or character, it makes them abnormal or corrupt.
NOUN **3** A warp in time or space is an imaginary break or sudden change in normal experience.
warped ADJECTIVE

warrant **warrants warranting warranted**
VERB **1** FORMAL If something warrants a particular action, it makes the action seem necessary. *The test is important and warrants a lot of preparation.*
NOUN **2** a document giving official permission to do something.

warren **warrens**
NOUN a group of holes under the ground connected by tunnels, which rabbits live in.

warrior **warriors**
NOUN a fighting man or soldier, especially in former times.

warship **warships**
NOUN a ship built with guns and used for fighting in wars.

wart **warts**
NOUN a small, hard piece of skin which can grow on someone's face or hands, caused by a virus.
warty ADJECTIVE

wary **warier wariest**
ADJECTIVE cautious and on one's guard. *Michelle is wary of marriage.*
warily ADVERB

was
a past tense of **be**.

wash **washes washing washed**
VERB **1** to clean something with water and soap, shampoo, etc.
2 to clean yourself using soap and water.
PHRASE **3** If you **wash your hands of** something, you refuse to have anything more to do with it.
wash up VERB **1** to wash dishes, pans and cutlery.
2 If something is washed up on land, it is carried by a river or sea and left there.
3 If someone's career is washed up, it is ruined.

washable
ADJECTIVE able to be washed without being damaged.

washer **washers**
NOUN a thin, flat ring of metal or plastic which is placed over a bolt before the nut is screwed on, so that it is fixed more tightly.

washing
NOUN clothes and bedding which need to be washed or are in the process of being washed and dried.

washing machine **washing machines**
NOUN a machine for washing clothes.

washing-up
NOUN If you do the washing-up, you wash the dishes, pans and cutlery used in the cooking and eating of a meal.

wasn't
contraction of **was not**.

wasp **wasps**
NOUN an insect with yellow and black stripes across its body, which can sting.

wastage
NOUN the loss or misuse of something: *a wastage of heat.*

waste **wastes wasting wasted**
VERB **1** to use too much time, money or energy on something that is not important or necessary.
2 If you waste an opportunity, you do not take advantage of it when it is available.
NOUN **3** material that is no longer wanted or material left over from a useful process: *nuclear waste.*
4 If an activity is a waste of time, money or energy, it is not important or necessary.
5 the use of more money or some other resource than is necessary.
ADJECTIVE **6** unwanted and unusable in its present form: *waste paper.*
waste away VERB If someone is wasting away, they are becoming very thin and weak because they are ill or not eating properly.

Synonyms: (sense 1) fritter away, misuse, squander

a b c d e f g h i j k l m n o p q r s t u v w x y z

A B C D E F G H I J K L M N O P Q R S T U V W X Y Z

wasteful
ADJECTIVE extravagant or causing waste by using something in a careless and inefficient way.
wastefully ADVERB **wastefulness** NOUN

Synonyms: extravagant, spendthrift

watch **watches watching watched**
VERB **1** to look at something for some time and pay attention to what is happening.
2 If you watch over someone or something, you care for them.
NOUN **3** a small clock usually worn on a strap on the wrist.
4 a period of time during which a guard is kept over something: *the night watch.*
watch out VERB **1** to keep alert to see if something is near you.
2 If you tell someone to watch out, you are warning them to be very careful.

watchdog **watchdogs**
NOUN **1** a dog used to guard property.
2 a person or group whose job is to make sure that companies do not act illegally or irresponsibly.

watchful
ADJECTIVE careful to notice everything that is happening.
watchfully ADVERB **watchfulness** NOUN

water **waters watering watered**
NOUN **1** a clear, odourless, tasteless liquid that falls from clouds as rain.
2 You use "water" or "waters" to refer to a large area of water, such as a lake or sea: *the boat floated on the waters.*
VERB **3** to pour water into the soil around a plant.
4 If your eyes water, you have tears in them because they are hurting or because you are upset.
5 If your mouth waters, it produces extra saliva, usually because you think of or can smell something appetizing.
water down VERB to make a liquid weaker by adding water; to dilute.
watery ADJECTIVE

watercolour **watercolours**
NOUN **1** Watercolours are paints for painting pictures, which are diluted with water or put on the paper using a wet brush.
2 a picture which has been painted using watercolours.

watercress
NOUN a small plant which grows in shallow water. Its leaves are eaten in salads.

waterfall **waterfalls**
NOUN water which flows over the edge of a rock and falls to the ground below.

watering can **watering cans**
NOUN a container with a handle and a long spout, which you use to water plants.

waterlogged
ADJECTIVE **1** something that is waterlogged is so wet that it cannot contain any more water.
2 A waterlogged boat is so full of water that it may soon sink.

watermark **watermarks**
NOUN a design put into paper as it is being made, which is only visible when held up to the light. Banknotes have a watermark to prove they are genuine.

watermelon **watermelons**
NOUN a large, round fruit which has a hard green skin and red juicy flesh.

waterproof
ADJECTIVE Waterproof clothing does not let water pass through to the body.

water-skiing
NOUN the sport of skimming over the water on skis while being pulled by a boat.
water-skier NOUN

watertight
ADJECTIVE Something that is watertight does not allow water to pass through.

waterway **waterways**
NOUN a canal, river or narrow channel of sea which ships or boats can sail along.

waterworks
NOUN **1** a system of pipes, filters and tanks where the public supply of water is stored and cleaned and from where it is distributed.
2 INFORMAL the parts in someone's body which form their urinary system. *He's had trouble with his waterworks.*

watery
ADJECTIVE **1** containing a lot of water or being thin like water.
2 pale or weak: *a watery smile.*

watt **watts**
Said "**wot**" NOUN a unit of electrical power. [named after James Watt (1736–1819), the inventor of the modern steam engine]

wave **waves waving waved**
VERB **1** to move your hand from side to side, usually to say hello or goodbye.
2 to move your hand to tell someone which way to go.
3 to hold something up and move it from side to side. *The doctor waved a piece of paper at him.*
NOUN **4** a ridge of water on the surface of the sea or a lake caused by wind, gravity or the movement of boats.
5 the form in which some types of energy such as heat, light or sound travel through a substance: *radio waves.*
6 a sudden increase of a feeling or activity: *a crime wave.*

Synonyms: (sense 3) brandish, flourish

 ► Many place names are connected with water. For example, "aber" means river mouth. ►

wavelength **wavelengths**
NOUN 1 the size of radio wave which a particular radio station uses to broadcast its programmes.
PHRASE 2 If two people are **on the same wavelength**, they understand each other and get on well together.

waver **wavers wavering wavered**
VERB 1 to move slightly. *The pen wavered in his hand.*
2 If you waver or if your confidence or beliefs waver, you are no longer as firm, confident or sure in your beliefs.

wavy **wavier waviest**
ADJECTIVE having waves or regular curves: *wavy hair.*

wax **waxes waxing waxed**
NOUN 1 a solid, slightly shiny substance made of fat or oil and used to make candles and polish.
2 the sticky yellow substance in your ears.
VERB 3 If you wax a surface, you treat it or cover it with a thin layer of wax, especially to polish it.
waxy ADJECTIVE

waxworks
PLURAL NOUN an exhibition of lifelike models of people made out of wax.

way **ways**
NOUN 1 a method of doing something.
2 The ways of a person or group are their customs or their normal behaviour.
3 The way you feel about something is your attitude to it or your opinion about it.
4 If you have a way with people or things, you are very skilful at dealing with them.
5 The way to a place is the route that you take to get there.
6 a direction. *She glanced the other way.*
7 "Way" is used in expressions such as **a little way** or **a long way** to say how far away in distance or time something is.
PHRASE 8 If something or someone is **in the way**, they prevent you from going where you want to.
9 You say **by the way** when adding something to what you are saying. *By the way, I've asked Eileen to drop in.*
10 If you **go out of your way** to do something, you make a special effort to do it.

Synonyms: (sense 5) course, path, route

we
PRONOUN A speaker or writer uses "we" to refer to himself or herself and one or more other people. *We are going to the Zoo.*

weak **weaker weakest**
ADJECTIVE 1 not having much strength or energy.
2 likely to break or fail: *a weak bridge.*
3 not very determined, and easily influenced by other people.
weakly ADVERB **weakness** NOUN

Synonyms: (sense 1) feeble, frail, puny

weaken **weakens weakening weakened**
VERB 1 If someone weakens something, they make it less strong or certain. *Could you make this coffee weaker, please?*
2 If someone weakens, they become less certain about something and give in. *She weakened and let me go to the party after all.*

weakling **weaklings**
NOUN a person who lacks physical strength or who is weak in character or health.

wealth
NOUN 1 a large amount of money, property or possessions belonging to a person, organization or country.
2 a lot of something. *The book contains a wealth of information.*

Synonyms: (sense 1) fortune, prosperity, riches

wealthy **wealthier wealthiest**
ADJECTIVE having a large amount of money, property or other valuable things.

Synonyms: affluent, rich, well-off

weapon **weapons**
NOUN 1 an object used to kill or hurt people in a fight or war, such as a gun or missile.
2 anything which can be used to get the better of an opponent. *Surprise was Mike's only weapon.*

wear **wears wearing wore worn**
VERB 1 When you wear something such as clothes, make-up or jewellery, you have them on your body or face.
2 If you wear a particular expression, it shows on your face.
3 If something wears, it becomes thinner or worse in condition.
NOUN 4 clothes that are suitable for a particular time or occasion: *swim wear.*
5 the amount or type of use that something has and which causes damage or change to it. *The boots showed evidence of heavy wear.*
wear down **VERB** If you wear someone down, you weaken them by repeatedly doing something or asking them to do something.
wear off **VERB** If a feeling wears off, it gradually disappears.
wear out **VERB** to become or make something no longer usable because of wear.

weary **wearier weariest; wearies wearying wearied**
ADJECTIVE 1 very tired.
VERB 2 If you weary of something, you become tired of it.
wearily ADVERB **weariness** NOUN

Other water place names: burn (meaning stream), ex (water), inver (river mouth), mere (lake).

A B C D E F G H I J K L M N O P Q R S T U V W X Y Z

weasel weasels
NOUN a small wild mammal with a long, thin body and short legs.

weather weathers weathering weathered
NOUN **1** the condition of the atmosphere at any particular time and place, for example, whether it is raining, hot or windy.
2 A weather forecast is a prediction of what the weather is going to be like in future.
VERB **3** If something such as rock or wood weathers, it changes colour or shape as a result of being exposed to the wind, rain or sun.
4 If you weather a problem or difficulty, you come through it safely.
PHRASE **5** If you are **under the weather**, you feel slightly ill.

weather vane weather vanes
NOUN a metal object, usually situated on someone's roof, which turns round in the wind to show which way the wind is blowing; also called a weathercock.

weave weaves weaving wove woven
VERB **1** to make cloth by crossing threads over and under each other, especially by using a machine called a loom.
2 If you weave your way somewhere, you go there by moving from side to side through and round the obstacles.
weaver NOUN

web webs
NOUN **1** a fine net of threads that a spider makes.
2 something that has a complicated structure or pattern. *His explanation was merely a web of lies and deceit.*
3 The Web is the World Wide Web.

webbed
ADJECTIVE Webbed feet have the toes connected by a piece of skin.

website websites
NOUN a publication on the World Wide Web which contains information or opinions about a particular subject.

wed weds wedding wedded
VERB; OLD-FASHIONED to marry.

we'd
1 contraction of **we would**.
2 contraction of **we had**.

wedding weddings
NOUN a marriage ceremony.

wedge wedges wedging wedged
NOUN **1** a piece of something such as wood, metal or rubber with one pointed edge and one thick edge which is jammed at the edge of something to stop it from moving.
2 a piece of something that has a thick triangular shape: *a wedge of cheese.*
VERB **3** to prevent something from moving by jamming it with a wedge.
PHRASE **4** If someone **drives a wedge between** people or groups, they create bad feelings between them in order to weaken their relationship.

Wednesday Wednesdays
NOUN Wednesday is the day between Tuesday and Thursday.
[from Old English *Wodnesdaeg* meaning Woden's day; Woden was the chief of the Anglo-Saxon gods]

wee
ADJECTIVE a word used especially by Scots to mean small.

weed weeds weeding weeded
NOUN **1** a wild plant growing somewhere it is not wanted.
VERB **2** to remove the weeds from a place.
weed out VERB If you weed out unwanted things, you get rid of them.

weedy weedier weediest
ADJECTIVE A weedy person is thin and weak.

week weeks
NOUN **1** a period of seven days, especially one beginning on a Sunday and ending on a Saturday.
2 the number of hours you spend at work during a week: *a 35-hour week.*
3 the part of a week that does not include Saturday and Sunday. *I live in town during the week, but spend most weekends in the country.*

weekday weekdays
NOUN any day except Saturday and Sunday.

weekend weekends
NOUN Friday night, Saturday and Sunday.

weekly weeklies
ADJECTIVE OR ADVERB **1** happening or appearing once a week.
NOUN **2** a newspaper or magazine that is published once a week.

weep weeps weeping wept
VERB **1** to cry because you are unhappy.
2 If a wound weeps, it oozes blood or pus.

weigh weighs weighing weighed
VERB **1** to be a certain weight. *He weighs 50 kilograms.*
2 to measure the weight of someone or something. *Weigh your parcel on these scales, please.*
3 If you weigh facts or words, you think about them carefully before coming to a decision or before speaking.
weigh down VERB **1** If a load weighs you down, it stops you from moving easily.
2 If you are weighed down by a problem or difficulty, it is making you very worried.
weigh up VERB If you weigh up a person or situation, you are making an assessment of them.

 ► Besides Wednesday, how did the other days of the week get their names?

weight weights weighting weighted
NOUN **1** The weight of something is its heaviness.
2 A weight is a piece of metal which has a certain known heaviness, used with scales to weigh things.
3 any heavy object. *Cor, this is a weight!*
4 The weight of something is its large amount or importance which makes it hard to fight against or contradict: *the weight of the law; the weight of public opinion.*
VERB **5** If you weight something, or weight it down, you make it heavier, perhaps to stop it from moving.
PHRASE **6** If you **pull your weight**, you work just as hard as the other people working with you.
weighty ADJECTIVE

weightlifting
NOUN the sport of lifting heavy weights in competition or for exercise.
weightlifter NOUN

weighty weightier weightiest
ADJECTIVE serious or important: *a weighty problem.*

weir weirs
Rhymes with "**near**" NOUN a low dam which is built across a river to raise the water level, control the flow of water or change its direction.

weird weirder weirdest
Said "**weerd**" ADJECTIVE strange or peculiar.
weirdly ADVERB **weirdness** NOUN

Synonyms: bizarre, odd, extraordinary

welcome welcomes welcoming welcomed
VERB **1** to greet someone in a friendly way when they arrive.
2 If you welcome something, you approve of it and support it. *She welcomed the court's decision.*
NOUN **3** a greeting to a visitor. *They received a warm welcome.*
ADJECTIVE **4** If you are welcome or made welcome at a place, you are received in a friendly way.
5 If you tell someone they are welcome to something or welcome to do something, you mean you are happy for them to have or to do it. *You're welcome to those shoes. I wouldn't want them!*
6 If something is welcome, it brings pleasure or is accepted gratefully: *a welcome cup of tea.*
PHRASE **7 You're welcome** is used to acknowledge thanks.
welcoming ADJECTIVE

weld welds welding welded
VERB To weld two pieces of metal together is to heat their edges and join them so that when they cool they harden into one piece.
welding NOUN **welder** NOUN

welfare
NOUN **1** The welfare of a person or group is their general state of health and comfort.
2 Welfare services are provided to help with people's living conditions and problems with money.

well better best; wells welling welled
ADVERB **1** in a good, skilful or pleasing way. *He draws well.*
2 thoroughly and completely. *Mix the ingredients well.*
3 kindly. *We treat our employees well.*
4 If something may well or could well happen, it is likely to happen.
5 You use "well" to emphasize an adjective, adverb or phrase. *She sat well back.*
ADJECTIVE **6** healthy. *Though I'm tired, I feel well.*
PHRASE **7 As well** means also.
8 As well as means in addition to.
9 If you say you **may as well** or **might as well** do something, you mean you will do it although you are not keen to do it.
NOUN **10** a hole drilled in the ground from which water, oil or gas is obtained.
VERB **11** If tears well or well up, they appear in someone's eyes.

we'll
contraction of **we will**.

wellbeing
NOUN Someone's wellbeing is their health and happiness.

wellingtons
PLURAL NOUN Wellingtons are long waterproof rubber boots.

Synonyms: Wellington boots, gumboots

well-known
ADJECTIVE known by many people, famous.

welly wellies
NOUN another name for a Wellington boot.

went
past tense of **go**.

wept
the past tense and past participle of **weep**.

were
a past tense of **be**.

we're
contraction of **we are**.

werewolf werewolves
NOUN In horror stories, a werewolf is a person who changes into a wolf.

west
NOUN **1** the direction in which you look to see the sun set.
2 the part of a place which is towards the west: *the west of England.*
ADJECTIVE OR ADVERB **3** in or towards the west.

A B C D E F G H I J K L M N O P Q R S T U V W X Y Z

westerly
ADJECTIVE OR ADVERB 1 to or towards the west.
2 A westerly wind blows from the west.

western **westerns**
ADJECTIVE 1 in or from the west.
2 of or relating to the developed countries of the western world, such as those of Europe and North America.
NOUN 3 a film about cowboys.

westward or **westwards**
ADVERB towards the west.

wet **wetter wettest; wets wetting wet** or **wetted**
ADJECTIVE 1 covered in water or another liquid.
2 If the weather is wet, it is raining.
3 If something such as paint, ink or cement is wet, it is not yet dry or solid.
4 INFORMAL If you say someone is wet, you mean they are weak and lack enthusiasm or confidence.
VERB 5 to put water or some other liquid over something or someone.
6 If people wet themselves or wet their beds, they urinate in their clothes or bed because they cannot control their bladder.
wetness NOUN

wet suit **wet suits**
NOUN a close-fitting rubber suit worn by divers or swimmers to keep their body warm in water.

we've
contraction of **we have**.

whack **whacks whacking whacked**
VERB to hit someone or something hard.
whack NOUN

whale **whales**
NOUN 1 a very large sea mammal.
PHRASE 2 If you have **a whale of a time** you enjoy yourself very much.

whaling
NOUN the catching and killing of whales.

wharf **wharves** or **wharfs**
Said "**worf**" **NOUN** a platform beside a river or the sea, where ships load or unload.

what
PRONOUN 1 "What" is used to ask for information. *What time is it?*
2 "What" is used in indirect statements and questions. *I don't know what you mean.*
ADJECTIVE 3 "What" is used to talk about an amount or kind of something. *They had to use what money they had. What music have you got?*
4 You use "what" to emphasize an opinion or reaction. *What a terrible thing to do!*
PHRASE 5 You say **what about** to make a suggestion. *What about a glass of juice?*

whatever
PRONOUN 1 "Whatever" is used to refer to anything or everything of a particular type. *He said he would do whatever he could. Whatever you decide, I'll be happy.*
CONJUNCTION 2 You use "whatever" to mean no matter what. *Whatever happens, you'll have to carry on.*
ADVERB 3 "Whatever" is used to emphasize a negative statement or a question. *You have no proof whatever.*

wheat
NOUN a cereal plant grown for its grain which is used to make flour.

wheel **wheels wheeling wheeled**
NOUN 1 a circular object which turns on a rod attached to its centre, often attached underneath other objects to enable them to roll along.
2 The wheel of a car is its steering wheel.
VERB 3 If you wheel something such as a bicycle, you push it along.
4 If someone or something wheels, they move round in the shape of a circle. *Cameron suddenly wheeled round and saw her.*

wheelbarrow **wheelbarrows**
NOUN a small cart with a single wheel at the front, used for carrying things in the garden.

wheelchair **wheelchairs**
NOUN a chair with wheels in which sick, injured or disabled people can move around.

wheeze **wheezes wheezing wheezed**
VERB to breathe with difficulty, making a whistling sound, usually because of a chest illness such as asthma.
wheezy ADJECTIVE

whelk **whelks**
NOUN a snail-like shellfish with a strong shell and a soft edible body.

when
ADVERB 1 "When" is used to ask what time something happened or will happen.
CONJUNCTION 2 "When" is used to refer to a time in the past. *I met him when he was six.*
3 "When" is used to introduce the reason for an opinion, comment or question. *How did you pass the exam when you hadn't studied for it?*

whenever
CONJUNCTION at any time, or every time that something happens. *I go riding whenever Mum says I can.*

where
ADVERB 1 You use "where" to ask which place something is in, is coming from or is going to.
CONJUNCTION, PRONOUN OR ADVERB 2 "Where" is used when asking about or referring to something. *I hardly know where to begin.*
CONJUNCTION 3 You use "where" to refer to the place in which something is situated or happening. *I don't know where we are.*
4 "Where" can introduce a clause that contrasts with the other part of the sentence. *A teacher will be listened to, where a parent might not.*

 ► Adverbial pun. "What a whale!" said Captain Ahab, superficially.

whereabouts
NOUN **1** The whereabouts of a person or thing is the place where they are.
ADVERB **2** You use "whereabouts" when you are asking more precisely where something is. *Whereabouts in Canada are you from?*

whereas
ADVERB "Whereas" introduces a comment that contrasts with the other part of the sentence. *Her eyes are blue, whereas mine are brown.*

wherever
CONJUNCTION **1** in every place or situation. *Mr Dawes heard the same thing wherever he went.*
2 "Wherever" is used to show that you do not know where a place or person is: *the nearest police station, wherever that is.*

whether
CONJUNCTION You use "whether" when you are talking about two or more alternatives. *I don't know whether that's true or false.*

which
ADJECTIVE OR PRONOUN **1** You use "which" to ask about alternatives or to refer to a choice between alternatives. *Which room are you in?*
PRONOUN **2** "Which" identifies the thing you are talking about or gives more information about it. *He's based in London, which is the largest city in Britain.*

whichever
ADJECTIVE OR PRONOUN You use "whichever" when talking about different alternatives or possibilities. *Make your pizzas round or square, whichever you prefer.*

whiff whiffs
NOUN a slight smell or hint of something: *a whiff of garlic; a whiff of scandal.*

while whiles whiling whiled
CONJUNCTION **1** If something happens while something else is happening, the two things happen at the same time. *She holds the nail while I hit it with a hammer.*
2 "While" introduces something which contrasts with the rest of the sentence. *Cratchit had many friends while Scrooge had none.*
NOUN **3** a period of time. *They'll be here in a while.*
PHRASE **4** If an activity is **worth your while**, it will be helpful or useful to you if you do it.
while away VERB If you while away the time in a particular way, you pass the time in that way because you have nothing else to do.

whilst
CONJUNCTION another word for **while**.

whim whims
NOUN a sudden desire or fancy, an impulse.

whimper whimpers whimpering whimpered
VERB **1** When children or animals whimper, they make soft, low, unhappy sounds.
2 If you whimper something, you say it in an unhappy or frightened way, as if you are about to cry.

whine whines whining whined
VERB **1** to make a long, high-pitched noise, especially one which sounds sad or unpleasant.
2 to complain about something in an annoying way, to whinge.
whine NOUN

whinge whinges whinging or whingeing whinged
VERB to complain about something in an annoying way.
whinge NOUN **whinger** NOUN

whinny whinnies whinnying whinnied
VERB When a horse whinnies, it neighs softly.
whinny NOUN

whip whips whipping whipped
NOUN **1** a thin piece of leather or rope attached to a handle, which is used for hitting people or animals.
VERB **2** to hit with a whip.
3 If you whip cream or eggs, you beat them until they are thick and frothy.
4 If you whip something out or off, you take it out or off very quickly. *She had whipped off her glasses.*
whip up VERB If you whip up a strong emotion, you make people feel it. *Mrs Murgatroyd whipped the crowd up into a frenzy.*

whippet whippets
NOUN a small, thin dog used for racing.

whirl whirls whirling whirled
VERB **1** to swing or turn round very fast.
2 If you say that your head or mind is whirling, you mean you are very confused or excited by something.
NOUN **3** You can refer to a lot of intense activity as a whirl of activity.

whirlpool whirlpools
NOUN a small circular area in a river or the sea where the water is moving quickly round and round so that objects floating near it are pulled into its centre.

whirlwind whirlwinds
NOUN **1** a tall column of air which spins round and round very fast.
ADJECTIVE **2** more rapid than usual: *a whirlwind tour.*

whirr whirs whirring whirred; also spelt **whir**
VERB When a machine whirs, it makes a long, low, continuous buzzing sound while it operates.
whirr NOUN

whisk whisks whisking whisked
VERB **1** If you whisk eggs or cream, you stir air into them quickly.
2 If you whisk someone somewhere, you take them there very quickly.
NOUN **3** a kitchen tool used for quickly stirring air into eggs or cream.

A B C D E F G H I J K L M N O P Q R S T U V W X Y Z

whisker whiskers
NOUN 1 The whiskers of an animal such as a cat or mouse are the long, stiff hairs near its mouth.
2 You can refer to the hair on a man's face, especially on his cheeks, as his whiskers.
INFORMAL PHRASE 3 **By a whisker** means by a very small amount. *Miranda won by a whisker.*

whisky whiskies; also spelt **whiskey**
NOUN a strong alcoholic drink made from grain such as barley.

whisper whispers whispering whispered
VERB to talk very quietly.
whisper NOUN

whistle whistles whistling whistled
VERB 1 to produce a sound or tune by forcing your breath out between your lips.
2 to make a loud, high sound. *The kettle whistled as it boiled.*
NOUN 3 a small metal tube that you blow into to produce a whistling sound.
4 A whistle is the sound someone or something makes when they whistle.

white whiter whitest; whites
NOUN OR ADJECTIVE 1 the lightest possible colour.
2 Someone who is white has a pale skin and is of European origin.
ADJECTIVE 3 White coffee contains milk or cream.
4 If someone goes white, their face turns very pale because they are afraid, shocked or ill.
NOUN 5 The white of an egg is the clear liquid surrounding the yolk.
whiteness NOUN

whiten whitens whitening whitened
VERB to make something whiter.

whizz whizzes whizzing whizzed; also spelt **whiz**
VERB 1 INFORMAL to move somewhere quickly.
NOUN 2 INFORMAL If you are a whizz at something, you are very good at it.

who
PRONOUN 1 "Who" is used when you are asking about someone's identity.
2 "Who" is used at the beginning of a clause to identify the person or people you are talking about. *He's a factory worker who wants to be a postman.*

whoever
PRONOUN 1 the person who. *Whoever wins is going to be very famous.*
2 no matter who. *I'm sorry for any friend of his, whoever it is.*
3 "Whoever" is used in questions to give emphasis to who. *Whoever thought of such a thing?*

whole wholes
NOUN OR ADJECTIVE 1 The whole of something is all of it.
ADVERB 2 in one piece. *He swallowed the cake whole.*
PHRASE 3 You use **as a whole** to emphasize that you are talking about all of something. *The village as a whole is a very friendly place.*
4 You say **on the whole** to mean that something is generally true. *On the whole, we should be glad that they're coming.*

wholefood wholefoods
NOUN Wholefoods are foods which have been refined as little as possible, do not contain additives, and are eaten in their natural state.

wholemeal
ADJECTIVE Wholemeal flour is made from the complete grain of the wheat plant, including the shell.

whole number whole numbers
NOUN an exact number such as 1, 5, 12 or 300, rather than a vulgar fraction, mixed number or a decimal.

wholesale
ADJECTIVE OR ADVERB 1 Wholesale refers to the activity of buying goods from the producer or manufacturer in large quantities and selling them again, especially to retailers. See **retail**.
ADJECTIVE 2 done to an excessive extent: *the wholesale destruction of the rainforests.*
wholesaler NOUN

wholesome
ADJECTIVE good and likely to improve your life, behaviour or health.

wholly
Said "**ho**-lee" ADVERB completely, entirely, totally.

whom
PRONOUN Whom is the object form of who: *the girl whom Albert would marry.*

whooping cough
Said "**hoop**-ing" NOUN an infectious disease which makes people cough violently and produce a loud sound when they breathe.

who's
contraction of **who is** or **who has**.

whose
PRONOUN 1 You use "whose" to ask who something belongs to. *Whose bag is this?*
2 You use "whose" at the beginning of a clause which gives information about something relating or belonging to the thing or person you are talking about. *There's the driver whose car is blocking the street.*
✔ Many people are confused about the difference between *whose* and *who's*. *Who's* is a short form of "who is" or "who has". *Who's that girl? Who's got my ruler?*

why
ADVERB OR PRONOUN You use "why" when you are asking about the reason for something or talking about it. *Why did you do it?*

wick wicks
NOUN the cord in the middle of a candle, which you set alight.

 ► Idioms: white horses, a white lie, a white elephant, a white flag, a white feather.

wicked
ADJECTIVE **1** very bad, evil.
2 mischievous in an amusing or attractive way. *She had a wicked sense of humour.*
wickedly ADVERB **wickedness** NOUN
[from Old English *wicce* meaning witch]

Synonyms: (sense 1) bad, evil, sinful

wicker
ADJECTIVE A wicker basket or chair is made of twigs, canes or reeds that have been woven together.

wicket wickets
NOUN **1** In cricket, the wicket is one of the two sets of stumps and bails at which the bowler aims the ball.
2 The grass between the wickets on a cricket pitch is also called the wicket.

wide wider widest
ADJECTIVE **1** measuring a large distance from one side to the other.
2 If there is a wide variety, range or selection of something, there are many different kinds of it.
ADVERB **3** If you open or spread something wide, you open it as far as you can.

Synonyms: (sense 2) broad, extensive, large

wide-awake
ADJECTIVE completely awake.

widely
ADVERB **1** over a great area. *The seed was widely scattered.*
2 by many people. *Horoscopes are widely believed.*

widen widens widening widened
VERB **1** to become bigger from one side to another.
2 You can say that something widens when it becomes greater in size or scope: *the opportunity to widen your outlook.*

widespread
ADJECTIVE existing or happening over a large area or to a great extent: *the widespread use of chemicals.*

widow widows
NOUN a woman whose husband has died.
widowed ADJECTIVE

widower widowers
NOUN a man whose wife has died.

width widths
NOUN The width of something is the distance from one side or edge to the other; the breadth.

wield wields wielding wielded
Said "**weeld**" VERB **1** to carry and use a weapon, tool, bat, etc.
2 If someone wields power, they have it and are able to use it.

wife wives
NOUN A man's wife is the woman he is married to.

wig wigs
NOUN a false head of hair worn to cover someone's own hair or to hide their baldness.

wiggle wiggles wiggling wiggled
VERB If you wiggle something, you move it up and down or from side to side with small jerky movements.
wiggle NOUN **wiggly** ADJECTIVE

wigwam wigwams
NOUN a kind of tent formerly used by some Native Americans.

wild wilder wildest; wilds
ADJECTIVE **1** excited and uncontrolled behaviour. *The crowd went wild.*
2 A wild idea or scheme is original and crazy.
3 Wild animals and plants live and grow in natural surroundings and are not looked after by people.
4 Wild land is natural and uncultivated.
NOUN **5** The wild is a free and natural state of living. *There are very few tigers now left in the wild.*
6 The wilds are remote areas where few people live, far away from towns.
wildly ADVERB

wilderness wildernesses
NOUN an area of natural land which is not cultivated.

wildlife
NOUN wild animals and plants.

wilful
ADJECTIVE **1** Wilful actions or attitudes are deliberate and often intended to hurt someone: *wilful damage.*
2 Someone who is wilful is obstinate and determined to get their own way, stubborn: *a wilful little boy.*
wilfully ADVERB

will wills willing willed
VERB **1** You use "will" to form the future tense. *Brian will be annoyed at missing the party.*
2 You use "will" when inviting or asking. *Will you have a glass of squash? Will you do me a favour?*
3 If you will something to happen, you try to make it happen by mental effort. *She willed the horse to win.*
NOUN **4** the determination to do something. *From an early age Delroy had the will to win.*
5 If something is the will of a person or group, they want it to happen.
6 a legal document in which you say what you want to happen to your money and property when you die.
PHRASE **7** If you can do something **at will** you can do it whenever you want. *He could wiggle his ears at will.*

English is the most widely spoken language in the world.

WILL AND SHALL
The verbs **will** and **shall** have only one form. They are used as auxiliary verbs to form the future tense:
We shall arrive on Thursday.
She will give us a talk on wildlife.
Shall is always used in questions involving **I** and **we**. Will is avoided in these cases:
Shall I put the kettle on?
Shall we go to the pictures?
Will is always used when making polite requests, giving orders and indicating persistence. Shall is avoided in these cases:
Will you please help me?
She will keep going on about Tom Cruise.

willing
ADJECTIVE **1** If you are willing to do something, you will do it if someone wants you to.
2 eager and enthusiastic: *a willing helper.*
willingly ADVERB **willingness** NOUN

Synonyms: (sense 1) game, prepared, ready

willow willows
NOUN a tree with long, thin branches and narrow leaves that often grows near water.

wilt wilts wilting wilted
VERB **1** If a plant wilts, it droops because it needs more water or is dying.
2 If someone wilts, they gradually lose strength or confidence.

wily wilier wiliest
Said "**wie**-lee" ADJECTIVE clever and cunning.
wiliness NOUN

wimp wimps
NOUN; INFORMAL someone who is feeble and timid.
wimpish ADJECTIVE

win wins winning won
VERB **1** to defeat your opponent in a fight, game or argument.
2 If you win a prize, you get it as a reward for succeeding in something.
3 to succeed in getting something you want. *They won an extension on the deadline for their project work.*
NOUN **4** a victory in a game or contest.
win over VERB If you win someone over, you persuade them to support you.

wince winces wincing winced
VERB When you wince, the muscles of your face tighten suddenly, because of fear, pain or distress.

winch winches winching winched
NOUN **1** a machine used to lift heavy objects. It consists of a cylinder around which a rope or chain is wound.
VERB **2** to lift, lower or pull someone or something using a winch.

wind winds winding wound
Rhymes with "**tinned**" NOUN **1** a current of air moving across the earth's surface.
2 air swallowed with food or drink, or gas produced in your stomach, which causes discomfort.
3 the ability to breathe easily. *After running a mile I got my second wind and started to relax.*
4 The wind section of an orchestra is the group of musicians playing instruments that you blow, such as trumpets, trombones, clarinets and oboes.
Rhymes with "**mind**" VERB **5** to twist and turn. *The road winds uphill.*
6 to wrap something round. *She wound the bandage round his knee.*
7 If you wind a clock or machine, you turn a key or handle several times to make it work. *You don't need to wind battery watches.*
wind up VERB **1** If you wind up a business, you close it down.
2 If you wind up somewhere, you end up there. *After a tiring journey we wound up in the grottiest hotel imaginable.*
3 INFORMAL If you wind someone up, you tease them to make them irritated.

windfall windfalls
NOUN **1** a sum of money that you receive unexpectedly.
2 a fruit, usually an apple, that has been blown from a tree by the wind.

wind instrument wind instruments
NOUN an instrument you play by using your breath, such as a flute, an oboe or a trumpet.

windmill windmills
NOUN a machine for grinding grain or pumping water. It is driven by wooden sails turned by the wind.

window windows
NOUN a space in a wall or roof or in the side of a vehicle, usually with glass in it so that light can pass through and people can see in or out.

windowsill windowsill
NOUN the ledge below a window, either inside or outside.

windpipe windpipes
NOUN the tube which carries air into your lungs when you breathe.

windscreen windscreens
NOUN the glass at the front of a vehicle through which the driver looks.

windsurfing
NOUN the sport of moving along the surface of the sea or a lake standing on a board with a sail on it.
windsurfer NOUN

windy windier windiest
ADJECTIVE If it is windy, there is a lot of wind.

wine wines
NOUN an alcoholic drink which is normally made from grapes.

A B C D E F G H I J K L M N O P Q R S T U V W X Y Z

String, brass, woodwind, percussion are the sections of an orchestra. How many instruments can you name?

wing wings
NOUN 1 A bird's or insect's wings are the parts of its body that it uses for flying.
2 An aeroplane's wings are the long, flat parts on each side that support it while it is in the air.
3 A wing of a building is a part which sticks out from the main part or which has been added later.
PLURAL NOUN 4 The wings in a theatre are the sides of the stage which are hidden from the audience.
winged ADJECTIVE

wingspan
NOUN The wingspan of a bird, insect or aeroplane is the distance from the end of one wing to the end of the other.

wink winks winking winked
VERB When you wink, you close one eye briefly, often to show that something is a joke or a secret.
wink NOUN

winkle winkles
NOUN a small sea-snail with a hard shell and a soft edible body.

winner winners
NOUN the person or thing that wins a prize, race or competition.

Synonyms: champion, victor

winnings
PLURAL NOUN Someone's winnings are the money they have won in a competition or by gambling.

winter winters
NOUN the season between autumn and spring.
wintry ADJECTIVE

wipe wipes wiping wiped
VERB If you wipe something, you rub its surface lightly (often with a cloth) to remove dirt or liquid.
wipe out VERB To wipe out people or places is to destroy them completely.
wiper NOUN

wire wires wiring wired
NOUN 1 metal in the form of a long, thin, flexible thread which can be used to make or fasten things or to conduct an electric current.
VERB 2 If you wire something or wire it up, you connect it so that electricity can pass through it.
3 If you wire one thing to another, you fasten them together using wire.

wireless wirelesses
NOUN; OLD-FASHIONED a radio.

wiring
NOUN The wiring in a building is the system of wires that supply electricity to the rooms.

wiry wirier wiriest
ADJECTIVE 1 Wiry people are thin but with strong muscles.
2 Wiry things are stiff and rough to the touch: *wiry hair.*

wisdom
NOUN 1 the ability to use experience and knowledge in order to make sensible decisions or judgements.
2 If you talk about the wisdom of an action or a decision, you are talking about how sensible, or otherwise, it is.

wisdom tooth wisdom teeth
NOUN Your wisdom teeth are four molar teeth at the back of your mouth which grow much later than other teeth.

wise wiser wisest
ADJECTIVE 1 Someone who is wise can use their experience and knowledge to make sensible decisions and judgements.
PHRASE 2 If you say that someone is **none the wiser** or **no wiser**, you mean that they know no more about something than they did before.
wisely ADVERB

Synonyms: (sense 1) judicious, prudent, sensible

wish wishes wishing wished
VERB 1 to want to do something. *We wished to return home.*
2 If you wish something were the case, you would like it to be the case but you know it is unlikely. *I wish I could fly.*
NOUN 3 something you desire or want.
4 Good wishes or best wishes are expressions of hope that someone will be happy or successful.

wishbone wishbones
NOUN a V-shaped bone in the breast of most birds.

wisp wisps
NOUN 1 A wisp of grass or hair is a small, thin, untidy bunch of it.
2 A wisp of smoke is a long, thin streak of it.
wispy ADJECTIVE

wistful
ADJECTIVE sadly thinking about something, especially something that you cannot have.
wistfulness NOUN **wistfully** ADVERB

wit wits
NOUN 1 the ability to use words or ideas in an amusing and clever way.
2 sense. *They haven't got the wit to realize what they're doing.*
PLURAL NOUN 3 Your wits are the ability to think and act quickly in a difficult situation. *Keep your wits about you.*
PHRASE 4 If you are **at your wits' end**, you are so worried and exhausted by problems or difficulties that you don't know what to do.

a b c d e f g h i j k l m n o p q r s t u v w x y z

A B C D E F G H I J K L M N O P Q R S T U V W X Y Z

witch **witches**
NOUN a woman claimed to have magic powers and to be able to use them for good or evil.

witchcraft
NOUN the skill or art of using magic powers, especially evil ones.

Synonyms: black magic, sorcery, wizardry

with
PREPOSITION **1** If a thing or person is with another, they are together in one place.
2 involving, concerning: *next week's game with Brazil; a problem with her phone bill.*
3 using or having. *She eats with her fingers. She saw a bloke with a moustache.*

withdraw **withdraws withdrawing withdrew withdrawn**
VERB **1** to remove something or take it out. *Dave withdrew his wallet from his pocket.*
2 to leave and go somewhere else. *The regiment withdrew to a town three miles away.*
3 to back out of something, to quit. *They withdrew from the conference.*
4 If you withdraw a remark, you say that you wish to change it or have it forgotten.
withdrawal NOUN

wither **withers withering withered**
VERB **1** When something withers or withers away, it becomes weaker until it no longer exists.
2 If a plant withers, it wilts or shrivels up and dies.
PLURAL NOUN **3** A horse's withers are the highest part of its back behind its neck.

withhold **withholds withholding withheld**
VERB; FORMAL If you withhold what someone wants, you do not let them have it.

within
PREPOSITION OR ADVERB **1** in or inside.
PREPOSITION **2** not going beyond certain limits: *within the rules; within fourteen days.*

without
PREPOSITION **1** not having, not feeling or not showing: *without emotion; without a break.*
2 not with or not accompanying. *The rats went without me.*

withstand **withstands withstanding withstood**
VERB When something or someone withstands a force or action, they survive it or do not give in to it. *These ships are designed to withstand Arctic conditions.*

witness **witnesses witnessing witnessed**
NOUN **1** someone who has seen an event such as an accident and can describe what happened.
2 someone who appears in a court of law to say what they know about a crime or other event.
3 someone who writes their name on a document that someone else has signed, to confirm that it is really that person's signature.
VERB **4** FORMAL If you witness an event, you see it.

Synonyms: (sense 1) bystander, observer, onlooker

witty **wittier wittiest**
ADJECTIVE amusing in a clever way.
wittily ADVERB

wizard **wizards**
NOUN **1** a man in a fairy story who has magic powers.
2 an expert at something: *a computer wizard.*
wizardry NOUN

wobble **wobbles wobbling wobbled**
VERB **1** If something wobbles, it shakes or moves from side to side because it is loose or unsteady.
2 If your voice wobbles, it trembles or shakes.
wobbly ADJECTIVE

woe **woes**
NOUN **1** LITERARY great unhappiness or sorrow.
2 Someone's woes are their problems or misfortunes.
woeful ADJECTIVE

wok **woks**
NOUN a large bowl-shaped metal pan used for Chinese-style cooking.

woke
the past tense of **wake**.

woken
the past participle of **wake**.

wolf **wolves; wolfs wolfing wolfed**
NOUN **1** a wild animal related to the dog.
VERB **2** To wolf food means to eat it up quickly and greedily.

woman **women**
NOUN an adult female human being.

womb **wombs**
Said "**woom**" NOUN A woman's womb is the part inside her body where her unborn baby grows; uterus.

won
past tense and past participle of **win**.

wonder **wonders wondering wondered**
VERB **1** If you wonder about something, you think about it and try to guess or understand more about it.
2 If you wonder at something, you are surprised and amazed at it.
NOUN **3** Wonder is a feeling of surprise and amazement.
4 something or someone that surprises and amazes people: *the wonder of science.*

Synonyms: (sense 4) marvel, miracle, phenomenon

 ▶ Joke. What do we call a witch on a broomstick? A flying sorcerer.

wonderful
ADJECTIVE **1** making you feel very happy and pleased. *It was wonderful to be together.*
2 very impressive: *a wonderful sight.*
wonderfully ADVERB

Synonyms: (sense 2) amazing, magnificent, remarkable

won't
contraction of **will not**.

wood **woods**
NOUN **1** the substance which forms the trunks and branches of trees.
2 a large area of trees growing near each other, a forest.

wooded
ADJECTIVE covered in trees.

wooden
ADJECTIVE **1** made of wood.
2 If you say that someone is wooden, you mean that they are rather stiff or lifeless in the way they do things.

woodland **woodlands**
NOUN land that is mostly covered with trees.

woodlouse **woodlice**
NOUN a very small grey animal that looks rather like an insect. It has seven pairs of legs, a segmented body and lives in damp places.

woodpecker **woodpeckers**
NOUN a climbing bird with a long, sharp beak that it uses to drill holes into trees to find insects.

woodwind
ADJECTIVE Woodwind instruments are musical instruments that are played by being blown into.

woodwork
NOUN **1** the craft or skill of making things out of wood.
2 the parts of a house, such as stairs, doors or window frames, that are made of wood.

woodworm **woodworm** or **woodworms**
NOUN **1** Woodworm are the larvae of a kind of beetle. They make holes in wood by feeding on it.
2 damage caused to wood by woodworm making holes in it.

woof **woofs**
NOUN the sound that a dog makes when it barks.

wool **wools**
NOUN the hair that grows on sheep and some other animals, and the material made from this hair.

woollen **woollens**
ADJECTIVE **1** made from wool.
PLURAL NOUN **2** Woollens are clothes made of wool.

woolly **woollier woolliest; woollies**
ADJECTIVE **1** made of wool or looking like wool.
2 If you describe people or their thoughts as woolly, you mean that they seem confused and unclear.
NOUN **3** a woollen garment, especially a pullover.

word **words wording worded**
NOUN **1** a single unit of language in speech or writing which has a meaning.
2 a remark or short conversation. *Could I have a word?*
3 news or information about something. *Is there any word on what happened?*
VERB **4** to express a feeling, idea, piece of information, etc. in words. *I'm not quite sure how to word this letter.*

wording
NOUN the way that something is expressed in words.

word processor **word processors**
NOUN an electronic machine which is used to prepare written material such as letters and books.
word processing NOUN

wore
past tense of **wear**.

work **works working worked**
VERB **1** to have a job which you are paid to do and to do the tasks that the job involves.
2 to control, handle or operate a machine. *It's easy to work a DVD recorder.*
3 If a machine, system or idea works, it operates properly, effectively and efficiently.
4 If something works its way into a particular position, it gradually moves there.
NOUN **5** employment, the state of having a job.
6 tasks that have to be done. *I've got a lot of work to do.*
7 something done or made: *a work of art.*
8 In physics, work is a transfer of energy, measured in joules.
PLURAL NOUN **9** A works is a place where something is made by an industrial process.
10 Works are large-scale construction activities.
work out VERB **1** If you work out the answer to a sum, you do the sum.
2 If a situation works out in a particular way, it happens in that way.
3 If you work out something such as a problem or disagreement, you find a way of resolving it.
4 to do systematic physical exercise or training. *She works out three times a week.*
work up VERB **1** If you work up to something you prepare for it.
2 If you work yourself up or work someone else up, you make yourself or the other person very angry.
worked up ADJECTIVE

A B C D E F G H I J K L M N O P Q R S T U V W X Y Z

workable
ADJECTIVE able to operate successfully or be used for a particular purpose: *a workable solution.*

workbench workbenches
NOUN a heavy table at which people do woodwork, metalwork or other practical jobs.

workbook workbooks
NOUN an exercise book or textbook used for study, especially a textbook with spaces for answers.

worker workers
NOUN someone who does a regular paid job.

workforce workforces
NOUN the number of people who work in a particular place.

workmanship
NOUN the skill with which something is made or a job is completed.

workout workouts
NOUN a session of physical exercise or training.

worksheet worksheets
NOUN a sheet of paper with exercises to be completed by a pupil.

workshop workshops
NOUN **1** a room or building that contains tools or machinery used for making or repairing things.
2 a period of discussion or practical work in which a group of people learn about a particular subject: *a theatre workshop.*

world worlds
NOUN **1** The world is the earth, the planet we live on.
2 Someone's world is the life they lead and the things they experience.
3 a division or section of the earth, its history or its people: *the ancient world; the Arab world.*
4 a field of activity and the people involved in it: *the world of dance.*
ADJECTIVE **5** "World" is used to describe someone or something that is one of the best or most important of its kind: *a world leader.*
PHRASE **6** If you **think the world of** someone, you like them very much.

worldly
ADJECTIVE Worldly people are knowledgeable about material things and daily events and are mainly interested in seeking wealth and pleasure.

worldwide
ADVERB OR ADJECTIVE throughout the world.

World Wide Web
NOUN the single worldwide computer network that interconnects other computer networks, allowing data and other information to be exchanged through websites, e-mail, news groups, etc.; the Internet.

worm worms
NOUN a small thin animal without bones or legs, which lives in the soil or off other creatures.

worn **1** the past participle of **wear**.
ADJECTIVE **2** damaged or thin because of long use.
3 looking old or exhausted.

worried
ADJECTIVE unhappy and anxious about a problem or about something unpleasant that might happen.

Synonyms: anxious, concerned, troubled

worry worries worrying worried
VERB **1** to feel anxious and fearful about a problem or about something unpleasant that might happen.
2 If something worries you, it causes you to feel uneasy or fearful.
3 If you worry someone with a problem, you disturb or bother them by telling them about it.
4 If a dog worries sheep, it chases them and bites them.
NOUN **5** a feeling of unhappiness and unease.
6 a person or thing that causes you to feel anxious or uneasy. *Her health is a big worry.*
worrying ADJECTIVE

Synonyms: (sense 5) anxiety, concern

worse
ADJECTIVE OR ADVERB **1** the comparative form of **bad** and **badly**.
2 If someone who is ill gets worse, they become more ill than before.

worsen worsens worsening worsened
VERB to become worse.

worship worships worshipping worshipped
VERB **1** If you worship a god, you show your love and respect by praying or singing hymns.
2 If you worship someone or something, you love them or admire them very much.
worship NOUN **worshipper** NOUN

Synonyms: (sense 2) adore, idolize, love

worst
ADJECTIVE OR ADVERB the superlative of **bad** and **badly**.

worth
ADJECTIVE **1** having a value of. *Our house is worth quite a lot of money.*
2 If something is worth doing, it deserves to be done.

worthless
ADJECTIVE having no real value or use.
worthlessness NOUN

worthwhile
ADJECTIVE important enough to justify the time, money or effort spent on it.

 ► There are about 3000 different languages spoken throughout the world.

worthy worthier worthiest
ADJECTIVE If someone or something is worthy of something, they deserve it.

would
VERB **1** "Would" is used to say what someone thought was going to happen. *We were sure it would be a success.*
2 "Would" is used to say that someone is willing to do something. *She would tell us if she could.*
3 "Would" is used in polite questions. *Would you like some lunch?.*

wouldn't
contraction of **would not**.

wound wounds wounding wounded
NOUN **1** an injury to part of your body, especially a cut in your skin and flesh.
VERB **2** If someone wounds you, they damage your body.
3 If you are wounded by what someone says or does, your feelings are hurt.

wove
past tense of **weave.**

woven
past participle of **weave.**

wrap wraps wrapping wrapped
VERB **1** to fold a piece of paper or cloth tightly around something to cover it.
2 If you wrap your arms, fingers or legs around something, you coil them round it.
wrap up VERB **1** to put warm clothes on.
2 If you are wrapped up in doing something, you are totally absorbed in it.
3 to cover a present in gift paper.
4 INFORMAL to finish doing something. *Let's wrap up here and go home.*

wrapper wrappers
NOUN a piece of paper, plastic or foil which covers and protects something that you buy.

wrapping wrappings
NOUN the material used to cover and protect something.

wrath
Said "**roth**" NOUN; LITERARY great anger.
wrathful ADJECTIVE

wreath wreaths
Said "**reeth**" NOUN an arrangement of flowers and leaves, often in the shape of a circle, which is put on a grave as a sign of remembrance for the dead person.

wreck wrecks wrecking wrecked
VERB **1** to break, destroy or spoil something completely.
NOUN **2** a vehicle which has been badly damaged in an accident.
3 If you say someone is a wreck, you mean that they are in a very poor physical or mental state of health and cannot cope with life.
wrecked ADJECTIVE

wreckage
NOUN what remains after something has been badly damaged or destroyed.

wren wrens
NOUN a very small brown songbird.

wrench wrenches wrenching wrenched
VERB **1** to give something a sudden and violent twist or pull.
2 If you wrench a limb or a joint, you twist and injure it.
NOUN **3** a metal tool with parts which can be adjusted to fit around nuts or bolts to loosen or tighten them.

wrestle wrestles wrestling wrestled
VERB **1** to fight somebody by holding or throwing them.
2 If you wrestle with a problem, you try extremely hard to solve it.
wrestler NOUN

wretch wretches
NOUN; OLD-FASHIONED someone who is thought to be wicked or very unfortunate.
[from Old English *wrecca* meaning exile or despised person]

wretched
Said "**ret**-shid" ADJECTIVE very unhappy or unfortunate: *a wretched childhood.*

wriggle wriggles wriggling wriggled
VERB **1** to twist and turn your body or a part of your body using quick movements.
2 If you wriggle out of doing something that you do not want to do, you manage to avoid doing it.
wriggle NOUN

wring wrings wringing wrung
VERB **1** to squeeze the water out of a cloth, mop, etc. by twisting it.
2 If you wring your hands, you hold them together and twist and turn them, usually because you are worried or upset.
3 If someone wrings a bird's neck, they kill the bird by twisting and breaking its neck.
4 If you wring something from someone or from a situation, you manage to get it with a lot of effort. *We will wring the information out of her.*

wrinkle wrinkles wrinkling wrinkled
NOUN **1** Wrinkles are lines in someone's skin, especially on the face, which form as they grow old.
VERB **2** If something wrinkles, folds or lines develop on it.
3 If you wrinkle something, you screw it up tight so that folds or lines develop on it.
wrinkly ADJECTIVE

wrist wrists
NOUN the part of your body between your hand and your arm which bends when you move your hand.

What do film directors mean when they say "It's a wrap"?

write **writes writing wrote written**
VERB **1** to use a pen or pencil to form letters, words or numbers on a surface.
2 to create something such as a poem, a book or a piece of music.
write up VERB If you write up something, you write a full account of it, often using notes that you have made.

writer **writers**
NOUN **1** a person who writes books, stories or articles as a job.
2 The writer of something is the person who wrote it.

writhe **writhes writhing writhed**
Said "**rieth**" VERB to twist and turn your body, often because you are in pain.

writing **writings**
NOUN **1** something which has been written or printed.
2 Your writing is the way you write with a pen or pencil.
3 a piece of written work, especially the style of language used. *This is very humorous writing.*

written
1 the past participle of **write**.
ADJECTIVE **2** taken down in writing.

wrong **wrongs wronging wronged**
ADJECTIVE **1** unsatisfactory or not working properly. *Something is wrong with the car.*
2 not correct, accurate or truthful: *the wrong answer.*
3 bad or immoral. *It is wrong to kill people.*
NOUN **4** an unjust action or situation: *the wrongs of our society.*
VERB **5** If someone wrongs you, they treat you in an unfair or unjust way.
wrongly ADVERB

wrote
past tense of **write**.

wrung
past tense and past participle of **wring**.

wry **wrier wriest** or **wryer wryest**
Said "**rye**" ADJECTIVE If you have a wry expression, you are laughing to yourself because you know more about the situation than others do.
wryly ADVERB

 ► Adverbial pun. "My first three answers were wrong," she said, forthrightly.

Xmas

NOUN; INFORMAL an abbreviation for **Christmas**. [in Greek, X is the first letter of *Christos* meaning Christ]

X-ray X-rays X-raying X-rayed

NOUN 1 a type of radiation that can pass through some solid materials. X-rays are used by doctors to examine the bones or organs inside a person's body. They are used at airports to see inside people's luggage.
2 a picture made by using X-rays.
VERB 3 to use X-rays to examine the bones or organs of a person's body.

xylophone xylophones

Said "**zy**-lo-fone" **NOUN** a musical instrument made of a row of wooden bars of different lengths. It is played by hitting the bars with special hammers.

X-rays got their name because X is used in mathematics for an unknown quantity.

A B C D E F G H I J K L M N O P Q R S T U V W X Y Z

Yy

yacht **yachts**
Said "**yot**" **NOUN** a boat with sails or an engine, or both, used for racing or for pleasure trips.
yachting NOUN

yam **yams**
NOUN a root vegetable which grows in tropical regions.

yank **yanks yanking yanked**
VERB 1 to pull or jerk something suddenly with a lot of force.
NOUN 2 INFORMAL A Yank is an American.

yap **yaps yapping yapped**
VERB If a dog yaps, it barks with a high-pitched sound.

yard **yards**
NOUN 1 an imperial unit of length equal to 36 inches or about 91·4 centimetres.
2 a large area often next to a building that is used for a particular purpose: *our back yard; a ship repair yard.*

yarn **yarns**
NOUN 1 thread used for knitting or making cloth.
2 INFORMAL a story that someone tells, often with invented details to make it more interesting or exciting.

yashmak **yashmaks**
NOUN a veil that some Muslim women wear over their faces when they are in public.

yawn **yawns yawning yawned**
VERB to open your mouth wide and take in more air than usual, often when you are tired or bored.

ye
PRONOUN 1 OLD-FASHIONED you.
ADJECTIVE 2 OLD-FASHIONED the.

year **years**
NOUN 1 a period of twelve months or 365 days (366 days in a leap year), usually measured from the first of January to the thirty-first of December.
2 a period of twelve consecutive months, or a period of a year, during which something happens or is organized: *the school year.*
PHRASE 3 If something happens **year in, year out**, it happens every year.

yearly
ADJECTIVE OR ADVERB every year.

yearn **yearns yearning yearned**
Rhymes with "**learn**" **VERB** If you yearn for something, you want it very much indeed; to long for.
yearning NOUN

yeast **yeasts**
NOUN a kind of fungus which is used to make bread rise, and to make liquids ferment in order to produce alcohol.

yell **yells yelling yelled**
VERB to shout loudly, usually because you are angry, excited or in pain.
yell NOUN

yellow **yellower yellowest**
NOUN OR ADJECTIVE the colour of buttercups, egg yolks or lemons.

yelp **yelps yelping yelped**
VERB When people or animals yelp, they give a sudden, short cry.
yelp NOUN

yen
NOUN 1 If you have a yen to do something, you have a strong desire to do it.
2 the main unit of currency in Japan.

yes
INTERJECTION You say "yes" to agree with someone, to say that something is true, or to accept something.

yesterday
NOUN OR ADVERB 1 the day before today.
2 You also use "yesterday" to refer to the past. *Leave yesterday's worries behind you.*

yet
ADVERB 1 If something has not happened yet, it has not happened up to the present time.
2 If something should not be done yet, it should not be done now, but later.
3 "Yet" can mean there is still a possibility that something can happen.
CONJUNCTION 4 You can use "yet" to introduce a fact which is rather surprising: *She never eats meat, yet she insists that she isn't a vegetarian.*

yeti **yetis**
Said "**yet**-tee" **NOUN** A yeti, or abominable snowman, is a large hairy apelike animal which some people believe exists in the Himalayas.

yew **yews**
NOUN an evergreen tree with bright red berries.

yield **yields yielding yielded**
VERB 1 If you yield to someone or something, you stop resisting and give in to them.
2 If you yield something that you have control of or responsibility for, you surrender it.
3 If something yields, it breaks or gives way.
4 to produce. *That tree yields wonderful apples.*
NOUN 5 an amount of food, money or profit produced from a given area of land or from an investment.

yoga
Said "**yoe**-ga" **NOUN** a Hindu method of mental and physical exercise or discipline.

 ▸ The letter Y probably began as a picture of a hook, possibly a thumbstick – or perhaps even a tree.

yogurt **yogurts**; also spelt **yoghurt**
Said "**yog**-gurt" NOUN a slightly sour thick liquid made from milk that has had bacteria added to it.

yoke **yokes**
NOUN **1** a wooden bar laid across the necks of two animals which are pulling a cart or a plough, to hold them together.
2 LITERARY If people are under a yoke of some kind, they are being oppressed: *the yoke of tyranny.*

yolk **yolks**
*Rhymes with "***joke***"* NOUN the yellow part in the middle of an egg.

Yom Kippur
Said "yom-kip-**poor**" NOUN an annual Jewish religious holiday, which is a day of fasting and prayers. It is also called the Day of Atonement.

yonder
ADVERB OR ADJECTIVE; OLD-FASHIONED over there.

you
PRONOUN **1** "You" refers to the person or a group of people that a person is speaking or writing to.
2 "You" also refers to people in general. *You can get lost quite easily in the city.*

you'd
1 contraction of **you would**.
2 contraction of **you had**.

you'll
contraction of **you will**.

young **younger youngest**
ADJECTIVE **1** A young person, animal or plant has not lived very long and is not yet mature.
NOUN **2** The young are young people in general.
3 The young of an animal are its babies.

Synonyms: (sense 1) immature, undeveloped (sense 3) babies, offspring, progeny

youngster **youngsters**
NOUN a child or young person.

your
ADJECTIVE **1** belonging or relating to the person or group of people that someone is speaking or writing to.
2 belonging or relating to people in general. *Cigarettes can damage your health.*

you're
contraction of **you are**.

yours
PRONOUN "Yours" refers to something belonging or relating to the person or group of people that someone is speaking to.

yourself **yourselves**
PRONOUN **1** "Yourself" refers to the person you are speaking or writing to. *Why can't you do it yourself?*
2 "Yourself" is used to emphasize the person you are speaking or writing to. *Do you want to go yourself?*

youth **youths**
NOUN **1** the period of someone's life before they are a fully mature adult.
2 the quality or condition of being young and often inexperienced. *The team is a blend of experience and youth.*
3 a boy or young man.
4 young people thought of as a group: *the youth of today.*
youthful ADJECTIVE **youthfully** ADVERB

youth hostel **youth hostels**
NOUN a place where young people can stay cheaply when they are on holiday.
youth hosteller NOUN

yo-yo **yo-yos**
NOUN a round wooden or plastic toy attached to a piece of string. You play by making the yo-yo rise and fall on the string.

Yule
NOUN; OLD-FASHIONED Christmas.

A B C D E F G H I J K L M N O P Q R S T U V W X Y Z

zany zanier zaniest
ADJECTIVE odd and ridiculous. *I love the zany humour of cartoons.*
[from Italian *zanni* meaning clown]

zap zaps zapping zapped
VERB **1** INFORMAL to kill or destroy someone or something, usually by shooting.
2 to move somewhere quickly. *I zapped over to Paris.*

zeal
NOUN enthusiasm and keenness.
zealous ADJECTIVE

zebra zebras
NOUN a type of African wild horse with black and white stripes over its body.

zebra crossing zebra crossings
NOUN a specially-designated road crossing place for pedestrians, marked with black and white stripes.

zero zeros zeroing zeroed
1 the number 0.
2 Zero is freezing point, 0° Centigrade.
ADJECTIVE **3** Zero means there is none at all of a particular thing: *zero chance.*
VERB **4** To zero in on a target is to aim at or to move towards it.
5 To zero a gauge or counter is to set the mechanism back to zero.

zest
NOUN **1** a feeling of pleasure and enthusiasm.
2 a quality which adds extra flavour or interest to something: *brilliant ideas to add zest to your room.*
3 The zest of an orange or lemon is the outside of the peel which is used to flavour food or drinks.
zestful ADJECTIVE **zestfully** ADVERB

zigzag zigzags zigzagging zigzagged
NOUN **1** a line which has a series of sharp angular turns in it.
VERB **2** to move forward by going at an angle first right then left. *The skater zigzagged round the ice rink.*

zinc
NOUN a bluish-white metal used in alloys and to coat other metals to stop them rusting.

zip zips zipping zipped
NOUN **1** a fastener used on clothes and bags, with two rows of metal or plastic teeth which separate or fasten together as you pull a small tag along them.
VERB **2** to fasten using a zip.
3 INFORMAL To zip somewhere is to go there very quickly. *I'll zip to the shops for some bread and milk.*

zodiac
Said "**zoe**-dee-ak" NOUN an imaginary strip in the sky which contains the planets and stars which astrologers think are important influences on people. It is divided into 12 sections, each with a special name and symbol, such as Leo, Capricorn and Sagittarius.

zombie zombies
NOUN **1** INFORMAL someone who does not seem to be aware of what is going on around them and who acts without thinking about what they are doing.
2 In black magic, a zombie is a dead person who has been brought back to life by witchcraft.

zone zones
NOUN an area that has particular features or characteristics: *a war zone.*

zoo zoos
NOUN a place where live animals are kept so that people can look at them and where they can be bred in safety.

zoology
Said "zoo-**ol**-loj-jee" NOUN the scientific study of animals.
zoological ADJECTIVE **zoologically** ADVERB
zoologist NOUN

zoom zooms zooming zoomed
VERB **1** to move very quickly.
2 If a film camera zooms in on something, it goes from a long view of something to a close-up picture of it.

zoom lens zoom lenses
NOUN a camera lens which can change smoothly in focus from long distance to close up.

zucchini zucchini or zucchinis
Said "zoo-**kee**-nee" NOUN a small vegetable marrow with dark green skin.

 ▶ The letter Z was a weapon, probably one using two sticks. *Zayin* was a word meaning weapon.

A short history of the English language

The history of the English language is the history of invasions from overseas. Over many centuries, successive invaders from northern Europe landed on British shores, fought the inhabitants and finally settled themselves. The languages they brought with them were absorbed into the English language.

The first of these invaders were the Celts, who came to Britain from Europe at least 3,000 years ago. English speakers now use very few Celtic words but many place names come from the words the Celts used for rivers and water.

In 55 BC the Romans invaded Britain and their language, Latin, was used here for more than 400 years, until the Roman legions had to return to Italy to defend the main part of their empire. It was the next wave of invaders who brought the language which was to become the basis of our English tongue.

The Angles, Saxons and Jutes migrated from the area we now know as the countries of the Netherlands, Germany and Denmark. For over 500 years Anglo-Saxon was the dominant language in England though it was influenced by Viking invaders from Scandinavia who brought their Norse tongue in the 8th and 9th centuries. They settled mainly in the north of England but their language gradually merged with Anglo-Saxon into what we now call Old English.

In 1066, William the Conqueror, Duke of Normandy, invaded England. Following his victory at the Battle of Hastings, he formed a new system of central government. French became the language of the ruling group. Old English was looked down on as a language for the peasants. But the language of the common people was too firmly established to die. It survived and over the years merged with French into what we now call Middle English. In the 14th century, this was accepted as the country's official language.

By 1450, many words sounded more as we say them today, and variations between different places grew less. With the coming of printed books, spelling, which had also varied greatly from region to region, became more standardized. It is from this period that we can date what we now call Modern English.

At the same time, exploration of the world was well under way. Words flooded into English from over 50 other languages. Writers such as Shakespeare experimented freely with language, inventing words, adding new prefixes and suffixes and making old words do new jobs. You can gain a good idea of the language of these times both from Shakespeare and the Church of England's Authorized Version of the Bible (1611).

Since then the English language has certainly not stood still. The flow of new words has continued uninterrupted – especially words to do with science and technology, which now make up well over half the English language.

During the 20th century the influence of America has been felt more and more, particularly through films and television. This peaceful invasion by American culture mirrors the invasions that began with the Celts 3,000 years ago. Each new generation coins its own words and phrases. Each generation has its fashions in language. The only difference is that today, thanks to instant electronic communication, things come (and often go) rather more quickly.

New words

As new inventions, discoveries and ideas occur, so new words enter our language all the time. Here are some examples from the last 100 years:

bhangra	download	radio	sitcom
boot up	email	mind-blowing	skateboard
bottle bank	fast food	morphing	slaphead
blitz	fax	multi-gym	snail mail
bra	gobsmacked	nerd	spam
bungee jumping	gridlock	photocopier	teenager
cellphone	hacker	quad bike	superglue
couch potato	hands-on	radio	television
credit card	helpline	ratbag	unleaded
database	Internet	rock'n'roll	windfarm
disc jockey	junk mail	rollover	yuppie
disco	karaoke	scratch card	zap

As language evolves, old words are given new meanings:

anorak	floppy	icon	smart
awesome	gay	mobile	soap
browse	goalposts	record	spam
disc	graze	sad	wrinkly

Words with unusual origins

Many words in the dictionary have unusual origins. For example, "checkmate", the move that ends a game of chess, comes from the Arabic *shah mat* meaning "the king is dead". Look up some of these words with interesting origins:

alphabet	denim	marathon	sandwich
Arctic	earwig	marsupial	sarcastic
atlas	gorilla	migraine	sinister
berserk	jubilee	muscle	slave
bogus	judo	newt	smack
bowel	juggernaut	nickname	soap opera
boycott	July	pedigree	starboard
bus	kidnap	quarantine	tadpole
catamaran	lens	radar	teddy
dandelion	lunatic	salary	vandal

Words from abroad

Many words (and phrases) have been introduced, virtually unchanged, from foreign languages into our language. For example:

Africa	banana, chimpanzee	**Ireland (Gaelic)**	leprechaun, smithereens
Australia	boomerang, budgerigar	**Italy**	macaroni, piano
Caribbean	cannibal, barbecue	**Japan**	judo, karaoke
Central America	chocolate, tomato	**Middle East**	alcohol, sofa
China	typhoon, soya	**Netherlands**	boss, coleslaw
Czech Republic	pistol, robot	**Portugal**	marmalade, palaver
Eskimo	kayak, anorak	**Russia**	cosmonaut, vodka
France	police, café	**Scotland (Gaelic)**	clan, slogan
Germany	hamburger, snorkel	**South Africa**	trek, apartheid
India (Hindi)	bungalow, shampoo	**Spain**	tornado, plaza
India (Tamil)	curry, catamaran	**Tibet**	polo, yak
Iran	caravan, sherbet	**Turkey**	tulip, yogurt

Many English words have their roots in other languages. Here are some examples. Look them up in the dictionary to see how their meaning has evolved.

Language of origin	Word	Original word/meaning
Dutch	**golf**	stick, club or bat
	hobble	to rock back and forth
	iceberg	ice mountain
	kit	jug, tankard or wooden container
	luck	happiness and good fortune
	skipper	to act as ship's captain
	snap	to snap or snatch
French	**advertisement**	*avertissement* meaning a warning
	dandelion	*dent de lion* meaning "lion's teeth"
	souvenir	to remember
German	**abseil**	*abseilen* means to "rope down"
	dachshund	literally, badger-dog
	kindergarten	literally, children-garden
	rucksack	back bag
Greek	**chaos**	gulf, abyss or empty space
	climax	ladder
	crisis	decision
	pentathlon	*pente* means five and *athlon* means prize or contest
	zone	belt
Hebrew	**amen**	truly
	rabbi	My master
	Sabbath	*shabbath* means to rest
Hindi	**juggernaut**	a huge cart carrying the image of the god Vishnu
	thug	thief
Italian	**casino**	little house
	confetti	sweets
	ditto	said
	lava	a flooded stream
	spaghetti	string
Latin	**audio**	"I hear"
	camera	a dark room
	circus	ring
	curriculum	racecourse
	et cetera (etc)	"and the rest"
	interior	inner
	medium	middle
	nausea	seasickness
	radius	the spoke of a wheel
	versus	against
	victor	winner
	video	"I see"
Turkish	**kiosk**	pavilion or palace
	yogurt	to blend

Tricky words

Here are 295 words that are often misspelt. Make sure you know their meanings as well as how to spell them.

absence
accelerator
accent
accidentally
accommodate
achieved
acknowledge
acquainted
address
advertisement
aerial
aggravate
agreeable
amateur
among
answer
Antarctic
anxiety
apparent
appearance
appropriate
Arctic
argument
arrangements
article
ascend
athletic
aunt
autumn
awful
bachelor
beautiful
because
beginning
believed
bicycle
breakfast
breathe
Britain
build
business
café
calm
captain
careful
catalogue
cemetery
certain
character
chemistry
chocolate
choice
Christmas
clothes
college
colour
comedy
coming
committee
comparative
comparison
competent
completely
conscience
conscientious
conscious
consistent
convenience
copies
course
courteous
courtesy
crept
criticism
cupboard
cylindrical
deceive
decide
decision
definite
descent
describe
desirable
desperate
different
dinghy
disappeared
disappointed
disastrous
discipline
disease
dissatisfied
doctor
does
efficiency
eighth
eliminated
embarrassed
enjoy
enquire
enthusiasm
envelope
equipped
especially
essential
etc.
everybody
exaggerated
excellent
except
exciting
exercise
exhausted
exhibition
existence
expenses
experience
familiar
fashion
favourite
February
fictitious
financial
forecast
foreign
formerly
forty
friend
gauge
genius
geography
government
grammar
grievance
guarantee
guard
guardian
guess
handkerchief
height
heroes
humour
hungry
hurriedly
hygiene
hypocrisy
imagination
immediately
incidentally
independent
indispensable
influential
instance
intelligence
interest
irresistible
jewellery
kept
knowledge
laboratory
led
library
licence
lightning
literature
longitude
lose
losing
lying
maintenance
marriage
mathematics
meant
mechanical
medicine
Mediterranean
meringue
miniature
minute
minutes
mischievous
murmur
mystery
mysterious
necessary
necessarily
neighbour
niece
noticeable
nuisance
occasional
occurred
occurrence
omitted
opinion
opportunity
originally
parallel
parliament
pastime
people
perhaps
permanent
permissible
perseverance
pharmacy
physical
physics
physique
planning
pleasant
police
possesses
preference
prejudice
present
privilege
probably
procedure
proceeding

Tricky words (continued)

proceeds
professional
professor
pronunciation
psychology
quiet
quite
really
received
recognized
recommended
referred
refrigerator (fridge)
remember
repetition
restaurant
rhyme
rhythm
said
satellite
scarcely
science
secondary
secretaries
seize
sentence
separate
sergeant
severely
Shakespeare
shining
siege
similar
sincerely
speak
speech
squirrel
straight
strength
successful
suppression
surprise
syllable
sympathy
symphony
synonym
taught
television
temporary
temporarily
tendency
themselves
thorough
through
tongue
tragedy
transferred
trouble
twelfth
unconscious
unnecessary
until
usually
vacuum
valuable
veterinary
view
Wednesday
went
whole
wholly
woollen
write
yacht
you're (= you are)

Spelling strategies

Here are the four main spelling rules.

- When the sound is "ee", it's I before E except after C: *believe, chief, receive, conceited.*
- Consonant Y changes to I: *carry* ➔ *carries, happy* ➔ *happiness, crazy* ➔ *crazier.*
- Knock off the E and add I-N-G: *hope* ➔ *hoping, slide* ➔ *sliding, cure* ➔ *curing.*
- Double the consonant to keep the vowel sound short: *sit* ➔ *sitting, hop* ➔ *hopped, mud* ➔ *muddy.*

To learn spellings: look, cover, write and check.

- **Look** at the word you have to learn.
- **Cover** it up.
- **Write** down how you think it is spelt.
- **Check** your spelling against the word you first looked at.

The golden rule to good spelling is: if you're not sure how to spell a word, check it in your dictionary.

Another useful approach is to use a mnemonic. A mnemonic is a phrase or sentence which helps you to remember how to spell tricky words. Here are some useful mnemonics.

because	**b**ig **e**lephants **c**an **a**lways **u**pset **s**mall **e**lephants
believe	never be**lie**ve a **lie**
rhythm	**r**hythm **h**as **y**our **t**oes **h**opping **m**adly
separate	separate has **a rat** in it

Key words

These words are used so often that they make up about half of all reading. If you know these, half your spelling will be right.

a
about
after
again
all
always
am
and
an
another
any
are
as
ask
at
away
back
bad
be
because
been
before
best
big
bird
black
blue
boy
bring
but
by
call
came
can
come
could
day
did
do
dog
done
down
eat
every
far
fast
father
fell
find
first
five
fly
for
four (4)
found
from
gave
get
girl
give
go
going
good
got
green
had
hand
his
have
he
head
held
help
her
hero
him
home
house
how
I
if
in
into
is
it
jump
just
keep
know
last
left
let
like
little
live
long
look
made
make
man
many
may
me
men
more
mother
Mr
Mrs
much
must
my
never
new
next
no
not
now
of
off
old
on
once
one
only
open
or
our
other
out
over
own
play
put
ran
road
rod
right
room
round
run
said
sat
saw
say
school
see
she
should
sing
sit
so
some
soon
stop
take
tell
than
that
the
their
them
then
there
these
they
thing
think
this
three
time
to
too
tree
two
under
up
us
very
walk
want
was
we
well
went
were
what
when
where
which
white
who
why
will
wish
with
woman
women
work
would
year
yes
yellow
yet
you
young
your
yourself
youth

The **singular** of a noun is the form used for just **one** person or thing.
The **plural** of a noun is the form used for **two or more** people or things.

Almost all the headwords in this, or any, dictionary are in the singular form. (The exceptions are words such as trousers or pyjamas which are not used in the singular form.) Plural forms of singular nouns are given on the same line as the headword.

Remember that apostrophes are never used to form plurals.

The usual way to show a noun is in the plural is to add *-s*:

pen ➔ pens
house ➔ houses
train ➔ trains

There are several exceptions to this general method of forming plurals:

- For nouns that end in "-ch", "-s", "sh", "-ss", or "-x", add "-es":

  pitch ➔ pitches
  bus ➔ buses
  gash ➔ gashes
  mattress ➔ mattresses
  fox ➔ foxes

- For nouns ending in a consonant + y, change "-y" to "-ies":

  baby ➔ babies
  pastry ➔ pastries
  party ➔ parties

- For nouns ending in a vowel + y, add "-s":

  donkey ➔ donkeys
  valley ➔ valleys
  Monday ➔ Mondays

- For nouns ending in "-f" or "-fe", change to "-ves" in the plural:

  loaf ➔ loaves
  half ➔ halves
  wife ➔ wives

  There are some exceptions to this rule:

  roof ➔ roofs
  chief ➔ chiefs
  safe ➔ safes

- Most nouns that end in "-o" add "-es" in the plural:

  hero ➔ heroes
  tomato ➔ tomatoes
  potato ➔ potatoes

- Some nouns have the same form in both the singular and the plural:

  one sheep, two sheep
  one deer, two deer
  one trout, two trout

Prefixes

A **prefix** is a letter or group of letters added to the beginning of a word to make a new word.

Prefix	Meaning	Example
ab-	away from, off, outside of, opposite to	abstain, abandon
ad-	to, towards, near or next to	adhere, advance
ambi-	both	ambiguous, ambidextrous
ante-	before	antenatal (before giving birth)
anti-	against, opposed to or opposite to something	anticlockwise
arch-	chief; principal; of the highest rank	archbishop
auto-	self or same	automatic, autograph
bene-	good, well	benefit, benevolent
bi-	twice or two	bicycle, bilingual
bio-	related to living things or people	biology, biography
cent-	one hundred	centimetre, century
circum-	around	circumference, circumstances
co-	together	cooperate, coordinate
con-	with, together	converge, contain
contra-	against or opposite to	contradict, contrast
cyber-	related to computers	cyberspace
de-	from, away, out of	deflect, deflate
deca-	relating to ten	decathlon
deci-	relating to tenths; also tens and multiples of ten	decimal
dia-	through, throughout or during	diameter, diagonal
dis-	added to the beginning of words to form antonyms	disappear, disconnect
equi-	equal	equivalent, equinox
ex-	out of	exhaust, exclude
extra-	outside or beyond	extraordinary, extra-terrestrial
fore-	before in time or rank; at or near the front	forehead, foresee
geo-	related to the earth	geography, geology
homo-	being the same; like	homonym, homograph
hyper-	very much or excessive	hyperactive, hypermarket
hypo-	under, beneath, below	hypotenuse, hypothermia
in-	in, into	include, income
in-	not: added to words to form antonyms	inappropriate, indirect
inter-	between	international, interview
kilo-	a thousand	kilometre, kilogram
mal-	bad or badly; wrong or wrongly	malfunction, malicious
maxi-	very large or long	maximum

Prefix	Meaning	Example
mega-	very great	megastore, megalith
meta-	a prefix indicating change	metaphor, metamorphosis
micro-	very small	microscopic, microchip
mid-	indicating the middle part of a place or a period of time	mid-Atlantic, mid-July
milli-	a thousand times smaller	millimetre, milligram
mini-	smaller or less important	minimum, minibus
mis-	wrong, bad or involving an error	misjudge, misspell
mono-	one; single	monologue, monopoly
multi-	many	multiply, multitude
non-	a prefix added to form antonyms	nonexistent, non-fiction
omni-	all	omnibus, omnivore
over-	too much	overeat, oversleep
para-	indicates an object that acts as a protection against something	parachute, parasol
per-	through; throughout	persevere, perspire
peri-	around; enclosing	perimeter
poly-	many or much	polygon, polyhedron
post-	after	postpone, post-war
pre-	before	prepare, prefix
pro-	supporting or in favour of	proposal, pronoun
pseudo-	false, artificial	pseudonym
quadri-	four	quadrilateral
quin-	five	quintet, quintuplets
re-	again	replace, rebuild
self-	done to yourself or by yourself; automatic	self-service, self-control
semi-	half or partly	semicircle, semidetached
step-	indicates people who are related through someone's second marriage, that is, they are not blood relations	stepfather, stepdaughter
sub-	under; below	submarine, submit
super-	over; larger or better	supersonic, supervise
tele-	far off	television, telephone
thermo-	related to, caused by or measuring heat	thermometer
trans-	across, through or beyond	transatlantic, transparent
tri-	three	triangle, tricycle
ultra-	extreme or extremely	ultraviolet, ultra-cautious
un-	added to the beginning of many words to form antonyms	unusual, unpleasant
vice-	deputy	vice-admiral, vice-principal

Suffixes

A **suffix** is a letter or group of letters added to the end of a word to form a new word.

These suffixes make **nouns**:

-er	buy	→	buyer
-or	inspect	→	inspector
-ism	magnet, vandal	→	magnetism, vandalism
-ment	encourage, impede	→	encouragement, impediment
-ness	good, happy	→	goodness, happiness
-ship	friend, hard	→	friendship, hardship
-tion	add	→	addition
-ion	convert	→	conversion

These suffixes make **verbs**:

-en	tight, length	→	tighten, lengthen
-fy	simple, terror	→	simplify, terrify

These suffixes make **adjectives**:

-able	drink, comfort	→	drinkable, comfortable
-ful	beauty, use	→	beautiful, useful
-less	help, worth	→	helpless, worthless
-ic	photograph, scene	→	photographic, scenic
-ible	reverse	→	reversible
-ish	red, Scot	→	reddish, Scottish
-ive	rest, prohibit	→	restive, prohibitive
-ous	danger, space	→	dangerous, spacious
-y	sun, sand	→	sunny, sandy

These suffixes make **adverbs**:

-ly	slow, bad	→	slowly, badly
-ally	automatic	→	automatically

This suffix makes nouns **feminine**:

-ess	prince, actor	→	princess, actress

This suffix forms a **diminutive** (small word):

-ette	disk	→	diskette

Other useful suffixes:

Suffix	**Meaning**	**Example**
-graphy	related to writing	biography, calligraphy
-less	without	worthless, shameless
-let	smaller	booklet, streamlet
-like	similar to, characteristic of	lifelike, warlike
-most	supreme or extreme	topmost, foremost
-ology	related to the study of something	geology, biology
-some	full of	troublesome, quarrelsome
-ward	turning to (adjective)	westward, homeward
-wards	turning to (adverb)	backwards, upwards
-wise	in a certain manner	clockwise, likewise

Full stops, question marks, exclamation marks, ellipsis

A sentence must begin with a capital letter and end with one of these:

- a full stop (.)
- a question mark (?)
- an exclamation mark (!)
- an ellipsis (…)

You can use an ellipsis (...) to:

- end a sentence which is interrupted or tails off:
  The award-winning actress sobbed: "Darlings, I'm lost for words, I…"
- show where words are missing from a quotation:
  "We will fight them on the beaches… we will never surrender."

Commas

Commas (,) are mainly used to:

- mark pauses in a sentence:
  She added, as my face turned red with embarrassment, "You are the weakest link!"
- separate items in a list:
  I bought tomatoes, beans, ham, potatoes and bread.

Semicolons

The semicolon (;) is used to:

- separate two clauses especially where there is a balance or contrast between them:
  I like bull terriers; they seem to like me.
- to separate parts of a complicated list:
  In the kennels were Tess, a white bull terrier; Jim, a mongrel who tried to lick everybody he met; Butch, a bulldog with a nasty temper; and Fifi, a poodle who slept most of the time.

Colons

The colon (:) is used to introduce lists, to introduce an explanation of a statement and, sometimes, to introduce a quotation.

Dashes

The dash (–) is used where the flow of a sentence is interrupted.
I caught sight of Wesley – who I hadn't seen for months – coming out of the car park.

Brackets

Brackets ( ) or [ ] are used to add extra information which is not part of a sentence.
Thomas à Becket was murdered by Henry II's knights (Brito, de Morville and two others).

Apostrophes

Apostrophes are used in two ways:

- to indicate omitted letters:
  can't, won't, let's, I'll, that's.
- to show possession:
  the boy's pens (the pens of the boy)
  the women's eyes (the eyes of the women)

Confusables

Be careful not to confuse these words. These pairs of words are frequently confused in written work, because they look alike or because they mean similar things.

affect effect
"Affect" is a verb.
The weather will not affect football matches.
"Effect" is usually a noun.
Late nights watching TV had a bad effect on David's SATs results.

always all ways
"Always" means all the time or for ever.
He was always at school on time.
"All ways" means in every way.
In all ways, she was an excellent sportswoman.

borrow lend
If I borrow your pencil, please will you lend me your ruler as well?

brought bought
"Brought" comes from the verb **to bring**.
I've brought some sandwiches in my lunch box; what did you bring?
"Bought" comes from the verb **to buy**.
They bought the last bike in the shop, which I had hoped to buy.

chose choose
"Chose" is the past tense of the verb **to choose**.
As Caroline chose the starter, I'm going to choose the main course.

clothes cloths
"Clothes" are what you wear.
Jack wore his best clothes to go out dancing.
"Cloths" are what you wipe things with.
She fetched some cloths from the kitchen to mop up the spilt tea.

does dose
"Does" comes from the verb **to do**.
"Dose" is a noun.
Does he need his dose of medicine now or later?

fewer less
"Fewer" refers to something you can count. "Less" refers to mass quantities which are difficult or impossible to count.
Jo had fewer potatoes and less rice than Jim.

its it's
"Its" is the possessive form of it:
The cat has hurt its paw.
"It's", with an apostrophe, is a short form of **it is** or **it has**:
It's green. It's been snowing again.

learn teach
"Learn" is what the pupil does.
She was slow to learn good manners.
"Teach" is what the teacher does.
Please teach me how to swim.

lose loose
"Lose" is a verb meaning to cease to have something because you cannot find it.
Don't lose your pocket money!
"Loose" is an adjective meaning not tight.
I fell off because the saddle was loose.

of off
The jug of milk fell off the table.

passed past
"Passed" is the past tense of **to pass**.
Four buses passed me without stopping.
"Past" is an adverb.
The bus went past me without stopping.

quiet quite
Although the party was quiet at first, it became quite noisy later on.

stationary stationery
"Stationary" means not moving.
The car ran into the stationary tractor.
"Stationery" is paper and pens.
The school had special stationery printed.

their there
The children took off their coats.
Put your boots over there.

weather whether
As the weather is showery, it's difficult to know whether to go to the seaside or not.

were where
We were trying to find out where they were catching all those fish.

Synonyms

A synonym is a word meaning the same, or almost the same, as another word. In writing, as a general rule, you should avoid repeating words too often, so it is important to know alternatives.

These are synonyms for some everyday words:

angry	annoyed, cross, hopping mad, furious, enraged, incandescent with rage
big	sizeable, large, huge, vast, enormous, colossal, mammoth, weighty, important
small	tiny, little, minute, miniature, microscopic, unimportant, trivial, insignificant
say	whisper, hint, mumble, mention, utter, remark, state, announce, proclaim, shout

Some words have a different meaning depending on their context. Consider, for example, the word "nice":

a nice person	pleasant, good-natured, charming, kind, helpful
a nice day	fine, sunny, warm, bright, pleasant
a nice meal	tasty, delicious, lip-smacking, scrumptious
a nice outing	enjoyable, lovely, agreeable, delightful

Antonyms

An antonym is a word meaning the opposite of another word. For example, the antonym of "cheap" is "expensive".

Antonyms are often formed by adding prefixes to root words:

im-	+	possible	➔	impossible
non-	+	sense	➔	nonsense
un-	+	usual	➔	unusual
dis-	+	pleased	➔	displeased
in-	+	complete	➔	incomplete
il-	+	legal	➔	illegal
ir-	+	regular	➔	irregular

The suffix "-less" is also used to form antonyms:

worth	+	-less	➔	worthless
hair	+	-less	➔	hairless
pain	+	-less	➔	painless

Homonyms

Homonyms are words that sound the same but have a different spelling or meaning. Examples include:

passed	past	
piece	peace	
there	their	they're
stationary	stationery	

Some homonyms which are often confused are listed on page 462.

Dates and time

Days of the week
Sunday
Monday
Tuesday
Wednesday
Thursday
Friday
Saturday

Seasons
spring
summer
autumn
winter

More time words
second
minute
hour
day
breakfast time
break time
playtime
lunch time
dinner time
bedtime
yesterday
today
tomorrow
week
fortnight
month
year
leap year
decade
century
millennium

Months
January
February
March
April
May
June
July
August
September
October
November
December

Parts of the day
dawn
sunrise
morning
midday
noon
afternoon
dusk
twilight
sunset
evening
night
midnight

Frequency
never
once
twice
rarely
occasionally
from time to time
sometimes
often
soon
frequently
usually
always

Telling the time
a.m.
p.m.
o'clock
half past
quarter past
quarter to
analogue
digital
clock
watch
timer

Important dates
anniversary
birthday
calendar
date
diary
holiday
term
weekend

Words about time
age
contemporary
consecutive
duration
era
eternity
future
historic
period
season
simultaneous
span
staggered

Continents
Africa
Antarctica
Asia
Australasia
Europe
North America
South America

Major rivers
Amazon
Danube
Darling
Mississippi
Nile
Thames
Yangtze

Oceans
Antarctic Ocean
Arctic Ocean
Atlantic Ocean
Indian Ocean
Pacific Ocean

Countries
Afghanistan
Albania
Algeria
Angola
Argentina
Australia
Austria
Bangladesh
Belgium
Bosnia
Bolivia
Botswana
Brazil
Bulgaria
Cambodia
Canada
Chile
China
Colombia
Congo
Croatia
Cuba
Cyprus
Czech Republic
Denmark
Ecuador
Egypt
England
Estonia
Ethiopia
Fiji
Finland
France
Gambia
Germany
Ghana
Gibraltar
Greece
Greenland
Hungary
Iceland
India
Indonesia
Iran
Iraq
Ireland
Israel
Italy
Jamaica
Japan
Jordan
Kenya
Korea
Kuwait
Latvia
Lebanon
Libya
Lithuania
Luxembourg
Macedonia
Malaysia
Malta
Mexico
Morocco
Myanmar
Namibia
Nepal
Netherlands
New Zealand
Nigeria
Northern Ireland
Norway
Pakistan
Paraguay
Peru
Philippines
Poland
Portugal
Romania
Russia
Saudi Arabia
Scotland
Serbia
Sierra Leone
Singapore
Slovakia
South Africa
Spain
Sri Lanka
Sudan
Sweden
Switzerland
Syria
Taiwan
Tanzania
Thailand
Tunisia
Turkey
Uganda
Ukraine
United Kingdom
United States of America (USA)
Venezuela
Vietnam
Wales
Zambia
Zimbabwe

Planets
Mercury
Venus
Earth
Mars
Jupiter
Saturn
Uranus
Neptune
Pluto

Measurement and numbers

Length
millimetre (mm)
centimetre (cm)
metre (m)
kilometre (km)
mile

Mass or weight
milligram (mg)
gram (g)
kilogram (kg)
tonne

Capacity
millilitre (ml)
litre (l)
pint (pt)
gallon

Roman numerals

I	one	VIII	eight	XV	fifteen	L	fifty
II	two	IX	nine	XVI	sixteen	C	hundred
III	three	X	ten	XVII	seventeen	D	five hundred
IV	four	XI	eleven	XVIII	eighteen	M	thousand
V	five	XII	twelve	XIX	nineteen	MM	2000
VI	six	XIII	thirteen	XX	twenty	MMI	2001
VII	seven	XIV	fourteen	XL	forty	MMX	2010

Cardinal numbers

1 one	16 sixteen
2 two	17 seventeen
3 three	18 eighteen
4 four	19 nineteen
5 five	20 twenty
6 six	30 thirty
7 seven	40 forty
8 eight	50 fifty
9 nine	60 sixty
10 ten	70 seventy
11 eleven	80 eighty
12 twelve	90 ninety
13 thirteen	100 one hundred
14 fourteen	1000 one thousand
15 fifteen	1 000 000 one million

Ordinal numbers

1st	first	12th	twelfth
2nd	second	13th	thirteenth
3rd	third	14th	fourteenth
4th	fourth	15th	fifteenth
5th	fifth	16th	sixteenth
6th	sixth	17th	seventeenth
7th	seventh	18th	eighteenth
8th	eighth	19th	nineteenth
9th	ninth	20th	twentieth
10th	tenth	21st	twenty-first
11th	eleventh	22nd	twenty-second

Fractions

half ½
third ⅓
quarter ¼
fifth ⅕
sixth ⅙
eighth ⅛
tenth ⅒

Decimals

0.5
0.333
0.25
0.20
0.167
0.125
0.1

AD	anno Domini ("in the year of Our Lord" in Latin)
AIDS	acquired immune deficiency syndrome
a.m.	ante meridiem, morning
anon.	anonymous
BC	before Christ
BSE	bovine spongiform encephalopathy
°C	degrees Centigrade or Celsius
cc	cubic centimetre(s)
CD	compact disc
CD-ROM	a CD made to be used with a computer
CJD	Creuzfeld-Jacob disease
cl	centilitre(s) (100 cl = 1 litre)
cm	centimetre(s) (100 cm = 1 metre)
cm^2	square centimetre
c/o	care of
CV	curriculum vitae
dB	decibel(s)
DAT	digital audio tape
DIY	do-it-yourself
DJ	disc jockey
Dr	doctor
DVD	digital video disc or digital versatile disc
EU	European Union
°F	degrees Fahrenheit
ft.	feet
g	gram (1000 g = 1 kilogram)
GM	genetically modified
GP	general practitioner
ICT	information and communications technology
ID	identification
IQ	intelligence quotient
ISP	internet service provider
IT	information technology
K	1000; kilobyte
kg	kilogram (1 kg = 1000 grams)
km	kilometre
l	litre
LED	light-emitting diode
m	metre(s)
mg	milligram (1000 mg = 1 gram)
ml	millilitre (1000 ml = 1 litre)
mm	millimetre (1000 mm = 1 metre)
MP	Member of Parliament
Mr	a title before a man's name
Mrs	a title before a married woman's name
Ms	a title before a woman's name
NHS	National Health Service
no.	numero ("number" in Latin)
OAP	old age pensioner
p	pence
p.	page
p.a.	per annum ("each year" in Latin)
PC	personal computer; police constable
PE	physical education
pH	potential for hydrogen
p.m.	post meridiem, afternoon
pp.	pages
PS	post scriptum, used to add an extra message to a letter
PTA	parent-teacher association
pto	please turn over
RE	religious education
Revd	Reverend
RGN	Registered General Nurse
RSVP	répondez s'il vous plaît ("please reply" in French)
SATs	standard assessment tasks
SOS	a distress signal (said to be short for "save our souls")
TV	television
UFO	unidentified flying object
UN	United Nations
USA	United States of America
VAT	value-added tax
v. or vs.	versus ("against" in Latin)
VCR	video cassette recorder
VDU	visual display unit
WPC	woman police constable
www	World Wide Web

The good writing guide for non-fiction

Know your stuff!

Before you start writing, you need to research your topic. Use as many different sources as you can find: books, newspaper or magazine articles and the Internet. (For more tips on how to use the Internet to help you with your work, see p. 474).

Take notes

One way to help you remember is to take notes as you go along. They aren't chunks of writing copied from a source. Notes should be short reminders to yourself about important things you want to include in your piece, such as dates, names or facts.

Plan your work

You need to give your work a structure, so that each point follows on from the next in a clear and logical way.

For example, a good structure to use for a discursive piece of writing is:

Introduction
Give a general view of the subject, with an outline of what you are going to say later.

Main body
This should be a series of paragraphs that clearly lay out what you want to say in a way the reader can understand. If you are asked to discuss a topic on which there are different views, make sure that you give points for and against each point of view, and give evidence for both.

If you are writing to persuade someone to take a particular point of view, give good reasons for your way of thinking.

Conclusion
This should summarise the points you have made in your writing, and give your final answer or opinion on your topic.

Write a draft

Once you have the structure of your essay in place, you can write a draft. Make brief notes of the points you want to include in each section.

Here are some things to check:

- Does each paragraph follow logically from the last one?
- Have you said too little, or too much?
- Have you strenghtened your argument with each point you made?
- Does your conclusion clearly give your answer or argument?

Write your piece

Follow your plan and you should find that your writing flows easily and smoothly! Here are some things to watch out for:

- Does each sentence make sense?
- Have you used a mix of different sentence lengths?
- Are the same, or similar-sounding, words repeated too near each other?
- Are any sentences too long or hard to follow?

Check and edit

Once your piece of writing is complete, read it through carefully. If you spot anything wrong, correct it.

Summary
- Research – from a variety of sources
- Make notes – keep them short
- Fill out your notes – make a draft
- Write your piece – use paragraphs that follow one another clearly
- Check and edit

A good presentation requires just as much preparation as a piece of writing. Remember, the more you research and practice, the less nervous you will be.

Research your topic
Whether you choose your own subject or not, it is important you are interested in it. It really helps you get your ideas across if you show your passion for the topic.

Find out as much as you can about the topic as possible, making notes as you go along. Remember you are not writing an essay that you are going to read out loud. Don't write out long quotes, keep your notes short, so they are easy to remember.

Plan the structure
Just like good writing, your presentation needs a beginning middle and end. You could follow this well-known piece of advice:

- Tell them what you are going to say.
- Tell them.
- Tell them what you've told them.

This doesn't mean repeating yourself! It just means explaining what you are going to talk about, delivering that information and summarising what you have said.

Presentation tools
Presentation tools help you remember what you are going to say and can keep your audience interested.

Cue cards
Use numbered postcards to note down the main points of what you are going to say. A presentation isn't a test of memory – lots of speakers use cue cards.

Props
It's a good idea to have things to pass around and show people. It keeps the audience engaged in what you are saying.

IT support
If you have access to a computer and can use PowerPoint, you can create a slide show. You could also use PowerPoint to include electronic illustrations, diagrams and graphs.

Practice your presentation
This is really important! Here are some things to watch out for:

- Is your voice too loud/quiet?
- Are you speaking too quickly/slowly?
- Are you keeping to your time limit?

Giving your presentation
Here are some tips on getting it right:

- Check you've got everything you need.
- When you start, check everyone can hear you.
- Go at a steady pace and give the audience time to look at your slides and props.
- Make eye-contact with people.
- Don't just read what is on your cue cards – you know more than that!
- Keep your sentences short and simple and emphasise the important things.
- At the conclusion ask if anyone has any questions.

One final thing to remember
Don't panic! Take a deep breath and do your best.

Word challenge

What's on the page?

You can play this game by yourself or with a friend.

- Slide a piece of paper into the dictionary and open it so you can only see the guideword at the top of the page.
- Write it down.
- Now make a list of the words you might find on that page (there are usually about 30).
- Put the words in alphabetical order and write a few definitions.
- Now check the real page. How accurate were you?

Writing down the alphabet

Find or think of a word which contains the letters ABC in that order, e.g. absence. Do the same for BCD, DEF and so on. It's not as easy as you think!

You can try these variations:

- go backwards through the alphabet.
- use four letters instead of three.
- choose the letters at random (you could select them using Scrabble tiles).

Guess the word

Play this game with a friend.

- Ask them to read the guide word from a page in the dictionary along with a definition of a word on that page.
- Try to guess what the word is.
- If you really want to show off, you can say what part of speech it is.

Word chain

Can you spot the link in this word chain?

outlaw – awful – ultimate – test – station

The first two letters of each word are the last two letters of the previous one.

Can you make a chain yourself? Try to build a 20-word chain. You can use the dictionary to help you.

Back to back

Some words can be reversed to make other words. Can you find any in this dictionary?

Here's a few examples to get you started:

plug – gulp
evil – live

Find the link word!

Each page in the dictionary has a fact file at the bottom. The fact file is always linked with a headword somewhere on that page.

Find the link word on these pages:

- p 22
- p 158
- p 179
- p 191
- p 337
- p 359

Answers to Find the link word!

p22 – audible
p158 – grievance
p179 – hyphen
p191 – inspire
p337 – scythe
p359 – soften

When we're speaking quickly, it's easy to lose a few letters in a word. Have you ever said "strenth" when you meant "strength", for instance? People will still understand what you mean, but you might forget about the lost "g" and leave it out by mistake when you come to spell it.

Sometimes you might find yourself adding or changing letters when you say a word out loud.

Here are a few tips to help you remember how to spell some tricky words without losing or adding any letters.

Arctic and Antarctic
Be sure to pronounce the "c" in the middle.

certificate
Make sure you pronounce the first syllable as "sur", not "sut".

constable
Make sure you say the first syllable as "con", not "cun".

deteriorate
Make sure you include the "or" sound in the middle.

drawing
Don't say it as if it had an "r" in the middle.

escape
Make sure you say the first syllable as "ess", not "ex".

extraordinary
Say it as two words, "extra" + "ordinary".

February
Make sure you pronounce the middle "r".

law
Don't say it as if it had an "r" at the end.

length
Make sure you pronounce the "g" in it.

library
Make sure you pronounce the second "r" in it.

longitude *Said* "**long**-it-yood"

maintenance *Said* "**main**-ten-ance"

mischievous *Said* "**miss**-chee-vus". Don't put an extra "i" in it.

particularly *Said* "part-**ik**-yoo-lar-li. Don't leave out the "ar" sound.

probably
Say it as it is, with an "ab" sound.

recognize
Make sure you pronounce the "g" in it.

specific
Make you sure you pronounce the initial "s". It is not the same word that's in "Pacific Ocean"!

strength
Make sure you pronounce the "g" in it.

tortoise
Say it with the first syllable "tor", not "toy".

undoubtedly
Say it with the middle syllable "ed", not "ab".

utmost
Make sure you pronounce the first "t" in it. It isn't a "p"!

Top tip
The word "pronunciation" is very often mispronounced! It has "nun" in the middle, not "noun".

Text messages

Texting is a really popular way of communicating by mobile phone. There is a limit on the number of characters you can use in each text, so a special shortened text language has developed. Here are some common text words.

@	at	**g9**	genius	**t**	tea
2	to or too	**l8**	late	**thx**	thanks
2day	today	**lo**	hello	**u**	you
2moro	tomorrow	**m8**	mate	**w8**	wait
4	for	**pls**	please	**wan2**	want to
A	Eh?	**r**	are	**wk**	week
b4	before	**q**	queue	**wrk**	work
c	see	**some1**	someone	**xlnt**	excellent
gr8	great	**spk**	speak	**y**	why

Here are some text phrases.

Asap	As soon as possible
Bcnu	(I'll) be seeing you
Cul8r	See you later
Ruok	Are you OK?
Thnkq	Thank you
Ti2go	Time to go
Bbs	(I'll) be back soon
Bfn	'Bye for now

What does this mean?

Lo. Thx 4 spkg 2 me @ work 2day. R u w8ng 4 som1 2 c u b4 u c me? Y?

Answer

Hello. Thanks for speaking to me at work today. Are you waiting for someone to see you before you see me? Why?

Smileys

Using smileys is a fun way to let someone know how you feel when you text or e-mail. Smileys are made using symbols on the keyboard that look a little bit like a face, if you read them sideways – like this:

:)

Smileys are also called emoticons. This is because they are signs, or icons, that show your emotions when you are writing. The first one is believed to have been used in 1979, and it was:

-)

It meant 'tongue in cheek', but it didn't catch on! It wasn't until 1982 that smileys really became popular, beginning with:

:)

to mean that something was funny.

Now there are lots of smileys, or emoticons. Here are just a few of them.

:- 0	surprised	**: - D**	laughing
;-)	winking	***:- I**	daydreaming
:-S	confused	**B-)**	wearing sunglasses
:'(	crying	**I– 0**	yawning
:- $	embarrassed	**O0o:-)**	thinking
(:+ (	scared		

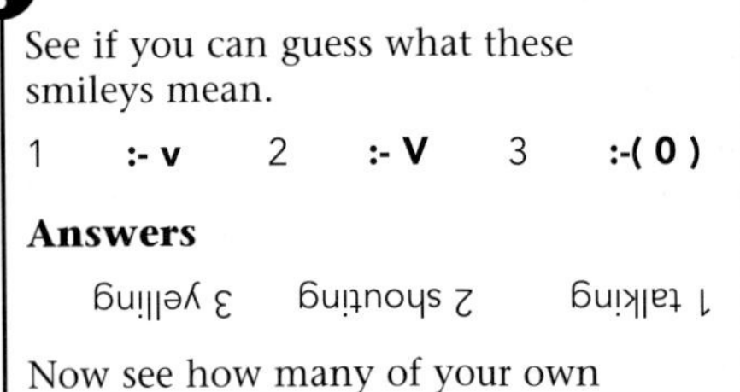

See if you can guess what these smileys mean.

1 **:- v** 2 **:- V** 3 **:-(0)**

Answers

1 talking 2 shouting 3 yelling

Now see how many of your own smileys you can make!

Palindromes

A palindrome is a word or phrase which reads the same backwards as it does forwards. It comes from a Greek word meaning "running back again". Here are some examples:

deed	gag	solos
did	kayak	toot
eye	madam	wow

There are lots of other palindromes. See if you can work out what these are.

1 What some people call their father
2 Flat and even
3 A member of a female religious community
4 12 o'clock midday
5 A quick look

Can you think of any more?

Sometimes whole sentences can be palindromes.

Madam, I'm Adam.

Was it a rat I saw?

Able was I ere I saw Elba.

(This is what the Emperor Napoleon is supposed to have said when he was exiled on the island of Elba.)

Palindrome answers

1 dad 2 level 3 nun 4 noon 5 peep

Foreign words

Lots of everyday phrases that we use in English are taken from other languages. Here are a few examples.

ad infinitum
Said "in-fin-**eye**-tum"
This comes from Latin, meaning "to be endless". If something goes on ad infinitum, it goes on and on, perhaps for ever.

ad-lib
This comes from the Latin phrase *ad libitum*, which means "at your pleasure". If you ad-lib a speech, you make it up as you go along, just as you please.

al fresco
This phrase is Italian and means literally "in the fresh". If you eat al fresco, you eat in the open air.

au revoir
Said "oh-ruv-**wah**"
This is French for "Goodbye for now".

bon voyage
Said "bon-voy-**arjh**"
This is French for "Have a good journey".

deja vu
Said "dayzha-**voo**"
This is French for "already seen". Sometimes people think they are re-living a situation they have been in before. Déjà vu is used to describe this experience.

en route
Said "on root"
This is French for "On the way". If you stop en route to a place, you stop on the journey there.

Weblinks

What is the Internet?

Millions of computers all over the world are able to communicate with each other. They are linked together because they are all connected to the Internet. The Internet is the word we use to describe this network of linked computers.

What is the World Wide Web?

The World Wide Web, or Web, is a way of getting information using the Internet. Search engines scan the Web for information given on websites.

What can I use the Internet for?

Dictionaries and other books can help you find information for school projects, or on topics that you're particularly interested in, but using the Internet is another great way to find what you're looking for. There's a lot of fun, interesting, exciting information out there – you just have to know how to get at it!

How can I use the Internet?

You can find information from the Internet by using a search engine. Search engines are pieces of software that can examine lots of websites for you, and they work by searching for "key words".

What is a key word?

The key word is the subject you want to find out about, but it helps to be specific. For example, if you type the word "sport" into a search engine, it will look for every single site containing that word – and there are lots of them! That's not very helpful. You can make the search narrower by giving the search engine more detailed information to work with. For example, if you really wanted to know about the route of the Tour de France in 2005, typing in "Tour de France route 2005" would set the engine searching for sites with all of those words in. That's much more accurate!

Can I make things easier?

If you know exactly what you want, typing the words inside inverted commas, "like this", will help. That way, the engine will search for exactly those words, in that order. For example, typing in "The London Eye" will only direct you to sites about the wheel overlooking the Thames, and will not give you details of the London Eye Hospital!

Internet safety

The Internet is great fun, but do remember that you need to take care and observe some rules to use it safely. You've probably heard about chat rooms and sites that allow you ask questions and discuss things. These can be helpful, but:

- don't give out your personal details (such as your name, address, telephone number) to anyone you meet online
- always use a nickname to long on with
- never arrange to meet up alone with someone you've met online
- talk to an adult you know well and ask for help if you're upset about anything that has happened while you are online.

Follow these simple rules and you'll be able to enjoy some really fun and useful information – online!

If you want to find out more about some websites that you might like, go to:
www.collins.co.uk/word_wizard

Page	Answer
14	Ideas: *First Day at School* by Tyrone Shoelaces; *Fall Down the Cliff* by Eileen Dover.
15	"Antonym" is the antonym of "synonym".
21	Ideas: gazelle, cheetah, whippet, bull, ox, elephant, antelope.
27	Barometer: pressure; thermometer: temperature; pedometer: distance walked; odometer: distance travelled by a vehicle.
33	A black sheep is a family member who is different from the others; black holes are regions in space with intense gravity; a black look shows you disapprove of something; a black mark is a mark against you when you have done something wrong.
37	They are all books written about life in the future.
41	Your breath.
44	A bull in a china shop is a clumsy person; a wolf in sheep's clothing is someone who looks innocent but can be harmful; a dog in the manger is a mean person who stops others from enjoying themselves.
50	Cardigans, sandwiches and diesel engines are eponyms: they are named after people.
60	The name of the word comes from the sound made.
61	Ideas: sick as a parrot; at the end of the day; once in a blue moon.
64	Help I'm trapped inside this dictionary (A=D, B=E, C=F, and so on).
71	Words deriving from *duco* are conduct, conduction and conductor.
74	Ideas: scoff, gobble, wolf, peck at, hoover, sip, guzzle, slurp.
82	Ideas: bomb, numb, tomb, plumb line, womb.
85	Ideas: score, redeem, employer, erase, secret, ethnic, icicle, lead, adaptor.
87	Purify, clean or cleanse, simplify.
88	A dead heat is a tie in a race; dead weight is something very heavy that does not support any of its weight; dead ringer is someone who is very like someone else; dead language is a language which is no longer spoken, such as Latin and Sanskrit.
94	Desert is a wild, barren, usually sandy, place; dessert is the sweet course of a meal.
102	Morning is a.m.; mourning is grieving for someone who has died. Dying is ceasing to live; dyeing is colouring hair or fabric. Singing is making music with the voice; singeing is scorching something.
109	Versatile means having many different skills.
110	Ideas: terror, ordeal, algebra, rake, keep, episode, death, throb, obstinate.
112	Herbivore: grass; carnivore: flesh/meat; omnivore:anything edible; nucivore: nuts.
116	Employees, payees and interviewees are all people who have the action of the verb done to them. Employees are employed, payees are paid and so on.
120	The words are all linked to the number ten.
131	February is often wrongly said and spelt without an "r" in the middle.
137	Commonest answers: a fleet of ships, a litter of puppies, a shoal of fish.
140	"The boy," said the teacher, "is a fool."
142	Form: hare; lodge: beaver; earth: fox (and others); holt: otter (and others); drey: squirrel; byre: cow; lair: several animals possible; burrow: rabbit; eyrie: eagle.
143	Deny.
147	Ideas: stable, leisure, rest, strange, gerbil, illegal, alcohol, olive, vest.
152	Glaciers are in the Antarctic; glaring error; gifted pupil; gladiators (in arenas).
157	Granny, sheepshank, bowline, clove hitch, reef are types of knots.

Fact file answers

Page	Answer
160	Guerrilla warfare; gruelling race; unconditional guarantee; security guard.
161	Muslims worships in mosques; Jews in synagogues; Sikhs in gurdwaras; Christians (including Baptists, Methodists, etc.) in chapels.
164	To be an old hand is to be experienced; to have the upper hand is to have an advantage; to have a free hand is to be allowed to do something in your own way.
165	Hard up is poor; hard cheese is bad luck; hard hearted is unkind or cruel; hard luck is bad luck; hard times are a time of poverty.
166	A hard copy is printed on paper. A soft copy is a computer file.
178	The bone in your upper arm is called the humerus. Humorous means funny.
179	A "man-eating chicken" is a chicken that can eat people. A "man eating chicken" is a man eating chicken.
181	Eligible is a good prospect to marry; illegible is not able to be read. Practice is a noun: *piano practice*; practise is a verb: *I practise the piano*. Colonel is an army officer; kernel is the centre of a nut.
184	An improper fraction is larger than one; fractions are usually smaller than one.
185	The opposites are impossible, unsure, irregular, misjudge and disappear.
187	Indigo is derived from India; attic from Athens; bayonet from Bayonne (France); canter from Canterbury; jersey from the island of Jersey in the Channel Islands.
194	A "computer anorak" is someone who is obsessed with computers and knows every detail about them.
197	Ideas: illogical, alternative, vice, cellar, article, lender, erase, semolina, name.
202	Junk mail is uninvited advertising through the post; a junk fax is uninvited advertising by fax machine; a Chinese junk is a flat-bottomed Chinese sailing boat.
206	The Torah is a holy book of the Jews, the Upanishads are holy books in Hinduism; Guru Granth Sahib is a holy book in Sikhism.
208	Ideas: fax, email, quad bike, digital, Internet, people carrier, banoffi pie.
209	NATO is the North Atlantic Treaty Organization; quango stands for quasi-autonomous non-governmental organization.
210	A leading light is a prominent person; a leading lady is the main female in a play; a leading question is a question that suggests a certain answer; a leading article is a newspaper article expressing the views of that newspaper.
224	"I" and "e" soften "g" to a "j" sound. In managing, the "i" softens the "g". In manageable, because the "a" would not soften "g", an "e" is necessary.
225	January: Janus; March: Mars; May: Maia; Thursday: Thor; Saturday: Saturn.
227	Phillumenists: match boxes; philatelists: stamps; numismatists: coins.
234	A minefield is a delicate subject which might go wrong unless handled carefully.
236	Knight, gnome, thumb, pneumatic, half, knit.
244	Ideas: odour, urge, gentleman, antelope, priest, stoop, operate, tease, session.
250	Edward Lear.
251	Bonbon literally means good-good.
253	Ideas: cease, sealed, editor, orphan, antic, icicles, estimate, test, stretch.
255	All the words are connected with the number eight. The Latin *octo* means eight.
258	To "put your foot in it" is an idiom meaning to say or do something unwise.
262	A "retail outlet" is a shop.

Page	Answer
263	A maiden over is a cricket term meaning an over in which no runs are scored; a maiden name is a woman's surname before marriage; a maiden voyage is a ship's first voyage in service; a maiden speech is an MP's first speech in Parliament.
266	A compass shows direction; a pair of compasses draws circles.
271	I had, I have, I shall have; I was, I am, I shall be; I thought, I think, I shall think; I flew, I fly, I shall fly.
272	All the words are connected with feet. The Latin words *pes* and *pedis* mean a foot.
274	Perch is a homonym. It has two meanings with the same spelling and pronunciation.
275	A cuckoo in the nest is an unwanted visitor or resident; a bear with a sore head is an irritable or angry person; a snake in the grass is a secret enemy.
277	Claustrophobia is fear of enclosed spaces; cynophobia is fear of dogs; xenophobia is fear of foreigners and strangers.
290	Because prefixes come before the rest of the word.
291	Speech, action, sight, sale, marriage.
295	To ob***ject*** is a verb meaning to say that you do not wish something to happen. An ***ob***ject is a thing.
298	Tom Cruise (Tom Mapother); Mark Twain (Samuel Clemens); Lewis Carroll (Charles Dodgson); John Wayne (Marion Morrison).
299	The sentence can be punctuated in two ways, giving very different meanings. *What do you think? I will feed you and clothe you for nothing.* *What! Do you think I will feed you and clothe you for nothing?*
306	Diwali is celebrated by Hindus; Hanukkah by Jews; Advent by Christians.
307	Rancid is smelling or tasting stale: *rancid butter*; valid means able to be used; livid is very angry; squalid is dirty through neglect: *a squalid house*; candid is honest.
308	An underdog is a person or team not expected to win; a dark horse is someone who has unexpected ability or success; to cry wolf is to ask for help when you do not need it; a lame duck is a person who is not as strong as they were or need to be.
315	Falsehood (or falseness), sadness, merriment, anxiety.
323	Ideas: hang out; greasy spoon; four-by-four; naff; to slag off; to suss out.
325	Henry the Eighth, 25, 144, The First Eleven, 2001.
327	The correct spellings are: deceive, thief, niece, ceiling, weird.
329	Ideas: also, soften, enter, erode, deceive, vermin, interval, alligator, ordered.
331	Eponyms: they have had things named after them.
332	Satchel: school books, etc.; carafe: wine; cruet: salt and pepper; compact: powder; caddy: tea; scuttle: coal.
335	Ideas: ache; bite; cross; dress; entrance…
336	These words are all to do with writing. The Latin *scriptio* means writing.
337	The letters of "chesty" can be rearranged to form "scythe".
338	Second sight is the ability to see into the future; second thoughts is changing your mind; second nature is something you are used to doing and find easy; second-best is not as good as the best.
339	Self-conscious is shy, embarrassed; self-made is successful through one's own efforts; self-possessed is confident; self-controlled is able to control temper and emotions.
345	Lambs and sheep bleat; horses neigh; cows low; bulls bellow; monkeys and dogs howl; elephants trumpet; monkeys chatter.

Fact file answers

Page	Answer
350	Black as night; cool as a cucumber; clear as crystal; mad as a hatter.
352	Apples and pears: stairs; mince pies: eyes; dog and bone: phone; trouble and strife: wife.
353	Scarper: to go (Scapa Flow); butcher's: look (butcher's hook); the Sweeney: Flying Squad (Sweeney Todd); titfer: hat (tit for tat).
354	Ideas: hail, sleet, drizzle.
355	Sluggish is slow and lazy; waspish is easily annoyed, with a cruel tongue; shrewish is bad-tempered, always telling people off; catty is unpleasant about other people.
357	If you are "snookered", you are in a bad situation you cannot get out of.
358	Association Football.
361	Ideas: shout, thorn, seat, stew, sink, file, strap, sever, miles, name.
363	A spectacle is an impressive sight; a pair of spectacles is glasses.
365	The name of the word comes from the sound made.
366	You could use any of these words to complete the exercise: spot, spotlight, spout, sprain, sprawl, spray, spread, spring, sprinkle, sprint, sprout.
368	Stag: hind; dog: bitch; fox: vixen; boar: sow; gander: goose; lion: lioness.
370	American pronunciation is "tom-**ay**-to" and "missul".
371	Pets, pest and sept are anagrams of "step".
372	Sternum is in the chest/breast; mandible is the jaw; scapula is the shoulder; femur is the thigh (leg); pelvis is the hips/waist.
373	The stomach digests food ; liver processes blood; kidneys remove waste from the blood; lungs transfer oxygen to the blood; brain controls thoughts and actions.
374	A storm in a teacup is a big fuss about a little issue; a windfall is unexpected money; seeing red is suddenly getting angry; feeling blue is feeling sad.
376	Ideas: carthorse, elephant, ox, lion.
379	The subway is what Americans call an underground railway.
381	The sentence is a mnemonic (verbal reminder) of the planets in order from the sun: Mercury, Venus, Earth, Mars, Jupiter, Saturn, Neptune, Pluto.
384	Ideas: halter, swallow, swat, wallow, want, warrior.
393	Piano means softly; allegro means lively; forte means loudly; stave is the lines on which music is written; clef is the symbols on the stave which indicate the pitch of the notes; pitch is the level of a note, high or low.
402	Ideas: zoo, boo, coo, moo.
403	Town centre, touch and go, Blackpool tower, tossing the caber, tough luck.
404	Ideas: terrifically, comically, specifically, medically, cynically.
409	To blow your own trumpet is to boast about yourself.
414	Ideas: bouquet, boutique, cougar, nougat, through, throughout, troupe.
422	PIN means personal identification number.
423	Criticize, shelve, teach, befriend.
429	Wishy-washy is pale, weak-looking; namby-pamby is weak, prim; fuddy-duddy is dull, conservative; a goody-goody is so anxious to do right that they annoy others.
434	Sunday: the sun; Monday: the moon; Tuesday: Tiw, a Germanic god; Thursday: Thor, a Norse god; Friday: Freya, a Norse god; Saturday: Saturn.
437	Lions roar; donkeys bray; monkeys chatter; seals bark; frogs croak.